# TOCQUEVILLE BETWEEN TWO WORLDS

# TOCQUEVILLE BETWEEN TWO WORLDS

*The Making of a Political and Theoretical Life*

SHELDON S. WOLIN

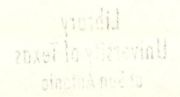

PRINCETON UNIVERSITY PRESS
PRINCETON AND OXFORD

Published by Princeton University Press, 41 William Street,
Princeton, New Jersey 08540
In the United Kingdom: Princeton University Press, 3 Market Place,
Woodstock, Oxfordshire OX20 1SY



Second printing, and first paperback printing, 2003
Paperback ISBN 0-691-11454-4

*The Library of Congress has cataloged the cloth edition of this book as follows*

Wolin, Sheldon S.
Tocqueville between two worlds : the making of a political
and theoretical life / Sheldon S. Wolin.
p. cm.
Includes bibliographical references and index.
ISBN 0-691-07436-4
1. Tocqueville, Alexis de, 1805–1859—Contributions in
political science. 2. Tocqueville, Alexis de, 1805–1859—
Contributions in democracy. I. Title.
JC229.T8 W65 2001
320'.092—dc21
[B] 00-065207

British Library Cataloging-in-Publication Data is available

This book has been composed in Adobe Garamond

Printed on acid-free paper. ∞

www.pupress.princeton.edu

Printed in the United States of America

10 9 8 7 6 5 4 3 2

*For*

*Arno J. Mayer*

# CONTENTS

᯾ ACKNOWLEDGMENTS

THROUGHOUT the final stages of this volume my friend Arno Mayer has done much to bring this volume to publication. His steady encouragement, wise counsel, tough-minded criticisms, and helpful suggestions have sustained me and contributed greatly to whatever value the work may have. Dedicating it to him is a small measure of my gratitude. The errors that remain are solely my responsibility.

For several useful suggestions and constructive criticisms I am indebted to Thomas Dumm and Roger Boesche and to the anonymous reviewer for Princeton University Press.

I want to thank the staff of Princeton University Press for its many courtesies and competent editorial advice. Thanks to Ann H. Wald for her early support of the manuscript and special thanks to Ian Malcolm for his help and encouragement throughout.

My principal source for Tocqueville's writings is the *Oeuvres complètes*, edited by J.-P. Mayer et al. (Paris: Gallimard, 1951–). I have cited it as *OC*. Limited use is made of the *Oeuvres complètes d'Alexis de Tocqueville*, edited by Gustave de Beaumont (Paris: Michel Lévy Frères, 1860–66). I have cited it as *OC* (B).

TOCQUEVILLE BETWEEN TWO WORLDS

# INTRODUCTION

ALEXIS DE TOCQUEVILLE has become a fixture in contemporary American political discourse, both within the academy and outside. Arguably there have been only two classics of American political theory, *The Federalist Papers* and *Democracy in America.* It is safe to say that today Tocqueville's masterpiece is invoked more often in support of some interpretation of present-day American politics than is the *Federalist,* even though the latter is commonly represented as the thinking of the Founding Fathers. While the *Federalist* is typically cited to shed light from the past on the present, as in current appeals to the "intentions of the Framers," *Democracy in America* is summoned not only to interpret the past and present but to augur the future.

Accordingly, I have tried to present a Tocqueville who is not so firmly in the French intellectual and political context of his times as to be irrelevant to ours.[1] Scarcely a week passes without some quotation from *Democracy in America* appearing in the popular media or in literary reviews. Although John Rawls may provide the common reference point for academic philosophers and Michel Foucault for postmodern literary theorists, Tocqueville may well be the more substantial presence in the public philosophy current in the media and in the rhetoric of politicians. To reflect on present-day American politics invites reflection on *Democracy in America* and vice versa.

Unlike Karl Marx, Tocqueville serves as a unifying rather than a divisive symbol, his magistral status owing much to the consensual function he has been made to perform. Interpreters have created a certain Tocqueville, one who slips easily into the main dialogue of American politics between self-designated liberals and conservatives, with each camp claiming him as its own. To the one he is a "liberal conservative" who values freedom as well as property rights; to the other he is a "conservative liberal" who is alert to the dangers of "too much democracy" and who commiserates with the burdens borne by political elites, not the least of which is the periodic invasion of the political realm by the masses.[2] Both sides assume that *Democracy in America* equals Tocqueville's "theory"; that a book about America is synonymous with a book about the United States; and that whatever Tocqueville ascribed to democracy applied to the United States. Each of these assumptions is, as later pages show, either wrong or in need of significant qualification.

Throughout this volume I have tried to keep three principal concerns in mind: first, to present a conception of what Tocqueville understood by political theory, how he experienced and practiced it, and how he tried to combine the theoretical life with the career of a politician;[3] second, to examine his conception of democracy as both a political and a theoretical project; and, third, to show that Tocqueville's writings and actions were preoccupied with the emergence of what would later be called the politics of modernity. I have projected his treatment of these concerns "backward" by relating them to his theoretical predecessors, particularly to Montesquieu, Rousseau, the *Federalist*, and Burke; and I have compared his ideas with those of certain of his contemporaries, like Marx and Saint-Simon. In chapters 1 and 2 I have tried to place these concerns in a historical context in order to emphasize the theoretical and practical challenges posed by the virtually simultaneous emergence of modern democracy and what I have called "modern power." They are, I believe, the indispensable context for an appreciation both of Tocqueville's achievement and of its failures.

The diverse character of Tocqueville's numerous writings, many of them unpublished during his lifetime, poses formidable questions about which of these, or all of them together, represents "Tocqueville's theory." Is "the theory of *Democracy in America*" to be considered the same as "Tocqueville's theory"? Such questions may seem Alexandrian, yet they point to the difficulties in applying the same notion of theory to all of his major works, each of which on its face is strikingly different from the others. Recent commentators have argued that the differences between the first and second installments of *Democracy* are so marked that it should properly be read as two distinct volumes. Even if one were able to resolve satisfactorily questions about the intellectual unity of *Democracy*, a more complicated problem concerns the theoretical and political character of Tocqueville's two late masterpieces, neither of which is ordinarily treated as a theoretical work and only one of which is considered to be "political" in intention. *Souvenirs*, a work that Tocqueville withheld from publication during his lifetime, is commonly classified as part autobiography, part memoir of the revolution of 1848. *The Old Regime and the Revolution* is widely esteemed as a classic of historical writing and often reputed to be the work of a detached man who, having been forced to retire from politics, discovered the scholarly rewards of archival research.[4] Its reputation has made it forbidden territory to the political theorist. Although there are subtle, even deliberate continuities between *Democracy* and *The Old Regime*, there are significant differences in their theoretical character and subtler ones in their politics. Each of Tocqueville's principal works represents a distinct moment in his public life and in the life of his country. This is not to represent what follows as a political biography or a study in "the life and times of Tocqueville." It can best be understood as a certain kind of biography: of political and theoretical choices made over time. Tocqueville's theory can be considered as the complex of those decisions extending not only over time but, peculiarly, over space as well.

In trying to conceptualize these differences we might note that "theorist" derives from the Greek *theoros*, which was the name for an emissary who traveled on behalf of his city to other cities or societies. A *theoria*, from which "theory" was derived, meant "journey."[5] Traveling is, of course, an encounter with differences. We might think of Tocqueville as a traveler in time whose *theoria* consisted of what he saw or experienced in his different journeys.[6] His journey to America convinced him that he had witnessed the future of Western societies. The personal recollections that formed the *Souvenirs* might be interpreted as an interiorized journey into the present of 1848. *The Old Regime* was a journey into the past, which, as it came closer to the present, was broken off. In the nature of things the same person's journeys to different places or times are never identical. They are never one *theoria* because a journey into difference brings surprises. And yet, when recollected in tranquillity, it is unlikely that they will be presented as wholly discontinuous. In Tocqueville's numerous introspective moments, continuities are insisted upon, even struggled for. Although he was acutely aware of living in an era of discontinuity, his *theoria* would maintain that in France one archetypal disruption, the revolution of 1789, was being replayed in the several revolutions over the next half century: disruption was the continuity. Although he would maintain that, over the years, the *theoros* had not changed,[7] his self-perception was of someone who was "incomplete," "incoherent," and whose "several parts were badly joined."[8]

THE abiding concern of Tocqueville's thinking, the referent point by which he tried to define his life as well as the task before his generation, was the revival of the political: in his phrase, *la chose publique.* The elevation of the political and the making of a public self were conscious gestures of opposition to the privatizing tendencies for which he, as much as any writer of his time, provided the authoritative critique. Tocqueville is commonly credited with having coined the expression "individualism" and, along with its companion term "privatization," having made them denotative marks of modernity.

Tocqueville might be the last influential theorist who can be said to have truly cared about political life. Few of his contemporaries did. Marx thought of politics as a form of combat. As for John Stuart Mill, he leaves the uncomfortable impression of a philosopher holding his nose as he writes about politics and attempts to remove its stench by having it submit to the deodorizing influence of experts. Neither Marx nor Mill could have composed the lament compressed in a note among Tocqueville's papers, "Absence d'un véritable parti conservateur de la vie politique . . ."[9]—roughly: the lack of a genuine conservative party in political life.

Tocqueville's notion of the political was not obscure so much as it was split between the heroic and the mundane: the one exalted the political as noble deeds, actions that were at once individual and altruistic, self-publicizing and public-spirited; the other was formed from his experience with the small-scale politics of American townships. The latter politics, confined to the daily concerns of ordinary citizens—roads, schools, taxes—was better described as participation than as action. Participation from *pars + capio,* taking a share rather than activating. The motives at work in participatory politics appeared unheroic and parochial. When judged against the heroic standard, the stakes were hardly such as to stir a sulking Achilles. The question raised by small-scale, participatory politics was not whether it was possible but whether it was interestingly political.

Tocqueville claimed to have witnessed a vibrant political life in America and he devoted his energies, both as a writer and as a politician, to nurturing *la politique,* the political, in France. The vehicle he chose for realizing the political—and I would emphasize that his choice was a halting one—was "liberalism." Yet it would be inaccurate to portray Tocqueville's political thought as though it were characteristic and emblematic of liberal thinking in general, even if it is assumed that the many varieties of liberalism could be reduced to some common denominators.[10] In the course of his parliamentary career French politics first lapsed into reaction, then into despotism. The issue that Tocqueville was driven to pose was whether liberalism was inherently flawed. It could not be *le véritable parti conservateur de la vie politique* because its conception of *political* liberty was too weak to resist the corruption encouraged when the content of freedom was defined by liberal economic values.There are, to be sure, very important points of contact between the evolution (in the neutral sense of that word) of his thinking and what is understood as liberalism but the same could be said of conservative elements. The complexity of his thinking had mostly to do with the difficult problems he engaged. Revolution and its aftermath, administrative centralization, the emergence of democratic politics, new forms of despotism, and increasingly self-conscious class conflicts did not readily admit to distinctively liberal or conservative solutions.

As an aristocrat he had to come to terms with a world that had once been interpretable in stability-charged and hierarchical terms. Now it was disappearing so rapidly that only traces remained. Caught between change and loss—loss of faith, of social status, and aristocratic privilege—Tocqueville was forced to deal with a world being shaped by those who, literally, were making a business of change and bore the responsibility for having destroyed much that he cared about. He would not only try to fathom the meaning of the diverse phenomena that would go by the name of modernity but he would also reflect on what had gone from, or was going out of, the world he knew and valued. I refer to this pronounced strain of antimodernism as *ancienneté.* It colors virtually all of Tocqueville's thinking, disposing him to dwell on contrasts between the Old and the New World, between past and present, between privilege and equality. If Tocqueville's theoretical formation begins with modernity in the form of American democracy, it culminates in *The Old Regime*, the fullest exposition of the idea of *ancienneté.* Tocquevillean theory had its own dialectic, burdened with dispossession and haltingly searching for the means of retrieval.

The English political economist Nassau Senior, who maintained a continuing correspondence and personal contacts with Tocqueville over the years, remarked on his friend's "talents for exploring the connection between thought and action."[11] Tocqueville is among the very few writers of major stature in the history of political theory—Machiavelli was another and in their contrasting ways so were Burke, Marx, and Mill—who could claim a relatively long political career. "The connection between thought and action," preoccupied or, rather, agonized Tocqueville throughout his entire life, not in the abstract but as *the* question of how he ought to spend his life. His private writings are virtually consumed by public themes and he constantly worries about how to act on his convictions. At the same time, he is committed to theorizing politically, not with an eye to satisfying professional conceptions of disinterested inquiry but from a commitment to a life of politics.

This study of the formation of a theorist, his theories, and his political engagements is possible because of the rich sources now available. One can follow Tocqueville through his creative travails and observe the gradual emergence of form, structure, and content, as well as theoretical consciousness itself. One observes someone self-consciously constructing himself into a political man while being constructed and limited by historical legacies whose disappearance he devoted his life to explaining. We can witness a theory and a theorist in the making thanks to the preservation of the diaries and notebooks in which Tocqueville recorded his observations, interviews, and reflections regarding his American journey; to the numerous letters that he wrote from America and, later, during the composition of *Democracy in America*; and to the preliminary drafts of that work. Any student of Tocqueville is indebted most of all to the careful and affectionate labors of a long line of scholars, from the pioneering researches of George Pierson, the editorial labors of J.-P. Mayer and his successors, and the more recent contributions of Seymour Drescher, James Schleifer, André Jardin, and François Furet. We are also able to gauge the extent to which the theory matched the intentions of its author;

whether there was slippage, loss of control, and unanticipated, even unwelcome, truths revealed; whether political aspirations and exigencies skewed theoretical vision, or whether the actor was undone by the theorist.

I hope to show that Tocqueville was a far more inventive theoretical mind than he is usually given credit for. His constructions are more complex than the easy accessibility of his writings suggests—or that his numerous contradictions deny. Beyond that, what, if any, are the connections between Tocqueville's pastness and our present?

This book makes two claims. The first is that *Democracy in America* represents the moment when democracy first came into focus as the central subject of a political theory. John Stuart Mill was right when he hailed *Democracy* as "the first philosophical book ever written on Democracy, as it manifests itself in modern society." Mill identified Tocqueville's crucial contribution by the phrase "as it manifests itself in society." Early modern political theorists, such as Machiavelli, Bodin, Hobbes, and Locke—none of whom were democrats or had ever observed an actual democracy—imagined democracy as a simple political structure or constitution dominated by the "common people." Thanks partly to Montesquieu's influence, Tocqueville succeeded in restoring the connective relationships between a distinctive type of politics and the social relations and cultural values and practices that transmitted definition and character to politics. Politics was not simply the "expression" of societal beliefs and practices but was as much constitutive of society as it was reflective of it. As a result of this comprehensive, interactive way of thinking, democracy presented a serious political problem precisely because it was a political conception in which the idea of a "whole" corresponded to the reality of an increasingly inclusive society. Previous societies were alleged by theorists to be "wholes" yet theorists also insisted that political rule was rightfully exercised by a select part, a monarch, an aristocracy, or a priesthood. The serious question of democracy was whether the political demands that it placed upon the Many, upon "those who work" (Aristotle), made its workability uncertain. Hence instead of presenting a simple question of its form(s), democracy might be a question of the political commitments of the Many.

My second claim is that Tocqueville's theory represents an important early engagement between liberalism and democracy. The eighteenth-century revolutions in America and France had been widely represented as the triumph of liberalism over monarchy and aristocracy. Tocqueville's encounter with American democracy turned an aristocrat into a liberal, albeit, as Roger Boesche has argued, of a strange sort. Tocqueville's self-description as "a new kind of liberal" reflected his strong conviction that freedom or liberty was the fundamental political value and an even stronger fear that the greatest threat to freedom was from a combination of political democracy and social equality.[12] Nineteenth- and twentieth-century liberals have responded warmly to Tocqueville's criticisms of egalitarian democracy, in both its political and social forms, and to his warnings about "the tyranny of the majority." That reading of Tocqueville boasts a distinguished genealogy: the political philosopher most responsible for making antidemocracy a staple of liberal theory was John Stuart Mill, the scion of English utilitarianism. Mill wrote one of the early tributes to *Democracy in America* and, more important, incorporated Tocqueville's critique of majority rule and egalitarianism into *On Liberty*, perhaps the most influential essay in modern liberal theory. Mill also drew from Tocqueville the idea that liberals ought to rethink the idea of aristocracy, thereby making explicit the elitist element that early modern liberals had disguised (tho' thinly) as "republican virtue." Elitism provided the conduit by which liberalism transmitted aristocracy into the postrevolutionary world. That required a redefinition of aristocracy, not as a caste with inherited privileges, but as the embodiment of educated taste, ideals of public service and philanthropy, and earned superiorities.[13]

Almost without exception, the appropriation of Tocqueville, whether by liberals or conservatives, fails to come to terms with the driving force behind his concern about the disappearance of aristocracy. For the political to take hold and be nurtured, there had to be a class that could serve as its historical carrier. Numerous commentators have emphasized his use of aristocratic notions in constructing a liberal critique of democracy but few have noted that Tocqueville's experience, even infatuation, with the American version of participatory democracy became the basis of a bitter indictment of middle-class liberalism in the *Souvenirs*. It was, he claimed, the inability of the bourgeoisie to temper self-interest with *civisme* that undermined the July Monarchy. If the bourgeoisie's politicians could not be depended upon to practice public virtue, liberalism might become a stalled ideology, content to stand behind constitutional arrangements whose purpose was to block the Many.

A broad aim of this volume, then, is to use Tocqueville's ideas as (con)texts for reflecting upon the passage of liberal society from early to late modernity. There is an important sense in which Tocqueville was engaged in a lifelong task of retrieving a receding aristocratic past in order to counteract the new forms of despotism. One possible task for today's theorist is to ponder his example and to undertake the task of retrieving a receding democratic present in order to counteract even more novel forms of despotism.

# PART ONE

## *The Abundance of Power*

# CHAPTER I
# MODERN THEORY AND MODERN POWER

## I

> *[T]he most striking characteristic of the times is the powerlessness of both men and governments to direct the course of political and social changes.*
>
> Tocqueville[1]

Tocqueville singled out "powerlessness" as the striking characteristic of the politics of the times. Yet those times might also be described as notable for the abundance and variety of powers rather than their scarcity and for actors overwhelmed by powers rather than lacking them. In this and the next chapter I want to develop the paradox of power and propose it as the political and theoretical context for interpreting Tocqueville.

From ancient to early modern times the theoretical problem presented by power lay in its finite amount and consequent social disorder as nations, families, singular actors, groups, and classes struggled for control of a scarce good and by its means the enforcement of their conception of good order.[2] The symbol of the politics of scarcity was the idea and institutions of privilege by which authority was bestowed on and power restricted to a relative few who were singled out on the basis of birth, an entitlement from a high authority, or great wealth. As late as the eighteenth century Rousseau began his reconstruction of the logic of society by positing a human condition afflicted by powerlessness: men find that "the power of resistance" offered by nature was greater than "the forces" that each individual could bring to preserve himself. Rousseau's solution of a social contract, whereby each incorporates himself into a community, admittedly did not create power. Instead "by aggregation a sum of forces . . . [would be] brought into play" by "the single motive force" of men "acting in concert." For "men cannot generate new forces, but only unite and direct existing ones."[3]

Beginning in the sixteenth century with Machiavelli, the hallmark of modern political theorists was a preoccupation with power or, more precisely, with the exercise of political power and with the conditions for maintaining and extending it. By the next century power talk ceased to be the monopoly of political theorists. Power became a concern shared with other theoretical forms, most notably in the natural sciences, and in the eighteenth century with political economy. By then the preoccupation of theorists had shifted from the acquisition of power to its production. The growth of modern science, the organization of it around technological applications, the phenomenal expansion of economic production, the development of ever more destructive weaponry, and the growing penetration by Western nations of the non-Western world all meant that powers of unprecedented magnitudes were reshaping the world, uprooting traditional social and political forms, and reconstituting nature.

Add to this list the enormous force potentially present in mass populations that had been aroused by revolutionary events (1776, 1789, 1848) and kept in motion by promises of material relief, the gradual extension of political and civil rights, the agitative activities of political parties, and even the halting efforts to organize workers—and the result is a kinetic society, a sociogram of forces of unprecedented weight and extent, actual and latent, thrusting ceaselessly, colliding and absorbing, but always transforming and being transformed. The exercise of power was no longer primarily associated with ruling. Instead, commentators noted how its diverse forms were reshaping the social world by altering the most intimate conditions of daily life. By comparison Machiavelli's pokings into the cruelties and vices of princes and into the mechanics of conspiratorial plotting seemed narrow and antiquated.

By the nineteenth century theorists were confronting a world of diverse powers and dominations, which humankind alone had brought into existence but no one had legislated. There were concentrated powers, like those of emergent industrial capitalism and the centralizing nation-state; diffused powers, such as those represented by small entrepreneurs, local notables, and an unorganized citizenry; and mysterious powers, which came into existence when large masses of people were aroused by appeals to liberty, patriotism, and nationalism.[4] Writers of a liberal persuasion had taken the lead in encouraging scientific, technological, and progressive political change. Initially they welcomed what seemed to be the benevolent direction of these great powers and defined the political task as one of replacing inherited practices with progressive values. Accordingly, liberals busied themselves with reform of the franchise and of parliamentary procedures, the abolition of slavery and of the poor-law system, the rationalization of administration, the establishment of a civil service based on the seemingly impartial principle of "merit," the strengthening of the "machinery" of justice and of local government, and the revision of taxation and tariff policies.[5] By midcentury liberals began gingerly to turn greater attention to issues of popular education, the condition of the working classes, social welfare, and the rights of women—that is, to inequities that appeared attributable more to the new society than to the old.

The recognition of a new class of problems coincided with a loss of confidence among liberals, as though they had suddenly come to doubt that a natural accord existed between the forces molding the age and the liberal view of the world. John Stuart Mill found consolation in the hope that a new era might be dawning in which "the progress of liberal opinions will again, as formerly, depend upon what is *said* and *written* and no longer upon what is *done.*"[6]

## II

Symptoms of liberal despair were but one manifestation of a common anxiety produced by a growing sense of helplessness amid a world bursting with new forces. A feeling that things might be getting out of control contributed to making avatars of many conservative writers. Some were driven toward racism, others to anti-Semitism, and many to virulent nationalisms. Helplessness was not, however, peculiar to those who looked backward. It affected even the futurists such as Saint-Simon and Comte who preached the urgent need for social "organization," authority, religion, and the revival of social hierarchy as necessary means for warding off social anarchy. Practically every major social and political theory of the nineteenth century, from anarchism to organizationalism, from liberalism to socialism, was tinged by the desperate knowledge that Western societies were being pushed, shaped, and compelled in ways that both fascinated and appalled.

The advocacy of violence by some revolutionaries expressed a kind of last gamble—that by shaking the vital center of society and grabbing its levers of control human beings could regain a hold on their destinies. While the putschist dreams of a Babeuf, Buonarotti, or Nechayev were marginal phenomena, there was an apprehensiveness broadly shared by radicals (such as Marx and Proudhon), conservatives, and liberals that an unplanned connection was being forged between bourgeoning power and irreversibility that would eventually spell an end to heroic, much less demiurgic, action. A future, whether in the form of Marx's communist society or Mill's representative government, was envisioned that required the detailed work of administrative clerks and faceless experts rather than political heroes.[7]

Historically, modern conceptions of theory were present at the creation of modern power, and in crucial respects modern power was the creature of modern theory. What, other than its sheer quantity, was modern about modern power and what was theory's role in its development?

## III

> *The bourgeoisie during its rule of scarce one hundred years has created more massive and more colossal productive forces than have all preceding generations together. Subjection of nature's forces to man, machinery, application of chemistry to industry and agriculture, steam navigation, railways, electric telegraphs, clearing of whole continents for cultivation, canalization of rivers, whole populations conjured out of the ground. . . . Modern bourgeois society . . . is like the sorcerer who is unable to control the powers of the nether world whom he has called up by his spells.*
>
> Karl Marx and Friedrich Engels[8]

This lyrical tribute to the sheer modernness of modern power was composed by the men who dedicated their lives to overthrowing that system or, more precisely, to dislodging the class in control in preparation for the full realization of the system's productive potential. Possibly no one before or since has equaled Marx's theoretical mastery of that system. His theory has largely set the terms for understanding how "such gigantic means of production and of exchange" had come into being and with what social, political, and economic consequences. Terms such as class struggle, social labor, concentration of production and ownership, the world system of production and markets, and the exploitation of the working class have all become established elements in the modern grammar of power, even among some who have rejected or sharply modified Marx's analysis.

The reason for this is not that the modern understanding of power is Marxist but rather that Marx's theory, as he himself recognized, both paralleled and intersected with the orthodox or hegemonic understanding of power as represented by classical economics and modern liberal political theories. Although he contested what he perceived as the ideological and ahistorical biases in the liberal conception of modern power, he not only shared but expanded its major assumptions: that economic forces were primary, that political life was secondary to the central problem of organizing the productive powers of society, that a rational society would see to it that politics was gradually displaced by public administration, and that technical education was emblematic of the cultural needs of a modern society.[9]

The reason why Marx's ideas are mentioned in a study of Tocqueville is that, like the classical economists he criticized, Marx centered the meaning of modernity around power: how it is generated by the exploitation and processing of the natural world and by the organization of human labor, and by what rules it is socially acquired and distributed. This way of inquiring into power has become so widely shared as to seem axiomatic. But, by and large, it was not Tocqueville's mode of understanding.

Although, like Marx, Tocqueville was convinced about the revolutionary nature of modern power, about the crucial importance of grasping it through historical categories, and, above all, about revolution as the defining experience of modernity, he differed sharply about the meaning, even about the location and form, of revolution and hence about the promise of modernity. Marx is customarily cast as the antithesis to modern liberalism, yet his ideas were as much an extension of liberalism as an attempt to remedy certain of its deficiencies, such as the subordination of science and technology to the dictates of the market and of moral and aesthetic values to money. The sharper his criticism of capitalism, the more it exposed a core of Enlightenment values that he shared with liberalism: the primacy of science, equality, progress, popular education, rationality, freedom, and humanity. The main difference was that Marx retained the revolutionary impulses that liberal capitalism preferred to sublimate into a vision of unending material progress.

To say that Marx was obsessed by revolution would be an understatement. The two polarities of his theory, the bourgeoisie and the proletariat, were each symbolic of revolutionary force. The bourgeoisie symbolized not only a new form of power but also the demise of privilege. The bourgeoisie, Marx never tired of saying, was a revolutionary class, the dynamic embodiment of the form of power that was continuously changing society. "The bourgeoisie cannot exist," he declared, "without constantly revolutionizing the instruments of production, and thereby the relations of production, and with them the whole relations of society."[10]

Modern power was thus a blend of three revolutionizing powers: science, technology, and capital; this distinctive composite was seemingly inexhaustible in its capability for change, protean in its forms, without inherent limits in its reach. The political task, in Marx's eyes, was to separate that form of power from the contemporary limitations represented by capitalist rule. The instrument was to be the proletariat, whose exploitation lent moral justification to its revolutionary role; whose oppression would produce the rage necessary to powering a revolutionary movement; and whose system-dependent, but power-creating, labor provides material reassurance that the secrets of power will be perpetuated and the continuities respected as in a dynastic succession. Thus the paradox: revolution is pitted against revolution, a titanic struggle between two world-changing, world-destroying powers.

That paradox was revealing because it uncovers a suppressed category in the constitution of modern power. As is well known, Marx believed that a revolution could only occur when capitalism experienced a profound "crisis."

Although Marx offered several theoretical explanations as to why such a crisis was inevitable, ranging from overproduction and underconsumption to falling rates of profit, my concern is not with the formal explanations but with their rhetoric and with the forgotten images they evoke. Crisis was equivalent to chaos, a "process of dissolution . . . within the whole range of old society." As Marx proceeds to describe that condition, he archetypically reintroduces early modern theory's favorite allegory of the state of nature. However, he historicizes it by treating it as the apocalypse of modern power rather than, as we shall see shortly, its genesis: "Society suddenly finds itself put back into a state of momentary barbarism; it appears as if a famine, a universal war of devastation had cut off the supply of every means of subsistence; industry and commerce seem to be destroyed; and why? Because there is too much civilization, too much industry, too much commerce. The productive forces . . . have become too powerful."[11] Marx's account only lacked a footnote to complete the historical circuit initiated by Hobbes's description of a condition where there was "no place for Industry . . . no culture of the Earth . . . And the life of man solitary, poore, nasty, brutish, and short."[12]

Marx's notion of crisis and catastrophe was, like the seventeenth-century notion of a state of nature, a rendition of experience into myth. It embodied the modern fascination with an identity that is fashioned only after a terrible experience in which mankind is driven to the edge of an abyss. Preserved in the myth is the trauma of a disastrous encounter with power. The state of nature in early modern thought depicts the consequences of arbitrary political power; crisis is attributed to the forms in which the political has been constituted. In contrast, the nineteenth-century version of the state of nature is located in a socioeconomic system subject to periodic disorders of unemployment, hunger, and poverty. In both cases mankind, having been chastened by the descent into darkness, emerges with a new wisdom, a new self-knowledge, about power veering out of control because men had not understood how it must be organized. The later solution was not to establish a settled framework, like a social contract or written constitution. As modernity proceeded, that framework was conceived less as an end in itself than as a necessary condition for a more extensive "order of things," to use Marx's phrase. What was beginning to be envisaged was a system for exploiting the power potentialities of modern science and industry, a system that held a promise of the continuous reproduction of power. Just as the early modern problem had been the unpredictability accompanying arbitrary rule, the problem of nineteenth- and twentieth-century capitalism was primarily associated with the unpredictable irruption of economic crises. The modern project was not to renounce the commitment to increasing power but to find a saving formula whereby it could be rendered ever more predictable, ever more obedient.

## IV

In the Homeric epics of classical antiquity the power of the gods was associated with the unpredictability of its exercise. The gods, the Greeks always said, used their powers in ways that defied human understanding. Their ways were capricious, devious, and artful precisely because they were not omnipotent. The Hebraic god, in contrast, displayed the unpredictability of a Greek god, but as the creator of the world, He had chosen to embody his omnipotence as order and so had separated day and night, water and land, man and beasts.

Early modern conceptions of constitutionalism—doubly derived from Hebraic notions of a covenant that had defined relationships of an omnipotent deity with a chosen people and from mediaeval notions about law and governance—emphasized the importance of setting limits to the exercise of power. In contrast, the modern constitution of power, as Bacon would insist, was designed for "increase." The success of the system of modern power, like the conception of a political constitution embodied in social contract thinking, depended upon certain conditions. But where contract theory was mostly concerned to find a formula for limiting political power and thereby reassuring the citizenry and insuring their obedience, the system of modern power wanted more than mere compliance or consent from its "citizens." It aimed, first, to enlist their skills and their energy, then, second, to adapt them to the new enterprise of developing power, not constraining it. The lure was the promise of continuous material improvement in the lives of everyone.

This vision of power was unique to modernity, enabling it, as Marx saw, to generate more power, more consistently, than any previous age. The explanation, according to Marx, lay in the development of "material forces of production." From this everything else followed. There were, however, other contributory considerations. One was the role of culture in the creation of the new system of power. The other concerned the constitutive force of theory, the means by which modernity came to constitute its peculiar conception of power and without which modernity, and Marx himself, would be incomprehensible.

## V

*For that gigantean state of mind which possesses the troublers of the world (such as was Lucius Sylla, and infinite others in smaller model, who are bent on having all men happy or unhappy as they are their friends or enemies, and would shape the world according to their own humours, which is the true Theomachy), this I say aspires to the active good of the individual . . . though it recedes furthest of all from the good of society.*

Francis Bacon[13]

Theory is, uniquely, modernity's way of constituting power; conversely, modern power has, uniquely, a theoretical constitution. For more than three centuries Western societies have invested material and intellectual resources in the cultivation of a certain kind of theoretical knowledge, knowledge that contains "explanatory power." It stands for the understanding or reasons why something is the case for a certain class of phenomena, which can then be applied to control, modify, make use of the world in order to achieve some human purpose. In contrast, the miracle for which Plato longed, a truth-loving ruler who would use his absolute power to reform society according to the true philosophy, was a confession of theoretical truth's own powerlessness. The preponderant opinion throughout antiquity conceived power primarily as action and registered prosaically in the facts of conquest or domination. It was believed that while the acquisition of power might be gained through "arts," such as rhetoric, the effective exercise of power was acquired from experience and depended on outstanding personal qualities such as "virtue" or "foresight." It was never conceived as something that could be generated continuously. Polybius thought that the Roman constitution had amassed more power than any previous political system and he attributed it to an artful arrangement that counterbalanced the tensions between social classes and their institutional representatives. Yet, according to Polybius, even Roman power depended on a highly contingent factor of threats from abroad that caused the rival classes temporarily to lay aside their animosities and unite their strength.[14]

Modern power, in contrast, was conceived theoretically—that is, its structure and attributes reflected materially the structure and attributes of theoretical knowledge as understood by the new theoretical consciousness represented in early modern physics, astronomy, and mathematics. Among the most important of these attributes that were written into modern conceptions of power were, first, unlimited power, unlimited because the knowledge that made power reproducible had selected nature as its object and conceived it to be a field of inexhaustible forces; and because nature was the creation of an omnipotent, omniscient, and immortal god, the forces were conceived to be, at one and the same time, lawlike in operation and inexhaustible, and hence knowledge of the laws of nature represented the possibility of tapping into the source of endless power. A second attribute involved abstract relationships and entities—for example, friction and gravity that could be conceived independently of local conditions or circumstances. A third and closely related attribute might be described, if clumsily, as "dehistoricization." Bacon, Hobbes, and Descartes associated the new theoretical sensibility with skill in handling ahistorical abstractions and attributed resistance to the practical applications of abstract reasoning to the prejudices engrained in habits and traditions.

Abstraction and dehistoricization conjoined to clear the way for a form of knowledge that could freely construct its objects and their relationships. Perhaps the greatest expression of these tendencies was that famous creation of modern theory, the free and equal individual. The modern individual did not become equal because of modern theory but he was first conceived as equal under its auspices. To be created he had to be conceived as other natural objects were: without regard to individual differences. Just as plants, animals, and minerals were said to have "primary" qualities that were displayed throughout the species and were to be the main signs of identity while "secondary" qualities peculiar to this or that specimen were set aside, so the signs of class, religious belief, local origin, and family could be held in abeyance and treated as secondary while the "nature" of the individual was accented along with the rights that belonged to each equally as part of his or her primary endowments.[15]

## VI

> *These times are the ancient times, when the world is ancient, and not those which we account ancient, ordine retrogrado, by a computation backwards from ourselves.*
>
> Francis Bacon[16]

The new ways of theorizing power were the achievement of a new theoretical consciousness. That consciousness was itself an artifact of theory, the self-conscious creation of several notable philosophers and scientists and of a few who, while notable, are better characterized as "the political theorists of modern power."

The idea of theory is older than modern science. A plausible genealogy can be constructed for it that extends at least as far back as ancient Greece and, if one were to describe theory more broadly as synoptic knowledge, even further. This is worth recalling because those who helped to create the modern theoretical consciousness believed that the condition of its emergence was the elimination of prior traditions of theory. A distinctively modern revolutionary tradition was forged in which destructiveness and innovation were inseparable, the one the necessary condition of the other.

The crux of that revolution was a rupture with the past, not simply as an incidental by-product but as a deliberate strategy aimed at the past as such. "Since something new is to be put in hand," Bacon claimed, "the safest oracle for the future lies in the rejection of the past."[17] A determinate past could then be replaced by an indeterminate future. The future stood for possibilities to be realized if progress was left unobstructed. Progress itself was the emblem for a form of power that required society to be in a state of permanent revolution, according to Hobbes: "So that in the first place, I put for a generall inclination of all mankind, a perpetuall and restlesse desire of Power after power, that ceaseth onely in Death. And the cause of this is . . . because [man] cannot assure the power and means to live well, which he hath present, without the acquisition of more."[18]

Later historians, after a vain attempt at ordering the new forms of power into a "first industrial revolution," then a "second," eventually gave up on enumerations and substituted names such as "steam," "electricity," "atomic energy," "electronic."

## VII

> *But it may be that most of the . . . [democratic societies' attempts at self-reassurance] could be told as the history of reformist politics, without much reference to the theoretical backup which philosophers have provided for such politics.*
>
> Richard Rorty[19]

Among the intellectual founders of modernity were Bacon, Descartes, and Hobbes, three philosophers whose lives spanned almost the entire seventeenth century. Their writings stated the conditions, prefigured the forms, furnished the ideology of modern power, and traced its major elements of individualism, egalitarianism, bureaucratic statism, and science-technologism. The missing ingredient of capitalism, or industrialism, would come later, but in Hobbes there were unmistakable intimations and in the others a strong presentiment of the practical applications of scientific knowledge such as to make the bent of their thought consistent with later capitalist practices and ideology.[20]

Understanding the modernity of these writers is an important preliminary to a crucial, though neglected, perspective that Tocqueville adopted. As we have noted, he claimed that, although Americans were philosophical innocents, they were natural Cartesians. Bacon, Descartes, and Hobbes each developed the identity of modern theory through a sharp contrast between what they considered to be true theoretical knowledge and what they represented as the ancient ideal of theory in the philosophies of Plato, Aristotle, and the mediaeval schoolmen.[21] This focus has misled later interpreters into treating the controversy as a dispute either between competing philosophical systems or between the champions of early modern science and the defenders of classical literature. Although these descriptions are not wrong, they tend to soften the radicalism of the moderns: they were bent on a cultural revolution or, more accurately, they focused on utilizing cultural forms and values as the means of promoting a revolution aimed not at justice or freedom or salvation but at a revolution in power made possible by truth but accomplished by the authority of the state.[22] Their project offered the first modern example of revolution long before the eighteenth-century political outbreaks in America and France.

The theorists of modern power were aware that the promises of modernity could not be delivered without causing great social disruption in human habits, skills, and beliefs. Yet they did not set out to cause political instability, much less social disruption. All of them were, theoretically, champions of political and social order who were self-consciously radical. Bacon had sensed the dilemma and protested the imputation that "to think or speculate out of the common way" was necessarily the mark of "a turbulent person and an innovator." Like the lord chancellor he had been, he proposed to settle the controversy by a distinction:

> But surely there is a great distinction between matters of state and the practical arts; for the danger from new motion and from new light is not the same. In matters of state a change even for the better is distrusted, because it unsettles what is established, these things resting on authority, consent, fame, and opinion, not on demonstration. But arts and sciences should be like mines, where the noise of new works and further advances is heard on every side.[23]

Although the modernizers launched their attack on a broad front, at the heart of their campaign was the allegation that ancient theoretical knowledge was practically useless. As Bacon remarked cuttingly, the ancient philosophers, like prepubescent youths, could talk but not generate.[24] "Truth" and "utility," Bacon insisted, are "the very same things."[25] Unless theory could promote the "commodity" or well-being of human life, Hobbes declared, it was "not worth so much pains as the study of [it] requires. . . . The scope of all speculation is the performing of some action, or thing to be done."[26] Two centuries later Tocqueville would be struck by how profoundly American culture had been shaped by that conception of knowledge: "In America the purely practical part of the sciences is cultivated to an admirable degree and the concern is with the theoretical side immediately necessary to application."[27]

A theory that could not be translated into practical works was adjudged incoherent according to modernity's new standard for mental activity. It was dismissed, not simply for its theoretical flaws but as "a waste of time," a notion that would have seemed incoherent to an antiquity that had associated theorizing with leisure. While virtually all ancient and mediaeval philosophers attributed a kind of power to truth, they did not mean a power to change man's relation to the natural world, much less a power to change the world itself. More often than not, they meant by truth a power that could change man's understanding of the true structure of the world and enable him to establish the right orientation toward an order of things that was believed to be the creation of divine or superior powers. Truth had to do with deference: with harmony, proportion, hierarchy, and proper place, not with efficacy. True power was represented by the orderliness of the natural world and the heavens: which was why Aristotle had said that philosophy begins in wonder that things are as they are.

Modern theory opened the route to a different conception of truth/power, a route that made truth a function of its organization and only secondarily a consequence of its correspondence to the structure of the world. "[I]n things artificial," Bacon declared, "Nature takes orders from Man."[28] All three of our theorists of power believed that the basic cause of the impotence of theory among the ancients was the lack of rigorous methods of investigation. Men spout absurdities, according to Hobbes, for "want of a clear and exact method."[29]

While they differed among themselves about the true conception of scientific method, the moderns banked their hopes about science and human power on the effective organization of scientific inquiry. All three authors wrote extensively, almost obsessively, about the rules of method that should constrain the mind to pursue the truth step by step, thus conserving intellectual labor while preventing the mind from "wandering into error," to use Descartes's phrase. Those who follow the scientific way, according to Hobbes, "proceed from most low and humble principles, evident even to the meanest capacity; going on slowly, and with most scrupulous ratiocination, viz., from the imposition of names they infer the truth of their first propositions; and from two of the first, a third . . . and so on, according to the steps of science."[30] The organization of thinking was intended to rivet truth to its practices.

Equally far-reaching, the concept of organization signified enclosure, surrounding inquiry within a comprehensive, all-embracing structure and subordinating it to an overall strategy. Although the development tended to be ignored by later philosophers concerned with the logic of discovery rather than its politics, it would transform inquiry from free speculation by a single investigator into a matter of coordinating, organizing, subsidizing, and dividing the labor of several. In Bacon's remarkable vision:

> [C]onsider what might be expected . . . from men abounding in leisure, and from association of labors, and from succession of ages: the rather because it is not a way over which only one man can pass at a time, as is the case with that of reasoning, but one in which the labours and industries of men especially as regards the collecting of experience may with the best effect be first distributed and then combined. For then only will men begin to know their strength, when instead of great numbers doing all the same things, one shall take charge of one thing and another of another.[31]

Paralleling the organization of inquiry was the political or, better, the administrative organization of science as a state function. What was needed, Bacon argued, was "an administration of knowledge in some such order and policy as the king of Spain in regard of his great dominions useth in State." This would mean centralized supervision of particular branches of research in "one council of State or last resort that receiveth the advertisements and certificates from all the rest."[32]

Like Aristotle, who had managed to persuade Alexander the Great to take time off from conquering the world in order to collect new specimens of flora and fauna from the East, Bacon, Hobbes, and Descartes grasped the importance of systematic organization to scientific progress and each pressed the rulers of his day to promote the cause of science. Each contended that, for its advancement, the new knowledge required the support of the new superpower just beginning to be tapped: the state and its treasury.

Bacon's famous aphorism, "knowledge is power," is typically quoted without reference to its context, which was that of state power. This was more evident in the alternative formula, which Bacon made while attempting to win royal favor for his project. There he referred to "the twin Designs" whereby "Knowledge and Power" would "meet." That conjunction seemed natural to the modern theorist, not just a matter of expediency or special pleading. For the project signified a premeditated union of two universals: the state, which in the modern conception existed to promote the common well-being of the whole society, and scientific knowledge, whose truths are universal and, equally, for the benefit of all. Bacon synthesized these notions in the phrase "the administration and governance of learning."[33]

The link with the state would soon be in place and by the eighteenth century the presence of "science policy" was widely recognized as the differentiating mark of the modern state. But it also signified the complete bureaucratization of one element of modern power, scientific research.[34] Now, with the role of the state accepted as necessary to the promotion of science, three tiers of organization enveloped the pursuit of truth: method, research conceived as a division of labor requiring administration coordination, and overall state control and direction.

## VIII

The concept of organization was modernity's version of the political and the means by which the political, in the form of science policy, was extended over nature. Both conceptions—organization as political and nature as the object of a political science—were revolutionary representations signifying the overthrow of established conceptions of order, one social and political, the other natural and theological. The campaign "to command nature in action" has become so deeply engrained in modernizing societies that it is difficult to grasp the revolutionary implications in Bacon's original injunction to treat nature not as "free and at large" but "under constraint and vexed; that is to say, when by art and the hand of man she is forced out of her natural state and squeezed and moulded."[35]

The concept of an organizational "revolution" might seem overdramatic. Unlike the civil wars of seventeenth-century England or the revolutions in America and France in the eighteenth century, it seems a quiet revolution without an object to overturn, no *infâme* to crush. I want to suggest the contrary, that the development of the idea of organization and its correlates of administration and bureaucracy was the theoretical overture that prepared the way to later insurrections. In its efforts to dominate nature, modern power kept encountering history in the form of traditional authorities, such as popes, universities, aristocrats, and judges. The symbolic representation of this moment was the famous rivalry between Bacon and Edward Coke: the one an arch-modernizer, champion of science and of an executive-centered state; the other, a critical reactionary, the champion of the "ancient" common law and of parliamentary rights. The idea that a new set of human relationships could be inserted wholesale into an ongoing society was understood to mean that what had existed theretofore would be expelled or dissolved. For in prescientific societies institutions were, so to speak, their history, and their history was a crucial element of their legitimacy. To break their hold, history, both sacred and profane, had to be discredited.

When the historical order was assaulted by religious dissenters, parliamentary politicians, and the middle and lower social orders, the theorists of modern power were quick to seize upon the moment of anarchy and to invent the state of "nature," thus assimilating society to nature and thereby legitimating in that domain the same unimpeded impulse to dominate and reshape. The symbolic moment, when modernity disentangled from tradition, was represented in Hobbes's response to civil war and revolution in his homeland. He had first sided with the traditional order associated with the royalists; when they were defeated, he fled with them into exile and served as tutor to the hereditary and rightful future king, Charles II. But when it seemed that the Protectorate of Cromwell, an unprecedented, despotic regime, was taking hold at home and that a new society might be in the making, Hobbes decided, as he put it, "to come ashore." In 1651 he published *Leviathan* where he set down the theoretical conditions for maximizing modern power in a revolutionary situation where hereditary and sacred authority had been overthrown and men were reduced to a state of nature. Accordingly, in *Leviathan* Hobbes wrote the prescription for legitimating any type of regime.

The powerful hold exerted on the theoretical imagination by the idea of the state of nature was attributable hardly at all to the allure of an aboriginal condition and only partly to the fears arising from the actual experience with revolutionary disorders. Rather it was the idea of a thought experiment in imitation of the biblical story of the Creation, an imagined revolution in which existing institutions were abolished as a preliminary to the total reconstruction of society and the political order.[36] The theoretical mind did not blanch from a prospect in which history was suspended and replaced by a moment of total reorganization. Theorists found it more congenial to waive risks and to conceive/construct a wholly new order than to contemplate a prospect where all seemed determined by what had gone before. Stated differently, the state of nature was the preliminary, hit upon in order to reconstitute the terms under which modern power could be liberated and modern man made secure. Accordingly, natural law and natural right were introduced not to reduce power in general but to check a certain kind of power, "arbitrary power" in Locke's phrase. Arbitrary power left men uncertain, anxious, vulnerable, and hence unable to concentrate upon the satisfaction of their desires by the cultivation of their powers. Unpredictable power (e.g., the royal prerogative) thrived on uncertainty (e.g., "emergency power") and had to be tamed, not destroyed, and made lawful by adhering to a certain prescribed course analogous to the "laws" followed by the powers of nature.[37]

The solution was to systematize power but without necessarily reducing it. Locke called the system "umpirage." Power would be made to conform to three essentials of the rule of law: a "settled, known Law," "a known and indifferent Judge," and an executive who would faithfully enforce the laws.[38]

The complex political and theoretical role still to be played out by the symbols of "history" and "nature" had been intimated in a phrase of Locke's when, in describing the nature of property and the value that labor creates in working the land, he remarked that "in the beginning all the World was America, and more so than that is now; for no such thing as Money was any where known."[39] America would serve as the setting for a new civilization that was all nature and little history and so the perfect site for an experiment in the democratization of modern power and its potential for making money "known"—and all of this in accordance with the laws of nature.

## IX

> *They say miracles are past; and we have our philosophical persons, to make modern and familiar things supernatural and causeless. Hence it is that we make trifles of terrors; ensconcing ourselves into seeming knowledge, when we should submit ourselves to an unknown fear.*
>
> Shakespeare[40]

Because the incorporation of science into the structure of state power represented a novel departure—for prior to the seventeenth century there had been little consistent state support for science—its revolutionary aspects were not immediately evident. The situation was far different in cultural matters. For the scientific reformers realized that at stake was not simply a question of whether, say, Galileo's theory was true, but rather the kinds of beliefs, values, and knowledge that were needed to sustain scientific pursuits on a permanent basis. The stakes were about what would later be called cultural reproduction—that is, continuously producing mind-sets, beliefs, and skills that would insure the perpetuation of scientific inquiry while supporting the purposes for which scientific knowledge was used.

Here the problem was not at all comparable with occupying a vacuum. All of the reformers insisted on the importance of instituting a new culture, a "grand instauration," radically different from the one traditionally transmitted in schools and universities.[41] Contemporary education, Bacon complained, taught "learning" rather than "knowledge." Classical philosophy, literature, and mediaeval scholasticism dominated the curriculum, while what little science was being taught was mostly erroneous, being primarily based on Aristotelian physics or Ptolemaic astronomy.

The problem with the learning represented by this curriculum was its allegedly static character: its truths were fixed and so later generations were condemned to repetition and to devising ever more ingenious commentaries rather than new knowledge. The stability or fixity of truth, which the ancient philosophers and mediaeval theologians had revered as its most important attribute, was the complement to the ideal of a motionless society. To a modern like Hobbes, nurtured on Galilean physics and enthralled by the metaphor of life as matter-in-motion, the ancient ideal of a static *summum bonum* seemed repellant. "Felicity," he declared defiantly, "is a continuall progresse of the desire, from one object to another; the attaining of the former, being still but the way to the later."[42] Modernity would be about human energy, about frustrated mobility ("motion is the continual privation of one place and acquisition of another"), and about negotiating bargains that would set minimal social constraints on entrepreneurial energies.[43]

Although all three (and especially Bacon and his secretary Hobbes) tried to influence political authorities to support scientific instruction and research by representing it as a mighty engine for producing wealth and increasing national power, their conception of culture was, at one level, antipolitical, at another, a political tactic: the first reflected their antipathy toward the participatory culture broadly represented by the Protestant conception of an actively involved church membership and most emphatically by the notions of churches as voluntary associations; the second was designed to avoid the accusation of being social incendiaries.

Theorists of modern power rejected the classical notion of culture as shared and publicly accessible, a preparation for participation in the polity, and hence inseparable from civic life.[44] Bacon, Hobbes, and Descartes were hostile to the participatory ideal; in their eyes loyalty and obedience were the sum of civic virtues. Modern power emerges in renunciation of a civic culture while encouraging a technocratic culture of service to the state, *une noblesse des polytechniciennes.* A technocratic culture subtly incorporates an element of a Protestant conscience that produces its own version of ambivalent loyalties. One commitment is to specialized knowledge, which is, at the same time, the modern self's version of its public identity; the other, a more attenuated political calculation, like the political obedience once grudgingly extended by Protestant believers to any political authorities other than their own. Bacon begins one of his works, "Believing I was born for the service of mankind," and that "I was fitted for nothing so well as for the study of Truth"; he nevertheless decided that because "a man's own country has some special claims" and because a high position in the state would give him "a larger command of industry and ability to help me in my work," it was essential that he "acquire the arts of civil life."[45]

The cultural revolution in the name of modern science was a revolution by elites, modernizing elites as they would later be called, who, while extending some of the benefits of power to the many, would retain control of the revolution by developing a discourse that was at once open and incomprehensible to laymen.[46] "The new philosophy," according to Bacon, ". . . does not sink to the capacity of the vulgar except in so far as it benefits them by its works."[47] This revolution was not intended, as Luther's had originally been, to make everyman a priest.

## X

The eventual defeat of the English revolutionaries after the civil wars of the first half of the seventeenth century symbolized the failure to establish a modern political culture. Cromwell's crushing of parliamentary power and of left-wing democratic movements destroyed an embryonic participatory culture so that when, toward the end of the century, John Locke set out a theory of modern power centered on a representative legislature and juxtaposed to it a strong executive, the effect was less to produce a participatory culture than a formula for a culture of legitimation. The social contract, with its central notion of a bargained agreement as the basis of political society, authority, and membership, was not intended as the foundation for a civic culture but as its substitute. It stipulated initial conditions and proposed a structure of complicity rather than of involvements.[48] The ghost of a participatory culture was preserved in Locke's justification of revolution, which was meant not as a threat to modern power but an indication of its political limits—but only of its political, not of its economic, technological, or intellectual limits.

The issue that was slowly gaining focus was whether human beings would be viewed as political beings who needed to be educated to care for common things as a principal concern in their lives or whether they were to be shaped to the specifications of modern power, as workers, employees, administered beings, and occasional citizens. Hobbes had outlined the contours of modern dependency: "The Value or Worth of a man is, as of all other things, his Price; that is to say, so much as would be given for the use of his Power; and therefore is not absolute; but a thing dependent on the need and judgment of another."[49]

Hobbes and Locke were crucial figures in the political theory of modernity and of its unique forms of power. Both tried to furnish a political form in which representation would be the key element. Hobbes called his absolute ruler "the sovereign representative," while Locke located sovereignty with a "supreme legislative" power which, in part, would be chosen by elections. Both writers tried to answer the question, What is representation supposed to represent? Their answers revealed the beginnings of the political dilemma posed by modern power. On the one hand, representation should reflect "real" social and economic powers in the society at large, which both writers understood in terms of class and social status.[50] On the other hand, both also endorsed the idea of equality of rights, although it is less clear how far each wanted to push that principle. The first or mirror principle was like the concept of representation itself, a legacy of the mediaeval notion of socially "weighted" representation of the "estates of the realm." But the trouble was that that principle would be rendered anachronistic by the forms of power about to be generated by modern science and technology.

Modernity was thus on the verge of introducing regressive institutions that could not represent politically the enormous magnitudes and types of power uniquely modern. The representation of power would take the form of "interests" and this would mean a certain distortion of modern power. The latter had to be fitted to what would later be called "interest politics." While the concept of "interests" was a rough way of updating the mediaeval idea of weighted representation, the interest principle would be continually dogged by modern principles of equality. Bentham's formula, "each man shall count for one," threatened to overwhelm weighted representation by demotic subjectivity, although James Mill would clumsily attempt to reinstate social weightiness by proposing forty-year-old middle-class males as the natural representatives of lower social classes, women, and children.[51]

The contradiction between equality and representation of inequalities was never worked out theoretically, but its practical political consequences were profound. Legislatures, which were assumed to be the natural center of representation, were gradually transformed by the growth of universal manhood suffrage, especially during the nineteenth century, so that it seemed to the male members of the middle and upper classes that equality would predominate through sheer numbers, thus endangering property and order and, most important, the rational basis of modern power grounded in expertise and technical knowledge.

In order to offset numbers, various techniques were introduced, including the rationalization of democratic subjectivity through the organization of electorates by political parties, the invention of organized interest groups to offset democratic will-formation in the legislature and the incorporation of those groups into the political process, control of "mass communications," and various techniques for refining bribery. But these had a profoundly irrational effect on politics. Diversity of interests as well as divergencies among the dominant social groups produced a cacophony of objectives that left governments bewildered. Politics appeared as the unending conflict between legitimate interests, mitigated only by shallow compromises, and sustained primarily by the fear that the irrational masses might brush aside the mediating devices and invade the political domain. Desperate for an instrumentality that would secure rationality and objectivity in politics, modern power holders turned from the more representative legislatures to the less representative executives and administrators, to the political forms that had survived the early modern monarchs who had invented them. It was not fortuitous that the expansion of the electorate during the nineteenth century was paralleled by the reform and rationalization of the civil service. In Hegel's view, modern power had to appeal from civil society to state bureaucracy in order to find the rationality congenial to its own nature. The tensions between the irrationality/egalitarianism of politics and the rationality/elitism of administration was never resolved. The rationality that had been the hallmark of the modern conception of power remained frustrated. The consequence would become evident only by the middle of the nineteenth century: modernity was politically unable to control its own powers.

How had this come about? How had the theorists of modern power conceived the political world so as to make it appear as an irrational threat to rational power?

## XI

> *On waxen tablets you cannot write anything new until you rub out the old. With the mind it is not so; there you cannot rub out the old till you have written in the new.*
>
> Francis Bacon[52]

If the new theoretical knowledge was, as its exponents claimed, universally applicable, then there seemed no inherent reason why politics and government should be exempt from rational principles. Descartes's observations on politics were particularly revealing of the temptations that plagued the moderns. Existing political societies, which at the time were predominantly traditional in character, were classified by Descartes as a species of imperfect works, necessarily irrational because shaped by many hands over time rather than executed by a single designer following a single design. Descartes praised a work, like the Spartan constitution, as rationally coherent because, in contrast to custom-bound societies, "one individual alone worked" on it and, as a result, could shape all arrangements "toward the same end." Descartes hastily added that it would be implausible "for any private individual to reform a state by altering everything" just as it would be to reform "the whole body of the Sciences, or the order of teaching established by the Schools." Which, of course, was exactly what Descartes attempted to promote—all of this to the accompaniment of repeated, perhaps even sincere disclaimers of any ulterior political designs.[53] Foreshadowed in Descartes' juxtaposition of the antihistorical to the historical, the rational to the traditional, were the terms that Tocqueville would invoke when confronting the antihistorical and abstract ideology of the revolutionaries of 1789 with the logic of ambiguities of a traditional society. In a similar vein, when Tocqueville defended the United States as an example of a stable democracy, he explained that it owed less to its formal constitution—and hence less to the Founding Fathers, the American Lycurgus—than to its *moeurs*, that is, to the habits, customs, manners, and inherited political and religious beliefs, to what could not be created by the fiat of abstract reason. America was a compromised modernity and because of that its experience might save the Old World from the uncompromised modernity represented by the revolutionaries of 1789 and by the Cartesian absolutism incarnate in Napoleon.

# CHAPTER II
# *THEORIA*: THE THEORETICAL JOURNEY

## I

> *I think that my taste for traveling grows by privation. I long to expand the horizon, to see new countries, new peoples, and new customs.*
>
> Tocqueville[1]

Alexis de Tocqueville made his political and theoretical mark in the world as the result of a voyage to America. Modern scholars have carefully traced every stage of his American journey and others have reconstructed in detail the evolution of the manuscript of Tocqueville's classic. Little if any attention, however, has been given to what might be called the theoretical aura surrounding his journey.

That a theory should have resulted from a journey to a foreign land placed Tocqueville's quest in a certain traditional genre of political discovery. Political theorists have always been great journeyers, as often to imaginary as to real places. The word "theory" comes from the Greek *theoria*, and the verb *theorein* (to see, observe). *Theoria* also had some associated meanings that suggested a variety of modes of seeing: journey, spectacle (e.g., a public festival), and even a diplomatic embassy.[2] Some of these implications were captured in a remark by the Jewish philosopher Philo Judaeus, writing in the first half of the first century C.E. He noted that men might journey for different reasons: some for profit, some "to see the sights of a foreign land," and others to benefit their countries.[3]

As early as the account of Atlantis in Plato's *Timaeus*, which, unlike the polities described in *Republic* and *Laws*, purported to be about a city that had once existed, theorists have constructed pictures of an ideal society, remote in space or time, removed from the material contingencies of "real" societies and of their historical vicissitudes. Tocqueville's journey, of course, differed from these imaginary accounts because he traveled to an "actual society." Before accepting that distinction as hard and fast, however, we should recall that "America" was only dimly understood. It had not been fully mapped geographically or completed politically. There was no professional political science to set the terms of understanding, and much about the new land appeared strange—its overpowering physical settings, its vast expanse of unoccupied land, its savage inhabitants, only some of whom were Indians—which may explain why no one before Tocqueville had considered America as a political subject worthy of theoretical contemplation.

Typically the *theoria* took the form of a story told by a traveler who has recently returned from a voyage to a distant and hitherto unknown land. Such travels should be considered not as "trips" but as an intimate part of the structure of a theory and so closely connected as to have the status of a metaphor for theorizing itself. A theoretical voyage imparts an element of action to theorizing that contrasts sharply with the equally ancient conception of *theoria* as contemplation, as the attempt of thought to imitate the unmoved mover god of Aristotle.[4] Typically the voyager describes the people of that place as happy, peaceful, economically self-sufficient, and virtuous because of their exemplary institutions and beliefs. His "description" serves a triple purpose of explanation, criticism, and prescription. He shows the causes that have produced the ideal condition and he identifies the principles (e.g., abolition of private property) behind those causes. The essence of utopias is that they should embody extractable principles, which can then be turned back upon the society from whence the journeyer has come: uncannily, virtually every feature of the discovered society, it is revealed, embodies a prescription or principle that can remedy the perceived ills of the traveler's homeland.

While journeying was employed as a metaphor for a special kind of knowledge that required both separation from "real" political life and contact with the ideal, it could also be a search for elements of the ideal that were actually incorporated in the life of some existing society other than the homeland of the traveler. The duality between the search for the ideal as such and the search for its actual embodiments was present in Plato. He compared his dialectical method to a journey in search of the ideal forms of truth, but in the *Laws* he made special provision for a *theoros* who would travel abroad and return with useful information about the political practices of other cities.[5]

Although this genre has a theoretical character, however, it does not present a formal philosophical argument. The ideal society is meant as the embodiment of a theory but the theory becomes, as it were, detachable from and eventually independent of the imagined society. Usually the traveler explains how various practices are representative of certain principles and how the several principles are interrelated. A unified theoretical structure emerges that can be restated independently of the imaginary setting that has served as a context of discovery. The persuasiveness of the theory does not require the defeat of rival arguments or empirical proof. Rather, the account turns on the skill of the traveler-theorist to depict a state of affairs that, though fanciful, nonetheless appeals to the experience of his readers—their beliefs, longings, fears, and grievances—so that they will not simply be charmed by his tale, or indulged in their fantasies, but conceive themselves living differently. Much depends on whether the theorist succeeds in preserving the line between theorizing and fantasizing while loosening the preconceived boundaries of reality and enlarging the possible.

## II

Use of the *theoria* allowed for an unqualified description of the "best society," one that would not have to make concessions to practicality and contingency. While this reason was undoubtedly a consideration for most, if not all, theorists in the construction of ideal states, it tends to place theories in a doctrinaire light and distracts attention from another feature that, ironically, bears a close resemblance to theory construction in the natural sciences, the supposed opposite of softheaded utopian speculation. Imaginary societies afforded an experimental field that served to unfetter the theoretical mind. The theorist could try out new practices or pursue the implications of a principle or, equally important, test the structure of existing society to "see" whether by omitting practices and beliefs that were regarded as "natural" or essential, the society would crumple. Ideal societies thus provided a means of testing both the limits of the actual and of the possible. Contrary to the common modern political judgment of "utopian" theories as ineffectual, some utopians actually succeed in one respect: they may have left the existing order intact but not unproblematical.

## III

> *[B]ut about stale travelers' wonders we were not curious. Scylla and greedy Celaenos and folk-devoring Laestrygones and similar frightful monsters are common enough, but well and wisely trained citizens are not everywhere to be found.*
>
> Thomas More[6]

Beginning early in the sixteenth century, the connection between theorizing and journeying acquired an additional dimension due to the voyages of discovery that brought Europeans into contact with vastly different cultures. The experience, or rather the reported experience, contributed to the unsettling of European assumptions about place, time, and the possible forms of human organization. As a result a quantum leap of the political imagination occurred. Mediaeval philosophers had no political utopias. Now, in contrast, Europeans could imagine themselves living differently, not necessarily by adopting exotic forms of life but by organizing in a consistent way the "rational" or "natural" possibilities immanent in their own societies.

The word "utopia" (literally "nowhere") was first coined by Thomas More to describe what he called "the best state of a commonwealth."[7] More represented his work as the account of a philosopher who has just returned from a voyage that, by the accident of shipwreck, had brought him to an ideal commonwealth on "the far side of the world." The Utopians live according to principles of Christian humanism and Plato's *Republic.* Their society is without private property or money; and education is the principal concern. By mingling "actual" characters and places with fictitious ones and combining direct criticism of certain social and political practices (e.g., private appropriation of the traditional commons) with descriptions of ideal institutions (prohibition of gold and silver as media of exchange), More was able to tease the received limits of plausibility and hence of possibility.

Another traveler's tale involving yet another shipwreck was contrived a century later by Francis Bacon. The *New Atlantis* revealed a different political imagination, one as far removed in tone and spirit from More's gentle Utopia as that happy land was from the Tudor England that in part More satirized. Despite the gesture toward Plato in the title of Bacon's work, it was not a story about saving cities or souls but an epitaph to the ancient endeavor to link virtue, knowledge, and power. For rule by philosophers Bacon substituted rule by scientists, and instead of the reign of justice and virtue he proposed the organization of research for the control of nature and the increase of human power. The *New Atlantis* was both a monument to the idea of mind-generated power and a constitution for that uniquely modern obsession.

## IV

By the late seventeenth century the type of political theory represented by Plato, More, and Bacon was being ridiculed, even though their "Model of an Eutopia," in Locke's dismissive phrase, differed from "normal" theories by a matter of degree rather than kind.[8] Locke's own "state of nature" with its "laws of nature" was hardly more "real" than More's commonwealth.[9] Utopians, such as More or, later, Fourier, may seem more "fanciful" because they depicted their ideal societies in far greater detail than, say, Machiavelli or Hobbes, yet "realists" and utopians alike shared certain theoretical assumptions.[10] They were all convinced that it was within the power of theory to describe a set of interconnected principles from which such a picture could be drawn; that such descriptions were meant to be a representation of a viable political totality; and that the representation of "the ought-to-be" as a "political whole" was the principal business of political theory.

Typically these representations were accompanied or, more precisely, preceded by a critique of existing society. Sometimes the critique was rendered in direct discourse, straightforwardly, as in Machiavelli's caustic description of princely rule in the *Discorsi.* Other writers took a more oblique approach, as in Montesquieu's account of despotism in *The Persian Letters.* Still others relied on abstractions, such as the "state of war" (Locke) or "state of nature" (Hobbes) to serve as a means of simultaneously characterizing and diagnosing the nature of the political and social evils in existing society.[11]

## V

Theory as radical critique and repicturization is attracted to the idea of a political journey because it provides an opportunity for the release of the theoretical imagination through an encounter with strangeness. Most theoretical journeyers attempt to convey a sense of astonishment at the remarkable arrangements they claim to have "seen." Astonishment is evoked by difference, by the contrast between what is familiar and what is true though garbed as strangeness. The evocation of difference signals a critical strategy. In claiming to have visited a "strange place," the theorist uses travel to provoke discontinuity: the strange place is isolated and separated from the "known" or familiar world. By "following" the author's journey, the reader is enticed into repeating the author's experience of difference, which works to unsettle familiar conceptions of time and place by picturing a better form of life in which truth is enclosed by a different organization of social space, a different distribution of human energies, and a different ordering of time. The purpose in "describing" an imaginary place as though it were real is to effect a reversal between the ideal place he has visited and the real place to which he returns: an ontological reversal of ideal/unreal and real/nonideal. The ideal because it is right becomes the real, while the actual because wrong is unreal. The ideal in every case represents the ultimate reversal: a society in which truth succeeds in humbling power.

Montesquieu's *Persian Letters* (1721), which he described as "a kind of novel," was a parody of the theoretical journey and of theory itself, and an intimation that the traditional genre was approaching exhaustion. Unlike the older theories of Plato, Machiavelli, Hobbes, and Locke, the *Persian Letters* did not depict an ideal or even a desirable society.[12] By implication Montesquieu disavows the notion that wholesale political and social transformation/regeneration is desirable or possible. This turn toward a more cautious conception of theory was even more pronounced in Montesquieu's great work, *The Spirit of the Laws* (1748). In *The Persian Letters* two nonideal societies are sketched, each in realistic or recognizable terms, but with their features artistically so heightened as to flirt with caricature. In one sketch contemporary France is visible, while in the other, a Persian harem is a disguised representation of the recent despotism of Louis XIV. A third theme represents a theoretical journey in reverse. It takes the theoretical traveler from the exotic to the real, from a homeland that becomes foreign to a foreign land that becomes "home"—although somewhat problematically. In the end the bizarre proves all too real: the harem embodies the deepest drives of absolutism, while the real proves bizarre and civilized society becomes a mass of absurdities.

In the story a Persian prince suspects that there are political intrigues against him at the royal court and he decides to go into exile. He secures royal permission to travel in order to gain instruction "in Western knowledge."[13] He journeys to Paris leaving behind his harem, a perfect absolutist regime devoted to satisfying the sensual pleasures of one man. In Paris he encounters a society at once enlightened and corrupt. The political point of the tale, which is developed in the letters exchanged primarily between the Persian and the inmates of the seraglio, lies in the ironic commentary on the condition of France only then emerging from the absolute rule of Louis XIV—exhausted, confused, and more than a little corrupted. Montesquieu parodies the theoretical journey. Instead of a triumphal return the antihero decides to remain in the West. His perplexities are unresolved. Meanwhile at home the harem is in revolt, its despotism clearly crumbling. The journey has enlightened the prince but has produced no clear vision of the good society. Theory appears as negative "social criticism." It hesitates to conceive society in transformative terms because it fears social upheaval as well as the concentration of power and purpose that transformation demands. In Montesquieu's parodic reversal theory's job is to expose "the perpetual contrast between the real things and the odd, naive, or bizarre way in which they were perceived."[14] Its political vision is deliberately unheroic: true politics is "a dull file which cuts gradually and slowly arrives at its end."[15]

Montesquieu's harem was unique for being a negative paradigm or dystopia, an "idealized" despotism that consumes itself without the assistance of a counterparadigm to reveal its flaws. It summarizes, nonetheless, two centuries of utopian thinking. It follows the tradition begun by More of depicting a society independent of time but located in a world that is otherwise identified through historical references. It has no prehistory and is not situated in history at all.[16] Its culture is logical rather than historical, the working out of the idea of despotism, of power divorced from restraints, and of sadomasochistic exploitation rather than civic affection.

## VI

Montesquieu did not follow the route of Locke or Rousseau and attempt to prevent despotism by relying on a social contract to stipulate the conditions and limits of rule. The radical, even revolutionary, element among modern contract theorists was the proposal to institute sweeping new political rules all at once. No less than they, Montesquieu abhorred absolutism but, unlike them, he abhorred equally the idea of an absolute break. Writing in the half century before the French Revolution, he gave little attention to the possibility of a popular revolution.[17] For Montesquieu revolution signified the alteration of certain fundamental relationships or beliefs that constituted the system called society. A society, in his view, consisted of multiple accommodations—of power, beliefs, laws, practices, manners—worked out over time or what he called "la perpétuité."[18] He tended to connect revolution with drastic reforms instituted by a ruler able to exercise absolute power. In this view the danger of revolution lay not in some combination of mass violence and irrational grievance but of absolutism and theoretic rationalism. In his formulation, which was to be repeated in Tocqueville's *Old Regime*, revolution involved two stages. The revolution is first initiated from above, which then provokes counterrevolution from below. According to Montesquieu:

> The prince who undertakes to destroy or change the dominant religion in his State, makes himself very vulnerable. If his government is despotic, he runs a greater risk of revolution than by any conceivable act of tyranny, which is no novelty in such states. Revolution occurs because a State cannot change religion, *moeurs*, and *manières* in an instant, and certainly not as quickly as a prince could ordain the establishment of a new religion. Moreover, the old religion is bound up with the constitution of the State while the new one is not.[19]

In this tightly packed passage Montesquieu was also contrasting the heightened tempos of modern power and the far slower ones of the political culture that sustains a constitution. We have already noted how Bacon had identified the difference between the busy, change-laden atmosphere surrounding science and invention and the stabler, settled character of political arrangements. Montesquieu reflected the divergence of the two, not just their differences. *Moeurs* and *manières* referred to the habits, customs, traditions, to temporally dependent practices that could not be legislated into existence by fiat. These sustained the actual operation of a political system and introduced accommodations that made it work, not efficiently but tolerably, a word that unfortunately does not carry the force and conviction with which Montesquieu invested it. His standard of good government was what he called "un gouvernement modéré," government whose power was not only exercised in a moderate spirit but moderated in the power actually at its disposal to do evil—or good.[20]

In pitting his cultural understanding of politics against the power drives of absolute rulers, Montesquieu challenged a whole range of modern notions and images and insinuated that the surface opposition between contractarian ideas and theories of absolutism might conceal some kinships. On the issue of political culture, as the example of Hobbes shows, modernity might be attracted to both despotism and liberal contractarianism, hopeful that somehow science might mediate those two forms of individualism, each the parody of the other.

What was the elective affinity at work between despotism and individualism? Both were modernizing mentalities whose outlook was deeply unhistorical, even antihistorical. Both were culturally radical in the specific sense of blanking out politics and political culture—despotism after the fact, contractarians beforehand in their state of nature. Whether the state of nature is portrayed as a violent state of war (Hobbes) or a more benign condition with certain "inconveniences" that harbor a possibility of turning nasty (Locke's "state of war"), in neither form was there a genuine discussion of political culture, of the skills, experience, habits, and practices needed for society to be *politique*. Instead, as in Hobbes's list of "natural laws," there are rules that should be followed, but they are all operative subsequent to the agreement and are treated as simple deductions from rational self-interest, not as acquired competencies. It is a political change from nature to civil society in which time serves simply as an abstract medium, as abstract as the place where the contractual "event" takes place. Political culture follows after the rules and institutions decreed by a sovereign power; it does not contribute to their constitution in a reciprocative way.

It is revealing of their attitudes toward political culture that for the theorists of modernity a tabula rasa should have been the favored image to describe the human mind. Strategically, the blank tablet formed the individual equivalent of the collective condition represented by the state of nature. In each case what was eliminated were cultural traits temporally acquired. A mental tabula rasa is a mind without the beliefs and dispositions that human beings are expected to have as a condition of acting in a recognizably human way; it is mind in a state of nature/innocence. Descartes's principle of radical doubt creates the tabula rasa by an act of will. Locke employed the notion in his famous account of how the mind formed ideas, but it was Hobbes who gave it the political cast that best revealed the extent to which the needs of modern power were defining the terms of culture.

Arguing against those who claimed that his principles of politics were too difficult for the "Common people" to comprehend, Hobbes insisted that "the

Common-peoples minds, unlesse they be tainted with dependence on the Potent, or scribbled over with the opinions of their Doctors, are like clean paper, fit to receive whatsoever by Publique Authority shall be imprinted in them."[21]

Although Montesquieu followed the convention of eighteenth-century theorizing and made mention of a state of nature, the concept does little or no service in his theory. It leads to no contract and creates no rights. It stands, rather, for human weakness arising from the nature of man, that is, from "laws" inscribed in his being. Natural man stands in need of protection, food, and sex. In short, he needs society.[22] He does not strike a bargain: society is not a choice but a necessity. And it is not a solution because society means inequality and the beginning of a state of war—that is, of social conflict arising from the effort of each to exploit social arrangements for his own ends as well as the more general conflicts between organized societies. Man is by nature a lawbreaker, not because he is driven to search for an elusive and precarious happiness (Hobbes), but because consistency of behavior is a social achievement rather than a natural endowment.[23]

For Montesquieu the great question was not how to harness the energies of this wayward and transgressive being, but what is it that makes civilized society possible despite the unpromising human material? Montesquieu's answer was inscribed man: man imprinted by a multitude of relationships ("laws"), some moral, some legal, some political, some physical, some scriptural, others geographical. The imprints were not the result of a contract or of a founding moment when society came into being. They were more in the nature of accommodations and understandings accumulated over time and without much premeditation. Unlike the Hobbesian dream of law-governed matter in motion, of power/freedom as the absence of impediments, and of order as the rational arrangement of power lanes, for Montesquieu resistance, barriers, and circumlocution were the necessary conditions of freedom and security and the essence of "un gouvernement modéré." The narrative of contract theorists typically began with the atomic individual and culminated in a bargain; Montesquieu presented a denser conception of society as a complex of received connections. Tocqueville will claim to discover a surprisingly dense society, one whose workings depended on Montesquieuean *manières et moeurs*, in the unlikely setting of a new world whose native theorists had conceived it to be a monument to contractualism.

In Montesquieu's scheme, nature was mediated by history, by the various arrangements that different societies made in order to live in the circumstances that the chances of geography and history had fashioned. Accordingly, Montesquieu was concerned with "cultural time" rather than efficient time, with the learned nature of politics, with what distracts power from the direct pursuit of its objectives and presses it into odd and bewildering configurations and prevents it from concentrating (in the double sense of consolidation and fixation). He does not conceive power in the instrumental terms that for the next two centuries would transfix the modern understanding of political rationality. Montesquieuean power operates in a world composed primarily of diverse social identities of class, status, religion, and region and only secondarily of means and ends. Accordingly, the ideal is of power as domesticated, adapted to relationships it inherits/finds rather than founds. It is a rationality at ease with indirection and obliqueness; it requires practice.[24]

## VII

Virtually all of Montesquieu's contemporaries as well as later commentators have agreed that the complex, unrationalized qualities that he ascribed to political formations were reflected in the shapelessness of his theory. The latter was as sprawling, ill-digested, and, even on occasion, inchoate as the former. It was a theory meant to promote political understanding, even subtle criticism of contemporary politics, especially for its despotic tendencies. It was made for a politics of indirection and obliqueness and at the opposite pole from a politics of unmediated rationality such as suggested by Helvétius, that "there is nothing better than the arbitrary government of princes who are just, humane, and virtuous."[25] Montesquieu's theory offered few formulas for political action and many for inaction. In its studied impracticality it was the perfect antithesis to the pragmatic criterion of a theory that we identified earlier in Bacon and Hobbes.

Although Montesquieu could not be characterized as a critic of the science of his day, the whole temper of his political theory ran counter to the modern culture of power we have been tracing: counter to the bureaucratic, centralized state, to aggressive individualism, and to the organized assault on nature. To state the same point somewhat differently, Montesquieu's practice of theory and his conception of society posed a challenge to the modern project of theory as pragmatics, as men-no-pause, as continuous action that seeks to link science-inspired technical reason with political power, to bring about a revolution in the quality and tempo of human life.

The stakes in the controversy between Montesquieu and his critics went well beyond the triumph of one mode of discourse over another to a choice between fundamentally different projects and modernities. Montesquieu's sociopolitical theory was the most complex effort in the history of Western theory to sabotage the accumulation of power and to make its exercise so exhausting as to leave it severely hobbled. Implicitly, if not intentionally, his theory was meant to counter the Bacon-Hobbes project of modeling society after the *logos* of science. He encouraged metaphors of a social topography full of so many creases, turns, obstacles, and entrenched bastions as to bewilder power and leave it unable to impose any architectonic vision. And it promoted a conception of the individual as a vectoral point where different norms converged and tugged so that the individual—diversified but not atomized—could never be the wholly reliable instrument of rulers or dominant groups.

Montesquieu's theory might be taken to represent the social forces that, threatened by the modernizing thrust of the centralized monarchies, tried to fashion "history" into a category of opposition to modern power. During roughly the second quarter of the eighteenth century in France the nobility and its ideological partisans appealed to the "ancient constitution" of France against what they perceived as the attempt of the monarchy to undermine the independence of the aristocracy. The so-called *thèse nobiliaire* claimed that in the dim past, before the encroachments of royal power had weakened the prerogatives and the independent institutions of the nobility, an original constitution had established the political power of the nobility and appointed nobles as the guardians of the constitutional order.[26]

Although the *thèse nobiliaire* was attacked for being little more than a disguise for special pleading, its basis in fact mattered less than its type of defense against modernizing power. Historical narrative was being developed as an alternative to abstract reason and its ahistorical state of nature. It spoke to a wide variety of endangered interests: class privileges of the nobility, regional and local elites who saw their *cursus honorum* disrupted by the appointment of agents from the center, local liberties of municipalities threatened by administrative centralization, provincial assemblies, and traditional economies that included local standards of weights, measures, taxes, and work regulations. The attempt to ground power in history rather than reason had the effect of exposing the abstract character of modernity's conception of the conditions requisite for power as itself a power tactic. Hobbes admitted that "there had never been any time wherein particular men were in a condition of warre one against another," yet in the next breath he stubbornly insisted that "this warre of every man against every man" was the proper theoretical starting point.[27]

What mattered about Hobbes's state of nature was not its historical warrant but its representation of human vulnerability due to the absence of a "common Power to feare."[28] In that condition, Hobbes emphasized, any man can be killed by any other. Thus power exists in the state of nature but it is so diffused as to leave everyone insecure. Similarly a society constituted without a sovereign authority would be in a virtual state of war comparable with that in the state of nature. Predictably, where no one is acknowledged to have the authority to impose a solution, social authorities will fight among themselves or league against the sovereign in order to advance their own interests. The state of nature, then, is not a state of powerlessness but an object lesson about the necessary condition for social peace. Just as in the covenant that ends the state of nature by requiring everyone to surrender the natural right to use his powers of doing whatever was necessary to preserve his life, so in society the prerequisite for making sovereign power effective involved the suspension of the historical rights or privileges of class, church, common law, corporations, and political institutions, such as a parliament. Because each of those claims represented a prior domain of power and their ensemble, the heterogeneity of power and the potential for obstruction, the sovereign was authorized to redefine them as he saw fit.[29] Accordingly, those claims had to be superseded to allow a certain structure of power to appear as logical: a Hobbesian "Sovereign Authority" or Locke's combination of legislative supremacy and a strong executive. Then the direction toward which society should be redirected in order to exploit the logic of power appears as a rational choice.

## VIII

*Is our theory any worse if we cannot prove it possible that a state so organized should be actually founded?*

Plato[30]

*I am at the point of believing this my labour as uselesse as the Common-wealth of Plato. . . . But . . . I recover some hope, that one time or other, this writing of mine, may fall into the hands of a Soveraign who . . . by the exercise of entire Soveraignty, in protecting the Publique teaching of it, convert this Truth of Speculation, into the Utility of Practice.*

Thomas Hobbes[31]

In contrast to the pessimism of premodern political thinkers regarding the possibilities of the theory of the good society ever being realized in practice, modernizing theorists were confident that the practical achievements of science could be duplicated politically and that a theoretical science of politics could give the moderns the means of bridging the gap between theory and actual practice. For Hobbes the practical powers that science had made available were transforming human life and proved that mind could actually change the world by "the arts of measuring matter and motion; of moving ponderous bodies; of architecture; of navigation; of making instruments for all uses; of calculating the celestial motions, the aspects of the stars, and the parts of time; of geography, &c."[32]

The revolution that was in the making, and that would soon spread to other domains of thought and activity, was the concept of revolution itself. To think of an absolute transformation had mainly been an indulgence of religious minds, typically with a predominant emphasis on the transformation of the personal lives of true believers along with a studied indifference toward the material betterment of society or political reform. Except for the isolated instance of a Thomas Münzer, who was universally condemned by the leadership of the Reformation, even the so-called "left-wing of the Reformation" had dreamed more of founding new communities separated from the world than of reconstituting existing societies.[33] It was precisely the example of science and technology that stimulated the theoretical imagination toward a radical breakthrough, to a vision of existing society continuously engaged in reconstituting its life form. The concepts of utopia and revolution were thus beginning to merge.

The opportunity for mind to remake the actual world came with stunning force with the outbreak of the English civil wars. Previously, as we have seen, modern theory had taken a highly cautious attitude toward political change and was overwhelmingly on the side of political authorities, although less enthusiastic about ecclesiastical establishments. This changed when the theoretical imagination became captivated by the daring scope and scale of reform attempted by the social forces grouped around Parliament, the New Model Army, and the dissenting sects. Following the outbreak of civil war in 1642 political theorists found themselves in a world astonishingly open, even to the most bizarre ideas and experiments. The monarchy was abolished, the House of Lords eliminated, and the church disestablished. Radical solutions were attempted: rule by the House of Commons, a written constitution, then a dictatorship. There were experiments in primitive communism, dreams of chiliastic redemption, even attempts to establish a democratic society.[34]

The symbolic moment when the theoretical revolution inspired by modern science was joined to political revolution came as Hobbes temporarily put aside his "Speculation of Bodies Naturall" in order to compose his "Doctrine of this Artificiall Body [politic]."[35] Clearly a theoretical mentality that believed in a pragmatic conception of theory would not invest in political inquiry unless convinced that men could treat politics as they had begun to treat nature—experimentally, practically, profitably, and ruthlessly. In order to think productively about politics, Hobbes declared, we should treat society as we would a watch, to "be taken insunder and viewed in parts . . . that they be so considered as if they were dissolved."[36] Revolution provided that opportunity of viewing a society "taken insunder," reduced to its "parts," and awaiting reconstruction. That spectacle launched a hopeful theoretic epoch that would last for more than three centuries.

## IX

Theoretical hopes and ambitions were aroused because modern revolutions appeared to have transcended the received categories of political thinking about revolutions. In antiquity revolutions were treated as catalytic agents, which of necessity followed the predetermined course inherent in a particular political form. Any given form would change into its "natural" corrective because any simple form was, by definition, based on a defining principle that excluded rival social claims. Monarchy would be overthrown by aristocracy because aristocrats, as the natural rivals of rule by one, resented being excluded from power; aristocracy would fear the rivalry of the rich, another small group of powerful men, who would feel that their wealth entitled them to offices; eventually the form of power represented by oligarchy would prevail only to be overthrown by the power of sheer numbers; the masses whose poverty and ignoble birth had previously barred them from power would impose democracy and the reign of equal power. Revolution was thus encased in a natural cycle of constitution changing, a succession of "revolving" forms governed by a logic that decreed that the new class and new form of social power furnish the corrective corresponding to the excesses of the previous regime.[37] But the conception was of a closed cycle; eventually the system would return to its starting point and begin again.

Modern revolutions seemed to have a greater potential for totally transforming society as well as political institutions and hence of permanently breaking the cycle. They hinted at a condition in which society was temporarily reduced to the equivalent of a state of nature or a tabula rasa. That condition of near zero signaled the end of the cyclical theory of revolution and its replacement by a conception of an absolute political beginning with no predetermined end.

Revolution/state of nature opened up a prospect of accelerated change that was wholly alien to classical notions. Time was now conceived as coming under human control rather than deriving its meaning from a prior order controlled by God. Revolution signified that time could be hurried along because it was no longer hostage to a myriad of authorities and their vested power of hereditary privilege and their monopoly upon the interpretation of truth. What might otherwise require extended negotiations could be accomplished within a comparatively brief moment. Thus there was being hatched the complement to the conception of modern power associated with the political theorists of modern science, Bacon, Descartes, and Hobbes. Certain kinds of time—eschatological ("the end of time"), customary ("time out of mind"), aesthetic ("timeless beauty")—could be annihilated by power or radically compressed, including time required for cultural practices to re-form around fundamental changes, to digest their meaning, and to develop the practices and skills that could harmonize the new with the old. While cultural practices redeem time, revolutions "take" time. By destroying the infrastructure of mediation, revolution, like science itself, seemed able to short-circuit history by destroying or neutralizing its cultural expressions.

## X

Yet men resisted the implications of time-consuming revolutions, as happened under the most admired constitution of eighteenth-century Europe. Notwithstanding the significant constitutional changes in the position of the monarchy and the role of Parliament effected by the settlement following the Glorious Revolution of 1688, Englishmen successfully persuaded themselves that they had maintained continuity with their political past—Locke would refer to the new king, created by parliamentary statute, as "our Great Restorer," while the House of Commons resolved in 1689 that James II "has abdicated the Government and that the throne is thereby become vacant"—thus conveniently overlooking the fact that the king had been deposed and forced to flee.[38] What would matter was not that political continuities were as much fiction as reality but that the most powerful social groups preferred the fiction and whatever measure of reality it might contain rather than admit a deep divide between past and present.

Nonetheless, it was reasonably clear that there had been a rejection of some of the most important institutions, myths, and beliefs relating to the identity of the political order as it had existed before 1640 and in its restored version of 1660. A political system with kingship "hedged by divinity" (James I) at its center, a structure of social classes with the aristocracy represented in a coeval branch of Parliament, and a religious establishment in which one church was recognized as supreme—all began to appear problematic, then contestable, and were eventually transformed by the end of the century. The changes were registered in, so to speak, the doubling of political life into a traditional or "old order," now receded into the past, an object of reminiscence and nostalgia. Alongside it, and steadily usurping its place in the national consciousness, although not without contestation, was the new order that had been "settled" by the events of 1688. European thought was about to be shaped by a new contrast, not between true believers and dissenters, or parliamentarians and monarchists, but between modern and ancient, the very contrast that Bacon and other theorists of modern power strove to establish in the European consciousness.

## XI

The self-prescribed category of the modern came to mean many things, among them an eagerness for new ways of thinking that were dismissive of custom and tradition as thoughtless. Locke had warned about "what gross absurdities the following of Custom, when Reason has left it, may lead."[39]

The belief that past and present were to be understood as a contrast between two different kinds of political order produced a reconceptualization of political time. The old order embodied a suspended and motionless time: movement was confined to the links between precedents. In the new order time was dynamic and superseding. The events of the last quarter of the eighteenth century seemed to mark, in the words of the motto of the New World republic, a *novus ordo saeclorum*, a new order of generations. Beginning first in America and then gathering momentum in France, the Western world was repeatedly shaken by revolutionary upheavals, which continued into the nineteenth century and spread far beyond Europe in the twentieth.

As men and women tried to comprehend the magnitude of events and their recurrence, some began to entertain a suspicion that revolution had not so much overthrown tradition as substituted for it. Tocqueville would later express bewilderment at "the mobility of everything, institutions, ideas, manners and men in a moving society which has been reconstructed by seven great revolutions in less than sixty years." And he would conclude wearily, "I do not know when this long voyage will be over . . . or whether our destiny is not to sail the seas eternally."[40]

Thanks to the frequency of revolution the theorist's journey had turned ironical, repeated beginnings rather than completed circles, "Persian" rather than Lockean.

## XII

Unlike those seventeenth- and eighteenth-century Englishmen who persuaded themselves that the Glorious Revolution had been a protest against the discontinuities introduced by innovating monarchs—and hence a true revolution must be one that enabled society to resume its traditional ways—others associated revolution with separation from the past. History came to signify not simply "the past" but the experience of irretrievable loss. Even American revolutionaries who had otherwise been confident of the progressive character of their rebellion against Britain became uneasy about cutting themselves completely adrift from the past. When constructing a defense for the constitution newly drafted at Philadelphia, James Madison had first argued heroically by recalling the example of the constitutions established by the individual states soon after hostilities had begun: "[Americans then] accomplished a revolution which has no parallel in the annals of human society. They reared the fabrics of government which have no model on the face of the globe." But in his peroration Madison faltered as if in the realization that it was one thing to invent a new political form and quite another to fling aside past beliefs and practices. And so he did the human thing and tried to have it both ways: Americans "have paid a decent regard to the opinions of former times" yet "they have not suffered a blind veneration for antiquity," and posterity would assuredly thank them for their "numerous innovations."[41]

The French revolutionaries ventured where the Americans had hesitated. They broke with the past and, if at first unintentionally, set about methodically eradicating its institutions and beliefs, abolishing not only the monarchy, aristocracy, and established religion but inventing new political forms and a new political culture, outfitted with its own religion, civic rituals, forms of salutation, and a new calendar to mark the new beginning.[42] So deep was the rift that they eventually drove between past and present that scarcely fifty years later when Tocqueville first began his historical inquiries into the prerevolutionary society, he professed to feel amazed at how his immediate forebears could appear so remote and unfamiliar.[43] The sense of loss, to which Tocqueville would frequently bear witness, and the fear that the past and the identities that it secured might be "lost," led to a certain shaping of "history" as a medium for expressing the experience of dispossession and as a counterlanguage of repossession.

As we have already suggested, around the mid-eighteenth century, however, the idea of history began to take on a different character. History came to be the medium of what might be called "cultural practices." The discovery of cultural practices exposed a whole layer of conduct and social skills that depended entirely on a conception of practice that challenged directly the received notion that subordinated practice to the realization of theory. In the new reading of the relationship, theory was post factum to practice, the interpreter of practice's contribution, not its prescriber, its consciousness rather than its conscience. The cultural conception was about conduct rather than action, about behavior that had to be practiced in order to be "followed" and hence required learning time. To say that a practice requires time before it is mastered is to say that practice acquires time in the course of acquiring mastery. In contrast, the theory-practice formula was about action as a cause, as Hobbesian motion, which produces an effect and refers back to what is not action, to theory. A cultural practice refers to itself, to prior instances. "Customs and manners," Montesquieu asserted, "are usages that the laws have not established at all, either because they could not or did not want to."[44]

Thus the received conception of a theory as a set of prescriptions to be objectified by practice was about to appear incoherent because it was ignorant of what was required to perpetuate and, above all, to maintain a society. "Men," Montesquieu claimed, "are governed by several things," and most of them appeared beyond the ability of theory to establish: "climate, religion, laws, principles of government, past examples, customs, manners."[45]

The controversy between history and theory was joined in the contemporary interpretations of the French Revolution.

## XIII

Almost from the beginning the French Revolution was intellectualized as uniquely a theoretical event, a collective assault inspired and promoted by theorists and directed against an old, historical regime. According to Burke, the revolution was "a revolution of doctrine and theoretic dogma."[46] Perhaps no event did more to fix the character of the revolution as *une cause théoretique* than the polemic between Edmund Burke and Tom Paine. Their exchange served to fix the terms of understanding that identified theory with revolutionary change in the present and utopia in the future and associated history with conservation of the past and grudging adaptation to the present.

Theory was depicted by Burke as goaded by a will to annihilate the past. The "state surveyors" of revolutionary France, he claimed, were inspired by "geometrical demonstrations" which rendered them insensitive to the historical nature of time and place. Notions such as "continuity," "tradition," "inheritance," and "prescriptive rights," which, Burke alleged, were held in contempt by the revolutionaries, were in reality the expression of nature. Nature was not an ideal condition representing some imagined Rousseauean past, nor was it the abstraction of Newtonian physics. History was man's nature: "By a constitutional policy, working after the pattern of nature, we receive, we hold, we transmit our government and our privileges in the same manner in which we enjoy and transmit our property and our lives."[47]

To Paine, the arch-rationalist with his fondness for depicting ahistorical states of nature and original contracts, and, above, all, his contempt for inherited privilege, authority, and power, theory was secularism's theology, a saving knowledge that could liberate men from the shackles of custom, prejudice, and mystery and inaugurate the age of transparent authority founded on equal rights, consent, utility, and "no secrets."

> What were formerly called revolutions were little more than a change of persons, or an alteration of local circumstances. But what we now see in the world, from the revolutions of America and France, is a renovation of the natural order of things, a system of principles as universal as truth and the existence of man, and combining moral with political happiness and national prosperity.[48]

The controversy between theory and history ran broad and deep. It cut to conceptions of action: revolutionary action was seen as constituted in the image of revolutionary theory; total criticism, total overthrow, total reconstitution. "The shortest way to reform" the political orders of Europe, Paine declared, was "to begin anew."[49] In opposition Burke and others staked out a genealogical theory of politics that had political action guiding itself by ancestral wisdom and mimicking the English common-law practice of deferring to precedent:

> Let us follow our ancestors . . . who, by looking backward as well as forward . . . went on insensibly drawing this constitution nearer and nearer to its perfection by never departing from its fundamental principles, nor introducing any amendment which had not had a subsisting root in the laws, constitution, and usages of the kingdom.[50]

The prudence and experience of the "statesman" was contrasted with the heaven-storming fervor of the revolutionist, and a politics of conservation was set over against one of sweeping innovation. At stake were opposing views of political knowledge: theory stood for universal truths acquired by emulating scientific methods, while history represented a collective experience of adaptation to local circumstance, a nationalized prudence.

## XIV

> *In that tremendous breaking forth of a whole people [in France], in which all degrees, tempers and characters are confounded, and delivering themselves, by a miracle of exertion, from the destruction meditated against them, is it to be expected that nothing will happen?*
>
> Tom Paine[51]

A line was about to be drawn between the modern and the antimodern. Paine and the French Revolution symbolized the demand for justice and equality, but they also connected that demand to ideas of progress, of science as the highest form of knowledge, secularization, and an irreligion that ranged from deism to agnosticism to atheism. Paine represented a moment when revolutionary thought attempted to unite democracy and science, thereby challenging the Bacon-Hobbes tradition adopted by the French philosophes, which had allied science with state power. In Paine's view, science would free mankind from fealty to the past, replacing adherence to venerated ways with a notion of action as "invention" and a new conception of collective achievement, "progress."

Paine's thinking also revealed how easily the democratic tendencies encouraged by revolutionary experience could be distracted by the lure of economic freedom and the apolitical values represented by civil society. Unwittingly, Paine shortchanged the very revolutions he so ardently defended. His thinking oscillated between two extreme images: between the victimization of "society" by aristocrats, monarchs, and the church and, at the other extreme, the liberation of society from oppressive restraints. What was missing was any substantive conception of the political, a lack that was in no small measure responsible for Paine's obscurity in both postrevolutionary America and France. The apolitical strain in his thinking was evident in his conception of the state of nature.

Unlike the prepolitical condition posited by Hobbes and Locke, Paine's state of nature did not serve as a tabula rasa on which the conditions for generating political power could be etched. It was, instead, the ideal condition of nonpower, an idyllic state of spontaneous relationships governed by natural reason and hence lacking any coercion. When Paine described the replacement of the natural condition by "government," the latter is represented as "the badge of our lost innocence." The task then becomes to reduce the scope of government by expanding that of society. "Society" stands primarily for socioeconomic relations; these signify the natural and the spontaneous, which, in turn, signify the noncoercive. Socioeconomic relations recreate innocence because they register "natural," rudimentary needs, such as food, clothing, shelter, and family life. All that remains is to "settle" the political.

Paine provides a glimpse of the emerging contrast between "the social" and "the political," the one standing for a natural democracy without artificial distinctions and wide disparities in power, the other for domination and unearned superiorities. The participatory expectations engendered by the revolutionary experience are, literally, captured, contained in Paine's proposal for a written constitution and confined to a system of representative government.[52] These serve—although Paine did not say as much—as the badge of a lost politicalness. It only remains to add that while the heirs of Bacon were busy incorporating science as an important element of state policy, Paine spent his last years vainly peddling various schemes for iron bridges, gunboats, and fortifications. He had projects, his rivals had policies.

Although Burke was not hostile to science, he was profoundly distrustful of its use to justify political experiments. The unpremeditated practices of "prejudice," "habit," and local custom were the means by which the members of a traditional society become adapted to a politics of deference to their superiors. Burke's idealized traditional society represented a counterutopia in which a privileged, public-spirited aristocracy ruled benevolently, where evils were inextricably interwoven with civilized advantages and not to be uprooted except when absolutely necessary, and where religion provided the "basis of civil society."[53]

## XV

The lines between history and theory had scarcely been drawn by Burke and Paine when they were dramatically dissolved by two developments that occurred within political theory. The first was the historicization of the theoretical consciousness, which began in the mid-eighteenth century and reached its culmination in Karl Marx.[54] Writers as diverse as Hume, Ferguson, de Maistre, Saint-Simon, Comte, Hegel, Coleridge, J. S. Mill, and Marx not only attempted to take account of historical events and in a broad way to use them to "prove" their theories, but, more important, they introduced historicized categories into the structure of their theories. Sometimes this took the form of a discovery that history followed certain "stages," as in Saint-Simon's distinction between "critical" and "organic" stages or Comte's "law of three periods" (metaphysical, theological, and positive-scientific) or Marx's various stages in the development of precapitalist formations and of capitalism itself. Equally crucial was the contribution to historicization primarily by Hegel and Marx. It consisted of the claim that no social phenomenon, such as the institution of property, and no mental category, such as experience, could be properly understood except by grasping the dialectics of its development, the contestations and incorporations that it underwent over time. History thus came to signify not so much "events" or "facts" that belonged to an external world called "the past," but the texture of a distinctive mode of understanding, a medium, which temporalized all that was within the human world and, at the same time, insisted that the traces and influences of much of what had gone before had not vanished but were still discernible and operative. Although Tocqueville did not self-consciously follow a dialectical method, he would introduce an antithesis between the "old" and the "new" and make its antagonisms the crucial element in his conception of history.

The second development involved the scrambling of the relationship between theory and revolution. Except for Proudhon and Marx, many of the major theorists were self-consciously antirevolutionary. Saint-Simon and Comte could fairly be said to have launched modern social science as a self-conscious antidote to the French Revolution, and the same holds for Hegel's conception of philosophy.[55]

The antirevolutionary character of early social science and its historicization of the social world were a response to a condition that suddenly seemed to be bursting with power. The French Revolution presented a kaleidoscope of powers—of upheaval, collective rage, and the mobilization of masses—that seemed to outstrip the received categories. Accordingly, the function of the newly invented social science became to demythologize revolution, to conceptualize it so as to render it inconceivable in the elemental and utopian form in which it had first appeared to the European generation of 1789 and to sublimate revolutionary idealism into technological utopianism. Social science would first treat the French Revolution as a "necessary" event that had removed a barrier to the progress of science and enlightenment. Then it was further reduced, from a preternatural event to a specimen of a genus, which, after being neutered, could be safely housed within a system of sociological categories and laws of social development. Later, in Durkheim's sociology, where revolution was redescribed in the clinical language of social pathology, a hint of primal terror was barely detectable but none of revolutionary hope.[56]

The development of social science witnessed the dissolution of the alliance between science and revolution that the revolutionaries of 1789 had promoted and Marx would vainly try to perpetuate.[57] As a cultural category, science gave up its critical role, which had associated it with radical change, and became integrated into and dependent on the political institutions being shaped by industrial capitalism and its revolution.

Social science also served as a medium for reintroducing concepts of social discipline, deference, and corporate solidarity, concepts that conservative writers like Burke, de Maistre, and de Bonald had identified with anti- and prerevolutionary regimes. Those concepts, it should be added, were ones that liberal thinkers beginning with Hobbes and Locke and continuing in the English Utilitarians were unable to generate from liberal assumptions about free, equal, and consciously consenting individuals. The great difference between social science and eighteenth-century conservatism was that while the latter was essentially reflective of agrarian, rural, and landed ways of life in which deference was connected with mutual obligations and a widely shared recognition of cooperation as a condition of survival, the new discipline issued from an entirely different conception of necessity, one couched in the form of technological imperatives and an entirely different conception of authority embodied in the figure of *l'industriel* (Saint-Simon), the one empowered to shape a rural population into an industrial one, "a captain of industry." Whereas the eighteenth-century radicals had seen progress as the condition for freedom, writers like Saint-Simon and Comte saw discipline as the condition of progress.

In keeping with this understanding Saint-Simon, Comte, and, later, Durkheim would endorse what some philosophes of the eighteenth century would have dismissed as regressive, the notion that a society based on the development and application of scientific knowledge must deliberately reestablish religion to inculcate morality and obedience. Although each of these founders of social science volunteered a sketch of what a religion should be like,[58] none was motivated by deep religious convictions, much less by a desire for the old ways. Rather they had perceived that modernity's version of science, technology, and economy had destroyed the "cultural capital" accumulated in previous centuries. The result was something akin to a latent potential for disobedience among the lower classes, permanent instability, and endless social dislocation. Religion was proposed as a stabilizing force that would somehow control the desires and resentments provoked by the permanent revolution being ushered in by modernity.[59]

The religion of social science denied the basic principle of a transcendent god and adopted, instead, the principle of immanence. The laws of nature inscribed in the structure of the universe were laws of power controlling the course of phenomena. Advances in knowledge of those laws meant advances in human power that would bring utopia within reach.

Curiously social science's concern to reconstruct religion as mass belief reflected both the demise of the theoretical journey and a renewed interest in utopias. Now, however, utopias were to be projections in time rather than journeys across space. This signified that the temporal orientation that governed action was the future rather than the present. As utopias became increasingly dominated by scientific (or pseudoscientific) conceptions—science symbolizing the predictive powers based on the laws of nature, which enabled mankind to control the future—they ceased to represent the strange and became, instead, the idealization of what was implicit, immanent. What seemed less a matter of concern was the fate of More's "well and wisely trained citizens."

# PART TWO

## *Encountering the Amazing*

# CHAPTER III
# DISCOVERING DEMOCRACY

## I

> *[The ancients] gave the name of democracies to those governments where the people had the same access to the magistracies and offices of state as the nobles. But of these we have none at this time in Europe.*
>
> Adam Smith (1763)[1]

Tocqueville was the first political theorist to treat democracy as a theoretical subject in its own right and and the first to contend that democracy was capable of achieving a genuine, if modest, political life-form. Although many political theories were composed after the ancient Greeks of the fifth century B.C.E. invented a theoretical discourse about politics, when it came to the topic of democracy discussion tended to be short on analysis and long on invective. "A popular state," warned Jean Bodin, a famous sixteenth-century theorist, "is always the refuge of all disorderly spirits, rebels, traitors, outcasts, who encourage the lower orders to ruin the great."[2]

Typically democracy was given perfunctory mention as one of the possible political constitutions along with monarchy, aristocracy, and their variants—and usually dismissed as the worst of the best forms, or, because of its ineffectualness, as the best of the worst.[3] The virtually unanimous opinion of all political theorists throughout antiquity, the Middle Ages, and early modernity was that democracy was inherently incapable of achieving, let alone, realizing, the political. The reason commonly given was that the common well-being of society, the moral quality of political life, the effectiveness of political rule, and the dispensing of justice—the main elements identified with the political—required uncommon abilities that were to be found among those who "stood out" by virtue of their noble birth, wealth, or military prowess. Political life with its recurrent threat of war and internal lawlessness required strong leadership, men who could and knew how to act. Thus the understanding was a peculiar combination of impartiality and discrimination. The political required that those who ruled should rule for the good of all; to have disinterested rulers, however, it was necessary to discriminate, to recruit rulers only from certain small segments of the population.

Democracy, from its first appearance in fifth-century Athens, challenged these assumptions. The political was identified, not with leadership, but with equalizing the context within which a leader, a Pericles perhaps, might emerge. It involved a radical change in the idea of deliberation. Previously deliberation meant taking counsel, seeking advice before acting, and invariably it was restricted to a small circle of skilled and experienced advisers. Democracy introduced the idea of participation, widening the circle of deliberants to include the citizenry while creating the idea of the citizen-speaker and thereby giving "the Many" an actual voice. To its critics these innovations merely confirmed the undiscriminating character of democracy. They saw democracy as introducing "confusion" by bracketing the differences that were of the essence of society and proclaiming a political in which differences of lineage or of wealth were not to be considered entitlements to precedence or the lack of them to be disqualifying. "Those who want to make all things equal," Bodin declared, "want to give sovereign authority over men's lives, honor, and property to the stupid, ignorant, and passionate, as well as to the prudent and experienced."[4] But equalizing also signified a new claim, that the political should provide the means of redress for run-of-the-mill members. In the traditional teaching, the suffering and deprivations experienced by most members of society were irremediable, being inherent in the human condition. Democracy posed for the first time the idea of the political as the means for combating the evils inherent in societies whose organization depended on the preservation, even celebration, of inequalities.

Among political writers from antiquity to early modern times the common synonym for democracy was the Many, a shorthand that conveyed both a contempt for the undifferentiated and a sense of the menace in collective power. A sixteenth-century English humanist phrased it in a way that showed how the animus had become enshrined as a continuity between classical and early modern republicanism. In *The Book Named the Governor* (1531), Sir Thomas Elyot claimed that the Latin word for the common people, *plebs*, meant in English "the commonalty, which signifieth only the multitude, wherein be contained the base and vulgar inhabitants not advanced to any honour or dignity."[5]

To the defenders of social hierarchy, democracy signified "leveling," a brute force that would overturn society and return it to a primal, undifferentiated condition. According to Elyot, it is "discrepance of degree . . . whereof proceedeth order" hence to establish equality would introduce "chaos" and "perpetual conflict" because it would subvert the structure of difference, status, and inequality that God had written into the whole fabric of Creation. Greek democracy, he noted, had instituted an "equality of estate [i.e., of condition]

. . . among the people" and the result was "a monster with many heads." Democracy's politics of *ressentiment*—or, in Elyot's phrase, "the rage of a commonalty"—aimed at leveling society's complex structure of subordination, and hence democracy was said to share the same impulse as the tyrant whose rule likewise depended on the elimination of all rival social powers. Of all the forms of rule, Elyot warned, "democracy is most to be feared." In their cyclical concept of constitutional change, ancient and early modern theorists made it virtually a convention for democracy to be described as a tumultuous prelude to tyranny.[6] The sequence of first democracy, then tyranny, had a special resonance in France where the course of the French Revolution had seemed to find its "natural" end point in the Napoleonic despotism. The democratic tendency toward tyranny would appear as a motif in Tocqueville's major writings. In no small degree due to his influence the connection would resurface in the twentieth century in the claim that "mass democracy" was a vital precondition for modern dictatorial rule.[7]

The allegation that democracy was complicit in the rise of tyranny—significantly, the reverse was rarely argued, Polybius being the exception—tended to obscure the fundamental difference not only between democracy and tyranny but the challenge that democracy presented to the other forms. Tyranny excluded all but the tyrant; aristocracy and oligarchies of wealth excluded all but the Few; in principle monarchy might open careers to talent and throw morsels to the bourgeoisie but only to check the Few, not to advance the Many. The potential explosiveness of democracy lay in a conception of the political whose first principle was that no one should be excluded—that is, whatever its inconsistencies, as in its practice toward slaves and women, democracy lacked a principled justification for exclusion.

## II

> *Monarchies and aristocracies are in possession of the voice and influence of every university and academy in Europe. Democracy, simple democracy, never had a patron among men of letters. . . . Men of letters must have a great deal of praise, and some of the necessaries, conveniences, and ornaments of life. Monarchies and aristocracies pay well and applaud liberally. The people have almost always expected to be served gratis. . . . It is no wonder then that democracies and democratical mixtures are annihilated all over Europe, except on a baren rock, a paltry fen, an inaccessible mountain, or an impenetrable forest.*
>
> John Adams[8]

The lack of theoretical interest in democracy is not surprising in one respect. From the decline of the autonomous Greek city-states in the fourth century B.C.E. to the emergence of the Italian city-republics of the thirteenth and fourteenth centuries there were no examples of actual democracies. Only by courtesy could the Italian republics be called democracies, for they were dominated either by the wealthy or by aristocrats.[9] The narrow political, social, and gender basis of these states, as well as of the Greek polities of antiquity may be one reason for the paucity of democratic theories—no one had ever seen an authentic specimen.

It is equally obvious, however, that the lack of actual exemplars had not prevented a Plato from imagining a society ruled by philosophers; or a Machiavelli from projecting schemes of political rejuvenation that, for inexplicable reasons, would rely on political adventurers; or Calvinists from envisioning a city managed by saints. Why did the theoretical imagination balk before "a government of the people, by the people, and for the people"?

In part the answer is that political theorists typically framed their notions of politics around a certain set of purposes or type of values that could only be realized by a small group or class. Well into the nineteenth century theorists continued to center their political ideals exclusively around elites—saints, priests, savants, warriors, scientists. Beyond whatever intrinsic merits those ideals may have had in the eyes of their proponents, the exercise had a practical-strategical attraction for theorists. Because most theorists had prided themselves on possessing a body of political knowledge whose difficulty made it inaccessible to the Many, the convenient, if tautological, conclusion was that only the Few who ruled had to be converted for theory to have a practical instrument for its realization. Accordingly, "virtue," "knowledge," "piety," or military skills were frequently made the focal point of the political societies projected by one or another theorist; the value of these values depended on the difficulty of their acquisition, on their uncommon character. As Hobbes pointed out, if "all things were equally in all men . . . nothing would be prized."[10] This ruled out "the Many" from consideration as the chosen medium of theoretical ideals. Even when a theorist managed to say a few good words about the "multitude," it usually turned out that he had merely found a political use for some very ordinary virtue or vice. Thus in *The Prince* Machiavelli had argued that the people provided a more suitable foundation for princely rule than would an aristocracy: "they demand no more than not to be oppressed," which meant simply security for their property and women.[11]

When measured by standards of excellence set by most ancient and modern theorists, democracy, in its undiscriminating, sheer ordinariness, seemed absurdly deficient. James Madison, often considered to be the "father of the

American Constitution," took the case one step further by arguing that democracy qua democracy could not properly deliberate, not even a democracy of philosophers. "Had every Athenian citizen been a Socrates, every Athenian assembly would still have been a mob."[12]

One of the major sticking points advanced in order to make democracy seem literally inconceivable concerned the practical difficulties of establishing a democratic constitution. Theorists found it unimaginable to think of a political society except as a distinct "form." Their assumption was that if democracy had to be a form of government, it must perforce be embodied in a constitutional framework. How, then, so the argument ran, could a multitude assemble and, once assembled, how could it actually compose a constitution? How could everyone deliberate about the details of laws and institutions, much less determine what common ends ought to be promoted? Where would they have acquired the experience or knowledge to resolve such problems?

These questions had posed no difficulties for the classical and early modern thinkers. They held that a constitutional founding required a single legislator with absolute authority to "impress" the best form on society. This belief in the Great Founder was not confined to defenders of monarchy, aristocracy, or rule by savants. It can be found among the so-called civic humanists, such as Machiavelli, Harrington, and Milton, as well as in a proto-/crypto-democratic writer like Rousseau. Among virtually all of these theorists there was a common fascination for the idea of a single Founder serving as the medium by which Mind impressed upon society its image of the Good Form. Oddly, Hobbes and Locke assumed that all men were capable of confronting the momentous decision of whether to form a political society; yet, like the other contract theorists, they were reluctant to admit that they were assuming a principle of demotic rationality that might be extended to include a decision to establish a democracy as the one form that embodied the assumption of popular rationality.[13] The American Founding Fathers would attempt to resolve the problem by contending that when "the people" had ratified the constitution presented to them, they had chosen a republican form in which democracy was only one element.

Tocqueville would challenge the tradition of discourse that had been unable to conceive democracy except as encased in a preconceived legal form. Although his account would seem at first glance to borrow from the classical notion of a political society as a way of life, he would part company by refusing to follow the classical analysis as it proceeded to encase that way of life into a constitutional form. He would reveal democracy to mean ways of life and multiple political life-forms.

## III

The distrust of the demos did not disappear with the advent of modernity but, instead, was received into English republicanism, one of the principal carriers of political modernity and the ideological center to many modern liberal theories.[14] In this connection it is important to bear in mind that republicanism in France carried revolutionary associations. To the French it came to mean sansculottism, the Jacobin Republic of 1793, the "Terror" of 1793–94, and the total mobilization of the population for war. French republicanism thus signified radical democracy and served to confirm the centuries-old distrust of the demos.

In 1832, while still in America, Tocqueville composed a long meditation on republicanism inspired as he contemplated the French Revolution, Bonaparte (a figure never far from Tocqueville's thinking), and the hostility between royalists and republicans. "If royalists could see the internal working of a well-ordered republic," he mused, they would realize that many of their fears were groundless. And if republicans were to confront the historical reality of republicanism in France, they could not but conclude that it had been the complete denial of liberty, the fundamental principle of republicanism. "[W]hat we called a republic [during the French Revolution] is nothing but a monster . . . covered in blood and filth." Although thousands of miles from any direct reminder of 1789, Tocqueville managed to work himself into a fury as he conjured up images of that upheaval: men "slaughtered in prison" by Danton; the proscription directed at the goods, families, and persons of helpless minorities; the censorship of opinion by the Directory; and the climactic despotism of Bonaparte. "[In] France we have seen anarchy and despotism in all its forms, but nothing that resembled a republic."[15]

The ideological strength of republicanism would be one of several obstacles that would subtly contribute to setting Tocqueville's theoretical journey onto a course different from traditional theoretical concerns. Tocqueville would not be describing "the best commonwealth" but one in which the main actors were not the rich, the highly virtuous, the educated, or the well-born but human beings whose manyness consisted in being none of the above. In short, the demos had succeeded to the republic founded by an elite and were shaping it into a democracy and, in the process, leaving the elite submerged.

## IV

> *This most sovereign and inclusive association is . . . the political association.*
>
> *The term "constitution" signifies the same thing as the term "civic body." The civic body in every polis is the sovereign; and the sovereign must necessarily be either One, or Few, or Many.*
>
> *[E]ither the name of citizen cannot be given to persons who share in the constitution [but whose interests are not regarded]; or, if the name be given, they must have their share of the benefits.*
>
> Aristotle[16]

While the ideal societies of classical, mediaeval, and early modern theories were defined in functional terms whose effect was to make politics a circle closed to all but the qualified few, most political theories were simultaneously claiming certain values of comprehensiveness to be fundamental to the existence of a "political" community. A sixteenth-century English writer and secretary of state, Sir Thomas Smith, represented the commonwealth as divided into classes whose members were citizens—gentlemen and yeomen—and those who were bondsmen "who can bear no rule nor jurisdiction over freemen," and who are considered "but as instruments and the goods and possessions of others." The latter, in addition to women, included "day labourers, poore husbandmen, yea merchants or retailers which have free lands, copiholders, and all artificers, as Taylers, Shoomakers, Carpenters, Brickemakers, Bricklayers, Masons &c." "These," according to Sir Thomas, "have no voice nor authoritie in our common wealth, and no account is made of them, but onlie to be ruled, not to rule other."[17]

Although Smith ends by conceding that some "lowe and base persons" occupy a public status, that anomaly is explained by an insufficient number of yeomen.[18] Accordingly, more inclusive conceptions began to alter the nature of comprehensiveness, but without surrendering the belief that political inequality was not a contradiction in terms. "A public weal," or rightly ordered society, according to Sir Thomas Elyot, "is a body living, compact or made of sundry estates and degrees of men, which is disposed by the order of equity and governed by the rule and moderation of reason."[19]

A political community, it was commonly argued, depended on shared values, things in common, and that the very essence of a rightly ordered society was to benefit all of its members, not just the few. "Our aim in founding the commonwealth," Plato had Socrates declare, "was not to make any one class especially happy, but to secure the greatest possible happiness for the community as a whole."[20] Yet, as Plato insisted, everyone should share in the happiness of a community but not in its politicalness. Shared happiness—or, more precisely, a share in happiness—was created as a surrogate for the political while power and decision remained privileged preserves, depoliticized in effect. Sir Thomas Elyot illustrated the point in his deliberately drawn distinction between the "common" and the "public." The former he associated with the democratic heresy of wanting to make all things common and shareable. A "common weal," he emphasized, is not a "public weal" or *res publica.* Public weal required that political office be correlated with social rank.[21]

From the perspective of modern theorists, the truly utopian element in Plato's *Republic* proved not to be the notion that men of knowledge should rule—that ideal would gradually be realized in the modern refinement of political knowledge to mean "silver" rather than "golden" knowledge, managerial and technical rather than philosophical—or that the Many should bear the primary burden of labor and produce according to the direction of others; but rather the ideal of a society as a shared austerity of rulers and ruled. Instead, shared happiness would prove as elusive and costly to the Many as its later functional equivalents, patriotism and nationalism.

Political utopianism, as the example of the *Republic* testifies, attempted to idealize the tensions between the conflicting principles of commonality and exclusivity. The most striking proof of that incoherence was the recognition by virtually every Greek political theorist, including Plato and Aristotle, that all constitutions were, in practice, stacked in favor of a particular class or person, that, indeed, the identity of a constitution not only resided in its partiality but, tautologically, the preservation of identity depended upon it: an aristocracy, for example, *had* to rule for the Few. To be sure, theorists tried to save the principle of commonality by claiming that in a rightly ordered constitution rulers would seek the "common good," but even in the "ideal" constitutions power remained, in principle, firmly lodged in the hands of a few.[22]

## V

*Democracy is the generic constitution . . . the resolved mystery of all constitutions.*

Karl Marx[23]

This incoherence lay undisturbed until what used to be known as the "Puritan revolution" of the seventeenth century led to the emergence of the Many as a political force or threat and its recognition as a new theoretical problem. The Many who, in large measure, had been activated by the Protestant Reformation, with its emphases on the actions and convictions of individual believers and the voluntary nature of church governance, became gripped by ideologies proclaiming a new day had arrived for the hitherto excluded:[24] "'[E]very man born in England,' insisted the Levellers, 'cannot, ought not, neither by the law of God nor the law of nature, to be exempted from the choice of those who are to make laws and for him to live under, and for him, for aught I know, to lose his life under.'"[25]

During the course of the English civil wars of that century a great many democratic notions were advanced not so much by systematic discussions of democracy as by the radical extension and connotations given to familiar terms.[26] The claims of conscience encouraged a belief that each individual had a right to be heard in public councils and a contribution to make to the common weal. "Every man by nature being a King, Priest, and Prophet in his own naturall circuite and compasse," argued a Leveller, no one could stand for him except by his consent.[27]

The topic of "church government," which involved questions about the election of ministers by congregations or about who was to determine the proper form of church governance, easily lent itself to political applications. At a more secular level, "the people," as a distinct entity, was extricated from the corporate, hierarchical community of mediaeval theory and asserted as the sole source of legitimate power and an actor in its own right. The political stake of ordinary beings was argued at length, and as a result a crucial awareness developed of a built-in conflict between the people and any system that claimed to represent and act for them. As one pamphleteer put it, it was illogical "for any man to imagine that the shadow or representative is more worthy than the substance, or that the House of Commons is more valuable and considerable than the body for whom they serve."[28]

The English civil wars of the seventeenth century, the American and French revolutions of the eighteenth century forced to the surface the incoherence between the commonality claimed for political society and the rejection of democracy. That tension and the compromise for resolving it found theoretical expression in the so-called republican tradition represented by English writers of the seventeenth century such as Harrington, Milton, and Sidney. While mostly anonymous individuals had been wrestling with concretely democratic ideas and practices, at the level of formal theory a remarkable effort was launched to republicanize the new democratic tendencies. In the process, republican theorists demonstrated the superior power of systematic thought to develop distinctive traditions of discourse whose influence would extend beyond their originating context. English republicans provided instruction to the American Founding Fathers, among others, on how to stabilize modern revolutions.[29]

Prior to the English revolution of the seventeenth century republicanism was commonly understood to be an alternative to kingship, and most republican theorists, like Machiavelli, were antimonarchical. But with the proliferation of populist ideas during the English civil wars republicanism had to redefine itself in the light of the revolutionary power and demands of the excluded. The compromise was prompted by the recognition that a principle that blatantly excluded a now self-conscious *populus* was practically untenable. A strategy had to be devised that would refine both the inclusiveness demanded by the Many and the claim to rule hitherto associated with distinctions of birth and wealth. English Republicanism, as many scholars have demonstrated, was deeply influenced by classical political theories, especially those of Aristotle and Cicero, but what has not been much noted was that, in the process of absorbing classical ideals, republicanism became the heir to classicism's antidemocratic ideology and perpetuated it as a tradition. Tocqueville would encounter its living form in America and he would construct an account that explained how republican theory was able to thwart democratic practice.

Republicans accepted the principle that the "people" were the ultimate political authority and should be granted some legislative representation. Typically, this amounted to little more than a modest enlargement of the electoral base of the House of Commons to accommodate a fairer and broader system of representation. But they held firmly to a belief that actual rule should be exercised by a public-spirited elite of the educated and virtuous, some, like Harrington and Sidney even preserved elements of aristocracy. Theirs was a conception more expediently demotic than democratic, dictated not because principle required that the people should be let "in" but more because there seemed no practical way of keeping them out.

In his utopia of *Oceana* Harrington made provision for a committee of the Council of Legislators to listen to any proposal submitted by anyone pertaining to the future form of government. The committee would then decide which proposals were to be forwarded—with no provision for popular protest. Harrington's summarizes the provision in a passage notable both for the candor with which it contemplates the manipulation of popular participation and for its anticipations of bureaucratic prose: "This was that which made the people (who were neither safely to be admitted, nor to be conveniently excluded from the framing of their commonwealth) verily believe when it came forth that it was no other than that whereof they themselves had been the makers."[30]

Equally important, the Many were beginning to be viewed as a valuable raw material for the two basic processes whereby the state could generate power, the army and the economy. According to Harrington, "In the institution or building of a commonwealth, the first work (as that of builders) can be no other than fitting or distributing the materials. The materials of a commonwealth are the people."[31]

The point was made succinctly in a document drawn up by the king's advisers on the eve of the English civil wars: "the good of democracy," it declared, "is liberty, and the courage and industry which liberty begets."[32]

Not surprisingly republican thinkers were especially concerned to integrate the army, the one institution that had been a consistent champion of greater democratization during the civil wars. The crucial problem in stabilizing politics and ending the revolutionary upheavals was, according to Harrington, gaining control of the militia.[33] The army signified control over an institution that, in its emerging character, was becoming more popular in composition and hence consisted mainly of those who had little or no political voice. Despite the efforts at democratic reform during the English, French, and Bolshevik revolutions, however, armies retained a hierarchical, antidemocratic character that illustrated perfectly the later theories of Michel Foucault concerning disciplinary/surveillance organizations.[34]

The theoretical task that followed from a republican perspective was not to define the polity in terms of the highest political ends possible but to preserve space for a political elite while developing institutional practices that could countervail the power of the Many. At the same time, members of the elite would, of necessity, be circumscribed in what they might accomplish because their primacy had to be veiled. They would, perforce, become pragmatists.

The same strategy can be seen at work among political theorists of greater fame and theoretical sophistication than the republicans and whose theories remain alive today. Hobbes, Spinoza, and Locke all make use of what might be described as "democratic principles"—such as the natural equality of human beings, the possession of equal natural rights, or the stipulation that legitimate authority must first be sanctioned by the consent of every individual member of society (save for women, children, and idiots) —yet none of those writers concluded in favor of a democratic form of government, much less of a democratic society. Each showed how a political system could be "based" on "consent" yet made safe from popular rule. The instrument was a constitution that provided the people with a limited corporate role while, at the same time, dissolving their collective identity into an aggregate of individuals endowed with the same rights but possessing strikingly unequal powers.

In the eighteenth century Rousseau, Paine, and Jefferson made sustained attempts to develop a more democratic conception of republicanism, although it is doubtful that Rousseau considered democracy to be a practical possibility. Paine and Jefferson were perhaps the only two political theorists, since the youthful Plato, who had actually seen a political society even approximating democracy and who, unlike Plato, largely approved of it. Despite their convictions about natural equality and equal political rights, however, both retained an important element of republicanism, Jefferson because he insisted on providing for a "natural aristoi" while declaring African slaves to be an inferior species, Paine because in the end he cared less about politics than about commerce and public enlightenment.

The genius of the Founding Fathers, who drafted the American Constitution, and of the authors of the *Federalist*, who supplied most of the categories for interpreting it, was to redefine republicanism as the transcendence of democratic localism through the creation of a national politics expressive of a nation-state and to prevent the tendencies toward democratic self-government that had emerged during the American Revolution from defining the national constitution. At a general level their achievement was to amalgamate late modern republicanism with early modern liberalism while preserving both the principle of inequality in its racial form and the illusion of political and social equality.

## VI

> *The effect of [a representative system] is . . . to refine and enlarge the public views by passing them through the medium of a chosen body of citizens whose wisdom may best discern the true interest of their country, and whose patriotism and love of justice will be least likely to sacrifice it to temporary or partial considerations. . . . [I]t may well happen that the public voice pronounced by the representatives of the people will be more consonant to the public good than if pronounced by the people themselves.*
>
> James Madison[35]

In America the tensions between republicanism and democracy had been repressed during the revolutionary years amid the general effort to mobilize popular support for the cause of independence and the military campaigns. Republicans were forced to appeal to broad, seemingly all-inclusive principles, such as natural rights, that appeared to place all "mankind" on an equal political footing. "Wartime democratization," which would be a recurrent phenomenon in modern politics, was hastened in America because of the peculiar circumstances of a war that was being waged without the presence of a state and its centralized power. Popular support was a necessity, and a broadened conception of participation was an obvious method of enlisting it. Further, the element of hereditary aristocracy, which English republicanism never fully disavowed, had been virtually nullified by American social conditions as well as by the revolutionary ideology directed against the British system in which aristocracy remained the dominant political class.[36]

The American Revolution thus would represent a turning point in the formation of republican identity. The historical enemy of republicanism, monarchy, as well as its ally, aristocracy, the traditional symbol of its elitist principle, had both been rendered impracticable and rejected theoretically. If republicanism were to survive, its theorists would have to conceive a new political form that could furnish elitism with a fresh principle of legitimacy and, while preserving the executive functions of monarchy, refashion its symbolism around a new office. In sum, republicanism would have to redefine its claims within a revolutionary milieu in which democratizing tendencies had become significant and republicans could no longer rely tacitly on the traditional antidemocratic institutions of monarchy, ecclesiastical establishments, and a hierarchical class structure based on inherited privileges, not the least of which was an officer class. Republicanism had thus to face democracy alone.

The new political form of republicanism had appeared in embryo during the American Revolution. A national political elite began to emerge and worked to develop what for the colonies was an entirely new political plane, nation-centered rather than local, focused upon the high politics of war, diplomacy, and large-scale public financial undertakings.[37] Just how deeply addicted to the heady stakes of power the new elite had become was exposed in a striking passage in one of Hamilton's contributions to the *Federalist.* There he warned what might happen if the aroused and enlarged ambitions of political men were frustrated by constitutional limitations restricting a president to a single term. "The peace of the community or the stability of the government" would be threatened by ex-presidents "wandering among the people like discontented ghosts."[38]

In the course of the revolution a new politics on a grander scale began to emerge. That development did not immediately find a suitably imposing public form, a public theater that might satisfy the ambitions of the increasingly self-conscious political class that had provided leadership for the revolution. Throughout the revolutionary war and in the years immediately thereafter the former colonies remained a loose cluster of thirteen political associations without a dominant center. The resources of political power were scarce and diffused among state and local bodies, while the few central institutions established under the Articles of Confederation were controlled by the states.

The formation of republicanism took shape as a reaction to what its theorists perceived as a condition of anarchy and weakness, a power vacuum created by the thirteen independent states whose internecine rivalries and democratizing tendencies had led to a condition but one stage removed from the state of nature. The republican strategy started first with a private initiative that led to the Annapolis Convention (1786). Although less than half of the states were represented, it was decided that in order "to render the constitution of the Federal Government adequate to the exigencies of the Union" the states should send delegates to a convention whose labors would then be transmitted to the Congress established under the Articles of Confederation and to the state legislatures. Once the delegates were assembled, what had been presented as an effort to amend the articles was tacitly laid aside in favor of bolder schemes for a structure of offices and powers that would enable the elites to carry forward the momentum they had generated during the war; that would create, in the form of a president, a monarchical institution expressive of republican values; and that would contain democracy by attracting it into the new system where its dangerous potential could be neutralized. Thus the new constitution would attempt to republicanize monarchy and democracy, revitalizing and modernizing the one while devitalizing and archaizing the other.

## VII

> *You say that the security of liberty lieth not in the people, but in the form of their government.*
>
> James Harrington[39]

After the convention at Philadelphia had finished its work, it was decided that the proposed constitution should be submitted to special ratifying conventions in the several states. While that strategy circumvented both the authority established by the Articles of Confederation as well as that of the state governments, it also gambled that the public would elect delegates who would support the experiment. Republican theory rose to the historic challenge and produced a justification of the new republican constitution that transcended the occasion. From its origins as a series of partisan tracts aimed at the electors of New York State, *The Federalist Papers* became the one undisputed classic of American political thought as well as one of the three documents whose exegesis was expected to reveal the true meaning of the Founding/Genesis of the new republic.

If the Declaration of Independence and its universalist principles were the expression of democratic tendencies and the Constitution was the embodiment of republicanism, the *Federalist* provided the justification for the sublimation of the one into the other. The essays by Madison, Hamilton, and Jay were remarkable for their lack of subterfuge. They staged an open confrontation between republicanism and democracy and championed republican principles as the remedy for the weak power-potential of democracy, its inherent tendency toward disorder, and its inability to operate on any but a small scale. Democracy was inadequate to the grand vision being staked out: of a political system that, while maintaining social stability, would be able to develop the power resources of a vast continent—"a republic for increase," in Harrington's definition of modern republicanism. One remarkable expression of that conception was the attention given in *Federalist*, nos. 70–72, to the president as an "executive" whose role was to impart "energy" to the whole government through an effective structure: "the true test of a good government is its aptitude and tendency to produce a good administration."[40] Monarchy was thus reconceptualized—as thaumaturgy sublimated into administration. Instead of a king who typically inherited power by direct descent, the *Federalist* envisioned a president who, while retaining the royal authority of a "center" in a system of power, would succeed to it by indirect election. The *Federalist* had not only re-visioned monarchy but, while preserving the idea that a political system required a center from which energy and direction would flow, adapted it to the enlarged political space of America: power would flow not top-downward, as in traditional theories of monarchy, but center-outward.

The process by which the president was to be selected was meant "to afford as little opportunity as possible" for political agitation. To prevent "tumult and disorder," the citizenry would be prevented from forming into a national constituency for the election of the nation's highest officer. Instead citizens were to be contained in the more manageable confines of the separate states, choosing electors who were likely to possess "information and discernment." The small body of electors would deliberate not in one nationally assembled group but in their respective states. "[T]his detached and divided situation will expose them much less to heats and ferments, which might be communicated from them to the people, than if they were all to be convened at one time, in one place."[41]

Republicanism could not, however, dismiss democracy as merely an impractical theory. The *Federalist* had to counter the criticisms of its opponents that the proposed constitution was biased in favor of the Few; that it would create a powerful centralized authority whose remoteness would eliminate the direct participation of citizens except as voters; that, in attempting to settle a republican constitution upon a vast continent, the republican form was being strained beyond its capabilities; and that monarchy would be restored in the unprecedented institution of the president.[42] Each of these criticisms represented either a more democratic conception of political life or a protest against a more restricted conception. Their common assumption was that politics was the activity of the Many and that political scales had to be adjusted to popular capabilities. As Aristotle had once observed of democracy, it is the form managed by those who spend most of each day in earning their livelihood.

In the *Federalist* response republicanism indicated that it was prepared to recognize the democratic principle of popular sovereignty provided that the republican principle of liberty, including private property, was protected from majority rule. The republican acceptance of popular sovereignty has to be understood for what it was, a bold tactic for nationalizing, and thereby rendering abstract, the idea of popular sovereignty while simultaneously preventing the possibility of democracy at the national level.[43]

## VIII

> *[Democracy is] a state of society where everybody more or less takes part in affairs.*
>
> Tocqueville[44]

The American controversy between republicanism and democracy is an important element in the background to Tocqueville's *Democracy in America.*[45] Although Tocqueville can be credited with having been the first to constitute democracy as a serious theoretical subject, almost every commentator has remarked on the great difficulties he encountered in attempting to state clearly what he or others meant by democracy. In part the difficulties were due to the originality of an approach that treated democracy not primarily as an institutional or legal "form" but rather as the reflection of certain beliefs and cultural practices. In part even a highly qualified defense of democracy had to fear offending his aristocratic family and friends, many of whom had suffered tragic losses from the democracy imposed by the revolution of 1789. An equally formidable obstacle was created by his use of an innovative technique that has won him much praise from later commentators. He conducted numerous interviews, almost all of them with representatives of the republican elite, several of whom were the descendants of the Federalist elite. Of necessity, the interviews were not conducted during the Golden Age of republicanism but the Bronze Age of Jacksonian democracy. Himself a member of a defeated aristocracy, Tocqueville was not unmoved by the sour judgments by the relics of another defeated elite, who patiently and eruditely explained that he was observing the decline of the American republic, its deformation into mob democracy.[46]

It was a crucial moment in Tocqueville's maturation as a theorist when he determined not to be the uncritical defender of republicanism. Republican hegemony depended upon being able to perpetuate its historical compromise with democracy whereby democracy reigned but did not rule and elites ruled but did not reign. Tocqueville would conclude that that republican strategy was doomed by an inherent contradiction between admitting the democratic principle of equal freedom for all in a society of unparalleled social mobility and then attempting to restrict political life to the Few.

Although Tocqueville's analysis of the American Constitution would rely heavily upon the *Federalist*, his own theoretical conclusions were frequently at odds with the vision of its authors. He would challenge their fundamental principle concerning the unquestioned supremacy and value of the national government and its inevitable accompaniment, the centralization of power. He would come to doubt that a state even existed in the United States, thus implying that the most important objective of the Founding Fathers, the creation of a national politics and a nation-state, remained unrealized—a view that would be confirmed by the Civil War. Above all, in his discovery and celebration of local democracy and its participatory politics Tocqueville would tacitly side with the Anti-Federalists. He would, however, go beyond their limited theoretical horizon and contest a fundamental conviction of the *Federalist*, that disinterested virtue embodied in a dutiful elite was necessary, or even possible, in a new society where there existed dazzling economic opportunities and few, if any, inherited fortunes. He would propose instead a question that would indicate he was closer to the universe of Marx, where class rule was the fact, than to the world of Madison where it was concealed by norms. Tocqueville would assert that from the beginning America "seemed destined to promote the development of liberty, not the aristocratic liberty of their mother country, but bourgeois democratic liberty of which the history of the world as yet did not present a complete model."[47]

America, then, might be the test not of whether a bourgeois republic was possible but whether the class that had made its way by the pursuit of wealth and status could develop into a politically serious class. Tocqueville's conclusion—written while he was sailing down the Mississippi and before he had begun the first volume of *Democracy*—was hopeful: "There is one thing that America proves conclusively and which I had previously doubted: it is that the middle classes can govern a state."[48]

# CHAPTER IV
# SELF AND STRUCTURE

## I

> *I am involved in a line of sentiments and ideas which go exactly against the grain of my contemporaries, almost without exception. . . . You cannot imagine, Madame, how painful and even cruel it is for me to live in this moral isolation; to feel myself outside the intellectual community of my age and country.*
>
> Tocqueville[1]

One of the recurrent debates among ancient and early modern political theorists concerned whether a life completely absorbed in the cultivation of thought, a *vita contemplativa,* was superior in virtue to a life devoted to attaining political fame, the *vita activa.* The contrary tugs between the two ideals would importantly define Tocqueville's quest for identity.

Among the philosophers of ancient Greece the two life-forms were depicted as mutually exclusive and incapable of being combined without detriment to both.[2] The dichotomy was reinforced by the belief that the contemplative or theoretical life was essentially a life of inaction; the idea that the demands of truth seeking could be fulfilled without reference to any practical impact on the world and, moreover, that if it did seek to act the likely consequence would be the corruption of both thought and the thinker.[3] Concerning God, the unmoved mover, whom Aristotle equated with the highest form of mind, it was said that "It is of Himself that The Intellect is thinking, if He is the most excellent of things, and so Thinking is the thinking of Thinking."[4] It was therefore proper for the thinker to remain self-absorbed and his life uneventful. In contrast, the active life was praised precisely because it aimed at public actions or military deeds that significantly affected the life of society. It was eventful, *res gestae.* Virtue, Cicero declared, depended on its use and its "noblest use is the government of the state and the realization in fact, not in words, of those very things philosophers, in their seclusion, are continually dinning in our ears."[5]

What it meant to make a life of one or the other involved confronting certain demands laid down in the prevailing conception of that life. A minimum requirement of a life-form is that it have an ideal structure to which the aspirant must measure up. Structure consists of the distinguishing qualities of that form rendered into enforced norms or requirements governing the practices peculiar to it. Many brave actors in the *Iliad* remain anonymous, unrecognized because unremarkable by the highly stylized structure of heroic action.

Throughout Tocqueville's political career French politics was affected by questions about the nature and identity of its form. Was it to be monarchical, or parliamentary and republican? Could it be a combination of the first two, or even a combination of democracy and socialism? When Tocqueville began his American journey in 1831, France was akin to a constitutional monarchy. The structure of politics was barely beginning to acquire the norms and practices associated with parliamentarism. Political groupings rather than parties provided an element of organization, while newspapers, journals, and public opinion were limited in their influence. In the years immediately preceding the revolution of 1848, structural elements of party and press received stronger definition, not least because of the emergence of socialism as a political force and of a flourishing political life outside of, and often in opposition to, the official system. The appearance of revolutionary conceptions of action offered a sharp contrast to their rival mode, that of the politician, the insider, whose skills of bargaining, negotiating, and winning favors for constituents defined the *vita activa* in prosaic terms that made the contrasts between it and the truth-seeking *vita contemplativa* seem irreconcilable.

The concept of a theoretical life had likewise changed significantly. Although European intellectual life during the first half of the nineteenth century had not as yet evolved into the sharply defined division of labor associated with "fields" and "disciplines" and there remained ample room for the gifted amateur, a distinctively modern style and temper were becoming predominant: secular, rationalist, and increasingly positivist and scientific in aspiration. New life-forms were being established, their practices and norms defined and reinforced by various institutions, such as scientific societies, academies, reviews and journals, and technical schools and universities. The undisputed importance of science and technology meant, however, that the "life of the mind" no longer looked to the contemplative ideal but sought knowledge that would remedy specific social evils, produce wealth, increase military power, and improve the general human condition. At first this led to an increasingly blurred line between the theoretical and the active life; it was replaced by a different distinction, between the theoretical and the practical. One important consequence of this evolution in life-forms was that the heroic impulse, the drive to achieve something Plutarchian, epical, which had been identified with the life of political figures—great warriors, statesmen, and founders of states and empires—was reversed: the great heroes, the doers of memorable deeds, were likely to be the creators of scientific theories (Newton,

Cuvier, Darwin) or literary "giants" (Shakespeare, Racine, and Goethe). At the same time, the growing role of engineers, bankers, agronomists, economists, inventors, and administrators—of those who would later be summarized as "technicians"—was testimony to the ways in which action was becoming defined almost exclusively in terms of specific tasks, mundane, routinized, and uneventful, with the result that the term "action" seemed grandiose, despite the efforts of Saint-Simonians to heroize engineers and bankers. This reversal in which the norms of performance for theory tended to demand heroic achievements and the norms of action tended to center upon the useful, was aided by the Romantic ideals of greatness preached later by Carlyle and Nietzsche. While Nietzsche heroized thought and banalized the technical action-forms, Carlyle praised both the "seer" and the "captain of industry."

Judged by the emerging conventions that were beginning to govern theory and action, Tocqueville was a nonconformist without being a rebel. He believed that neither life-form was worth pursuing in isolation from the other. "[I]t is not through mediocre sentiments and vulgar thoughts that great things are ever accomplished."[6] At the same time he became convinced that, with the advent of modernity and of equality as its accompaniment, both theory and action had settled into mediocrity. Although responsive to the agonal ideal of the Romanticists, he was unmoved by the model of heroics represented by great scientific achievements. An autodidact in theory, he remained disengaged from the methodological controversies that captivated so many of his theoretically gifted contemporaries. When Mill sent a copy of his *Logic*, Tocqueville, after some delay, wrote a polite note of praise and invited Mill to apply "la logique" to "the study of man," employing "la méthode" to "the matters which you mention." In reply, Mill solemnly noted—possibly to Tocqueville's consternation—that "you share my ideas on the proper method for perfecting social science."[7]

## II

*I cannot forgive Descartes.*

Blaise Pascal[8]

For reasons that were as much personal as political and theoretical Tocqueville was led to confront the question of structure in the form of method, although without addressing it squarely. The agonies of doubt, the political revolution of egalitarianism, and the search for the right form of presenting political truths led him to Descartes, author of the first and possibly the most authoritative text on method. The major influence that served to unite

Tocqueville's concerns and to direct them toward Descartes was Pascal, Descartes's sworn adversary.

It was Descartes who had declared that "in the search for the truth of things, method is indispensable";[9] who had furnished the most radical philosophical rationale for making inquiry a function of a methodical structure; and who had passionately argued that methodism was a commitment requiring a profound intellectual and spiritual reorientation of the inquirer, not just a bland acceptance of certain "steps" or techniques.

Tocqueville's first theory, *Democracy in America*, took shape as the reprise of a Pascalian confrontation with Descartes. "The method" of Descartes, he flatly stated in *Democracy*, had been "openly adopted or secretly followed by all the nations of Europe" and it had provided the ideological framework for the critical and revolutionary ideas which had seized eighteenth-century France.[10] Cartesianism was, for Tocqueville, a main key to understanding modern man and the democratic mentality. The "new science of politics" that he would proclaim was intended as an alternative to Cartesianism; the phrase, "science of politics" was possibly borrowed from the *Federalist*, but Tocqueville inverted the usage.[11] Unlike the authors of the *Federalist*, who appealed to the authority of modern science as a support for their republican principles, Tocqueville's science would be antimethod because anti-Cartesian.

## III

> *But like one who walks alone and in the twilight I resolved to go so slowly, and to use so much circumspection in all things, that if my advance was very small, at least I guarded myself well from falling.*
>
> René Descartes[12]

Descartes's conception of method can be said to have been fashioned as a response to two great and interconnected questions: why is the mind of man prone to err, and how can the mind be reconditioned so as to overcome its weakness and serve as a reliable instrument of inquiry? The initial problem, thus, was set not by some event in the world or some question about the structure of the world, but by the nature of man as expressed in the usages of the mind. The major obstacle to scientific investigation was the self, not the self with its native endowment of reason, but the self as it had been historicized and socialized, the self as defined by inherited beliefs, prejudices, and opinions and as fashioned by diverse carriers of social meaning—family, church, community, school. The self was overloaded, as it were, with excess meanings. The Cartesian discipline aimed to unburden it, reduce the self to mind, and then persuade it to submit to an order in the form of procedures and techniques. Accordingly, the self had first to purge itself of the beliefs that were the source of its errors—and of its identity.

The first and most dramatic step stipulated for the Cartesian truth seeker was the one most likely to torment a Tocqueville: to embrace the method of radical doubt. All that an initiate had hitherto believed or taken for granted should be treated as suspect. "That in order to examine into the truth, it is necessary once in one's life, to doubt of all things, so far as this is possible." Any belief to which there attached "the slightest trace of incertitude" must be stripped away so that the mind, now cleansed, would be able to recognize only what is indubitably clear and distinct.[13]

Once the inquirer had dispensed with the inherited *bricolage* that had served to mediate the external world and his own inner ruminations, he would be in a position to know himself truly. As an unmediated self he would be in the ideal position to be his own judge as to what principles and beliefs to accept. He could thereby become the artificer of his own consciousness, maker of himself. This way to truth, Descartes claimed, is universally accessible, for the differences among men are not due to differences in natural endowments but to the "different ways" or methods they have followed in their thinking. "Good sense is of all things in the world," according to the opening sentence of the *Discourse on Method*, "the most equally distributed."[14]

When the initiate had completed the rites of purgation he was ready to submit to the procedures of inquiry and follow their dictates. Fourteen explicit rules were enumerated to guide the understanding step by step. Cling to them tightly, Descartes exhorted, "as he who entered the labyrinth had to rely on the thread that guided Theseus." Lacking method the mind was apt to be led by "blind curiosity" and to squander its energies "along unexplored paths."[15]

## IV

> *If I had to class human miseries, I should put them in this order:*
>
> *First. Illness.*
> *Second. Death.*
> *Third. Doubt.*
>
> Tocqueville[16]

> *[M]en cannot do without dogmatic beliefs, and I would even maintain that they should have them.*
>
> Tocqueville[17]

The most powerful and influential tradition of modern theory was inspired by the hope of creating models of inquiry fashioned in emulation of mathematics and modern science. For thinkers such as Hobbes, Descartes, and Spinoza, doubt regarding the reliability of the senses and of received knowledge was installed as the pivotal experience of modern thinking.

That starting point, which, in may ways, was also the central concern of the theological tradition whose influence modern theory was most anxious to combat, appears all the more striking because, as in the theological tradition, doubt ends in the promise of absolute certainty. "We can be certain of nothing," Spinoza remarks in his commentary on Descartes, "until we have a clear and distinct idea of God."[18] Owing to its confidence in the methods of scientific and mathematical reasoning, this version of modern theory, unlike theology, looked upon doubt as intellectually fruitful rather than anxiety fraught. Accordingly, doubt was deliberately provoked and radically pursued, yet always conducted within the framework of assurance provided by the rituals of method. Rules of method were supposed to reduce the possibilities of error while maximizing the probabilities of theoretical truth. The installation of the methodical at the center of the enterprise of modern theory meant that, in principle, every theorist would take the same journey, although not necessarily to the same destination.

Tocqueville was a true modern in his belief that doubt was central to modern man. But there the resemblance ended. If the methodical was aesthetically repugnant—it smelled of uniformity—doubt was Tocqueville's demon. In reading his correspondence, one is struck by repeated references to doubt or, more exactly, to its torments. Tocqueville confronted doubt after having first known certainty. He never regained the one or willingly chose the other. It pursued him from adolescence to maturity, nagging at his self-confidence and upsetting his expectations of what the world was or should be. Throughout his life the order of evils, quoted in the preceding epigraph, remained unchanged except that toward the end he had elevated doubt to the second ranking.[19]

Doubt became Tocqueville's equivalent of hell. In Dante's vision hell had its circles of increasing gravity. For Tocqueville they were, in sequence, three: personal, political, and theoretical.

In the first circle, doubt stood for the state of confusion produced by the subversion of certitude, that is, of accepted truths that were, in Tocqueville's view, a necessary condition for personal happiness.[20] Writing to a close acquaintance, Tocqueville lamented the lack of "solid ground" for belief and implored his friend, "If you know a recipe . . . for God's sake!, give it to me." If belief were simply a matter of will, Tocqueville confided, he would have become "devout" a long time ago. He had once discussed his fears with a priest but left dissatisfied, still dogged by the "passionate craving for certitude," which led only to "a black hole without bottom in which opinions swirled around."[21]

In the second circle, Tocqueville came to regard doubt as producing disbelief and thereby undermining one of the main supports of traditional society. Doubt was, in his eyes, a prime cause of social instability and a contributory factor to modern revolutionary movements. Doubt emptied the world of meanings that had depended on certain associations with places or traditional relationships between persons. Doubt was thus the symbol of a world coming apart, of a collapse of meaning that might herald social dissolution. Although Tocqueville would occasionally express the fear that doubt was a harbinger of social disorder and thus seemed to be echoing the alarms of conservatives like Burke and counterrevolutionaries like de Maistre, he was less concerned with the danger of anarchic violence, at least until 1848, than he was with the danger of subjectivism. Doubt, in his view, threw the individual back on his own resources, drove him inward, and hence was the accompaniment to an unhealthy preoccupation with the self and to the neglect of the public realm.

Finally, in the third circle, theory would be dedicated to the replenishment/restoration of meaning by reestablishing control over the disjointed world brought into being by radical doubt. Radical doubt would be combatted but, ironically, its influence would infect the structure of the theory being formulated to exorcise it.

## V

> *My work is oppressed by a feeling of imperfection. Before my eyes I am haunted by an ideal that I cannot reach. . . . There is another intellectual malady which also afflicts me without end. It is a frantic and unreasonable passion for certainty.*
>
> Tocqueville[22]

The first circle traced by doubt originated in an experience during adolescence that Tocqueville claimed had left a permanent mark.

Tocqueville's major biographer, André Jardin, was the first to draw attention to a letter of 1857 that allows us to date retrospectively the moment when Tocqueville first experienced the devastating effects of doubt and to learn how Tocqueville related his continuing fears of doubt to his theoretical life.[23] The significant passages begin with a theme that frequently recurs in Tocqueville's correspondence with close friends and forms the prelude to doubt, an insufficiency of personal power: often "my sentiments and desires are higher than my powers."

> I believe that God has given me a natural taste for great actions and virtues, and that the despair of never being able to reach these objectives, which always hover before my eyes, the sadness of living in a world and at a time which responds so little to these accomplishments . . . is a great cause of the interior malaise that I have never healed.

Tocqueville then remarked that his "passion for success and renown" had been rekindled by the acclaim that had followed the publication of *The Old Regime and the Revolution.* His insatiable "craving" for more success was, he believed, related to "a mind which yearns for certainty but cannot know it; who more than anyone has need of it and is less able to take it in stride." When experiencing this kind of "blackest melancholy" and "despair," he was often "repossessed" by an incident, a kind of negative epiphany, that had occurred when he was sixteen. He recalled being seated in a library surrounded by books; while contemplating the variety of conflicting opinions, shelf upon shelf, he was suddenly overwhelmed by a feeling of "extraordinary violence" that "penetrated his soul." It was an all-pervasive, "universal" doubt that shook the foundations of his world. That experience, he noted—of "being lost in an intellectual world that was revolving constantly and reversing or upsetting all the truths on which I have based my beliefs and actions"—returned to haunt him in later life. The letter closes with Tocqueville alluding to "the new situation" created by the death of his father.[24]

The influence of doubt upon Tocqueville's development as a theorist was enormous. It was a vital element in certain of the major mythemes that helped to shape *Democracy in America.* The mytheme of the "abyss," the tyranny of the majority, and the saving role of religious beliefs in a democracy were all connected to the interplay of doubt and belief, the predominance of one or the other being decisive in determining whether modern societies would gravitate toward a moderate democracy or toward despotism. Which brings us to the second circle, of doubt and society.

Tocqueville never questioned his own inference that, because an individual without a solid bedrock of certain beliefs must find existence intolerable, a society, likewise, required a fund of shared certitudes. For doubt, when widespread, paralyzes the ability to act and leads to feelings of helplessness. Democracies, he concluded, are particularly susceptible to the corrosive effects of doubt because they encourage the union between the modern sentiment that each should think for himself or herself and the egalitarian epistemology implied by the axiom of doubt that no belief is privileged, either by authority, revelation, or social convention.

Accordingly, he would argue in *Democracy* that "men have an immense stake in having fixed ideas about God, their souls, their general duties toward their Creator and their fellows." But these "necessary truths" are beyond the capacities of minds engrossed in the cares of everyday life. Because such truths are cast in a general form, it would be dangerous to let each follow his "unaided reason." "General ideas relative to God and human nature are therefore the ideas above all others on which it is better to restrain the habitual action of private judgment. . . . Only minds truly free from the ordinary cares of life, truly penetrating, subtle, and highly trained can plumb the depths of these truths that are so necessary."[25]

A connection was being forged by Tocqueville between private judgment, doubt, and general ideas at the same time that an opposition was posited between socially necessary truths—that is truths that ought to be as widely shared as possible, but whose hidden and obscure basis remained unfathomable except to subtle and penetrating minds. Thus, he remarks that Democracy's vices "can be demonstrated by obvious facts while its salutary influence is exercised in a way that is insensible and, so to speak, hidden."[26]

The opposition that Tocqueville constructed was a prime example of how he was able to transmute his personal emotions and despair into theoretical representations. He would give it a marvelously inventive form of a contrast between two of the dominant presences in modern French intellectual history, Descartes and Pascal: the one its greatest scientific philosopher and the author of the classic account of scientific method; the other no less a mathematician but also poetic metaphysician, naturalistic believer, sensitive scientist—and, in the end, essentially unclassifiable.

For Tocqueville Descartes was the negative exemplar of private judgment, doubt, abstraction, and the claim that "Good sense or Reason is by nature equal in all men";[27] Pascal was the positive exemplar of truths necessary but not easily demonstrable, a Vergil to Tocqueville's Dante. Because of their actual importance in the organization of Tocqueville's thinking about America, the Descartes-Pascal antithesis needs some elaboration. There is, after all, something astonishing about the spectacle of a young French aristocrat observing a half-savage society through constructs inspired by two of the Old World's most sophisticated philosophers. Tocqueville's Descartes and Pascal would represent two contrasting modern archetypes of theorizing, one eagerly modern, the other only equivocally; one mostly indifferent to context, the other highly sensitive to it.[28]

## VI

> *But because . . . I wished to give myself entirely to the search after Truth, I thought that it was necessary for me . . . to reject as absolutely false everything to which I could imagine the least ground of doubt.*
>
> René Descartes[29]

> *When doubt depopulated the heavens . . .*
>
> Tocqueville[30]

Tocqueville's struggles with doubt not only affected the categories and substance of his thinking but his conception of theorizing as well. He projected the struggle onto a theoretical plane by employing Descartes and Pascal as the symbols for two contrasting modern archetypes of theorizing, one eagerly modern, the other only equivocally.

Pascal had shown how it was possible to believe in a god-dependent universe, that is, to preserve meaning while surrounded by doubt; Descartes had so undermined the foundations of belief, throwing each back on his or her own private reasoning, that those, like Pascal, who did believe and were self-conscious about the implications of doubt were compelled to treat their beliefs as a gamble. When juxtaposed, Descartes and Pascal revealed how, in the modern world, belief and doubt had exchanged places: belief was now the expression of marginality, like aristocracy in the political world.

There was, of course, historical warrant for this pairing. Throughout his writings Pascal had engaged in a running criticism of Descartes and in the course of it had drawn a portrait of two contrasting intellectual temperaments, *l'esprit de géométrie* and *l'esprit de finesse.* The former, which, is Pascal's Descartes, proceeds systematically from principles far removed from ordinary life; the latter, which is less a regimen than a sensibility, "a thinking reed," responds to principles grounded in ordinary life and are to be "felt" or intuited rather than "seen," grasped as a whole without following "technical rules."[31]

The two temperaments represented contrasting conceptions of the self, or, more precisely, of self-confidence. The Cartesian presents a controlled self, translucent, autonomous; its errors traceable and, in principle, corrigible, its possibilities calculable, and its prospects in a mathematicized world infinite. Tocqueville would find every element of this self repugnant. For him, and for his mentor Pascal and their distant teacher, Augustine, the self was ultimately shrouded in elements of mystery, a mystery compounded for Tocqueville by an admixture of Christian despair and post-Enlightenment disbelief. There is a passage in *Democracy* striking not only for its deeply Pascalian vein but startling for its revelation of the intellectual temperament that would attempt to interpret the New World:

> I need not traverse earth and sky to discover a wondrous object woven of contrasts, of infinite greatness and littleness, of intense gloom and amazing brightness, capable at once of exciting pity, admiration, terror, contempt. I have only to look at myself. . . . [Man] gropes forever, and forever in vain to lay hold of some self-knowledge.[32]

The Pascalian temperament views the beliefs on which one based or, better, staked one's existence, as a risky but welcomed action; the Cartesian prefers the assurance of the slow and steady: "But like one who walks alone and in the twilight I resolved to go so slowly, and to use so much circumspection in all things, that if my advance was very small, at least I guarded myself well from falling."[33]

When Tocqueville attempted to describe to John Stuart Mill his own procedure for composing, the result was virtually an ideal statement of the sort of methodological disorder that Descartes's *Rules for the Direction of the Mind* was intended to cure:

> I am never precisely sure where I am going or whether I will ever arrive. I write from the midst of things and I cannot see their order as yet. . . . I want to run but I can only drag along slowly. You know that I do not take pen in hand with the prior intention of following a system and of marching at random toward an end; I give myself over to the natural flow of ideas, allowing myself to be borne in good faith from one consequence to another.[34]

The Cartesian regimen, distrustful of the world in the mediated forms it assumes in the socialized consciousness, seeks to alert the inquirer to the nonrational basis of the beliefs fostered by custom and authority; at the same time that it discredits the generality sought by those agencies, it devalues the exceptional, the unique, that which is the product of special circumstances. In order to make objectivity possible the Cartesian must suspend historicized time and politicized space. It refuses authority to those privileged moments that narrative history treasures when the meaning of events is revealed or great matters settled.[35] In contrast, Tocqueville would insist that insight, even objectivity, depended on chance conjunctions of time and place that had to be seized before they dissolved. The theorist does not stipulate the conditions for objectivity beforehand and then follow them faithfully; rather truth is recognized in the ripeness of time when meaning lies exposed.[36] Truth seeking is dependent as much on *when* one sees as on *what* one sees and *how* one sees. These requirements, especially that of timing, are critical when theorizing aims at eliciting a response in action.

More unorthodox still, truth seeking also depends on *who* Is seeing. Or stated more sharply, Tocqueville insisted upon the special, unreplicable character of his vision of democracy in America. Instead of the Cartesian argument that a method stands for the idea that truth is more likely to be uncovered by an approach that subordinates the self to impersonal standards, Tocqueville emphasized the exact opposite, calling attention to a particular self and its attributes. He would claim that a personal and historical uniqueness had made his theoretical vision possible. His was a privileged self, claimant to a special historically constituted vantage point.[37] He spelled out for his English translator the conditions that had made his particular theory possible:

> Others ascribe to me alternately democratic or aristocratic prejudices; perhaps I might have had one or the other if I had been born in another century and in another country. But as it happened, my birth made it very easy for me to guard against both. I came into the world at the end of a long revolution which, after having destroyed the old order, created nothing that could last. When I began my life, aristocracy was already dead, and democracy was still unborn. Therefore, my instinct could not lead me blindly toward one or the other. I have lived in a country which for forty years has tried a little of everything and settled nothing definitively. It was not easy for me, therefore, to have any political illusions. . . . I had no natural hatred or jealousy of the aristocracy and, since that aristocracy had been destroyed, I had no natural affection for it, for one can only be strongly attached to the living. I was near enough to know it intimately, and far enough to judge it dispassionately. I may say as much for the democratic element. . . . In a word, I was so nicely balanced between the past and the future that I did not feel instinctively drawn toward the one or the other. It required no great effort to contemplate quietly both sides.[38]

These notions found expression in *Democracy.* Early on in that work Tocqueville exhorted his countrymen. Now is the moment, he urges, for grasping the nature of democracy before the inevitable democratic revolution comes to France; and now, while the evidence of its formative period is still visible, is the moment for analyzing America: "Near enough to the epoch when American society was founded to know in detail its elements, far enough from that time to judge what those germs have produced, the men of our day seem destined to see further than their predecessors into human events."[39]

Thus in Tocqueville's account the vision and power of a theory were inseparable from the biography of the theorist: from who he is, what he is, and when he is. Biography, unlike method, is unique and untransferable. Attempts to replicate it or found a school upon it make no sense. The power of the vision to encompass and penetrate two worlds, one dying the other emerging, depends on the theorist being conversant with both worlds but fully implicated in neither. The defeat of the old aristocratic world had deprived him of his privileges but not of his history. Aristocracy had become disembodied, detached from political actualities, thus freeing it theoretically. Because he had been formally disinherited by the new world but actually advantaged by the old, a unique detachment was possible: too much the stranger to the new world to identify with it, too aware of the demise of the old to indulge in political necrolatry.

No longer politically indentured, the aristocratic theorist could contemplate the meaning of aristocracy in radically different theoretical terms. Aristocracy would no longer signify the "best," as it had for Plato, Aristotle, Cicero, and a line of republican theorists, including Jefferson. Aristocracy would now become a metaphor for loss, for the things passing out of the world, from manners to virtue, from taste to disinterestedness. It would come to bear witness to loss in a world so thoroughly numbed by relentless change as to be unable to discriminate between change of fashion and loss of meaning.

Although Tocqueville's letter to Reeve made it appear that he was merely giving a matter-of-fact retrospective, the letter can also be construed as marking a first attempt at constructing a public image of himself as an impartial thinker. Or, alternatively, as an experiment in self-deception. Others before him had done the same. Plato not only constructed himself but Socrates as well. The construction of a theoretical persona, a self to fit a lofty conception of a theoretical office, entailed a degree of disingenuousness on Tocqueville's part. He claimed that his detached view of aristocracy and democracy was made possible by the absence of any family or personal interest that might give him "a natural and necessary affection toward democracy. I have no particular motive to love or hate it." And, symmetrically, he professed to have "no natural hatred or jealousy of the aristocracy," nor any natural affection toward it because "one can only be strongly attached to the living." The inversion represented by that formulation is startling.

Given the harsh treatment of the French aristocracy, including Tocqueville's family and relatives, by the revolutionaries, the question for a Tocqueville was not whether he had "a natural and necessary affection for democracy," much less a "natural hatred or jealousy of the aristocracy," but whether he preserved a natural hatred for democracy and a natural affection for aristocracy. After reading *Democracy* one might also be skeptical of Tocqueville's declaration that it would be fruitless to consider reviving aristocratic institutions "because one can only be strongly attached to the living." There are, Tocqueville would show, many forms in which aristocracy might be perpetuated without calling for the restoration of the Old Regime, just as there are many ways of coming to terms with democracy short of truly embracing it.

These contrasting modes began to make their presence felt while Tocqueville was puzzling out the key to understanding America. "One of the most striking features of American institutions," he noted in his journals, "is that they form a perfectly logical chain." Yet, he insisted, it is "*profoundly* superficial minds" that, after praising "logic and uniform laws," proceed to comment on the lack of them in most societies. "Then they can create theories in which these two merits are exhibited." To grasp the nature of America, one should not look for a system but for the historical absences that allowed Americans to build an apparently simple system. "[T]hey have been able to build their social edifice on a tabula rasa."[40] America might display the geometrical spirit but it required an inspired intuition to understand its origins and not be misled by social contract rhetoric into believing that Americans had effected a kind of transubstantiation that had enabled democracy to pass from the state of nature into political society without benefit of inheritance.

Tocqueville would transform the Descartes of Pascal's philosophical criticisms into an ideological form, Cartesianism, and represent it as a crucial element in the modern ideology of equality, revolution, and democracy. A Cartesian society would display discontinuity, disconnection, loneliness—in short, the abyss of a collectivity without a shared identity. At the same time, like the Cartesian investigator, its actors would begin with the self but, instead of asking how the self might be shaped into a reliable instrument of inquiry, it asked how can I advance the interests whose acquisition defines who I am in the world?

When Tocqueville came to write the second part of *Democracy*, his remarkable analysis of the culture of democracy was based on the premise that Americans, without ever having read Descartes, had produced a Cartesian culture by simply following out the implications of an egalitarian society. "That should not surprise anyone."[41] Democracy would be Cartesianism operationalized, a political society that had traded meaning for uniformity, the political analogue to reductionism. In place of genuine diversity, it substitutes mere subjectivism, its version of Descartes's *cogito* principle, "I think, therefore I am." Democracy, like Cartesianism, would seem the realized condition of that Pascalian void opened up by modern revolution and carried to extremes in America, a society without a common identity. "American society is composed of a thousand diverse elements recently assembled. . . . There is no common memory, no national attachments."[42]

For Tocqueville Pascal was the finest expression of a culture that prized the rare and the exceptional. If Descartes symbolized the idea of a method that was in principle available to all, Pascal stood for the inimitable mind whose "burning love of truth" represented "a rare, creative passion," an exaltation of the theoretical life into an *imitatio Christi*, a self-immolation in the cause of truth: "When I see him, if I may put it this way, tearing his soul free from life's cares to commit himself entirely to this quest, and prematurely breaking the bonds which tied him to the body, so that he dies of old age before he was forty, I am astonished, and I know that no ordinary cause was at work in such an extraordinary effort."[43]

In Pascal's *Pensées* Tocqueville found, and responded to, themes of suffering, sadness, and solitude, of yearning for a hidden god. These he shaped into a conception of the theorist as a suffering servant in a democratic age when the theoretical life faced a culture of practicality that made a Pascalian theorist both necessary and unwelcome. "The majority lives in perpetual self-adoration; only strangers or experience can bring certain truths to the attention of Americans."[44] But strangers, Tocqueville would claim, are the deviant thinkers in a democratic society. Democracy tolerates but it also punishes ruthlessly. Unlike the old-fashioned despots who struck at the body but left the soul free, it strikes "directly at the soul." Democracy says: you are free to think as you please and to retain all of your rights but "henceforth you are a stranger among us . . . a polluted being."[45] That fate revives an earlier question: why should the god who presides over history permit once again the sacrifice of the unique and precious to the undiscriminating Many? Perhaps Pascal is again Tocqueville's teacher, but this time a Pascal with an element of defiance of one who "rallies . . . all of the powers of his intelligence to discover the most hidden secrets of the Creator."[46]

## VII

> *I was then in Germany, to which country I had been attracted by the wars which are not yet at an end . . . the onset of winter detained me in a quarter where, since I found no society to divert me, while fortunately I had also no cares or passions to trouble me, I remained the whole day shut up alone in a stove-heated room, where I had complete leisure to occupy myself with my own thoughts.*
>
> René Descartes[47]

In his treatise on philosophical method Descartes describes how he deliberately shut himself off from the world and sought solitude in order to subject all of his opinions to close scrutiny and to begin the hazardous business of divesting himself of his acquired beliefs and bypassing received authorities so that he could, as far as prudently possible,[48] create a tabula rasa on which to reconstruct the foundations of reliable knowledge. And yet, beginning with Tocqueville's negative epiphany, the individual encounter with doubt in the solitude of a library, and continuing with his voyage to America, there were striking parallels between, on the one hand, Tocqueville's theoretical progress, which was possible only because of his decision to leave the familiar certainties of France for the unknown America, and, on the other, Descartes's decision to put aside inherited beliefs and traditional values.

Tocqueville, as we have seen, broke with family and close friends in order to journey to a strange land where his most frequent experience was that of silence and solitude and where he, too, would find much of his intellectual, spiritual, and social legacy unsettled by the encounter with emptiness and loneliness.[49] Shortly after returning from America he summed up his post-Cartesian wisdom: "there is no absolute truth or good in human affairs."[50]

Later in his life when he turned to writing his *Souvenirs* of the revolution of 1848 and, again, when toward the end of his life he began *The Old Regime and the Revolution*, the first theme mentioned is solitude. Solitude not as the Cartesian quest for certainty but as the setting for recollecting loss—of his political career by the revolution of 1848, then of a whole way of life denied him by the revolution of 1789. Unlike Descartes, Tocqueville would be profoundly anguished by the heavy price exacted by modern self-examination, particularly in its political and social implications. And unlike Descartes the past seemed more precious and modernity more troubling. But perhaps the most crucial confrontation with his own "Cartesianism" would involve the distinctive characteristic of Tocqueville's style of theorizing, his dependence on general ideas to convey theoretical meaning. His genius was inseparable from his use of general ideas yet he regarded them as the *damnosa hereditas* of Cartesianism, perpetuated in the glib ideological formulas of revolutionary intellectuals in France, and institutionalized in American democracy in the Protestant culture of private judgment. Ironically, however, general ideas were to be Tocqueville's signature and would prove to be one of the crucial means he would employ for overcoming the paralyzing form that doubt often takes for the theorist, the form of empirical facts.

## VIII

*Tocqueville was not a theoretician but rather had more contempt than appetite for political speculation.*

Jean-Claude Lamberti[51]

*[A] book the essential doctrine of which it is not likely that any future speculations will subvert, to whatever degree they may modify them, while its spirit, and the general mode in which it treats its subject, constitute it the beginning of a new era in the scientific study of politics.*

John Stuart Mill[52]

*So we must abandon any searches for the coherent system of a philosopher and concentrate instead on capturing the pluralism and diversity of Tocqueville's mind.*

James T. Schleifer[53]

Unlike predecessors such as Thucydides, Cicero, and Machiavelli, Tocqueville did not come to theory from a background of firsthand political experience. Unlike his contemporaries—Hegel, Marx, and Mill—Tocqueville did not come to politics with a theoretical preparation. Nor was he beguiled, as were Marx, Mill, and Comte, with the prospect of setting the study of society on a systematic basis.

More than temperament important political stakes figured in Tocqueville's aversion to highly systematic thinking and brought him closer to Burke than to Mill. Historically, the opponents of the French Revolution had accused the critical thinkers of the previous century of being the accomplices of revolution and attributed their revolutionary ideas to an infatuation for logicomathematical modes of thought. The revolutionaries before the fact had inspired a misguided attempt to impose a new system on forms of life which were better comprehended through historical and political terms and more closely attuned to the needs of political action than of scientific investigation. Tocqueville resisted the conjunction of two forms of modern power, revolution and a scientific conception of theory. He conceived a political realm that would remain interminably ambiguous and historically burdened rather than one potentially transparent and awaiting liberation from the past.

Tocqueville did not so much "develop" into a political theorist as feel his way toward becoming a politically engaged theorist and eventually into a theoretically minded politician. He became a political theorist in the course of his travels through a new political world. There he was gradually impelled to theorize in order to convey the staggering impact of the new republic upon his inherited conceptions of a political society. In attempting to assess the meaning of what he had observed, he began to employ abstract and general ideas. Aside from the significance of the move from observation to theorizing, that development was fraught with political significance, both for the construction of *Democracy* and for all of Tocqueville's subsequent writings.

Shortly after Tocqueville had returned from the United States he wrote anxiously to Beaumont: "My ideas become enlarged and generalized. Is this good or bad?"[54] Why was he apprehensive?

Generalization and abstraction are forms of theoretical action that represent the phenomenal world in a certain distinctive way that erases particularities and idiosyncrasies. They are modes of escaping ambiguity. When Tocqueville remarked that his ideas had become "enlarged and generalized," he was calling attention to the political character of general ideas, to how generalization and abstraction extend the power of theory to identify and survey an otherwise impossibly broad field and fix its meaning by emphasis and reduction. At the same time, as the anxiety of his query to Beaumont hinted, there was an affinity between generalization, abstraction, and systematic, logical thinking, and perhaps with the radicalism of the philosophes and the revolutionary visionaries of the 1790s. Generalization empowered the theorist but, in a Tocqueville, it also produced guilt. How, then, to employ generalization yet avoid its political pitfalls and historical associations?

## IX

> *Aristocracy naturally leads the mind to contemplation of the past and settles it there. Democracy, in contrast, gives men a kind of instinctive disgust for the old.*
>
> Tocqueville[55]

The theoretical form that we know as *Democracy in America* resulted from a political insight stimulated by the contrast between the New and the Old. The crucial element, and source of stimulus, in virtually all of the contrasts was a certain absence. For example, Tocqueville would use the absence of aristocracy and of feudal institutions to explain the comparative benignity of the American Revolution. What is striking about the nonparallel was that the institutions in question were no longer prominent in France. The comparison was between a society in which a certain institution barely survives as an anachronism and one where it never existed. The comparison thus served as a teaching about loss, about the role of what has disappeared, and about why it was important to discover or to contrive what might serve in its stead. As Tocqueville wrote, "At the moment when an aristocracy is dissolved, its spirit still hovers over the mass, and its instincts are perpetuated long after it has been conquered."[56]

Tocqueville's remarkable insight was that the structure that generalization and abstraction impart to a theory has a certain analogous relation to the structure of action that increasingly comes to be characteristic of the modern state bureaucracy. State power is most effective when its population is made subject to the same general rules; it becomes halting when forced to deal with numerous exceptions, particularly when the exceptions have power resources independent of the state. Accordingly, bureaucracy, like generalization, wants to override exceptions, abstract them out, smooth the ambiguities. Tocqueville countered by drawing attention to the absence of centralized administration in the United States and to the contrast it presented to a society that was heavily administered from the center. The American federal system, with its crazy-quilt of multiple overlapping jurisdictions, complex division of authority, and "extraordinary decentralization," was a masterpiece of political ambiguities, a trade-off between communal liberties and efficiency.[57] Tocqueville perceived the strength of American particularity in resisting administrative generalization as a reminder of French loss pointing backward to a time when France was a decentered society. Later Tocqueville would make its re-creation the principal theme of *The Old Regime.*

Once he became convinced that the actions and institutions of Americans were comprehensible as the creations of a distinctively egalitarian politics and culture, the shape of theory had to accommodate the tensions between generality of meaning and the countering influences of particularity, between transparency and ambiguity. Egalitarian was, in Tocqueville's eyes, synonymous with sameness. It was the democratic analogue to bureaucratic rule and to theoretical generalization and abstraction. Abstraction meant factoring out many of the sort of differences that Tocqueville cherished. This caused him to hesitate over using "enlarged and generalized" ideas even though the radical homogeneity of a democratic society seemed to "naturalize" the use of explanatory abstractions such as equality, democracy, and what Tocqueville called the "social condition." That discovery, of the correspondence between a theoretical structure based on abstraction and the actuality of a democratic society, he would explore more fully in the second installment of *Democracy in America.* To a sensibility inclined toward the antidemocratic, the affinity between certain abstractions and the suppression of differences by a democratic society suggested that while abstraction was a necessary element for a theoretical understanding of democracy, it was also susceptible to certain specific pitfalls inherent in the reliance upon abstract generalization. There is a moment in *Democracy* when he seems to want to rein in the temptation to generalize. He reminds himself that "there is nothing more unproductive for the human mind than an abstract idea. I shall therefore make haste towards the facts."[58]

The homogeneity of egalitarian America invited a generalizing that might produce true statements of broad relevance. At the same time, however, those statements, like democracy itself, might lead to the suppression of deviant "facts," exceptions to the rule. The exception(al) or rare was the phenomenal equivalent of aristocracy, of what was vulnerable and precious. Hence, although the tendencies expressive of a democratic society were recognized and incorporated theoretically, they had to be resisted by discovering countervailing practices or beliefs. A theory of democracy had to be constructed of tensions between general tendencies and particular countertendencies. The reverse would be true of Tocqueville's theory of aristocratic society—particular tendencies and general countertendencies—in his last great work on the Old Regime. The political expression of the theoretical resistance to democracy, while explaining and even partly justifying it, would be the incorporation of antidemocratic elements into liberalism in the hope of preventing or, at least, containing the emergence of a politically active and self-conscious demos.

## X

Present-day readers most often read *Democracy* as one book, although it was actually published in two widely separated installments of 1835 and 1840.[59] Tocqueville himself insisted that "the two parts complement each other and form a single work."[60] Recent commentators have claimed, however, that the differences between the first and second installments of *Democracy* are so marked as to indicate a major shift in Tocqueville's expository strategy, from political institutions (part 1) to social practices and cultural values (part 2), and hence justify treating them as two distinct works. Perhaps, however, it is less a matter of "two *Democracies*" than of two Tocquevilles, a younger and politically inexperienced Tocqueville who traveled to America but wrote the first part after his return and an older Tocqueville who by the time he had completed the second had been elected to the National Assembly. The difference between the two parts may result not from one being "abstract" and the other "concrete" but from a tension between a growing frustration with contemporary politics and an increasing sense of theoretical mastery. Tocqueville implied as much when he wrote to Mill about the somewhat cool reception that critics had accorded the second part. His "original sin," Tocqueville suggested, was to demand too much of a readership ill-prepared for a general discussion that ranged between France and the United States. "Only those accustomed to the search for general and speculative truths" would be intrigued by the parallels.[61]

## XI

> [Democracy in America] *is the first philosophical book ever written on Democracy, as it manifests itself in modern society.*
>
> John Stuart Mill[62]

> *Tocqueville was at once analytically lucid and systematically ambiguous.*
>
> Seymour Drescher[63]

*There is no point in searching in the United States for uniformity and permanence of viewpoint [in administration], minute attention to details or perfection of administrative procedures; what one finds instead is an image of force, a trifle wild it is true but full of vitality; of life that is not without mishaps but also is full of movement and striving.*

Tocqueville[64]

Modern understandings of theory are still in thrall to Hobbes's ideal of a theory as an interconnected and logically consistent "whole" in which clarity of basic concepts is regarded as essential. The emphasis on clarity is the accompaniment to the modern assimilation of theory to a mode of "construction" that depends on "conceptual rigor" to produce the interlocking building blocks of which a theory is allegedly made. Tocqueville's theory, in contrast, would be panoramic rather than architectonic. He often described himself as attempting to "paint" a "general condition" (*état*). Instead of arguing or explicating his ideas, he tended to *display* them as images on a broad canvas, as effects that were visually and aesthetically, rather than logically, compelling.

Tocqueville's main concepts were, to the despair of later commentators, remarkable for their diverse meanings. Instead of pouncing upon the contradictions, evasions, and ambiguities in Tocqueville's formulations, however, it may be more revealing to query their implications and to suspend conventional notions about the primacy of theoretical orderliness to consider what might be learned from a body of ideas that is at once highly theoretical yet disorderly. Such a theory will often seem confusing, on the verge of collapse, forced, and artificial. It may also compensate with dazzling insights and unsuspected truths produced by its refusal to constrict a particular idea by one invariant meaning. As we shall see later, Tocqueville refused to confine "democracy": sometimes he uses it to characterize a whole society, at other times its politics and culture, and at still other times as the opposite of aristocracy. The interesting question is not about logical or methodological shortcomings but rather, What was it about the world that might elicit a certain theoretical disorderliness?

In part, as suggested earlier, theoretical disorderliness was a consequence of the tensions internal to the theory, a result of the search for the ambiguities that might disrupt generality. Perhaps, too, disorderliness was a means of registering the multivalency natural to a society freer than any existing hitherto. New World disorder was not the product of uncontrolled anarchy but, like the surprisingly conservative politics of Americans, within the normal range of the theoretical order designating "democracy." Democracy's theoretical character derives from its generality. It pervades the whole society yet it assumes a variety of expressions. Sometimes it appears as volatile, other times as rigid, sometimes as deviant, other times as envious to the point of refusing any superiority, most times as devoutly law-abiding, but sometimes as violent in the extreme. Democracy does not display that one-dimensional character attributed to it by ancient and early modern theorists as the revenge of the have-nots elevated to a constitutional form: in America democracy has no domestic enemies. Because it is modern, it has to be tracked in the different manifestations made possible by modern freedom. Modern freedom signifies the social openings possible when, for the first time in Western history, a great society has come into existence in blissful innocence of the notion of prescriptive privilege.

As far back as the history of theory extends, mind had been provoked to seek an understanding of society by the contrasts in status, wealth, power, and knowledge and their conflicting claims. In the face of rampant particularity, generalization was difficult to sustain, theologians excepted. The coming of modern democracy meant the leveling of extreme differences, or at least the reduction of their status from the "natural" or "inevitable" to one in need of defense. The extension of democracy to most domains of New World society, to the social, the economic, the cultural and educational, as well as to the political meant that the social landscape presented fewer reference points. A different system of reference was needed in order to interpret democracy.

Aristotle's Lyceum is said to have collected 158 different species of political constitutions; Tocqueville was convinced that the political world, insofar as it was becoming modernized, was being reduced to one. He had discerned a modernity that was driven by a will to dehistoricize, to rationalize disappearance. His theoretical reaction was to repopulate the world through an imaginary of loss. Certain contrasts were superimposed on American democracy, such as old and new, aristocracy and democracy, not solely from ideological inclination but as much from theoretical necessity. He was among the first to sense that modernizing is potentially totalizing. It expunges the rival contexts that give meaning to particularity. The theoretical expression of its monopoly is the triumph of generality, not as a category imposed on a recalcitrant reality, but as the epitaph for a subjugated, dehistoricized reality. Generalization is that form of statement that is the context and allows no other. Its political counterpart *is* democracy subordinate to egalitarianism, while its governmental counterpart, or temptation, is administrative centralization.

Tocqueville did not set out to compose a conception of democracy as multivalent. It was thrust upon him in astonishment at the spectacle of a world seized by unending change, by the pure realization of the modern in a world so new as to be barely separated from its natural condition. But thrust upon him in alarm as he contemplated the threat of democracy to the history-ridden societies long removed from the state of nature, from that pure condition of generality and abstraction represented in the "laws of nature."

## XII

*My object here is not to seek for new truths, but to show in what manner facts already known are connected with my subject.*
Tocqueville[65]

As we approach the moment when Tocqueville begins the journey that will culminate in a theory, certain recurrent features of theories bear mentioning. Every political theory constructs a conception of the political as a province of common concerns to its members and to the authorities entrusted with its care. A theory constitutes the political by providing a structure of presentation that allows or elicits a certain existence/expression to the political. Structure does not so much dictate substance as align it while determining its order of priority.

The idea of a theoretical structure provides a way of exposing the inevitable gap between, on the one hand, the theorist's aspirations toward control and, on the other, the chosen theoretical form and the content that it is able to encompass and represent. Content may work against form's attempt to circumscribe meaning and subvert what the theorist intends to demonstrate: structure and control, illusion and elusion.

At the center of Tocqueville's first theoretical structure was a primary principle. He called it "a premier fact." It served to connect, explain, and signify each of the main parts of the theory.[66] This "same fact," he wrote, "from which each particular fact seems to derive . . . [forms] a central point where all my observations terminate."[67] A "premier fact" thus exercises a certain kind of power: it brings into being other facts, which, in turn, depend on it. Elsewhere Tocqueville referred to such facts as "generative facts" to indicate their sovereign/paternal status. The "parts" of the theory connected by the premier fact constitute a second element consisting of concepts, categories, and relationships/facts. For Tocqueville among the most important of these were: liberty, centralization, participation, majority tyranny, individualism, Cartesianism, and political culture.[68]

These and other Tocquevillean concepts—tyranny of the majority, equality of social condition, and despotism—acquire an enhanced meaning by virtue of their relation to the "premier fact" of equality. The acquired meaning will differ from received usages. For example, instead of being merely a type of constitution, as in traditional theoretical discourse, Tocqueville's "democracy" represents a form of necessity that generates and is generated by new political and social forces; but democracy also stands for the universalization of political rights under broadly egalitarian social circumstances. Where Marx would identify necessity with economic and technological forces, Tocqueville would give it a political character, an emanation of democracy. He depicts democracy not only as a form of government but as a massive social pressure resulting from the actions of countless free individuals, of "millions of men marching at the same time towards the same point on the horizon: their language, religion, customs different, but their end in common."[69] Democracy represents the weight of diffused power, a massiveness that is quantitative in character because derived from the uniformity that, paradoxically, accompanies individualism. It literally depresses: "It seems to me that a sudden heaviness weighs down on me, and that I am dragged along in the midst of shadows that surround me."[70]

Within Tocqueville's theory democracy was in the nature of a major theme as well as a conceptual category. Indeed, rather than a series of arguments, Tocqueville's theory consists of a series of master themes. I call them "mythemes" (borrowing from Lévi-Strauss). The function of mythemes is to establish the basic meaning-pattern of the theory. The mythical is not a category of impotence; powerlessness is the burden of a specific mytheme, the archaic. The mythical is power-laden; hence a mytheme stands for a materialized idea that, in Tocqueville's usage, operates as a force in the world. "Equality of condition" is such a force; it is "irresistible" and "universal" in its sway. Its influence is everywhere. "Democracy" is itself a mytheme: it gives a general meaning to the emerging shape of the modern world; its influence, too, is all-pervasive. "Despotism" is another mytheme, a threat rather than an actual presence but a possible fate. Mythemes originate in ordinary facts but they acquire an enlarged domain and become portents of some huge fate, such as that depicted in Tocqueville's famous vision of a world whose fate can be like either that of the autocratic despotism in Russia or that of the democratic despotism intimated by the United States. Perhaps the most pervasive of all mythemes concerns disappearance and the recollection of it. I shall call it "the archaic" or archaism. Although it may be politically powerless, Tocqueville will try and lend it theoretical significance. The archaic is made to intrude constantly, upsetting the present by the remembrance of things past. It can be illustrated by Tocqueville's studiedly casual remark that what is true of the disappearance of aristocratic manners is true of aristocracy generally: "It is not necessary to attach too much importance to this loss; but it is permissible to regret it."[71]

As employed here a mytheme is not a construction that ignores historical fact nor is it intended as a criticism of Tocqueville's use of such facts. Rather "myth" is intended to carry the force of "preter" suggesting "more than, beyond" historical fact. In Tocqueville's use the mytheme is the characteristic element that connects what is most distinctive in Tocqueville's thinking, the politically inspired blending of theory and history.

In describing the structure of Tocqueville's theory I may have left the impression of a static system. Nothing could be more misleading: it would lose not only the most salient qualities of Tocqueville's thinking—its fluidity, suppleness, and, above all, its vivid imagery—but the strategic element that serves to transmit Tocqueville's intentions to his theoretical structure and to shape it accordingly. By the strategic element I mean the deploying of certain theoretical notions as images to produce a desired political effect. It can be illustrated by a letter of Tocqueville to his brother in which he outlined his proposed discussion of the crucial notion of centralization. His *idée mère*, or what I have called a mytheme, concerns the "General Influence of the Democratic Ideas and Sentiments . . . on the Form of Government." He writes of his intention to show "*theoretically*" how they promote centralization. Then he hopes to turn to the circumstances that promote it, noting that they "do not exist in America and exist in Europe." Then, "by *facts*" he will show that centralization is growing in Europe as the power of the state increases and that of the individual grows less. He plans to follow this with a definition of the type of democratic despotism that might come to Europe and then consider what legislation could be introduced "to struggle against this tendency of the social condition." A last chapter would offer counsel on how to make "use" of equality but not "compete" with it.[72]

Of all the elements in Tocqueville's theory, the strategic one is most obviously in the service of Tocqueville's politics. A strategy is not external to a theory but an important determinant of a theory's structure. It influences choices (e.g., among facts) and the distribution of emphasis (e.g., deciding what is primary). Some of Tocqueville's strategies are devised to situate himself in relation to the contending forces of his day, others to define the nature of his intervention, and still others to promote his political fortunes. Some of the elements of strategy were evident in the closing words of Tocqueville's introduction to *Democracy*: "in writing [this book] I did not intend to serve or to combat any party. I have attempted to see, not differently, but further than the parties; while they are preoccupied with tomorrow, I have wanted to reflect on the future."[73]

That lofty disclaimer was a kind of prolegomenon setting the stage for the conflict that would tear at Tocqueville throughout his public life. At one and the same time he wanted to establish a theoretical self "above" politics and "outside" the partisan contests for determining the present, and he wanted a political self that could pursue a political career according to the same lights as traditionally defined the *vita contemplativa.* He wanted to turn the impartiality of theory, its vocation of truth telling, into the effectiveness of the actor without compromising the true and independent self who aspired to play the mediator.

# CHAPTER V
# DOUBT AND DISCONNECTION

## I

*This mission would flatter the pride natural to a young people who would see arriving for their sakes travelers from the old society of Europe who think that they have something to learn there.*

Louis Serunier, French minister plenipotentiary to the United States, 17 May 1831[1]

In April 1831 Alexis de Tocqueville set sail for the United States in company with Gustav de Beaumont, who, except for an occasional moment of political estrangement later, would remain his lifelong friend. Their declared purpose was to investigate various experiments with penal institutions in the United States. Although Tocqueville later remarked that that study had been "a pretext," he was not implying that from the outset he had intended to write what we know as *Democracy in America*.[2] He and Beaumont were genuinely interested in penal reform and shortly after returning to France they produced a book on it. Tocqueville would maintain an interest in prisons throughout his parliamentary career.

What had to be disguised was not a theoretical project—for as yet he had none—but a political ambition. Two years before their departure he had exhorted Beaumont that "we must make of ourselves political men."[3] But in the interval his chances for a political career were stymied, a fact that had an important bearing on his decision to leave France. Official doubts existed about his personal enthusiasm for the Orléanist regime and even more doubts about the political loyalties of his family and friends.

His forebears had served the Old Regime, suffered persecution at the hands of the revolutionaries of 1789, and maintained an ultraroyalist reserve toward Louis Philippe, the Orléanist monarch installed after the expulsion of Charles X. Tocqueville's father, brother, and some of his closest friends were stoutly antiliberal, unyielding in their distaste for parliamentary politics and, on occasion, even tempted to plot against Louis Philippe and in favor of a Carlist restoration.[4]

Matters came to a head in 1830 when, as a junior magistrate, Tocqueville was required to swear an oath supporting the Orléanist regime, which had assumed power following the July revolution of 1830. Tocqueville faced his first political *crise de conscience.* He took the oath in the face of strong familial disapproval. His closest friend described the act as dishonorable and even traitorous.[5] Tocqueville promptly made another vow, that "if at any moment the new dynasty should prove incompatible" with the true interests of the nation, he "would conspire against it." But to his future wife he wrote, "I am at war with myself."[6]

Shortly thereafter he decided upon his American journey. To Beaumont he wrote that "it is impossible to play any role whatever here."[7] Tocqueville had become a political émigré of sorts, a casualty of yet another revolution which he nonetheless defended—though without enthusiasm—as better than anarchy or a republic.[8] In a letter to a close friend announcing his decision "to forsake the laziness of private life and to embrace the hectic existence of a traveler," he described himself as abandoning private life for a journey "invested with a public character."[9]

Through no fault or act of his own, but owing to the contingencies of genealogy, Tocqueville began as an outsider to his own society. He was about to have that status doubly confirmed by his two voyages, one to an alien land, the other the return to a homeland where aristocracy had lost much of its political status. He would find on returning that among his family and friends earlier doubts about his own political reliability were revived as, disbelievingly, they watched him commend the democratic heresy to his own countrymen.

A few years before leaving for America he had composed an extended self-analysis. He saw himself as "proud" and "easily offended," even resentful of his more articulate contemporaries. "Every day I am aware of a need to be first that cruelly torments my life." He feared, too, that his legal studies would turn him into "a legal machine . . . incapable of judging a great movement and leading a great action."[10]

Over the next two decades Tocqueville would be deeply involved in French political life, but it would be his American journey that compelled him to define his politics, his public persona, and himself. The unique form which that self-clarification took has not been fully appreciated because the specificity of reference in the title, *Democracy in America,* has tended to mislead readers into thinking that it is simply an account of the American political system written for the edification of Frenchmen. Tocqueville's *theoria* or theoretical journey was really three journeys, one to America, another a return to France, and the third an interior journey. All three journeys were bound together.

## II

*It is unusual for two men of distinguished social position, father and son, to publish books on the same subject only a few years apart—with the son's work becoming instantly famous, and the father's ignored and soon forgotten. Such is the story of the two Tocquevilles. . . . It is strange that Alexis seems never to have mentioned his father's books.*

R. R. Palmer[11]

Tocqueville can fairly be described as having been hemmed in by familial traditions of aristocratic conservatism and of loyalty to a principle of legitimacy derived from inheritance rather than based on choice or consent. His American journey turned into a quest for an identity of his own, distinct from the one that was automatically his by birthright. The American adventure, according to Beaumont, "worked a complete change in [Tocqueville's] manners, transforming him from a somewhat cold and overly reserved" person into "an affable and gracious" one.[12]

At first American culture came as a shock. He saw no strict traditions of filial and familial obligation, only freedom: freedom to choose one's moral, religious, and political beliefs; to choose vocations and locations; and then to change any and all of these traditionally stable referents of Old World existence. Unnerved at first by the modern notion of freedom as choice, not of casual preferences concerning ephemera, but of first-order beliefs and primary ties, Tocqueville paused to lecture himself sternly that "life is neither a pleasure nor a grief but a serious duty imposed on us, and to be taken on and to be seen through to the end to our credit."[13]

His Old World resolve was, however, unprepared for the magnitudes he encountered. The vast size of America, the scale of its political undertaking, the dreams of fabulous success entertained by ordinary citizens, the intensity, even brutality, of life upset his expectations and confidence in the categories he was about to employ. A theorist who had journeyed to a largely natural world, where man's presence was intermittent rather than dominant, likely to be fleeting rather than lasting, would not have come easily to Marx's vision, or that of many of his contemporaries, of a world with man's signature triumphantly written upon it. For Tocqueville theory would have to come to terms with a "force superior to man."[14]

America had liberated Tocqueville but it had also left him exposed, or, as he frequently put it, "solitary," surrounded by an oppressive "silence." At home the Old World hierarchies of class, status, and patriarchy were not only social voices giving directions/directives, but defenses, forms of power, and these democracy denied. In America he would see himself as confronting a new kind of power, not the power of singular leaders or the power made available by institutions, but powers that were vast and impersonal, a product of historical confluences unplanned by human agents. Democracy would signify the presence of a ubiquitous, collective power, mild yet irresistible. Its operation would be invisible, subterranean, though its effects would be manifest throughout society in its control over the behavior, practices, and beliefs of the members.

A few months after arriving Tocqueville wrote an impassioned letter to a close friend, arguing at length that "the irresistible democratic movement" in America had destroyed a native "aristocratic tendency" and swept all social distinctions before it. But, he insisted, in France we are also being "pushed by an irresistible force" toward "unlimited democracy." The choice was between "absolute government or a republic."[15]

## III

As he continued a journey that would take him to western New York State, Quebec, Michigan, down the Mississippi to New Orleans, across the deep South, and then northward to Washington, New York, and Boston, the absolute contrasts gradually began to work a change in his opinions. A growing respect and wonder at the civilization emerging from virtually empty space and the efforts of its very ordinary inhabitants produced in Tocqueville an inward turn:

> Paternal power which cuts such a grand figure in the classical republics that theorists have seen it as the source of their greatness and longevity is almost reduced to nothing among American institutions.
>
> American laws seem to look with as jealous and as suspicious an eye on the power of a father as on all other powers that can burden human liberty. Paternal power is an aristocratic institution. It makes old men into a privileged governing class. It gives them a sort of patronage by making their descendants depend on them; all such things are antipathetic to democracy.[16]

The aristocratic convictions that Tocqueville had brought with him, including deference to family authority, began to relax. He wondered about the chastity of the young in America, the freedom of American women, the simple but practical religiosity of Americans, the apparent unimportance of social distinctions (except for "*money* . . . the first of all social distinctions in America"),[17] the easy marriage between members of different social stations (much to his family's dismay Tocqueville would later marry an Englishwoman of no particular social distinction), the "thirst for gain," and the constant and dizzy changes in personal fortunes.[18] He was staggered by the spectacle of an entire society where few were born where they lived, and fewer still wanted to live where they were born.[19]

Not surprisingly Tocqueville experienced strong feelings of disorientation that approached an identity crisis. To an intimate he confided: "There is no being in the world I know less than myself. I am endlessly an insoluble problem to myself. I have a very cool head, a rational, even calculating mind; but there are also ardent passions which carry me away without convincing me."[20]

America, where lineage was forgotten and the links between generations uncoupled by westward migrations, was both an exhilarating revelation of a personal life unburdened by the past and also an equivocal symbol of a potentially sterile freedom that allowed men to live unencumbered lives inevitably ending in soured ambitions. A note of defiance crept in when Tocqueville contrasted the American with the French family. In America, he noted, the son becomes independent very early and the father accepts it easily. Aristocrats, he continues, who have tasted American or democratic freedom "do not want to return to the respectful but cold formalities of the aristocratic family. They would freely retain the domestic habits of democracy provided they could reject its social condition and laws but they cannot."[21]

Tocqueville was not, however, tempted to disown his patrimony. The American experience would force him to reflect upon aristocracy rather than merely reflect or reject it. He would use his aristocratic identity to constitute his theoretical vision. When transmuted into a perceptual category, aristocracy importantly determined theoretically how he would conceive the political world, measure it, and what he would admit into it. Theoretical discovery, political identity, and inheritance were to be fused.

## IV

In America he had seen what few of his species had, a world where his kind not only did not exist but where the fundamental principle of equality implicitly pronounced him to be extinct.[22] In France, Tocqueville noted wistfully in his American journal, "birth still puts an almost insurmountable barrier between men." In America, however, birth "carries no right and no disability, no obligation toward the world or towards oneself."[23] America might have to be described as a theodicy if the otherwise inexplicable triumph of equality over superiority were to be justified and the aristocide of the French Revolution rendered comprehensible.

Tocqueville's surprise at encountering a society without a social hierarchy and the impact it had on his thinking can be measured in two formulations.

In a draft of *Democracy* of 1835 he classified aristocracy as a "natural association." But in the published volume he asserted that "there is nothing more contrary to nature" or "repugnant to natural equality" than an aristocracy.[24] His attempt to understand the strange land provoked him to a self-understanding: America becomes the "other" once removed, not the revolutionary society that had sought to destroy his kind, but the other of a more complex relationship to him: of a total silence of ignorance, as though his kind had never been. Aristocracy had disappeared with as little trace as the once busy settlements that the relentless wilderness had reclaimed. America was pure nature without history because without aristocracy.

The unsettling encounter with a society that represented his own annihilation proved to be the most fundamental experience in Tocqueville's theoretical development. At one level it forged a deeper political connection between France and America than the jejeune ambitions of exploiting theory to advance his own political career. At another level it had a personal bearing. The annihilation of aristocracy released its sons. The new age might not be better but it offered fresh opportunities. The last page of *Democracy* would end on that note: "We should not strive to make ourselves like our fathers; rather we should strive for that type of greatness and happiness which is proper to ourselves."[25]

## V

> *Ceremony of 4th July . . . Perfect order that prevails. Silence. No police, Authority nowhere. Festival of the people. Marshall of the day without restrictive power, and obeyed, free classification of industries, public prayer, presence of the flag and old soldiers. Emotion real.*
>
> Tocqueville in Albany, New York, 1831[26]

In a letter written about a year before he embarked on his American journey, Tocqueville set down his conception of the condition of the individual in the civilized society of the Old World.[27] The terms he used, while Rousseauan, are rich in hints of a developing sensibility that would be attracted to American freedom but offended by the social constraints developed to contain it:

> Society is all pervasive; the individual takes the trouble to be born; for the rest, society takes him in its arms like a nurse; it watches over his education; it opens before him the road to fortune; it sustains him on the march; it takes away from him all perils; he advances in peace under the eyes of this second Providence; this tutelary power which has protected him during his life watches, finally, over the disposition of his ashes; this is the fate of the civilized man.[28]

This description of Old World society strikingly anticipates the benevolent despotism he would associate with democracy. It identifies enveloping control, not with a harsh political system, but with the pressures of "society." American democracy would be represented not by its famous written constitution—Tocqueville would allot surprisingly little attention to the document and its institutions—but by the primacy of society over the state. More precisely, it was democracy as the expression of a complete life-form—religious, cultural, social, economic, and political—that would fascinate Tocqueville because in the new land men had first experienced the space and freedom to do as they wished. The result was not, as many Europeans believed, anarchy tempered by vast distances but a mixture of tendencies, some welcome, others not, but the overall direction irresistible; and beneath that judgment there was, on Tocqueville's part, a deep-seated fear.

While the unboundedness of life in America was liberating, it was also terrifying. The notion of terror has not figured in most accounts of Tocqueville's thinking, possibly because its object seems less than compelling to modern sensibilities and possibly, too, because Tocqueville's terror was in the nature of a displaced religious emotion, and hence expressive of convictions that the French Revolution had newly encoded as a sign of counterrevolutionary proclivities. Tocqueville was not a practicing believer in the institutional sense but he was far from being a resolute atheist or agnostic or skeptic. He might be called an uncertain theist who was assailed by religious anxieties arising from a nagging worry that the universe was being governed either by a dying deity, a god who, like the absolute monarchs, had lost his potency, or by a god who had changed his mind, and transferred his favor from aristocracy to the multitude. His deepest fear was that the deity might be neither and that men were condemned to live in an abandoned world, a chance arrangement devoid of any immanent meanings. Late in life he would confess to Madame Swetchine, his religious confidant, that "I find human existence in this world inexplicable and in the other terrifying."[29]

Several passages of *Democracy* allude to the "awe" or "fear" that he experienced in America. The introduction to *Democracy* declares that "this entire book has been written under the impress of a kind of religious terror."[30] Accordingly, his choice of language alternates between conviction and uncertainty, two feelings that would compete throughout his life. Uncertainty gropes for a theological vocabulary and produces a phrase at odds with itself, "a kind of religious terror": the terror of a mind that accepted the same structure to things as a true believer but could not bring itself truly to believe the theological explications of that structure any more than it could renounce belief. It could only hesitate before the Pascalian wager. The religious vocabulary of a hesitant believer allowed for appeals to a power believed to govern human existence but without the confidence of traditional theological rationales or the elaborate means that ritualized faith possessed for entreating or communing with that power.

## VI

> *It seems that the habit of changing place, of turning things upside down, of cutting, of destroying, has become a necessity of [the American's] existence.*
>
> Tocqueville[31]

The focus of fear is the possibility that a change had been decreed in the course of things that radically altered the terms of existence. The terror of the "providential fact" is the possibility that God is on the side of revolution: "perhaps, after all, the will of God was to diffuse a mediocre happiness over the whole of mankind, and not to concentrate a large amount of happiness on some and perfection on a small number."[32] Apprehensiveness about a fundamental shift in the order of divine dispensation injected a persistent element of uncertainty in Tocqueville's political judgments. During the composition of *Democracy* he vacillated less in his evaluation of democracy than in his own feelings about it. While he complained to his English translator that he had been made to appear more critical of democracy than he actually was, to Mill he wrote that although "democratic ideas" were "the only ones which have a future in modern society," he did not look upon the results of the democratic revolution as "the Israelites looked on the promised land." We must move toward it "without hesitation, without enthusiasm . . . [and] without weakness."[33]

Far from being comforted, then, by the possibility that God had willed the regime of equality, Tocqueville seemed tormented by a repressed gnosis that could not be uttered as he contemplated the chilling prospect of a society composed entirely of equals, a vast agglomerate of similarities on a scale never before witnessed. That spectacle produced an ambivalence that haunted, enriched, and inhibited Tocqueville's theory and had its source in a complex of convictions that had prompted him to ascribe a providential quality to the growing and universal dominion of equality. His phrase in *Democracy*, "It may be God's will," expressed perfectly the combination of hesitancy and conviction that would issue in ambivalence in the face of a newly emerging world that, absent a divine sanction for it, would be a horror. He would cling to the belief that behind the universal groundswell of equality there had to be a benign deity who, too, was a liberal of new kind: "I cannot believe that God has for several centuries been pushing two or three hundred million men toward equality just to make them wind up under a Tiberian or Claudian despotism. Truly that wouldn't be worth the trouble."[34]

Tocqueville's apprehensiveness was aroused by what he perceived as the peculiar dynamics unleashed by an egalitarian society. Equality did not merely declare that all were free; it rendered them free. In releasing human beings from the restraints of a traditional society, equality had energized them. Each was now free to pursue the interests of the self without trailing a host of inherited obligations. Social life became charged as though by a million dynamos driven by an "immoderate" zeal for quick wealth and gripped by a collective frenzy: "perpetual instability of desires, a continual need to change, a total absence of old traditions and customs, a commercial and mercantile spirit."[35]

The terror was compounded by the spectacle of a huge continent being attacked with ferocious energy, a single-mindedness of small purposes that paradoxically, transformed nature while leaving men unchanged. The fury of American life, Tocqueville frequently noted, was that of a civilized people, not a savage people, yet it was being performed dumbly on the plane of nature rather than articulated through historical consciousness as it warred against that which lacked a vocabulary of protest: nature, Indians, slaves. The aggrandizement of the continent resembled a revolution transferred from the plane of history to that of nature, and the pioneer seemed, in Tocqueville's eyes, a kind of Jacobin destroyer; "the habit of changing place, of turning things upside down, of decapitating them, of destroying has become a necessity of his existence."[36]

The enormous power unleashed in society was made possible by the development of a culture whose prerequisite was being satisfied in the recurrent dramas of abandonment. The first act in establishing the collective identity of Americans had been to leave behind their native lands. The second was to consummate it by a rebellion that forever separated them from the mother country. Early in their individual lives Americans freed themselves of most of the bonds that Europeans took for granted; for Europeans history had become their nature. It was not that Americans were ignorant of the allegiances due family, home, social station, or locale. Rather they felt free to leave those attachments behind. Life was given meaning by "moving on," by restarting time with a "new beginning" rather than by cultivating human relationships whose meaning depended on "staying in place" and letting time give continuity and meaning to human life. The final act was the establishment of the reign of equality. Men become alike not by imitation but by dissociation from "the ideas and sentiments peculiar to a caste, profession, or family." Culture becomes minimized and the result is that human beings "arrive simultaneously at what is closest to the essence of man which is the same everywhere."[37] Man thus becomes renaturalized and, as such, the natural enemy of an order based on artificial distinctions and artful masks.

## VII

> *Have all ages been like ours and have men always dwelt, as in our day, in a world where nothing is connected?*
>
> Tocqueville[38]

Tocqueville's anxieties were hastened by the peculiar atmosphere created by abandonment. Writing from America to a friend, he described its oppressiveness: "Above, below, around us a profound solitude and complete silence reigns. Eventually it weighs down and oppresses the soul."[39] The image that most recurs when Tocqueville described this Cartesian condition of freedom and disconnectedness was the Pascalian abyss. Early in *Democracy* he depicted a postrevolutionary society as cut loose from its moorings, adrift with its gaze fixed upon the remains of a prerevolutionary society, and unaware that it is moving toward its own demise: "caught in the midst of a rapid current, we rivet our attention on the ruins still in sight while the stream carries us backward toward the abyss."[40]

The abyss is made to serve as a mytheme symbolic not of emptiness but of emptiedness, of a universe whose plenitude had been drained of meaning by the disappearance of all familiar landmarks denotive of difference, limitations, and the connectedness of a traditional social order. Disconnectedness brings loss of meaning when the human ties that supply life with a bottomless fund of interpretable experience are deliberately snapped.

The abyss is a metaphor of loss meant for Frenchmen, a reminder of the destructiveness set in motion by the Great Revolution and a warning that society is edging toward the precipice of meaninglessness.

The image of being carried "backward" was a discordant one to an age accustomed to rhapsodize progress. Tocqueville's theory would be shaped by his efforts to combat historical loss and the disconnectedness it produced. He would deny the death of the past by preserving it, so to speak, in solution and transmuting the dead past into specific theoretical concepts, such as "feudalism" and "aristocracy" or, simply, as "the old," incorporating them into his theory, and then deploying them to illuminate their opposite, democracy. The past would become a mediating device, standing between extreme egalitarianism and his version of a limited democracy, and thus serve to check and modify the drive toward egalitarianism generated by the French Revolution. Tocqueville's uses of the past would lend a subtly counterrevolutionary character to *Democracy* and add an enigmatic edge to his frequent claim that the French Revolution was not yet over.

# CHAPTER VI "... THE THEORY OF WHAT IS GREAT"

## I

> *I have long had the greatest desire to visit North America. I shall go see there what a great republic is like; my only fear is lest, during that time, they establish one in France. . . . [Upon returning] you know just exactly what a vast republic is like, why it is practicable here, unpracticable there. . . . On returning to France you certainly know yourself possessor of a talent that you did not have on leaving. If the moment is favorable, some sort of publication may let the public know of your existence and fix on you the attention of the parties.*
>
> Tocqueville[1]

> *Since we see . . .*
>
> Aristotle[2]

When Karl Marx left continental Europe and took up the life of exile in London, the hub of world capitalism, his immediate theoretical task was to choose among the many partly finished theories he had begun earlier. There was the theory in the *1844 Manuscripts*, with its combination of Hegelian dialectic, Feuerbachian psychology, and first foray into political economy; the theory of historical materialism sketched in *The German Ideology*; the theory of revolution first presented in the *Communist Manifesto*; and the detailed and systematic theory of political economy that would become the *Grundrisse* and, later, *Das Kapital*.

When Tocqueville came to America he had no theory, no theoretical vocation. After his return he confided to a friend, "I did not travel there with the idea of writing a book, but the idea of a book came to me."[3] On this point Tocqueville was not quite accurate in his recollections.[4] He had discussed with Beaumont the possibility of a joint work before going to America. Nevertheless, there is an important sense in which Tocqueville had not misremembered.

Originally Tocqueville looked upon political writing as a passport to political life. His decision to go to a strange and primitive land to gain a political reputation seems almost calculating when compared with his touching belief that writing a book was a natural way of gaining a political foothold. Throughout his life political motivations would importantly shape Tocqueville's theoretical work, and for much of his life he would claim that his basic allegiance was to the life of action. To his first political mentor, Royer-Collard, he vehemently denied that he intended to follow the career of "author" and avowed that once *Democracy* was completed he would not write again—unless "a great occasion" arose.[5]

Rather than blocking his efforts to find a theoretical formulation, Tocqueville's political commitment would profoundly shape it and all of his subsequent writings. By the same token, theorizing became Tocqueville's way of clarifying his own political commitments. The American journey proved to be a remarkable political education. It brought the French travelers in contact with the many specimens of the American citizen, particularly with representatives of America's political elites. Tocqueville's notebooks, in addition to providing an early example of the use of questionnaires and prestructured interviews, are a registry of unending surprise. "The bearing of this fact is immense," Tocqueville notes. "This observation needs confirmation. . . . 'How did you get proof of this fact?' I asked him."[6]

The lack of a theoretical orientation at the beginning of his journey is suggested in a letter written just prior to his departure for America. There he describes the kind of book he had in mind. "We want to examine in detail and as scientifically as possible everything in the vast society of America which everyone talks about but no one knows."[7] The same note of gathering as much detail as possible was reaffirmed six months later when Tocqueville wrote to his father describing what he and Beaumont had to do before being able to identify their questions. "We are forced to decompose the society a priori, to seek out the elements of which it is formed." He complains of the "mass of details" that threatens to overwhelm him.[8] He concludes that if he is ever to write a book on America, it will happen only after he returns home and has a chance to study the documents he has collected.[9]

The struggle to collect and then master the details of the varied, strange, and huge phenomena assembled under the name "America" was a crucial development in Tocqueville's journey toward a theory. He would soon discover a powerful tension between details or particular facts and the creation of a theory that is supposed, at one and the same time, to reflect/acknowledge facts and to illuminate them by means of general statements, to assert no more than the facts will support, yet to say more than the facts themselves say. There are always more details than a theory can master and always some that it cannot account for. A theory, Tocqueville would learn, has not only to go beyond where the facts are, but go against where the facts have been, turn against the facts in a sense. But to do that a theorist must fashion a form of discourse that will enable him to modulate the facts, and on occasion even ignore them, trusting that in the end the theoretical achievement will have established a plane where factual objections seem petty. However sincere his intention of retaining a firm connection between the discourse of theory and the discourse of facts, the one mode of discourse will, nonetheless, remain vulnerable to the objections of the other, and so the ultimate weapon of theory will always be, quite literally, brilliance—that is, enlightening the facts so that they speak to *concerns* about which they themselves are mute.

While in America he and Beaumont found that daily they were forced to rethink their generalizations and basic categories. They encountered human beings who lived without reference to historical memories; for whom little in their world remained fixed for very long; and who simply shrugged off the destruction of nature, that sacred category of Enlightenment and Romantic thought, as "a necessity of existence." They found private associations of unprecedented power, a politics without deep passions, a people who had "principles" but not "*vertu.*"[10] "We are," Tocqueville wrote ruefully, "most certainly in another world here."[11] Yet one worry remained constant and nagging: whether "the material and special advantages of the United States" did not make it the exception to, rather than the focus of, a theory.[12]

What Tocqueville felt he lacked most was a controlling and connective structure. He desperately entreats a friend to enter into a discussion of "theoretical matters" (*de choses théoriques* ) and implies that he needed help in formulating his project.[13]

## II

> *It is not fitting that I should appoint myself the censor of my times. It is a role that I have no right to play and that my age makes at once inappropriate and ridiculous. It is only after one has done something extraordinary that one has a right to complain if one's contemporaries pay no heed.*
>
> Tocqueville[14]

By the first part of the nineteenth century there was a well-established genre describing the extraordinary qualities of politics and social life in the United States, and many European writers had tried their hand at it, including Harriet Martineau, Dickens, and Tocqueville's famous cousin, Chateaubriand. But theirs was a literature of observation, of curiosity and comment, rather than theory. That genre was hardly a choice at all for Tocqueville because the idea of a travelogue could not satisfy certain powerful visionary and self-dramatizing impulses that were to shape his conception of theory and politics. While he lacked a clear notion of theory he did have a standard: theory would have to possess the quality of political *grandeur*.

## III

> *It is a time, above all, of self-interrogation. Why did he come to such a place? With what hopes? And to what end? . . . Or does it follow upon some more radical decision—one that calls in question the system within which one was born and has come to manhood? . . . Or did my decision bespeak a profound incapacity to live on good terms with my own social group? Was I destined, in fact, to live in ever greater isolation from my fellows? The strange paradox was that, so far from making me free of a "new world," my life of adventure tended rather to thrust me back into my old one, while the world to which I had laid claim slipped through my fingers.*
>
> Claude Lévi-Strauss[15]

How, then, does a traveler turn *theoros?* When does a travelogue become a *theoria*?

At the outset the answer to the question of how a traveler becomes a theorist seemed straightforward to Tocqueville. It would mean using the method of comparison and to compare and/or contrast America with France while drawing political lessons from the similarities and differences.

But this solution encountered immediate difficulties. The exceptional circumstances of America—geographical isolation, the ease with which an individual could become a landowner, and the rich political heritage of self-government—made it difficult to extrapolate lessons or even generalizations. It was one thing to contrast the practices of one country with those of another. It was quite another to relate a practice to "democracy." Was democracy simply a synonym for America and, ipso facto, were all or most of its practices democratic? Or did American practices deviate in important ways from democracy and, if so, what was the democracy from which it deviated—a theory? If so, whose theory? Well-informed Americans were anything but reassuring, insisting that "the American experience proves nothing." A month before departing for home Tocqueville was forced to admit that while "some parts" of the American system might usefully be adopted by another society, "only an ambitious or foolish man could, after seeing America, maintain that in the actual state of the world, American political institutions could be applied elsewhere than there."[16]

America thus seemed like a perfect case of Montesquieuean particularism rather than Enlightenment universalism; its uniqueness threatened Tocqueville's political and theoretical ambitions. In Montesquieu's case the emphasis on the distinctiveness of political societies had produced a cautionary politics: "I do not write," Montesquieu had declared, "to censure anything established in any country whatsoever." An enlightened ruler, he counseled, should always be satisfied with a lesser good if there were doubts about a greater one.[17]

The problem beginning to take shape for Tocqueville was how to retain a Montesquieuean respect for the cultural embeddedness of political institutions, their setting, and yet open it to a cross-cultural politics. A comparative theory of politics thrives on differences and contrasts—and chokes on uniqueness. But a theory that doted on uniqueness ran the risk of making America into a fascinating curiosity irrelevant to France. There had to be some quality to American democracy that deeply mattered to France politically. American democracy would have to be conceived so as to be of serious, even urgent, moment for France and conversely the political condition of France had to be conceived so as to be receptive to the significance of America. Before America could be rendered politically relevant, it had to be transformed into a theoretical object. Unfortunately, the strictly empirical character of America was its uniqueness, a "fact" that Tocqueville repeatedly encountered on his travels. Paradoxically, the only way by which contact could be established between two countries whose empirical histories were so extraordinarily different was to theorize them. Thus the practical character of the project depended on first establishing its theory.

In order, therefore, to create connections between two historically distinct societies Tocqueville had to commit himself to an activist style of theorizing. To his father he wrote:

> By selecting the materials [one might] present only those subjects that had a more or less direct relation with our political and social condition. A work of this kind could have, at one and the same time, a permanent interest and a topical one. That is the sketch: but will I ever have the time and do I have the necessary talents to complete it?[18]

Although Tocqueville would write hopefully to his brother—"we are assembling some magnificent materials and if we should discover in ourselves the talent to put them to use, we shall without question create something new"—despair was never far from the surface.[19] To be sure, he had succeeded in identifying several promising themes: the importance of social equality, associations, decentralization, inheritance laws, and political education. Further, certain general observations began to seem of more fundamental importance than others. He detected among Americans "a sort of refined and intelligent selfishness [that] seems to be the pivot on which the whole machine revolves." And he mused that "America has established municipal [i.e., local] liberty before establishing public [i.e., national] liberty." He discovered, too, that without provoking anticlericalism or encouraging obscurantism religion could play a constructive role in a republic, instructing the citizens about morality while helping to restrain their natural appetites.[20] As these preliminary observations suggest, the emerging shape of Tocqueville's theory was being guided by an *ancien régime* sensibility. His phrase "municipal liberty" (*la liberté municipale*) carried echoes of old historical controversies in France between municipalities and the crown, as well as between the nobility and the king.

Yet an overall, synoptic view that would hold together the disparate observations, the center that would tie a network of notions into a conceptual whole, remained elusive. The concept of self-interest seemed a possible centering point or "primary fact" of a theory, but the more exalted politics he was beginning to envisage would be demeaned by such an ignoble motive and make the American example appear as little more than bourgeois politics on a grand scale. In a broad if oversimplified sense, we might say that Tocqueville's difficulties arose from his attempt to combine a conceptualized aristocratic sensibility and a democratic content. The theoretical notions that Tocqueville had expected to find were utterly defeated by the facts, and he was left groping for a new hold.

## IV

The despair and the veriest hint of what was to come were present in an unpublished essay, "A Fortnight in the Wilderness." The passage that follows is lengthy but it allows a reader to see a theoretical preconception unraveling and a structure of perception, stimulated by the overpowering visual impressions of the raw land, being brought to focus upon the uniformity of American civilization and a culture shaped by a struggle with nature rather than history:

> Everything there is abrupt and unforeseen; everywhere extreme civilization and wild nature meet and in a way confront each other. It is something that one cannot even imagine in France. As for me, in my traveler's illusions . . . I was imagining something different. I had observed that in Europe, the more or less isolated a province or a town, its wealth or poverty, its smallness or its extent, exerted an immense influence upon the ideas, manners [*moeurs,*] the entire civilization of its inhabitants, and often made the difference of several centuries between various parts of the same area.

> I had imagined that it would be like that in the New World, even more so, and that a country only partially populated as America is ought to present all of the conditions of existence and ought to offer an image of society in all of its ages. America, I supposed, was the only country where one could follow, step by step, all of the transformations that the social state has caused man to undergo and where it was possible to discern something like a vast chain descending ring by ring, from the wealthy patrician of the town to the savage in the wilderness. In a word I counted on finding the whole history of humanity framed within a few degrees of longitude.
>
> Nothing is true in this picture. Of all the countries in the world America is the least appropriate to furnish the spectacle I was seeking. In America, even more than in Europe, there is only one society. It could be rich or poor, humble or brilliant, commercial or agricultural, but everywhere it would consist of the same elements.[21]

Instead of encountering a great chain of social being, graduated by qualitative differences and temporal disparities, Tocqueville found himself in the presence of a vast civilization of sameness, mainly striking as a reproduction of the unremarkable on a grand scale. In the background an uncomfortable truth: no traveler had ever won fame for recounting his observations of a civilization and culture of banality. By ordinary criteria America seemed a profoundly unpolitical society. What kind of political theory could there be for a society where one was immediately struck by "the absence of government"?[22] What kind of politics was worth reflecting upon when men of talent abandoned politics for economic pursuit; when the fundamental principle of republicanism, devotion to the public good, had ceased to operate as a regulative principle of conduct; when "in reality, in order to prosper, America has no need for skillful direction, profound designs, or great efforts. But only liberty and still more liberty."[23] How does one theorize the unremarkable?

If it could not be enthusiastically praised and recommended, could it, nonetheless, be exploited and used strategically? Could the remarkable reside in the unrelievedly unheroic character of American political life? Did the incredible energy of Americans, the ceaseless changes it brought about, and the grandiloquent rhetoric accompanying it conceal an unexpected moderation, even conservatism?

## V

*What strikes me most about our times is not that we make so much of trifles, but that we do not conceive the theory of what is great.*
Tocqueville[24]

Early on in his travels Tocqueville wrote contemptuously, "Here there are no common memories, no national attachments. What then is the one bond that unites the different parts of this enormous body? *Interest.*"[25] The question of how to come to terms with banality nagged at him from his earliest political awakening to the end of his life. It arose because of his conviction that for politics to be authentic it had to be heroic, larger than ordinary life. In a letter of 1840 he remarks to Beaumont. "You know what a taste I have for great events and how bored I am with our bland, democratic, bourgeois stew."[26] Throughout his life Tocqueville would retain a deep disdain for the pettiness of bourgeois politics.

Tocqueville's revulsion at interest politics preceded his voyage to America but the American experience would confirm the lifetime task he would set for himself of redeeming politics from the triviality and baseness of an interest-oriented age. He formulated it in an early letter:

> All are becoming more and more devoted to their personal interests. Those who only desire power for themselves or glory for their country can rejoice at such a spectacle. . . . I certainly do not scorn political convictions . . . as mere instruments. . . . I try not to have two worlds: a moral one, where I still delight in all that is good and noble, and the other political, where I lie with my face to the ground, groveling in the muck which covers it. . . . I try not to separate what is inseparable.[27]

Tocqueville's extravagant language for depicting his ideals of action may strike a late modern reader as overwrought. But its seeming excess points to an influence on Tocqueville's political thinking that is so unexpected that commentators have mostly overlooked it. If we ask, What was the inspiration for such an outsized or heroic notion of action, a notion that would permanently shape an aristocrat's thinking and leave him frustrated by the limited possibilities of liberal politics? the answer is, the French Revolution.

Tocqueville made the French Revolution serve not only as the crucial moment of modern history, as marking the decisive turn from a world of rank, stability, and quality to one of uniformity, *stasis*, and quantity, but also as the standard of what is possible when men subordinate self-interest to principles. "Fifty years ago today," he wrote in 1842, "our fathers drove themselves to found something greater than what we see."[28] Yet the one thing that the revolution would never be for Tocqueville was a call to revolutionary action.

The revolution has to be a silenced referent, a suppressed norm whose denial preserves the heroic without the revolutionary—passion without object/ consummation. It would produce an outburst remarkable for its Nietzschean intensity:

> I would have preferred a revolutionary condition a thousand times more than our present misery. . . . Will we never again see a fresh breeze of true political passions . . . of violent passions, hard though sometimes cruel, yet grand, disinterested, fruitful, those passions which are the soul of the only parties that I understand and to which I would gladly give my time, my fortune, and my life.[29]

By political action Tocqueville meant more than the disinterested pursuit of the public good that had been the hallmark of republican writers. Genuine action had to be bold, risk-taking, passionate, large-scaled, and, above all, deeply principled. Great actions were the secular complement to theoretical heroics: both asserted meaning against a banal world. Neither conceived of politics primarily in policy terms.

Typically Tocqueville would signal the presence of authenticity by introducing the word "great" (*grand*). His conception of greatness was sharpened in the course of reflecting on American political parties in the Jacksonian era:

> What I would call great political parties: those which are attached to constitutive principles and not to their consequences, to generalities and not to particular cases, to ideas not to men. Such parties have in general nobler qualities, more generous passions, clearer conventions, and a franker, bolder look than the other [parties].

In contrast, "petty political parties" were without "political faith," self-interested, weak, and timid. The great parties "overturn society" while the petty parties merely ruffle its surface.[30]

Tocqueville would lament the decline of "great parties" in the United States and the failure to reproduce statesmen of the stature of the generation of Founding Fathers, and, revealingly, his numerous portraits of Bonaparte were always tinged by an element of admiration for an actor who had imposed his will on society and dominated the politics of his age. "Has there never been," he wrote plaintively to his political mentor, Royer-Collard, "a political world where one could see the reign—I do not for a moment say, of virtue—but of some great passions and which would lead to something other than the interests of yesterday?"[31] In an echo of Plato's *Republic*, where the politically rebuffed philosopher is given the consolation of always dwelling in an ideal polis laid up in heaven, Tocqueville would fantasize about "putting myself . . . in a small ideal city, populated with the men I love and respect, and living there."[32]

## VI

How to make of America the stuff of epical theory? Although other writers might find it in the westward migrations and the struggles against nature and wild savages, Tocqueville needed some loftier theme that would embody ideas and convictions rather than physical prodigies. Somehow he would have to transfigure America, not in its physical magnitudes, which were naturally overpowering, but by idealizing its origins, what he would call its "point of departure." He would make America worthy of its theoretical role by sanctifying it with intimations of a divine element, some special endowments in its beginnings that would explain to a postrevolutionary, divided France what democracy might be if it were dissociated from revolutionary origins. The American citizenry, he would claim, was "the most enlightened in the world" and its "practical political education is the most advanced."[33]

At the same time, however, Tocqueville wanted a theory that would convey useful, practical knowledge to his countrymen. Early on, while in America, he worried about the seeming contradictions between the conflicting requirements of theory and practical action. "Nearly all political precepts," he mused, "have something so general in their formulation, so theoretical and so vague, that it is difficult to draw the least advantage from them in practice."[34]

What would a "useful" theory be like and how could that purpose be made compatible with an epic theory? Do practical requirements demand a pedestrian concreteness and specificity that could only result in a limping epic? Equally important, if he was capable of composing a practical theory, was that to be the real test of the value of his theory? A practical theory asks to be judged by whether its prescriptions could succeed when applied. But in what sense, if any, might an epic theory be accounted "successful" or are the standards by which to judge it very different? Does an epic theory seek to subscribe to standards, or to prescribe them? Or is it merely a yearning for acclaim?

A further and equally vexing problem: does an epic theory presuppose that the politics it describes will likewise be of epic proportions? It is one thing for an epic to have a Ulysses or an Achilles for its subject, quite another if it is all Lilliputians and no Gulliver: the one demands heroic diction, the other teeters always on the edge of low comedy because of an element of incommensurability in the fit between the theory and its subject matter. Tocqueville would concede democracy meant a society with "less luster than in an aristocracy . . . the sciences less lofty . . . less passionate feelings, gentler manners . . . less brilliant, less glorious."[35] To persuade his countrymen that democracy was their fate compelled Tocqueville to struggle with defining a conception of theoretical role that would accord with the modest politics of democracy while somehow preserving the heroic element that democracy rendered anachronistic. A frustrated epic becomes traceable by its ambiguities.

Nonetheless, uniqueness can suggest possibilities other than mimetic ones. This realization started Tocqueville on his theoretical way. "The more I see of this country," he confided to his father, "the more I find myself persuaded by this truth: that there is nothing absolute in the theoretical value of political institutions, and that their efficiency depends almost always on the original circumstances and the social condition of the people to whom they are applied."[36] If there was no absolute value to any political institution, then neither monarchy nor aristocracy was intrinsically superior to democracy. The subversive implications of this last point depended, however, on a theoretical decision that, without dismissing the uniqueness of the American phenomenon, would try and find points of contact between it and the Old World. Tocqueville would decide *not* to write a book about the United States but, instead, to write a book in which American society and its politics would serve as a prism through which a more universal political plane could be viewed and a deeper temporality experienced.

The decision to write a book about America but for France would, however, force him to go even further theoretically, to a plane that was not exclusively French or American. As he put it in a letter to Mill: "But beginning with the notions that French and American society provided me, I wanted to paint the general features of democratic societies of which no complete model exists."[37] That theoretical plane would be constituted as much from political motives as from purely theoretical considerations. While in America Tocqueville wrote down some reflections that indicated the depths of the political passions that were shaping his theoretical concerns. If only, he argued, royalists could see "the internal operation of a well-ordered republic," where there was respect for property rights, law, and liberty, and where the "true reign of the majority" operated and "everything progresses naturally and easily."[38] Tocqueville would attempt to reveal such a republic that would persuade monarchists of its benignity and disabuse republicans of its loftiness.

## VII

Political commitment would, however, aid rather than block the theoretical development of his American project, causing the formulation to shift from a political book focused solely upon "the great republic across the ocean" to one that, while exposing the basic political principles, practices, and structure of an entirely new society, would situate it in a theoretical context that connected the New to the Old World.[39] The realization that a political act was being made by theoretical means came almost as a revelation to Tocqueville:

like Molière's *bourgeois gentilhomme*, he was startled to discover he had been writing theory. After completing the first volume of *Democracy*, he described it to Beaumont as "un ouvrage philosophico-politique."[40] A few weeks later, after a flattering review had appeared, Tocqueville enlarged further, if retrospectively, the theoretical character of his work: "You know that I have worked on America a little like Cuvier [the great geologist] on ante-diluvian animals, making use at each step of philosophical deductions and analyses."[41]

That Tocqueville appeared to have discovered a philosophical character to *Democracy* after he had returned to France suggests that, although he had evolved a theoretical outlook while in America, he had not fully mastered it until he had settled down to write at home. This is partially confirmed by some remarks in the introduction to *Democracy*. There he recounts the stages in the evolution of his thinking. His first paragraph records the vivid impact that equality of condition had made "during my stay there." The third paragraph makes an implied reference to a period of extended observation before his return ("So the more I studied American society . . ."). The next paragraph seems to assume his return, "Later, when my thoughts turned toward our hemisphere . . .", and then that paragraph is followed by the statement, "It was at that moment that I conceived the idea of this book."[42] The theoretical journey thus depended as much on going home as on venturing abroad, as much on familiarity as on strangeness.

## VIII

> *I live in a profound solitude, buried in one idea. . . . I can only speak of Democracy.*
>
> Tocqueville[43]

The breakthrough had come when Tocqueville designated a center around which he would develop a theoretical structure and when he came to conceive of a theory as a structure with a supporting center. He described the experience in the introduction to the first volume of *Democracy* when he discovered a connection between a "local fact" and a universal and "irresistible" force. The latter was represented by "equality of conditions" and by the astonishing degree to which it prevailed among Americans. Equality of conditions functioned as the modern equivalent of the *logos* in ancient Greek philosophy, as the underlying organizing principle of the universe. What entitled this fact to be considered the predominant or "principal fact" was its all-pervasive character: it shaped the "public mentality," the complexion of the laws, and the actions of the governors as well as the habits of the governed.

Once he had grasped the determinative role of equality of condition and its wide-ranging potential as an explanatory force, Tocqueville's thoughts then turned to the Old World and he saw "something analogous to the spectacle that the new world presented to me . . . [of] democracy . . . rapidly advancing toward power." That conjuncture produced a kind of epiphanic moment: "At that moment I conceived the idea of the book that is about to be read."[44]

The primary fact of equality thus connected two of the main concepts in Tocqueville's theory, the New World and the Old, thereby establishing the relevance of each to the other. The language that Tocqueville employed to describe his discovery, "equality of conditions," appears at first glance an unfortunate choice because it obscured the dynamics he was concerned to convey. His description of equality as "rapidly advancing toward power" revealed equality to be a metaphor for a new kind of power. Not Marx's power of the forces of production, or Saint-Simon's power of organization, but power that first seems merely quantitative, as the power of sheer numbers that had burst the bounds of the traditional societies in the Old World. In the New World, however, where no resistive order had existed, quantity had turned into something more formidable.

E-quality = equal-ity: Equality was a condition wherein certain shared values and beliefs were operative, not merely "held," and hence were in the nature of a political, social, and moral force. Equality penetrated the daily lives of the vast majority of the society and left little or no room for sharply different cultural formations or political forces. Tocqueville would repeatedly compare it to a "weight" that "pressed down" and evoked the sensation of suffocation. Equality of condition would turn out to mean equality as the condition for the exercise of a peculiarly modern form of power, one in which coercion was a negligible element, the placing of power in a sovereign center was not a prerequisite of its effectiveness, and, most paradoxical of all, massive power could not be assembled and "used" as kings once "drew" on their authority.

We shall return to Tocqueville's account of equality in the New World and his prescriptions for dealing with it in the Old, but first we need to identify the several moves by which he established the theoretical structure of the work and advanced its political objectives.

## IX

The first move took him from writing a book about the practices of American democracy to composing a theory about democracy in America. "In America," he declares in the introduction to *Democracy*, "I saw more than America:

I sought the image of democracy itself, its inclinations, character, prejudices, and passions."[45] America as a descriptive field was thus made subordinate to a theoretical construction, "democracy." That decision would also allow for a more general applicability of whatever political truths he could distill; the concept of democracy would shift the emphasis away from America's uniqueness, thereby releasing democracy from dependence upon a particular place (the fate of "Athenian democracy") and enabling it to function as the symbol of an emerging condition about to become universal. That transformation of the empirical particularity of America into "the image of democracy" could be called Tocqueville's theoretization of democracy "in" America. As he put it in a letter to Mill, "America was only my framework, democracy was the subject."[46] He insisted that "what is democratic" should not be confused "with what is merely American."[47] By distinguishing democracy from America the theory would not be tied to a particular embodiment: he would be able to say something "of interest not only to the United States, but to the entire world, not to one nation but to all mankind."[48]

The overcoming of the empirical uniqueness of America was registered in the title that Tocqueville finally chose for his work, not *Démocratie américaine* (American democracy) but *Démocratie en Amérique* (Democracy in America). At one point he had even considered the title, "The rule [*empire*] of democracy in the United States."[49]

Critics would later complain about the vagueness and contradictions in Tocqueville's use of the term "democracy." Such complaints, however, confuse the presumed importance of a standard usage for interpreters with the risk taking inseparable from theorizing a novel condition.[50] Tocqueville was after something other than unambiguous meaning. He would exploit the concept of democracy so as to display ambiguities because he believed them to be politically relevant for the audience he wished most to reach. He wanted democracy to appear as multivalent, not confined to an original meaning and certainly not rigidly restricted to its American version. Perhaps there was a convergence between Tocqueville's political requirements and real ambiguities in democracy, such as a high level of local political involvement that testified to the civic skills of the citizens and the vulgar quality of national leadership in the Jacksonian era. Perhaps because of the unprecedented freedoms it allowed to so many, democracy was destined to produce contrasts that its critics would seize upon as contradictions.

The problematic character of democracy was of crucial political importance to Tocqueville for it signified the possibility of choice in a world increasingly given over to massive forces. Ambiguity was the modern equivalent to what contingency had meant for the ancient theorists and Machiavelli, the *fortuna* that made political action possible, freedom a necessary condition of genuine action, and democratic *virtù* its sufficient one. Ambiguity also afforded Tocqueville a tactical advantage in addressing a French audience that remained deeply divided in its feelings and beliefs about the revolution of 1789.[51] Democracy could not be presented as a sharply distinct choice, *en bloc*, without alienating most shades of French opinion. It had to be constructed not as a holistic choice between all or nothing but as numerous choices within the broad limits of a given, that some form of democratic equality was inevitable.

The second of Tocqueville's moves was less obtrusive but equally portentous theoretically. On more than one occasion he confessed that in writing *Democracy* he had scarcely mentioned France, yet he had not written a page without thinking of his homeland.[52]

> What I have sought particularly to highlight in the United States and to have it well understood is less a complete portrait of that foreign society than its contrasts or resemblances with ours. . . . That continual return to France, which I did without calling attention to it was, in my view, one of the principal reasons for the success of the book.[53]

"That continual return to France" involved the construction of "France" into a "world," an "Old World" occupying a common theoretical plane with the New. While each world was, in an obvious sense, a geographical entity, each assumed the character of a symbolic form signifying more than distinct national identities. Neither was meant as an exact miniature of a specific society. Each would be a selective distillation whose significance would be revealed by the contrasts between the two societies. "It is always, either by contrast or by analogy with the one that I succeeded in giving an appropriate and accurate idea of the other."[54] Neither world was conceived as fixed in its form or meaning. The New World would have to struggle to remain new, that is, democratic *and* free, and not resolve that tension by opting to be democratic and unfree. The Old World was dying and in the throes of a transformation into a democratic world, but in the process its politicians and citizens might be tempted to surrender political freedom in exchange for private freedom to pursue primarily social and economic ends.

The implications of that construction for Tocqueville's conception of a theoretical role will be taken up later but here we need to emphasize the theoretical achievement: the creation of a new plane of universality that first transformed the empirical United States into the representation of "democracy" and elevated it to an abstract plane where it could make contact with a theoretically transformed "France." While in America Tocqueville had been struck by near ideal laboratory conditions for the experiment in democracy: geographical isolation and a bounteous nature allowed democracy to unfold without distortion or the burden of a long history. The task of bringing the two societies into theoretical juxtaposition was begun while Tocqueville was in America:

> What is really interesting in America is to examine the inclinations and instincts of democracy left to itself and to see to what social condition it forcibly leads the society which it dominates. Such a society is particularly interesting for the French who are perhaps marching toward despotism, perhaps towards a republic, but certainly toward an unlimited democracy.[55]

The France that Tocqueville would create was a society whose unified historical character had experienced diremption by revolution, class enmities, suspicions between believers and doubters, and hardened ideological positions, yet was strangely torpid in its social and political life. The cause, Tocqueville believed, was traceable to the destructiveness that accompanied the appearance of democracy in France: a revolution that "overthrew everything that has stood in its way, shaking all that it did not destroy."[56] What had been destroyed in France was the political life of civil society, a theme he would later take up in his great work on the Old Regime. The consequence was the strengthening of the state. If France was to be depicted as the state without political society, America would be political society without the state. That complementarity of absences would inspire the purpose that Tocqueville would follow more consistently than any other, the re-creation of the political life of French civil society and criticism of the centralized state.

The third move involved the enlargement and complication of the concept of revolution. Tocqueville's account of American democracy would downplay its revolutionary origins in the hope of repeating that operation for France. The United States would be treated as a society that had achieved democracy without a violent political revolution—he virtually ignored 1776—even though the state of that society represented the most extreme example of egalitarianism.[57] France, in contrast, was a society traumatized by revolution, the extreme case of a society left divided and condemned to instability. Tocqueville would discern a providential march toward equality or democracy at a universal level where America's revolution in democracy could serve as a lesson for stabilizing French revolutionary equality. Democracy would thus be pressed into serving as accomplice to an obliquely counterrevolutionary teaching.

In the course of using democracy for that purpose Tocqueville discovered something about modern democracy that would place it in a very different light from ancient and early modern conceptions. In the received understandings democracy was associated with radical tendencies, such as the confiscation of the property of the wealthy classes or the elimination of inequalities based on merit or "virtue." These tendencies were usually attributed to democracy's elevation of freedom to the principal political value. Although Tocqueville adopted the older equation of democracy with freedom, he would reveal democracy to have a conservative character, not only in its moral and religious fundamentalism but in its respect for political fundamentals as well. The demos whose appetites and passions had haunted Western political thought from Plato to the *Federalist* was about to be reconceived as a moderating force.

The fourth move: In the course of his journey he became more and more impressed by the extent to which American politics could only be accounted for by habits shaped by the broader culture of society, especially by the moral teachings supplied by religion. This importance of culture would be grasped only incompletely in the first installment of *Democracy* in which Tocqueville would mainly treat legal and institutional frameworks. In the later installment, however, he would turn to the culture that informed and sustained them and defined the character of them as practices. The explanatory importance that he would assign to political culture as the key to the stability and self-restraint, which, in his eyes, would recommend democracy, would necessarily shift attention from heroic action to the culture of citizens.

The problem Tocqueville would raise might be put this way: two of the master ideas of Enlightenment theory, the idea of the market (Adam Smith) and of administrative organization (Saint-Simon), operated mostly without the idea of civic virtue and often against it. Political culture was introduced as a third form of ordering, appealing to history rather than, as was the case with conceptions of the market and of bureaucratic organization, to rational action. The concept of culture was primarily the work of conservative thinkers, such as Montesquieu, Hume, Burke, Coleridge, Fichte, and Hegel and of reactionaries such as de Maistre. The intellectual genealogy of culture provokes the question, Was it a way of restoring civic virtue to a central place in democratic politics or, instead, would its politics be as banal as the politics of markets and no less reactionary than the rule of administration? Was it to be the means of promoting political quietism in what has been called "the age of democratic revolutions" and hence the conservative alternative to popular political education?

## X

Like many theorists before him—the aristocrat Plato with his disdain for Athenian democracy, the republican Machiavelli observing the Medicean conquerors of Florence—Tocqueville would write as though in the presence of a deep political rupture which it was his personal fate to represent theoretically and his duty to heal politically.

Throughout his life he felt dogged by an acute sense of estrangement. He attributed it to his membership in an aristocracy that the French Revolution had not completely eliminated and the Restoration had not fully revived. Unlike his theorist predecessors, however, Tocqueville was not only at odds with the political developments of his era but caught off guard by the scope and rapidity of the changes conventionally ascribed to the advent of modernity. His development as a theorist involved acquiring a conceptual vocabulary for dealing with modernity. "Democracy," "New World," and "revolution" would be among the more important ones. That vocabulary was striking for the nuance of archaism shading terms such as "Old World," "Old Regime," and "aristocracy." These were expressions not only of estrangement and of living amid discontinuity but of an inconclusive opposition.

Confronting change, division, and instability Tocqueville set for himself the role of mediator. He would try to overcome the political estrangement of his class by mediating between it and a postrevolutionary politics struggling for identity and stability. By writing *Democracy* he would attempt to prove that an aristocrat could give a just and sympathetic account of an antiaristocratic society while persuading his own class that its fears of democracy were exaggerated. He would, at the same time, try to introduce a measure of sobriety to the intellectual enthusiasts for democracy, warning them that democracy lacked "poetry and *grandeur*" and was sustainable only "under certain conditions of enlightenment, of private morality, of beliefs that we do not have."[58]

Yet estrangement, in both the political and theoretical sense, let alone the personal, was not like an illness, a condition to be overcome and eliminated altogether. It was, instead, to be preserved as essential—to the power of theory to furnish insight, to the resolve of political actors to resist the excesses not only of democracy but of modernity, and, not least, to the self struggling to find a harmony between establishing a public self that satisfied private aspirations without revealing them. Although Tocqueville on numerous occasions and in public as well as private venues would insist that a basic condition for political reconciliation in France was an acknowledgment of the impossibility of restoring the Old Regime, in the structure of his theory the death of the past was, in effect, denied by preserving it as a theoretical element. The facts associated with a dead past and the living resentments about their passing were resuscitated through concepts such as "feudalism," "honor," "*grandeur*," and "aristocracy" and contrasted with democracy, more often than not to the disadvantage of the latter.

While the past was being restored as a theoretical device/disguise, when Tocqueville entered the French political world he came to realize that he would be forever trapped in the alien world of bourgeois politics that he was attempting to persuade his peers to accept, his sense of class identification was strengthened. He would forever be the *theoros* in a strange land.

# CHAPTER VII
# MYTH AND POLITICAL IMPRESSIONISM

## I

*Powerless against that which has been done, the will is an angry spectator of all things past.*

*The will cannot will backwards; that it cannot break time and time's desire—that is the will's most lonely affliction.*

Nietzsche[1]

Tocqueville's theoretical structure was not shaped to produce the triumph of certainty over doubt or truth over error but to avert a plunge into the abyss of meaninglessness. Meaninglessness signified the appearance of new magnitudes of power that threatened to deplete the social world of its meaningfullness.

For Tocqueville the meaning-full resided in singularity, in the uncommon, in what stood out by virtue of having been cultivated: historicized singularity. The threat to plenitude of meaning resided in a certain overpowering that proceeded according to a rule of sameness. The overpowering threatened the variety of human expressions possible when a society was richly differentiated yet modestly empowered in all of its dimensions—political, social, cultural, and economic. Meaninglessness signified the defeat of particularity by repetition, reproduction, and, ultimately, domination; it was the condition of being *overpowered*—in both meanings of the word: overwhelmed by power(s) and overwhelming powers. Human beings responded to sameness by identifying with, while re-cognizing themselves in, the forms of power engaged in reproducing and enforcing a sameness that erases historical differentiations: sameness stands for the dehistoricized.

The second threat was to the possibility of significant individual action. The powers shaping the world and preempting the public space being opened by modernity, whether powers of the state, industry, or opinion, were collective and anonymous. They seemed bent toward preventing the individual actor from standing out.

Modern power: one could not withstand it or stand out amidst it.

Tocqueville's preoccupation with the disappearance of singularities and significant action can be understood as an encounter with the theodicy of modernity, the promise that the suffering inflicted by power would eventually be redeemed by even greater power and relief from suffering. Although the generation before him had witnessed possibly the greatest expression of revolutionary power in Western history, revolution's promise was eventually overshadowed by its parody, collective mobilization for war and in support of dictatorship. Similarly the Enlightenment's search for universal/uniform truths was parodied by the power of the centralized, increasingly bureaucratized (uniform rules) and militarized (uniformed men) nation-state and its fetishization by theorists such as Fichte and Hegel, now harnessed with the explosive uniformizing ideology of nationalism. Not least was the astonishing growth in economic power, its conception of well-being defended by a new theoretical vision, political economy, marking the transformation of politics into policy, the idea-lization of material processes, the revenge of the material for centuries of subordination to the metaphysical and the theological. Materialized under the name of capitalism, the new theory was helping to reconfigure the conditions under which human life was being lived and the perceptions by which it was being understood. Conceptually, materially, and irrevocably western Europe was being uncoupled from its past while America was destined/doomed to living without one.

The theoretical issue posed would be central in Tocqueville's formulation of his ideas: whether theorists would assume the task of normalizing the appearance and presence of these huge powers, preserving their impressive and triumphal character while rendering them familiar and, above all, demonstrating their manageability, or whether the powers would be revealed to have certain unsettling and unnatural qualities that portended a continuous discontinuity in the human condition.

## II

If the task of a normalizing theory could be described as the demythologizing of power, the task of an abnormalizing theory might be described as the remythologizing of power. Demythologizing would represent modern theory's turn toward scientific modes of inquiry and away from theological and metaphysical explanations and from notions of occult powers; remythologizing, represented in the route taken by Tocqueville, did not mean rejecting scientific knowledge or embracing the occult. Rather, in the post-Enlightenment age remythologizing was a critical claim that genuinely sought to engage the demythologizers by making a case that they had underestimated the exactions demanded by modern power just as they had overestimated its benefits.

Demythologizing would be the direction followed by Saint-Simon, Comte, Bentham and Company, and Marx.[2] Saint-Simon and Comte would develop theories of history as a progression from ages dominated by superstition, religion, and metaphysics to ages of increasing enlightenment culminating in scientific knowledge. Among the most suggestive examples of the normalization of what might seem the natural stuff of mythologizing was the notion of revolution itself. From a series of events that, to horrified contemporaries such as Burke, signaled the unholy destruction of an entire civilization, revolution was quickly adopted as the official emblem of modernity and impressed into serving as a description of economic change, scientific advances, and new aesthetics. The widespread use of "revolution" signified that sweeping changes were becoming commonplace, that disappearance had become an everyday occurrence. Tocqueville would devote a chapter of *Democracy in America* to the theme of "Why Great Revolutions Will Become Rare."[3]

Yet, as the writings of Saint-Simon and Comte testify, the demythologizers were not wholly secure in a totally demystified world. Both writers came round to the belief that society needed a form of religious myth, albeit one adapted to a scientific age, and both proposed versions inspired, in varying degrees, by Christianity. Although Marx proved to be among the greatest of all unmaskers of myth, particularly of political economy, its most sophisticated form, he also composed one of the great rhapsodies to the massive, transforming power of modern capital, science, and technology.[4] That the demythologizers felt compelled to reintroduce a mythical element at odds with the prosaic character of their reality principle suggested either that modern power could not, of its own accord, generate meanings that could satisfy a modern sensibility still in thrall to premodern and classical aesthetics, or that the reintroduction of myth signified the limits of a mode of understanding. The most elaborate attempt to demonstrate that it could was made by Marx and Engels in their concept of ideology. In their most sweeping formulation, the modes of production—which they considered to be the principal source of power—gave rise to forms of belief, from the most sophisticated to the least, and these transmutations in turn came to reflect and reinforce the distribution of power among classes.[5] Marx and Engels also believed that a proletarian revolution would usher in a classless era in which conscious human direction of modern power would spell the end of ideology and the emergence of truths that would reflect reality instead of distorting or obscuring it.

Tocqueville's project for confronting a world that was becoming less meaningful but more powerful as it became demythologized required a theory that could accomplish a reversal, a remythologizing of the world.

## III

> *When doubt had depopulated the heavens, and equality had reduced each man to smaller and better known proportions, the poets were unable to imagine what they could put in the place of the great concerns lost with the aristocracy.*
>
> Tocqueville[6]

Along the way to becoming a theorist Tocqueville fashioned his own instrumentalities for remythologizing the world that revolutions had brought into existence. These instrumentalities occupied a prominent part in the structure of Tocqueville's theory and in the strategy for reclaiming the meaning-full and averting the abyss.

The sense in which Tocqueville sought theoretical control over his chosen subject matter was not, however, expressed in the ancient metaphor of imposing theoretical form on political matter. Beginning with Plato and continuing through medieval writers and early moderns such as Machiavelli, Hobbes, and Spinoza, a number of theorists had embraced theoretical schemes whose purpose was to order the dynamics of political and social life, to channel them by means of arrangements designed to ensure the structure of purposes which they thought society should embody. Although some writers, such as Aristotle, Machiavelli, and Locke, allowed for a greater flexibility in institutions and thus encouraged a broader expression of social differences than, say, Hobbes, their arrangements, nonetheless, were concerned with "closure," with delimiting the range and number of differences. Locke would defend a principle of toleration but it would exclude atheists, Catholics, and Jews. In the political schemes of virtually all theorists from antiquity to early modernity, the laboring classes, agricultural workers, artisans, and mechanics were consigned to silence, and women were treated either as mute facts of nature (Locke's "day-laborers and tradesmen, spinsters and dairy maids")[7] or as somewhat unnatural creations of art, while non-Europeans were exhibited as exotica. The silence imposed on certain races, classes, occupations, and gender increased the freedom of theorists to develop abstract structures that discounted the potential power of the silenced and, instead, subsumed or redefined them under other categories, such as "wages," "household," and the like. (Who was more satirized by the "noble savage," the nobles or the savages?) Theorists were thus able to control the proliferation of certain sources of power by reascribing their meaning. The result was to deposit a tension peculiar to early modern theory and politics.

Although it was widely acknowledged by theorists—and even celebrated—that in large measure politics was about the representation of interests and governance was about the reconciliation of conflicting interests, and it was admitted as well that the interests of laborers and of women might be different from those of owners and husbands, the conclusion was almost universally resisted that laborers and women should be admitted into the institutions that represented, regulated, and promoted interests. John Stuart Mill was the exception, something that could not be said of his teachers, Bentham and James Mill. Modern theory was more typically advice on how to stabilize society in the interests of modern power and its bearers. This involved postrevolutionary theorists in a strategy of reconceiving the "laws of nature."

Revolutionists of the seventeenth and eighteenth centuries had identified the laws of nature with universal principles of right from which they deduced natural rights and invoked their authority to subvert traditional prescriptive society. Postrevolutionary theorists sought to trade on the authority of modern science in developing a conception of scientific laws of nature that would serve the cause of order rather than revolt. Instead of nature as the source of right, nature represented regularities in physical phenomena and hence a realm of predictability. The new science of society aspired to be the science of stability for societies threatened with destabilizing effects—namely, the irregularities of social unrest and revolt accompanying the revolutions in economy, technology, warfare, and state-organization. Chaos versus cosmos.

Tocqueville resorts to a bewildering variety of theoretical devices in order to generate a plenitude of meanings, to overproduce, as it were, or as I put it earlier, to remythologize the political. With that reading taken into account, one can grasp the main thrust of his worries about democracy and the resulting characterization of it. Unlike most previous political theorists who had associated democracy with anarchy and disorder, that is, with a riotous display of diversities, Tocqueville sees it as threatening to squelch what is rare, unique, and different, with creating a world of "silent and empty spaces." His response is a theory that is constantly generating excess meanings, over and beyond whatever specific point he is making.

The replenishment of meaning would profoundly affect Tocqueville's presentation of American democracy. He had to emphasize its sameness, its thrust toward mediocrity, its banality, to depict it as a threat to singularities. Yet, if one examines the entries in his American notebooks, one finds him constantly registering the opposite impressions. He is "amazed," "overwhelmed" by the extraordinary character of America and Americans. Although much of this was preserved in the final form of *Democracy*, much was filtered out. One of the most striking examples was the contrast between the notebook impressions of Ohio and the description that appeared in *Democracy*. In the latter Tocqueville emphasizes the contrast between the effects of free labor in Ohio when compared with those produced by slavery in nearby

Kentucky.[8] In the notebooks, however, the entries depict Ohio as a radical democracy and the famous phrase that he would use in *Democracy* appears, "the experiment of a democracy without limits."[9] The omission of Ohio's radical democracy had the effect of making the state's progressive practices toward the Negro, which Tocqueville admired, appear unrelated to the democratic political culture that had made those practices possible.

America had to be presented as a particular kind of threat to plenitude of meaning. American society did not eradicate meaning. The singularities of class and of intellectual creativity that had typified the Old Regime in France had never taken hold. Americans, instead, tended to abort meaning, discouraging it from appearing. The threat Tocqueville wanted to confront lay in France, but this forced him toward a dilemma: while he wanted to warn his countrymen of the dangers of democratization illustrated by America, he also wanted to use America to demonstrate the possibility of moderating the effects of democratization. The theoretical devices he developed were, as a consequence, designed to demonstrate how meaningfulness might be, if not fully restored, at least protected.

## IV

> *I would prefer to place the eye on the end [of an eyeglass] which enlarges; in my life I have always needed to look at whatever I am doing in this way in order to make it worth doing.*
>
> Tocqueville[10]

The moment of theoretical control, when Tocqueville is fully aware that he is in possession of a theory and so can express what a theoretical journey means, occurs at the end of the first volume of *Democracy in America.* It takes the form of a remarkable metaphor that describes a traveler ascending a hill and the coalescing of a vision of a city that lies below him. It is a double vision in which we, the readers, are positioned to watch Tocqueville as he "sees" theoretically. As the metaphor unfolds, the reader "sees" Tocqueville's theoretical power developing and expanding and observes the necessary conditions of that development and the visual transformation of the world by a vision that grows more unified before the eyes of the reader and through the eyes of the theorist. The newly visioned reader shares Tocqueville's experience of theoretic empowerment and thus becomes a different kind of reader, a theorist's companion:

> I should like to unite the whole from a single point of view. What I shall say will be less detailed, but more certain. I shall perceive each object less distinctly; but I shall comprehend with more certainty the general facts. I shall be like the traveler who has

> left the walls of a vast city and climbs the neighboring hill. As he goes farther, the human beings he has left behind disappear before his eyes; their dwellings are blurred; he can no longer see the public squares; he can hardly make out the great thoroughfares, but his eye follows the contour of the city more easily. For the first time he sees the shape of the whole.
>
> It seems to me that in the same way I have discovered the whole future of the English race in the new world. The details of this immense tableau are lost in the shadow, but my glance captures the whole, and I conceive a clear idea of it.[11]

Here in compressed form are virtually all of the major elements in Tocqueville's conception of theory and of the theorist. The theorist is compared with a traveler, that is, he does not fully belong to the city he is observing. He is a sojourner, perhaps from a very different city, who is outside it and above it. Heights and distance are crucial metaphors in the language of theoretical power. They provide a critical perspective but they are also symbols of superiority. Heights symbolize loftiness of purpose as well as a privileged vantage point. Distance signifies detachment, the absence of self-interest. He can "see" the city better than its denizens. A theory resembles, if not a revelation, an illumination: "for the first time he sees the shape of the whole." The ancient metaphor of light/truth and darkness/ignorance is hinted at: "the details . . . are lost in shadow." Theory promises to "unite the whole from a single point of view," that is, it circumscribes the city as a creator-god would a world. The paradox of theory is that specific details (human beings, dwellings, and squares) are suppressed by being reduced to the point of indistinctness, while their general meaning emerges more clearly: mere details must be sacrificed, as it were, to the good of the theoretical whole, the healed whole.

The nature of theory is also delineated by the metaphors within the larger metaphor. The city being referred to is not the United States or France but democracy, the political form that more than any other was historically associated with city-states and which will have that genealogy confirmed in the forms of local self-government encountered in the towns of New England, which Tocqueville was quick to compare with the Greek polis.[12] The politicalness of the city alone forms the focus of perception. Its political character makes for a whole and a fitting theoretical object.

Politicalness is also the locating mark of the utopian element in Tocqueville's vision of America, not as the United States but as "democracy." He would not hesitate to pronounce Americans to be the most advanced in their political education. Puritan New England would play a special role as the agent of Tocqueville's remythologization of America's beginnings: "Democracy such as antiquity had not dared to dream broke away fully grown and fully armed from the midst of the old feudal society."[13]

The democratic point of departure shaped American society from the beginning and gave it a theoretical coherence unlike that of any previous society, "the new spectacle of a society homogeneous in all its parts."[14] The traveler ascending the hill did not create the city, however much he may have helped to reveal it.

Thus a theoretical vision that seeks a unified, coherent system of meaning finds a unified, coherent society. But that vision, at the same moment, begins to undercut itself. At the end of the chapter celebrating the theoretical coherence of America's New England beginnings, Tocqueville qualifies it by saying that the Puritans were not free to found a society relying solely on their own point of departure because no one "can disengage themselves totally from the past."[15] The unified vision of a new world will be haunted by the dirempted vision of two worlds and, ultimately, finds that its intelligibility depends on a world it has left behind rather than lost.

## V

*In order to succeed I shall frequently be forced to retrace my steps. But I hope that the reader will not refuse to follow me since the roads which are known to him will lead him to some new truth.*
Tocqueville[16]

Unlike Marx who developed his mature theory of capital by means of a running engagement with classical economics—and he never concealed his intellectual debts to Steuart, Smith, and Ricardo—Tocqueville made no effort to associate his sweeping claims with previous theoretical contributions that might have prepared the way for him. Instead of acknowledging that prior theoretical achievements had made his discoveries possible, he claimed that because he had been born between two worlds, he could see into them both in ways that others, coming from different origins, could not and that his journey to America was perfectly timed: that it was not just a question of what one saw theoretically, or even how one saw it, but, equally crucial, when. And that suggested some deeper power at work:

> Near enough to the period when American societies were founded to know in detail their elements, yet far enough from that time to judge what those seeds have produced, the men of our day seem destined to see farther into human events than our forefathers. Providence has given us a light denied to our fathers that allows us to see the first causes, in the destiny of nations, that the darkness of the past had obscured for them.[17]

Thus Tocqueville placed himself within his own myth, proclaiming a uniqueness that gained him entry into his own mythical world. His uniqueness coincided with the unique circumstances he would be surveying: the true nature of a society is not theoretically accessible at any moment the theorist might choose. There was a time right for theorizing, Tocqueville was saying, when the crucial beginnings of a society were still decipherable, when "the truth" is no longer "hidden."

## VI

*Paint, not the object, but the effect it produces.*
Stéphane Mallarmé[18]

The ascent of Tocqueville's *theoros* is an escape from details in order to achieve a panoramic vision. Unlike his contemporaries whose theoretical structures were methodically built on premises and hypotheses while professing deference to facts, the structure of Tocqueville's theory was shaped to organize impressions, developing what he called "tableaux" and "spectacles." The model he followed was not that of the scientist but of the painter. The theory he created might be called "political impressionism."

Of the impressionistic quality of Tocqueville's work, one can say: it employs and evokes images, abounds in sweeping generalizations, is richly allusive, dwells on the quality and style of political performance, and persuades by exhibiting rather than demonstrating. It is not uncommon for readers of Tocqueville to come away with "strong impressions" or "striking insights" because of the theory's visual effects. The reliance on visual impressions became an abiding feature of Tocqueville's mode of theorizing. Its presence was clearly evident in his last, and in many ways his greatest, work:

> [I]n studying our old society, I have never let the new order *pass from view.* I have not only wished to *see* the disease of which the sick man died, but also how his life might have been saved. My aim has been to *draw a tableau* strictly accurate and at the same time instructive. Every time that I have encountered among our ancestors some of those masculine virtues I have set them *in relief.* . . . [T]he vices . . . I have taken care *to put in the limelight.*[19] (emphasis added)

Through various devices Tocqueville would seek to engage the reader in a visual form of experience analogous to the way that a painter enlists the participation of the viewer. That analogy may be pushed further: a visual theorist is like a painter who, to attract the attention of the viewer and to entice him into the painter's way of seeing things, tries to establish his canvas as a field or setting against which selected objects are to be placed in a certain "light."

A theory that attempts to remythologize and relies on political impressionism at a time when the main theoretical tendencies favored scientific approaches will most clearly expose its heterodoxy in its conception and treatment of facts. In a letter to his translator Tocqueville confides that his temperament "for a time prevents my seeing things in their true perspective; external objects seem to me to be sometimes larger and sometimes smaller than they really are, just as fancy paints them."[20] A theory that attempts to "see" facts will use them differently than a theory that *handles* facts or assembles them as proof. In the prevailing theoretical understanding facts were intimations of unsuspected connections between phenomena, but for Tocqueville facts represented the direction of things. To employ facts to serve visual effects rather than a demonstrative purpose is to use them to reveal not only the unsuspected relationships but the ineluctable, in the present and past, and to identify their portents for the future. Impressionism, in the expansive mode it assumes with Tocqueville, would be his means of imaging facts so as to render them serviceable for a mode of theory inclined toward mythologizing and, as we shall see, drawn toward prophecy in a world no longer attuned to that mode of warning and promise but instead seeking its knowledge of the future in scientific predictions.

In *Democracy* there is a highly revealing passage where Tocqueville used the contrasts between two distinct styles of painting, the idealism of Raphael and the realism of David, to assert the transcending truths of imagination over the mimetic truth of facts ("details"):

> I doubt if Raphael made such an elaborate study of the detailed mechanisms of the human body as do the draftsmen of our day. He did not attach the same importance to rigorous exactitude. . . . for he claimed to surpass nature. He wanted to make of man something superior to man, to embellish beauty itself.
>
> In contrast, David and his pupils were as good anatomists as they were painters. They copied the models before their eyes marvellously well, but rarely did their imagination add anything more. . . . Renaissance painters generally looked for towering subjects and far removed in time so that their imagination could have a vast field. Our painters can produce exact details of private life . . . and copy trivial objects.[21]

Tocqueville was aware that when translated into theoretical practice these notions would make him vulnerable to fact-oriented critics. In *Democracy* he pleads for understanding from the reader:

> [I]n the whole work *une pensée mère* binds all its parts together. But the diversity of subjects treated is very great and it will not be difficult to oppose an isolated fact to the ensemble of facts which I cite, or an isolated idea to my ensemble of ideas. I hope to be read in the spirit that has guided my labors, and that my book will be judged by the general impression which it leaves, as I have formed my own judgment not on any single consideration, but upon the mass of considerations.[22]

## VII

*I have only taken in his conversation what accorded with all the notions I had already received.*

Tocqueville[23]

Tocqueville's use of facts has been the object of much criticism by later historians who have taxed him with oversimplifications and numerous errors of commission. He has been accused of exaggerating the democratic vitality of the New England township; of willfully misunderstanding the effects of inheritance laws in discouraging the growth of an American aristocracy; of underestimating the power of the central government while overestimating the strength and authority of local institutions; and, most egregiously, of ignoring the darkening shadow of industrialization.[24]

Anticipating that he might be vulnerable to such criticisms Tocqueville tried to deflect them by protesting that he had "never knowingly succumbed to adapting facts to ideas, instead of submitting the ideas to facts."[25] That disclaimer, with its suggestion that he and his critics were in general agreement about the proper handling of facts, glossed over the disagreements inherent in a deviant theoretical enterprise. While publicly professing adherence to prevailing conventions—which were far less standardized than they would shortly become—Tocqueville appeared to realize that he had a different, more political, conception of truth telling. In the closing paragraphs of his introduction to *Democracy*, he pleaded for an understanding reader who would judge the book theoretically, by its "general impression," and bear in mind that "the author who wants to make himself understood is forced to draw out all of the theoretical consequences from each of his ideas, often to the limits of the false and the impracticable."[26] In later years when he began his researches for *The Old Regime*, his departures, especially from the conventions of professional historians, were expressed with even greater deliberateness. He complained that if he were to abide by the historians' notions regarding the use of facts, he would be prevented from "mixing facts with ideas." A colorist, as it were, had to be free to apply the "color" of "philosophy."[27] Tocqueville was not, however, defending a notion that a theoretical history had a license to distort or invent facts. Instead he was claiming that a certain specular/speculative enhancement, which he refers to as "philosophy," was essential if the facts were to be "seen" in their true meaning, or, more precisely, their true political bearing.[28] Far from dismissing the importance of facts, Tocqueville attached the utmost importance to them, elevating them to the central role in his theory—but only after redefining their function in a theory. Facts were the means of *displaying* theoretical meaning rather than serving primarily as supporting proof for theoretical statements.[29]

In the metaphor of the traveler, Tocqueville had referred to "particulars" and "details" becoming "lost" or "obscure" as the traveler made his way to his privileged vantage point. That formulation was indicative of Tocqueville's impatience with a certain type of fact, "details," that made the world appear prosaic and could be invoked to banalize the sort of panoramic generalizations that were to be the staple of Tocqueville's mode of theorizing. Details were, at best, considered a low order of facticity.

Tocqueville was concerned with identifying/creating a particular type of facts, facts that, in his eyes, operated as forces in the history of society. The type of facts to which he attributed the utmost importance he referred to as "general," or "universal," or "central facts." The names given to these facts were meant to convey power; these facts held sway. That species of facts did not follow the logic of "such is the case that . . ." Instead they were given a thematic or, more exactly, mythematic character. Tocqueville would refer to the mythematic as *une pensée mère* or *une idée mère.* They identified the powers that were shaping the political world *generally* by reproducing themselves—*à la mère*—in diverse forms. As such they were crucial elements in Tocqueville's project of remythologizing the political and prophesying the future.

## VIII

*You are a counsellor, and by that virtue, no man dare accuse you.*
Shakespeare[30]

The generality of power represented by the mythematic fact resided in its connecting role. Such a fact revealed a broad range of phenomena to be interrelated and explicable by the *virtue* of the general fact. A general or mythematic fact possessed "virtue" in the older meaning of that word as denoting the power inherent in a supernatural or divine being. A general or universal fact is an empowered entity that shapes details by animating their particular identity and causing them to reflect its meaning. The power-laden, mythematic character of a general fact is conveyed by a passage in *Democracy* in which Tocqueville suggested that certain similarities exist between American Indians and Germanic tribes of the feudal era. "It is not impossible," he declared, "to recover a small number of generative facts [*faits générateurs*] from which all others flow."[31]

Generative facts produce preponderant tendencies. Tocqueville typically introduced them when he was depicting powerful historical forces. The following passage is his description of a "universal, master fact":

> [I]n each century one meets a singular and dominant fact to which all the others are connected; this fact nearly always gives rise to a basic idea [*mère pensée*] or to a principal passion which succeeds in attracting to it and carrying with it all feelings and ideas. It is like a great river toward which each of the tributary streams seems to run.[32]

The trend toward equality was the prime example of a generative fact that had acquired the status of a general conception. That status was derivative of the place assigned the fact in the order of significance proposed by the theory. That order, in Tocqueville's conception, required a controlling center from which power over other facts emanated and to which the theorist returned to assert his control. The opening paragraphs of *Democracy* establish its theoretical center by designating "equality of conditions" as "the generative fact [*le fait générateur*] from which each particular fact would seem to descend, and I found myself constantly returning to it as the center where all of my observations would terminate."[33]

The aim of Tocqueville's decision to locate equality of conditions at the center of his theoretic structure was to enable the phenomena of democracy to emerge and appear interconnected. While the justification for selecting equality was its observable effects throughout society, the decision to select it and trace its ramifications was made possible by a theoretical eye sensitive to equality's impact upon inequality. Whereas a general fact calls attention to the condition of the external social world, its discovery and significance call attention to the special qualities of the observer:

> Among the novel objects which drew my attention during my journey to the United States, none struck me more vividly than equality of conditions. I discovered easily the prodigious influence which this primary fact exerted over the course of society; the direction it gives to public opinion and a certain emphasis to the laws, new maxims to those who govern, and new habits to the governed.[34]

Within Tocqueville's theoretical structure, equality of conditions functioned as the fundamental concept that enabled the theorist to characterize a wide range of social and political phenomena. Its status signified that the theory has made contact with the *logos*, the ontological principle of power shaping the postrevolutionary world. Accordingly, equality is not only a status sanctioned by a formal legal principle of right but a "virtue" that invades the innermost regions of the human psyche. "The passion for equality penetrates all reaches of the human heart and fills it in entirety." So overwhelming is its power that "all men and all powers which wish to struggle against this irresistible power will be overthrown and destroyed by it."[35] By virtue of its power a general fact poses a danger that justifies intervention by a mediator, by one who is specially discerning and specially chosen.

Not long after Tocqueville returned from America and before he had settled down to writing *Democracy*, he journeyed to England. There he discovered that not all societies manifest general facts and are, therefore, less accessible to theoretical understanding. England struck him as "a vast chaos." "There is not a single principle from which consequences follow quietly; there are some lines which crisscross, a labyrinth in which we are absolutely lost."[36]

In America the power of theory was greater because general facts were more prevalent:

> In America all laws originate more or less from the same idea. The whole of society . . . is based on just one fact: everything follows from one underlying principle. One could compare America to a great forest cut through by a large number of roads which all end in the same place. Once you have found the central point, you can see the whole plan at one glance. But in England roads cross, and you have to follow along each one of them to get a clear idea of the whole.[37]

Thus the more democratic a society, the more theoretically transparent or generalizable; the less democratic, the more opaque and less generalizable. The first case has the potential for a strong theory; the second, the potential for a less comprehensive, less totalizing theory. The power of theory, in Tocqueville's conception, seemed to depend on the presence of general facts, the type of facts that a democratic society displayed in abundance and that, in their generality or scope, posed the greatest danger to individuality and diversity. Generality thus presented theory with a powerful new weapon in the form of a dangerous political symptom. The novelty lay in the reversal being effected. Previously theorists had identified political danger with the arbitrary or tyrannical, with that which demanded exception from general rules of law or conventions of morality. The sway of generality would not abolish tyranny but refashion it in its own image.

## IX

> *[T]he oldest things seem new when shewn as you shew it* [sic], *in all kinds of previously unsuspected relations to all the other things which surround it.*
>
> J. S. Mill[38]

Tocqueville's metaphor of the traveler ascending the hill also indicated that the form of theory would be a mix of epic and prophecy. "I have discovered," he claimed, "the whole future of the English race in the new world." Epic and prophecy are both highly visual forms. They want their audience to "see" the deeds being recounted or the fate that is in store. So they "display" (*illustré*) and depict generalizations as a way of explaining them. A characteristic usage in this connection was Tocqueville's phrase *jeter un coup d'oeil général.* It appears throughout *Democracy* and in practically all of his later publications and in much of his correspondence. The phrase resists a graceful translation: *un coup d'oeil* means a "surveying," and *jeter* implies an active, assertive character, a "casting" (in the double meaning of that word: to set and to assign) of the surveying glance over its field of objects while setting them in place. When employed as a synonym for theorizing, *jeter* suggests the commanding of objects, fitting them into their "right" places, empirically as well as normatively.

Visual representation as theoretical ordering or control was best exemplified in two favorite metaphors of Tocqueville's, "tableau" and "spectacle." "Tableau" was an expression of Tocqueville's striving for a visual ordering of relationships. As in the metaphor of the traveler ascending the hill, it creates distance between the theorist and the objects being described, which is then reexperienced by the reader. Once again details are sacrificed in order to produce effects and to assert the unity of the connected elements being represented. As Tocqueville explained to Reeve, "I refer to the *ensemble*; the tableau is painted only to be seen from afar. A mass of details has been deliberately omitted."[39]

A tableau is distinguished by several elements: its pictorial character fixes its subjects, positions them in relation to each other, and establishes meaning by the vivid effects that their arrangement produces upon the understanding. Writing to a friend shortly after returning from America, Tocqueville first mentions a wide range of detailed observations about American life and society and then he remarks, "there is in the tableau a mass of defective materials but the whole seizes the imagination."[40] For a tableau to form a "whole" it must be centered so that whatever is included within its boundaries acquires meaning by a relationship established between itself and the center. The notion was captured by a terse notebook entry inserted by Tocqueville while journeying to England and Ireland in 1835. It related to the striking contrast between "apparent equality" and "the real privileges of the wealthy": "Central idea: all the facts lead my mind back to it."[41]

Before arriving at a "central idea," Tocqueville would endure several false starts until "a flood of light was cast which allows one to form general ideas."[42] His notebooks show him pondering facts, discarding some, rearranging others, and trying to survey his field of phenomena from a variety of vantage points. He described this later when he began his work on the French Revolution: "I investigate; I experiment; I try to grasp the facts more closely than has yet been attempted, and to extract from them the general truths which they contain."[43]

Thus the first step in composing a full tableau was to find specific facts that, so to speak, shared a common inclination, a shading that pointed toward a general idea. Once the general idea has been outlined it could then be expanded and serve as a center drawing other facts into the frame of the tableau. The next step was described by Tocqueville in a letter written while he was working on the final volume of *Democracy.* The particular problem he was wrestling with concerned the influence of democratic ideas and sentiments upon the government. "With the support of the whole edifice of my book," he wrote, "I have begun by establishing theoretically" that democratic beliefs lead the people to concentrate power in central authorities. "Now," he continued, "I want to prove by *les faits actuels* that I am right. Already I have a great many general facts (for these are the only kind that I can use) but I would like more."

Tocqueville's conclusion to the letter affords a fine glimpse of the theoretical mind struggling for the higher ground of general ideas so that it may "see" things in new relationships and in deeper significance:

> You will note that I am trying to get above the viewpoint of administrative centralization which primarily consists of replacing the secondary powers by the central power. I do want to show that, but also how the state successively seizes everything, putting itself from all directions in place of the individual or placing the individual in tutelage, governing, regulating, *uniformizing* everything and everybody. It is surely a grand tableau and a great subject. But my materials are not yet sufficient; my imagination and reality go beyond what I can express and make understandable.[44]

That passage provides a nice illustration of how a theoretical structure arises from a complex of decisions. Tocqueville begins with a determination of the particular problem; then he proposes a guiding theoretical notion distilled from certain general facts; and, finally, he seeks to compose a full picture, a tableau, that will reveal the great and general significance of particular facts. The theoretical structure of *Democracy* would be primarily composed of facts of a broadly general character, such as equality of social condition, centralization, the influence of the majority, social mobility, liberty, and localism (i.e., the power of local governments, the political life of citizens). The general facts would then be used to constitute a number of tableaux, each serving to draw the reader into Tocqueville's theoretical field by sensitizing him or her to relationships between various phenomena (actions, events, practices, beliefs) and a general fact, such as equality, and the shaping of the former by the latter. A theory thus becomes a means of educating civic perceptions.

## X

A tableau is the direct expression of the creative power of the theorist. He discovers or creates connections that had remained hidden or badly understood. It represents a different element than Tocqueville's other favorite metaphor of control, the "spectacle." In a letter to a friend in which Tocqueville tried to explain their disagreements, he wrote that "you are impressed by the spectacle before your eyes and me by the tableau which is before mine."[45]

Tableau and spectacle both have theatrical as well as theoretical connotations; both are visually arresting. There are, however, important differences. A spectacle presents a panorama intended to provoke awe or amazement. Its extraordinary character strains the theoretical imagination as it seeks to compress hugeness, as when it tries to render the spectacle of the French Revolution. A tableau, however, produces comprehension by revealing unsuspected connections that, at first glance, may have seemed implausible.

Tableau and spectacle also signify a contrast between what is within human power and what is not, and, correspondingly, between what is created theoretically and what is theoretically reflected. In large measure, a tableau is staged; a spectacle is revealed. Here, for example, is Tocqueville presenting in tableau form the extraordinary energy and efficacy of Americans, the mastery that they display over their world:

> However powerful and impetuous the flow of time [in America], imagination anticipates it and is already taking possession of a new universe. The tableau is not big enough for it. There is not a country in the world where man more confidently seizes the future, where he so proudly feels that his intelligence makes him master of the universe, that he can fashion it to his liking.[46]

Thus a tableau, both for theorist and actor, celebrates the expression of power. Despite its large scale, it is nonetheless limited in what it can convey. As the foregoing quotation suggests, it is not "big enough" for the epic character of its subject, "taking possession of a new universe." Spectacle attempts to remedy that shortcoming.

# CHAPTER VIII

# THE SPECTACLE OF AMERICA

## I

> *For the Greeks* theoria *had a double sound of "looking" or "viewing," from* thea *"spectacle," and* horan, *"to see." The word, compounded of these two elements, expresses a religious love of spectacle which was peculiar to the Greeks.*
>
> C. Kerenyi[1]

> *Socrates: The prayers and the spectacle were over, and we were leaving to go back to the city.*
>
> Plato[2]

The idea of a theoretical spectacle is as old as the idea of theory; indeed, spectacle is one of the meanings associated with a *theoria.* Plato had described philosophers as those for whom "the truth is the spectacle which they love."[3] For Tocqueville, too, spectacle and truth were intimately related, but unlike Plato, who was primarily enthralled by the pure intellectual splendor of the Idea, its immaterial beauty, Tocqueville was dazzled by the massive overwhelming power of the spectacle of a new political world. The New World assumed a purely physical form at the very beginning of *Democracy in America.* Here he surveyed the topography, the awesome natural wonders, the richness of material resources, and the natural drama of mountains, pristine rivers, tangled forests, and total silence. And yet it was presented, not as a series of scenic wonders in a travelogue, but as a theorizable object set off within a natural frame.

The opening sentences of the first chapter are rich in theoretical code words, even though what is being visualized is the "exterior configuration of North America." It presents "general features which it is easy to trace at first glance [*au premier coup d'oeil*]." These were imbued by Tocqueville with overtones of the biblical account of Creation, a recurrent mytheme of *Democracy*: "A kind of methodical order presides there in the separation of land and water, of mountains and valleys. A simple and majestic design is revealed even in the midst of a confusion of objects and among the extremely varied tableaux."[4]

Tocqueville then focuses his object more specifically, merging theoretical with physical boundaries, the theoretical design with the providential: "Placed in the center of an immense continent where human industry can extend itself without limits, the Union is nearly as isolated from the world as if it were hemmed in on all sides by the Ocean."[5]

Thus framed as a separate world America can then be depicted as the scene of an extraordinary theoretical spectacle. Everything—the freedom of action, the energy of the inhabitants, their expectations—was outsized. Traditional assumptions about time, space, and human limits had been exploded.[6] For the first time in Western history it seemed that human action had found a Promethean setting where the only limitations on action were those of the individual actor.

Like earlier theorists who claimed to have discovered a land that embodied a theory—and thus the utopias they were reporting were, in reality, a claim to a uniquely theoretical spectacle—Tocqueville would make the same case for his America: "It is there that civilized men have attempted to build society on new foundations while applying for the first time theories hitherto unknown or deemed inapplicable; they are presenting to the world a spectacle for which past history had not prepared it."[7]

Tocqueville was not content to allow that spectacle to be construed as the triumph of low material concerns of land, wealth, and social mobility. It had to be mythicized as the embodiment of ideas and elevated beyond the ordinary: "It is an intellectual movement which can only be compared to the discovery of the new world three centuries ago; and one can easily say that America has been discovered a second time."[8] The American "was already master of the most important secrets of nature, united with his fellowmen, and instructed in the experience of fifty centuries."[9]

Implicit in the rich spectacle of America would be the equally remarkable spectacle of the theory that reported it. In presenting the spectacle of America, the theory itself becomes an object to compel admiration and wonder.

## II

> *There is a country in the world where the great social revolution . . . has very nearly reached its natural limits; it operates there in a simple and easy fashion, or rather one could say that this country sees the results of the democratic revolution which is going on among us, but without having had the revolution itself.*
>
> Tocqueville[10]

The spectacle of America was expressed theoretically in one of Tocqueville's great metaphorical constructions, *le Nouveau Monde.* Tocqueville was being only slightly immodest when he remarked that "America had been discovered a second time," implying the first time by explorers, the second by a theorist.

His America was both a distinctive world and, more importantly, a new one—that is, Tocqueville's discovery was as much about the phenomenon of the new as about democracy. The "new" referred primarily to life without a past and its inherited rancors. An American "has nothing to forget."[11] The new man can live wholly oriented toward the future. His is a society without inherited positions or striking differences among its inhabitants, a democratic/egalitarian civilization shaped by its emergence from and struggle with primeval nature, a striking mix of individualism and collectivism plus a politics that seemed more improvisation than practice—a society "without roots, without memories, without prejudices, without routines, without common ideas, without a national character, more than a hundred times happier than ours."[12]

Because it had never been old, the United States was *a* new world but not *the* new world. It had features uniquely its own and unreproducible elsewhere, most notably its natural resources and the untraumatic origins of its democracy. It was newness without poignancy or shock. "This new society which I want to paint and judge continues to evolve. Time has not yet fixed its form; the great revolution which has created it still continues."[13] Because it had no past to distract it, the United States could devote itself to the reproduction of the new, to being a purely modern civilization:

> The American inhabits a land of prodigies; he is surrounded by constant movement, and every movement seems an advance. In his mind the idea of the new is closely linked to the ideas of the better. Nowhere does he see any limit that nature could impose on human effort; in his eyes, that which does not yet exist is simply what has not been attempted.[14]

Although the Old World was becoming new, it had a past to overcome or, more accurately, a past that had been overcome by revolution, that peculiarly modern act by which world creation is accompanied by world destruction, a loss of customary reference points. "The past no longer illuminates the future, and mind proceeds in shadows." The effects of the democratic revolution "cannot be compared with anything previously seen in the world." The main features of the "vast tableau" could be identified: good and evil would be more equitably distributed; great wealth would disappear and small fortunes grow; no great prosperity but less misery; less energy and gentler manners; the individual will shrink, the state expand.[15]

The new would be Tocqueville's replacement, although far from being his synonym, for "the best," the term that had been at the center of most premodern and many modern theories of governmental forms. Its use would signify a shift of emphasis in the understanding of politics, not only from the qualitative to the quantitative, but from the qualitative in the moral sense to the qualitative in a temporal sense.

## III

*The new world which is emerging is partly entangled under the débris of the world it has toppled.*

Tocqueville[16]

The theoretical meaning of the New World depended on a contrast with another equally distinct but more complex construction, the Old World. If "the great advantage of Americans is to have arrived at democracy without suffering through democratic revolutions, and to be born equal instead of becoming equal," each of those traumas had been endured by the Old World.[17] Unlike the New, the Old World had been riven by revolution so that its past was set over against its present rather than succeeded by it. For aristocracies usually succumb only after "a prolonged struggle" that leaves behind "implacable hatreds among the different classes." The dispossessed aristocrats become "as strangers in the new society," ill at ease and resentful.[18]

Modernization had come to the New World without the sufferings caused by imposed equality and the leveled relationships it brought along with its newly collectivized power. In the Old World the revolution introduced equality and universality of right by seeking to eliminate the politics and culture of inequality; it had thus attempted to establish "natural" right and restore a "natural" condition by abolishing a historical one. Aristocracy, which had once thought itself to be the expression of "natural" inequality, was condemned as artificial. America, in contrast, did not have to constitute nature artificially. It *was* a natural condition unmediated by historically grounded oppositions to hierarchy, religious establishments, and hereditary privileges. It was the embodiment of the modern state of nature, a suppressed war of each against all but tempered by unlimited possibilities. The absence of history had left nature exposed, and it became the object of human power and striving. "The Americans only arrived yesterday on the land they live on, yet they have already overthrown the order of nature to their advantage."[19]

Although Tocqueville furnished his Old World partly with inherited elements and partly with ones imposed by the French Revolution, the theoretical meaning he gave to it centered almost entirely on its *ancien régime* features, especially the aristocratic ones. If the New World could be summed up by the general insignia of equality, the Old was epitomized in particularity. Thus in the New World the individual claimed identical rights from a "general" fund of rights for all citizens; in the Old World before the revolution the aristocrat "possessed in himself a particular right."[20]

## IV

> *Those who live in aristocratic societies never conceive of themselves in terms of general ideas and that is sufficient to give them a habitual distrust of those ideas and an instinctive disgust for them.*
>
> Tocqueville[21]

> *I have a too pronounced penchant for general ideas.*
>
> Tocqueville[22]

Why is it impossible to imagine a political theory without generalizations? To the theorist, generalization can, of course, mean different things. It can refer to the logical practice of deducing common features from a selection of particulars or to statements about a class of objects. A scientific theory or even an economic theory *confines* generalizations to what holds or is "true" or "law-like" under certain specified conditions. Generalizations, if not suspect, usually require "qualification"—that is, their power is limited but within those limits it is secure. But in a political theory, such as Tocqueville's, generalizations are employed to *expand* a domain of assertion. The basic structure of his theoretical formulations, accordingly, would be shaped to culminate in generalizations that were visually expansive rather than logically constrictive, imagistic rather than *pointilliste.*

To state it this way is to call attention to the political impulses/motives congealed (rather than concealed) in a political theory. Generalization means exerting sway over a certain domain of objects denied qualification except as afterthought. Like metaphor, it is an instrument of theoretical control—although not that alone. For that we need to recall that the "general" implies or refers to a whole, to some grouping of whose coherence generality is the expression or representation.[23] That mode of referring is a way for the mind to exercise power. It reduces a mass of particulars to instances in a grouping at a level devised or assigned by the mind: at that level the power of the mind is most perfectly exerted. This understanding was captured in the phrase of a nineteenth-century writer, when Sir David Brewster referred to "a method of great generality and power."[24]

General facts came to represent for Tocqueville the junction where theory most securely connects with the nature of the democratic world. He was convinced that general facts explain more in an age of leveling because, not requiring qualification, they have a greater sway than in an aristocratic age. The institutions of equality enforce a greater uniformity, thereby rendering citizens more generalizable as theoretical objects as well as objects of rule-making powers.

Tocqueville's worries about generalization were not epistemic but political. When theory introduces abstractions, it factors out differences. That action might seem unnatural when abstractions are used to read a highly differentiated social order, but that same operation is "naturalized" when the object is a deeply homogeneous society. The homogeneity of egalitarian America invited the production of statements of broad relevance. Yet the temptation to generalize might also occasion statements that, like democracy itself, work to suppress certain "facts" that are "exceptions to the rule." The exception(al) or rare was the phenomenal equivalent of aristocracy.

Tocqueville was observing America at a time when the sectional differences were beginning to stir that would tear the Union apart. At the same time, as a French citizen, he was cognizant of the historical struggles between local authorities and the centralized monarchy in which the aristocracy had mainly been on the side of the former against the "generalizing" power of the state. These intertwinings of theory, epistemology, history, and politics produced a constant anguish in Tocqueville because his generalizing theoretical impulses were at odds with his particularizing political and historical loyalties.

Tocqueville was aware of the contradictions but a number of basic considerations, some theoretical, others political, made him want to have it both ways. Theoretically Tocqueville became convinced that the sacrifice of particulars was, to some degree, a sine qua non of theorizing. It was as though the loftiness of the enterprise justified *une théorique raison d'état* in overriding particular differences; otherwise the scope of theoretical vision would be too constricted. In a note written to himself while completing the final volume of *Democracy*, Tocqueville revealed how self-conscious he was of the tensions:

> Last chapter. General survey of the subject. General estimate of the effects of equality. I can only tackle this summary in an open and noble manner, otherwise it would seem out of place and incomplete. I must appear [as] wanting to compress into a narrow frame the whole picture that I have painted, [as] brushing aside details by closing my eyes to them [as] no longer being interested in America which opened the way for me.[25]

Tocqueville would be strongly committed to the value of the "general" and would make it emblematic of his theoretical style. It was of a piece with his highly pictorial, imagistic practice of theory and his urge for depicting sweeping panoramas of developments covering centuries. It fitted, too, with a prophetic bent, always trying to peer into the future, not to make precise predictions about events but to describe the fateful condition that Western societies might drift toward if their political leaders were unable to act in time. Yet Tocqueville took offense when several critics complained about the abstract character of the second installment of *Democracy*.

Tocqueville seemingly had placed himself in a quandary in which his theoretical structure conflicted with his inherited political values.[26] To resolve it he would attempt a conception of theory that would do justice both to generality (= democracy) and to particularity (= aristocracy), thereby qualifying the theory's own power. The politics of methodology whereby Tocqueville will seek to find ways of restricting the scope of the general, and thereby of the power of the theoretical statement, by associating the particular with resistance, would find expression in the role he laid out for those whom he considered to be the custodians of the human spirit in the age of democracy and secularism. In the second part of *Democracy* he summons philosophers, poets, and historians to a "holy enterprise." In an almost eerie anticipation of the "aesthetic policies" of socialist realism, Tocqueville warns of the ways democracy would corrupt their callings: poets will be encouraged to compose ballads extolling collective life; the historian will feel the pressure to explain events by impersonal forces and he will respond by picturing the individual actor as reduced to helplessness; and the philosopher will find it difficult to persuade people that the future has legitimate claims on the present. Poets, historians, and philosophers should, therefore, set themselves against the democratic grain. The poet should be concerned with the permanent nature of man rather than the glory of the collectivity; the historian should emphasize the efficacy of individual action, and the philosopher should restore that "love of the future" that encourages men to look "beyond their present desires."[27]

The injunctions laid upon the intellectual elites have a peculiar, almost religious resonance—"the permanent nature of man," "love of the future" (which was not about calculation but about inheritance and possibly the afterlife), and "beyond present desires." Those overtones, combined with the defense of the particular, pose yet again the question of the nature of a theory that might aspire to generality while defending particularity. The answer lies in the form in which Tocqueville put the question: is there an ideal theory that accomplishes both and, if so, who is the exemplar of it?

## V

> *I must attempt to get away from particular points of view in order to take a position, if possible, among the general points of view which depend on neither time nor place.*
>
> Tocqueville[28]

How, and for whom, was it possible to combine the general and the particular while doing justice to both? Tocqueville's formulation of the problem took the following form: the ordinary theoretical mind was able to classify objects on the basis of their similarities and differences, and to distinguish parts from wholes. But it seemed unable to comprehend, at one and the same time, similarities *and* differences, parts *and* wholes. Where, then, was a theoretical model for such a feat to be found?

From the same note cited in the preceding epigraph Tocqueville concludes with an injunction to himself, "See as much as possible through the thought of God and judge from there."[29] The archetypal theorist was God and the paradigm of perfect theoretical knowledge was embodied in God's way of thinking. God sees "the resemblances that make [an individual] like his fellows" just as he sees "the differences which isolate him from them."[30] To see as God would see, to think as God would think, would mean being able not only to see into the future, but to grasp at one and the same moment the particular and the general, the individual and the collectivity, aristocratic singularity and democratic generality/equality. It would mean not sacrificing the particular to the general, as was the wont of democracy, or the general to the particular, as was the vice of aristocracy. In an astonishing passage toward the close of *Democracy*, Tocqueville wrote, "I strive to penetrate into the viewpoint of God, and it is from there that I seek to consider and to judge human things."[31]

Although Tocqueville admitted that the human mind could not equal the divine in the simultaneity of its grasp of the general and the particular, he insisted that it was possible to approximate that achievement without surrendering the theoretical power inherent in generalizing. General ideas enable the mind to abstract from the welter of particulars the recurrent or common features and to convert these into general concepts and social laws. They enabled the human mind to fight clear of "the immensity of details" in the world—the bête noire of the theorist—and "to pass judgments on a great many objects at once."[32] But that power also has, not so much a weakness as a certain despotic element that produces injustice in its treatment of particulars as well as a loss of specificity: "General ideas do not testify to the strength of the human intellect but rather to its insufficiency; for in nature there are no beings exactly alike; no facts precisely identical; no rules indiscriminately and in the same way applicable to several objects at the same time."[33]

The task was to create a theoretical counterpoint between general and particular, using the latter to restrain the despotic tendency in the former. The solution, the theoretical construction of two worlds mentioned earlier, mimicked one of the oldest forms of mythmaking, world creation. By juxtaposing them it was possible to disrupt generalizations through a strategy of revealing similarities and differences between the two worlds as well within each. It could be shown that within the new or democratic world there were institutions based on principles contrary to or dissimilar from those associated with an egalitarian society but significantly similar to those in an old or premodern world. For example, if the American legal system were surveyed from the vantage point of the ancient legal institutions of the predemocratic world, the status and function of American courts, judges, and lawyers would reveal striking similarities with the prerevolutionary French *parlements* (courts) and the *noblesse de robe*.[34] One could then conclude that "the American aristocracy" was located "in the judiciary and bar."[35] Thus the general, represented by quantity and majority rule, was qualified by a particular representative of the aristocratic principle. Another example: voluntary associations and local governments opposed to centralization played a role comparable with the *corps intermédiaires* in the Old Regime in France.[36]

In pointing up the similarities between Old and New World practices Tocqueville was not only deepening empirically the New World by suggesting the existence of discontinuities within it, but also dissolving the monolithic character that democracy had in the eyes of conservative groups in France and replacing it with a qualified or moderate democracy.

## VI

Tocqueville's struggle to combine generalization and particularity was the theoretical reflection of contradictory tendencies in his politics, not just of strategies. He never truly embraced democracy; he never truly renounced aristocracy. The converse was also true. He came to recognize the limitations of aristocracy and to appreciate the virtues of democracy. But there was no lasting equilibrium. He would declare, "the good of mankind is the only objective worth pursuing," but in the next breath he confessed that "while I love mankind in general, I constantly encounter individuals whose baseness revolts me. I struggle daily with contempt for my fellow creatures."[37] A few years later he described himself somewhat differently to Mill: "By taste I love liberty; by instinct and reason I love equality."[38] Although Tocqueville would struggle, often successfully, to see the world through democratic eyes, to do justice to democracy's merits, democracy would always remain foreign, his subject matter rather than his element.

The vision of Tocqueville's *theoros* became more focused as the city receded. Aristocratic perception, if threatened by its object, egalitarianism, will defend a certain unbridgeable theoretic distance. It might sympathize, even understand, but never merge or identify. An exact contemporary, Ralph Waldo Emerson, formulated a conception of theory that contrasts as sharply as possible with Tocqueville's traveler. "The act of seeing," Emerson declared, "and the thing seen, the seer and the spectacle, the subject and the object are one."[39] It was not that Tocqueville's conception of theory excludes the activist character of thinking celebrated by Emerson; rather they were separated by Tocqueville's wariness about idealism's project for overcoming the subject-object distinction, which seemed to dissolve differences and to surrender critical distance.

Tocqueville's vacillations about the value of democracy were testimony to the contrary pulls of what he had observed in America and what, as an aristocrat, he had been bred to see, and to a genealogy defined by a historical rupture. The result was a theoretical mind attracted to contrasts, moving restlessly between democratic realities and aristocratic idealities, equality and distinction, commonplace and rarity, innovation and tradition, a present that lived for the future and a past that was being embalmed.[40]

His aristocratic eye would make for attentiveness to the value of discriminations, subtleties, nuances, gradations, idiosyncrasies, in a word, to all manner of particularities. The aristocratic mode of perception would be a rich source of insight, supplying endless contrasts and colors in an increasingly monochromatic world. It would also be a basis for resistance, insisting that democracy submit to being understood by its Other, by principles that were not only predemocratic but antidemocratic. Aristocratic perception, when it was able to transcend nostalgia, encouraged a theoretical sensitivity to the special claims of differences, less as a matter of right or of empirical observation, than because of the potential resistance embodied in cultural differences now jeopardized by a world inclining toward sameness. "When conditions are very unequal and the inequalities are permanent, individuals gradually become so dissimilar that one can say that there are as many distinct humanities as there are classes."[41]

With its built-in political biases disguised as the scientific quest for regularities, generalization serves as the discursive complement/compliment to social equality and as such finds the democratic mentality congenial. Methodologically it favors abstract universals ("All men are created equal [and] endowed by the Creator with certain unalienable rights") and thus appears as an ally to those critical of tradition.

At the same time, the general may also be the discursive medium of absolute monarchy. According to Aristotle, the democratic and the tyrannical mentalities have certain affinities.[42] Each is a leveler: democracy has its equal citizens, monarchy its "subjects." Hobbes had captured the idea in the remark that "all honor and dignity" vanisheth before a sovereign who could be either a single ruler or a people.[43] Tocqueville would amalgamate the two into "democratic despotism": for both democracy and absolutism the Other was aristocracy. The antitheses were also embedded in his epistemology. Although generalization finds congruence with democracy, it also reveals in its inherently abstract quality an urge toward domination. If particularity is the site of resistance, generalization is a sovereignty over a realm of particulars/statements. The abstract is monarchical and incorporate, the particular is disaggregated but potentially pluralist.

One measure of a sharpening in Tocqueville's theoretical focus was his learning how to exploit the division between the two modes of perception. This comes through in a self-addressed note written while he was preparing the second part of *Democracy*; despite its cryptic quality, the note reveals a political purpose being inserted and a self-conscious exploitation and manipulation of his chosen contrasts: "Danger of allowing a single social principle to take over absolute direction of society without contestation. The general idea that I have wanted to underscore in this work."[44]

The political and theoretical task was becoming defined as finding ways to employ particularity, the epistemological equivalent of aristocracy, to frustrate egalitarian uniformizing. Like Aristotle before him, Tocqueville came to believe that democracy worked safely only when some provision was made for institutions that restrained or blocked the full realization of the logic of democracy. More often than not, such institutions served as the functional equivalents or stand-ins for aristocracy. As the historical successor to monarchy, democracy is made to perpetuate the animus against aristocracy, while aristocracy is allowed to linger on, not as a social class but as the symbol of a heroic politics of resistance.

*Democracy in America* abounds with references to aristocracy: to its codes, its mode of life, as a form of society, and its institutions. If, as Tocqueville averred, he never wrote a page of *Democracy* without thinking of France, it was equally true that he never thought about democracy without writing about aristocracy. The result was that democracy emerges importantly through the contrasts with aristocracy. By incorporating aristocratic images of power, public service, family relationships, belief, taste, and sensibility and by underscoring their differences from the democratic counterparts, Tocqueville, in effect, "restored" theoretically what the French Revolution had attempted to abolish politically.

Although he always disclaimed any attempt to revive aristocratic power and glory, he never ceased attempting to reincarnate it as a theoretical and structural principle to combat what he perceived as the totalizing tendencies in the democratic ideology. Tocqueville would represent democracy as the harbinger of a new kind of holism, without social hierarchy, a collectivism independent of socialism and even hostile to it. "[D]emocracy is . . . either on the march in certain domains or is fully extended in others. It is in the *moeurs*, in the laws, in the opinions of the majority."[45] Unlike a ruling aristocracy, which asserts its superiority by jealously guarding its social distance from other classes, democracy rules by permeation. It seeps into all of the major life-forms of society—social, cultural, religious, moral, as well as political. Its paradox, Tocqueville would discover, was that, unlike socialism, which posited a collectivism logically and ontologically prior to individual liberation, democracy would invert the sequence with collectivism emerging out of extreme individuation.

## VII

The singularity cherished by aristocratic modes of theorizing was easy enough to appreciate when contrasted with the monotony of egalitarianism. It assumed a more problematic quality, however, when used against liberal bourgeois notions of individualism then gathering around doctrines of self-interest and acquisitiveness. Aristocracy, as the particular, displayed a flaw similar to that of bourgeois individualism: a pride in its own uniqueness, which prevented it from rising above the limitations of class interests to be the symbolic representative of the political. The aristocrat, like the bourgeois, symbolized the irrevocability of social divisions and of apartness. While the aristocratic might temper independence by noblesse oblige and paternalism, its virtues were at cross-purposes with the most fundamental element of the political, its irreducible commonality. Aristocracy reveals itself as inherently flawed by an insufficiency of generality or, rather, the French Revolution had first exposed it as a failing, then punished it as a crime.

Democracy, as bourgeoisified in the postrevolutionary era, would reveal itself to Tocqueville as likewise inadequately endowed with concern for the political but, unlike aristocracy, it threatened to become overgeneralized. Democratic equality is one way of promoting commonality, but bourgeois individualism can undercut equality while bourgeois competitiveness destroys both equality and solidarity. The consequence is the perversion of generality and the prelude to democratic despotism. That dire condition is immanent in the democratic form of apartness, individualism, an overparticularization that withdraws from the public domain and thereby allows power to generalize itself, to extend its rules without encountering differences. Where traditional societies included distinctions of wealth, birth, and status, within the political, democratic societies attempted a separation of the public and the private realms with social distinctions forbidden in the one and sanctioned in the other.

## VIII

> *In the main, only the affairs of our time interest the public and interest me as well. The grandeur and singularity of the spectacle which our world presents absorb too much attention for one to attach much value to those historical curiosities which satisfy idle and erudite societies.*
>
> Tocqueville[46]

The effect of a spectacle is to diminish the individual actor who cannot but be dwarfed by comparison with the gigantic movements conjured up by Tocqueville. In that vein he wrote to a friend in the midst of a diplomatic crisis, "the spectacle at least is great, for we can look at things and forget the men."[47] Not surprisingly, democratic men are frequently described by Tocqueville as "very small" or "weak."[48] One of the most notable omissions from *Democracy* is any analysis of individual American politicians or statesmen, save for the unflattering references to President Andrew Jackson. Small actors were only capable of petty politics.

Sometimes Tocqueville seemed to attribute the trivial character of political action in America to the stature of the men who had succeeded the heroic Founders, other times to the defeat of great passions by the prevalence of self-interest and calculation. But the main thrust of his writing was to see the American spectacle as a collective action, not of a corporate general will but of a huge aggregate of scattered individuals. The epical character of collective action is massive movement rather than a movement by the masses-as-actor. It is the "march" of equality, or the movement of opinion, or the social tendency imparted by millions of uncoordinated individuals each bent on his or her own affairs. In America individuals seem "powerless," while society seems to proceed by "free and spontaneous cooperation." It is not that individual actors are without influence, only that it is far smaller than in aristocracies and hence difficult to discern.[49] Direction without a Director(y).

This contrast between great movements and puny men not only left the future of action in doubt but equally the future of that form of theory which conceived its role in close association with action. It was one thing to remythicize the world but quite another to state what practical or, better, vocational implications followed from that. Marx, no stranger to myth, attempted to unite a theory of epical forces, capitalism, with a theory of epical action, proletarian revolution. Although initially he declared that theorists could change the world by a "critical theory" that would expose its flaws, he was eventually led to claim that theory foresaw an epical "crisis" of contradictions gathering within capitalism, making the system contribute to its own destruction, thereby lightening the burden of action and allowing it to be a bit more opportunistic, somewhat less Promethean and potentially more Leninist. Nonetheless, Marx retained a certain complementarity between epical vision and heroic action.

Tocqueville chose to approach the problem of theory and action not as Marx would by situating theory in intimate relationship with the material *forces* of the world, but by way of a discussion of the potential power resident in "ideal" factors, specifically, in the status and character of literature and history in America. History provides theory with the necessary grounding in mundane reality; literature, and especially poetry, supplies the imaginative, elevating element so crucial to epics. His choice of those particular topics signified that theory was not to be allied with the demos, the political correlative to Marx's proletariat, or with the productive forces of society but concerned instead with cultural beliefs and values, with what the ancients called *paideia* and Marx called "superstructure." That alignment did not signify an alliance with emergent power but the reverse: the theorist was to employ the discourse of culture to restrain rather than educate the demos. That, however, required the theorist to invent surrogates who might carry on theory's work under another name. Surrogation was necessary to cope with the consequences of what theory had disclosed but was unable to reverse. The theorist's instruments of disclosure (generalization, central facts, spectacle, epic, and tableau) and his basic categories (equality of conditions, democracy, tyranny of the majority) were shaped to represent the true nature of the threat in the democratic reality, and to educate those threatened by it, not those who were its bearers.

## IX

Tocqueville's heroic intentions not only shaped his American spectacle and the tableaux that composed it but determined as well the form of his judgments about what was significant, general, and preponderant in the New World. These intentions were expressed in two distinct types of epic, which Tocqueville would intermingle. One was biblical-prophetic, the other classical. America's beginnings, he declared, "seem to breathe at once an air of antiquity as well as an aroma of the Bible."[50]

The biblical-prophetic strain combined Tocqueville's sense of personal mission, his chosenness, with a growing awareness that his theoretical preoccupations were with the future of the political condition created by the modern revolutionary movements represented by America and France. The present was not ignored but rather to be understood in terms of the future dangers implicit in those movements. Tocqueville's understanding of the present was not the banal one as located between past and future. Rather he was coming to recognize that the meaning of the present was conditioned by revolutions, which were continuing and hence a persisting element in the composition of the present.

Throughout *Democracy* Tocqueville adopts the stance of a prophet and, as he unrolls one vast historical and social panorama after another, a reader feels the presence of one who has been privileged to glimpse the future of Western societies. Repeatedly Tocqueville recreates "scenes which pass before our eyes," sketches long centuries during which certain changes gather force, and projects the future shape of things, as in his famous prophecy about America and Russia.

Prophecy thus reemerges as epic, spectacle as tableau, as the epical act of the theorist and the collective epic of a people converge. America is exalted into a phenomenon whose extraordinary nature demands an extraordinary idiom: "The founding of New England presented a new spectacle; everything about it was singular and original. . . . [America had] sprung full-blown and fully armed from the midst of an ancient feudal society."[51] Throughout *Democracy* Americans are depicted as larger than life, their actions verging toward the preternatural. The society is gripped by restlessness, continuously agitated as no society has ever been; the mobility of Americans is, likewise, without parallel, as is their individual isolation; their energy is Herculean, as is their destructiveness. Yet the question nags, Epical but in what sense?

*Democracy* is not a tale of solitary heroes performing astounding deeds. In part the epic is collective or, better, disorganized, unpremeditated collectivism: countless and mostly anonymous individuals, without plan or organization, subduing a vast and dangerous wilderness, founding cities, raising the material level of the Many beyond anything in the past, and promoting an unprecedented degree of equality. It is an epic in which quantity has turned into quality, and quality into quantity. Before America existed, men had practiced some measure of equality and some democracy. The same was true of most of the other attributes of American life. Never before, however, had so many practiced the same things at the same time in the same place. Similarly, earlier men had loved liberty, political participation, and free institutions; but now these qualities had become bred into an entire society so that the sheer collectivization of these values and practices rendered them qualitatively different.

## X

Tocqueville did not distinguish sharply between epic and prophecy but moved unselfconsciously from one to the other. Both served the ends of his visual politics. Both enlarged the scale of things and vivified their meaning. In the introductory chapter Tocqueville depicts in broad strokes the great historical movements that over the centuries had been preparing for "the great democratic revolution." He paints a panorama of the rise and fall of classes, the destruction of the feudal system, the upheaval of Protestantism, the collapse of monarchy, and the relentless march of equality. That majestic sweep is sustained in the next chapter. There Tocqueville portrayed the overpowering physical presence of America: the awesomeness of the land, the dark mystery of its forests, the land bursting with rivers, and all so utterly different from the smooth topography and carefully tended landscapes of the Old World. In no respect was the European sense of scale more confounded than by the endless stretches of available land. To the land-starved European it could only be compared with another miracle of divine dispensation: For "just when" the Old World appeared to be suffering from overcrowdedness, Tocqueville declaimed, "North America was discovered, as though God had kept it in reserve and it had just risen from beneath the waters of the Flood."[52]

Not surprisingly, when Tocqueville turned to the beginnings of New England and of American political institutions, he would find inspiration and warrant for his biblical and classical themes. He accepted the Puritans' self-designation as the new children of Israel, and he elaborated their myth of the reenactment of the triumph of Exodus. They had conceived a society in righteousness in the promised land, had fought for its survival, and had dedicated it to the achievement of an "idea." The Puritans, Tocqueville declared, were not "a mere troop of adventurers gone forth to seek their fortune beyond the seas, but the seed of a great people that God has released to a predestined land."[53] The mark of their chosenness was not, for Tocqueville, in any revelation or theological truth but in the unique political endowments they had brought with them from England. A prior "political education" had made them "more conversant with the notions of right and the principles of true liberty than the greater part of the peoples of Europe." They had become accustomed to the practice of municipal self-government, "that fruitful germ of free institutions." Like the ancient Israelites, the Puritans devoted themselves to "the triumph of *an idea*," and in their legislation they laid a basis as sure and true as that in the Mosaic law.[54]

Once Tocqueville had established the theme of America as the embodiment of an "idea," he enlarged it and made America the fulfillment of the dreams of theorists since antiquity of finding a land where, self-consciously, theory had been converted into practice: "In that land an experiment was made by civilized men in building a society on a new basis, and of applying there for the first time theories hitherto unknown or deemed impracticable; they presented a spectacle for which the world had not been prepared by the history of the past."[55] While prerevolutionary Europe had been reveling in its "splendor," boasting of its "literature," and practicing a torporous politics in which only a tiny minority was engaged and almost no one understood "the principles of true freedom," there, "in the wilderness of the New World," "the boldest theories were reduced to practice."[56] The American theoretical genius was not, however, exhausted in its beginnings. The constitutions later adopted by the several states were direct expressions of theories and many of the principles have become "axioms in the political science of our day."[57] Similarly, the Supreme Court embodied a theory that had been foreshadowed in Europe but was "actually put into practice in America."[58] The system of federalism set out in the Constitution was "a wholly novel theory" and now "may be considered a great discovery in the political science of our day."[59]

The epical qualities with which Tocqueville selectively invested certain aspects of American politics were necessary complements to the impulses governing his theoretical efforts. Heroic theory required at least some corresponding political elements; otherwise, as he once remarked, the theorist "falls flat." In retrospect, the epical enlargement of American political beginnings helped compensate for the triviality of democratic politics.

## XI

Triviality, while it threatens to trip up the epical theorist, has the opposite effect on one important audience that Tocqueville had specifically in mind. In a letter of 1835 Tocqueville described the "political purpose" of *Democracy* as "a double effect on the minds of men of my time." To those who idealize democracy he would show that it does not have "the elevated qualities" that they imagine. But to the more important audience, the audience closest to Tocqueville's own social origins and intellectual tastes, "for whom the word *democracy* is synonymous with upheaval, anarchy, despoliation, and murders," he would show that it was possible to have a democracy that could govern society and would respect property, rights, liberty, and beliefs. Democracy might not do much to cultivate certain "beautiful faculties of the human soul," yet "it had attractive and impressive sides." Although a democratic society would lack "poetry and greatness," still it was possible to establish one that would have "order and morality."[60]

The epical impulse, though confounded by banality, would nonetheless find partial expression but not without deepening the ambiguities of the work. *Democracy* would depict a utopia, a society that had no strictly empirical correlate in either the United States or France. Some recent commentators have sensed the presence of a utopian element in that work, but in their efforts to laud Tocqueville's forward-looking analysis, specifically as an intimation of Weberian ideal types and hence a forerunner of modern political sociology, they have missed the point.[61] Late moderns tend to recognize and even empathize more easily with the versions of utopia created by Tocqueville's near contemporaries: with the utopias of economic plenty (Owen and Marx), of sexual gratification (Sade or Fourier), or of scientific managerialism (Saint-Simon).

*Democracy* includes an element of political utopianism or, more precisely, a utopia of the political. It is identified as a possibility unique to the political condition ushered in by modern egalitarianism and, for that reason, its utopian character is less than ideal: equality is a given in the modern world—a necessity, not a choice. The democracy represented by Tocqueville was the best that modernity might realistically hope for, provided that it could learn or be taught how to value political life for its own sake. Modernity as such, untutored, would fixate upon the pursuit of economic interests rather than cherish the political for the satisfactions peculiar to it. Thus, absent political democracy, the course of modernity would take a very different turn.

Although Tocqueville did not identify democracy with the most exalted political life, a life of disinterested service to the common good and the striving for a politics of *grandeur*, he found in it a plenitude of civic vitality, an intensity of involvement in common concerns by large numbers of citizens, and a lack of bitterness among social groups that was unmatched. He found its "model"—by which he meant a "real" object for imitation rather than an abstract heuristic construct—in the forms of democracy practiced in the New England towns. Among their citizens he recognized a new political animal, not the rustic, virtue-loving member of Rousseau's community of the general will, but an ordinary being who learns to acquire a political identity, first and foremost, out of physical necessity and self-interest, but then, as civic concerns gradually become an integral part of his life, to find that he cannot do without them.

There was an additional element of utopianism that both complemented and served as a necessary condition of democratic participation. America presented the unique spectacle of a society, which for most purposes was without a state, without the centralized organ of control and intervention with which Europeans were familiar. The institution of the state that, beginning in the sixteenth century, had come to dominate European society and to define the meaning and locus of politics had not been transported to America. Like the absence of feudalism, the absence of the state encouraged the belief in the American idyll. "One of the happiest consequences of the absence of government," Tocqueville declared, ". . . is the development of individual powers, something which is never lacking in such cases." Although France could never hope to reproduce a near stateless society, it could make "the most important concern of good government to habituate people to gradually doing without it."[62]

The America of part 1 did not teach Tocqueville the importance or value of the political but confirmed what he already knew. It did teach him that any hope for reviving the political in the modern world depended on promoting democratic participation. In accepting that principle, even in a qualified form, Tocqueville seemed to be aligning himself with one important tendency in that multifaceted and often contradictory phenomenon, the French Revolution, and to be implicitly rejecting an important element in his own political genealogy and its ideology. To a degree he was, but he was also concerned, as we have seen, to reassure those who remained stubbornly opposed to the democratic changes inspired by 1789. As a result his project became to show how participation might moderate democracy while extending it. He envisioned an ambivalent republic where civic-mindedness would keep the bourgeois spirit at bay, confine it to the countinghouses, while elements of aristocracy would work to leaven and diversify democracy. In the remark that closes out the crucial second chapter of *Democracy*, he lays down the basic principles on which New World democracy was formed: "The tableau which American society presents is, if I can put it this way, covered with a democratic coat, but beneath it from time to time the old colors of aristocracy break through."[63]

# PART THREE

## *The Theoretical Encapsulation of America*

# CHAPTER IX SOCIAL CONTRACT VERSUS POLITICAL CULTURE

## I

*There are three men with whom I spend some time every day: Pascal, Montesquieu, and Rousseau.*

Tocqueville[1]

Among the many aspects of American political life none impressed Tocqueville more than the rich stock of political ideas on which Americans had relied in establishing their institutions, winning independence from Britain, and conducting their politics. He was especially admiring of Puritanism for its combination of moral rigor and ideals of self-government. It is striking, however, that Tocqueville made no explicit reference to the contract theorists of seventeenth-century England or to its great exponents, Hobbes and Locke.[2] Although by the time of Tocqueville's arrival in the United States the appeal of contract theory had declined, its principles had not been discarded but were identified with the constitutional system founded in 1789. The written Constitution was taken to embody the contractualist principle of legitimacy, that government ought to be founded on and bound by an explicit document. Further, the ratification process by which it had been adopted was perceived as fulfilling the basic contractualist requirement of the consent of the governed. From the viewpoint of democracy, however, the crucial point was that neither contract theory, nor the Constitution, nor the *Federalist*'s interpretation of the Constitution had ever defended democracy, much less developed a theory of it, and, in consequence, debates about democracy had to operate within a largely unsympathetic ideological context.

In the course of formulating the first comprehensive theory of democracy, Tocqueville would free the discussion of democracy from the framework of constitutionalism and from the contractualist tradition customarily used to interpret it. He would largely ignore conventional concerns about institutional forms, such as the separation of powers, checks and balances, and federalism. Instead he would concentrate on the moral and religious influences that had produced a new type of political being, the democrat who was able to exercise power with skill and, more surprisingly, with moderation. That focus would, as we shall see, allow Tocqueville to overcome one of the most striking omissions in contract theory, the problem of political culture and political education in a democracy.

At stake was a crucial question of foundations. Was the basis of a free and self-governing society to be found in a primordial document or in the more modest practices and beliefs of daily life? Paradoxically, Tocqueville would pioneer the latter approach, but the route by which he would undermine contract theory had been suggested by Jean-Jacques Rousseau. The latter's influence was decisive in sensitizing him to the problems of political culture and education. Yet while Tocqueville was familiar with this last great statement in the contract tradition, he had also absorbed the arguments of its most powerful opponent, the more traditionalist Montesquieu.

## II

*But if it is true that a great prince is a rare man, what about a great legislator? The former only has to follow the model that the latter should propose.*

Jean-Jacques Rousseau[3]

The founding of new institutional systems and the political education of kings, warriors, aristocrats, parvenus, gentlemen, even condottieri had been major themes of political theorists beginning with Plato and continuing through the eighteenth century. The connection between the two topics hung on a hope that a properly educated ruler, ruling class, or even a Machiavellian bandit could be persuaded to use his position of power to introduce a politics based upon true principles of statecraft and/or justice. Founding was appropriated and conceived as an extension of theory with the theorist disguised as a wise legislator.

Among the premodern writers, such as Plato, Aristotle, Cicero, and Aquinas, it was agreed that, once established, the maintenance of the system depended on restricting politics to a small number of actors. Consequently, virtually the same repertory company reappeared in slightly different makeup over the centuries and, not surprisingly, able to learn the parts as the theorist's script dictated. Machiavelli's *Discorsi* broke ranks by claiming that a republic depended for its preservation on the broad support of the citizenry, yet he assumed that politics would remain confined to a small circle of actors.

That thematic which restricted political founding and political maintenance to an elite group of players was first challenged during the English civil wars of the 1640s and the American and French revolutions of the following century. Those events breached the charmed circle of court politics. Through notions such as the equal rights of citizenship, a broadened franchise, government based on the consent of the citizens, legislative supremacy, and the sovereignty of the people, the revolutionaries sought to reconstitute authority on the basis of a more enlarged conception of who should share in the act of founding the political and in conducting the politics of its preservation. These revolutionary notions helped to inspire a succession of social contract theorists—notably Hobbes, Locke, Rousseau, and Paine—who attempted to repair the theory-founding connection by granting theoretical representation to popular revolutionary forces. By giving symbolic expression to popular power through ideas, such as "the right of revolution" and "the will of the majority," theorists appropriated revolution and then reconstituted it mythically as the act of founding.

But now that the new sovereign was the demos, where did political education figure in the connection between founding the political and maintaining it? The same instrument by which revolution was appropriated also served as the principal text of political education.

The social contract not only explained/legitimated the "right" of revolution and the establishment of a new political order but provided a vehicle for a new conception of political education, a new structure of understanding in which the emphasis was not on knowing how to rule but on recognizing what it meant to be ruled in a nonarbitrary way. The theory consisted in almost equal parts of a new myth and a reasoned argument. The main point of this education was to instruct the signatories in the meaning of the fundamental political category that the contract symbolized, the act of consent. The action of consenting to the terms of the contract created two central myths/fictions: that consent produced "one Body Politick" (Locke), "a reall Unitie of them all" (Hobbes), "a moral and collective body" (Rousseau), and that it created "citizens" out of mere signatories.[4] Consent thus pointed in two directions, one sacramental, the other dissolvent. The first evoked ideas of corporate solidarity, of persons bound together as "We, the people"; the other tacitly divided the "people" into public beings (citizens) who shared in power and private beings whose rights protected them against public power. Undergirding both ideas was the conception of the contract as a "settlement" that aspired to fix permanently the terms and limits of politics and, tacitly or explicitly, placed barriers to political movements arising from popular grievances or aspirations.

The idea of contract also introduced a discourse of exchange that attempted to settle the terms of nonarbitrary power while connecting the political to the newly conceptualized world of the economic.[5] Contract theory proposed to educate the signatories about the terminology of exchange: about the meaning of promises, rules, obligations, rights, what they entailed, and what constituted violations. The main concern for each signatory, according to the theory, was to fix the terms of what he should cede of his "own" to the new authority and what he should gain in return. Own-ership presupposed a world of ownable objects, not just real property but owning legal rights, owning up to one's promises. Owning succeeds lineage, fear of theft succeeds fear of illegitimacy. The identity of objects now derives from being owned, potentially or actually. The owner is the one who confers being upon those objects. He individuates in order to possess.[6]

## III

*If my dear love were but the child of state,*
*It might for Fortune's bastard be unfather'd . . .*
*It fears not policy, that heretic,*
*Which works on leases of short-number'd hours,*
*But all alone stands hugely politic.*

Shakespeare[7]

The first stage of this development was represented by the theories of Hobbes and Locke. Its motto might be said to have been liberty (rights), equality (in the state of nature), and paternity. The problem as they framed it reflected a certain male trauma associated with inheritance. How was legitimacy—that is, the descent of the ownership of power—to be established? In a chapter he entitled simply, "Who Heir?" Locke declared that "the great Question" was "not whether there be Power in the World, nor whence it came, but who should have it."[8] The revolutionary notion, which Locke defended and Hobbes had pioneered, was that contract or agreement was to be substituted for hereditary right as the answer to the "great Question." That answer was not, strictly speaking, based on notions of paternalism but of paternity, of fears about the lineage of power, about its possible bastardy or illegitimacy. We need, Locke declared, "another Original of Political Power, and another way of designing and knowing the Persons that have it."[9] Hobbes and his successors envisioned "another Original of Political Power": a society formed around an original contract between adult males that was intended to settle the question of legitimate authority by deriving it from consent. Each would acknowledge paternity of the new power as his issue, to be "his own," his "representation."

The crucial move made by the post-Hobbesian contractualist was to make "arbitrary power" the main charge against absolutism but Hobbes had anticipated the move and handled arbitrariness by treating it as a species of illegitimacy. Illegitimate power was "disowned" as bastard power while legitimate power was owned—that is, acknowledged as genealogically proper. "[E]very Subject is Author," as Hobbes put it, "of every act the Soveraign doth." Sovereign actions would be recognized as done in my "name" and "as if" they were my progeny: "he that acteth [for] another is said to beare his Person."[10]

The appeal of the theory depended on establishing consent as the decisive symbol of membership. Consent legitimated not only political authority but legitimated the individual who consented. He became a citizen, one who obeyed legitimate authority and could, in turn, expect to be protected and secure in his legitimate rights. The focus on consent left in obscurity, however, the question of informed consent. What resources had the protocitizen been able to call upon in making the original judgment to consent? Whence the political competence of previously unaffiliated individuals, their access to political experience on which to have made the momentous judgments about authorizing a power of life and death over themselves or of abiding by the legal rules issued by judges and legislators? In reality, the contractualists had abstracted the idea of a consenting individual from any context of practice and had left undeveloped the potentialities of participation implied in the contractualist's admission of the constitutive role of the "people." The omission made it easier to dissociate consent from substantive participation and to insert any number of surrogates, the favorite being, of course, the elected "representative." The direct answer to the question of competence was illustrated by the fact that until well into the nineteenth century in France, England, and (to a lesser degree) the United States property requirements for voting were widespread: ownership implied "possession" of the qualifications for making informed political judgments.

Modern theoretical efforts at justifying postrevolutionary authority revealed the real dilemmas involved in founding a society based on the incorporation of democratic impulses and rhetoric without any intention of establishing democratic power. In arguing that all legitimate government must rest on the explicit consent of those who chose to join in the formation of a new political society, the contractualists joined consent with "choice" or, more precisely, with the idea of rational choice; indeed, writers, such as Hobbes and Locke, who otherwise thought poorly of the reasoning capacities of ordinary beings, especially those from the lower social ranks, had to declare all "men" possessed of sufficient reason to grant or withhold their consent, otherwise there would be no new "Original of Political Power."

That argument unintentionally exposed the disjunction: a conception of a society in which all male adults were to become citizens who, according to the implication of the theories, although not according to their explicit arguments, were then to assume a larger role than hitherto in political affairs. In the state of nature prior to the contract, that role and its implied politics had not existed and hence could not be known. Thus an instant citizenry, the vast majority of which had actually been excluded from any part in public life but which, nonetheless, was supposed to "know" how to deliberate the terms of the original contract, what it meant to be bound by a political promise, how to participate in public affairs, and how to make the ultimate judgment that an existing government should be disobeyed and possibly overthrown by force.[11]

Hobbes had recognized the problem and much of *Leviathan* was devoted to instructing its readers about the meaning of terms such as "promises," "covenants," "rights." That response suggests the limits of own-ership were being pressed by demands for a broadened conception of citizenship. Yet Hobbes had clearly meant his teaching for the political and intellectual elites; when it came to instructing the people, he compared "the Common-peoples minds" to "clean paper" and proposed that they be indoctrinated with the political equivalent of a catechism containing the principles of obedience to authority.[12]

The result was a radical oversimplification of the stakes involved, one that was perpetuated by later theorists as a matter of doctrine. They started from the end of the problem of membership rather than the beginning, from an act of choice by politically "empty" homunculi, and never worked backward to explore the tacit knowledge presupposed by what Harrington, in a typical reductionism, had called "choosing."[13] For him, literally, the problem was a piece of cake. Imagine, he wrote, two girls faced with the problem of dividing a cake so as to assure each an equal share. The answer: let one divide the cake and the other have first choice. Harrington's homely illustration of the people's role in choosing proved prescient of the form choosing would take. The solution was not to educate in the principles of rational choice but to preset a structure that would of itself produce rationality. The effect was to transform the status of certain principles of contract theory from arguments to mechanics of construction that exploited the role of self-interest.

## IV

*It was a fine spectacle in the last century to see the impotent attempts of the English to establish democracy among themselves . . . the people, stunned, sought democracy and found it nowhere. Finally, after many movements and many shocks and jolts, they ended up with the very government that had been proscribed.*

Montesquieu[14]

The divorce between reason and the political skills of collective action had the effect of rendering reason abstract while political skill was never formulated as the project of popular political education. The result was the worst of both worlds, an untutored but formally sovereign people who looked and sometimes behaved like a mob.

Not surprisingly, the social groups dominating the politics of postrevolutionary societies found it politically less risky to adopt the myth that political society was founded *on* the people rather than *by* them. That formula tacitly conceded that someone other than the people had done the founding. Did a democratic society presuppose some form of tutelage, perhaps a selfless elite who would educate a mass of politically inexperienced individuals into becoming "the people" and thereby justify a constitution and its politics, not because it was democratic, but because it was making progress toward that goal? Or did democracy mean a politics of keeping the demos at bay, of managing them by the arts of the politician?

One might expect Rousseau to have attempted to resolve some of these questions for he has often been cited as the most important democratic theorist during the period between the English revolutions of the seventeenth century and the French Revolution of 1789. In fact, however, Rousseau insisted that democracy demanded a level of civic virtue that was beyond ordinary beings and that there was a fundamental reason why democracy could not be the object of a Founding.[15] "Men would have to be prior to law what they ought to become by means of law."[16]

Rousseau was thus pointing to the circularity of any attempt to establish a democratic form of government without presupposing from the beginning that, somehow, the people already possessed the virtues and skills needed to operate it. In that context Tocqueville's emphasis on the political inheritance brought by the early American colonists prior to their "contract" offers a more intelligible starting point. Although Rousseau seemed to renounce the project of theorizing a democratic political society, he embarked on a theoretical venture that would mislead some later critics and defenders into interpreting him as a theorist of democracy. What caused the confusion was that Rousseau seized the problem of political virtue that had exercised theorists from Plato to Montesquieu, but where invariably they had posed it as a question of educating an elite governing class, Rousseau treated it as a matter of making an entire people virtuous. By that staggering reformulation of the problem of civic virtue he created a different vision, not of democracy, but of how human beings should be fashioned into citizens without becoming democratized. The immediate object of founding was to establish a political system, but the long-term project was to found the people themselves: "One who dares to undertake the founding of a people should feel that he is capable of changing human nature, so to speak; of transforming each individual, who by himself is a perfect and solitary whole, into a part of a larger whole from which this individual receives, in a sense, his life and his being."[17]

Rousseau conceived of virtue not as mere conformity to external norms, but rather as their internalization. To that end the role of institutions is not to represent the various "orders" of "society," as they had in the Middle Ages—Rousseau detested representative government—but to reconstitute the demos as the citizenry: "I had seen that basically everything is tied to politics, and that, however one tried, no people would ever be anything except what the nature of the government would make it be."[18]

Rousseau's citizens were crammed into a mold of rustic simplicity and natural virtue and then thrust into a round of civic duties inspired in equal parts by the cheerless models of ancient Sparta and Calvin's Geneva.[19] The main values are solidarity and community, leaving politics tightly controlled and minimized. Rousseau's citizen looks like a political animal; he attends the assembly, votes in accordance with the idea of a general will, and is loyal to his polity. But he is forbidden to discuss political matters outside of formal assemblies or to form "partial associations" ("factions").[20] His political education thus closes the circle opened by the revolutions of the seventeenth century. The politically virtuous citizen is to be the creature of a discipline intended to prevent the recurrence of the revolutionary impulses that had provoked the discourse of the social contract.

## V

Rousseau's democracy without politics was prefigured by the innovations he effected in the social contract. While retaining contractualist language, its meaning was radically transformed from a negotiation into a political sacrament,[21] from an agreement among signatories into a rite among communicants, from the founding of a political society to transubstantiation into a *corpus mysticum*:

> Each of us puts his person and all his power in common under the supreme direction of the general will; and as a body we receive each member as an indivisible part of the whole.[22]

> [I]n place of the private person of each contracting party, this act of association produces a moral and collective body . . . which receives from this same act its unity, its common *self*, its life and its will.[23]

The transformation of discrete persons into a collectivity, Rousseau declared, takes place "instantly" (*à l'instant*)—a pronouncement that works as a magical incantation for obliterating human differences and for causing the problem of prior political competence to vanish. It is easy to see why Tocqueville might read seventeenth-century New England in Rousseauean terms, New England with its town meeting democracy, civil religion, covenantal myths, and heavy sense of community—more Genevan than Rousseau's Geneva.

Rousseau's citizens, unlike Tocqueville's Puritans, could not draw upon a prior legacy of a community preformed by Scripture and church-disciplined self-government. Enter Rousseau's Great Legislator, who can fairly be described as the master theorist of social mysteries. The Legislator creates a people "instantly" and thus "solves" Rousseau's own paradox noted earlier, that the political qualities of a democratic people cannot be presupposed, that they cannot be what they are supposed to become—and that they are unqualified to fashion themselves. His solution depended on altering fundamentally the role of political culture. Instead of being constitutive, culture has to be reified, prefabricated to be fitted to a created people. "The true constitution of the State" had to be engraved "in the hearts of the citizens" by means of "*moeurs*, customs, and especially opinions." These work to reanimate the state with "fresh force," while "preserving a people in the spirit of its institutions."[24] Culture becomes coercive, primarily a system of social reinforcement rather than of access to the range of experiences preparatory to the acquisition of competence and of a sensibility regarding matters of common concern. "By what means, then, are we to move men's hearts and make them love their fatherland and its laws? Dare I say it? Through their games as children; through institutions, though useless in the eyes of superficial men, form cherished habits and unbreakable bonds."[25]

The incongruity between the godlike action of the Great Legislator (the theorist) and the development of a democratic community was exposed in the inconclusive answer that Rousseau gave to the natural question, How does a Legislator acquire the authority to give laws to a people and to form the people when no prior "people" existed to authorize a lawgiver?[26] Rousseau's response was to contrast the current situation with that of the past when legislators could speak in the name of the gods and command obedience. Today, lamentably, no such mystique was available, no language existed for the "wise" to speak to the "vulgar." Rousseau concludes enigmatically that "the true political theorist" (*le vrai politique*) understands that this is no longer possible.[27] But, as Tocqueville recognized, in New England the ministers of local congregations knew very well how to speak to the vulgar and were certain about who was authorized to do so.

## VI

Montesquieu and Rousseau presented Tocqueville with conflicting theoretical and political possibilities.[28] For Montesquieu a society was not a tabula rasa awaiting inscription by a single theoretical intelligence but a historically constituted system of patchwork adaptations among diverse elements of habit, custom, *moeurs*, religion, climate, and geography. These elements were shaped by a variety of "laws": natural, divine, legal, and political but without a single lawgiver. Each law shaped a different aspect of human social existence by encouraging habits, manners, traditions, and responses appropriate to the mode of being represented—for example, by economic behavior or religious beliefs. Over time these domains became adapted to each other to form a distinctive set of accommodations, a *bricolage* of usages and expectations of subjects and rulers, an ethos rather than a force. Accordingly, a constitution was not a document or a covenant but a maze of interconnections that Montesquieu referred to as a "labyrinth," which no single actor or generation had authored and which no one could redesign without inviting calamity. Montesquieu's advice to politicians was: be curious, cautious, and accepting.[29] His was a nonregenerative politics. Theory's ambitions, in turn, were reduced from the architectonic to the admonitory. That meant, among other things, a flat rejection of the myths of a social contract, state of nature, and a Great Legislator. At the same time the problem of how or whether political competence came to be acquired ceased to be a mystery. Competence was acquired through the different types of experience in the range of practices within a particular system, or, more precisely, within the corporate bodies composing the system.

Tocqueville was in accord with Montesquieu's skepticism about the relevance of the Legislator to a historically complex society:

> Occasionally, after many efforts, the legislator succeeds in exerting an indirect influence upon the destiny of nations and then his genius is celebrated. However, it is often the case that due to the geographical position of the country, a social condition emerged without his assistance. Customs and ideas whose origins are unknown, a point of departure with which he is unacquainted, exercise an irresistible influence. He struggles in vain against it and is carried along in its wake.[30]

Although he retained Rousseau's identification of the Legislator with theory, he accepted a more chastened version, although not one quite as unheroic as Montesquieu's: "The legislator resembles a man who navigates the seas. He may direct his vessel but he cannot change its structure, create the winds, nor prevent the ocean from swelling beneath him."[31]

Montesquieu's lessons of political prudence tempered by inaction seemed insufficient, however, for an unstable society like France still struggling through the trauma of 1789. His prescriptions took for granted the very institutions of church, monarchy, and nobility that the French Revolution would attack, and his theory could represent society's irreducible interconnectedness because its author did not have to reckon with the consequences of a new individualism.

Tocqueville's reservations about Montesquieu were expressed through the two metaphors discussed earlier, the abyss and the divide. The first signified the loss of meaning that accompanies the destruction of traditional referents—customary norms, political privileges and duties, religious authority—while the divide represented the discontinuity in collective identity, the repudiation of the Old Regime definition of France and its replacement by a political and social order that disavowed the ideal of connectedness based on hierarchies. The newly emerging society not only rejected the Montesquieuean ideal of a pluralistic corporate society, but, once the revolution was over, renounced Rousseau's dream of a solidaristic political community. The new condition was characterized in *Democracy* in a passage that Tocqueville clearly intended more for France than America:

> [I]n our day when all class distinctions have been confounded, where increasingly the individual disappears into the crowd and is easily lost in the midst of a common obscurity . . . , what even can public opinion do when there scarcely exists 20 people held together by common bonds; when there is neither a man, nor a family, nor a corporate body, nor a class, nor a free association which can represent public opinion and act in its name?[32]

The challenges represented by the abyss and the divide seemed to demand a conception of action and theory more interventionist than Montesquieu's and a conception of society that would break with both Rousseau's solidarism and Montesquieu's corporatism. Instead, despite his imaginary antithesis of the New World/Old World, Tocqueville would seek out certain cultural practices in the democratic New World that were formative of those civic virtues which limited the excesses of individualism. Invariably he would liken these practices to some Old World institution, such as religion or aristocracy.

Accordingly, Tocqueville set for himself the difficult task of trying to mediate two opposing conceptions of politics, on one side, a Montesquieuean conception of a nonregenerative, nonthreatening politics entrapped in culturally complex forms, which he presented as an account of the politics of New World democracy. The politics he would seek to contain was the politics of democracy, which would produce a peculiar reversal in the respective roles of theory and action. Tocqueville would identify equality in America not as a simple value but as a driving passion toward uniformity, a force that threatened to overwhelm social differences and distinctions. To contain it Tocqueville would call upon mores, traditions, habits, and especially religious beliefs and invest them with the power of controlling and blunting the drive toward equality. Thus the roles of culture and action would be reversed: culture becomes the heroic but anonymous force, restraining the politics of equality but at the cost of reducing the scope of action to the routines of ordinary life, to practical questions of roads, schools, and the like. At the same time, Tocqueville clung to a more positive, Rousseauean notion of political action that proclaimed its commitment to the regeneration of Old World politics, felt frustrated by the subordination of the political to a politics of material self-interest, and aspired to be the agent of a higher, nobler theoretical purpose—and yet, notwithstanding the grandeur of these aims, to remain nonrevolutionary. These contrary pulls would produce in Tocqueville a conception of action that strained against the frustrations of petty politics and toward greatness, and a conception of theory that was epical in form but resigned to being antiarchitectonic in substance.

## VII

The conflicts between action and culture confronted Tocqueville as soon as he began to construct his theory of American democracy. Was the United States to be explained in Montesquieuean terms as the successful transplanting of Old World beliefs, customs, and institutions; or was it more dramatic, more Rousseauean, the actual creation of a new society virtually ex nihilo? There was undeniably the contra-Montesquieuean fact that at the beginning and during its westward expansion America truly resembled a tabula rasa—indigenous peoples aside. Several colonies had been founded on charters that could be construed as original contracts—John Locke, no less, had drafted one for the Carolinas;[33] numerous communities had been created de novo; and all of this community building actually took place in the same wilderness that had inspired Locke's famous state of nature.

Tocqueville's own construct, *le nouveau monde*, was premised on the reality of an American tabula rasa:

> In coming to America Americans have brought with them what was most democratic in Europe. When they arrived, they left on the other side of the Atlantic the greater part of the national prejudices in which they had been reared. They became a new nation, adopting new habits, new customs, something of a national character.[34]

Moreover, the idea that a nation might be the work of a great Lawgiver seemed to have been realized by the Founding Fathers of the American Constitution. The identity of a whole society appeared to have been transformed during a brief moment. A remarkable group of public-spirited statesmen, "the finest minds and the noblest characters ever to have appeared in the New World," had proposed an entire constitution and then, like Rousseau's Great Legislator, had withdrawn from the scene, leaving it to the people to ratify or reject it. "But what was new in the history of societies was to see a great people" ponder the document, then "submit to it voluntarily without costing humanity a single tear or drop of blood."[35]

Thus Tocqueville seemed to be supporting the view that America was a living example of a society whose founding moment was a matter both of historical fact and theoretical achievement. In making the point about the absence of a feudal past and the newness of America, Tocqueville appeared to be acknowledging the existence of a most un-Montesquieuean setting for politics.

But if that were true then an Old World reader might conclude that the New World was either irrelevant to the historically defined societies in which he and she lived or, worse, a dangerous example that might encourage revolutionaries to forcibly impose their tabula rasa upon a historical society, returning it to a state of nature where it could be reconstructed according to principles of natural right. Had not Robespierre and other radical leaders of the French Revolution appealed to Rousseau in order to justify a violent attempt to establish a new political and social order that would change human nature?

## VIII

> *The new federal government began to function in 1789, after two years of an interregnum. Thus the American revolution ended at the precise moment when ours began.*
>
> Tocqueville[36]

> *It is not only to satisfy a curiosity, otherwise legitimate, that I have studied America; I wanted to find some lessons from which we could profit.*
>
> Tocqueville[37]

Tocqueville attempted to mute the revolutionary implications of the idea of a founding and to use it for conservative, antirevolutionary ends. This would involve a complicated strategy of exploiting the Americans' distinction between the national and the local. Tocqueville portrayed the local as the work not of an inspired lawgiver but of an inspired people, the New England Puritans. The national was represented as the creation of the Founding Fathers: a constitution for a new national government. "It is only at the birth of society that it is possible to construct a completely logical system of laws." That level preserved a theoretical character similar to Rousseau's idea of a founding but, by Montesquieu's lights, it represented a limited achievement because it lacked its own accompanying and supporting culture of appropriate beliefs, habits, and values. The Founders had been forced to accommodate two "irreconcilable theories" at the center of their work, a prior, historically grounded system of thirteen independent states and a contrived system of national sovereignty.[38] By necessity, the work of founding had to be superimposed on a political culture developed over a century and a half, a Rousseauean constitution standing on a Montesquieuean base, so to speak.

The creative moment seized by the American Founders had a different resonance to an Old World whose experience of founding was the French Revolution of 1789, which had created some democratic moments only to have them overwhelmed by civil war, terror, dictatorship, and foreign wars. The revolution appeared to have abolished Montesquieu without installing Rousseau. It had settled for a "restoration" with a pseudomonarchy, an uncertain aristocracy, an embittered clergy, and a tentative constitution.

Accordingly, the task was to define what of American democracy was politically relevant to France, given the formidable differences of geography, political systems, and mores. Tocqueville developed his conception of the political possibilities of a theoretical project within the framework of a specific claim, that "A new political science is necessary for a wholly new world."[39]

The new political science was inspired by the New World but it was intended for the Old. It was conceived as a praxis, a practical science of politics rather than as a prescription for founding.[40] Praxis had, however, to be elevated to a suitably lofty plane, idealized, even mytheoretical in character, and yet be the achievement of a people and not of a Great Legislator.

## IX

*Providence has not created mankind entirely independent or completely enslaved. In truth, Providence has traced a circle of fate around each man beyond which he cannot pass; but within its vast limits man is powerful and free, and so are peoples.*

Tocqueville[41]

Tocqueville's new science was not a science of prediction nor a mere echo of Aristotelian or Montesquieuean political science. It was something more unexpected: a practical science textually embedded in and surrounded by a prophetic element that was integral to Tocqueville's theory. Although the new science was tied to the particular, to the specific maladies and tendencies of democracy, prophecy foretold a universal condition, revolutionary egalitarianism, and elevates the new science while supplying it with a meaningful context.

Prophecy is about powers that cannot be resisted and of things that will come to be: prophecy puts determinism in a more elevated key. Tocqueville refers to the mysterious and hidden ways in which human actors and events have been forced, contrary to their intentions and even their interests, to promote the spread of equality. The mood he fosters is, like that of ancient prophecy, one of apprehensiveness, foreboding. "The entire book being offered here has been written under the influence of a kind of religious terror produced in the soul of the author by the view of that irresistible revolution which has advanced for centuries and which continues to advance in the midst of the ruins it has made."[42]

Prophecy envelops the whole of Tocqueville's work, contextualizing it. The introduction to *Democracy* depicts the broad historical movement toward equality and foresees its complete triumph; the conclusion to the first part lays out the claim "that before me lies exposed the whole future of the English race in the new world."[43] The final chapter of the work sketches the future character of life in a democratic world.

Prophecy serves Tocqueville as the alternative discourse to science; unlike the latter, which cannot discriminate among its users, insisting only upon the subordination of the investigating self to the objective norms of rigorous method, prophecy bestows a "chosenness" upon its agents, singling them out from all others. Yet like scientific discourse prophecy adopts a language of determinism, of states of affairs that are bound to be, "the great revolution" that is "still continuing" and the "new society coming into being."[44] Prophecy in the age of positivism—Comte was Tocqueville's contemporary—will use the language of "fact" while trying to invest fact with sacred rather than natural necessity. "It is not a question of reconstructing an aristocratic society but of how to make liberty emerge from the democratic society to which God has consigned us."[45] Prophecy invests a theory with a certain aura of the unarguable.

As he invites the reader to ponder the spectacle of all "being pushed pell-mell in the same direction . . . in spite of themselves, working in concert . . . blind instruments in the hands of God," Tocqueville makes the same confession as the ancient prophets, that his powers of foretelling are greater than his ability to understand the ultimate "why" of things, and he ends on the appropriate note of submission:

> If patient observation and sincere meditation have led men of the present day to recognize that the gradual and progressive development of equality is both the past and the future of their history, that discovery alone gives to this development the sacred character of the will of the Sovereign Master. In that case the attempt to halt democracy appears as a struggle against God Himself, and nations have no alternative but to adjust themselves to the social condition imposed by Providence.[46]

But Tocqueville's submission had been preceded by the protestations of a Job who cannot abstain from arguing with the higher power whose plan he has discerned. The final pages of *Democracy* find Tocqueville confessing that he cannot survey a world rendered more uniform without being "saddened and chilled" and "tempted to regret that state of society which has ceased to be." He finds it painful to accept the Deity's decision to destroy aristocracy and to prefer the happiness of the Many to that of the Few. He has a quarrel with God: "What seems to me decadence is thus in His eyes an advance; what wounds me is agreeable to Him."[47]

The grounds for his submission are that, ultimately, the regime of equality is more just than regimes of hereditary inequality: "its justice is the source of its greatness and beauty."[48] Despite his disclaimers Tocqueville would wage tacitly a "struggle against God." The new science will provide several prescriptions for checking and limiting the rush toward democracy. Most of these can be grouped under the heading "a new political science for a new world." We shall examine these later; here we need only note that, unlike his prophecy about the triumph of democracy, he would not claim that his political science was divinely sanctioned. The contrary was true. The new science is the reassertion of an epical form of theoretical action that both submits to God's decrees and selectively combats some of them. Providence had decreed democracy, the new political science would try to contain it. Tocqueville would close *Democracy* on a note that combined the submissiveness of prophecy with the heroic motif of epic:

> I, who have reached the utmost limits of my journey, and grasping from afar, but at the same time, all of the diverse objects which I have contemplated along the way, I am full of fears as well as hopes. I see mighty dangers which it is possible to exorcize, mighty evils which may be avoided or alleviated, and I am strengthened in the belief that for democratic nations to be virtuous and prosperous, they require but to will it.[49]

## X

While the new science is enclosed by prophecy, it is also in contention with it. The new science exploits the traditional theological claim that while God controls history, He also allows humans a measure of free will. Tocqueville takes advantage of the openings that prophetic theory discloses as preordained. The closing lines of *Democracy* will affirm the incomplete character of necessity: "The nations of our day cannot prevent conditions from becoming equal; but it depends on them whether equality leads to servitude or to liberty, to enlightenment or to barbarism, to prosperity or to misery."[50]

It is, Tocqueville claimed, a modern conceit to argue that some political or social fact is irresistible and no longer suitable for deliberation because no action can negate or reverse it.[51] To say that democracy is a closed question should not imply that there was no point to reflecting upon it. It is in the nature of reflection to want to continue the process of thinking. One reflection invites/stimulates another. For Tocqueville, when the new science has identified necessity, it has defined the new terms for reinstating deliberation, not so that we may defeat necessity but so that we may decide on what, if anything, can be done within its limits. We deliberate how we may adapt or adjust to, or possibly modify necessity. Thus necessity does not mean, as it had for Marx, the end of politics and the beginning of administration; it was for Tocqueville the threshold of politics and, potentially, the recovery of it from administrative centralization—that is, from the political equivalent of a *bienfaisant* monotheism.

The principle that institutions were contingent formed the raison d'être of the new science. It meant that endless permutations of democracy were possible because the success of the American democracy was not tied to its rich natural resources or even to the ready availability of land. If a distinction is drawn between "the institutions of the United States" and "democratic institutions in general," it is possible "to imagine a democratic people organized differently than the Americans."[52] The alternatives that Tocqueville imagines were all conservative versions of democracy: a democracy, for example, where the majority respected "the order and stability of the State" and restrained its instinct for equality sufficiently to entrust executive authority to a particular person or family. Or a democracy where national power was more centralized than in the United States and the people would exercise far less direct influence on national affairs and, instead, each would participate "in his own sphere."[53] Clearly these imaginaries belonged to *Démocratie en France*, the tacit companion of *Démocratie en Amérique.*

These possibilities were implicit in what was the abiding lesson of America for all democracies, that devices for curbing rule by the majority were essential. That might seem to be the same lesson taught earlier by the authors of the *Federalist* and enshrined in the constitutional principles of the separation of powers, checks and balances, representative politics, and judicial review. But that reliance on constitutional machinery, the "auxiliary" checks of which Madison wrote, was not the principal lesson that Tocqueville sought to convey. The *Federalist* had viewed society, not as the nurseries of political education but as a dangerous seedbed for ideological "factions" or economic interests inimical to the rights of private property. A major objective of constitutional safeguards ought to be to prevent factions from forming a majority and, failing that, to obstruct as much as possible a majority from setting state policy. The *Federalist* had argued for protecting the central government from civil society at large by creating strong institutions that were either removed from popular control by elections, such as the Supreme Court and the federal court system, or else, like the president and the Senate, were elected indirectly in the hope that "popular passions" might be screened out. The *Federalist* made little effort to conceal its hope that "wiser" and "better" elements would control the indirect elections. Although Tocqueville agreed strongly that there should be "obstacles" to majority rule, he entered a crucial qualification that not only distinguished his position from that of the *Federalist* but also indicated that his use of aristocracy was not meant to revive a ruling class but to make a point. Calling the idea of "mixed government" "a chimera," he declared: "It is not, I believe possible to preserve liberty by mixing several principles within the same government so that they will really be opposed to one another."[54]

If democracy were a civilization or political culture, its threat had to be confronted and resolved within society by democracy setting limits to itself. Majority tyranny was only secondarily the problem of majority rule; it was primarily the problem presented by a homogeneous civilization, a totally democratic culture. Accordingly, Tocqueville's science of politics displays an emphasis significantly different from that of the *Federalist*, away from the center and from national constitutional structures and toward locally grounded practice and usage, which homogeneity had made powerful but which nonetheless restrained it: "I think that in the democratic centuries which are opening before us, individual independence and local liberties will always be the product of art. Centralization will be the natural government."[55]

## XI

> *Now most people would regard the good as the end pursued by that study which has the most authority and control over the rest. Need I say that this is the science of politics?*
>
> Aristotle[56]

> *My aim has been to show, by the example of America, that laws, but especially* moeurs *can allow a democratic people to remain free.*
>
> Tocqueville[57]

Tocqueville's new political science, like the term itself, was inspired by the *Federalist.*[58] It stood for practical applications derived from general theoretical principles. The idea becomes clearer if compared with classical notions rather than with the nineteenth-century conceptions inspired by modern scientific methods. It is not so much the numerous points of contact that Tocqueville's new science had with Aristotelian political science as that the classical reference point exposes more clearly the tensions in Tocqueville's thinking created, on the one hand, by the pressures of postrevolutionary politics and, on the other, by certain received principles regarding the values of political life. That tension simply did not exist for Tocqueville's social scientific contemporaries. To make the contrasts more pointed, it is, I believe, more fruitful to argue that the revealing contrasts are not the broad ones between the modern and the classical but, more pointedly, ones that juxtapose the modern-revolutionary and classical-order. The distinction does not rest on any claim that revolution was unknown to the premodern or ancient world. Rather it is uniquely modern for revolution to be first established as a "right" and then as a virtual synonym for a permanent condition of change.

Aristotelian or classical political science was a science of a different "right," of right order (*eunomia*), of the right juxtaposition of social classes in relation to the "ends" of political society. Its aim was to delineate how a political community might be arranged so that its members could achieve the noblest life possible. It was a science of fine actions for the few who aspired to the highest virtue, and essentially a political education prepared for an aristocracy of intellect and an aristocracy of political and military skills. But it was also a science of exclusion and inclusion, of who should be included in the citizen body and who among the citizenry should be eligible for office. Its scope was architectonic, reaching to and comprehending the individual, the household, social classes, economic relationships, law, justice, war, and education, and ordering each and all toward the purposes identified with the best polity or, failing that, the lesser constitutions defined by wealth rather than goodness, by the rule of law rather than the striving for excellence.[59]

Aristotle was sensitive to the possibility of democracy assuming different forms and he identified at least five, four of which were granted a certain grudging respect because they set the law above the citizenry.[60] Yet he insisted that democracies represented rule by the "baser" elements of society and belonged to the types of constitution classed as "perverted" because ruled in the interests of the dominant class. The constitution best suited to the majority of men, that is, the constitution that embodied the best way of life for men with limited potentialities, was the "polity." Its proper basis was in those of middling wealth, who, by Aristotle's reckoning, were distinguished by an ability to listen to reason and by their modest ambitions.[61]

Although Tocqueville's new science accepted Aristotle's claim that the main political division was between aristocracy and democracy, that division was rendered complicated, cut athwart, as it were, by a division unknown to Aristotelian political science, a division between the new and the old, between the revolutionary and the prerevolutionary. The work of the democratic revolution, Tocqueville asserted, "cannot be compared with anything previously seen in the world." As a result, "the past no longer illuminates the future and the mind proceeds among shadows."[62] He is left with the hard conclusion, which he insisted upon but could not always honor: "It is necessary to guard against judging emerging societies with ideas drawn from those which no longer exist." It may be "honorable" to judge the new societies by the old, but it is ultimately a "sterile" exercise because the two are incomparable.[63]

These injunctions did not prevent aristocracy from serving several functions within the structure of Tocqueville's theory: as a contrast to precipitate the meaning of egalitarian democracy, as an archaic source of inspiration for devising countervailing institutions to moderate democracy, and as the archaeological reminder of the price exacted by the revolutionizing power of modernity. Aristocracy finds its expression/refuge in the new science, that is, as the knowledge that, while reconciled to the coming of democracy and the demise of aristocracy, seeks to combat excesses and dangers that are best discerned by an aristocratic eye. The incorporation of aristocracy as both an evaluative and an analytical category was less a confession of prejudice than of desperation for a reference point that, by its sharply contrasting practices and values, could convey the awesomeness of a new world where human powers were being unleashed, not as a single moment of mass upheaval but as a steady state.

Tocqueville recognized that the saliency of aristocracy had been fatally weakened once modernity insisted on treating it as a class defined by interests rather than as an elite distinguished by public virtues. His image of aristocracy would be ambiguous: both an ideal of noble character, refinement, and public virtue and a fallen class, admitted to be archaic and even judged as deficient. Its normative status is retained, yet it functions primarily within a sociological analysis focused upon the implications of equality—as though the most useful terms for illuminating democracy were the archaic ones of its historical opposite. Aristocracy thus remained alive hermeneutically while being interred politically.

## XII

Tocqueville began his inquiry into democracy from an Aristotelian distinction between a society in which a few men aimed at fine actions and the noblest ideals and one in which many lived according to modest goals, most of which were material:

> What do you want of society and its government? We should be clear about that.
> Do you want to elevate the human spirit to a certain loftiness, a generous way of viewing the things of this world? Do you want to inspire men with a contempt for material things? Do you want to nurture deep commitments and thus prepare for acts of profound devotion?
> Are you concerned with refining *moeurs*, elevating manners, and causing the arts to shine? . . .
> Do you want to organize a people so that they will exercise powerful influence over all others . . . and leave a great mark on history?
> If, in your view, such be the main objectives of society, do not choose democratic government.[64]

Democracy, in contrast, represented a social condition in which living well was defined in predominantly egalitarian and materialistic terms:

> [I]f instead of a brilliant society, it is enough for you to live in a prosperous one, and . . . if for you the main object of government is not to achieve the greatest power or glory possible but to provide for each individual the greatest well-being, then you should equalize conditions and establish a democratic government.[65]

Tocqueville's new science assumed that although the rise of democracy had rendered the question of the best political order irrelevant as a practical choice, it was crucial that it be preserved as a critical counterpoint. This was because the focus of the new political science was to be strikingly different. Its focus was not, as Aristotelian political science had been, on scarce goods, like excellence and honor, but on mediocrity, on what was within the reach of the Many.

Mediocrity, like democracy, was depicted not as a choice but as a fate, a condition resulting from the dominance of aspirations lying between the ignoble and the noble. The very considerations that made American democracy what it was, a moderate, free, egalitarian, moralistic, law-abiding, proprietary, and enterprising society, also defined the limits of virtue and vice, individuality, intellectual imagination, aesthetic sensibility, patriotism, public spirit, and national *grandeur.* To be sure, Tocqueville's new science preserved the idea of noble action—promoting the common good, defending immaterial values, and serving the nation—but only as one highly tenuous element among others in the complex motivations of actors whose outlook was essentially bourgeois rather than aristocratic and who were, therefore, "naturally" drawn to economic vocations, material values, and personal happiness.

## XIII

Tocqueville's new science was distinguished by its preoccupation with a phenomenon whose sheer magnitude was unknown to the classical science of the political. His was to be a science of the new as such, in part because he believed that the changes that had taken place in the New World were universal in bearing and hence important for his countrymen to understand, and in part because newness itself, and the powers of change that produced it continuously, both of which had hardly figured in Aristotelian political science, or even in Montesquieu or Rousseau, had become defining qualities of the modern democratic condition. In premodern times the new was typically the monopoly of the Few. In modern times, however, the new was becoming a collective experience.

When Tocqueville discovered the power assumed by the new in a democratized culture, it marked a move beyond the *Federalist,* whose authors had been solely concerned to check the new in the form in which they recognized it, that of temporary electoral majorities. For Tocqueville, however, a democratized culture resembled a template signifying the inseparability of polity, economy, literature, religion, education, and manners, and hence a more far-reaching power than that of occasional majorities. The frightening power of America, which Tocqueville felt he had glimpsed, was so unique as to make the traditional categories that political thinking had developed to account for extraordinary power—for example, absolutism, tyranny, despotism, arbitrary power—appear suggestive only to a degree.

The orienting concern of the new science, therefore, would be to explain how it was that, despite the presence of a totalizing demotic culture, American democracy had avoided becoming its own victim. The new science would reveal how a democracy managed to restrain its own potential for excess and thus offer a praxis designed to work within democratic society, retaining its advantages and counteracting its evils. It would be a practical political science designed to show the actual relevance of American democratic experience to a France struggling to become a postrevolutionary society.

Did the assumption that France could learn from America mean that Frenchmen would be forced to innovate where Americans had merely practiced?

## XIV

*If morality were strong enough by itself, I would not consider it so important to rely on utility. If the idea of what was just were more powerful, I would not talk so much about utility.*

Tocqueville[66]

Like the theory of which it is a part, the science of the new sets out to emulate the paradigm of the Divine Mind. It is constructed around a strategy that Tocqueville identified with the way God worked His will. That strategy was revealed in the second volume of *Democracy*.

When men wish to realize some great end, Tocqueville declared, they concentrate on the means and, as a result, they are tempted to want to mobilize the whole society on its behalf, "forcing all men to march in step toward the same goal." God's way is different. He "introduces endless variety into actions" and "combines them in such a way that they all tend toward the achievement of a great design. . . . Men think that they prove their greatness by simplifying the means. God's object is simple, but His means vary infinitely."[67]

Like God, Tocqueville would set a simple goal for the new political science, to moderate democracy; his means would likewise be varied, combining some discoveries of New World politics with some practices retrieved from the archaic or prerevolutionary past.[68] The new science, while instructing about the "new evils" that accompany democracy, also encompasses a more unconventional purpose of showing how to "secure the new benefits which equality can offer."[69] A democratic regime has the possibility of spreading enlightenment and material comfort to all members of society; of encouraging softer habits and fewer great crimes; and of endowing all of its citizens with the unique dignity that comes from possessing equal political rights.[70]

Clearly Tocqueville had set for himself a complex task: of instructing the French about America and simultaneously addressing France's political condition while touting democracy's potential moderation. The difficulties of execution were compounded by his claim to have discovered an authentic political society. That claim provoked a crucial question: was the moderate character of American democracy the work of a controlled or of a self-controlling democracy (e.g., the New England township)? But if neither term fit the raucous, demos-driven politics of Jacksonian America, then the emphasis on moderation seemed prompted less by a perception of America than by a concern to find a solution to the political instability of France. Tocqueville's new science appeared more tailored toward controlling the degree of democracy to be admitted into an old world rather than confronting a self-contradicting democracy, which was at once vibrant in its politics and ferociously antiegalitarian in its treatment of Indians and cruelty toward its slaves. The new science preferred to echo a long line of political theorists from Plato to Montesquieu and the *Federalist*: "Each government carries within it a natural vice which seems inherent in its very life principle; the genius of a legislator consists in discerning that clearly."[71]

The "vice" of democracy was, of course, majority rule. From Aristotle to Rousseau, political theorists were unable to imagine how democracy's vice could be remedied except by some external, nondemocratic deus ex machina, such as Harrington's Lord Archon or Rousseau's Great Legislator. Were Tocqueville's new science to follow that route, it would be less a science of democracy's *political* possibilities than a science of democratic *politics* aimed at reassuring the old governing groups while instructing the emerging political class about the consequences arising from the pressures of an enlarged electorate and the increasing role of organized parliamentary groupings.

That he did opt for that route seems to be suggested in a passage striking for its uncharacteristic crudity: "the leaders of the State" and "the most powerful, intelligent, and moral classes of the nation" have failed "to take hold" of democracy in order "to direct it." As a result, democracy "has been abandoned to its savage instincts . . . like children deprived of parental care who educate themselves in our town streets and know nothing of society except its vices and miseries." Instead of attempting to suppress democracy, it fell to enlightened leaders to bring about "changes in the laws, ideas, habits and *moeurs*" so as to give "the democratic revolution" an appropriate culture.[72] A political culture begins to appear less as the matrix deposited by the interaction between practice and the political lore acquired by the citizen than as public tutelage of the citizenry. Yet, on Tocqueville's own showing, the practice of democracy *was* political education. Participation, discussion, and deliberation provided the forms and settings for the process by which members, in educating themselves and each other, truly became citizens. By that account, democracy did not require an elite to instruct it in the ways of its own politics. Tocqueville went even further and broke with the long-standing tradition in political thinking that saw no remedies to democracy's ills except from some wise and disinterested "outside" agent who could somehow dilute a democratic system with a "mixture" of non- or antidemocratic principles. In an unpublished fragment he wrote:

> Use Democracy to moderate Democracy. It is the only path open to salvation to us. To discern the feelings, the ideas, the laws which, without being hostile to the principle of Democracy, without having a natural incompatibility with Democracy, can nonetheless correct its troublesome tendencies and will blend with it while modifying it. Beyond that [i.e., reliance upon reactionary principles] is foolish and imprudent.[73]

What emerges is that, although Tocqueville was enamored of the democratic political, of the ideal of a civic spirited community in which citizens were earnestly engaged in defining the common good and their responsibilities toward it, he was skeptical of the possibilities for achieving the political through democracy's politics. This ambivalence colors his discussion of participation, the topic for which he is most famous. On the one hand, he glowingly describes American participatory practices as surpassing the achievement of ancient democracy and extolls the lofty political character displayed by Americans in their passion for political life and in their simple affection for their communities: "[In] democratic republics . . . it is not only one section that undertakes to improve the state of society; the entire people takes on this concern. It is not a matter of providing only for the needs and comforts of one class but of all classes at the same time."[74] On the other hand, he insists that demotic politics is rooted primarily in self-interest. That claim has the effect of making the spirit of the political appear as artificially grafted onto less elevated concerns. In the end the politically best that can be achieved is to follow the American practice of "self-interest rightly understood" which encourages the citizen to recognize how and when the long-term common interest of the political might be combined with his own politics of self-interest.

That uneasy compromise points to the growing difficulties experienced when theory tried to reconcile the premodern ideal of political action with modern mass participation. That ideal had been based on the twin notions that it was possible to perform actions that were morally or politically significant and that politically significant action was the work of disinterested individual political actors. Montesquieu had asserted not only that virtue was the crucial quality of a democratic society but that "political virtue is the renunciation of oneself which is always a very painful matter."[75] The coming of modernity in both of its revolutionary forms, economic and political, changed all of that. It was no longer possible to conceive politics based on the virtue of the few and the deference of the many or to assert, as Montesquieu did, that democracy was "the love of equality," which could only be maintained if there was "the love of frugality"—and that would require the force of laws.[76] Montesquieu's enforced frugality was the ghost of republican virtue: theorists could no more easily contemplate a democracy unleavened by a republican elite than some publicists of the 1990s could resist the notion that because certain "wise men," representative of the American elite, had been in high office during the postwar years, the "republic" had managed to contain communism.[77]

Theory confronted a politics weighed down by the equality of all, narrowed by the self-interest of each, and threatened by the promise of material plenty for all. The *levée en masse*, whereby revolutionary France conscripted a national army, was emblematic of a shift that would see the hero displaced by collective action or else treated as its mouthpiece.[78] The questions being posed were, Once the moment of "revolutionary idealism" had passed, how, if at all, could the political be experienced or realized through collective action? Would it be confined to exceptional moments, such as wartime or a national crisis? And if the political was a fugitive experience, did that mean that in modernity the political would be experienced only as a rare moment of collective action and that majority rule would merely serve as a counting device? And, if so, had Tocqueville gotten matters backward: instead of being the inexorable wave of the future, democracy was, from its first appearance, an endangered species? Or perhaps Tocqueville had glimpsed that democracy's entrance into the world and its eventual triumph opened the possibility of it serving as the basis for an antidemocratic democracy. If so, then democracy might be both an endangered and an endangering species.

Before those questions could be answered, however, the idea of collective action was being challenged from within by the social revolution being effected by modernity.

Social power in the postrevolutionary world had shifted from the aristocracy to the middling classes, from the class whose ideology was public virtue to the class whose ideology was private self-interest. In Tocqueville's eyes, that shift had produced in France a paradoxical situation of a triumphant social class, the bourgeoisie, whose political and social power operated pervasively, even oppressively; yet the society was not a cohesive collectivity but a loose collection of separate individuals content if protected in their personal rights. Thus power seemed disaggregated, divorced from will: the majority was not a corporate entity, like a committee or an assembly, which first deliberated about a course of action and then proceeded to enact it. The majority might appear as an imposing cultural power, anonymous, homogeneous, and pervasive, yet because of the anonymous ways by which culture is formed, the majority cannot recognize itself as as an actor, much less as *the* actor.

Modernity's idea of action as expressed through revolutions had been collective and political but its postrevolutionary, liberal notions of action were (self-)centered and economical rather than political. Instead of mass action with a common enemy, classical political economy posited a bewilderingly large number of individual actors, each with his own agenda—and each, if not the enemy, then the competitor of the other. That potential for anarchy was repressed by investing [*sic*] actors with rationality to guide their self-interest and by inventing the market as a framework for the exercise of rationality. Rational self-interest would bring social harmony because the actor's own reasoning would force him to recognize that if he wanted to advance his own interests, he must meet the needs and desires of others. The free market, freed from the political, its only "laws" being the impersonal ones of the market itself, induced negotiation between buyers and sellers and assured the most efficient use of social and natural resources. The economic, so to speak, socialized its actors despite itself and in spite of the political.

Tocqueville recognized that the power exerted by this new, modern principle of social action extended beyond the marketplace and operated throughout society, in politics as well as in private associations and personal relationships. One result was to introduce a profound tension, even contradiction, between two basic principles of democracy: "The two great social principles which . . . rule American society . . . [are], first, the majority . . . is always right and there is no moral force above it. Second, every individual, private person, society, community or nation is the only lawful judge of its own interest."[79]

Clearly, a majority that is considered always right will be in frequent conflict with individuals and groups intent upon defending or promoting their particular interests. Either majority rule becomes a virtual impossibility in a society where the self-referentialism of interests is legitimated, or it becomes a rhetorical cover for whatever private interest is most capable of organizing power and exploiting the idea of majority rule for its own ends. In this context, where action is being played out politically but generated socially, how is it possible for the new science to emulate the Divine Mind—or the more prosaic mind of Adam Smith and the "unseen hand?"—so as to "combine" the "endless variety" of social, apolitical, and self-interested actors "in such a way that they all tend toward the achievement of a great design" while bearing in mind that the Divine Mind has apparently willed that the world should become democratic and dominated by a mediocrity driven by self-interest?

## XV

*America demonstrates that virtue is not, as has long been claimed, the only thing which can maintain republics.*

Tocqueville[80]

Montesquieu had written that a "popular state," more than any other type of system, required a greater degree of virtue because the whole responsibility for governing, from enacting laws to executing them, lay with the people.[81] But he had also taken note of changes in the language of civil discourse whose effects were subversive of civic virtue. "Unlike the political men of Greece," he declared, we no longer see virtue as the main "force" that sustains popular government: "Today political men speak to us of manufacturing, commerce, finance, wealth, and even luxury."[82]

Tocqueville found that while America confirmed Montesquieu's insight a thousandfold, it disconfirmed his claims that virtue was the "force" that sustained a democracy and that without the practices of frugality equality would give way to inequality. In a society where inherited wealth and social status had never figured importantly, economic pursuits defined the nature and terms of life. In particular, economy rather than politics drew the energies of the ambitious, for it was there that the stakes and risks seemed most challenging. Where, then, in a world dominated by economy, was politics and where was the political successor to the civic-minded aristocracy? In France the bourgeoisie was emerging as the dominant economic class but it had yet to exhibit, at least to Tocqueville's satisfaction, the passion or ability for great politics that was the mark of a true political class. Although Tocqueville noted in his travel journals that the Americans seemed to have proved that the bourgeoisie could govern,[83] he made no effort to incorporate that insight into the text of *Democracy*. In part, the silence may have reflected the influence of the survivors from the old Federalist elite; in his interviews they rarely failed to lament the passing of the political generation that had created the republic. More likely, however, silence may have resulted from a belief that the politics of democracy did not necessarily require a virtuous political class.[84] Democracy eliminates *grandeur* and the *agon* from the political; but it enlarges the political to accommodate all. Both of these developments are the result of the revolution affecting the location of power.

## XVI

> *In America free customs* [les moeurs libres] *have created free institutions; in France it is free political institutions that have to create the practices.*
>
> Tocqueville[85]

In the "aristocratic centuries," Tocqueville noted, the political problem was to establish state power in the face of "the numerous social powers that played on the individual." In those days there were a few powerful individuals and a "feeble social authority." Unity and uniformity were unknown. The men of those days reacted by curtailing individual freedom and "subordinating particular interests to the general good." The result was a "nearly all-powerful" sovereign and dependent individuals.[86]

The new world of democracy changed all of that. Politics was relocated from an absolute center and diffused throughout society. Even power's forms changed in ways that would have astonished ancient or mediaeval thinkers, accustomed as they were to locating power in some person or class. Authority in the modern world is no longer personified in a king or a great family. It is anonymous, as diffused as politics itself, yet nonetheless powerful. Its form is cultural, its agent the unconscious majority, its expressions intangible rather than material, its power more the conditioning resulting from simultaneity of belief rather than from self-conscious concerted action.

An equally far-reaching change had taken place in the relationship between politics and administration, one that dramatized the contrast between the Old World's version of modernity and the New World's. The early modern centralization of state power had been accomplished largely at the expense of local and provincial authorities, which, historically, had practiced a politics of consultation, negotiation, and discussion with local notables and ordinary inhabitants. The modern state spelled the displacement of local politics by bureaucratic politics. The New World represented a dramatic reversal, whereby politics had been established to the exclusion of administration. "*Grandeur* is not in what the state administration does, but what is accomplished without it or outside it."[87] Administration is rendered almost "invisible": "The constitution of administrative power in the United States presents nothing centralized or hierarchical; this is what makes it go unperceived. The power exists but its representative is nowhere to be seen."[88] Local bodies, voluntary associations, and private corporations had spontaneously assumed the functions that Old World modernity, in the name of rational expertise, had assigned to the state.

Among the goals of the new political science was the strengthening of the rights and status of the individual against the new anonymous power represented by the majority. Yet the new science is strongly antiprivate and wants to draw the individual back into public life, not the public life clustered around state institutions but scattered throughout society. Modernity has given society a profoundly political character by multiplying the sites of political life outside the centralized state. "Society" does not signify the "private realm" of family, church, personal relationships, and work. It includes governmental institutions in the village, city, county, and state; religious bodies, educational institutions, newspapers, and voluntary associations that have "no explicit political object" but nevertheless have profound political consequences.[89] Society is political societies.

Democracy transforms society, penetrating all aspects of its life, "customs, opinions, and forms of social life; it is to be found in all of the details of social life as well as in the laws."[90] Ultimately democracy is more than a set of institutions. It is a new civilization.[91] "[I]n the United States the constitutive principle of the republic is the same as that which governs the greater part of human actions. As a consequence the republic penetrates . . . into the ideas, opinions, and all of the habits of Americans at the same time that it becomes established in their laws."[92]

A civilization is a common identity defined by shared habits, customs, usages, and responses: it is community in its most extended and generalized form. What gives coherence to that ensemble of cultural practices is the "dogma of the sovereignty of the people," which Tocqueville described as "the last link in a chain of opinions which binds the whole Anglo-American world." That metaphor was meant seriously. In America, Tocqueville noted, the sovereignty of the people has gone as far as "the imagination can conceive."[93] "It is really the people who give direction, and even though the form of government is representative, it is clear that the opinions, prejudices, interests, and even the passions of the people encounter no lasting obstacles which prevent them from finding expression in the daily direction of society."[94] Popular sovereignty "binds" because it serves as "the last link" that connects "civil and political society." The first link, however, is the fundamental principle to which Americans steadfastly adhere and practice throughout the reaches of their society:

> Providence has given to each individual, regardless of who he is, the amount of reason necessary for him to conduct himself in the matters which concern him exclusively. . . . [T]he father of a family applies it to his children; a master to his servants; a township to those under its administration; a county to the townships; and the state to a county; and the Union to the states.[95]

But was the American completely immersed in civilization; was his political culture to be understood solely through Montesquieuean categories of *moeurs*, settled practices, and intellectual and spiritual inheritance combined with an amount of reason sufficient to his and society's needs? Although that formulation might serve in describing settled communities whose inhabitants had distanced themselves from nature, it was inadequate when it came to the American who had not come to society from the state of nature but the reverse, and for whom nature was not the harmonious condition rhapsodized by Rousseau but thc nature "red in tooth and claw" that Darwin was investigating. Just as the long exposure to violence during the Peloponnesian War had conditioned the character and fate of Athenian democracy, to understand the democratization of the political in America it would be necessary to consider the implications of the democratization of violence that accompanied the steady advance toward the frontier. As we shall see, Tocqueville would journey from the civil society of New England to the state of nature in (what was then) the West.

# CHAPTER X
# THE CULTURE OF THE POLITICAL: "THE RITUALS OF PRACTICE"

## I

*When I compare the Greek and Roman republics to the republics of America, the library manuscripts of the first and their coarse populace, to the thousand newspapers which furrow the second and to the enlightened people who live there; when finally I plunge into an attempt to judge the one by the other and to foresee what will happen by what happened 2,000 years ago, I am tempted to burn my books and to apply only new ideas to a new social condition.*

Tocqueville[1]

*For our part we stopped, struck with astonishment at the spectacle.*

Tocqueville[2]

Commentators have largely approached *Democracy in America* as a solitary text to be understood within its own boundaries. The contents of the work are so rich that nothing seems to have been lost by working within those limits. Nonetheless, I want to attempt to enlarge its field of meaning at the expense of its boundaries by starting from "outside" *Democracy.*

This involves approaching it as a work flanked by two other works, both of which precede it and are intimately related to it. One consists of the notebooks in which Tocqueville recorded his thoughts and observations as he traveled throughout the United States and Canada.[3] Numerous entries in the notebooks reappear verbatim in *Democracy.* The other work, *Du Système Pénitentiaire aux États-Unis*, appeared in 1832, three years before *Democracy.*[4] Unlike the notebooks, *Du Système Pénitentiaire* appears as discontinuous, a world of unfreedom, strangely at odds with the temper of an author who repeatedly extolled liberty as the supreme value. Because the latter was written after Tocqueville's return to France, I postpone discussion of its contents until a later chapter and focus briefly on the notebooks.

Collectively the notebooks form a journey through the United States and lower Canada, perhaps the truest example in the history of political theory where three of the meanings of *theoria*—journey, spectacle, and theoretical observation—come together. Tocqueville's *theoria* takes him to cities and towns where he encounters an impressive level of political and cultural sophistication. His interviews are remarkable not only as a registry of the judgments and ideas of influential Americans, including a former president, but for the fact that their beliefs contributed importantly to the contents of *Democracy.* It marked the first time in the history of political theory that the subjects of a theory were, to a significant degree, contributors. With only slight exaggeration, the first volume of *Democracy* could be said to be a democratic achievement. The interviews are accompanied by Tocqueville's observations and reactions, including several that confirm how much his preoccupation with France was interwoven with the construction of *Democracy.*[5] This part of the journey might be summarized as a politicohistorical record of Tocqueville's inquiries into a new political culture, a distinct civilization, which he sees as emerging from an older one.

> The Americans, in coming to America, brought with them what was most democratic in Europe. When they arrived they left on the other side of the Atlantic the greater part of the national prejudices on which they had been nurtured. They became a new nation taking on habits, new *moeurs,* and something of a national character.[6]

The *theoria* also encompasses a journey that takes Tocqueville into wilderness areas where few settlers had ventured, the exact opposite of the civilized, historically grounded political culture of settled communities. That part of his journey into an unsettled world was recorded in two essays which he wrote while traveling, "Voyage to Lake Oneida" and "A Fortnight in the Wilderness." The first essay recalls Tocqueville's feelings and thoughts as he visits an abandoned site on a small island where a refugee couple from the French Revolution had struggled to make a new life for themselves. It might be described as nature overcoming history for hardly any traces remained of their existence, the vegetation having effaced any reminders. The second essay recounts a journey into the wilds of northern Michigan. There he encounters a "spectacle" that, literally, staggers his imagination for he actually experiences the condition that the political theorists of the seventeenth century and of the Enlightenment could only hypothesize: he has entered the state of nature, complete with noble savages. It is, however, a temporary state of nature. For poised at its edges is "another European," whom Tocqueville carefully distinguished from the French Canadian and described as "one who attaches himself to the earth, and seizes from savage life everything that he can. His struggle against it never ceases; every day he strips it of some of its attributes. Piece by piece he transports into the wilderness his laws, habits, usages, and, if he could, the smallest refinements of his advanced civilization."[7]

History and nature form two of the principal mythemes in the structure of *Democracy.* The first chapter of *Democracy* establishes the mytheme of nature; it will have its counterpart in the second chapter where the mytheme of history enters in the form of the political heritage that the colonists brought to the new land. Nature stands for the extraordinary gift that Americans have taken rather than received. Only slightly less extraordinary is the energy with which they have assaulted nature. Every day that campaign helps not only to redefine nature as resources and property but to shape the American character. Nature and history form the contrasts that frame *Democracy* and provide the settings in which the worst and the best in America are set against each other.

Tocqueville begins by describing nature in epical terms, the pristine grandeur of a purely natural world before the European settlements. Nature is represented by the incredible forests, which, though untouched by man, form a scene not of idyllic peace but "a field of violence and destruction"[8] of and by nature that will be mimicked by the settlers: a tangle of broken limbs; fallen trees, some suspended in mid air; mounds of debris and decaying vegetation; "savage majesty" mixed with a primal "chaos."[9] Yet nature is so inexhaustible in the New World that forms of life continuously emerge through the openings amid the decay: "As in the forests subjected to man's domination, death strikes here without surcease. . . . But in the midst of this debris the work of reproduction goes on continuously. . . . Thus in some way death comes to the aid of life. Brought face to face, they seem to have wanted to mingle and confuse their works."[10]

Tocqueville is struck not only by the immensity of the forests, which reminds him of nothing so much as the unending emptiness of the ocean, but by "a silence so profound, a stillness so complete that the soul feels itself penetrated by a kind of religious terror."[11]

The chapter hints at an even darker theme as Tocqueville pauses briefly, even elegiacally, over the fate of the Indians, the New World's natural inhabitants, a people whose courage, pride, and stubborn love of freedom are declared to surpass any of the "famous republics of antiquity" but whose fate was to occupy the land without "possessing" it, whose vices and virtues—including a "certain aristocratic *politesse*"—"delivered them to an inevitable destruction."[12] And unlike the forest, the Indian will not return to reclaim his place once civilized man has moved on in quest of more promising prospects. What he cannot reclaim is his culture; it will have been shattered by contact with civilization.

Nature is also the setting for the appearance or rather the reenactment of Rousseau's representation of the natural equality of mankind. But with a difference. Those parts of the forests "cleared" by man resemble the society he has left behind: all trees are equal when leveled to stumps; all men are equal when "there is one society only":

> It could be rich or poor, humble or brilliant, commercial or agricultural, yet it is everywhere composed of the same elements. The standard of an egalitarian civilization has been impressed on it. The man you left behind in the streets of New York you will meet again in the midst of the most impenetrable solitude: the same dress, the same mentality, the same language, the same habits, the same pleasures.[13]

The crucial phrase, "an egalitarian civilization," would have struck many of Tocqueville's class as oxymoronic. For them civilization was the creature of history, an accumulation of great literature, the refinement of aesthetics, the cultivation of manners and sensibility, the pride of long and honorable lineage, and of the unending struggle to enforce law upon societies never far removed from lawlessness. The achievements of civilization were assumed to be primarily the work of exceptional men and to depend upon such men for their preservation and perpetuation. The idea of an "egalitarian" civilization was an idea without an illustration. The revolutionaries of seventeenth-century England and eighteenth-century France seemed unable to describe equality except in terms of what they hoped to get rid of from an inherited past: rank, privilege, and power monopolized by the Few. America, which had no "feudal past," according to Tocqueville, was in the unique position of being able to develop a positive conception of equality that would apply to far more than equality before the law or equal political rights.

According to the narrative constructed by theorists of the state of nature, man would step out of the state of nature, cease to be natural man in order to form civil(ized) society, and thereby acquire identity as a citizen. In Locke's phrase, man "abandons" a state whose peculiarity is that, in a historical sense, it is contextless: it has no institutions, settled practices, no memories. Nothing is "received." Accordingly, its abstract, ahistorical character allows it to be governed by the equally abstract and ahistorical elements of human reason and the laws of nature. Tocqueville's American, however, would not exit from nature but enter it and bring the civilization that destroys nature and corrupts its representative, the Indian. Seemingly the American brings a context but, paradoxically, the culture of equality reproduces the uniformity characteristic of Locke's laws of nature: "everywhere composed of the same elements." Later, when Tocqueville treats the phenomenon of centralization, a comparable process of abstraction will reappear: destructive of historical context, of practice, memory, continuity, and particularity.

What kind of man is it who proceeds to attack nature with a preternatural ferocity, to corrupt natural man, and "to whom the future of the New World belongs"? Tocqueville represented the frontiersmen as "a restless, calculating, adventurous race which acts coldly in a way that is explicable only in terms of a passion that traffics in everything without excepting even morality and religion."[14] For the most part that encounter between history and nature was postponed until the final chapter of *Democracy* as Tocqueville presents a mytheme that narrates the application of theories derived from an inherited political culture to nature, to a setting with no preexisting political culture, an apparent tabula rasa. America will illustrate how theory and practice can be constructively combined and relieved of the odium resulting from the alliance between theory and revolutionary action, which Burke and others had made complicit in the horrors of the French Revolution.

## II

> *The Anglo-Americans were wholly civilized when they arrived on the land which their posterity now occupies; they had no need to learn, it was enough that they should not forget. It is the children of these same Americans who, each year, move into the wilderness with their homes, the knowledge, which they have already acquired, and a respect for learning. . . . In the United States society has no infancy; it was born to maturity.*
>
> Tocqueville[15]

What had enabled the invaders to possess the land? Chapter 1's closing paragraph provided an answer that served as the threshold between the natural and the political epic. The invader was "civilized" man. He was "destined to build society on new foundations," employing the modern resources and skills that would enable him to possess rather than merely occupy. These included "theories previously unknown or considered unworkable."[16]

The people who inscribed themselves upon the tabula rasa represented history in the form of considerable political experience combined with the most advanced political ideas of their age. Freed from the historical constraints of the Old World they could press ideas, such as equality, liberty, and individualism, far beyond anything hitherto attempted. There "the great social revolution seems to have nearly reached its natural limits."[17] The movement toward equality, according to Tocqueville, had its origins as far back as the eleventh century and had grown apace since then. The Americans were thus participating in history, as Europeans understood that notion—not interrupting it.

Thus even though his *theoria*/journey was to a "real" world, Tocqueville would insist from the beginning that the society he had observed embodied a new and remarkable political theory, one that the first settlers had self-consciously used as a model. That claim was meant to distinguish the new society from a primitive utopia. Although the setting was natural in the extreme, the settlers themselves were carriers of an advanced civilization.

In these early pages of *Democracy*, Tocqueville introduces a radical revision of two traditional mythemes. One narrates the political action that, more than any other, had been the stuff of epic, the commanding action of founding. The other establishes the identity of the founder-hero. Tocqueville deviated from his theoretical predecessors by presenting a founder who was not a Moses or a Solon but a people. The people found a new society not by a single memorable act, as Lycurgus did when he imposed a constitution upon the Spartans. Instead of a single great moment, founding consists in the continuity of practices. What they will establish is equally unprecedented. The New World democracy will not be, as the democracies of antiquity or of modern France had been, the creatures of revolution but will issue, instead, from the prior political habits, ideas, and character of the people.

In the past, when political theorists had sketched their ideal commonwealths, they had imagined a sequence of two distinct stages: first the presentation of the theory, then the shaping of a society and people by the laws and institutions prescribed by the theory. The only way in which they could conceive the two stages to be joined was by entrusting absolute power to a lawgiver (Rousseau), or a prince (Machiavelli), or a suggestible young tyrant counseled by a theorist (Plato's *Laws*) to impose an ideal form upon naive matter. In these formulations theory was prior to power and power prior to the social, cultural, and educational practices required for its support.

## III

The emphasis on political culture was perhaps Tocqueville's single most important theoretical choice. Its consequences were stunning for it enabled him to reverse the received theoretical perspective upon democracy and to break with the centuries-old conception that political societies were to be understood as entities created and structured by constitutions. That theoretical opening was prepared by the bold claim that culture, which most writers treated as the unique characteristic of old societies, was to be found in its most highly developed form in the New World. Because the American citizenry was proclaimed to be "the most enlightened in the world" and its "practical political education the most advanced," the culture of American democracy could only be a late development, the end product of Western political experience rather than a precocious beginning.[18] It embodied an inheritance of political skills and their popularization which no rude population could ever have contrived by itself.

Unlike his contemporary, Benjamin Constant, who enlisted the democracy of ancient Athens as a cautionary example of the dangers to freedom when a society rates public life as its highest ideal and private life as lower, Tocqueville insisted that Athenian democracy, as well as republican Rome, was an aristocratic republic rather than a democracy and hence largely irrelevant.[19] Moreover, the factor that rendered the comparisons misleading was that the ancient "democracies" included a "gross populace"; America, in contrast, was remarkable for the widespread and high level of popular enlightenment. In New England "every citizen" was instructed in the basic elements of human knowledge, religion, and the history of his country and its constitution. America, Tocqueville declared, could not be judged by what had happened two millennia ago nor could predictions about its future be drawn from antiquity.

For Tocqueville the difference between the ancients and the moderns did not lead to Constant's praise of the freedoms that protected private life and warnings about politicization but instead to questioning privatization and exposing its threat to freedom. Tocqueville would contend that the great value of America's example, as well as its astonishing achievement, was a citizenry more, not less, political than the Greeks. By inverting what had become the modern priorities of private over public, the Americans had developed a politics that was not restricted to a narrow, bounded domain, but was a way of life. Politics vitalized the whole society, transmitting its energies to civil society rather than reflecting the impulses coursing through civil society. The energy generated by democratic politics "then passes" from the political world "into civil society." And that, Tocqueville suggested, may be the "greatest advantage" of democratic government.[20] Democracy "diffuses throughout the social body a restless energy, a superabundant force, an energy which would never exist without it . . . [and] can do wonders."[21] No one who has not observed "the political activity" prevailing in America can appreciate its intensity. The ubiquity of politics produces a continuous "tumult" and "clamor." That "everything is in movement" is connected with the domination of political concerns over the lives of Americans. Except for the wealthy, all classes are caught up in it and even women take an active part. "To be involved in political concerns . . . , to take part in the governing of society and to talk about it is the most important matter and, so to speak, the only pleasure that an American knows."[22]

## IV

*Democratic government, which is founded on such a simple and natural idea, presupposes, however, a highly civilized and knowledgeable society. At first glance one would think that it belonged to the earliest ages of the world; but looking more closely, one quickly discovers that it could only come last.*

Tocqueville[23]

*The founding of New England presents a new spectacle, everything about it being both remarkable and original.*

Tocqueville[24]

Not surprisingly, when Tocqueville turned to the beginnings of New England and of American political institutions, he would find inspiration and warrant for his biblical and classical themes. He accepted the Puritans' self-designation as the new children of Israel and he elaborated their myth of the reenactment of the triumph of Exodus. They had conceived a society in righteousness, ventured alone to the promised land, had fought for survival and won. Like the ancient Israelites the Puritans were dedicated to "the triumph of *an idea*" and in their legislation they laid a basis as sure and true as that in the Mosaic law.[25] The Puritans, Tocqueville declared, were not "a mere troop of adventurers gone forth to seek their fortune beyond the seas, but the seed of a great people that God has released to a predestined land."[26]

Once Tocqueville had established the mytheme of America as the embodiment of an "idea," he enlarged it and made America the fulfillment of the dreams of theorists since antiquity of finding a land where, self-consciously, theory had been converted into practice. There "in the wilderness of the New World . . . a system of legislation without precedent was improvised by the human imagination."[27] The American theoretical genius was not, however, exhausted in its beginnings. The constitutions later adopted by the several states were direct expressions of theories, and many of their principles have become "axioms in the political science of our day."[28] Similarly, the Supreme Court embodied a theory of judicial power that "actually put into practice" an idea that Europeans had only barely grasped.[29] The system of federalism set out in the Constitution was "a wholly novel theory" but now "may be considered a great discovery in the political science of our day."[30]

## V

The American political culture was both a founded culture and a deeply derivative one, and the American a new *historical* figure. As the inheritor of a European political legacy, the American had been born a political adult rather than a child. "Thus in the United States, society had no infancy, being born at a virile age. . . . [Americans] have no idea of the virtues or vices or the crude habits and the naive graces of a newborn civilization."[31] The first settlers brought the most advanced "democratic and republican theories," an austerity of manners, "wonderful elements of order and morality," a strict legal code, and all of "the general principles upon which modern constitutions rest": citizen participation, especially in the voting of taxes, the accountability of officials, individual freedom, and trial by jury.[32]

The crucial importance of the English legacy—and, for Tocqueville, virtually all Americans were viewed as English in origin—was that the first colonists were accustomed to freedom and political participation before they felt the full impact of the equality encouraged by their social condition. "Among Americans it is liberty that is old; equality is comparatively new."[33] The reverse was true in Europe where equality had been introduced by "absolute power" and "under the eyes of kings"; it had "penetrated into the habits of the people long before liberty entered into their thinking."[34]

## VI

> *Puritanism was . . . as much a political theory as a religious doctrine.*
>
> Tocqueville[35]

Tocqueville's Puritans were remarkable for possessing an articulate political theory and a sharply delineated, self-conscious conception of political liberty as a strict moral discipline. They were, in Tocqueville's portrait, a theoretical people who governed their religious life and their political practices in accordance with a distinctive system of ideas. The "principles of New England" spread to adjoining regions, and eventually penetrated "the entire American world."[36] Democracy had to be understood theoretically because its American origins had been powerfully shaped by "the most absolute democratic and republican theories."[37]

What made the epic of democracy theoretical was not that it had been conceived by an individual theorist or embodied in a specific theory but that ideas about freedom, law, and self-government, which hitherto had existed mostly as theoretical speculations, were actually applied in America and put to the test.[38]

Tocqueville's idealized description of the township (*commune*) had a didactic purpose of showing the level of political utopia of which democracy is capable. Democracy can never achieve the best political state for its egalitarianism would always inhibit superiorities of all kinds. Yet there is a democratic best. The township could be used as a "model" because there the basic principles of democracy are "thrown into sharper relief and hence are easy for a stranger to observe."[39] Accordingly, Tocqueville presents the township as a realized theory, a coherent whole intellectually and practically: "In New England the communal institutions form a complete and regular *ensemble*; they are old; they are strengthened by laws, strengthened even more by *moeurs*; and they exercise a prodigious influence over the entire society."[40] Although the democratic best fails to incorporate Aristotle's criterion of "fine actions," it is superior by another equally Aristotelian measure of the political. Democracy is the form in which the citizen and the political seem naturally coterminous: the whole has become an inclusive whole, instead of a whole in which a part is predominant.

Tocqueville's township is to his theory what the polis was to ancient Greek theorists, the best representation of the political. His selection of the township as the starting point of *Democracy* forms a striking parallel with Aristotle's *Politics*. Aristotle's analysis began from the family and culminated in the polis or city-state, the highest, most inclusive, and most sovereign of all associations. The city signified the limits of the political. Tocqueville built on the Aristotelian premise, which had been all but forgotten with the emergence of the early modern nation-state and theories of state sovereignty: that the city is the nursery of politics and "the spirit of the city [is] inseparable from the exercise of political rights."[41] "Communal institutions are to liberty what primary schools are to science; they put it within the people's grasp."[42]

Unlike Aristotle, however, Tocqueville would venture beyond the township to confront the antipolitical, the modern state, but he would conclude that only a democratic conception of a citizen could redeem the politics established within that essentially antidemocratic constitution. "Today the most powerful, and perhaps the only available means for interesting men in the welfare of their country is to make them participate in its government."[43]

## VII

*The republic has the deepest roots. . . . America is par excellence the country of provincial and communal government.*

Tocqueville[44]

The township served as Tocqueville's principal vehicle for challenging the claim of the state to be the highest embodiment of the political. In selecting the township as his beginning point, Tocqueville was, in effect, decentering the tradition of political thinking begun by early modern theorists such as Machiavelli and Hobbes and perpetuated by later moderns such as Bentham and Austin. That tradition had developed two centers, which it treated as polarities. One was the individual, the other the state. Tocqueville's township belonged to an older tradition that antedated the appearance of the nation-state. It is a tradition historically grounded in the experience of autonomous or quasi-autonomous corporations, sodalities, communes, and city-states whose beginnings have been identified by scholars and theorists as mediaeval.[45] Historically these associations were self-governing rather than democratic but they were explicitly decentralist in character and implicitly anti-statist. Their defenders typically asserted that associations were "natural," "spontaneous," or "voluntary," arising from some deep-seated human impulse to seek an association with others in order to satisfy basic human needs and to achieve certain shared purposes. With some qualifications, this conception might be broadly described as naturalistic. In that respect the tradition perpetuated the Aristotelian conception of the polis as the culmination of a powerful human impulse to want to secure life itself and the advantages made possible by diverse human contributions within a delimited space. That conception also served a polemical purpose of providing a contrast to political rule. The latter could then be represented as a dominion imposed by an external authority upon grudging subjects.

In choosing the New England township as paradigmatic, Tocqueville was, in effect, availing himself of a different tradition, that of the church community. The latter was based on conceptions of membership, participation, and authority that were deeply at odds with French Catholic teachings on these same matters.[46] This congregation-centered, activist tradition, which was brought to America by the Puritans, Independents, and (later) Pietists, emphasized belief as the unifying and distinguishing center of a life-sustaining form in which all should share. Members chose to join a church in order to live together, as well as worship, in accordance with the inspired truths of Scripture. The founding of a political community would be, therefore, a sacred act that merged association and congregation into a community aspiring to sanctify its common life, as well as the lives of its individual members. Protestantism had thus found its own formula for civic virtue.

For Rousseau the idea of a dissenting community was incoherent. Although the New England community was sacramental in character, as Rousseau had striven to make his conception, the former had legitimated an element of discordancy by making allowance for the possibility of a "tender conscience" unable to countenance the current orthodoxy, even of dissenters.

Tocqueville's account combined these two traditions. For the English "township" he usually employed the French word *commune* with its mediaeval and Aristotelian overtones. Thus he declared the township to be "the only association which is so perfectly natural that it forms wherever men congregate."[47] At the same time he saw it as the Puritans had, as God's work. Man "makes kingdoms and creates republics, but the township seems to issue directly from the hands of God."[48]

## VIII

What is the sense in which the township is "natural"? Is it because it owes its existence to the cooperative effort of many rather than to the fiat of a Great Legislator?[49] Is the American the modern successor to Aristotle's "political animal" whose nature can be fulfilled only within the limited confines of the polis? Is the natural what man adapts to or is it what is fitted to him? Or has the natural become an anachronism in modernity?

The township is natural because it is where the immediate interests and most elevated concerns of ordinary beings are located.[50] It attracts the citizens' deepest loyalties and stirs their strongest emotions. The further removed from his government, the weaker the individual's sentiments toward it. A central national government could elicit only "a vague and ill-defined sentiment," because as yet men's interests were little affected by the actions of that remote center.[51] The township is where the individual lives and from that intimacy comes the possibility of affection for a place and from affection loyalty. The township is a political form because everyday concerns and mundane interests are lifted above their ordinariness and rendered in a different idiom than that of the household or marketplace, the idiom of power and of respect for the handling of it. It is "the center of the ordinary relations of life that are expressed in the desire for esteem, the press of real interests, the taste for power and fame."[52] The immediacy of its politics has the not inconsiderable virtue of restraining the democratic appetite for generalization. A politics geared to immediate concerns has a natural respect for limits because the implications of a law are more readily grasped. In contrast, generalized concerns—concerns whose contexts have been bracketed—are the unnuanced stuff on which Old World bureaucracies feed.

The township accepts that modern man is *homo economicus* but it assumes that he can become interested in political liberty and develop, at least in part, into *homo politicus.* Given the American preoccupation with economic pursuits and the axiomatic status of individual self-interest, how is it that "in the midst of the township a real political life prevails, active, wholly democratic and republican"?[53] How does the democratic individual come to be?

## IX

Tocqueville described his first impressions of the tumult, excitement, and energy that suffused American political life and reflected the involvement of each citizen in the practical decisions of the community:

> Hardly has one alighted on the soil of America when you find yourself in a kind of tumult; a confused clamor rises from every side; a thousand voices assail your ears, each expressing some social need. Around you everything is in movement: here the people from one district are meeting to discuss whether they should build a church; there they are busy choosing a representative; further on, the deputies of a village are rushing to town in order to advise on some local improvements; in another place the village farmers have left their furrows to discuss plans for a road or a school. One group of citizens assembles for the sole purpose of declaring their disapproval of the government's direction while others assemble to proclaim that the men in office are the fathers of their country.[54]

To the affections and sentiments that familiarity encourages the township brought a circumscribed politics, a politics of reduced scale corresponding to the modest scope of the citizen's interests and abilities. The citizens come to acquire a "practical wisdom of everyday life and the science of small events that goes by the name of good sense."[55] At the same time, their material interests are naturally connected with the place so that interest and affection become intertwined.

> The New Englander is attached to his township because it is strong and independent; he is interested in it because he shares in its management; he loves it because he has no complaint about his condition . . . he involves himself in all of the happenings of communal life; in the restricted sphere which is within his reach he learns to govern society; he becomes used to those forms without which liberty can advance only by revolutions, and penetrated by their spirit, acquires a taste for order, understands the interrelation of powers, and in the end acquires clear and practical ideas about the nature of his duties as well as the extent of his rights.[56]

Smaller scale meant smaller temptations. The insignificant amounts of money, power, and prestige were unlikely to stimulate dangerous passions. "These passions which so often trouble society change character when they are exercised near the domestic hearth and the family circle."[57] Municipal politics was, undeniably, petty politics, yet it was sufficiently personal in its impact to stimulate the citizen's concern yet not of a complexity to exceed his grasp or his moral capabilities and sympathies.

Circumscribed politics had the additional advantage of a visual character. Men could see that their political involvements made a difference; they could gauge the manifest consequences of their own actions or inactions as well as those of others and thus come to grasp the reciprocal bearing of individual interests and common concerns.[58]

## X

> *The great object of the lawmaker in democracies thus must be to create common affairs which* force *men to enter into contact with one another.*
>
> Tocqueville[59]

The township, while small, was not as inward-looking as the family or the individual. It had a truly public life that called upon its citizens to contemplate problems broader than the household—"an appetite for general undertakings"[60]—and to mingle in public assemblies. It was the principal bulwark against privatization.

Thus the township struck a delicate balance: small enough to encourage affection between its members and large enough to require that they think in terms more comprehensive than the self, the family, or the workplace. The political culture that sustained what Tocqueville called "communal liberty" was fragile and "easily destroyed."

> It rarely occurs and is rarely created: it grows by its own accord. It develops almost secretly in the midst of a semibarbarous society. It is the continuous action of the laws and of *moeurs*, circumstances and especially of time which helps to consolidate it. Among all the nations on the European continent, it can be said that there is not one that understands it.[61]

Because communal politics drew men out of the confines of household and economy, and, above all, because it encouraged them to work together, politics became the single most important force in combatting the disconnectedness of modern life.[62] Whether politics would be able to overcome atomization was by no means assured. The paradox at the heart of democracy was that, while political participation promoted solidarity, the idea of popular sovereignty, which provided the justification for it, was based on an anticorporate individualism, which taught that each is the best judge of his own interests and needs.[63]

Tocqueville concluded that it was futile to attempt to root out modern individualism. In an earlier age society and politics were both dominated by rich and powerful individuals who "took pleasure in professing that it is glorious to forget the self and that it is proper to perform good actions disinterestedly, as God himself did."[64] Now, however, "disinterested patriotism" and civic virtue "are finished."[65] What is natural for modern man is self-interest, self-centeredness wrapped in a distinctive ideology and embedded in a culture in which "beliefs" were being replaced by "arguments," "feelings" by "calculations." Tocqueville described that ideology as "*interest* that comes out into the open and *calls itself a social theory.*"[66] The only political possibility was "to connect the idea of rights with personal interest, the only stable point in the human heart."[67]

By "rights" Tocqueville understood primarily political rights and that emphasis issued from his most fundamental conviction, that without a vibrant participatory culture there was nothing to recommend democracy and everything to fear from it. The American had not suppressed selfishness but had refined it; in the process he demonstrated that consciousness could be expanded, so that the ego came to recognize that its own interests were often best served by promoting the common interest. Tocqueville referred to this as enlightened selfishness. Although he held to this view throughout *Democracy*, he expanded on the dangers of egoism by connecting it to the appearance of "a new idea." "Our fathers," he declared, "were only acquainted with egoism," but now "individualism" has emerged.[68] Egoism is "the impassioned and exaggerated love of the self which leads a man to relate everything to himself and to prefer himself above all else." Unlike egoism, which is driven by "blind instinct," individualism develops from a "calm and considered feeling" that "disposes each citizen to isolate himself" from the larger society and to retire into the "little society" composed of his family and friends. Individualism thus blocks the expression of "public virtues" and eventually it undermines all of the virtues and is "absorbed" into egoism.[69]

Individualism was, Tocqueville concluded, peculiar to democracy, a product of the disconnectedness inherent in a society of equals. It is the institutionalization of Cartesian solitude as "each is forever being thrown back upon himself alone and is threatened with being shut up completely in the solitude of his own heart."[70] The only remaining link is interest.

The huge task assigned political participation is to combat individualism. Accordingly participation is given an enlarged meaning, one coextensive with the life of the various political jurisdictions, which, in America, were historically and normatively prior to the state. Participation does not denote a single action (e.g., electing) but a web of multiple involvements. It is not a deduction from the principle of popular sovereignty but constitutive of it. It is nothing less—or more—than individuals taking care of the everyday needs of their community, that is, deliberating and acting together on matters in which each feels concern because these make up the life of the community.

Participation is represented in the numerous modalities of connectedness distinctive to those who conceive of themselves as equals. Participation has to do with the terms on which equals associate and deal with power, with what traditionally had produced the distinction/distance between rulers and ruled. Thus its stakes were far larger than voting. Beyond even the contribution of participation to the political education of citizens or to the development of human capacities was the challenge that the democratic way of associating human beings presented to the logic of modern power.

## XI

The logic of what might be called "high modern power" was the theoretical achievement of liberal political economists. The writings of Adam Smith, Bentham, James Mill, Ricardo, and Jean Baptiste Say established a discourse in which the main point of politics was to formulate rational state policies that would best encourage, while only minimally regulating, the possibilities for material wealth in a domain they named "the economy." The economy came to signify the locus of the distinctively modern modes of action and power largely independent of political control. Industry, commerce, invention, capital, labor, and agriculture represented forms of organizing, directing, and rewarding human activity concerned with the generation of wealth. High modern power had come to be the representation of intricate social cooperation and its distinctive mode of association, the division of labor. The latter represented social cooperation and association that stopped short of community. Modern power has its distinctive prerequisite in a new type of person, the "individual" who converts dissociation from community into a matter of a right to cultivate individuality. But a person can achieve individuality only by submitting to the efficient use of himself or herself in the form of the division of labor.

The division of labor was a decision about how to organize and generate power by connecting human beings through the structure of tasks. The individual was assigned a set of circumscribed operations ("specialization"); the coordination of those operations was a matter of prior design by managers. While the many would "perform," the director would "see" that the operations would be "carried out"—the performers were defined as being, by their condition, unable to "see" beyond their minute tasks.

It was, in effect, industrial theater, ritualized drama of need and power. In this equation, power was the product of combined efforts, but those who contributed their efforts did not decide the combining or the defining. As a matter of law and constitution, they were precluded from the realm where power was being discussed and decided in general terms, in terms that, formally, were political because applied to the "whole" operation. The political character of power was, as it had been under royal absolutism, importantly a matter of prerogative, this time of managers rather than monarchs. As a consequence the common lay beyond the comprehension of those who produced and thus did not form an element of their experience, a deprivation that was strongly reinforced by the precariousness of their employment. Unlike the status of citizenship, the division of (the) labor(er) involved a status that could be easily lost and—because of the unstable nature of an economy, whose ideal was intense competition—often was.

In contrast, local political life in America followed a different principle of power and refined it to "an art": not to divide power but to "disperse" it (*d'éparpiller*), not to associate individuals in order to generate power greater than the sum of the individuals but according to the principle of "interesting the greatest possible number in *la chose publique.*"[71] Toward that end, and over and beyond the periodic enlistment of voters "to perform government actions," Americans have a variety of local officials who identify themselves with the community and thus "a large number" of individuals "share in local power," not as directors but as coactors. There were, Tocqueville emphasized, no distinguishing marks of uniform or title to set officials apart from ordinary mortals. They were more like citizens taking turns in performing public duties. However slapdash the methods of local governance, it involved citizens in the exercise of substantive power rather than in obedience to decrees decided elsewhere. The township exercised real power and enjoyed genuine autonomy without which—and here Tocqueville was thinking of France—there would be only "administered beings, not citizens."[72]

Tocqueville extended his point about the democratic modes of power by confronting the usual criticism, then and now, that it was an inefficient way of exercising power and far inferior to what could be accomplished by centralized authority employing professional functionaries. Tocqueville did not deny the validity of the criticism but argued for "*political*" rather than "administrative" criteria.[73] Democracy could not bring efficiency, stability, concern with detail, or "perfection of administrative procedures"; instead, expect "untidy budgets" and a "lack of uniformity." It could bring, however, some priceless advantages, "an image of force, a little savage perhaps, but full of power" and "a life, while not without mishaps, yet full of movement and initiatives."

Thus the value of political participation was not confined to government in a narrow sense; it animated civil society as well. In America if an individual conceived of some project that directly affected the welfare of society, he did not turn to the state for assistance. Instead he publicized it and encouraged others to join him. Although the state might do it better, in the long run the "sum" of such efforts brought advantages far beyond any which governmental action might produce.[74] Perhaps the strongest contribution of participation was to preserve patriotism in an age where self-interest has produced men who "find their country nowhere." In modern times the attachments to place have weakened, "the prestige of memories has vanished," and, Tocqueville emphasized, these cannot be revived. It is only by having "each man . . . take an active part in the government of society" that he will take the public good to be identical with his own well-being. It is not a pretty patriotism for it borders on "greed," yet it produces in the individual a powerful attachment to country because its achievements are seen as the result of his efforts.[75] The crux of democratic patriotism is the connection between the vitality of political participation and the strong emotions of patriotism. "The American system, at the same time that it shares municipal power among a large number of citizens, does not hesitate to increase communal duties. In the United States it is rightly believed that the love of the fatherland is a kind of cult to which men are attached by rituals of practice."[76]

The clear implication was that if patriotism were divorced from political participation, it might become fixated upon leaders as nation bearers.

## XII

*[The colonists] had been accustomed in the homeland to taking part in public affairs; they were familiar with the jury system; they had freedom of speech and press, individual liberty, the idea of rights, and usages to rely on.*

Tocqueville[77]

Tocqueville's focus on the township has usually been accounted a simplistic infatuation with "New England town meeting democracy" and hence with the most inimitable of American institutions. But that interpretation misses both the significance of the focus as well as the status of the township in his thinking. The township forms the crucial context of the version of democracy that Tocqueville eventually recommended. It represents the politicizing of democracy, the redirection of its dangerous tendencies of egalitarianism and privatism and their transformation by political education. The township was not so much the faithful reproduction of democracy as its crucial qualification.

The township was, however, a theoretically uncertain foundation on which to base expectations about the future course of democracy in America, much less in France. Tocqueville's principle that participation was the means of making citizens out of individuals was a tacit acknowledgment that the Puritan moment, when the self and its material interests had been subordinated to the norms of the community, had passed, perhaps not yet in New England, but, as Tocqueville recognized, it had never taken hold in the American South or in the rawer cultures of the western states.

While the South presented a special case, crucial to America although irrelevant to Europe, the West was of great importance. It allowed a glimpse of democracy "in its most extreme form" and thus displayed more vividly the symbiotic relationship between individualism and equality. The inhabitants arrived there "only yesterday" and "each is ignorant of his nearest neighbor's history"; there is, as yet, no "natural aristocracy" and there are no great fortunes.[78] The American westerner has thus arrived naturally at that fully liberated state which Europeans had struggled toward so painfully. A liberated state alone revealed the natural individual, undefined by custom, status, traditional religion, or allegiance to a sovereign, and forced to interpret the world unassisted.

To keep these denaturing influences on the self at a distance, the individual appealed to inalienable rights, which were his "by nature." Natural rights enabled him to defend himself against history's efforts at inscription and to accept only those, or the portion thereof, with which he agreed. Although in principle the individual could choose to define his self as a being whose nature required a strong and demanding measure of political involvements and welcomed the prospect of sharing in a common life, the task of choosing and defining placed an enormous burden on the self. That burden was exacerbated by the weakness of the agencies that had served/shaped the interpretation of the various life experiences the individual had faced, not least those emanating from the all-consuming and ruthless pursuit of material gain. He lacked the interpretive context of culture, a hermeneutical past—a being neither modern nor premodern but disinherited. Elsewhere in America the influence of religion remained strong and politics occupied the center of communal life, and so the self could find some relief from its own omnipresence: "It happens that by ambition a man comes to care for his fellows, and that, in a sense, he often finds his self-interest in forgetting himself."[79]

As that new man, poised at the edge of modernity and looking beyond, comes into focus, the polis/township suddenly appears in a different relationship to that being, not as too small but as too large, too demanding in its politicalness, too inconclusive for a temperament becoming attuned to a new culture of opportunity, and too outward for a being who finds endless fascination in exploring his own self and takes pleasure in a restricted circle of intimates, "wholly absorbed in permitted pleasures."[80]

## XIII

> *It is incontestable that in the United States the taste for and usages of republican government were born in the townships and essentially in the provincial assemblies.*
>
> Tocqueville[81]

Before *Democracy* the idea of culture had come to signify not only a field of investigation but a shift of emphasis, away from the role of rulers, ruling classes, and warfare to "society" and its constituent elements of classes, families, associations, corporations, and ecclesiastical establishments. In this new perspective authority was conceived as, if not derivative from society, at least dependent upon it for its moral legitimacy and material support. Although that conception had been intimated in the sixteenth and seventeenth century by writers defending the freedom of religious congregations, the conception of legitimacy as pluralistic was appropriated in the eighteenth century by inventors of a traditionalist conception who viewed society as historical in nature rather than juristic or theologicophilosophical. In prerevolutionary France it was deployed in defense of the nobility against the monarchy and its centralizing policies. In Great Britain it was formulated most notably by Burke as a defense of monarchy, aristocracy, and the European status quo against the revolutionary ideology of 1789. In both forms "society" was employed primarily either to justify resistance against monarchical encroachments on the traditional prerogatives of the nobility or to defend inherited privilege, customary rights, and an exclusionary politics against revolutionary demands for their abolition.

Although the champions of traditionalism argued that nobility encouraged independence, they were unable to persuade an increasingly skeptical public that independence necessarily meant political disinterestedness and was other than a form of special pleading for a politics of privilege. Traditionalism became equated with an unchanging culture of obedience to superiors at a time when inherited cultures were being undermined by modernity's most distinctive and powerful tendency. The extraordinary revolution in conceptions of change stimulated by developments in technology and transformations in systems of economy not only altered how and where people lived but how they perceived their immediate circumstances. In political terms change might be defined as the gap being experienced between the effective power of the instrumentalities of social control available and the dissociative effects produced by secularizing ideas, the new technologies (i.e., profane sources of power), and their accompanying behaviors.

In their different ways monarchical centralization, now revitalized by theories of benevolent despotism, by ideas about administrative reform and the importance of expert public servants, and, at the opposite pole, revolutionary movements demanding both political rights and educational opportunities were in agreement that the cultural nexus binding together society and the political order was rapidly dissolving, that change was as much a necessity as a choice. New terms of order had to be invented for negotiating the two polarities emerging, of official policy or ordered direction ("central intelligence"!) and popular movement seeking to invent forms of a political by which to privilege common aspiration and grievance rather than exceptional lineage, wealth, or talent.

## XIV

> *The importance of customs* [moeurs] *is a universal truth of which study and experience constantly remind us. I find that it occupies the central position in my thoughts; all my ideas come back to it in the end.*
>
> Tocqueville[82]

In Rousseau's envisioning of the requirements for a political culture and, curiously too, in that of the *Federalist*, the state was designated as the primary symbol of the political and its main carrier. The role of culture was to support the state by nurturing citizens who would serve it loyally, bravely, and competently.[83] Thus culture waited on the constitution of the state and was to be its servant. The new statists viewed society uneasily, with a mixture of respect for its moral authorities and suspicion of it as the nursery of associations ("factions" to the *Federalist*) and the gathering place of popular "passions."

The Americans, in Tocqueville's account, had reversed the classical sequence. America began with a political culture rather than a state. A national state followed after and depended on a preexisting political culture, one that was provincial and local. Its founding was represented in its political culture, not its constitution. "America," he noted in his journal, "created municipal liberty before it created public liberty."[84] "Political liberty" meant full participation in and involvement with political life. It presupposed a political culture in which citizens took for granted "the idea of rights and the practice of asserting them . . . against the invasions of the State."[85] Political culture was but a "résumé" of the "provincial patriotism" attached to the several state governments. Its support of the late arrival of a national state was necessarily equivocal.

Although in his treatment of the role of culture Tocqueville may be Montesquieu's student, he should not be considered his disciple. He was the first to explore firsthand the actuality of a democratic culture and to claim that a political culture could be both democratic and conservative, politically free although not strictly virtuous. His achievement was to transform completely the concept of culture, to lessen without deprecating its association with learning, refinement, and sensibility while demonstrating that under the conditions being introduced by modernity, the political role of culture would be played out by the people—or, more ominously, through them.

The moment when Tocqueville perceived the importance of culture to the American system occurred early in his journey and coincided with a significant change from an initial and largely unsympathetic impression of political life in the new society to a more favorable view. He had discovered that "habit," the most hallowed term in the lexicon of traditionalism, was the key to the unexpected stability he found in American political life. Writing to a friend in 1831, he remarked that if one managed to look beneath the apparent simplicity of American institutions, one would appreciate their prerequisites, "a long habit of liberty, and a mass of *true* enlightenment which can be acquired only rarely and over a long time."[86] Tocqueville's democratization of culture and along with it the political was qualified by the crucial role of *moeurs* in customizing the new: "In the course of this book if I have not succeeded in persuading the reader of the importance which I attach to the practical experience of the Americans, to their habits, opinions, and, in a word, their *moeurs*, in maintaining their laws, I will have failed in my main object."[87] *Moeurs* referred to the habits and customs, the transmitted experience, which human beings employ in their daily political and social life and which become engrained in their conduct. In explaining the success of Americans in operating complex political institutions while preserving an enviable degree of stability, Tocqueville insisted that *moeurs*, rather than laws or material conditions, were responsible.[88] More precisely, the transmutation of laws and legal practices into *moeurs* was the key to the American political culture.

Tocqueville's favorite example of the power of *moeurs* was the circulation throughout society of the legal culture represented by lawyers, judges, and the jury system. "Public men" in America, Tocqueville explained, are typically lawyers and naturally apply "legal habits and turn of mind" to public affairs. At the same time, most ordinary Americans have experienced jury service and by means of that "free school" have become accustomed to legal language and adopted it "as a sort of popular language. . . . The juristic spirit, born within schools and courts, is diffused little by little beyond their confines; it infiltrates the whole society, descending into the lowest ranks till finally the whole people have contracted some of the habits and tastes of a magistrate."[89] Tocqueville went on to claim that the jury "is the most powerful way of effecting popular rule, and also the most effective means in teaching [citizens] how to rule." It teaches them to respect the courts and the idea of right; it teaches men "equity in practice" and the acceptance of responsibility for their actions, and it makes them aware of their duties to society while feeling that "they have entered into its government." In the process "it combats individual egoism which is corrosive of societies."[90]

Without displacing the *importance* of participatory institutions *moeurs* introduced an entirely new conception of democracy as rooted in, and corresponding to, the democracy of daily life. At the same time, the notion of *moeurs* allowed Tocqueville to nuance his conception of a democratic culture with traditionalist tones. He made a special point of claiming that his usage represented "the meaning which the ancients had attached to the word *mores*."[91] The "habits of the heart," as Tocqueville called the *moeurs* of engrained feelings and sentiments, constituted only one part of his meaning.[92] *Moeurs* were also represented by "habits of the mind." These included current opinions as well as the "*ensemble* of intellectual and moral beliefs of a people," the most crucial of which were religious; next in importance were those imparted through public instruction.[93] In a society of free individuals, who were often separated from the influence of family and native community, religion furnished the most effective restraint upon democratic passions and ambitions.[94] The family in general and women in particular played the major roles in transmitting the influence of religion. *Moeurs* mediated the effects of individualism and equality, which, despite their apparent opposites, encouraged a drift toward privatism. The regime of general equality meant that there was no "natural" class that could legitimately claim the role of defending society and individuals from the state; the reign of individualism with its corollary of self-interest meant that few would care to accept that role. *Moeurs* served to counteract the influence of egoism; they were at the center of the political education that Americans received; and they shaped the culture, political and communal, for the practice of liberty. In this respect they did not operate solely as external signs, signifying appropriate behavior or the right understanding; they were deeply internalized as well. According to Tocqueville, the "hardly noticeable power" of lawyers, for example, "envelops the whole, penetrating into each of the classes which compose society, working secretly, operating ceaselessly on a society unaware of it, and eventually models it according to its desires."[95]

The careful and sustained attention that Tocqueville gave to *moeurs*, as well as the extraordinary powers he attributed to them, were dictated, one might even say were swelled, by the magnitude of the problems they were meant to remedy: they confronted not only the excesses inherent in democracy or the antipolitical tendencies inherent in the rival culture of self-interest and individualism, but they were expected to counteract the powerful influence of the complex of elements that Tocqueville identified as the "social condition." The latter represented the main source of his fears.

## XV

> *In order to understand the legislation and* moeurs *of a people, one has to begin by studying its social condition.*
>
> Tocqueville[96]

Underlying *moeurs* themselves was this more fundamental social determinant that promoted further democratization. "The social condition is usually the product of circumstances, sometimes of laws, most often a combination of the two; but once it has come into existence, it may itself be considered as the prime cause of most of the laws, customs, and ideas which control the behavior of nations; what it does not produce, it modifies."[97]

The most important thing to be said about the "social condition" of Americans, Tocqueville noted, was that it was "eminently democratic." He was referring not to equality of rights or equal citizenship but to a democratic "social" state in which wealth, "mental endowments," and opinions all gravitated toward "a certain middling standard." This meant that democracy in its egalitarian mode suffused society.[98] In illustrating the thoroughgoing effects of the combination of laws and circumstances, Tocqueville cited the effects produced by early American legislation abolishing primogeniture, the right of inheritance assigned exclusively to the firstborn male. What was striking was not so much the exaggerated effects he ascribed to the legislation as the impassioned tirade that the whole subject itself aroused in him. He interpreted that prohibition as the deathblow to the establishment of an American aristocracy as well as a powerful encouragement to social atomization. Laws of inheritance, he declared, have "an unbelievable influence" over the social condition of a people. They cast their influence over generations unborn as they parcel out power and property and promote equality. The laws abolishing primogeniture "grind up or smash everything in the way and pulverize it into a pile of fine and shifting dust and that is the foundation for democracy."[99]

Clearly the abolition of primogeniture was a sensitive subject for one whose class had suffered confiscation and worse from the revolutionaries of the past century. It aroused resentments that were always just below the surface. Such legislation, he insisted, dissolves the ties between generations and undermines the unity of the family because "land no longer represents the family."[100] It simultaneously dehistoricizes, levels, and encourages a self-centered individualism. "It has destroyed the last trace of ranks and of hereditary distinctions and has everywhere imposed one level."[101] In contrast, where primogeniture rules, "the family represents the land, the land represents the family; it perpetuates its name, its origins, its glory, its power, its virtues. It is an imperishable testimony to the past, and a precious surety of an existence yet to come."[102]

The American social condition, then, is one characterized by extreme equality and disconnection. There "the work of destruction" has been virtually completed. Its effects can be seen in a wide range of social phenomena: in the equality of wealth, learning, and education; in the fact that everyone works and that science is pursued as a practical trade; and that large numbers "share virtually the same notions about religion, history, science, political economy, legislation, and government."[103] "Thus in its social condition America presents the strangest phenomenon. The men there are closer to equality in their fortunes and intelligence, or, in other words, more nearly equal in their power than they are in any other country in the world, or than they have been in any other century in historical memory."[104]

It is easy to see why *moeurs* were second in importance only to the notion of equality. If equality functions as the providential fact around which the meaning of American democracy revolves, *moeurs* are the counterfactuals that link men together by a network of political practices and habits, modifying the effects of a society of resolute individualism whose members "are indifferent and treat one another as strangers. Aristocracy links all citizens, from peasant to king, into one long chain. Democracy breaks the chain and sets each link apart."[105]

Tocqueville thus began the line of theoretical speculation that associated modernity with atomization and proposed the paradox that the greater the degree of individualism, the more the homogenization; the more the homogenization, the greater the loneliness.

Accordingly, *moeurs* serve as equality's therapeutic and democracy's essential *paideia*. All of Tocqueville's hopes concerning the possibility of educating democracy, of exploiting its advantages and offsetting its dangers, depended first and foremost on the complex of elements that *moeurs* represented.[106] *Moeurs* represented the informal curriculum of basic skills necessary to the political education of the democratic citizen. But, for Tocqueville, their crucial political function was to envelop the conception and practice of rights. The liberal idea of natural rights, which pictured the individual as owning rights independently of society, and the democratic idea, which extended equal rights to all, were redefined in the contextual character supplied by *moeurs.* Thus, Tocqueville claimed, at the same time that the American is taught that he is the possessor of political rights, he is also taught that he should respect the rights of others and the authority of magistrates: rights thus were modulated from their individualistic starting point to a social conception that takes account of others.[107]

Tocqueville's conception of *moeurs* was aristocratic, not in the class or status sense of that term, but in the sense in which the notion of an ancient, hereditary aristocracy belonged to a larger family of premodern conceptions that shared, as their most crucial element, a certain corporateness that worked against atomism. The political expression of that corporateness Tocqueville called "communal liberty." "It is the continuous action of laws and of *moeurs,* circumstances, and especially of time which helps to consolidate it."[108]

*Moeurs* thus imparted a Burkean dimension to America. They were the means of readmitting history and tradition into a political society short on both. As Tocqueville emphasized, their transmission, absorption, and application demanded "time": they were not the work of a day, nor could they be encapsulated in a few rational precepts. Political habits literally "take" time: they take it from the rounds of private life. In their furthest reach *moeurs* were the essential strands of a distinct civilization in which all shared certain basic ideas so strongly that they had crystallized into habits. "Civilization is the result of a prolonged social endeavor which occurs in the same place and has different generations transmitting it to those which follow."[109] But like the other entries in the vocabulary of aristocracy—inequality, history, intermediate bodies, social rituals—habits, traditions, and manners possessed a certain irregularity, an uncodifiability, that presented obstacles to what Tocqueville called "uniformizing" tendencies. They served not only to civil-ize democracy, but their lack of concise definition made them an invaluable ally in resisting the centralized state. The crucial question left outstanding was whether *moeurs* and their allied notions—manners, traditions—could survive the heightened tempos of modernity. If both a traditional society and a democratic society needed time for cultural practices to take hold, would a democratic culture prove any more impervious than a traditional one to the corrosive effects of rapid change? What had an emerging culture of change to do with a culture of *moeurs,* or a democratic society with a modernizing one?

The easy answer is that change itself is a culture and that modern democracy is its congenial political form. Tocqueville would view the Negro slave and the Indian as belonging to the same ill-fated company as the aristocrat, those whom modern history first makes remote, then exotic or incredible. They were testimony that a culture of change is also a culture of loss.

Change is rhetoric's euphemism for the work of power in its various forms—of direction or policy, of intellectual excellence, of moral guidance and spiritual authority, of wealth. Change signifies the establishing of new conditions favorable to the production of power and its exercise by the representatives of the new. What democracy stands to lose to modernity and to its attempts to scientize power are the practices of participation and their context of social equality. These appear as hindrances to the operative conditions required by the forms of power that had previously been viewed as anathema. The task of culture, accordingly, is to devise categories that will discredit the "hinderers" and hindrances (e.g., as ineffectual or irrational) and, simultaneously, will legitimate the new powers and their bearers. The striking quality of high modern powers, soon to become evident, would be the absence of *moeurs*, of the practices of the received, among the cultural conditions deemed necessary to the efficient production and effective exercise of the new powers.

# CHAPTER XI
# FEUDAL AMERICA

## I

Unintentionally and reluctantly *Democracy in America* reveals an America in political crisis. In the early decades of the nineteenth century Americans were actively challenging, and in 1861 would eventually overthrow, the political legacy of the Founders and dispute the classic ideology of the *Federalist.* Tocqueville had not come to America to investigate that crisis, yet he became deeply fascinated and troubled by it. He had witnessed an America during a prolonged debate about collective identity and he came close to writing a book on that subject. He did devote the last chapter of the first volume to that crisis, and it is by far the longest of any in *Democracy*, composing nearly one-fourth of that volume.

The crisis over secession and slavery eventually led to the Civil War and the dissolution of the Union. It was one of several concurrent crises, each a variation on the theme of member: dismemberment, membership, and remembering.

It was a crisis in the state: in doubt was the ability of Americans to preserve and develop the institutions of central authority that the Founders had set out to establish over the member states. The complex system attempted simultaneously to divide and limit the powers of the national government (federalism, separation of powers, and checks and balances) while establishing an effective central authority *and* preventing it from becoming the instrument of majority rule.

Further, there was a crisis in the concept and practice of membership in a democracy. Whether slavery was to be perpetuated or abolished, either course held far-reaching implications. One course would mean incorporating into the body politic a distinct but enslaved people, which, in the eyes of dominant opinion, North and South, lacked a political culture or, in Tocqueville's notion, the mores of liberty. The other course meant perpetuating a standing contradiction to the American public philosophy of freedom and equality. Either way, the notion of a body politic capable of integrating radical differences, let alone celebrating them, seemed destined to give way and to settle for a condition in which the Union was a formal, juridical entity legitimating a strong state.

Finally, there was a crisis in national identity as it related to the symbolism of the Founding. The meaning of the national portrait in *Democracy* was that the machinery of 1789 was not operating according to design and that the great project of creating a national political culture had faltered. Given these various crises, Tocqueville's main conception, the development of democracy as equality, suffered from both exaggeration and underemphasis. Far from being the widely pervasive fact of American social life or widely shared norm he insisted upon, equality was a deeply contested issue that would lead to the destruction of the Union and, despite the outcome of the Civil War, to the perpetuation of racism as a social fact. By the end of the twentieth century Tocqueville's confident claim, that "one cannot foresee the time when permanent inequality of condition could be established in the new world," had become problematic.[1] Tocqueville's recognition of the pervasiveness of racism in Jacksonian America and his doubts that it could be eradicated presented him with a difficult tactical problem. Given the persistence of slavery and a slave-owning "aristocracy," how could America be represented as a democracy? And how could localism be recommended as the best hope for a moderate democracy when localism harbored the most stubborn defenders of slavery? And in those circumstances was a weak national government a blessing?

Given his political objectives of explaining how egalitarianism had been moderated and liberty preserved and extended, Tocqueville had to contain the crisis within the chapter. To do otherwise, to elevate the problematic status of nationhood in the United States into a major theme, would have cast doubts upon those positive features of American democracy which he had highlighted in order to reassure his anxious and skeptical countrymen. At the same time, however, the anomaly represented by the southern states strongly affected Tocqueville, which, while it made him uncertain about the future of the Union, paradoxically elicited from him an unexpected positive democratic sympathy.

## II

> *The middle ages were a fractious era. Each people, each province, each city, each family was strongly inclined to assert its individuality. In our day a contrary tendency is evident as people seem to march toward unity.*
>
> Tocqueville[2]

Measured by the aspirations of its Founding Fathers, America appeared in Tocqueville's rendering as only a qualified success and, by certain of their most cherished hopes, a failure. It had a "powerless and passive State,"[3] a

Jacksonian mob, and ardent zealots for nullification who appeared undeterred by the possibility of a dismembered Union. Contrary to the Founders' hopes, the defining fact about governance in America turned out to be not the steady consolidation of a centered political nation but an arrested development with regressive elements reminiscent of the anticentrism of the Articles of Confederation. Instead of the choice of representative government, which the *Federalist* had championed, the system portrayed by Tocqueville was the one its authors had denigrated.

In writing his *Old Regime* Tocqueville would exhume a feudal society in prerevolutionary France and discover a quasi-democratic politics. But in *Democracy* he identified quasi-feudal elements within a democratic order of things: a lively politics of small-scale, fierce provincial loyalties, a strong sense of local citizenship, dispersed power, an "aristocracy of the bench and bar," a rural rather than an intellectualized religiosity, a profusion of political associations and voluntary groups, and a weak central authority. To a very great extent, much of the first volume of *Democracy* combines discovery with puzzlement over a society without a state. Most of the aspects of American democracy that found favor with Tocqueville shared the common quality of being, in his eyes, in accord with aristocracy's historic struggles and defeat by monarchy. His "feudalism" appears at its most tortured—and suggestive—when he discusses the American "federal government." In trying to unravel the puzzle of American federalism, Tocqueville complained that "the human mind invents things more easily than words."[4] Admitting defeat, he concluded that "the new word which ought to express the new thing does not yet exist" and settled for the idea of "an incomplete national government."[5] Those elements of American politics that he singled out approvingly formed a progression starting with the decentralization of power and administration, the "spirit of locality," the entrenched powers (especially in matters of taxation) of state and municipal governments, and the strength of the jury system; then proceeding to a corporate quality as expressed in the profusion of political and private associations and in the lofty status of lawyers, judges, the law itself, and the predominantly local character of economic life; and culminating in the pervasive influence of religion on all aspects of American life, public and domestic.

The luster of American newness was thus being dimmed by the premodern categories that Tocqueville applies to its democratic institutions. At times his America, especially in its New England idyll, appears more like a lost political world than a preview of the future. His opposition to postrevolutionary modernity was expressed most strongly in a preoccupation to the point of obsession with perpetuating the mediating instruments between local existence and "higher" authorities, with the institutions and associations that opposed, deflected, or modified the aggrandizements of a concentrated authority. In a democracy that concentration was potentially present in the doctrine of the sovereignty of the people and the supremacy of the majority. But Tocqueville suggested that when democratic energies are localized and "customized," the effect is to eviscerate the nation-scale democracy implied in majority rule or popular sovereignty. By local democracy the people temper their own power—in effect, silently dissolving as one corporate body. "The people," that compacted unity which Tocqueville dreaded, is thus safely dispersed into the everyday activities of diverse kinds of self-government. "The municipal bodies and the county administrations form so many hidden breakwaters which check or part the flow of the popular will."[6]

## III

The decentered corporativism that Tocqueville attributed to the new nation provides good reason to reconsider his famous aphorism, that the success of American democracy was due in great measure to the fact that it was established without having to combat the carry-overs from a feudal past as had the European revolutionaries.[7] To be sure, Tocqueville did in fact assert that America had no feudal past to eradicate. Contrary to that assertion, however, his theory disclosed something even more striking, that America had a feudal present and, moreover, its feudal elements provided the basis for commending American democracy to his countrymen. Historically the presence of a strongly entrenched feudalism had been synonymous with a weak central administration, with an "incomplete national government." While this combination may have been cause for Tocqueville's claim that the French could learn from the American example, it was precisely the combination of southern plantation feudalism and an "incomplete" national government that would make secession possible and civil war near interminable.

By "feudalism" I do not mean that Tocqueville's America was a fantasist's representation of a mediaeval "society of fealties" replete with a hereditary social structure, hierarchical system of reciprocal rights and duties between lords and vassals, a manorial economy based on serfdom, and a universal moral and ecclesiastical authority. Although some plausible parallels could be drawn between the slaveholding "planter society" of the antebellum South and a feudal economy, a possibility not lost upon some of the southern apologists for slavery,[8] Tocqueville's feudalism expressed itself in the representation of dispersed power, a loose political system in which the most significant units—in terms of power, loyalties, and active individual involvement—were local in character, hence far smaller than the nation-state.[9]

Although Althusius and Montesquieu were exceptions, modern political theorists were typically distinguished by their abhorrence of dispersed power. A "scattered people" was, as the story of the Tower of Babel had taught, a weak people, the equivalent of a dismembered body politic. Machiavelli singled out for praise Theseus, the legendary founder of Athens, for having gathered together a dispersed people.[10] When advising a new prince about what he must do to retain power over cities formerly free, his advice was "to disunite or disperse them" (*disuniscono o dissipano*).[11]

During his travels Tocqueville frequently remarked on the absence of a controlling center in American political society and the exhilarating effects it had in encouraging individuals to initiate undertakings that a European assumed belonged to the province of the state. Hobbes's theory had been one sustained effort to contain such centripetal forms of social power by vesting in the sovereign a complete monopoly of legitimate political power. He compared "factions" and "unlawful corporations," whether "gypsies," "papists," or trading monopolies, to "Wens, Biles, and Apostemes engendered by the unnatural conflux of evill humours."[12] In contrast, Tocqueville was moved to pronounce "the most important concern of a good government should be to accustom its people gradually to doing without it."[13] Local autonomy, in the form of "provincial" and "communal liberty," was vital to "national greatness and prosperity."[14]

The crucial element in Tocqueville's feudalism was aristocracy. Aristocracy is represented as the instinctive opposition to any form of massed power, monarchical or popular. Although the pride or confidence of self-worth natural to aristocrats prevented them from coalescing their powers, it made them adversaries of rulers who tried to monopolize power and honors.[15] Tocqueville, himself a lawyer, found an aristocratic counterpart secreted in America in the values, outlook, and functions of lawyers and judges. "Hidden at the bottom of the soul of legists is something of the tastes and habits of the aristocracy." They have a natural contempt for the multitude and form a "corps" that is opposed to "the revolutionary spirit." They prize "order" and "authority"; they have "a liking and respect for what is *ancien*" and they make a ritual of following "the legal decisions of their fathers."[16]

The American penchant for abandonment of family and birthplace signified a distinctively modern society dominated by discontinuity rather than "based" on its opposite. Tocqueville's ascription of a guild character to the American lawyers, together with the introduction of feudal/aristocratic mythemes, was part of a strategy for introducing an element of historicity into a new, ahistorical society. Practices and institutions extended over generations and social groups that drew their identity and power from continuities were modes of resistance to modernity. In Tocqueville's account of America the Puritans assume special significance precisely because they were historical beings who brought the political ideas and practices of the Old World to a prehistorical, natural land. No more than the aristocracy of the Old World were they portrayed as faultless—Tocqueville was aware of the harshness and bigotry of the early colonists. They were redeemed in his eyes because they represented not the new joining the new but, instead, archaic survivals, not only in their piety and discipline but in their democratic political practices.

Paradoxically, insofar as his democracy is political, it is potentially an archaism. It rubs against the grain of a New World inclined toward unpolitical concerns and the severing of elemental connections that hindered the pursuit of happiness.

## IV

> *I am firmly convinced that an aristocracy cannot be founded anew in the world; but I think that by associating ordinary citizens can constitute very rich bodies, very influential and very strong, in other words, an aristocratic being.*
>
> *In this way one could gain many of the greatest political advantages of aristocracy without its injustices or dangers.*
>
> Tocqueville[17]

Tocqueville's archaism was more an ontological than a genealogical category. In singling out judges, local institutions, and the mediating associations of civil society, he represents them as theoretically rather than historically connected to institutions of an earlier era. Judicial institutions and political associations were participants in the mythematic form of which aristocracy was the defining element. Aristocracy stands only partly for a social class distinguished by special privileges; it is also the perduring (and idealized) representation of distinctiveness, antimaterialism, and diffused power. Aristocracy thereby manages to survive its demise as a political class but only by being cast in an antidemocratic role without making clear what stake democracy had in tolerating, let alone defending, its other. However, were a class to emerge whose power and wealth contradicted the democratic principle of equality, should it be viewed as the legitimate heir of aristocracy or as a mere pretender? In the second volume of *Democracy* Tocqueville opined that if aristocracy were to reappear in a democracy, it would be in the form of the industrialists; yet he could not bring himself to admit that they had anything in common with preceding aristocracies. They were "*un monstre*" among aristocracies. Nonetheless, they did not present a danger to democracy and for the same reason that they did not qualify as a genuine aristocracy. They were insufficiently feudal.[18] They displayed a lack of "a corporate spirit" among themselves and a callous disregard for the welfare of those dependent on them. Tocqueville cautioned, however, that if social inequalities were to increase significantly, the threat posed by the new class would justify reconsideration.[19]

Tocqueville's "archaic sensibility" was partly a class inheritance and partly the intellectual influence of Montesquieu.[20] But, as we have noted, the comparisons and contrasts he makes between democracy and aristocracy or feudalism serve both perceptual and strategic ends in his theory of democracy: the latter could only be "seen"—that is, truly understood—in juxtaposition to the former and hence "depends" upon it politically as well as methodologically. Because democracy is the Many, the undifferentiated, it so thoroughly dominates and oppresses all that is within political space, it can only be understood—and combatted—by introducing a contrast from the "outside." The most striking use of feudal elements to illuminate/combat democracy occurs in the penultimate chapter to volume I, "The Main Causes Tending to Maintain a Democratic Republic in the United States." There Tocqueville momentarily transcends America in order to work out on a purely theoretical plane his main lesson about what made for a moderate democracy. He concentrates on presenting two tableaux: one recreates a past, the other forecasts a future. At that level, unencumbered either by the demands of empirical exactness regarding America or by specific references to French history or politics, the feudal tendencies emerge more openly.

The first tableau might be labeled "feudal monarchy." It represented the prerevolutionary regime and was designed to show how society, conceived as a political constitution distinct from the state, could restrain absolutism and thereby avert revolution. It was a theoretical representation of a structure that had proved effective in combatting central authority by the means available to an undemocratized society. This tableau was not presented as a precise description of the institutions of any particular historical period, although Tocqueville clearly thought it depicted realities of the French past. It was an abstract creation located in an equally abstract, constructed "past." Tocqueville wants to show, as his mentor Montesquieu had, how a monarchy that is absolute in theory can be controlled in practice if its power is mediated by a wide array of autonomous institutions. According to his account, "The blows of its authority were softened" and "the spirit of resistance preserved" by "the prerogatives of the nobility, the authority of sovereign courts, the rights of corporations or the privileges of provinces." Although those institutions of corporate freedom, Tocqueville conceded, often worked against individual freedom, they nonetheless kept alive the love of communal liberty. The constitution of that regime also contained other "barriers" to absolutism, less publicized but equally powerful. They were "religion, the affection of the subjects, the benevolence of the prince, honor, spirit of family, the prejudices of the provinces, custom, and public opinion." These contained royal authority within an "invisible circle" of habits and customs.[21]

Tocqueville presents his feudal monarchy as a heuristic device for understanding the democratic present. His assumption was that the kind of present that exists is most clearly revealed through its opposite, aristocracy, because the condition for the existence of the present had been the historical destruction of democracy's other. The claim that is being made is that absolutism of the past possesses some important similarities with a possible despotism in the future and that a future despotism could no more be effectively combatted by unadulterated democracy than had the despotisms of the past by purely aristocratic means. At the same time, the idea of "feudal monarchy" reflected the same sort of tensions as his "incomplete State": the incongruous combination of elements of centralization and decentralization. Bearing in mind that during the 1830s France was a monarchy, albeit a constitutional one of sorts, feudal monarchy served as a veiled suggestion not for a reversion to feudalism but for an "incomplete State" with its combination of democratic elements tempered by functional equivalents for feudalism.

The second tableau depicts the stark opposite of feudal monarchy: the wholly anomic condition that follows upon revolution. Royal honor has ceased, the nobility has virtually disappeared, "all classes are jumbled together," municipal and provincial liberties have been lost, and "there is no common bond not even among a *score* of people."[22] It is the return to a kind of primal chaos, the undifferentiated condition that is the preliminary to despotism. What is it, then, that prevents the slide into the abyss? What is it in America that succeeds in limiting a people whose individualism is fed by a situation that encourages a sense of limitlessness? What except myth has been the typical response to chaos?

## V

Elements of the first tableau were retrieved and preserved in Tocqueville's reconstruction of America. The thematic of that reconstruction might be described as "the feudalization of America." Its pre/antimodern spirit is best represented by the way in which he introduces American religion or, better, American religiosity as one of the principal supports of the "democratic republic in the United States." "The eighteenth-century philosophes," he wrote, "had a very simple explanation" for the expected decline of religious enthusiasm: once freedom and enlightenment were spread, religious beliefs would weaken. Tocqueville then remarks maliciously that "it is boring but the facts do not at all agree with the theory." He recalls that upon arriving in America "it was the religious atmosphere of the country that I found most striking."[23] Americans were free, enlightened, *and* religious.

Tocqueville wanted, however, to do more than persuade his countrymen that religion and democracy could coexist, more even than that religion was the essential inhibitory ingredient in democratic self-restraint. He undertook to demonstrate that the influence of religion in America rivaled that of pre-Enlightenment Europe, without, however, reproducing the resentments of "a religion of the State," which had provoked French revolutionaries into dissolving the religious establishment. He was thus proposing a revisionist view of the political role of religion. Americans were depicted as being constrained by an all-pervasive spiritual power without a state-controlled religious establishment. "America is still the place where the Christian religion has retained the greatest real power over souls. . . . [B]y regulating *moeurs* and by regulating the family it helps to regulate the State."[24] In Europe, he noted, "nearly all social disorders" are traceable to the family and "the nuptial bed."[25]

Tocqueville's depiction of religion in America was a political construction rather than a historical description. He pays virtually no attention to the crucial matter of church governance, or to specific articles of faith or ceremony, or to the enforcement of discipline. He appears only slightly acquainted with the evangelical fervor of "great awakenings." His religion is constructed as akin to an ideology or a set of internalized cultural restraints. It was not so important, he noted, that "citizens prefer the true religion as that they profess a religion."[26]

Tocqueville looked upon religion in America in much the same objectifying way that ruling groups had in the past, as a means of restraining the Many, with the crucial difference that in this case the Many were not the dominated and excluded but the sovereign majority. Because in theory it was sovereign, the majority had to be made inhibited in its passions, even in its sexual appetites.[27] In Tocqueville's account the political influence of religion persuades the sovereign people to deny its own powers, to be the name that does not know its strength.

Institutionalized religions in America, Catholic as well as Protestant, appeared to Tocqueville to have attained the advantages of a premodern religious establishment minus its disadvantages. They dispensed moral influence without accumulating political power. The representatives of American churches supported freedom yet remained committed to religion's traditional role of defending order, which in the modern age meant accepting the separation of church and state and relinquishing any political ambitions.[28] American Catholics, he averred, were the most republican and democratic of all.

The priesthood aside, Catholicism, he contended in an argument increasingly strained, is naturally congenial toward democracy: it levels all men toward a plane of equality, more so than Protestantism which "inclines men less toward equality than independence."[29]

Clearly these emphases upon the reconciliation of religion and politics were intended primarily for a readership whose society had been wracked for centuries by conflicts between church and state over fundamental matters of loyalty, jurisdiction, and revenues. Clearly, too, Tocqueville was using America to mediate that conflict by showing that it was possible for a democracy to live in harmony with religion and for religion to be a major force in the moral life of society. The last thing he wanted to import from America was the religious analogue of Cartesianism: private judgment, subjectivity, and the political analogue of individualism.

## VI

> *Among the laws which rule human societies, there is one which seems more precise and evident than all the others. If human beings are to remain or become civilized, it is necessary that the art of association is developed and perfected in the same degree that equality of condition increases.*
>
> Tocqueville[30]

Tocqueville's "feudal" sensibility brought his greatest theoretical discovery in America: the myriad of ad hoc associations spontaneously organized by citizens for a variety of public purposes, from matters of education and roads to concerting influence on behalf of moral causes (temperance), social reform (abolition of slavery), or economic aims (tariff rates). Political associations were likened to "large, free schools where all citizens come to learn the general theory of associations."[31] "The free action of the collective power of individuals," as he called the phenomenon, was declared critical to resisting the tyranny of the majority as well as the trend toward centralization. In this respect he found it analogous to "the secondary bodies" that had served as buffers against the centralizing power of the old monarchy.[32] Significantly, under political associations Tocqueville included state and local governments, calling them "permanent associations."

Tocqueville's praise for associations marked an important difference with the view of feudalism and associations set out in the *Federalist.* Hamilton described "feudal anarchy" in virtually the same terms as a centralizing monarch of the seventeenth and eighteenth centuries might have: as "continual opposition to the authority of the sovereign."[33] Hamilton and Madison attempted to identify the system of the Articles of Confederation with feudalism, but they also suggested that an element of feudalism had been perpetuated in the new constitution by the broad powers reserved to the separate states. The reason for that, they conceded, was that, like feudalism, local powers, at least for the present, had a stronger hold on the affections of the people than a remote central government.[34] The *Federalist*'s animus against feudalism closed off a possible exploration of the positive role of associations, just as Tocqueville's archaic sensibility led to an opening of that possibility and eventually to a defense of associations in their own right, independent of feudal overtones.

Although in the first volume of *Democracy* he tended to feudalize what the Founders had federalized, in the second volume associations transcend the feudal and are praised for bringing men out of themselves by teaching them the need to subordinate themselves to others and to join in common actions.[35] Tocqueville's fundamental point is that the experience of political associations would be carried over into private associations and thereby reduce "the perils of liberty." Thus private associations are viewed as a somewhat mixed blessing, as suggested by the favorable view of them taken by the state: they divert attention from public affairs and drain off discontents.[36]

The emphasis throughout much of the first volume of *Democracy* leaves the impression that political life in the states and localities has a natural vigor that contrasts sharply with the ineffectiveness of the central government. "The sovereignty of the states envelopes each citizen, in a variety of ways, and affects every detail of daily life."[37] The national government's claims to sovereignty are, he declared, those of "an abstract entity," "a work of art . . . huge and distant," which evokes only "a vague and ill-defined sentiment." In contrast, the sovereignty of the individual states was "natural."[38]

Tocqueville similarly feudalized the press and political associations, treating them as elements in a general dispersion of power that mitigated and offset the effects of an egalitarian social condition and of the massed power potentially present in the doctrines of popular sovereignty and majority rule. Although he recognized that a good part of the agitation over tariffs was attributable to the press and to associations and that it served to fan secessionist sentiments, he argued that the sheer proliferation of newspapers and associations minimized their demagogic effects.

Tocqueville was particularly fascinated by newspapers, not only for the ease with which they could be established in America but because, by nurturing a decentered politics, they helped to discourage the type of political and cultural monopoly that the intellectuals of eighteenth-century Paris had exerted over the French aristocracy:

> The United States has no dominant capitol; both enlightenment and power are diffused into all parts of this vast country; the rays of human intelligence, instead of

> radiating from a common center, cross each other in every direction; Americans have not fixed the general direction of thought, any more than public affairs, in one place.[39]

## VII

Tocqueville's discussion of association has been much admired by later commentators who have seen it as a confirmation of the values of "American pluralism" and as the logical extension of the argument first developed by James Madison in *Federalist*, no. 10. However, that interpretation undervalues Tocqueville's originality by obscuring the extent to which his analysis subverted that of Madison's. It fails to recognize that Tocqueville's "pluralism" originated in an archaic sensibility rather than from a perspective that accepts interest in politics as natural. That sensibility is feudal and anti-individualistic. For that reason it takes issue with an influential modern tradition that categorized associations as expressions of "faction" and, as such, conspiracies against the "common good." Although Madison, like Tocqueville, was eager to use "factions" to splinter majorities into impotence, he had not conceived of them as barriers against the state but the reverse: the national government was to withstand the "pressures" of faction. Nor did Madison see any participatory value to spontaneous organizations of citizens, or any contribution to the development of a civic personality. Tocqueville regarded associations as a valuable way of connecting people by overcoming some effects of individualism; Madison, in contrast, valued them for the disconnections and antagonisms they nurtured, which made a majority "unable to concert and carry into effect schemes of oppression."[40] What remained unexplained by Tocqueville's account of associations was how a society in the grip of egalitarianism nonetheless managed to produce diverse associations that checked each other and the state.

# CHAPTER XII MAJORITY RULE OR MAJORITY POLITICS

## I

*Democracy is rule directed to the advantage of the poorer classes.*
Aristotle[1]

*But above all of the institutions and outside of all of the forms [of American political society] there resides a sovereign power, that of the people, which can destroy or modify them according to its will.*
Tocqueville[2]

One of the great mythemes in *Democracy* is the appearance of the people as full-fledged political actors continuously involved in the exercise of power and in deliberations about the well-being of their communities. Instead of politics being the medium for acts by outstanding individuals or a tiny "band of brothers," it was action that was political even though no one "stood out." Before the extraordinary achievement of ordinary beings could be recognized, certain traditional assumptions had to be, if not discarded, at least suspended. The American achievement, by Tocqueville's reckoning, was to demonstrate that in its politics democracy might at least approximate a level of disinterestedness that qualified it as a genuinely political regime. But what exactly was a *democratic* politics? How was it to be practiced and by what means?

Beginning in antiquity theorists had typically defined democracy as a form of the political by which the people ruled for their own advantage.[3] If that definition was a commonplace, it was invariably stated with a certain awkwardness. Most theorists believed that a democratic political was self-contradictory.[4] The political concerned what was right, good, or proper for the whole of society, and that could only be discerned by those who could claim long experience and training in military, diplomatic, or legal matters. Aristotle was so certain that democracy was inherently incapable of grasping the political that he argued there could never be a "good" democracy because its rule would be biased in favor of the poor. The only thing to recommend democracy, he declared, was that it was incapable of great harm.[5] The animus against democracy was expressed as contempt for mere numbers and as admiration for distinctions of prowess, knowledge, and lineage, which democracy must necessarily discriminate against if it sought to promote equality in general and the interests of the poor in particular.[6]

From its first appearance in ancient Athens, democracy signified an invasion and takeover of the modes of action that "naturally" belonged to aristocrats and men of wealth. Its politics began in grievances, in class conflicts, in protests about the use of political power by those of high birth and great wealth to favor their kind. It crystallized in demands for political equality that eventually democratized the major institutions (such as assemblies, executive councils, and juries) and the eligibility requirements for office and voting. These were seen as the substantive means by which the people could act and exercise power and, in the process, "realize" the form of democracy.

What practices were established for such a rough-and-tumble politics? Did they promote democracy or attenuate it? Athenian democracy developed the practice of depending upon "leaders" who, in turn, employed the arts of rhetoric to "persuade" assemblies and juries, compete with rivals, and "lead" the citizenry.[7] Thus while democracy invented citizen participation and the practice of public debates, it paralleled and intersected these with the invention of a politics of politicians and "followers" that promoted a rhetorical democracy of speakers and listeners, of the Few who structured the issues under discussion and the Many who decided them.

On its face, the greater inclusiveness of democracy, although far from complete, seemed to be more consonant with the idea of the political as the common good than did regimes based on elites.[8] In fact, however, the efforts at democratizing power regularly provoked conflict and opposition, suggesting that democrats, too, were capable of unfairness. This seemed confirmed by the further fact that neither the democrats nor their opponents developed a conception, much less a practice, that acknowledged the legitimacy of "opposition." Defeat might mean exile, banishment, or proscription for those who had lost. However, as Thucydides' striking descriptions of public assemblies show, opposition could take the form of engaging in public debates about proposed policies or laws without suffering reprisal.

Although it would be an exaggeration to describe these developments as "party politics," it could be said to be their omen. The theoretical question posed by the recurrence of opposition was not whether it was fully legitimated but rather: what did opposition, division, and contest mean for the assumption that a political society formed a whole? What was/is the democratic significance implied by the presence of organized partisanship? Is partisanship merely social differences now finding expression as a consequence of greater freedom and participation? Or is it an implicit, although unformulated, challenge to the holistic conception of the political? What kind of political is it that partisanship aspires to, one that is simply embodied in neutral rules of the game? What kind of neutrality is possible in the context of partisanship—Hegel's combination of monarchy and bureaucratic rationality or Hamilton's of a president and skilled but unelected officials?

## II

There was no democratic polity in Europe from roughly the end of the fourth century B.C.E. until the French Revolution but there was a significant historical experience of a new form of divisiveness. The religious struggles that began in sixteenth-century Europe and continued throughout much of the next century introduced a novel—and explosive—element into the politics of that era: the injection of systematic "beliefs" into a politics that heretofore had mostly concerned class conflicts, rivalries among elite families, or dynastic ambitions. During the English civil wars of the 1640s ideas about democracy and religion—about, that is, forms of popular belief—began to intermingle and to shape the politics of democracy and to enlarge its identity, from being primarily a protest against material injustice and political inequality to becoming a symbolic form, a vessel of the truth. Although the concept of "ideology" did not become current until the mid-nineteenth century, it was clear that already "idea" and "belief" had combined to produce the phenomenon of large numbers of individuals from the "lower ranks" of society motivated (later they would be said to be mobilized) by common convictions into acting to promote them, if necessary by political revolution.[9] They became, at risk, agents of the immaterial, a role previously reserved for priests, philosophers, and kings by divine right.

Although there were strong anticipations during the English civil wars, the first modern conception of the people as developed actors is found in John Locke's *Treatise of Government.* It stands as a bench mark, not because subsequent writers adopted his formulas but because both in his omissions and in his emphases he sketched out the stakes. Locke's contribution was to rescue the notion of the people from the opprobrium of a destructive mob whose only modes of action were revolutionary violence and expropriation of private property and to put in its stead a theory of majority rule, which, potentially, could become annexed to a democratic politics. More precisely, he introduced a comprehensive conception of the majority that expanded it beyond the episodic: Locke's majority was, successively, a constituent power, a form of rule, and a revolutionary actor. In his ideological justification of the revolution of 1688, Locke had not only made the majority the central political actor but he had gone further. By connecting the idea of "the" majority with the idea of ruling in a parliamentary system based on free elections, he normalized the idea later postrevolutionary writers would most fear, of a revolutionary mass transmuting into a ruling majority.

In its first appearance Locke's majority materializes as representing the sovereign will of society at the crucial moment when political society is instituted according to the terms of a contract. Crucially, in the Lockean myth the first action that men would take in deciding to exchange the state of nature for civil society is not to agree to a contract but rather to agree to be bound by the decisions of a majority. The constituent majority does not disappear, however; it is held in reserve as a revolutionary force ready to act in the event of a constitutional crisis provoked by the threat of tyranny.[10]

Locke's majority is a provocative mixture of might and right. When men consented to "*make one* community," their action signified that "the *Majority* have a right to act and conclude the rest."[11] At that moment the majority served as the sole repository of legitimating authority. The source of its own legitimacy was simply its nature as a kind of primitive force. The majority, Locke declared, signifies "a Power": it represented the preponderant force latent in precivil society, a coalescence of the physical power and goods of a majority of potential members.[12] It is "the power of the community . . . to act as one Body." The unity of action attributed to the majority was "necessary" because it was "necessary to that which is one body to move one way; it is necessary the Body should move whither the greater force carries it which is the *consent of the majority*."[13] The reason for locating the "greater force" in the majority becomes clear. The majority's role was not to be limited to formulating the terms of the contract. Majority rule, as the embodiment of consent, is the fundamental political principle and continuously operative: it is a form of rule, not an episodic intervention. The precivil majority is perpetuated through its practical representations, the majority of an electorate and the sitting majority of an elected legislature.[14]

Locke's majority principle attained its fullest and least qualified form in democracy: "The Majority having . . . upon Mens first uniting into Society, the whole power of the Community, naturally in them, may imploy all that power in making Laws for the Community from time to time, and Executing those Laws by Officers of their own appointing; and then the *Form* of the Government is a perfect *Democracy*."[15]

Thus Locke was formulating a conception of continuous majority *rule*, not merely a theory of a discontinuous majority, which like a deus ex machina suddenly materializes on the extraordinary occasion when men exchange a prepolitical condition for a political one, or when they revolt against the antipolitical condition of despotism. One might draw from Locke's argument the conclusion that because majority rule is the "perfect" expression of democracy, any deliberate limitation on majority rule was a limitation on democracy. At the same time, however, Locke had reduced democracy to a set of practices, expurgated of any trace of being the bearer of a systematic ideology. His majority, in turn, has been emptied of ideology and become an ideological cypher that might lapse into a mere convention.

## III

In the aftermath of the American and French revolutions, conservatives and moderates feared that the majority now had at its disposal the legal means of achieving revolutionary ends without having to resort to revolutionary means.[16] The origins of those fears lay in the revolutionary experiences of 1776 and 1789 when large segments of populations hitherto outside the political circle had edged closer to its center. It is well to recall that the American Revolution had become an element in the French political consciousness of the late eighteenth century and that the French Revolution, in turn, was a major source of bitter divisions of the 1790s between Jeffersonian Republicans and Federalists.[17] To the American Federalists and the French upper classes, majority rule conjured up the specter of a revolutionary populace and the imminent likelihood that majority rule would become the means of perpetuating revolution. The *Federalist* had responded by fashioning a conception of the majority as discontinuous. It attempted to use constitutional structure to drive a wedge between majority and rule and to create in the process a rhetorical politics "based" on the people rather than on actual majority governance.

For the Madison of the *Federalist*, who feared the focused might of a majority, the task was to exploit the difficulties attendant upon assembling a majority and, should it succeed in assembling and representing itself, to introduce numerous checks preventing it from being realized in legislation, or, if it should succeed, the rites of passage through successive institutions would have "filtered" out its extremisms. The barriers that Madison emphasizes, other than the vast distances, were ones that Locke had described as "the variety of Opinions and contrariety of Interests which unavoidably happen in all Collections of Men."[18] However, Locke had drawn attention to these as difficulties inherent in any attempt to gain unanimity and, therefore, a pragmatic justification for adopting the majority principle and recognizing that it "passes for the act of the whole" and therefore may exercise "the power of the whole."[19] Locke, in other words, did not look upon the multiplicity of interests and opinions as prophylactic against majority rule but rather as the justification of it, implying that it was not utopian to assume that the existence of multiplicity would not necessarily preclude a majority from being mustered in the ordinary course of politics.

In the light of later thinking about the relationship between majorities and political parties, Locke's conception of the majority encountered serious difficulties: did Locke's majority represent a monolithic formation of settled duration or was it contingent and temporary, continuously being reconstituted? When Locke discussed "the dissolution of government" by the rebellion of its subjects, he employed the phrase "the body of the people." Were the two concepts, "the people" and "the majority," synonymous, or was the former an edited version of the latter? The difficulties with the concept became apparent during the last decades of the seventeenth century when English political writers began to discuss the majority and parties. They began from an assumption that both notions referred to phenomena whose nature it was to divide the members of society into opposing or contesting groups.[20] Although the vocabulary of writers was full of references to "factions" and "parties" and those usages were most likely inspired by the divisions prominent during the recent civil wars (cavalier and roundhead, parliamentarian and royalist), it was also true that the idea of divisions was strongly influenced by the astonishing multiplication of sects during the century and by the attempts of public authorities to favor some religious groups and to persecute others.

In the second of his *Two Treatises of Government*, Locke failed to pose the question of whether majority power was limited by religious freedom and whether specific religious beliefs were a major element in the composition of the majority. His silence was surprising, not only because the issue of religion was a volatile one in the English politics that preceded the forced abdication of a Catholic king in the Glorious Revolution of 1688 but also because nearly two decades earlier he had composed a first draft of his famous *A Letter concerning Toleration.* In the published *Letter* there was no mention of majority rule, much less a conception of a compact majority will. Instead the actuality of religious diversity dominated his discussion and the danger he evoked was of state-enforced religious orthodoxy. Locke maintained that, except where politically subversive ideas were advanced under the "specious show" of religious doctrines, religious beliefs and associations should be treated as private matters.[21]

One significant consequence of removing the state from religious conflicts was to reinforce one of the oldest traditions in political thinking and one most recently maintained by the defenders of monarchy: that the state was above partisan controversies, that it was the representative of a mythic ideal of the undivided, of the common good. As such, the idea of the state as above politics seemed to demote the majority from being the representation of "the body of the people" to being simply a partisan association. When the rich religious pluralism of Locke's *Letter* is placed alongside the homogeneous majority of the second *Treatise*, the suspicion arises that the condition for the existence of the latter was the absence of the former.

Madison seized upon that possibility to argue that the great number of diverse sects and interests served to diminish the danger of majority tyranny. Madison's formulation compelled him to disavow the myth of the state as the guardian of the undivided. There was no "whole," only diverse interests and "mutual animosities" that "divided" society "into different classes, actuated by different sentiments and views." While "the principal task of modern Legislation" was to regulate "these various and interfering interests," the task itself "involves the spirit of party and faction in the necessary and ordinary operations of Government."[22] Madison's argument included economic interests in the same category as "different opinions concerning religion, concerning Government and many other points, as well of speculation as of practice."[23] Far from being a neutral guardian of the common good, the Madisonian state was explicitly committed—"as the first object of Government"—to protecting the "different and unequal faculties of acquiring property," property being "the most common and durable source of factions."[24] Thus the state would be charged with a complex mandate of protecting inequalities and diverse beliefs while ensuring equal rights—and this by a state whose neutrality was compromised from the beginning by its porosity to interests.

As historians have suggested, when eighteenth-century politicians and theorists in Britain and America confronted the phenomenon of political parties, their response, with very few exceptions, was to group parties with religious sects, especially of the fanatical sort. From that understanding one of two conclusions tended to be drawn: either that parties were dangerous and ought to be outlawed, or that diverse parties were, like religious beliefs, inevitable, "sown in the nature of man," as Madison would put it. In a free society, parties, like sects, had to be tolerated.[25] Yet in the Tenth *Federalist*, Madison was already suggesting that conflicts between proliferating varieties of property, rather than forms of belief, were the principal source of political disturbances. If that was the case then, unlike "the" majority of Locke or Rousseau's General Will, there were majorities in the United States rather than "a" majority. A majority might be one of mere numbers or of beliefs, or it might refer to local majorities in the townships, counties, and states. By Madison's own showing, "the" majority was a fiction and, at best, a temporary alliance. Even Hamilton pointed out that "many of those who form the majority on one question may become the minority on a second, and an association dissimilar to either may constitute the majority on a third."[26] The various constitutional provisions for controlling and thwarting the majority—indirect election of the Senate and the president, appointment of the Supreme Court by the president and Senate, checks and balances, and the separation of powers—were justified by attributing two particularly dangerous qualities to majorities, passion and interestedness. Because of "the impulse of sudden and violent passions," the possibility of an "unjust and interested majority" posed in Madison's eyes a continuous threat to property rights.[27]

The majority was thus the latent revolutionary force that Locke had defended as a check on tyranny, but for Madison it was a danger that had to be thwarted, even if it meant preventing or severely weakening the majority from ruling. And that was the crux of the problem which Madison's argument raised without squarely addressing. He had shown that, in view of the extraordinary diversity of sects and interests in the projected Union, there was little chance of majority tyranny; yet his contributions to the *Federalist* then proceeded from the opposite assumption, extolling all the safeguards in the new constitutional system designed to guard against majority tyranny. The conclusion, which appears inescapable, is that Madison and the other contributors to the *Federalist* were mainly concerned to block not the hobgoblin of majority tyranny but the possibility of majority rule.

By "ruling" one could mean who sets policies and national objectives; but one might also take ruling to mean who grants or withholds legitimacy from those who are "responsible" for setting policies and objectives. By the first understanding the question is who *governs*? By the second the majority may reign without ruling.

It is revealing that toward the end of his life Madison revisited the question of the nature of the majority. Before then he had severely qualified his state-oriented position in the *Federalist* by joining with Jefferson to promote the principle that a state legislature could declare a federal statute unconstitutional if it believed that the statute violated the original compact of the Constitution to which the states were the consenting parties. A local majority could thus invalidate a national majority. In 1833 Madison drafted a letter on "Majority Governments" in which he posed an even direr prospect than nullification: suppose a "constitutional majority" in the national government (i.e., Congress and the president) proceeds to pass a significant law that is strongly opposed by a "popular majority" in the nation? In that circumstance, Madison declared, the "force" of public opinion represented by the popular majority, provided "justice" is on its side, should prevail. The alternative is to amend the Constitution or "subvert" it.[28]

The difficulty to which Madison's suspicion of majorities and of parties led was that even at the end, when he defended a conception of the majority, it was conceived as a negative checking power, not as a means of realizing the policies favored by a majority. One might even argue that the idea of a "popular" majority checking a "constitutional" majority might be a covert means of preventing a perfectly legal majority from enacting a policy. One can project from Madison's concern to frustrate ruling majorities how a Tocqueville might be struck by the presence of an imperfectly realized state.

## IV

Tocqueville takes up the problem of the majority by asserting, in effect, that Locke had won and the Founders and the *Federalist* had lost. The terms he uses to describe American democracy are strikingly similar to Locke's formulation of a "perfect Democracy" where the majority rules as well as reigns:

> In America the people name those who make and execute the law; the people make up the jury which punishes violations of the law. Not only are the institutions democratic in principle but in all their operations. . . . So it is really the people who are directing, and even though the form of government is representative, it is clear that the opinions, prejudices, interests, and even the passions of the people can find no lasting obstacles preventing them from being manifested in the continuous direction of society.
>
> In the United States, as in all countries where the people reign, it is the majority which governs in the name of the people.[29]

Tocqueville's rapturous account of local democratic political life in America ill-prepares a reader for the numerous warnings about majority rule scattered throughout the text. The spirit of his discussion is conveyed by the chapter title, "The Omnipotence of the Majority," and by the heading of one of its sections, "Tyranny of the Majority." Characteristically, the chapter begins with a sweeping assertion: "It is of the very essence of democratic governments that the rule of the majority should be absolute; for in democracies there is nothing outside of the majority hence nothing to resist it."[30] The glaring disjunction between the model of civic culture found in the township and the dangerous concentration of power in "the" majority seems all the more curious in the light of Tocqueville's own claim about the weakness of the American central government. The obvious question was, How could a majority tyrannize by means of a state that was said to hardly exist?

One answer might be that Tocqueville accepted uncritically the Founders' argument about the dangers of majority rule. A different explanation might be that the disjunction between Tocqueville's picture of a highly moral and self-disciplined local democracy and an immoral, uncontrolled majority tyranny was the product of a split theoretical vision. After having observed America, he theorized about it while contemplating France. From a French perspective still deeply affected by recent revolutionary events, majority rule and political parties appeared in a harsh light but, as I shall try to point out, one that Tocqueville accepted unquestioningly when he analyzed American politics. The result was that when he approached the topic of political parties he overlooked their antimajoritarian possibilities. By exploiting the robustly factional character of American politics, parties were creating a fluid politics of temporary coalitions that destabilized the meaning of majority by depriving it of a coherent identity over time. The democratic problem was not the omnipotence of the majority but its evanescence.

Tocqueville's characterization of the majority as omnipotent and potentially tyrannical was based upon the state legislatures, not the national government.[31] In effect, locally, American democracy was Lockean rather than Madisonian. Despite having praised Americans for their self-restraint in local politics, Tocqueville denounced the "moral authority" by which the majority attempted to justify its rule. The majoritarian claim was alleged to be twofold, that there was more "enlightenment and wisdom" in a numerous assembly than in one man; and that the "interest of the greatest [*sic*] number" should prevail over that of a lesser.[32] In Tocqueville's view, this reasoning was responsible for the "impious and detestable maxim" that the majority has "the right to do everything."[33] Roundly denouncing the maxim, he appealed to a self-evident universal principle of "justice" that protects the opinions and interests of the minority against impositions by the majority. He concluded that in America there were insufficient legal safeguards against the tyranny of the majority. He offered no evidence of a tyrannous majority in the country as a whole; on the contrary, he suggested that constitutional safeguards were operating effectively.[34]

## V

The explanation for the unconvincing quality of Tocqueville's discussion is most probably that he had published the first volume of *Democracy* without having clearly formulated his "solution" to the problem of majority rule. When he wrote that majority rule was "absolute" because there was "nothing outside it," he was trying to formulate his main concern, which was not with "rule" as the expression of a will, but with a certain "sway" (*empire*) that was exercised over the American mind by virtue of the "weight" of uniform opinions, beliefs, and values held simultaneously by millions of widely scattered individuals and the complete absence of an aristocratic tradition of corporate distinctions (i.e., an "outside"). The danger was not that a legislative majority might ride roughshod over minority rights but a strange lack of opposition to the dominant set of values—and this despite an unprecedented degree of liberty and fully guaranteed rights of expression. He insisted that there was no country in which there was less intellectual independence and freedom of discussion than in America. His explanation was that in a democracy the majority combined physical, moral, and legal authority. Democracy's vaunted inclusiveness did not extend to the critic who espoused unorthodox views; he would eventually feel the whole weight of the community against him.[35]

Tocqueville's democracy, then, was not a simple description of government by the people but an account of the complex nature of the immaterial power that conditioned it. He identified it as an influence diffused throughout civil society, something closer to a mode of social and cultural domination that a half century later Durkheim would call the "collective consciousness" and another half century later Gramsci would call "hegemony." Its peculiarity was that, unlike traditional forms of domination in which a specific actor or organized group exercised power by means of legal rules, physical coercion, or the credible threat of it, the new form resulted from what Tocqueville identified as "the invisible and intangible power of thought" affecting millions of beings scattered over vast distances.[36] It produced similarity of result without simultaneity of contact.

## VI

Clearly, Tocqueville had moved away from the notion that the dangerous element of a democracy was a majority will as such. He was beginning to see the political behavior of democracy as the expression of a "deeper" cultural phenomenon. That insight would be more fully realized in the second volume of *Democracy* where Tocqueville all but abandoned the notion of the tyranny of the majority in the traditional sense and transfigured it into a cultural formation. The kind of power that Tocqueville had claimed to discover in America was less strictly a species of domination than of predominance. The former implies a settled, coherent direction, resembling the type of hegemony Gramsci ascribed to capitalism or like the enveloping ethos that ancient and early modern theorists had associated with oligarchy or democracy. Tocqueville, however, warned about confusing "stability with force, or the greatness of a thing with its duration." In America the power that governed was unstable and constantly shifting direction. The crucial point remained that "its force was always irresistible."[37] While admitting that American majorities had not acted tyrannically, Tocqueville insisted nonetheless that the "omnipotence of the majority" presented the gravest single danger to American freedom. That conclusion signaled the invention of a new battleground for the defense of freedom against majoritarian democracy, a shift from

Madisonian constitutional devices to cultural formations, from strategies for preventing the coalescence of a majority to shaping or countering its beliefs and values.

Tocqueville's discussion of democracy at the national level provided one of those instances where his personal animus, this time concerning majority rule, led to some discoveries whose importance would, over time, become apparent. That discussion served to reveal a profound lack of fit between, on the one hand, a conception of democracy whose identity was inseparable from majority rule and, on the other, the concentration of powers, authority, and technical functions associated with the state and the forms of politics beginning to cluster around those functions. In attempting to cope with the state the vices and limitations of the majority become exposed and the question arises of whether and to what degree a democracy of continuous majority rule was compatible with the modern state and vice versa.

Tocqueville set the problem differently from those who criticized the majority because of its necessary crudity as a form of decision making and its ignorance of high matters of state. He took the tack of connecting the will of the majority to the democratic political culture and asked how such a culture was likely to affect the performance of certain functions and requirements of government. His conclusion was that majority rule produced several distinct weaknesses: the laws are unstable; able men are discouraged from politics; administration is chaotic; public expenditures tend to increase and resources are frequently wasted; policies are often ineffectual because the public is unable to stay the course when, as in the case of wars, there are demanding undertakings of extensive duration and sacrifice; government has difficulty in persuading the society to make provisions for a distant future; and, most strikingly, democratic governments are inept at foreign policy. The common thread in all of these deficiencies of democracy was that, while at best majorities can be aroused in support of weighty matters, such as prison reforms, over time their passions subside and they lose "interest."[38]

## VII

*Individual partialities and local attachments are secondary and quite unimportant compared . . . with the* INTERESTS AND PERMANENCY OF THE REPUBLICAN PARTY.

Leaders of New York
Democratic-Republican Party, 1823[39]

Today, more than a century after the publication of *Democracy*, it is official doctrine among "industrialized democracies" that a political society is to be judged as certifiably democratic if it has free political parties and free elections. Today's parties are commonly described as having the functions of mustering majorities in support of a party's program and candidates and of containing conflicts. They are rarely described as instruments of an omnipotent majority and they have clearly shed their revolutionary genealogy. The externalization of majority to party is the corollary to the domination by "party professionals." In late modernity the role of parties consigns majorities to a constructed existence episodically governed by the electoral calendar. The truly modern political party has reduced the Lockean majority to public opinion and voters, a distinction that suggests that the two elements need not coincide. Although this hapless majority now seems inevitable, it did not occur to early critics that parties, instead of being the servants of majority rule, would become its embalmers. The question of whether democracy would be realized as an operative political force or rendered harmless was answered in the evolution of parties.

When Tocqueville set sail for America in 1831, French parties in the sense of permanent organizations and disciplined parliamentary groupings hardly existed. In contrast, American party formations had come into existence with the republic and the partisan struggles over the ratification of the Constitution; thus early on parties gave notice of evolving into a major element in a politics of competition.[40] Citizens were exhorted to take sides, to identify with a party, its leaders, candidates, slogans, policies, and values. Oddly, American political elites were long in coming to the realization that parties might be a powerful means of containing the demos. Instead, both Jeffersonians and Hamiltonians regarded them as partisans who prevented the true common interest from being promoted and protected.[41] For the democrat the natural question raised by the appearance of parties was whether they could become the instrument of popular democracy. Equally important was the possible impact of a politics of competition on the quality and character of citizen politics. The invention of an abstract plane where a remote politics would be played out in ways that, while they might be presented as merely a larger replica of local politics, were radically discontinuous and implied a conception of the citizen as a rooter limited to choosing sides.

The context in which Tocqueville sets parties served notice of his intention to discredit them as potential instruments of a national democratic politics of majority rule. The discussion begins with an assertion about the uncontested supremacy of majority rule in America; it closes with a description of the majority of citizens as "surrounded" by political parties that allegedly kept the country in a state of constant agitation—a modern tempo that Tocqueville found foreboding.[42] The implication was that parties were a breeding ground for majority tyranny.

Although Tocqueville launched his account by characterizing parties as "an evil inherent in free governments," the conception of parties that unfolds seems, nevertheless, not only opposed to Madison's politics of interests but ambiguous toward Tocqueville's own politics of localism and citizen participation.[43] To one intent upon finding a place in politics for principled political action and big stakes, both interest politics and local politics seemed inherently unheroic. That Tocqueville's concern about parties should have focused on the place of ideas and that action should be inflated and conceived in highly charged terms reveal how deeply the revolution of 1789 had figured in Tocqueville's political and theoretical consciousness. For much of his life the epic of 1789 would serve as the standard of actions motivated by grand ideas, with actors performing on a large stage, and fighting for even larger stakes. If parties were threatening to become the principal vehicle of politics, and if revolution had revealed that heroic actions were still possible, then how better to test party's implications for thought and action than by connecting their origins to modern revolutions?

As his starting point, Tocqueville proposed a distinction between a political and a social revolution.[44] There were moments in a nation's history, Tocqueville averred, when it was "tormented" by such great evils that it begins to consider "a total change in its political constitution." There were other times when "an even deeper malaise" existed and the fundamental structure of society seemed "compromised." The latter are "the moments of great revolutions" and "grand parties." Tocqueville did not explicitly identify such moments, but it seems reasonable to suppose that the political revolution referred to the actions of the American colonists and that the social revolution referred to France. Although Tocqueville's construct of "grand parties" seems more an account of social movements, the contrast he was seeking was between times of fundamental transformation of political and social institutions and times when society is changing slowly, when wide agreement exists on fundamentals and a limited vision prevails ("ne porte pas ses regards au dela d'un certain horizon"). "The latter are the times of intrigues and small-minded parties."[45]

Tocqueville used the contrast between "grand" and "petty" parties to set out two contrasting conceptions of politics.[46] They represent the kind of alternative politics a feudal or archaic outlook might generate in desperation, yet they also hint at the role of what some contemporaries were labeling "ideologies." Grand parties, he declares, are attached to principles rather than consequences; to generalities, not to particulars; to ideas, not to men. They are noble and generous. Then, however, Tocqueville adds an important qualification: while it makes the contrast seem more gestural than substantive, it also implies that ideas might serve the ideological role on which Marx and Engels would later expand: "particular interests, which always play the greatest part in political passions, is here [in grand parties] more skillfully concealed under the veil of the public interest."[47]

Petty parties generally "lack political faith . . . and lofty purposes." They are selfish, cold, and timid. Grand parties convulse society; petty ones merely agitate it. When the Federalists and the Jeffersonian Republicans were contesting for power, America had grand parties: the one representing aristocratic principles of restraint on democracy, the other championing the cause of democracy. "Today there are no grand political parties in America." Even the parties that threatened the Union "rested not on principles but on material interests" such as tariffs. Ideas were merely an afterthought, exploited for show rather than substance.[48]

## VIII

Tocqueville's brief and inconclusive discussion of political parties reflected both an uncertainty about the subject and a deep repugnance toward the phenomenon that would become a permanent element in his political outlook. The uncertainty came from the limitations of a feudalist orientation. Its emphasis on local politics and local elites left no obvious role for national parties. A feudal politics tends to fragment issues, contextualize them to reflect the peculiarities of local circumstances. National parties, in contrast, nationalize politics by crafting "issues" whose broad generality and deliberate vagueness rarely can be realized as "policy."

Tocqueville's admission that even grand parties were based on material interests left the implication that disinterested, public-spirited action on a grand scale was incompatible with party politics of any kind—except under revolutionary conditions. Political action had been supplanted by political acting and by actors of lesser stature than the public-spirited Founding Fathers. Alexander Hamilton had once solemnly warned that a great national political theater, such as the one conceived by the Framers, was essential to public tranquillity.[49] For Tocqueville, however, the dramaturgy of Caesar denied in America had produced the anticlimax of a Jackson, whose instincts Tocqueville judged to be more comfortable with restricting national powers than enlarging them.[50]

## IX

Tocqueville's account of parties opened up two problems. The first concerned the possibility that the condition of parties was connected with, perhaps even a function of, the "incomplete State." Although the constitutional powers of the national government seemed far-reaching, the number of issues proved to be few. Lacking the opportunities to exercise its powers, the central power had signally failed to develop the one capability deemed essential to the modern state, the power to enforce uniform rules throughout the entire society and, equally important, by its own agents.[51] "The federal government," Tocqueville concluded, "is plainly getting weaker."[52] If that were the case, then the phenomenon of incompleteness was deserving of more than Tocqueville's lame conclusion that the United States seemed to enjoy the advantages of both a large state and a small one.[53] Perhaps what he had captured, but under-described, was a new political form, different from the one being embraced by virtually all modernizing states.

As Tocqueville himself recognized, thanks to geographic isolation, American national politics was peculiar in that concerns of foreign policy, diplomacy, warfare, standing armies, and administrative action hardly figured to the extent that they did for European governments and that ever since Washington's Farewell Address most American political leaders were committed to avoiding "foreign entanglements" and wars. Was this an "incomplete politics" complementary to an incomplete state, a different politics determined to forsake the road to a politics of *grandeur* or simply the afterthought of a preoccupied people, one driven by an obscure obsession to abandon what they had just built in order to drive farther west?

The second problem connected with Tocqueville's discussion of parties concerned the implications of a weak party system, in the context of an incomplete politics and an incomplete state, for majority rule and the conception of the citizen. Clearly the possibility of mustering an effective majority nationally would be greatly diminished if parties proved to be a source of frustration for the majority. Some would even argue that a weak party system was welcome precisely because it frustrated the majority by denying it its natural vehicle and, as a result, strengthened the hand of the more cohesive state administration. Thus the incomplete state was potentially a lopsided state with an executive emboldened by the corresponding weakness of a disheartened citizenry, while the national legislature, as the logical extension of the majority, was doomed to remain in a state of disorganization and unfulfilled promise because of the weakness of parties. The opposite of the incomplete state, the lopsided state, Tocqueville would designate democratic despotism, an administered society without citizen politics.

The crucial question thus concerned the fate of the New England–style citizen. What kind of democratic citizen would be encouraged, even constructed, by a lopsided state and its antipolitics? Tocqueville gives some clues in his description of the condition of the public during the election of a president. He describes it as "a moment of national crisis" whose intensity resides in its symbolic rather than its institutional significance. Although the presidency is not an office of great power or patronage, it does affect "all of the citizens." "Any interest, however petty, assumes great importance once it becomes general."[54] In this case, however, the "general" is not, as in the politics of the township, an object of public deliberation emerging from the attempt to elicit a common interest among particulars, but the name for a Roman spectacle that evoked, for the moment, a huge national theater and an excited mass. Presidential candidates turned into "symbols" and became "the personification of theories."[55]

> Long before the appointed moment arrives, the election becomes the greatest, indeed the sole matter occupying men's minds. Factions redouble their ardor; every artificial passion which the imagination can create in a happy and peaceful society is aroused to produce this great day.
>
> For his part, the president no longer governs in the interest of the State but of his reelection. He prostrates himself before the majority . . . [and] strives to anticipate their caprices. . . .
>
> As the election approaches, intrigues are quickened, and agitation grows more lively and widespread. . . . The whole nation falls into a feverish state. . . .
>
> True, as soon as fortune has decided, this ardor is dissipated, and everything is calm again. . . . But shouldn't one be astonished that the storm should have arisen at all?[56]

The phenomena that Tocqueville was uncovering—the citizen-spectator, the politics of excitement, the potentially lopsided state—served both to highlight the extraordinary character of American citizenship and to reveal its fragility.

The Americans had invented not "a" citizen but a potential for a multiple civic personality. The secret of Americans, Tocqueville declared, was "to give themselves a political life for each portion of territory . . . [and] then to multiply to infinity the occasions on which citizens could act together."[57] His phrase, "a political life for each portion of territory," was a telling one. Americans had exploded the traditional concept that had confined the citizen to a single identity, the *polites* to the *polis*, the *civis* to the *civitas*, the mediaeval burgess and early modern burgher to the city, or *le citoyen* to the revolutionary nation. The American was simultaneously a citizen of the township, county, state, and nation. Each represented a wider, somewhat different level of generality, a more extensive coordination of diversities, a broader outlook suggestive of "democracies," rather than Democracy, in America.

But deprived of the grand issues seized by a nationalized politics and with talents drained by the allure of a grander stage, could the humdrum character of these multiple engagements rival the hyperexcitement of political spectacle? Would spectacle undermine the delicate synthesis of communal altruism and individual self-interest, overwhelming the one while attaching the other to more effective media of influence and turn the multiple civic personality into a multiple-personality disorder?

One testing ground for answering these questions would be the institution that was second only to the New England township in Tocqueville's affection. What might be the likely effects of the nationalizing politics of presidential elections upon the vaunted role of the public and private political associations? As Tocqueville recognized, they represented, at best, a politically ambiguous experience of membership because of their homogeneous composition. They were organized to concert wills that were predisposed to agreement.[58] Unlike the politics of a township, an association was not a grouping in which members learned to deliberate their differences in order to develop cooperative action. Their membership was organized around sameness and hence exposed to a narrow political education. Tocqueville saw their politicalness primarily in the potential resistance that connected individuals might present to state power and majority tyranny. Although they might help to preserve "the common liberties," it would be because they were intent on "defending private interests," not because of their civic virtue.[59]

Associations were politically important, even crucial, yet they were not substitutes for the political but its beneficiaries. Americans, Tocqueville noted, bring their political habits into private life rather than the reverse. If, however, the truly political layers of citizenship were to languish, then associations might well be transformed. Instead of being centers of resistance and instead of their habits and *moeurs* being shaped by the political life of the township, they would look toward the arena of politics defined by the state and accordingly pattern themselves to compete as rivals for the favors of the state. Because their aim was to further private interests, Tocqueville's original maxim would be reversed: instead of civic habits modifying the drive of private interests, the private would condition the public.

## X

Nationalizing, state-focused politics might also have grave implications for the emotional identification of citizens. This had become a crucial matter ever since the French Revolution had created a cult form of the nation.[60] In the

United States multiple layers of citizenship and membership combined with the feudal politics of an incomplete state to produce an American patriotism rather than a nationalism:

> Public spirit in the Union is in a way only a summing up of provincial [i.e., local] patriotism. Every citizen of the United States transports, so to speak, the concern inspired in him by his local [*petite*] republic into love for the common fatherland. In defending the Union, he defends the growing prosperity of his district, the right to direct its affairs in the hope of promoting plans for improvement which should enrich himself: in short, all the things which, ordinarily, touch men more than the general interests of the country and the glory of the nation.[61]

Tocqueville believed that because the Union was so vast and "somewhat vague," it had not developed its own patriotism. "Individual egoism," which he identified as the crucial element in modern patriotism, did not find itself reflected in the nation.[62] The American, instead, is able to see himself in the township, county, and state because his participation in their affairs enables him to perceive the connection between the "general prosperity" and his own happiness. He comes to regard the former as the product of his own efforts and will defend all of these entities against outside criticism.[63]

Tocqueville did not press these multiple forms of identity by contrasting them with the aggressive nationalism that later characterized the French Revolution. A few years after the final volume of *Democracy*, however, Americans were seized by the fervor of "manifest destiny" and showed in the subsequent war with Mexico what kind of dynamic could be generated when democracy experienced the "higher" patriotism of the nation-state. Was patriotism to be the pseudodemocratic element vital to the emergence of the lopsided state, one of the means of assuring the citizenry a measured "sense" of participation?

The obverse side to Tocqueville's corporatist reading of American pluralism was that it called into question the identity of Americans as the direct offsprings of a union consecrated by the Constitution and the subjects of a strong nation-state. The national identity, the habits of "looking toward the center," had not developed as strongly as the Founders had hoped, while the centrifugal forces had grown stronger than they had feared. As the symbolic assertion of control over future generations "The Founding" was experiencing the crisis of passing from history to faith as the possibility of disunion loomed ever larger. The question being pressed by the nullifiers was, Was it more natural for America to develop as an unaggregated society than as a society of "united states" governed positively by a central power? On the other hand, could the new nation abandon its creation myth, with its promise of order, except by embracing its traditional opposite, chaos?

# CHAPTER XIII
# CENTRALIZATION AND DISSOLUTION

## I

It seems fitting that in the closing pages of volume I of *Democracy in America,* entitled "Conclusion," Tocqueville should introduce his allegory of the traveler who pauses at the top of the hill and finds that the city below has come into full focus, its outline settled at last. The tableau of a settled regime, of a firmly theorized object and its confident claim to have grasped "the whole" of the new political society is at odds with the chapter of which the "Conclusion" forms the final section. Throughout virtually all of that chapter Tocqueville worried that the powerful tendencies of secession and slavery had produced a deeply divided city and might eventually dissolve it into several independent sovereignties. The theorist's confident vision of the city—written after his return to France—appears in striking contrast to his earlier confession of a failed vision in the same chapter. On no less a question than whether the Union would survive he admitted to no answer: "The future is hidden and I cannot pretend to lift the veil."[1]

That Tocqueville should suppress the di-vision in favor of a holistic vision is understandable. The threat of a southern secession was never mentioned in any of the chapters preceding the final chapter of volume I. The silence allowed Tocqueville to develop his conception of American democracy undistracted by the danger being posed to the Union, to its collective identity as a democracy, and to the coherence of Tocqueville's theory. Similarly slavery and racial genocide do not make an appearance until that same final chapter. The problem raised does not concern bad faith on Tocqueville's part—which in any case is to be denied—but rather, What is the relationship, if any, of slavery and genocide, to the conception of democracy that Tocqueville had delineated? Are they historical anomalies or integrally connected with democracy? Similarly with the ideas of secession and nullification: were they peculiar to the southern states or were they more closely related to democratic notions than either their defenders or opponents would admit?

These questions begin to emerge when Tocqueville turns to discuss centralization in volume I, part 2, chapter 8, prior to taking up the racial divisions. In place of earlier expressions about the settled character of American democracy there are suggestions of a challenged, irresolute democracy unsure of its identity. Reflecting that uncertainty Tocqueville begins to ask, What significant changes might democracy experience and, while still retaining something of a democratic character, what new features might it acquire and what old ones discard? The problem of possible mutations becomes in its American setting a question about the tensions between a social condition and a political form and the possibility of a reversal concerning which was the "settled." The social condition, while seemingly a vast field for human striving and an endless source of disturbance, was in reality a settling force. Its endless economic opportunities and absence of social barriers reinforced equality and promoted the irreversible, unambiguous democratization of society. In contrast, the political form, which was usually represented as "settled," was displaying cracks in its "foundations," ill-fitting elements that over time had become so glaringly incongruous that, unless replaced, were likely to disfigure forever, even undermine the democratic regime. The context in which he situates the idea of a changing *political* democracy is the polarity of centralization and decentralization.

Centralization was a topic that seems, at first glance, yet another example of Tocqueville discovering America only to find France. To a Frenchman with deep roots in the Old Regime centralization symbolized monopolization of power, the antithesis to the dispersed power of feudalism; an absorption of political attention toward a center; and an administrative mode of governance that steadily penetrated and regulated the most intimate areas of the lives of individuals. For Tocqueville administrative centralization was a distinct form of power, indeterminate in its boundaries, invasive in its reach, and disruptive of smaller, largely self-contained forms of political life. In its postrevolutionary manifestation it signaled the coming of the complete modern state and a pseudoaristocracy of officials.

In volume I of *Democracy* Tocqueville tried to formulate the underdeveloped character of the state in America and the overdevelopment of the state in France by means of two images of centralization. One represented the American national government, the other the French state. The first he calls "governmental centralization." It is not peculiar to the United States but a response to the existence of certain general interests, such as foreign affairs, that are of obvious concern to all parts of a nation. When the regulation of those matters is concentrated under "a directing power," then governmental centralization exists. In contrast to the limited scope of governmental centralization, "administrative centralization" is descriptive of an arrangement where local interests and the concerns special to a locality are controlled by central authorities.[2]

The great danger, Tocqueville concluded, was that the two forms might be combined to produce, in my language, a complete state. In the United States, according to Tocqueville, although the Constitution provided the potential for an extreme concentration of governmental power in the national government, this had not materialized. There was little centralized administration and "hardly any trace of hierarchy."[3] Instead, administration was deliberately decentralized; the application and enforcement of the laws was distributed among numerous agents whose authority was carefully delimited.[4] In the eyes of some critics the undeveloped character of administration demanded reform, but Tocqueville remained committed to localized power—at least as long as he could postpone the questions of slavery and secession. Inefficient central administration could be viewed positively, as the expression of a society that assigned responsibility for its prosperity not to the state but to the citizens. "The collective force of the citizenry," Tocqueville declared, "will always be more powerful in producing social well-being than the authority of government."[5]

Tocqueville defended the notorious inefficiency of American public administration as inevitable and justified because expressive of the myriad of cooperative actions by which citizens laboriously went about defining their common interests. It was the price paid by a participatory culture when it contested the assumption that the common good was principally the preserve of state action.[6] "Administrative centralization enervates a people who submit to it. Its relentless tendency is to diminish the spirit of the city among them."[7] In the United States, Tocqueville noted, "there is nothing centralized or hierarchical in the constitution of administrative power. . . . [T]here is no central point on which the radii of administrative power converge."[8]

Although Tocqueville's concerns ultimately were with France, the power of his contrasting, even anachronistic, imagery illuminated American society where centralization was strikingly absent and provided another example of how Tocqueville's way of theorizing could be suggestive just when it seemed to be committing something akin to a category mistake. The absence of bureaucratization in the United States and its unmistakable presence in France combined with the presence of highly decentralized, participatory politics in the United States and its relative absence in France would be played off in ways that reveal in both societies tendencies, dangers, and possibilities otherwise unsuspected. Stated more strongly, if secessionist America had left the status of equality and decentralization ambiguous, and, as a consequence cast doubt upon the irresistible march of equality, which Tocqueville had confidently prophesied at the outset of *Democracy*, then French centralization might prove a more accurate harbinger of the form which democratization might take.

Were the spatial limits of the city a metaphor for its political limitations? The American polarity of centralization/decentralization represented a fault line that ran through American history from colonial opposition to the British crown, through the Articles of Confederation and its governance by thirteen sovereign states, the Anti-Federalist opposition to the proposed Constitution, the Nullification Controversy of 1798, the threatened secession of New England states (Hartford Convention of 1812), and the states' opposition to the National Bank during the Jacksonian presidency. Recall as well that the *Federalist* had associated democracy with small scales and contrasted it unfavorably with large-scale centralization, thereby setting democracy and decentralization against republicanism and centralization. Over time equality would gravitate toward centralization in hopes of enforcing "equal protection" for all, while localism and self-government would become associated with inequality and the defense of slavery. The polarity of centralization and decentralization would thus effectively split democracy from within, setting equality on a course different from and opposed to local self-government.

## II

> *Centralization, a democratic instinct; instinct of a society which has succeeded in extricating itself from the individualistic system of the Middle Ages. Preparation for despotism.*
>
> *Why is centralization dear to the habits of democracy? Great question to* delve into *in the third volume of my work. . . . A* major *question.*
>
> Tocqueville[9]

In a democracy an obvious method for concentrating power would be to cultivate the majority and enlist its hopes and energies in support of central authority. That course, however, had been rendered virtually impossible by the terms of the Constitution. Tocqueville's treatment of centralization in volume 1 reflects the unintended consequences resulting from the success of the Founders in rebuffing democracy at the national level. By frustrating majority rule from ever gaining control of all of the various branches of government simultaneously, especially of the judiciary and the administrative branch,[10] they encouraged an even stronger identification of the demos with local institutions and suspicion of the center. Tocqueville recognized that if the majority were unable to assert its power nationally through administration, it could take advantage of the decentralized system to effect its purposes through state and local institutions. Tocqueville seized on that possibility and declared that centralization was primarily a phenomenon of state and local governments. The state governments, he claimed, were as centralized as an absolute monarchy.[11] The peculiarity was that centralization mainly assumed a legislative rather than an administrative form. And this because the citizenry identified with the legislatures and granted them the power to serve the will of the majority. Local majorities, which one might have expected to serve Tocqueville as institutions of resistance, appeared as miniature versions of centralized power and the state legislatures as the potential instruments of majority tyranny.[12] Decentralization, instead of providing the natural habitat of democracy, might work to distort its expression causing it to side with inequality and pseudoaristocracy. Further, the majority, frustrated at the national level, might withdraw, leaving the central state weakened and unable to preserve itself except by reducing its dependence on democracy.

There is an ambivalence in Tocqueville's discussion of centralization as he finds himself being drawn in a direction he dislikes. The ambivalence is caused by the collision between his natural tendency to defend local autonomy (present in America, absent in France) against state centralism (present in France, absent in America) and the American setting where localism was seen as the stronghold of slavery and centralism as so weak that the national government allowed the evil to persist. The "logic" of democracy seemed turned upside down: decentralization might strengthen local self-government and inequalities without promoting participatory politics, while majority rule and equality might throw in their lot with centralization, abandon participatory politics, and accept a diluted politics as a substitute.

## III

> *[B]efore [a hundred years have] elapsed, I think that the territory occupied or claimed by the United States will be populated by a hundred million inhabitants and divided into forty states . . . for that very reason, the continuance of the federal government is merely a happy accident.*
>
> Tocqueville[13]

The incomplete character of the state began to appear as a fatal weakness and the near autonomy of the several states as a dangerous threat.[14] The result was a sudden reversal on Tocqueville's part and a suspension of feudal reflexes sympathetic to corporate resistance to central authorities. He treats the southern elite with aristocratic contempt and roundly condemns resistance to central power by the states. He criticizes the nullificationists, saying that when the majority has spoken the "duty" of the minority was to "submit."[15] He defends as aristocratic the proposal to recharter a national bank and stigmatizes the Jacksonian opposition to it, which was based in the states, as democratic.[16]

The complexities Tocqueville was encountering stemmed mainly from his fundamental belief that "ideal" concerns were not only loftier than material ones but somehow more powerful in their hold on human behavior. This surfaced in his insistence that differences of culture, rather than the opposing material interests represented by northern manufacturers and southern slave owners, were at the heart of the dispute.[17] While the controversy "attacks" the order of Union "indirectly," he declared, it strikes at its most vital element, "*moeurs*."[18] In contention were two strongly entrenched and opposing political cultures, one localist and secessionist, the other and more recent identified with the Constitution and the national government. Although increasingly during the period of the composition of *Democracy* the controversy was perceived by Americans as one between two cultural blocs, represented by the northern and the southern states, Tocqueville clearly recognized the existence of several distinct political cultures. New England political culture differed from that of Ohio and Ohio from Kentucky; the cultures in the newer western states were not those of either the North or the South; and the "middle class" culture of the North contrasted with the "aristocratic" culture of the South.[19]

If the political reality was several political cultures within a society represented by an incomplete state, then the cultural differences crystallizing around the issue of slavery appeared as a threat to order rather than the resistive stuff of freedom: incompleteness produced a state too feeble to enforce a national standard of right, even in the face of attacks upon rudimentary democratic values of freedom and equality. Culture, instead of serving as the supporting matrix of political order, turns out to be its nemesis, while majority rule, instead of being a latent tyranny, might be a badly needed source of cohesion.

Clearly, if the Union were to fall apart, the didactic aim of his volume would founder. An account of a successful democracy might attract a curious readership but an account of a failed one would only confirm a widespread prejudice. To save the project Tocqueville mustered a degree of optimism about the future of the Union by retrieving the concept of culture, only this time with an emphasis on the positive value of homogeneity rather than heterogeneity. There existed, he announced, a national culture of consensus consisting of certain beliefs that were shared by virtually all Americans. "There is unanimity about the general principles that ought to govern human society."[20] The points of agreement were many: though divided by sects, Americans all "look upon religion in the same way." Americans "uniformly" believe in the sovereignty of the people, liberty and equality, freedom of the press, the right of association, the jury system, and the accountability of governmental officials. They look to public opinion as the final arbiter in matters of right and wrong. They believe that each person should be free to govern himself and that if each follows his self-interest "rightly understood," he will do what is right. And they are convinced that the future holds the promise "of something better though still hidden."[21]

Nevertheless, after conferring upon consensus a near unanimity, Tocqueville was forced to conclude that the federal government is "tending to weaken daily and the sovereignty of the Union itself is in peril." The cause of his pessimism is indicated by the place it occurs, in the chapter analyzing racism and genocide.

## IV

> *In America one encounters other things than an immense and complete democracy; the peoples who inhabit the new world can be considered from more than one point of view.*
>
> Tocqueville[22]

The last or tenth chapter of part 2 of volume 1 of *Democracy* is entitled "Some Considerations on the Present Condition and Probable Future of the Three Races Which Inhabit the Territory of the United States." It is at once the lengthiest, the most revealing, and the most enigmatic of the entire work.[23] Recent commentators have noted that the chapter was not in the original draft and have suggested that the preceding chapter, the ninth, represents the true conclusion to the first volume.[24] Perhaps, however, the alleged anomalous character of the chapter is best understood in terms of the anomaly of slavery within a democracy.

The last few pages are headed "Conclusion," but they are far from being a summation of the volume. They are integrally connected to chapter 10, which, it is no exaggeration to say, portrays a society in which violence is deeply woven into the fabric of its material existence, as distinct from its ideological self-representation. Recall that this chapter is immediately preceded by four chapters that appear to be summarizing the whole work. They deal with the "real advantages" of democratic government to American society, the omnipotence of the majority and what restrains it, and the main causes tending to maintain "a democratic republic in the United States." In none of those chapters do racial relations receive more than passing mention.

On two vital matters chapter 10 undermines the point of all that has preceded it by suggesting that the federal union may likely dissolve under the strains of sectionalism and thus end the brief episode of the "first new nation." And it suggests further that it is deeply misleading to speak of "democracy" in the United States when all Americans knew, and most approved, of the enslavement of one race and the extermination of another.[25] Thus a neofeudalism, in the form of sectional antagonisms and of socioeconomic rivalries between a southern landed "aristocracy" and a northern manufacturing class, threatened to end the experiment of a democratic nation-state while the historical record of democracy's treatment of Africans and Indians, of enslavement and genocide within and by a democratic political society, pointed to an unsettling possibility—that to describe the United States as a "democracy" might have required serious qualification from the beginning. The laws and *moeurs* that Tocqueville had lauded as the factors that curbed the excesses to which democracy was prone were also the folkways that incorporated slavery and justified the destruction of the native population.[26]

> What is happening in the South of the Union seems to me both the most horrible and the most natural consequence of slavery. When I see the natural order of things overthrown and I hear humanity cry out in vain against the laws, I confess that my indignation is not aimed at the men of our day, the authors of the outrages; rather my hatred is concentrated against those who, after more than a thousand years of equality, have reintroduced slavery into the world.[27]

Thus, although democracy existed in parts of America, the term did not describe the political constitution of the United States. Or rather, the legal Constitution did not describe the whole of the United States. "The democracy of the United States" was not merely flawed but profoundly contradictory from its beginnings. The plight of Africans and Indians had added democracy to the category of the incomplete and, as southern apologists soon realized, made for a curious mix. Some ingredients—localism, paternalism, inequality—seemed feudalist, while others evoked the example of Athenian democracy, with its mélange of equal male citizens, slaves, and subjugated populations abroad.[28] Tocqueville records John Quincy Adams as asserting that, except for slavery, southerners were more equal than northerners who, while equal before the law, were divided between "upper classes and working classes."[29] Given the racial and class inequalities and their seeming insolubility, the irresistible march of equality and, along with it, of democracy had suddenly become problematical in the extreme. American democracy might appear either as a work in progress or as one in regress.

At the beginning of the chapter Tocqueville explains, lamely and with a touch of embarrassment, that in previous pages he had not had time to consider "the Indians and the Negroes" or to discuss the possible survival of what he calls "the Anglo-American confederation." It was, in other words, possible to discuss "democracy in America" with only passing reference to the problem of "three races" because two of them had never been included.

They had also been thrust "outside" in a theoretical sense by Tocqueville. He had not made their presence an operative influence insinuating itself in complex ways into the assumptions that Americans had about power, treatment of dependents, and social classes—something he would rectify in his treatment of the status of women. Nor, more extremely, could his theory of America as the society where equality of social condition was most advanced account for the presence, let alone the expansion, of slavery or for the relentless violence against "the red men." Was it at all possible to assign equality the commanding place in the formation of American social and political life while that democracy sanctioned the grossest form of inequality? Less advanced democracies, such as France and Great Britain, had either abolished the institution of slavery or soon would—although, admittedly, they had kept at an imperial distance the destructive effects of rule over their own "Indians." How could Tocqueville recommend American democracy to the world while acknowledging that slavery was so deeply embedded in American society that he doubted equality between the races would ever be realized?[30]

Tocqueville had to face the question of whether the condition of the "other" two races was an anomaly that democracy would inevitably correct or a manifestation of some other driving force within modern society, as deep as racism. A nation so uniquely blessed in its material resources, economic opportunities, absence of inherited class antagonisms, and with a rich legacy of self-government, nonetheless sanctioned slavery and obsessively expelled the natives from one treaty-guaranteed area to another. America provided a sober lesson, not in the possibilities of democratic politics, but in the unlimited possibilities of a condition even newer, perhaps more compelling, than democratic politics, a democratic economy that opened to all an opportunity to exploit. "The misfortune of the Indians is to have come into contact with the most civilized people, and I would add the greediest in the world."[31] One educated American, speaking the authentic Lockean language about God having given the earth to rational exploiters, put it simply to Tocqueville: "I think that civilized man has the right to take the land of the savages for they do not know how to draw a profit from it."[32] Was the curse of America not that of egalitarianism driven to extremes, but something within the genius of a people whose vaunted pragmatism had allowed them to accept slavery into the original constitution and to trust thereafter in political compromisers, such as Henry Clay, to put off indefinitely the day of reckoning?

## V

*I then spoke to him [John Quincy Adams] about the more immediate dangers to the Union and of the causes which could lead to its dissolution. Mr. Adams did not reply but it was easy to see that on this point he had no more confidence than I about the future.*

Tocqueville[33]

Tocqueville tried to preserve the relevance of democracy in America while condemning the horrors of slavery and genocide in its midst by drawing a distinction between democracy and the United States and then identifying the problem of the three races with the latter: "These matters [racism and disunion], which touch on my subject, do not enter into it; they are American without being democratic; and it is democracy which I have been especially concerned to portray. So at first I have put them to one side; but now I must return to them in closing."[34]

In treating the problems of race as an American problem, Tocqueville first approached it through the question of whether the Union could survive the sectional conflicts, which, in addition to slavery, also included controversies about preferential tariffs favoring domestic manufacturers, the right of states to veto federal laws and court decisions, the desirability of a national bank, the admission of new states to the Union, and the resulting shifts in regional power. He concluded that the Union was in fact beginning to come apart. The power of the central government was becoming more ineffectual as that of the states increased.[35]

Tocqueville had consistently called attention to the "artificial" nature of the Union and of its uneasy relationship to the states, not only because the national Constitution recognized the autonomy of the states but because the civic culture of the Union remained undeveloped and mostly parasitic off that of the states.[36] The dilemma of the American experiment seemed to be a federal system that could not develop an effective central government without threatening the states or preserve the political integrity of the states without weakening the center and straining the Union. A quarter-century after the final volume of *Democracy* appeared the Civil War resolved the dilemma by "saving" the Union, strengthening the central government, radically reducing the power of the states, and working a revolution in the *moeurs* of the American citizen: instead of a participating member of a polis, he would be a voter.

Tocqueville sensed that American democracy was in crisis. Although it was possible that strong ties of economic interest as well as of patriotic pride might enable the Union to survive, civil war and "the dismemberment of the

Union" had to be contemplated as a distinct possibility: "by injecting war into the midst of the states presently confederated, and along with it permanent armies, dictatorship, and taxes, might in the long haul compromise the fate of republican institutions."[37] If that occurred, Tocqueville thought, the Union would dissolve into a number of armed federations of states or several regional alliances. He insisted, however, that that eventuality would not necessarily mean the experiment had failed. "[O]ne need not confuse the future of the republic and that of the Union."[38] Republicanism was so deeply rooted as to be able to survive the disintegration of the Union.

Significantly, the theme of republicanism is given its most extended treatment in the course of the chapter whose thematic of racism would seem its antithesis. The section on republicanism has an eerie serenity about it, as though Tocqueville had somehow forgotten the terrible treatment of the two races. In those pages republicanism supersedes democracy as defining the identity of American political culture. Republicanism is lauded as a "conciliatory" system, deliberative, "orderly," based on "the enlightened will of the people." "The republicans of the United States value *moeurs*, respect beliefs, and recognize rights."[39]

In the penultimate pages, before its conclusion, the chapter moves sonorously: history reveals that societies have evolved from aristocracy toward democracy, "[b]ut a people starting from a civilized state and democracy gradually encouraging inequality of conditions, and ending by establishing inviolable privileges and exclusive statuses, that would be a novelty in the world. Nothing indicates that America is destined to furnish the first example of such a spectacle."[40]

That expression of optimism seems unearned. That Tocqueville could envision both the dissolution of the United States into several republics *and* the perpetuation of slavery poses a question he did not raise: while slavery was clearly contradictory to egalitarian democracy, was it incongruous with republicanism? Was slavery, in other words, one of those issues which exposed the differences between democracy and republicanism as well as the difficulties of trying to weld them together? Historically, republican theory had always been marked by a preference for aristocracy/agrarianism and a corresponding bias against egalitarianism/commerce. The slaveholding states were precisely those states which, as Tocqueville recognized, were dominated by elites whose culture was commonly characterized as aristocratic.[41] The issue posed by slavery was, therefore, the reverse of what Tocqueville had seen as the genius of America, the willingness of democracy to qualify itself by adopting republican restraints upon majoritarianism. Now the issue was whether republican aristocracy would yield to democratic egalitarianism and accept the abolition of slavery. At the same time, however, while slavery appeared as oppression *by* an aristocracy, the treatment of the Indians was the oppression *of* an aristocracy. Tocqueville admiringly remarked upon a natural nobility among those Indians who had as yet not been debased. Accordingly, if slavery was the crime of aristocracy, perhaps racial genocide was the crime of common men.

## VI

> *Seeing what passes in the world, might one not say that the European is to the men of other races what man himself is to the animals? He fashions them to his uses, and when he cannot bend them, he destroys them.*
>
> Tocqueville[42]

Tocqueville's concern to preserve republicanism from both the dissolution of the Union and the stigma of slavery should not be allowed to obscure his profound abhorrence at the condition of the two races and at the moral degradation it inflicted on both masters and slaves, conquerors and conquered. Although that abhorrence makes his sanitized republicanism appear all the more unconvincing, it does not call into question the importance or passion of his comments about the "three races" and their "condition." There are no more powerful passages in *Democracy* than those in which the French aristocrat and critic of the French Revolution denounces the dehumanization of two races by their alleged superiors. Thus he writes bitingly that by their Indian policies Americans, "with marvellous ease," have accomplished "calmly, legally, philanthropically" what the Spaniards achieved by atrocities. "It would be difficult to destroy men with more respect for the laws of humanity."[43]

The principal notion that Tocqueville relies upon in analyzing that condition is "tyranny." But he transforms that idea, enlarging it well beyond traditional connotations of arbitrariness or lust for power while separating it from his own creation, the tyranny of the majority. In the case of both the Africans and the Indians he is concerned with the impact of what we would call "cultural genocide," or the destruction of a people's culture, and with why the vulnerability thus created prepares for a peculiarly modern species of tyranny. The African has been stripped of his language, religion, and family. He "is suspended between two societies," black Africa and white America, "and isolated from both peoples." The Indian has been stripped of traditions, language, "his chain of memories," his family, and his natural spaces.[44] The white man has reduced him to a lower stage of civilization than when the two races first met. Because their condition is one of helplessness, the slave and the

Indian, like nature itself, invite a violence that in its limitlessness differs from war or torture. The slave's status gives little or no protection except as a species of property; the Indian is a party to treaties with the states and federal government that are enforced when it pleases the conqueror; nature's plenty serves merely to incite the "settler" into becoming an itinerant exploiter.

The American southerner, unlike the ancient slave owner who had relied primarily on physical force, has created *une force nouvelle.* The old tyrannies enslaved the body, the new ones strike at the soul. The southerner has "spiritualized despotism and violence," destroying the will to be free by means of legal measures designed to remove even the hope of abolition while denying the Africans the rudiments of an education.[45] Slavery is thus not simply an institution but a method of producing a distinct species. The slave is a human being who is first broken, then reconstructed as ignorant, abject, hopeless, cultureless, and dangerous, hated alike by himself and by his creator.[46] Although slavery is recognized to be economically inefficient, the southerner cannot let go of his creature. His choice is stark, either to free the negro, "mingle" and intermarry, or continue to repress.[47]

The fate of the Indian is more revealing. While the African has been exploited to maintain a leisured aristocracy, the Indian is the victim of the dynamic embodied in a new kind of being, who not only subdues nature but makes it the medium of a different politics than that celebrated in the New England township. It is the politics of a will-to-power that is driven by an urge to level and is stronger than any radical revolutionary will. The fate of the African and Indian is its testimonial. Originally each of those peoples had been creatures of nature, living in intimate relation with the land. Yet they were more than natural peoples. They had "native cultures" and their own histories preserved in stories, legends, and myths. The frontier settler and the slave owner had destroyed both the nature and the history of those peoples.

## VII

> *At the time of which I write 13 million civilized Europeans are quietly spreading themselves over these fertile wildernesses whose resources and extent they have no precise knowledge. Three or four thousand soldiers drive the wandering native tribes before them; behind the armed men the woodcutters advance and penetrate the forests, driving off the wild animals, exploring the rivers, and preparing the triumphal march of civilization across the wilderness.*
>
> Tocqueville[48]

What kind of a being was this, and what kind of tyranny was it that he directed at nature and history? Was it peculiar to democracy or to modernity?

He is best revealed in the frontier settler rather than the slaveholder. The latter is now settled, cultivating and cultivated, defensive rather than aggressive. The frontier type is less a settler than an unsettler. He comes from nowhere and he travels light.

> The emigrant shows a restlessness of spirit which is quite extraordinary; the land never remains with those who have cleared it. When it begins to produce the pioneer sells it and plunges again into the forests. It seems that the habit of changing places, of turning things upside down, of felling, of destroying, has become a necessity of his existence.[49]

Although this man had a history in his New England beginnings, he is now immersed in nature, dwelling in a Cartesian solitude, outfitted with little save a Bible, an ax, and newspapers.[50] A reversal of the *politikon zoon* who, Aristotle claimed, could only be fulfilled in a political community. His is a life without rituals and forms, pure modernity unrelieved by *moeurs*. In his brief lifetime he has witnessed an "empty" wilderness first dotted with a dwelling, then cleared, then populated, and now "a huge city." He has lived among tribes who now "live only in history." He has seen rivers change their course and the climate alter. He has annihilated history and replaced it by change: "Often born under another sky, placed in the midst of an ever moving tableau, borne by an irresistible torrent which sweeps along everything around him, the American has no time to attach himself to anything, he is only accustomed to change, and ends by regarding it as the natural condition of man."[51]

There is, perhaps, something darkly circular about inheriting a tabula rasa and briefly inscribing upon it, then striving to reproduce it. Proceeding in a void of his own creation, he can become the supreme pragmatist and rational calculator, for there is little around him with a prior claim. New World man focuses "on the single aim of making his fortune." His own family loses its identity and merges into "a vast egotism": he regards it as but an extension of himself. His is "a restless, calculating, adventurous race which does coldly what ardent passion alone would explain, which traffics in everything, not excluding even morality and religion."[52] Nature for him is not external, however. It becomes incorporated as the experience of actual infinity, of the unlimited. That is how modernity incorporates nature: as democratized infinity wherein nothing is privileged; as the giver of natural equality and equal rights to all, without regard to the distinctions attributed to history. And when the new man will have exhausted the last democratic vista, what then? "It is a nomadic people whom the rivers and lakes cannot halt, before whom the forests fall and the prairies become shaded; and who, after having reached the Pacific Ocean will retrace its steps to trouble and destroy the societies which it will have formed behind it."[53]

Slavery, genocide, a restless power that reaches its limits and then turns on its own: a certain democracy would eventually exhaust its moral potentialities but persist as a self-righteous, dangerous infinity. The democracy that emerges in these final pages gains a final bloated form, a power of unprecedented and mythical proportions. Recall that the concluding section of the last chapter begins with Tocqueville's famous metaphor of the traveler who ascends the hill to gain a better prospect of the city below. By the end of the section the city has disappeared, swallowed up by "something entirely new in the world, the dimensions of which the imagination cannot grasp."[54] Tocqueville prophesies an insatiable power, an Anglo-American imperium encompassing not only the southwest and Mexico, but extending throughout the entire New World.[55] This power, he predicts, will face another great power, Russia. The two giants, symbolizing two contrasting ways of life, will confront each other, each astraddle a world. As Tocqueville recites the contrasts, the crucial point lies in the transmutation of democratic values into a democratized economy of opportunity. Participatory democracy disappears into sheer energy and the will-to-power. Suddenly there comes into focus the full implications of a land of plenty, of the dynamic of human energy let loose without hindrance. The American symbolizes the war against nature and "barbarity," the Russians against men and "civilization" itself; the American relies on the "plowshare," the Russian on arms; the American is propelled by self-interest: power emerges spontaneously from free individuals and their good sense; the Russian concentrates "all of the power of society" in a single individual; the principle of the one society is freedom, of the other servitude.[56] In the end the appeal of "democracy" in America appears no longer to depend on the promise of a new political but rather on a contrast with despotism.

# CHAPTER XIV THE IMAGE OF DEMOCRACY

## I

> *First of all I think it necessary to distinguish carefully between the institutions of the United States and democratic institutions in general.*
>
> Tocqueville[1]

As he neared the completion of the first volume of *Democracy in America*, Tocqueville confronted serious difficulties in delivering on the promise that his study would not only be "interesting" but "profitable" to Frenchmen. Certainly the differences were formidable. In the United States there were no hindrances, natural or political, to the development of democracy; no social class or political party analogous to the embittered victims of the French Revolution, no *revanchistes* who rejected the existing political system and toasted its collapse or overthrow. Material scarcity and the class conflicts arising from the unequal distribution of scarce material goods, which had haunted ancient democracies and early modern republics, hardly existed in the new land. Its democracy knew neither "proletarians" nor "peasants."[2]

Further, by Tocqueville's own showing, the key to developing a successful democracy was political education. That, in turn, depended on vigorous participatory institutions, precisely the element that had been left in limbo in France by two centuries of royal and revolutionary centralization.[3] Thus the two societies were not synchronous: local political culture was firmly in place in America before a nation-state was founded and before the extraordinary geographical and economic expansion of the early nineteenth century had been set in motion. American democracy had not had to face the dilemma created by the contradictory temporal requirements of cultivating democratic habits and beliefs and building a centralized state, while struggling to adjust to the increasing tempo of modern change.

## II

*I know that I am treading on burning coals. Each word of this chapter will offend in some way the different parties which divide my country. I shall say, nonetheless, what I think.*

Tocqueville[4]

While negotiating these perplexities, Tocqueville was at the same time attempting to define his own role, part political educator and part mediator. His mission, as he conceived it, was to construct a version of democracy that might attract a consensus in a society that remained badly divided. That would not represent the same task as constructing a theory *of* American democracy. Instead it would be the more abstract undertaking of envisioning a democracy theoretically. As he had explained in the introduction to volume 1, he had not aimed at an exact representation of American politics. He had sought "more"—"an image of democracy itself." That image would be constructed by seeing through America to a deeper layer of meaning: "in America I have seen more than America; I have sought the image of democracy itself, its tendencies, character, prejudices, its passions so that we might know what we might hope or fear from it."[5]

But "more than America," "democracy itself," might mean less than America. Although the theoretical and political problems of finding what relevance American democracy had for France posed a formidable hurdle, Tocqueville's principal difficulty, the one that ended by blurring both the political and the theoretical point of the first volume of *Democracy*, lay not with the pragmatics of applying it to France but with conceptually grasping "democracy in America" before attaining to "an image of democracy itself." That failing was due to a theoretical shortfall between an understanding of theory as capable of comprehending a "new world of democracy" and the realization that, while in some important respects the United States had extended the idea of democracy and of equality further than any previous society, in other important respects that society was crucially, perhaps fatally, unevenly democratized.

Take, for example, Tocqueville's formulation that Americans were willing to alter "secondary" matters "but they are very careful not to touch fundamentals."[6] That formulation had an unmistakable resonance to a France that had made fundamentals—such as religion, secular education, the franchise, and the monarchy—the center of bitter and prolonged controversy, thus depriving the society of a stabilizing consensus: disagreement over fundamentals left change as the main continuity. Yet at the same moment that he was trying to instruct his divided countrymen on the value of consensus and of its exemplary presence in the United States, Tocqueville was aware that it was precisely on matters of fundamentals that Jacksonian America was passionately embroiled—in disputes about the meaning of the Union, of its Constitution, and of the rights of property versus democratic equality. Under virtually every major category by which Tocqueville had hoped to explain American democracy—culture, education, political virtues—there proved to be wide variations among the several parts of the Union.

Not surprisingly, commentators have remarked on the confusingly different notions of democracy to be found in the work. One reason for the apparent muddle was Tocqueville's discovery that there was no single democracy in America from which to draw lessons. The aristocratic republicanism of the slave states was as distant from New England democracy as both were from the raw democracy of the western states.[7] In addition, there was the national democracy superimposed on the entire country. The extent to which Tocqueville's theoretical scheme began to unravel as he moved toward a conclusion for volume 1 was reflected in the formal organization of *Democracy*.

Tocqueville's conclusions and recommendations do not come in the form of a summarizing final chapter to the first volume. As I have already intimated, the final chapter comes close to subverting the entire enterprise for it is a devastating finale that reveals the dangerous depths of antidemocracy in the United States. Instead of being a proper conclusion, the last chapter is a potential epitaph. The more positive conclusion occurs in the chapters immediately preceding the last chapter where Tocqueville summarizes the advantages and drawbacks to democracy. There American democracy appears as ambivalent rather than problematic.

A sense of the difficulties being encountered by Tocqueville can be gotten by recapitulating the order of the first volume of *Democracy*, which divides almost equally into two parts. Part I and its eight chapters explain the system of political localism and extol the civic democracy of the New England township, a community at once political and moral. Throughout these pages Tocqueville's prose is passionate and intense as he seizes the possibility that within modernity itself, and despite the powerful attraction toward private concerns and pleasures, politics might nonetheless be restored as the defining center of social life and as essential to the development of human capacities. He sees/constructs a politics that is at once exuberant and virtuous, bursting with an energy that infects all of social life, catalyzing its members into prodigies of construction—of new communities, daring economic ventures ("there is a heroism in the way Americans conduct commerce"),[8] and a new nation. In that vision lay the possibility that human beings can learn to act politically/disinterestedly without first becoming godlike or being born to rule. "In no country of the world do men make such efforts to promote the well-being of society."[9]

The possibility of political revival, which Tocqueville would carry back to his countrymen, had initially been inspired not by the political totality summed up as the "United States" but by a civic democracy whose politics was localized, schooled in the stern public morality of Puritanism, and conducted over relatively small stakes of power, money, and prestige. That picture, possibly the first favorable representation of a contemporaneous democracy since Pericles' funeral oration, becomes overlain with the portrait of another and more problematic democracy when Tocqueville turns in the later chapters of part I to consider "government by democracy" in the more abstract setting of a nation-state with all of the parts of a scattered society as its domain. Although it, too, is a species of democracy, the tenor of Tocqueville's response to it was markedly different. The political passion and excitement stirred by the New England idyll of communal democracy dwindles into a mostly perfunctory description of the national Constitution and of the powers attached to the offices and institutions of the national government. Tocqueville concluded that American *moeurs*, strong religiosity, and experience enabled the system to work, and that with the exception of the courts, there was little that was applicable to France. Surveying the federal system as a whole, he professes amazement at its complexity and at the ability of ordinary citizens to comprehend it. His amazement is the expression of a discovery—that the federal government is an altogether different, far less admirable species of democracy from that represented by communal democracy.

But was it sustained by a distinctively national political culture, as suggested by Tocqueville's admiring remarks about the ability of the citizens to grasp a complex system? or did the national political culture merely mimic the rhetoric of local democracy without its substance? If the latter, then a "nationalized democracy," without a strongly developed culture of its own, would suffer the worst of both worlds, of being dependent on local cultures, which might well run the gamut from extreme to sober democracy to antidemocracy (as they did in the United States), or appearing to be so distant from local concerns as to attenuate severely the active involvement of citizens and thereby making possible a nationalized democracy and a thin culture of inattentive citizens.

## III

> *If it should ever come to pass that a democratic republic like that of the United States were founded in a country where the power of a single man had already established administrative centralization and caused it to penetrate the customs, as well as the laws, I would not hesitate to say that in such a republic the despotism would be more intolerable than in any of the absolute monarchies of Europe. One would have to go to Asia to find anything comparable.*
>
> Tocqueville[10]

In the second or concluding part of volume 1, Tocqueville begins to explore the implications of there being no single "democracy in America" but rather a certain discontinuity in democratic culture between the national system and the local ones as well as between the several local systems. That perception becomes the basis of a negative paradigm of democracy, a nationalized democracy. The term, which is mine, is not synonymous with either a national government or a national constitution. Nationalized democracy represents an amalgam of impressions, most of them critical, which Tocqueville draws from various levels of government, including the national, and then combines into an imaginary whose purpose is to allow him to generalize about the pitfalls of democracy relevant to his countrymen.

In the crucial passages,[11] he argues that the American case is valuable because, unlike Europe where democracy is contested by competing and opposing principles, in the United States "the people dominate without obstacles." It is thus a pure example, "democracy in the grip of its own propensities." At the same time the imaginary is haunted at its edges by an unidentified presence, the excesses of the French Revolution. Thus Tocqueville rounds out his claim for the value of the American example by once more invoking an "irresistible movement," which is carrying Europe "perhaps toward despotism" or "perhaps a republic" but "certainly toward a democratic social condition."[12] "A democratic social condition," or what I have called nationalized democracy, is an abstraction that enables Tocqueville to press the "logic" of democracy to what he conceives as its theoretical limits.

To be sure, Tocqueville recapitulates what he finds politically impressive about American democracy: the public-spiritedness in local matters, the respect for law, the inhibitions imposed by the strong religious beliefs, the ability to improvise instead of relying on administrative interventions, the extraordinary energy that a free society encourages in its members, and the self-respect that political participation promotes. Yet at almost every step Tocqueville attaches qualifications that make his praise seem grudging. Thus the secret of American democracy is to connect political rights with self-interest so that the individual becomes committed to the nation, not from "duty" or "pride" but "from greed."[13] Some measure of popular participation is recommended because it is possibly the only way of getting democratic individuals interested in "their country's fate."[14] The advantages of the American system seem to exist despite the actors and their intentions and owe much to the unique fact that in America mistakes are always "retrievable."[15] "At the bottom of democratic institutions there is a hidden tendency which makes men promote the general prosperity in spite of their vices and errors . . . in democracies men produce the good without having thought about it."[16]

In its generality nationalized democracy presents an actuality that corresponds to its abstract theoretical character. Nationalized democracy is *unqualified* in the double sense of that word: its citizens are not distinguished by their political competence, and their behavior is unconstrained by *moeurs.* Its character is drawn, in part, from what Tocqueville had identified as the disadvantages of American democracy. Despite all he had said in praise of American political enlightenment, he now insists that democracy cannot raise the level of enlightenment "above a certain level" because intellectual progress depends on those who "can live without working."[17] At the same time, the "envy" natural to democracy causes its citizens to discourage superior men from holding office and as a result the talented and the virtuous devote themselves to private pursuits.[18] Above all, democracy imposes the most pervasive conformity upon its citizens. By "an invisible power" the majority "silences" independent thought. Although, admittedly, the majority has used its power "well," the danger lies in the mere existence of this "irresistible power": it is a "continuous fact while its good use is only an accident."[19]

Nationalized democracy is literal democracy, unmediated, a novel political form where the people actually "reign" and the majority "rules."[20] It is made possible by a shallow, generalized culture and "a democratic social condition." The members of society have become more or less alike according to the several measures of property, education, manners, tastes, and values, and hence "more equal in power" than in any other country or epoch.[21] This homogeneity is the matrix from which the "despotism of the majority" issues. Nationalized democracy threatens to be a total presence, more enveloping than anything imagined by absolute monarchs: "the opinions, prejudices, interests, and even passions of the people find no lasting obstacles preventing their manifestation in the every day life of society."[22] At the end of volume I, Tocqueville's America has the status of a discovery about a possible future. Democracy generalized, freed from the immediacy of local restraints and affections and released to be reconstituted on a national plane, belongs to a different political species, which might be called "spasmodic democracy." It stands for a form of pure governance in which power is dissociated from popular influence, save for the periodic spasms of elections. That remoteness enables its governors to constitute, define, and grapple with large-scale problems (war, diplomacy, international economic relationships, etc.) that have no counterparts in the everyday experience of citizens and seem manageable only if the number of decisionists is few and if they have experience in these somewhat abstract matters. The increasingly abstract character of the political, while unconducive to popular democracy, lends itself to republican elitism.

Thus part 2 begins with the basic principle of the negative paradigm of democracy, a strong assertion about the reality and broad scope of majority rule in America. Building on the national plane he had established by his discussion of constitutional structures, he begins to treat the "national" as interchangeable with the general and the abstract. He turns first to political parties and, as I suggested earlier, his treatment begins by being national and American, but quickly changes and becomes general, abstract, and critical. The same pattern is repeated where the press and political associations are treated as countervailing to nationalized democracy; he moves from practices that are widespread in American society to an abstract formulation of those practices which would evoke a meaning that Frenchmen could connect to their own political history.

## IV

> *What a happy land this new world is, where man's vices are nearly as useful to society as his virtues!*
>
> Tocqueville[23]

What I have been describing is Tocqueville's attempt to discover, not empirical America, but that "image of democracy" to which he had referred in his introduction. That image was a theoretical composite designed to show what was worthy of emulation in the "democratic republic" (positive paradigm) and what were the dangers and drawbacks to nationalized, majoritarian democracy (negative paradigm). The remainder of volume 1, that is, chapters 5–10 of part 2, was devoted to analyzing democracy on this more general plane where its admirable elements could be sorted out from the dangerous ones. The fundamental question that his procedure provokes is: what explains Tocqueville's profound equivocation, not about democracy in the abstract but about the United States in the concrete? Is the problem simply one of trying to find the right way of presenting the American experience to Frenchmen or is it the problem of the American experience itself, the problem of trying to pin down just how democratic it really was?

The awkward title for chapter 5, "The Government of the Democracy in America," captures the point of Tocqueville's strategy of both detaching democracy from America and yet connecting it, but also implying that "government" represents a set of tasks or functions with objective criteria of performance independent of any particular system. Invariably those criteria involve some combination of aristocratic and meritocratic values. Chapter 6 sets out "the real advantages which American society derives from a democratic government." In part, that chapter tries to redress the very lukewarm appraisal of democracy's capacity for governance by a strong account of "public spirit" in America, including the respect for law that prevails when rights are widely shared and the remarkable energy those entitlements generate. Chapter 7 poses the problem of majority tyranny, while chapter 8 discusses the ways that Americans have "tempered" it. Chapter 9 attempts to summarize "the principal factors" that "tend to maintain the democratic republic in the United States." Here Tocqueville considers the relative weight of "accidental" and "providential" factors, of laws, *moeurs*, religion, education, habits, and experience. The chapter is crucial not only for suggesting how much of the American experience is imitable but also for focusing that question not on "democracy" but on a moderated version, "the democratic republic." Chapter 10 is, by its author's own admission, an anomaly. It treats what is peculiar to America, its racial problems, and at the same time it adds crucial elements to the discussion of the republican character of American democracy.

## V

> *Those who, after having read this book, were to conclude that in writing it I am proposing that the laws and* moeurs *of Anglo-Americans should be imitated by all nations with a democratic social condition, would have made a great mistake. . . . I am very far from believing that we should follow the American example and imitate the means which they have used [to remain free]; for I am not unaware of the influence exerted by the nature of a country and of antecedent conditions on political constitutions.*
>
> Tocqueville[24]

The general aim of his strategy was to compress a minimalist version of democracy from the maximalist example represented by a nationalized democracy, where "democracy is allowed its full reach." This required that he treat the association between democracy and the United States as contingent, thus making it possible to "imagine a democratic people organized differently from the American people."[25] By challenging the notion that the United States was the archetypal form of democracy, a space was created for a different image of democracy. "The political constitution of the United States seems to me," he would write, "to be one of the forms that democracy can give to its government."[26] The distinction between democracy and its governmental form, between "a democratic people" and its "institutions," was meant to support a basic thesis, that a society whose social condition is egalitarian or postaristocratic is not predestined to reproduce American practices or to adopt any other institutional prescription as the "natural" one for a democracy.

Having methodically identified the desirable features of American democracy and, at the same time, having developed a profile of the undesirable ones drawn partly from America and partly from the French revolutionary experience, Tocqueville proceeded to juxtapose the one model to the other and draw out their implications.

Selective aspects of the American experience were separated from the American example and incorporated into a new form.[27] Political rights, jury service, and voluntary associations are singled out, but the emphasis falls on the institutions and practices that serve to qualify majoritarian democracy. Two-stage elections (as in the election of senators), a strong and independent judiciary, and the restraints supplied by religion and morality all operate to moderate democracy.[28] It can be summed up as "republican democracy," a phrase that recurs frequently throughout the first volume of *Democracy* and always with favorable connotations. Only toward the end of the last chapter of the volume, however, does Tocqueville insist on the primary importance of the republican element and tries to expand on its meaning. It would be more precise to say that he tries to apotheosize it because his discussion starts by raising the possibility that the Union will be "dismembered" by a war between the states. He insists that need not "compromise the fate of republican institutions." "The future of the republic," he declares, "should not be confused with that of the Union." The latter is described as "an accident," a creature of the law; the republic, in contrast, has "deeper roots" and is "the natural state of Americans."[29] The move that disengages the republic from the American democratic form, and especially from the rancorous politics of the Jacksonian era, begins with the definition that "in the United States what is understood by a republic is the slow and quiet action of society upon itself." It is, Tocqueville emphasizes, a "regular condition truly founded on the enlightened will of the people."[30] A republicanized democracy will be self-limiting by practicing "self-control."[31] It is not a society whose predominant characteristic is of a democracy that has pushed equality to extremes but a people that has combatted "the weaknesses of the human heart and corrected the natural defects of democracy."[32]

> It is a conciliatory government in which proposals have time to ripen, and are discussed with deliberation, and executed only when they are mature. . . . In the United States "republic" means the tranquil reign of the majority. . . . But the majority itself is not omnipotent. Above it is a moral order of humanity, justice, and reason, and in the political world prior rights.[33]

The republicanized democracy imagined by Tocqueville would not be the democracy that had emerged historically in America but one chastened by the French encounter with its revolutionary form:

> Is it impossible to conceive of a government based on the real will of the majority, but of a majority that represses its natural instincts toward equality in favor of order and a stable State, and consents to investing one family or one man with the attributes of executive power? Can't one imagine a democratic society where the force of the nation would be more centralized than in the United States, where the people would exercise a less direct and less irresistible sway over general matters, and where, however, each citizen, endowed with certain rights, would take part in the proceedings of government within his sphere?[34]

That formulation could be described as a minimalist version of democracy. It requires the majority to act against "its natural instincts toward equality" and to "favor" "order and a stable State," the code words for hierarchy and traditional authority. The majority should abstain from "general matters" of national politics and disaggregate itself into individuals content to participate in local politics.

For the majority to accept this solution would require a very different majority than the active, sovereign-minded one that Tocqueville had found in America. How was it possible to conceive of a majority surrendering its own political potential and "repressing its natural instincts"? Tocqueville's solution was to put the question differently: "The great political problem of our time is the organization and establishment of democracy among Christians."[35] The "organization" of democracy assumed that democracy, that is, the demos, was the object to be organized, not the subject doing the organizing. Democracy could not be properly organized by majority rule with its susceptibility to popular passions and sudden enthusiasms. The project had to be carried out gradually; the nature of the means was such as to require considerable time and the knowledge of those who understood the dangers as well as the advantages of democracy. A republicanized democracy would be a "Christian" democracy because of what the Americans had demonstrated about the power of religion to restrain the demos. While American democracy had given the demos two forms of power previously denied it, the power to make its own laws and the independence that widely distributed economic opportunities gave to all, republicanized democracy would exploit *moeurs,* the form of power that the demos barely comprehended, much less knew how to wield but which Tocqueville confessed was so "central" to his thinking that "all of my ideas come back to it in the end."[36] *Moeurs* broadly covered "the *ensemble* of intellectual and moral dispositions" that shape men's emotions as well as their mental habits.[37] The power of *moeurs* was stronger, he maintained, than the power of either laws or geography, the latter a tacit reference to the unprecedented natural wealth in America.[38]

## VI

> *Thus Europeans exaggerate the influence that the geographical location of a country exercises over the staying power of democratic institutions. Too much importance is attributed to laws, too little to* moeurs.
>
> Tocqueville[39]

Was it possible, Tocqueville asks, to sustain democratic institutions by appropriate laws and mores but without the support of the geographical and material advantages operative in America? "[I]f geography cannot take the place of laws and *moeurs,* can laws and *moeurs* take the place of geography?"[40] Clearly, if in a democratic age customary beliefs and modes of behavior were to be controlling of the citizenry, what was at stake was the character of the demos and the identity of the arbiters of *moeurs* and the means by which the desired habits of behavior would be transmitted. Instead of being the principal actors, the demos would serve as the bearers of certain ideas of right and morality whose effect would be to create a democracy characterized by individual self-denial and collective self-restraint. A new political domain was thus being defined, the domain of popular beliefs, of beliefs "held" by the populace but created by others. This domain where power is exercised over democracy would become the main subject of the second volume of *Democracy.*

# PART FOUR

## *Persona and the Politics of Theory*

# CHAPTER XV
# TRAGIC HERO, POPULAR MASK

## I

*My desire [is] to write something good and pure, complete and forever above me.*

Tocqueville[1]

The first installment of *Democracy in America,* consisting of two volumes in the 1835 edition, was an immediate success and French critics promptly compared Tocqueville with the great thinkers of the past.[2] Its enthusiastic reception did not, however, satisfy Tocqueville's ambitions, quiet his torments, or goad him into rapidly completing the remainder of the work.

Tocqueville had returned to France in February 1832. Another three years elapsed before volume 1 of *Democracy* was written and another five before volume 2 appeared. Judging from certain remarks in his introduction to the first volume, he did not initially intend to work on a second volume.[3] The increase in distance between theorist and subject matter and the lapse of time between immediate impressions and eventual composition were to have a disruptive effect on the continuity of Tocqueville's theory.

As we have seen, the closing chapters of the first volume had left ambivalent impressions about the success of American democracy, even about its survival, thus suggesting an element of political uncertainty and perhaps theoretical disarray. If we are to understand what might be meant by "Tocqueville's theory," it is, at this point, as natural to interrupt our account of *Democracy* as the actual composition of it was in fact interrupted. The principal justification for interruption is that shortly after completing the first volume Tocqueville entered the world of politics. That decision to fashion himself into a politician meant, among many other things, that his personal preparation for the second volume was different from what it had been when he embarked for the New World. It also meant that in undertaking a second installment of *Democracy* he would be facing a theoretical situation of more restricted possibilities. The first volume, now published, confronted its author as a brute fact occupying a certain theoretical space, reflecting a relatively recent, unrepeatable experience and presenting to the world a certain fixed image of America. In a second volume theory would necessarily reflect a different experience and Tocqueville would be forced to situate himself in relation to a preestablished, if uncertain theory rather than begin with the theoretical equivalent of a tabula rasa.

## II

> *Some bursts of real happiness which from time to time issue from the midst of an habitual* malaise, *a great many discouragements, irritations, some disgust, and then sudden and shining hopes: that is the ordinary course, in an abbreviated but faithful epitome, of my history. It all makes, in the depths of my solitude, for a very troubled existence, agitated by violent and conflicting passions.*
>
> Tocqueville[4]

Before completing the first volume of *Democracy*, Tocqueville extended his political education by a journey to England and Ireland in 1833.[5] Although his brief stay did not fundamentally alter his viewpoint or assist him greatly in formulating his theory of democracy, it did alert him to the diverse forms that centralization might take and reinforced his conviction of the value of local institutions of self-government. Equally important, he was exposed for the first time to the stark class and power relationships being forged by capitalism, although he confessed to Beaumont that he was unsure of their implications.[6]

He was forcibly struck, too, by the persisting political and social influence of the English aristocracy. While the power of the English aristocracy in contrast with the French confirmed his belief that the latter was a spent political force, it also caused him to revise the political role and theoretical representation of aristocracy. Politically and theoretically aristocracy could no longer serve as it had from the beginning of Western theory and practice, the constitutional function of a competing and equilibrating force. Once it had mediated between princes and the middle classes, but now "the people" had emerged as actors, princes had given way to ministers, and aristocrats were merging into elites. Genealogy can offer only a futile resistance, the mannered opposition of "high society."[7] The revolution had disrupted the history of aristocracy, rendering it discontinuous and causing aristocracy to surrender its most crucial value, continuity. When it reemerges, its public element has been taken over by meritocratic elitism. The latter is, in theory, discontinuous.

For Tocqueville, paradoxically, the fact of its political demise freed aristocracy theoretically. As pure idea it assumed even greater importance in the second volume of *Democracy* than it had in the first.[8] This was because he began to see democracy less as a specific form of government by which the majority ruled—centralized administration had superseded the power of the majority—than as a generalized pressure that dissolved individual identity into the anonymity of "society." Democracy now stands more pronouncedly for the undifferentiated, the regression into a more primal state. Aristocracy is reaffirmed, not only as a social class but as the principle of individuality and resistance.

## III

*[I]t is necessary, whatever the cost, that I finish this book; between it and me there is a duel to the death; it is necessary that I kill it or that it kills me; I can no longer live as I have since beginning the project.*

Tocqueville[9]

When after considerable procrastination Tocqueville resumed writing, much had intervened that would affect his focus and emphasis. Personal preoccupations about his future career, marriage and domesticity, the broadened perspective supplied by England, and the continuing uncertainties about the direction of French politics all contributed to a growing distance between himself and America that led to self-doubts and complaints that the task of finishing the work had become a "nightmare."[10] He experienced wild swings in mood, from despair to exhilaration, from defeat to triumph. More than once after pronouncing the work to be virtually finished, he would begin yet another radical revision. More than once he swore never again to undertake a large work. His theoretical agonies occasioned further self-examinations: what he was trying to do theoretically seemed at odds with what he thought he should be politically. To confidants he gave frequent reports of his struggles toward self-clarification, of his restlessness, of unfulfilled ambitions, and bedeviling pride.[11]

These travails might be interpreted as a resistance to a life in which theorizing would be the defining center. This interpretation is supported by the unusual amount of attention that Tocqueville would devote to discussing the nature and status of theory in the second volume of *Democracy.* Although commentators have generally ignored the problem, of the twenty-one chapters that compose part 1 of volume 2, seven (1–4, 9–11) are concerned with some aspects of theory. Chapters 1–4 deal with the role of ideology in a democracy and with what one might call "the theoretization of everyday life" or "everyman as theorist." Chapters 9–11 address several of the most fundamental topics that theorists have engaged since antiquity: the relation of theory to practice, the differences between "pure" and "applied" theory, and the status of theory under different types of regimes. In the course of his discussion Tocqueville seems most deeply affected when he describes the heavy burden assumed by those who, like Pascal, were driven by a "disinterested passion" and "a pure desire to know."[12]

Despite his praise for those who had pursued a life of pure intellectual commitment, such a life seemed unable to satisfy Tocqueville's need to overcome doubt and to test himself by the demands of political action heroically conceived. As he struggled against becoming a confirmed theorist, his frustrated political aspirations became the shaping force of his theoretical formulations. As in composing the first volume whenever progress on the second lagged, he attempted to rekindle his spirits by fantasies of a great deed that would capture the central movement of his times:

> I work frequently with passion, rarely with pleasure. My work is oppressed by a feeling of imperfection. I am haunted by an ideal I cannot reach, and when I am weary with trying, I halt and retrace my steps, full of discouragement and disgust. My subject is truly the greatest, greater than myself, and I am tormented in seeing how little use I am making of ideas which seem to me good ones. There is another intellectual malady which gnaws at me endlessly. It is a frantic and unreasonable passion for certainty.[13]

## IV

When at last the final volume appeared in 1840, its reception was respectful rather than enthusiastic. The common complaint was of its abstractness. Tocqueville acknowledged that he had placed heavy demands on the reader and had probably disappointed those who, expecting a more extended treatment of America, found it difficult to follow a line of thought that forced them to journey back and forth between France and the United States.[14]

Scholars in the late twentieth century have found more striking differences in the second volume, so much so that some have argued that, instead of composing a sequel, Tocqueville had produced a different version of *démocratie.* The proponents of the *deux Démocraties* argue that, America practically disappears in the second volume and that different emphases appear, such as the importance given to centralization and despotism, a less simplistic conception of equality, and a more obtrusive preoccupation with France. It has been asserted that "two different frameworks for the book" are evidence that in the second volume Tocqueville was concerned to distinguish/separate revolutionary equality from democratic equality and thereby make clear that the evils ascribed to the latter were really the fault of the former.[15] In response other scholars have warned against overstating the differences so as to underplay the strong continuities.[16]

Whether volume 2 represents a different "book" depends on what one understands the requirements of a "book" to be and whether one assumes that a criticism of a book is automatically a criticism of the theory advanced in it. Stated differently, the boundaries of a theory and its structure need not coincide with those of a book. By its physical character a book imposes boundaries on its contents; it signifies a completed project while a theory may contain "tendencies" that point beyond its own current representation—as with Plato's dialogues. In Tocqueville's *Democracy* there are pointers in the direction of his *Old Regime* just as there would be interconnections, many of them explicit, between that last theory of Tocqueville and his first. It is possible, then, that the second volume contains emphases and directions, even conclusions, that appear to challenge those in the first volume, yet these may be attempts to enlarge the theory by drawing implications only half appreciated when first glimpsed.

I am suggesting an alternative conception of theory in which discontinuities, redistributions of emphasis, latent tendencies are "normal." A striking illustration occurs in the penultimate chapter of volume 1 immediately preceding the discussion of the "three races." There Tocqueville has finally managed to endorse the idea of "a democratic republic," an idealized version of what he had found in America. He all but confesses that he had not clarified that conception in the previous pages or even prepared the reader for it and had hardly grasped its importance himself:

> Among the causes [of the phenomenon of the democratic republic] there are several toward which, in spite of myself, the direction of my subject was carrying me and I touched upon only in passing. There are others which I have not been able to deal with; and still others with which I have dealt extensively that have been left behind virtually buried in details.[17]

To enter sympathetically into the thought world of a Tocqueville we need a conception of theory more tolerant of disorder than the usual notions of a book. Although such a conception would eschew the overly dramatic notion of a rupture, it would aspire to encompass both the continuity of preoccupations figured into the second volume and the differences that frequently unsettle them. What was at stake was an attempt to theorize a world beset by radical political, social, and intellectual changes. To say that the final installment of *Democracy* is focused on France is illuminating only if we understand that "France" serves also as a surrogate for modern politics. The boldness of that attempt is suggested by a contrast: both his near predecessors, Montesquieu and Rousseau, presented conceptions of society as a bounded, stable entity and his near contemporaries, the Utopian socialists and Comte, projected future societies, bounded and stable, even as their creators were acknowledging the unsettling influences of science, modern technology, egalitarianism, and secularism. Precisely because the modern world was the site of forces whose distinctive element was that their consequences were continuously generating further consequences—new scientific discoveries spinning off yet more discoveries, technologies that led to refinements only to have these superseded by a better, more efficient technology, and philosophies that were as fecund as technology in producing refinements (Young Hegelians, Left Hegelians, neo-Kantians)—the uncontrollable proliferation of consequences made the ideal of theoretical order seem incongruous at best for modernity's polyvalent world and repressive at worst for a self-subverting one.

## V

A conception of theory in which elements of "completion" or finality, of consistency and continuities are deemed all-important seems even less appropriate when we bear in mind that "Tocqueville" signifies not only a theory but a politics or, more precisely, a theorist who wrote the first volume while inspired by political aspirations but wrote the second after he had become a political actor who had lost some powerful illusions. Our project requires allowance for a second or changing Tocqueville. Although Tocqueville did not significantly change his political beliefs from the time that he completed the first volume and when he had completed the second, he did change his estimate of the value of politics and, especially, of its possibilities for significant action.

As we have already noted, personal crises were recurrent in Tocqueville's life but rarely were they simply personal. Tocqueville's genius or demon was to intermingle the personal, political, and theoretical so that when crises occurred, they typically took the form of a frustration of some personal ambition, some political hope, some theoretical vision. More often than not, he would manage to achieve the theoretical vision but fail to satisfy the personal or the political. That feeling of a lack of coherence to his life was directly related to—indeed, was a registry of—his encounter with French politics, the dimension of his life that most commentators have ignored in detailing the differences between the two volumes.

The Tocqueville who confronted the task of completing *Democracy* would bring a range of political experiences and theoretical resources that he did not possess in 1831 when he set sail for America, or even in 1835 when the first installment was published. They would produce an interior dialogue between the political and theoretical life that would go to the question of personal identity; they would also produce profound tensions and a troubled vision of democracy. At home he would encounter politics as defined by parliamentarism and energized by the pursuit of material interests. Tocqueville was resolved to make a political career for himself, to become a politician in an unheroic milieu. That resolve would inject a tactical and politicizing element into the structure of *Democracy.* "France" will be not a general reference point but a political construction in which Tocqueville's emphases and suppressions will be shaped by a political vision threatened by a growing repugnance toward what his contemporaries were defining as normal politics. Within his theory there would be contrary tugs. Tocqueville would enlist theory to advance a conception of the possibilities of political revival and thus politicize it. Theory as the guardian of an ideal political would, at the same time, provide refuge from a politics that struck him as partisan and mundane. Struggling to work out his ideal conception of the political in *Democracy* and, at the same time, to relate it to the modest practical possibilities of everyday politics produced tensions. Theory becomes not a solution but a consolation:

> I feel that I hold the most important idea of our time; its grandeur elevates me, but my own inadequacy brings me down. . . . In the midst of all these tribulations I feel a great happiness: in my mind I work over a vast field where no preoccupations of personal interest come to trouble me, where it runs freely and where it nourishes only the feelings of honest thoughts.[18]

## VI

> *The man who takes action in his own country cannot hope to understand the world outside: the man who takes all knowledge for his ambition must give up the idea of ever changing anything at home.*
>
> Claude Lévi-Strauss[19]

Writing to a close friend, Tocqueville implied that some change in his understanding of himself as a theorist had occurred between the two installments of *Democracy.* He describes it by a contrast between "a casual observer" (*un promeneur*) and "a serious traveler" (*un voyageur sérieux*).[20] The former is satisfied with surface appearances, the latter gazes "into the depths of society."[21] We might interpret "surface" to refer to the political novelty of democratic government, the obvious topic for any traveler to the new land. "The depths of society" implied a nonobvious, deeper level of being: inarticulate beliefs, unwritten codes of conduct, and anonymous forces—in short, hidden, immaterial interconnections that were of profounder significance than formal institutions in moderating or exacerbating democratic politics and to which Tocqueville would try and give expression in his account of the role of manners, morals, sentiments, and beliefs. The serious traveler had not only discovered civil society but made contact with an ontology of power beneath the surface of politics and potentially controlling over it. Civil society would be the site of the modern struggle over the shape of the political.

What had intervened to cause Tocqueville to hint that while in America he had been *un promeneur* but now, with his journey over, he had become *un voyageur sérieux*?

For one thing, he undertook a serious theoretical preparation of a kind he had not done prior to his American journey. In preparing the second volume of *Democracy*, he began a careful reading of, and argument with, some of the major political theorists of the past. He continued to draw upon Pascal, Montesquieu, and Rousseau;[22] but he read deeply in Plato and Machiavelli as well.[23] In addition, he turned to the great writers of the Old Regime, to Bossuet, Fontenelle, Saint-Evremond, Voltaire, Duc de Saint-Simon; they would be the silent sources for his construction of a "high" culture of aristocracy to stand alongside, and in judgment upon, his construction of egalitarian culture.[24] Along with the classics of political theory and French literature, he turned to Plutarch, the ancient writer whose memorable stories of great statesmen, military heroes, and founders had over the centuries fed the imagination of numerous dramatists, theorists, and historians, as well as of young gentlemen who dreamed of political greatness.

Tocqueville's reading of the past masters of political theory is of special importance in assessing the theoretical character of the concluding volume of *Democracy*. That experience was not primarily a matter of completing a liberal education or of learning the grammar of theory or of amassing intellectual debts (and thereby acquiring a certain intellectual genealogy). It had to do, instead, with his continuing attempt to thresh out the vexing question of the relationship between the moral and agonal *grandeur* of the political and the mean and egotistical motives at work in politics.

While at work on the second volume, Tocqueville shared with his friend Kergorlay some thoughts about one of his persistent concerns, the theorist's uses of religion. In the course of a letter that seems almost "Nietzschean," it becomes clear that he has been musing about theoretical strategies and what they reveal about motives. He notes that prophets are "an unbelievable union of selfishness and charity." They are "obscure" men aspiring to become "famous" yet driven by a love for their fellow men. They "dress up" moral teaching "in a religious and prophetic form" that appeals to the "tastes of the masses." For Tocqueville the prophet was a moralist with a touch of the *politique*, one who adapts his teaching to his audience without corrupting the one or the other. Tocqueville goes on to say that in later ages prophets are succeeded by philosophers who also embody a blend of *egoisme* and charity, but in their case *egoisme* is predominant, though disguised. Tocqueville found it striking that the motives of philosophers have been overlooked and suggests that they ought to be subjected to closer scrutiny. Unlike the prophet, the philosopher systematizes morality in order to discredit religion. The philosopher and the prophet have been the two main types that have tried "to moralize humanity." There is no "third way" of teaching morality and hence all that we can do is to try and counteract the one by the other. Tocqueville closes the letter by confiding that he had been impressed by a maxim of a prerevolutionary writer, that men first act and then create "principles that rationalize their actions." That, he concludes, is particularly true of revolutionaries.[25]

Elements of the prophet and the philosopher of morality were clearly present in Tocqueville's own makeup, as he was acutely aware, although he identified his *egoisme* as aristocratic pride rather than plebeian selfishness. The unresolved dialectic of *egoisme* and idealism, politics and the political, was crystallized for Tocqueville by his reading of Plato and Machiavelli, the theoretical representatives of that polarity.

Although he judged Plato a great moralist and a "poor politician," Tocqueville remained strongly drawn to Plato's subordination of politics to a stern standard of the common good. He also found the austere economy of *The Republic*—the strictures against money, wealth, and display—reinforcement for his own growing distaste for the aggressive self-interest of the bourgeoisie. Revealingly, in the sole reference to Plato in *Democracy*, Tocqueville pictures him as struggling against "the materialism" of his times.[26] For Tocqueville Plato was exemplary of the theorist bearing witness against those social and moral forces which had to be resisted before a purer politics could gain recognition.

Machiavelli represented the opposite extreme of a politics so obsessed with gaining and holding power that it loses sight of the goal of political renewal.[27] In *The Prince* the Florentine presented himself as the consummate politician, yet in the end, in Tocqueville's reading, his was merely "a very complicated machine" for wickedness. Tocqueville responded more positively to Machiavelli's *History of Florence*, perhaps out of sympathy for Machiavelli's melancholy over the political decadence of his native city. The raw politics depicted there—brutal, violent, egotistical in the extreme, and, above all, secularized—was, in Tocqueville's reading, an object lesson of the "pure" politics that follows when a people loses its religion. If Machiavelli had sought to limit the damage that wicked actors inflict, if he had tried to restrain their evil inclinations, he would then have deserved fame.

Tocqueville's commentary imposes a great silence on Machiavelli's complete subordination of religion to the ends of statecraft. Tocqueville would come close to adopting a similar position but, and it is a large qualification, without Machiavelli's reversion to pagan models of civil religion. Revealingly, Tocqueville seemed chilled by the bleakness of a Machiavellian world, "the world [as] a great arena from which God is absent."[28] Certainly the role of religion in American democracy was one of the few topics for which Tocqueville's praise was unqualified, although, ironically, the positive contribution of American Christianity, of maintaining the democratic republic without injecting a contentious clericalism, could qualify it as a Machiavellian civil religion.[29]

## VII

*In politics it is necessary to be pure, more than in other things.*
Tocqueville[30]

These theoretical and intellectual concerns converged—and collided—when Tocqueville decided to enter electoral politics. He would remain actively engaged in politics throughout the completion of *Democracy* and beyond. The experience would be unsettling, bringing its own full measure of doubts, uncertainties, and crises of identity—political as much as personal. What first appeared in 1837 as the golden moment when politics and theory, the active and the contemplative lives, were to be joined proves instead to be a source of nagging anxieties. Tocqueville came to suspect that theorizing and action were alternative, perhaps mutually exclusive forms of challenge and gratification, not simply alternating modes of activity to be picked up or laid aside as the occasion warranted. Perhaps, too, the true antithesis was not between theory and action but the less grandiose one between theory and politicking. During the time that he published the first installment of *Democracy* and finished the last, he vacillated frequently about whether he should forgo a career of writing and concentrate primarily upon politics.

His uncertainties were a response not only to competing ideal life-forms, one contemplative and the other active, but to the tensions within them as well. The theoretical had come to symbolize the defense of an ideal political, the plane where politics was transfigured and made the vehicle of truth and right, where it acquired an ultimate significance, and where the theorist embodied the will to disinterestedness and the pure passion for freedom and the common good. Theorizing embodied the hope that politics could be redeemed from the struggle for power and material interests. Writing to a friend about the "torment" of his unfinished volume, Tocqueville remarks: "That fixation poisons all the pleasures I feel at returning to the world of general ideas after having languished several months among the miserable small particulars of the last session [of the Chamber]. Immersed in the book and in general ideas render me . . . like a stranger to what is passing in the world."[31] As long as theory was the defender of the political against politics, Tocqueville could not renounce theory; and as long as theory could not realize the political by the efforts of the theorist alone, he could not abandon politics.

In the midst of his electoral campaign he wrote to Beaumont about his disgust and disdain for politics and lamented the distractions preventing the completion of *Democracy*, a concern he claimed was more important to him than the election.[32] Once, during his first electoral campaign, when Tocqueville was challenged to produce evidence of having performed some political action, his reply was that "the publication of a political work" was "a serious action, significant and irrevocable."[33] But to his parliamentary mentor, Royer-Collard, he vigorously disclaimed any intention of becoming an "author" and averred that, upon finishing *Democracy*, he would never write again unless a great occasion demanded it.[34]

The life of theory seemed insufficiently performative, unable to fulfill that part of him that craved the chance to run risks for the sake of lofty, disinterested ideals and to win praise from those he respected. Writing to Beaumont in the midst of a war scare, he remarked that the books they had written would in all likelihood be forgotten amid the excitement. "It is a poor calling, after all, that we are following, if one can only influence men when they are tranquil. You amuse them and they leave you when they want to act."[35]

As long as he was unable to gain entry into the real political world, he was prepared to follow a theoretical vocation but to pursue it with a political passion. The second volume of *Democracy* would be importantly shaped by that passion without fully satisfying it. In midpassage he confided to his close friend Kergorlay:

> Do not believe . . . that I have a mindless enthusiasm, or any enthusiasm whatever, for the intellectual life. I have always placed the life of action above everything else. But I cannot agree that when the way of action is closed, one should not muster all of one's energies for thought. After all, isn't it thinking, in its purest forms, that endlessly shook the world for three centuries? And is there a more powerful mode of acting than writing?[36]

That letter, written shortly before Tocqueville finally won a seat in the Chamber of Deputies, assumed that "the life of action" was synonymous with politics and that politics was the name for the public forum where issues of great gravity to the common well-being were contested and fundamental principles of morality and of the meaning of the political itself were defended and resolved. What was most lacking was what he described as "the first symptom of public life, the frequent contact of men with each other rather than just meeting each other. There is never any kind of joining together, no place where a large number of men can freely exchange opinions and thoughts."[37] As he imagined it, politics was meant to be the heroic dramatization of competing visions of the good. But he would quickly discover that he had entered not a Plutarchian politics of memorable deeds, but politicking: a politics of politicians that imposed severe limits on action, prescribing its modes and confining its aims while inflating its rhetoric.

> I cannot tell you . . . the disgust I feel at seeing all the public men of our day trafficking and pursuing the smallest interests of the moment in matters that are in my eyes as serious and sacred as principles. . . . [It] makes me ask myself if in this world there is something other than interests and if what one takes for sentiments and ideas are not merely interests which act and speak.[38]

The politics Tocqueville had to engage was the politics of modernity: bourgeois, liberal, parliamentary, organized around parties and elections, defined by material interests, fought by coalitions and alliances, and settled by negotiations. He would discover that the "way of action" remained "closed," even when one was "in" politics.

## VIII

> *[Plutarchs' actors] are not perfect . . . but they are great, and it is the* grandeur *one hungers for in a century such as ours.*
>
> Tocqueville[39]

Tocqueville would set out on a political career nursing the same lofty notions about heroic politics whose demise he had explained in the first volume of *Democracy* and now revivified by reading Plutarch. He was exhilarated by the opening of his electoral campaign and by the encouragement of his supporters. He wrote feelingly of the "bond" forged between himself and the place he would represent. A "mist" had dissolved, he testified; and he felt as though finally he had found his true identity and the opportunity of following his true calling, of redeeming politics by elevating it above the mere pursuit of material interests.[40]

Before Tocqueville's plunge into politics, his persona was defined by political desire but sublimated into a world created by thought and publicly identified with its creation. Now the aristocratic theorist of antiaristocracy was about to acquire a political persona and seek to sublimate his theoretical desire into political creation: no longer the distance of the voyager-observer, no longer the representative of privilege in a land of equals.

To help sort out these crosscurrents, I want to draw on Bakhtin's intriguing distinction between the "epic and tragic hero": the first wants to externalize "an absolute past," while the second is the wearer of "popular masks" and a chameleon of sorts. All of the hero's possibilities are identified with his social position and all of his hopes are "for the memory such a self anticipates in its descendants." His being depends on "a single and unified world view" and "tradition" and the "distancing" from the present world that it brings. When that world is shattered—and the chief enemy of its destruction is laughter—the way is open for "popular masks," and for a radically different being, one who has "ceased to coincide with himself" and so is free "to assume any destiny" and improvise any plot. Unlike the tragic hero who always perishes, the man of masks always has an unrealized potential, a surplus that overflows all forms: "popular masks . . . never perish."[41]

Tocqueville in America approximates the tragic hero: distance "upon" one society, distance "from" another; tradition absent in the one society but brought to bear upon it from the other, albeit a tradition that had been shattered. Now, as candidate, the hero approaches a role that, by its nature, demands connections with others, even dependencies, and offering, temptingly, a popular mask.

At the start of his campaign Tocqueville issued an open letter in which he set out to instruct his fellow citizens in the proprieties that ought to govern the relationship between candidates and electors. The performance was remarkable for its rigidity and arrogance: a tragic hero in the extreme. His circular began not with an appeal but a provocation. He proclaimed his intention of rejecting any obligation that might compromise his political independence. "I shall not ask you to give me your vote," adding that he presumed they would reciprocate by not asking for his. "A soliciting candidate," he warned, would be a "weak deputy." Voters and deputies alike should be guided solely by conscience and he would, therefore, promise to remain independent of party. When he turned to substantive matters, his views echoed the ambivalence in *Democracy*. We live, he warned, in "a new, unprecedented era" when "traditional habits and old laws" are no longer adequate. His conclusions, however, were cautious in the extreme. France did not need to be transformed into a republic but to develop free institutions. This required the extension of liberty (i.e., the right to vote) "slowly, gradually, and with infinite precautions." France has had its fill of revolution and change; it needed "repose."[42]

In the course of the campaign an offer of assistance was tendered by Tocqueville's cousin, Count Molé, then serving as Louis-Philippe's prime minister. In the exchange of correspondence that followed, Tocqueville stiffly declined the offer, saying that he wished "to be freely elected," free "to vote according to his conscience," and free to pursue an "independent position."

Molé's response to what he perceived as "literary" fastidiousness was a direct and sharp rebuke accompanied by a concise lesson in the realities of a parliamentary game in which groupings were all-important. "A man who chose to act only when he was sure of being right, without doubt or compromise, would do nothing, even in private life. He must sit with folded arms." One must fight, Molé concluded, for the principles and goals of one's chosen political group, but its support was not "a yoke which need hurt your pride or delicacy."[43]

When the votes were counted, Tocqueville had been defeated. By flaunting his independence, he had probably assured the result, although he attributed it to "the power of money . . . unhandicapped by noble birth and seconded by the popular hatred against the nobles." Rebuffed, he turned for solace to his unfinished work on America, but not before reassuring Beaumont that he looked forward to completing *Democracy* and gamely insisting that "the future is ours."[44] He would return to the theoretical life and, citing the example of Plato, consoled himself with the thought that the greatest and most influential writings throughout history have been those which appealed to lofty religious and moral principles.[45] Yet the hurt ran deep and he felt that his heroic ideals had made him a marginal man. "I have a temperament crammed with a heroism which hardly belongs to our age. I fall completely flat when I come out of these dreams to find myself faced with reality."[46]

The "reality" on which he vented his resentment was the politics of his time, the "disgusting" scramble for place among the politicians and their preoccupation with "the pettiest interests of the moment."[47]

Nonetheless, with the end of his theoretical labors in sight, he decided to run again for the Chamber in 1839. This time he was successful, and it marked the beginning of a parliamentary career that lasted until 1851. Initially he exulted in his "honorable and great success" and promised to be "an honest and disinterested politician" rather than "a great statesman."[48] A year later disillusionment set in: "The side of human nature disclosed by politics is, indeed, miserable. . . . Perfect purity and disinterestedness are unknown. . . . I have entered public life; I like its excitement, and the great interests involved in it stimulate my mind; but there are many things absolutely wanting in it, without which I cannot live."[49]

Although disillusion and contempt for the sterility and tedium of politics remained a constant theme in his letters, there was a growing intensity to his outbursts as he realized that he had caught the contagion of the game. He could not suffer to be in it or to endure the thought of being outside it.

> I am much afraid that if I were compelled to give up the excitement which is so often trying to me, in order to bury myself in the retirement which I value so highly,

> it would end by becoming insipid. Is the fever of public life, then, essential to my moral temperament? I am inclined to think so; and yet I often suffer cruelly from it.[50]

Tocqueville's torment was the greater as he was nagged by the thought that perhaps at bottom the political and the theoretical life were irreconcilable. He complained to Royer-Collard, who himself combined the two roles, that

> there is no action, and what is politics without action? To live in a public assembly in order not to work efficaciously for *la chose publique,* is not to act and not to unify those who alone have the power of acting . . . is this not manifest nonsense? . . . Is it not to transfer one kind of life to another, *l'observation théorique* to the life of action, to the great detriment of both?[51]

Although some of Tocqueville's sentiments cited here were expressed after he had completed the second volume of *Democracy,* they are all consistent with a desire-and-revulsion response to politics that agitated him as he was writing. There is a revealing passage in a letter to Royer-Collard written after Tocqueville's successful election and first experiences in the Chamber. "Until now I have been unable to return to my book and that has been a cause of great annoyance. For what I have seen of the inside of the political world over some months has made me feel the need to revise certain parts of the work that I had thought were finished."[52]

A New World that once had been seen from the outside, an Old World freshly seen from the "inside," and the inspiration for revising "certain parts" of *Democracy*—or *pour France*?

# CHAPTER XVI THE DEMOCRATIZATION OF CULTURE

## I

*After having examined the influence which the fact of equality exerts over men's opinions and sentiments, which more of a philosophical than a political undertaking, I finally come to the influence these opinions and sentiments, thus modified, have on the course of society and government.*

Tocqueville to Royer-Collard[1]

In the preface to the second volume of *Democracy in America* Tocqueville insisted that "the two [volumes] complement one another and form a single work."[2] The difference between them, he explained, was that the first volume had dealt with the laws and political *moeurs* shaped by the "democratic social condition" in America, while the second would focus on the "multitude of feelings and opinions unknown to the old aristocratic societies of Europe" and on "the new relationships" encouraged by that condition.

That he intended a shift in emphasis in volume 2 was suggested in a letter written to Royer-Collard before its completion. Now that he had a better sense of "the book as a whole," it struck him as concerned more with "the general effects of equality upon *moeurs* than the particular effects which it had produced in America. Is that a bad thing?"[3]

The phrase "the general effects of equality" implied an abstraction suggested by his American observations and one confluent with developments, equally abstracted, in the Old World. The second volume of *Democracy*, then, would not aspire to be a Second Journey to the New World. It would be a journey to a world coming-to-be. America would serve as its anticipation but emphatically not as its archetype. Instead of being the focus, America would provide a reference point for a broader configuration. "Democracy" remained the subject but its scope was greatly extended, no longer tied to modern notions of a formal institutional structure or mode of governance. This was suggested in a draft of a preface which he prepared for the second volume:

> A democratic people, society, epoch does not mean a people, society, time where all men are equal, but a society, people, epoch where there are no longer fixed castes,

> classes, privileges, exclusive rights, permanent wealth, immobile property in the hands of families; where all men can incessantly rise and fall and involve themselves in everything.[4]

By what it omits the draft draws attention to what had been missing in all of his attempts to explain the purpose of volume 2: any reference to the participatory democracy and vital political life that he had described so warmly in the first volume. Although four chapters in volume 2 are devoted to "associations," the topic does not constitute a formative theme. Rather, when considered in the context of the entire volume, the participatory idea and its practices appear overwhelmed, and not just by the sheer amount of attention given to other topics. Forms of participation are not viewed, as they were in volume 1, in the context of a society that prized them, but in a setting where they ran against the grain of an indifferent society.

Tocqueville was justified in claiming that the two volumes formed "a single work." It is less certain that they are united by the same "democracy." The first words of Tocqueville's foreword to volume 2 are: "The Americans have a democratic social condition [*état*] which naturally inclines them towards certain laws and certain political *moeurs*." That, he declares, was the subject of "the work about American democracy which I published five years ago."[5] Sandwiched between the two statements quoted here is an obscure paragraph in which Tocqueville asserts that many of the "sentiments" and "opinions," which were "unknown in the old aristocratic societies of Europe," were generated by that "social condition" and resulted in the destruction or modification of "relationships" that once existed and in the substitution of new but not equivalent ones. And that, he tells the reader, is the subject of the second volume.

The tortuous language cannot seem to name its subject directly. He declines to utter "France" or "revolution," although he describes his subject as the destruction of the culture of the "old aristocratic societies of Europe" and the emergence of a new culture; yet, except for a few fleeting references to England, no European country is even briefly discussed in volume 2. His obscurantism comes not from uncertainty about the identity of his subject but about its awesomeness: world creation, first intimated in the New World, then in the Old, creations of a novel form of power that is overpowering and anonymous. Although that power has always been present in the history of political society, it has assumed new forms in the modern world. Notions such as "democracy," "equality," "social power," "modern," and "culture" are crucial aspects of it, and Tocqueville would employ them all, yet neither separately nor collectively can they be said to comprehend it fully. And if the new powers are not fully grasped in thought, then it is unlikely that they can be effectively controlled in practice. And if they cannot be fully understood in theory or controlled in practice, then the terms of both would be rewritten in the light of a world that cannot be radically reshaped but only negotiated.

## II

The theory associated with this journey was received less enthusiastically. To contemporary critics, and later ones as well, it seemed to lack a main thread so that in the end it remained unclear what its author had established. In blaming the work's obscurity on its "abstract" character, critics were reacting to the remarkable facility with which Tocqueville skims a wide range of cultural subjects—literature, poetry, religion, manners and morals, architecture, history, science, and philosophy—but rarely analyzes specific examples or mentions specific authors. Thus he writes at length about religion in the United States without identifying any of the numerous sects or denominations, except for Catholicism.

The abstract quality—or as Tocqueville put it, "philosophical" character—of volume 2, its lack of empirical references, contrasts with volume 1, in which his theoretical flights usually began from a description of some concrete American practice or institution; not infrequently there were statistical references. Accordingly, although it is possible to provide a relatively brief statement that might give a reader some sense of volume 1, few commentators have ventured to do the same for volume 2. It is, I believe, true to say that volume 2 does not aim at an exact description of any existing state of affairs. It selects certain tendencies, which are then projected to form a set of possible alternatives. The world of volume 2 is, therefore, more radically constructionist than the New World of volume 1. This is owing to his belief that, unlike volume 1, where he was able to *describe* a political society that, by a combination of circumstance, political inheritance, and religious influences, had mostly succeeded in domesticating the forms of power accompanying the democratic revolution, he was now prophesying the emergence of a world in which those same powers loomed larger than present means of controlling them and he, the author of *Democracy*, has no well-defined alternative. At a theoretical level volume 2 is an anticlimax—which may be one reason why posterity can offer snippets of wisdom from that volume but not neat summaries. It does not promise to reshape the world of huge and unprecedented powers but to moderate them.

On what terrain might the democratization of society be engaged?

## III

*The unity, ubiquity, omnipotence of the social power, and the uniformity of its rules form the striking feature that characterizes all of the political systems created in our time. They reappear as the foundation of the most bizarre utopias. The mind pursues those images even as it sleeps.*

Tocqueville[6]

The absence of any reference to "politics" and the "political" in the resumés by which Tocqueville tried to communicate his intentions was a strong indication that the significance of democracy was to be worked out in a different context than the political or, alternatively, that the political was to be contextualized differently. The new location of democracy was announced in a passage which could serve as the motto of volume 2: "The appearance of civil society has not been less given to change than the physiognomy of the political world."[7] The changes in civil society have been so fundamental, Tocqueville contends, that the contrast between the present Old World and its past approximates the original contrast between America and the Old World. His guiding assumption was succinctly formulated: "In the long run political society cannot fail to become the expression and image of civil society."[8]

That formulation is the anticipation of the central concern in volume 2, an increasingly democratized civil society. To appreciate Tocqueville's achievement we need to recall that in the centuries after Aristotle no political theorist had elaborated a concept of a politics in which mass power predominated. When Mill declared that Tocqueville was the first to theorize modern democracy and its politics, that claim holds for volume 1 of *Democracy*; in volume 2, however, a different claim is plausible, that he was the first to theorize democracy as the dominant cultural force.

This required the bracketing of democracy as a political structure (elections, legislation, policy) in order to explore or, better, to project a formation of power beyond anything intimated in the ancient experience of democracy or by modern theories about it. Although he would describe it as democratic or egalitarian, his account burst the limitations of his own vocabulary to announce the gathering of a pervasive force whose reach extended not only into the most intimate areas of existence, shaping family life, the character of the feminine, and sexual mores, but energized economic behavior while turning aesthetics into a category of production and making a fetish of private life. Accompanying the transmutation of democracy from the political into the sociocultural would be the emergence of a distinctive mentality, a strange type of consciousness expressive of two contradictory tendencies, a Cartesian individualism oddly coupled with a Rousseauean homogeneity: a being at once self-centered yet other-directed, a being eagerly attacking the world in search of opportunity and also retreating from it to seek sanctuary in private life.

Tocqueville referred to the power created by democratization/modernization as "social power." It amounted to the discovery of a new field of power and a new theoretical domain, one strikingly different from the economic and technological emphases of many of his contemporaries. The new field had been charted tentatively in the first volume of *Democracy* in the importance attributed to customs, *moeurs*, and religion in shaping and restraining the political behavior of Americans; now, however, he would be concerned with the effects of democratization on customs, *moeurs*, religion, and all of the modes of behavior, belief, and symbolic expression. The principal assumption of volume 2 was that unlike the United States, where, save for the southern states, democracy had totally enveloped a whole society without, however, submerging the primacy of political identity, the Old World was being rapidly democratized, culturally and socially, without first having been politically democratized. Indeed, "the revolution" has gone further in France than in any other European country.[9] Democratization represented the movement of an entire society toward a state of affairs in which the vast majority shares the same beliefs and aspirations, enjoys the same pleasures, is fixated upon practical concerns of which the pursuit of wealth is uppermost, and instinctively resists any criticism of its norms.

Paradoxically, as society becomes more democratized, the political potential of democracy remains undeveloped. Majority rule, which had represented the idea that the demos could rule, now is disembodied, no less a force though anonymous and unselfconscious. It is "the general will of the greatest number" but it assumes the form of "the intellectual dominion of the greatest number." Democracy as political praxis dissolves and becomes incarnate in "a strange power," "public opinion." "It does not promote its beliefs by persuasion; it imposes them and causes them to penetrate the souls by a kind of immense pressure of the mind of all upon the intelligence of each."[10]

Thus the democracy that began in America as distinctively political in its structure becomes a diffused power, less consciously shaped by an active demos than by its interaction with the new forms of power represented by public administration and private industry. Democracy is on the verge of losing its political identity, of becoming merged into modernization, unable to compete with the domains promising ever greater material benefits and more exciting challenges.

The transmutation of democracy from a political identity to an ethos of modernity would be delineated bifocally, so to speak. Tocqueville would bring into focus what once was close at hand but now distant (i.e., the United States) and then alternate it with what once was distant but now close at hand (the Old World).

## IV

Tocqueville's shift of emphasis from conventional political institutions to social beliefs and institutions represents a move with a long pedigree in the history of political ideas. In some historical eras "civil society" has been a conceptual rallying point for protesting state centralization and religious or cultural policies aimed at imposing uniformity of belief.[11] At such moments civil society has stood for political pluralism or the demand for autonomy or semiautonomy of groups, associations, and municipalities. Variations on the notion appeared in the aristocratic resistance to the French monarchy in the half century before the outbreak of the revolution; in numerous separatist movements of the nineteenth and twentieth centuries; in the so-called "pluralist movement" among early twentieth-century British intellectuals and the Guild Socialism of the post–World War I years; and, more recently, in the opposition to Communist rule on the part of some Central and East European intellectuals, workers, and religious groups after World War II. Most champions of the notion of civil society have used the diversity and voluntarism that they perceive as the hallmarks of civil society—culture, religion, local institutions, and history—to fashion a critical construct for dissolving various holisms such as "nation," "the state," "church universal," and "society" that signified a homogeneous collectivity.

The dominant tendency among theorists of civil society has been to view the state as the principle enemy of free associations and to attribute its enmity to its alienation from society; Tocqueville's concerns grew out of the question as to what the sources of state power were such that it could stand over against the society it was supposed to protect. Did the state not represent society and draw its resources and authority from that source?

Tocqueville proceeded to shift the focus *initially* from the state to society itself and to the phenomenon of a society permeated by a democratic culture. Although Tocqueville never quite establishes a steady distinction between "civil society" and "society," it is possible to read his "society" as signifying generality in the form of relations, beliefs, habits, sentiments, and *moeurs* that are operative throughout a determinate nation and that reinforce similarity. "Civil society" refers to differentiation, to what distinguishes the practice, say, of the religious beliefs of Catholics from Protestants, or the aesthetics of the aristocrat from that of the bourgeois. Stated differently, society embodies "social power" by virtue of repetitiveness and exercises it as "weight" that "presses down," imposing uniformity. Civil society, when differentiated, signifies the discontinuous. The crucial development that Tocqueville traces might be described as the collapse of civil society into society, of particularity into generality, and as smoothening the discontinuous.

The traditional problem was thus turned on its head: society could potentially pose as much of a threat, perhaps even more, than the state. Or, more precisely, the threat lay in the *social* developments signified by democracy: these were connecting state and society, creating a continuum where there had been important elements of resistance, of breaks in the circuitry of power. Aristocratic power and culture had once represented discontinuity, identified neither with king nor commoner nor bishop. The cultures of ancient democracies and early modern republics had all been defined and dominated by the culture of elites, leaving "low" or popular culture without official recognition, unselfconscious, and uncelebrated. In America Tocqueville claimed to have discovered a society enveloped by a common culture that overwhelmed and isolated the elites. There "temporary distinctions" rather than social classes existed.[12] Tocqueville believed that the advent of egalitarianism and democracy meant that civil society was becoming more of a single piece. The homogenization of civil society, the blending of civil society differences into broad social uniformities, prepared the way for the accommodation of a nation to the mode of power peculiar to the centered state, that of generalized applicability.

Tocqueville used America to depict what a democratized civil society might be like by specifying the democratic and egalitarian content to the Montesquieuean notions of "manners, *moeurs*, customs, and opinions." He included under civil society not only the family, churches, public and private associations, the status of women, relationships between workers and owners and between masters and servants, but the arts, rhetoric, literature, and the status of theoretical inquiry. The discussion proceeds throughout by means of a binary contrast. His reference point, the term that assigns meaning, as well as value, to the artifacts of civil society, is contained in his phrase, "multitude of feelings and opinions . . . unknown to the old aristocratic societies of Europe." Democratic civil society is to be revealed by its contrasts with a form in which an aristocratic culture flourished and democratic ways were alien. Aristocracy is compressed into an analytical device, an outside perspective for an observer confronting an unprecedented form of totality. The totality of democracy is thus engaged by an analysis that exploits its opposite, by an antidemocracy that tacitly claims a superior understanding of egalitarianism because aristocracy's own self-consciousness, even its power, had—unlike democracy—depended on the presence, rather than the elimination, of its opposite.[13]

## V

How, then, to understand an entity as uncentered and powerful as civil society? Was it to be explained by civil society and society becoming indistinguishable, less civil and more social? If so, how could something as seemingly amorphous and acephalous as civil "society" be a field of forces capable of producing startlingly similar social beings and a "type of oppression . . . resembling nothing that has ever existed in the world before"?[14]

In the power-packed language of his preface to the second volume Tocqueville gives some clues to the mode of understanding he thinks appropriate to the phenomenon. The "democratic revolution," he wrote, is "an irresistible fact." It is "neither desirable nor wise to struggle against it." His subject is described as "immense"; it "comprehends the greater part of the sentiments and ideas which have caused the new shape of the world."[15] It is futile to struggle against a power that, by bringing into existence a new world, is comparable to the demiurgic deities of ancient mythologies. Accordingly, Tocqueville brings a mythical mode of representation to bear on the Old World. The newness of the New World depicted in volume I was more the product of nature than of art; the Old World, in contrast, had been coerced into the new by a "democratic revolution." That power had a precise historical embodiment, the French Revolution, but, astonishingly, Tocqueville refuses to name it, preferring to employ surrogates such as "democracy" and "equality."[16] The reason is that he wants to depict a massive movement continuing and anonymous, not to trace back current conditions to antecedent actions or individual actors. He wants to dwarf actions and actors, submerge them in what is neither action nor actor, but an enveloping ethos.

The mythical character of his subject is intimated in the choice of chaos, a recurrent theme of mythology, as a starting point. Modern chaos is the condition produced by revolution and democratization. Tocqueville's exact word for it is "confusion." Confusion does not mean disorder but the absence of striking or significant differentiation, an order that is egalitarian rather than distinction-sensitive, that does not forcibly suppress differences, such as birth, wealth, or intellect, but refuses to honor them or to concede that they are privileged. The differences exist but are accorded no standing, and because they are properties of the Few, their owners feel isolated. Even in the United States, Tocqueville asserted, the rich retreat to private life and rarely enter politics. Confusion exists when differences exist, even mingle, but no one has special claims.

A striking example of how revolutionary change is made to echo biblical myths occurs in Tocqueville's account of the changes in language brought about by democracy. When societies are divided into classes, Tocqueville writes, each class develops its own linguistic meanings and usages but when "men are no longer held in their place" and they proceed to mix together, when "castes are destroyed and classes change and are confused all the words of the language become mixed up as well."[17] "The continual restlessness which reigns in the midst of a democracy" is manifested in the constant introduction of new words and leads to an "endless change of language, as in other matters."[18]

His account is reminiscent of another myth about confusion and power. According to the biblical story of the Tower of Babel, Yahweh intervenes when He sees mankind projecting massive power (the Tower) that will predictably be used to challenge His domination. The amassing of human power was made possible because the men of Babel spoke "one language"; so Yahweh proceeds to undermine their unity by dispersing them into diverse linguistic societies.[19] Pluralism is thus associated with weakness, uniformity with power; but paradoxically the power that introduces pluralism is stronger than the power that employs uniformity.

While Tocqueville notes that democracy "changes words" even when there is no apparent need and that the "genius" of democracy is its fertility in inventing "new words" and "ideas," the explosion of plurality is not, in the case of democratic society, the sign of weakness but the expression of power. In democratic societies "it is the majority which makes the laws about language, as in everything else." What is being reflected through the majority, however, is another, all-pervasive power, the power of a new form of civic culture. "The majority is more occupied with business than with learning, with political and commercial interests than with philosophical speculations or *belles-lettres.*" Consequently, "most of the words . . . will mainly serve to express the needs of industry, the passions of parties, or the details of public administration."[20] Thus, social "confusion" has produced a linguistic profusion indicative of, and subservient to, industry, politics, and bureaucracy, the three major forms of power in the age of democracy and equality, each power in its way a promoter of uniformity. As we have seen, Tocqueville's quarrel with God is that He seems now to have reversed Himself, siding with uniformity and concentrated human power. Democracy the beneficiary of a grand betrayal or of a deity turned administrator?

Profusion is associated with the quality of being congenial to mass taste and ability, the opposite of what is rare or exceptional. Paradoxically profusion signifies paucity rather than plenty. The breakdown/destruction of class barriers and distinctions of status and the resulting spread of equality to the various social domains (work, family, religion, cultural creation) signifies the appearance of what is distinctively democratic and modern, the domination of generality. "General facts explain more things in democratic than in aristocratic centuries."[21] Equality, it bears repeating, is a generalizing and economizing phenomenon as well as a political value. Generality stands not only for a type of all-inclusive statement that marginalizes the exception but structures the distinctive shorthand by which modern man believes. One can represent Many, and the Many one.

## VI

> *Among democratic peoples, then, the public has a strange power of which aristocratic nations cannot even conceive. It does not use persuasion for its beliefs but imposes them and causes them to penetrate into souls by an immense pressure of the collective mind* [l'esprit de tous] *upon the intelligence of each.*
>
> Tocqueville[22]

The first eight chapters of volume 2 are about belief; it would not be an exaggeration to claim that their dominant theme concerns belief and its democratic modalities.[23] I want to suggest that those chapters and much of volume 2 constitute an alternative formulation of the phenomenon of ideology and the ideological mentality that is as distinctive as Marx's and perhaps more nuanced. In volume 1 Tocqueville had defined *moeurs* comprising not only "the habits of the heart" (feelings, sentiments, and passions) but also the "notions," "opinions," and "the sum of ideas that shape mental habits."[24] That conception of *moeurs* was, as Tocqueville made clear, governed by a specific concern with identifying "the elements [in *moeurs* ] which are favorable to the maintenance of political institutions."[25] In America the most important element was religion. We might call this the conservative function of belief or ideology-as-system-maintenance.

In volume 2, however, Tocqueville's concern is with generalized belief as a form of power which does not so much support a system as impart a dynamic potentially dangerous to "the maintenance of political institutions" and to much else. In Tocqueville's discussion there were two specific reference points for his conception of the dynamics of mass belief: one is religion, the other, the revolutionary beliefs of the French populace in the last quarter of the eighteenth century. Although the Americans have a fondness for general ideas, Tocqueville claimed that it was the French during the period of "our Constituent Assembly and Convention" who displayed a "passion" and "blind faith" in "general ideas" and "any theory."[26]

When ideas become generalized beliefs, they acquire in the process a certain weightiness, an oppressiveness that is compounded by their anonymous nature. Their terror is the terror of the undifferentiated. It surfaces in Tocqueville's discussion of pantheism, a philosophy whose "great progress in our day" is the result of a "powerful [*durable*] cause."

## VII

> *Among the different systems used to explain the universe, pantheism seems to me to be the one best suited to seduce the human mind in democratic eras.*
>
> Tocqueville[27]

The abolition of monarchy by revolution had involved not only the murder of a monarch and the death of a political form but the destruction of an important cosmological analogy. In premodern times the relationship of kings to society had been conceived as analogous to God's relationship to His creation. In both cases the myth functioned as an unequivocal (because single and unified) principle of order, a guarantor of the world's continuity, and a center from which power radiated sustenance. Aristocracy, in contrast, was considered analogous to polytheism with its several competing centers and consequent differences.[28]

What was the cosmology projected by democracy? Assuredly not the riotous atheism of nonbelievers, a free-for-all of anarchic forces. Tocqueville would claim that democracy's "principal effect on philosophy" was to promote "pantheism." Tocqueville's usage should not be measured by a strict philosophical formulation—an impossibility given the many historical varieties of that doctrine. Possibly he may have been thinking of Spinoza's conception of a total system in which every being is reflective of an order that derives from one substance, God. Tocqueville's pantheism was closer to an ideology, a projection of a mass belief-system. It represents the cosmologized mirror of democratic despotism. It "has made great progress in our day" because when social conditions become more equal, human perceptions are altered. As individuals become more equal, they become "more similar, weaker, and smaller." As a result the mind no longer thinks primarily in terms of "citizens" but of collectivities, such as "the people" or "the species." As conditions become more equalized, "individuals seem smaller and society greater. . . . [E]ach is lost in the crowd and only the huge and imposing image of the people itself is perceptible."[29]

That description of the individual's experience of massiveness, which likens it to being swallowed up, absorbed into the indiscriminate, creates the impression of a democratic social condition as boundless, oceanic. Each no longer is attracted to particulars but to aggregates. Under the sway of democracy, the mind seeks to enclose a multitude of objects "at once" and to discover "a single cause." Driven by "a desire to dissolve all differences" and mediations, the democratic mind wants to dissolve even "the primary division of things" between "creation and creator" and so it comprehends "God and the universe in a single whole." At the same time the mind seems "to embrace a crowd of diverse objects at once; its constant aim is to connect a multitude of consequences with a single cause. . . . It is obsessed by the idea of unity. " The result is the destruction of "individuality" and hence pantheism's "secret charms" for those living in democracies.[30]

Pantheism's vision is a terrifying one: its god is a preview of democracy's despotism. Difference is reduced to mere parts which are swallowed by "an immense being who alone remains eternal in the midst of continual change and incessant transformation of all that composes it." Pantheism is thus the myth of modernity, of a realized totality in which stability and assurance coexist with continuous change.

Those who remain committed to "the true greatness of man," Tocqueville exhorted, "must join together and struggle against [pantheism]."[31]

## VIII

> *It is impossible to conceive anything so petty, so dull, so full of wretched interests, in a word, so antipoetic as the life of a man in the United States.*
>
> Tocqueville[32]

Although Tocqueville's achievement was deeply dependent on the prior explorations of Montesquieu, Rousseau, and Burke, he alone demonstrated the relationship between the importance of culture as expressing a conception of politics in which the dominant power was anonymous and the arrival of a modernity that diminished politics while professing to expand it. His three predecessors had both translated culture into an idiom composed mainly of terms denotive of stability—for example, habit, custom, mores, fundamental laws. While Tocqueville continued to employ that same vocabulary he tried to incorporate the social dynamics he had observed in America. Modern energy—a phenomenon unknown to Montesquieu and Rousseau—he saw as revolutionizing culture by generalizing it through the medium of equality and promoting individual self-consciousness without individuality.

The power of culture and the expression of its modernity was its bewildering combination of two opposing tendencies, one political, the other antipolitical: culture united human beings, bound them together, while it also isolated them from each other. Culture defuses the tensions between the political and antipolitical, between solidarism and anomie, produced by modernity's unlimited potential for recurrent social dislocation. It sublimates revolution into a continuous succession of changing artifacts. "Revolutionary" is familiarized as a normal predicate in aesthetics, economy, science, and technology. Culture is socialization into modernity through symbolic rebellion: a frantic dash to keep pace by rejecting the past. In the process the slower rhythms of life that were suited to the deliberative character of political life, especially of democratic politics, give way to ever quickening tempos that favor execution over deliberation.

## IX

Throughout the analysis Tocqueville employs interchangeably "democracy" and "equality" to describe the new cultural formation and "aristocracy" and "freedom" as the terms of contrast that serve as controls delimiting the meaning and significance of democratic beliefs and behavior. In part that usage is to be interpreted in the light of Tocqueville's frequent lament that he lacks the words to describe a wholly new set of phenomena. Clearly democracy and equality are made to encompass an enormous range of phenomena that would later be distinguished. For example, other writers would identify democratic ways of thinking as ideological; democratic obsession with the pursuit of wealth as the expression of capitalism's ways or simply as economic behavior; the democratic penchant for embracing change as a species of "modernization." These later distinctions serve, however, to underscore the boldness of Tocqueville's attempt to offer a theory of a unified culture that was far more than an inventory of topics, such as literature, art, theater, rhetoric, science, education, manners, and beliefs. He develops a conception of a new type of person who thinks, feels, believes, admires, hates, strives, worships differently from his forebears.

Democracy is, then, as much a revolution in cognition and sensibility as in politics. The new being is not a passive register of relationships and beliefs but a different kind of participant. The new being is the reflection point where social influences converge and then are, in effect, reflected back into "society." Thus the American, existing amid an unprecedented condition where the opportunities for acquiring wealth seem boundless, responds with boundless energy: he is in a hurry and because of that he cannot pause to contemplate, although he may be beset by the anxieties that have often produced contemplation. As a result he seizes on "general ideas" that represent abridgments, enabling him to deal rapidly with a wider range of situations or possibilities, "to discover common rules for everything."[33] Generalizations concentrate "a great many things in a small volume and give a large return quickly."[34] At the same time, he is a proud member of a society of equals where no one is privileged; accordingly he can rely on general ideas, say, about human behavior, in the confidence that, because all are alike, what applies to one applies to all. And acting on that principle, he helps turn a value into a fact.

Tocqueville was groping for a kind of homology between what could be loosely called a novel type of governance, despotism, and a novel type of mind. Tocqueville views the latter as a distinctive construction, a social and not altogether self-conscious creation. Far from the acutely self-conscious substance that modern philosophers labeled "mind," it is a collective mentality that thinks of itself along lines that are defined by the play of social influences upon it: what the mind believes accords with what society conduces. Far from feeling itself in thraldom to society, the mind feels more powerful because it believes that its discoveries are the result of its own efforts and at the same in harmony with prevailing beliefs.

The power it feels is directly related to generalizations, the form of knowledge peculiarly congenial to the age of democracy. Under predemocratic conditions of inequality human beings perceive themselves as dissimilar, virtually different species. As a consequence the mind is reluctant to hazard generalizations while the notion that all mankind might share a "common nature" seems implausible and, to the aristocrat, repugnant. In a democratic society, where the individual finds himself surrounded by beings more or less like himself, he easily thinks in more general terms, such as "humanity as a whole." Upon encountering others, the democratic mind displays the same expansive, aggressive behavior as it had in the frontier wilderness. The process by which he thinks is described in power-laden terms by Tocqueville: the mind becomes enlarged (*s'agrandisse*) and expanded (*se dilate*). Generalization becomes not a category but a symbolic aggression, not a preference but "a need to discover common rules for everything, to capture a great number of objects by the same formula, and to explain an *ensemble* of facts by a single cause."[35] Soon the abstractions take over speech itself, making it "run quicker" by personifying the abstractions and making them into agents while relaxing reference to any concrete "fact."

## X

His construction of the new man and, as we shall see, of the new woman, begins from observations, then proceeds to generalizations about the United States, and ends typically in a claim that what he has described applies more generally to societies that are in the midst of being transformed by the same type of tendencies operating in the United States. At the same time Tocqueville took special pains to emphasize that the state of culture in America was not necessarily the predestined form that culture need assume in other "democracies."

In a chapter significantly entitled "Why the Example of Americans Does Not Prove That a Democratic People Cannot Have the Aptitude or Taste for the Sciences, Literature, and the Arts," Tocqueville warns against confusing "what is democratic with what is merely American" and reminds his readers that "the situation of Americans is completely exceptional," that no democratic people will be similarly placed. "We must cease looking at all democratic nations through the American type and instead attempt to see them according to their own traits."[36]

That formulation was an announcement of an approach to the tasks of political theory in which the challenge is to identify the dominant direction of historical forces, in this case, "democracy," and then, within those limits, to propose possible permutations. Theoretical activity is not architectonic in the sense of legislating an ideal society completely outfitted with laws, institutions, and norms. Rather it is tactical and imaginative, taking its point of departure from a dominant tendency in which there seem to be valuable elements and sufficient plasticity in the undesirable ones that allows for their modification or control. Tactically minded theory is on the alert for contingency.

In that vein Tocqueville not only intimates the constructions that would later be called "ideal types" but the idea of "thought experiments" as well.[37] Thus in his discussion of literature Tocqueville begins with: "I suppose an aristocratic people among whom letters are cultivated. . . ." After developing a picture of a literature controlled by aristocratic sensibilities, he then switches to its opposite: "Let us now return to the tableau and consider its other side. . . . Imagine ourselves in the midst of a democracy where ancient traditions and present education have sensitized it to the pleasures of the mind. Ranks are intermingled and confused; knowledge as well as power has been infinitely divided and, if I may dare to put it this way, scattered in all directions."[38]

Theorizing alternative democracies meant discounting the notion that the American experience of democracy was decisive and authoritative: "Equality can be established in civil society without reigning in the political world. . . . There can be a kind of equality in the political world without any political liberty at all."[39] This opened the way for the possibility of a democratic society that cultivated intellectual as well as material values. Hypothetically, if a society were to abolish privileges and make men equal in enlightenment and independence, large and unequal wealth would nonetheless reappear. It would accrue to "the most capable," and the likelihood was that some part of the wealthy class would be drawn to "the pleasures of the intellect" and toward "the infinite, the immaterial, and the beautiful." The limiting case was of a democratic society that prevented "natural inequalities" from emerging. Again, hypothetically, in a society where caste and class privileges have been abolished along with the laws of inheritance, no one would have the leisure or inclination for "the pleasures of the mind."[40] In contemplating that prospect Tocqueville compares it to living in a dark and suffocating space where occasionally light breaks in but quickly disappears. "A sudden heaviness overcomes me" and "I struggle in the darkness to find an opening."[41]

In these imaginaries the democratic politics of volume I was demoted to the status of a variable, displaced, projected on the plane of culture. At the same time, there is the suggestion of a meritocracy ("the most capable") beginning to occupy the place being vacated by aristocracy. Culture emerges as an invented terrain where the demos is most disadvantaged. For while the demos has long memories of economic exploitation and political domination, it has little or no experience of engaging in cultural politics.

Tocqueville's juxtaposition of aristocracy to democracy implies a theorist who occupies a privileged location outside and above both tendencies. The role of theory in a democratizing culture is suggested in a chapter where Tocqueville describes the salutary effects of religion in turning "the soul of Americans toward spiritual delights." First he pauses in order to inquire how that worthy goal might be conceived as a political project. That opens the way for the ancient conception of theorist as masked legislator: "The essence of the lawgiver's art is to anticipate the natural bents of human societies in order to know where the efforts of citizens might need support and where it is necessary to restrain them. For those demands are different at different times." Tocqueville then illustrates how different conditions dictate different theoretical strategies: had he been born in an aristocratic age when spiritual beliefs caused men to accept their economic misery passively, he would have done his utmost to awaken in them a consciousness of their needs and to exhort some of them to pursue scientific studies with the aim of finding the best means of "satisfying the new desires." "I should try," he concludes, "to arouse them to the quest for prosperity."[42] When democracy prevails, however, "the legislators have different concerns." Men do not need to be exhorted to pursue prosperity but to be recalled from it, else there is the danger of man's "most sublime faculties" withering from disuse.[43]

## XI

How might a tactically minded theory operate in the world of powers constructed by mytheory? Mytheory insists that the world is being irreversibly shaped by the power of democracy and that, if uncontested, its power will eventually culminate in democratic despotism. But what exactly is the nature of the power attributed to democracy and what is mythical about it?

As we have noted, Tocqueville has moved away from the identification of democracy with simple majority rule and, instead, has posed the problem in terms of cultural norms that democracy imposes without deliberation or recourse to formal political processes. That formulation was, however, an imaginary future constructed by projecting certain drives that Tocqueville believed to be immanent in democratic egalitarianism. They might be described as those drives expressed in conventional forms, such as literature, architecture, poetry, or in manners. In those familiar, even respectable, incarnations, the drives could be described as bourgeois. In every department of culture Tocqueville's unvarying prescription was for uplift, for setting higher aims than democratic impulses aspired to. But there was another side of Tocqueville's democracy that retained elements of its revolutionary origins, that was affiliated with the mythic rather than the prosaic. In that genealogy democracy drew from the lower depths, from the underclasses of the poor, deprived, and desperate and became the carrier of their primitive passions. Thus Tocqueville writes of his fears that in a democratic society poets will lose touch with reality and "depict entirely imaginary countries" and present "immense and incoherent images, overwhelming descriptions, bizarrely composed, with fantastic beings issuing" from the poet's uncontrolled imagination.[44]

The dread of revolution was preserved in Tocqueville's description of a democratized culture. He had been able to ignore democratic anger, its blind urge for revenge and for reparation when he had focused on American democracy in volume 1. He had accepted his own thesis that democracy was successful in the United States because it had not been the creature of revolution. Although his faith wavered when he contemplated the destructiveness and violence of the frontiersman, he managed to persevere in his portrait of American society as mediocre and essentially conservative.

Tocqueville's fear of primal powers surfaced in the second volume of *Democracy.* It was signaled by a curious formulation that occurs at the close of the penultimate chapter of volume 2. "Let us have for the future that salutary fear that makes for vigilance and the defense [of liberty] rather than that kind of soft and passive terror which makes the heart sink and weakens the will."[45]

A choice between "salutary fear" and "passive terror" seems to turn upon a fine distinction between two forms of fright.[46] The contrast to which Tocqueville seems to be alluding is a stereotypical one between a masculine fear and a "soft and passive" feminine fright, between a fear that is consistent with resolve and one that undermines the will, between a fear that ultimately will resist and one that easily submits. The subtext here, the source of fear, is the Many, not in the guise of majority rule or democratic despotism but in the specter of mass "pleasure" and "materialism." Behind these and driving them is mass "passion." "In democratic times men need to be free in order to procure more easily the physical pleasures for which they never cease to long."[47] When popular appetites are not disciplined by education or "the habits of liberty," "men are carried away and lose control of themselves at the sight of the new goods they are ready to grab." They lose all interest in public affairs and are ready material for a despotism that promises to fulfill their desires.[48]

Was this true of Americans, that they were sacrificing civic life to personal pleasures? Tocqueville's reply in volume 2 is equivocal and hardly reassuring: although Americans have "a passion for material enjoyments" that is "violent," it is not "blind." Reason, "though powerless to moderate it, directs it nonetheless." The American possesses an astonishing ability to be wholly absorbed in private concerns but then, in the next moment, to become totally absorbed in public affairs. He is able to switch, alternately, from "the most selfish greed" to "the highest patriotism." Americans are able to sustain the contradiction because they have come to recognize that "freedom" and "prosperity" are interconnected. Tocqueville suggests, however, that the combination of materialism and *civisme* is unstable: "The human heart cannot really be divided in this way."[49]

The place occupied by fear was related to the transformation of the image of democracy in volume 2. Passion transforms equality from a demand for political rights, a demand that in principle is satisfiable and limited, into an amorphous social force without limit. The consequence is that the abundant opportunities, social fluidity, and torrential energy associated with American democracy are transformed—as their venue is being tacitly transferred from the New to the Old World. From being favorable conditions for political life they become elements fueling a dynamic that converts equality into an object of fear. The prospect is that the sovereign masses, now released from the inhibitions imposed by traditional authorities, can indulge unrestrainedly in the enjoyment of material and sensual pleasures. Democracy is Babylonian rather than Athenian.

## XII

> *From the moment when common matters are treated in common . . . when public values rule, there is no man who does not feel the value of mutual goodwill and all seek to win it by attracting the esteem and affection of those among whom they must live.*
>
> *Those passions which freeze the heart and divide men must then retreat into the depths of the soul and hide there. Pride must disguise itself; scorn dare not show itself. Egoism is afraid of itself.*
>
> Tocqueville[50]

Tocqueville's description of passion is presented in language that is psychological, erotic, and suffused with sensual imagery. Equality appears as democratized desire. The place of the chaste bodies politic of New England, for whose members politics was disciplined, self-denying, is taken by "the body social." *Le corps social* emerges quivering with rapacious desire. "[O]ur contemporaries have a more ardent and tenacious love of equality than of liberty" and at certain moments "it may swell to delirium." The "barriers" between persons having been erased, "men hurl themselves as on a conquest, and they cling to it as a precious treasure that others want to ravish. The passion . . . penetrates into every corner of the human heart, expands, and fills the whole."[51] Unlike the "sublime pleasure" that political liberty affords to those "few" who are willing to sacrifice for it, equality's gratifications resemble those of a wanton, "free" and "immediate," its "charms" easily available in countless ways.[52]

Although Tocqueville had identified passion as the driving force of great actions and deplored its absence from politics, now, when the passions of the lower social orders were stirring, he became fixated upon the "ardent, insatiable, eternal, and invincible" passion for equality. His countrymen, he complained, would tolerate "poverty, servitude, and barbarism" rather than "endure aristocracy."[53]

The dilemma, as he framed it, was that political liberty and equality appealed to different social classes. "Political liberty occasionally gives some sublime pleasures to a few citizens. Equality furnishes daily a multitude of small pleasures to each person."[54] Although only the Few can truly appreciate political liberty, the passion for equality drives men to demand political liberty and, as a result, political liberty in the modern world has to acknowledge equality for its basis. "The extreme case" is where all participate in government and have the right to do so. This would be "the most complete form of equality possible on earth" and is "the ideal toward which democratic peoples are tending."[55] If political liberty fails to enlist equality for its cause, however, equality will be co-opted by despotism.[56] If the political world is moving toward domination by the undifferentiated (complete equality), differentiation (political liberty) must find the means of containing it while protecting itself. But how can political liberty, which signified exclusiveness in that its values are truly appreciated only by the few, and equality, which signified inclusiveness, be accommodated to each other?

## XIII

> *For my part, I doubt that men can ever support complete religious independence and at the same time entire political liberty; and I am persuaded that if he has no faith, he must be servile; and if he is free, he must believe.*
>
> Tocqueville[57]

For political liberty to come to terms with equality, the "ardor" of equality had to be cooled. The first tacit assumption of that strategy was that equality was synonymous with the Many, the undifferentiated. The absence of significant differences allowed for a widespread similarity of response. A passion that grips some would likely be transmitted to all. The undifferentiated thus stood for a system of diffusion. The second tacit assumption was that the alliance was possible because liberty, too, was cooled before it reached the "extreme case" of equal political participation by all. Political liberty is mainly exercised through representative government, a free press, strong judiciary, and civil associations. To fit in with forms of liberty in which emphasis was placed on checking and frustrating, the democratic passions of the Many would have to be toned down, even repressed, and discouraged from direct expression without, however, differentiating them. This had to occur within society rather than through political processes. The obvious means was religion—or at least it seemed to Tocqueville the obvious remedy, given the deep impression left on him by the wholly salutary role of religion in the United States. Americans were portrayed by him as religious as a matter of fact rather than of doctrine and, for the most part, without fanaticism. Oddly, of all the possible lessons of American institutions that Tocqueville sought to apply to France, he should have taken the most idiosyncratic.[58]

In volume 1 he had praised Americans for their high regard for religion and emphasized the contribution that religion had made to public and private morality. In a crucial section of part 2, chapter 9 on "The Main Causes That Make Religion Powerful in America," however, Tocqueville engages in a tortuous discussion of why, despite the crucial contributions that "the intimate union" of religion and liberty had made to the stability of American democracy, he, as "a professed Catholic," could not recommend the American example to his countrymen. The peculiarity of the American example was that the principle of the separation of church and state coexisted with the pervasive influence of religion upon society and politics. It was as though America had preserved a premodern practice that intermingled religion and politics while formally embracing the modern doctrine of their separation.

For religion to flourish in France, however, institutionalized political entanglements and dependencies had to be avoided. Tocqueville accepted that the Americans were correct in adopting the separation of church and state. His decision to accept the principle of separation did not go to the heart of his views, however. For one thing, in the United States the principle, while important, was not crucial because, unlike France, there was no "church," merely churches and sects. What mattered was not so much separation as toleration.

Yet diversity of religious beliefs is never championed by Tocqueville. He wants a coherent set of beliefs, even dogmas, because he wants religion not merely to "maintain a democratic republic," as he had put it in volume 1, but to help contain, even offset it. Hence, in volume 1 he would ask of religion that it provide reassurance to "the longing for immortality that equally torments every human heart" and stand aside from the "agitation" and "instability" that is "natural" to life in a democratic society;[59] in volume 2 he wants a more complex relationship of engagement. This required a strategy that would use the modern principle of separation in order to preserve the church rather than protect the state. *The* church's survival was vital to perpetuating antimodernist principles, especially ideals of the eternal and permanent, but religion had become too important to be left to the church alone. And it should always be born in mind that throughout volume 2 Tocqueville habitually refers to "religion," rarely to "religions." Once again his discussion will not be American or French but located on a plane where it can contend with the projected forces of modernity.

In volume 2, therefore, Tocqueville is less concerned with the solace furnished by religion than with its utility as a method, perhaps the principal one, of social control. In both volumes of *Democracy* Tocqueville had been careful to explain that he would be discussing religion from "a human point of view."[60] This involved more than treating it from a political perspective and asking how religion might contribute to morality, self-restraint, and order. It meant nothing less than asking the question, What kind of religion had to be fashioned to meet the political crisis created by equality? That question involved making religion into an object, manipulable theoretically and politically. What warrant was there for treating Christianity, especially Catholic Christianity with its powerful ecclesiastical traditions of hierarchy, dogma, and authority, as a political object?

## XIV

*How could a society fail to perish if, when social ties are relaxed, moral ties are not tightened? And what is to be done with a people which is master of itself if it does not submit to God?*

Tocqueville[61]

*Although it is of great moment to man as an individual that his religion should be true, that is not the case for society. Society has nothing to fear or hope from another life; what is important for it is not that all citizens profess the true religion, but that they profess a religion.*

Tocqueville[62]

In answering these questions Tocqueville inserts a little noticed digression which is meant to justify the concessions about to be imposed on religion. He will show that Christianity, the sacred, has been deeply influenced and affected by profane circumstances. Accordingly he describes the changes in Christian beliefs, which the political and social circumstances "prepared without doubt by Providence," had caused over the centuries. At the beginning the Roman world was "united" under Caesar, and countless individuals obeyed the same laws and "each of them so weak and small compared to the greatness of the emperor that all seemed equal when compared to him." Humanity was thus readied to receive "in a quick and easy way" the general truths taught by Christianity."[63] However, with the breakup of the Roman empire mankind became divided and subdivided and "new tendencies" appeared, including the introduction of "a nearly idolatrous cult" of "angels and saints" by "each people, each city, and almost by each man." Fortunately, the idea of a sole creator-god was preserved and just when it seemed Christianity might disappear into "the religions it had once conquered," "the barriers" between nations and citizens began to fall away and humanity spontaneously turned toward "the idea of a unique and all powerful being who dispensed equally and in the same way the same laws for each person."[64]

Clearly Tocqueville is drawing on the same mythical history that, in volume 1, had declared equality an irresistible "providential fact." Curiously, however, a kind of democratic centralization, by his account, had saved Christianity for the modern world.

The astonishing aspect of his treatment of religion in volume 2 is not the expression of Tocqueville's religious alienation, or the predictably repressive role he assigns religion. It is his insistence that if religion is to succeed in moderating the ideology of a democratic society, it must make major concessions to modernity and, in particular, to the zeal for "prosperity." Unlike the

United States where religion was the single most important element in a web of restraints—legal, constitutional, moral, and geographical—on the power of majorities, in France revolutionary equality was uncontained. In the absence of *moeurs*, practices, and habits of democratic self-restraint, the main burden of controlling it fell upon the church. The men who have made revolutions on behalf of equality, Tocqueville warned, were "inspired" by a "savage taste for lawlessness and independence" that produced "violent changes in the status of property and persons" and "much anarchy and license because they were brought about by the least civilized part of the nation against the most."[65] Religion's task should not be confined, therefore, to saving souls; it must combat a pathology rooted in the release of mass desires.

Democratic passion was, in part, the "anxious longing" of disconnected individuals and, in part, an obsession with material good that produces "a complete and brutal indifference to the future."[66] Democracy has inverted the Enlightenment faith in progress and its implicit futurist orientation. The liberated moderns are absorbed in the enjoyment of the present and its possibilities, and indifferent to the future. Having renounced the past and encouraged by modern skepticism to doubt traditional beliefs about an afterlife and the need to prepare for it in the present, "they give themselves over completely to the desires of the moment." They live "amidst the tumult of democracy," "an immense competition open to all" where "wealth is accumulated or lost in a moment" and where "the image of chance in all its forms" dominates the human mind. The resulting "social instability encourages the natural instability of desires."[67]

## XV

> *Every revolution, then, has more or less the effect of throwing men back upon themselves and opens to each man's mind a space that is wide and nearly without limits.*
>
> Tocqueville[68]

The tactical directions of Tocqueville's thinking about religion dominate as he confronts the dilemma of how to enforce religious beliefs when the post-Enlightenment elites are more skeptical than the masses. In 1836 he had confided to a friend that he was dedicating himself to reconciling those "who value morality, religion, and order" with those "who love liberty and legal equality."[69] He had in mind in the first group those aristocrats who could be considered unrepentant defenders of legitimacy and the church, diehard opponents of the revolution; in the second, those aristocrats and bourgeoisie who, with some qualification, accepted the political results of the revolution in the narrow form of constitutional monarchy, guarantees of civil liberties, and the extension of electoral privileges to the propertied.

Notably absent as an object of mediation were the working classes and the poor. They are assumed to be the extreme form of the undifferentiated even though, arguably, as a class they were the most sharply differentiated. Although the undifferentiated are not objects of persuasion in *Democracy*, they are the concerns of a persuasion aimed at the higher classes. This comes out most clearly if we ask, What kind of god is suited to a democratic age? The question might seem, at the least, impertinent and yet it is warranted by Tocqueville's remarkable, almost Whitmanesque advice to poets writing for a democratic audience. He makes the poet into a surrogate for the mytheorist in the democratic age. In an astonishing passage in which Tocqueville mixes indifferently what the poet imagines a god to be with what God chooses to reveal, the reader becomes privy to the spectacle of a god being deliberately tailored to fit the times.

The democratic poet, Tocqueville asserts, is under the sway of the general, the massive. He is compelled to deal, not with the rare and exquisite, but the human species itself. Conditioned by large subjects, he will begin to look upward, beyond his own country. There he will find a huge and towering God, one commensurate with the new scales ushered in by democracy. Because democracy destroys "intermediary powers" (sc. aristocracy and ecclesiastical hierarchies), "God," Tocqueville remarks, "reveals himself more and more to the human spirit in His full and complete majesty."[70] The no longer hidden God allows the democratic imagination to see the divine plan by which God leads the species. That plan requires that the poet/theorist be warned away from a major theme in premodern theology and Milton's poetry alike, the depiction of gods, angels, and demons struggling for possession of the earth. That would render the democratic imagination lifeless. The new political theology and its strategy are set forth by Tocqueville: "But if they link together great events and trace them back to God's general design for the universe, and without showing the hand of the sovereign master, penetrate his thought, they will be admired and understood, for the imagination of their contemporaries will instinctively follow this route."[71]

The phrase, "without showing the hand of the sovereign master," is startling for its suggestion of a complex relationship between the theorist and a deity who has revealed himself through the theoretic/poetic imagination yet is hidden away from the mass of human beings. Why would a mind as agonized by uncertainty as Tocqueville's want to offer a formula for a god for the democratic age? Or is the question a Nietzschean one: what resentments are rankling the aristocratic theorist as he surveys the banality of a democratic world and muses on a previous world shattered by an upheaval so profound that it must have been, if not divinely ordained, then tolerated? And does that have the unintended effect of reintroducing democratic despotism at the celestial level?

## XVI

The topic of religion, perhaps more than any other, reveals how culture is being shaped into a construct which contains, as it were, directives to the ruling groups instructing them in the type of powers available for shaping and containing democracy. It is well to bear in mind that when Tocqueville refers to "the majority" in this context, he is typically not referring to the "whole society" or "all of its members" but to a select portion that enjoyed the privileges of citizenship and, in one way or another, was politically active or interested.

Volume 2 offers counsel to religion concerning how to adapt and survive, especially when coping with an age preoccupied with material well-being and beset by unprecedented collective power.[72] Although he professes to be unable to shed a "Catholic" viewpoint, his prescriptions are astonishingly deferential to popular sensibilities in what he describes as "secondary matters." Religionists must remember that it is "the majority that establishes belief." They should not "unnecessarily run against the generally prevailing ideas or the permanent interests of the masses. . . . [I]t is necessary, then, to placate the majority in all matters which are not contrary to faith." If religion is to retain its hold it must resist any attempt to "overcome" or "abolish" the desire for "well-being" which is "the most striking and indelible trait of democratic ages."[73]

At the same time Tocqueville was insistent, if not consistent, that there must be fixed dogmas, not least because of the urgency to combat "materialism." Thus the best safeguard against "democracy's taste for physical pleasures" was the teaching that "the soul is immortal."[74] Although he allowed that Americans had acted wisely by incorporating religious inhibitions into their political culture, he insisted that the main forms of religiosity had made too easy an accommodation of otherworldly values to material success—with the result that Americans lacked the element of asceticism that the times required.[75] The fault lay with the nature of American spirituality. Americans, he observed shrewdly, react spiritually against their own materialistic excesses, but it is "an enthusiastic, almost wild spirituality." "Religious madness is very common there."[76] Its origins are, however, in the soul itself. Implanted in the soul is "a taste for the infinite and a love of what is immortal." The soul wearies of "sensual pleasures" and hence in a society strongly gripped by material pleasures the reaction of the soul is to seek the most extreme forms of religious excitement and ecstasy.[77] The dangers of religious extremism are not as apparent in a society of great natural wealth and opportunities, but under conditions of relative scarcity religious emotionalism could be explosive. The task of official or mainstream religion should be to sublimate hyperactive belief by promoting a high-minded asceticism:

> [T]he lawgivers in democracies and all upright and educated men should tirelessly seek to elevate souls and to direct them toward heaven. It is urgent for all who are interested in the future of democratic societies to unite and, acting in concert, to make continual efforts to diffuse throughout society a taste for the infinite, an appreciation of greatness, and a love of spiritual pleasures.[78]

The task of concocting an antimaterialist ideology for the demos depends on new political elites being able to set an example of self-denial. That project quickly takes on the character of a civil theology, part Jansenist rigor, part Jesuitical strategy: "What I am going to say will damage me in the eyes of politicians. I believe that the only effective means by which government can honor the dogma of the immortality of the soul is for each [politician] to act daily as if they believed it themselves."[79]

Unlike the masses who, Tocqueville points out, remain deeply attached to the old religion, the educated classes are infected by disbelief. Disbelief was a product of the individualism that had become rampant in all departments of life. If skepticism is communicated to the demos, the potential for disorder in a society already confused by revolutionary doctrines may reach the flash point:

> During the 50 years that France has been transformed, we have rarely had liberty, but always disorder. In the midst of this universal confusion of ideas and that unstable condition of general opinion, among that incoherent mixture of just and unjust, true and false, right and fact, public virtue has become uncertain and private morality shaken.[80]

## XVII

> *Is it true that here [in the United States] morals* [moeurs] *are as chaste as people pretend? . . . To what do you attribute the incredible power over the passions that prevails here?*
>
> Tocqueville[81]

The moral authority with which Tocqueville endows religion and the importance attributed to it as a stabilizing influence on American democracy have seemed so comprehensive that interpreters tend to overlook the instrument by which the influence of religion and its authority was actually enforced.[82] As a result the crucial role of women is underemphasized and, along with it, a revealing window into the nature of the dangers he was attempting to ward off.

Tocqueville's American woman forms a major subtext reflective of his near obsession with the masculine passions of the demos as well as his lack of confidence in external mechanisms of control, such as a constitution. The American woman crystallizes a shift in emphasis, from the dangers of majority rule conceived as conformism to the passions of the demos. His concern is to find means of control that rely upon internal rather than legal or institutional checks. In reality, they prove to be externally generated and orchestrated.

In modern times, in the era of Sade, whom Tocqueville knew, the inner life and the understanding of it had been dramatically changed. The religious soul had now to compete with an eroticized psyche. A wide range of French thinkers, including Fourier, Georges Sand, and Comte, had begun to discover various forms of power in sexual relationships and to explore the possibilities of "organizing" them. Eros was becoming theoretically objectified, the first step toward its manipulation.

Tocqueville's introduction to this new potential for social control came in a revealing moment recorded during his American travels. While interviewing a distinguished southern legislator who boasted that, compared with the behavior of the English, marital fidelity among all classes of Americans was superior, Tocqueville with uncharacteristic tactlessness blurts the question: "But in your opinion what explains this extreme chastity of morals? I tell you frankly that I cannot regard you as a *virtuous* people."[83]

In answer to his own question Tocqueville developed the construction of the virtuous woman and presented it as an American achievement, one of the few American social artifacts that he recommends unreservedly for emulation. Tocqueville's strategy for controlling the demotic passions is to concentrate virtue in one sex, passion in the other, and repression in both. In the course he exposes an unsuspected layer of sexual politics in his theory. For the question of virtue boils down to a question of woman's virtue; and her virtue is her chastity.

Tocqueville claims that the American woman was the product of a systematic and premeditated upbringing and education that predestines her to be the principal instrument for, literally, domesticating democracy.

Her education begins when, as a young girl, she is permitted a degree of freedom that contrasts sharply with the chaperoned, sheltered upbringing of French Catholic girls. The latter, Tocqueville observes, are first "cloistered" and then "without guidance or assistance are abandoned amidst the disorders inseparable from a democratic society."[84] "Stage by stage" the American girl, in contrast, is allowed to think, act, and speak independently and to move freely about society. Her "chastity" is thus deliberately placed "in danger." She comes to see "the vices and perils" in a clear light, learns to face them without "fear" or "illusions," and eventually acquires "full self-confidence in her own powers." Americans "have calculated" that "the chances of repressing in women the most tyrannical passions of the human heart" are improved if women are taught "to combat them themselves." The central point of "the incredible efforts" used in "defending the chastity of women" is to encourage the independent individual "to regulate herself."[85]

In contrast to her European sisters, with their "naive and artless charm," the American has lost that "virginal guilelessness that accompanies surging desire. . . . Like the European girl she wants to please, but she knows precisely what the price is. She may avoid evil, but at least she is aware of what it is; she has pure morals rather than a chaste mind."[86]

## XVIII

Tocqueville frames the American woman wholly in the context of marriage and the family. The discussion is a mixture of modern, premodern, and antimodern elements and it proves highly revealing of Tocqueville's personal perplexities about sexuality and sex roles, as well as repressed elements of his sexual identity. The American woman is portrayed not simply as virtuous but as an ideal that combines both sexes: "American women, who often seem manly in their intelligence and truly virile in their energy, preserve a great delicacy in their personal appearance and always remain feminine in their manners, although sometimes they show the minds and hearts of men."[87]

Although he portrays the American woman as "a strong man," Tocqueville insists that she nonetheless welcomes her domestic yoke.

> I have never observed that American women consider conjugal authority as a fortunate usurpation of their rights, nor do they believe that they abase themselves in submitting to it. On the contrary, it seems to me they find a kind of glory in freely relinquishing their will and they identify their dignity with yielding to the yoke themselves rather than escaping from it. That, at least, is the sentiment expressed by the most virtuous; the others remain silent, and in the United States one never hears an adulterous wife noisily proclaiming the rights of women while stomping on the most sacred duties.[88]

The larger-than-life, selfless qualities of the American woman are an extension of the crucial role of the family in transmitting religious values. It is not the congregation, much less the ministers (for most of them Tocqueville had undisguised contempt), but ultimately the mothers of families who perform that function. Consequently, the status of women, "their habits and opinions," is "a matter of great political importance."[89] Because women do not vote or hold office and rarely participate in public life—and Tocqueville was very cool toward all of these possibilities—their "political" importance attaches to the family, which emerges as a microcosm of repressed democracy. In the first volume Tocqueville had observed that although religion often fails to "restrain" American men from "temptations," "it reigns supreme over the souls of women, and it is women who shape morals."[90] In volume 2 the point is made even more emphatically: "and now that I am nearing the ends of this book in which I have shown so many of the considerable achievements of Americans, if I were asked what, in my view, has contributed most to the remarkable prosperity and growing power of this nation, I should reply that it is due to the superiority of its women."[91]

## XIX

The American woman is hailed by Tocqueville as a triumph of democracy, yet he does not choose as his model the remarkable women who endured the harsh rigors of frontier life, although he had given a sensitive portrayal of them in his travel notebooks.[92] Nor is his construct a composite of middle-class and working-class women. Traces of the stereotypical New England woman are evident, as are those of the coquettish southern belle, but no suggestion of the bluestocking intellectual. Instead a monster of impregnable virtue, modern perhaps in her momentary liberation from Old World constraints but unrebellious and ultimately subservient. What might that woman tell us about Tocqueville's conception of freedom? Tocqueville himself claimed that the remarkable self-control found among Americans was not a special case but part of a "consistent" system of discipline. "In this, as in so many other circumstances, they are following the same method."[93] The method Tocqueville discovers is about control.

Although the American education of girls is not without "danger," producing an unimaginative creature who is all judgment, apt to be "cold and proper" rather than "a tender loving companion of men," these are "secondary evils" in comparison with the "greater good" they serve. "A democratic education," he insists, "is necessary to protect women from the perils with which the institutions and mores of democracy surround them." A point has been reached "where we no longer have a choice."[94]

Tocqueville's new model woman was constructed for one purpose, to control democratic man without challenging his "authority." When the free and independent girl enters marriage—her unquestioned destiny—she assumes the life the European girl had known from the beginning, "virtually a cloister."[95] Rule and regularity are insisted upon, Tocqueville explains, because among Puritan-influenced peoples and trading nations "regularity" of life is taken to be a sign of "purity of morals." The American woman is, therefore, confined within "a small circle of concerns and domestic duties" from which "she is prevented from venturing outside." She finds the strength to submit because of "the manly habits received from her education." Democracy, Tocqueville remarks approvingly, has elevated women "morally and intellectually to the level of man" while preserving a desirable social and economic "inferiority."[96] American practice is deliberately contrasted with those who reflect "the gross, disorderly imagination of our age" and who argue that men and women are "not only equal but similar." The latter would decree the same duties, functions, and rights to both sexes and have them "share in everything." The end result, in Tocqueville's view, would be "timid men and unseemly women."[97] To avoid that dilemma Tocqueville justifies a double standard of sexual freedom. Men are not likely to be chaste; hence, "courtesans" are inevitable and are less damaging to society than "intrigues." Fortunately, the democratic obsession with business renders men less romantic and diminishes sexual appetites.[98]

## XX

> *Democracy relaxes social bonds but it tightens natural ones. It brings kindred closer together at the same time that it separates citizens.*
>
> Tocqueville[99]

The American family is the culminating institution in which Tocqueville merged the function of the American woman, the devitalization of democratic passions among both men and women, and the moral instruction of its members. Yet his conception of the family lacks the political coherence of homology that characterized two earlier models of the family, Filmer's patriarchal monarchy or Locke's contractual agreement. In the one case kingship is embodied in the father's undisputed authority; in the other subordination is legitimated by the protoliberal idea of consent between the sexes for the practical purpose of procreation.

Tocqueville's American family is as politically charged as Filmer's or Locke's, but instead of serving as a means of socializing its members into the larger political system, it is constructed to counter it. It is not an anticipation of democracy but a check whose influence is directed at moderating democracy while resisting the extension of democracy into the structure of the family. Americans are praised for

> never having supposed that the consequence of democratic principles would be the overthrow of marital authority by introducing a confusion of authorities within the family. . . . [T]he natural head of the conjugal association is the male. . . . [Americans] believe that in the small society of man and wife, as in the larger political society, the object of democracy is to regulate and legitimize necessary powers and not to destroy all power.[100]

Tocqueville's conception of family and of women amounts to the construction of anomalies intended to counter democracy. It politicizes each but simultaneously depoliticizes them: the woman submits to the yoke of domesticity, the man is neutered sexually but finds a restored masculinity in his undisputed authority over his family, and the family provides training in authority and obedience. Revealingly, Tocqueville offers another justification for his conception of the depoliticized family by appealing to the then fashionable notion of the division of labor. "The Americans have applied to both sexes the great principle of political economy that dominates today's industry." The division of functions, he notes, justifies a separate "sphere of action" for each sex. Tocqueville describes the division in sexually charged and threatening terms: women are not permitted to direct "the external relations of the family, or engage in negotiations or penetrate into the political sphere." They are compensated by being spared the heavy physical work endured by laborers. "If American women are never allowed to escape the peaceful circle of domestic concerns, they are also never forced to do so."[101]

In Tocqueville's picturization of women and the family, freedom disappears into an internalized notion of self-government. The focus is on the government of the self rather than government by the selves. Accordingly, the pressures resulting from social equality are now seen in a positive light. They have helped to make American morals stricter than elsewhere in the world because public opinion is an "inexorable" guardian of morals. And because equality encourages marriages between "similars," unions tend to be more lasting.[102]

The disappearance of freedom into social control was reflective of Tocqueville's near panic whenever he contemplates the moral chaos accompanying democracy. Despite the "unparalleled force that has been driving European nations toward democracy," relations between men and women "have not become more regular and chaste." Morals generally have become more lax.[103] Tocqueville reverses the usual contrast between Old World order versus New World anarchy and offers up America as the solution to the modern problem of assuring stable family relations when women were beginning to demand equal rights and greater sexual freedom.

But these developments have also resulted in a reversal of the moral status historically associated with the various social classes in France. While the general effect of the French Revolution was to encourage "moral disorder among the middle and lower classes," paradoxically the aristocracy, which had been "very dissolute" during the eighteenth century, is now discovered by Tocqueville to have been miraculously transformed. Its members have turned inward, forsaking court and city for domesticity and the contemplative life. They have become "respectful of religious beliefs, fond of order, quiet pleasures, domestic joys and contentment."[104] In short, "the most antidemocratic class of the nation now represents the best example of the kind of morality one might reasonably expect of democracy."[105]

Although Tocqueville did not write that the aristocracy had become the bourgeois ideal incarnate, he did suggest that it had become a model of social if not political conduct.

## XXI

The alleged problem of controlling the appetites of the demos is as old as the emergence of Athenian democracy (fifth century B.C.E) and the response to it in the political theories of Plato and Aristotle. The populist passions for easing credit and debtor laws had been a major worry of the property-minded framers of the American Constitution. Historically, "culture" has been the preoccupation and contribution of thinkers such as Montesquieu, Hume, de Maistre, Burke, and Coleridge, who are usually considered conservative. A continuous theme among them had been the habit-bound, nonrational character of loyalty, obedience, and consent. Culture, they argued, could not be created out of whole cloth for it was preeminently the product of experience tested by time. In contrast, theorists considered liberals, such as Locke, Bentham, and the authors of the *Federalist*, emphasized rational coherence as the essential desideratum. They conceived institutions as constructions rather than practices, as embodiments of principles rather than habits, and as requiring public ratification rather than tacit acceptance.[106] If adopted, habits and sentiments would subsequently form around them.

As already noted, Tocqueville became disenchanted with the utility of constitutional forms early on, regarding them as secondary to, and dependent on, cultural practices. We have also noted his intellectual debts to Montesquieu and Rousseau, and one can add his familiarity with Burke's writings, all of whom contributed to shaping an approach that emphasized cultural factors rather than rational constructions. Unlike Burke, who had defended an existing culture being challenged by revolution, or de Maistre, who dreamed of restoring a prerevolutionary culture, Tocqueville conceived a postrevolutionary culture that would be antirevolutionary. The paradox, however, was that in a society such as France, where a culture had been significantly changed by revolution, an antirevolutionary culture must, of necessity, be a political construction. It must become reified before it can be the object of theoretical and political manipulation—and of systematic economic exploitation.[107]

A conception of a democratic culture that is not the evolving creation of the demos, that judges the demos as incapable of self-discipline, is more inclined toward guardian democracy than self-government. The cultural teaching of *Democracy* was "French" rather than "American," aimed at the ruling elements of the aristocracy and the bourgeoisie who had acquired a measure of detachment upon religion and could bring some objectivity to the problem of political culture and thus appreciate the importance of religion as an antidemotic force.

Not surprisingly, echoes of Plato were evident in the politics of culture that Tocqueville was beginning to stake out. The great task that falls to "philosophers and rulers," he opined, is "to make [men] see that despite the perpetual movement that envelopes them," worldly prosperity depends on "long term projects" and hence on repressing "a thousand mundane petty passions." "Once men become more accustomed to taking the long view of what is likely to happen to them in this world," they will be led to "break out of their limitations and to look at what is beyond . . . and without realizing it, they will be led to religious beliefs."[108]

The very point of Tocqueville's conception of a culture whose purpose was to make democracy safe for the world was not to prepare democratic man for political action but to neutralize him. Tocqueville's account of the genesis of culture and its diffusion leaves a strong impression that those who are its objects are simply respondents. The elements of culture—Tocqueville's litany of *moeurs*, manners, habits, and beliefs—are traits and characteristics of conduct that are received rather than developed, that impress themselves upon the members of society, configuring them into systemic patterns that make for social stability.[109] The power exercised through culture requires that those who are to be influenced should not be conscious of the molding influences or engage in public controversies about them. The project of theorizing culture as a "whole" is to create a great social unconsciousness.

## XXII

> *Democratic peoples are passionate about generic terms and abstract words. . . . In order to make discourse run more rapidly [democratic writers] personify the object of abstract words and make them act like a real individual. They will say, "The force of things wills that capacities govern."*
>
> *I can best illustrate my meaning by my own example: I have often used the word equality in an absolute sense; I have even personified equality in several passages, and I have found myself saying that equality did certain things or abstained from others.*
>
> Tocqueville[110]

The democratization of culture is ironic: the demos is its carrier, its user, to some lesser degree its maker. Eventually it would become trained to be culture's consumer. When Tocqueville introduces culture, he consistently sets it into a bipolar field where the running contrast is between an idealized aristocracy and a less-than-idealized democracy, between a culture that prizes uniqueness and refined taste while despising commercialism and a culture that turns literary pursuits into an "industry."

Tocquevillean culture thus becomes a tactic in the symbolization of lack. In portraying anonymity it means to evoke its opposites: scarcity, preciousness, the unattainable. In Tocqueville's idea of culture the aristocratic implies the superior, the "refined"; democratic culture represents rawness, vulgarity in behavior and belief, that which lacks cultivation even when, as Tocqueville noted, a strong emphasis on education is present.

Although the demos has learned by hard experience about "power" and yearned for "justice," the idea of "culture," like the word itself, is not part of the common vocabulary of the demos. Although the demos may have actually developed rich cultures of its own, it has not as yet caught on to the fact that in making culture a coherent entity the upper strata had suddenly found themselves in possession of a new weapon of political control.

At a historical juncture when democracy seems the only palatable political form, culture becomes the stuff of political strategems for insuring a kind of tolerable democracy through the establishing of a domain where the new bourgeois society feels unconfident and yearns to be edified while the poor are excluded from what they do not "appreciate." "Culture" thus becomes the domain of the discourse of political reversal. The vanquished, who, as "aristocracy" were once dominant, attempt to reestablish not class superiority but superior status over the dominant bourgeoisie by co-opting the domain of yearning that the aristocrat Saint-Simon had dubbed "the spiritual."

Suddenly the democracy that had been the harbinger of modernity now is threatened with becoming its casualty. Like aristocracy it would be pronounced archaic, although unlike aristocracy, which successfully transformed its principle of exclusiveness into elitism, democracy's defeat followed after its revolutionary triumph. Democracy appeared to have survived—and in the next century wars of unprecedented destructiveness would be fought to make the entire world safe for it. But the apparent universal triumph of democracy would be the triumph of a certain democracy, a democracy that, like aristocracy, would be trans-formed, have its shape and substance altered. Lost in the process was the civic democracy Tocqueville had celebrated in volume 1. The transformation had been prefigured in the "cultural democracy" of volume 2. It culminates in a prescription remarkable for the aroma of reaction exuded by its incoherence:

> The political world changes; henceforth it is necessary to seek new remedies for the new evils.
>
> We should fix limits to the social power, extensive but clear and firm; private persons should be given certain rights and guaranteed their undisputed enjoyment; to conserve the little independence, power, originality which remains to the individual; to raise his position in society and maintain it against society. Such seems to me to be the chief object of the legislator in the age we are entering.[111]

If this passage could serve as the epigraph to cultural democracy, the epitaph to political democracy was provided in a book review Tocqueville wrote shortly before the revolutionary outbreak of 1848. There he proposed a distinction between "pure" and "representative" democracy. The first stood for political systems in which the people "retained the exercise of power in their hands" and have formed a "body" that "governs." Representative democracy consisted of representative assemblies. Pure democracy, which the Swiss had instituted in some of their cantons following their revolution, Tocqueville declared "a passing phenomenon," "an object of curiosity," a relic of the Middle Ages, rather than "a useful subject." He predicted, accurately as it turned out, that while representative democracy would continue to gain ascendancy pure democracy would decline, lingering on as "the last and respectable remains of a world which no longer exists."[112]

Thus the fate of participatory democracy helps to define the meaning of modernity and its politics. Unable to nurture a democratic political life, modernity assigns it a fleeting existence—of protest, outrage—but never a settled condition; always a losing struggle to preserve what seems increasingly anachronistic. The danger Tocqueville foresaw, however, was not that democracy might be reduced to a rearguard action but that it might acquiesce into becoming the basis of an unprecedented despotism, one that does not actively suppress democracy but exploits it.

# CHAPTER XVII
# DESPOTISM AND UTOPIA

## I

> *What then is the majority, taken collectively, except an individual who has opinions and more often interests contrary to those of another individual, called the minority? . . . My strongest reproach to democratic government, such as it has been organized in the United States, is not . . . its weakness, but its irresistible force. What I find most repugnant about America is not the extreme freedom which rules there, but the few guarantees against tyranny.*
>
> Tocqueville[1]

If "political" or "communal liberty" was the great discovery of the first volume of *Democracy in America*, the theory of modern despotism was perhaps a greater theoretical achievement: the intimation of a postdemocratic "beyond" that did not yet exist.[2] In the first volume Tocqueville had raised the possibility that despotism might emerge from American democracy, that is, grow naturally out of it rather than be imposed on it. The unlimited discretion that Americans allowed their elected magistrates might enable one of them to exploit the dogma of the unlimited authority of the people to establish despotic rule.[3]

When Tocqueville resumed the discussion of despotism in volume 2 he did not cast it as a response to the breakdown of institutions, or to a crisis that provoked a demand for a "strong man"; or to the emergence of a charismatic leader, such as Andrew Jackson.[4] In fact, despotism did not represent a specific response but a configuration resulting from certain tendencies in the symbolic life of democracy and their cultural repercussions in the psychic lives of individuals. To grasp it required the equivalent of a conceptual revolution.

In one of the last chapters of the second volume, "What Type of Despotism Democratic Nations Have to Fear," he remarks that although he had recognized in volume 1 that a democratic social condition furnished a potentially fertile ground for despotism, he had assumed that the despotism would be similar to the kind of "oppression" that had weighed upon "several of the peoples of antiquity." Now, however, "after five years of new meditations, my fears have not at all diminished but their object has changed."[5] Tyranny remained the most pressing danger but it did not lay in the potential excesses of majority rule or in the threat of a new-style democratic Caesar: "the type of oppression which threatens democratic peoples has no precedent; our contemporaries will find no image of it in their memories. I myself have vainly sought for the expression which would exactly capture the conception I have formed."[6]

Why was it difficult to name despotism? Over the centuries political theorists and historians had not been at a loss in describing or agreeing about the characteristics of despotism.[7] The despot gathered all power to himself; would not tolerate rivals; eliminated political life; ruled by personal whim; lived extravagantly while demoralizing economic life; and, as Montesquieu emphasized, used cruelty to create a climate of fear that paralyzed opposition and stifled cultural creativity. These conceptions were all inconceivable without the dominating figure of the despot himself. The state of society was a projection of him. Everything flowed back to him; everything flowed from him. Despotism as the abnormality of power.

But what if, instead of being enslaved, men were formally free; instead of economic misery and bleakness there was a vibrant economic life; instead of a single person indulging his pleasures, all enjoyed the prospect of endless gratifications? What if, instead of cruelty, there was benevolence; instead of fear and uncertainty, there was security; and instead of personal caprice, there was order and predictability? How, amid such contradictory evidence, was it possible to declare it a despotism? Where was the despot, where the unfreedom and the invasion of private sanctities? Where was the oppression, if tyranny, instead of appearing as the opposite of the normal, appeared to be its embodiment—the tyranny of norm-all?

These anomalies appear puzzling as long as thought remains in thrall to the ancient idea of despotism as one of the possible "forms of government or constitution," albeit a "perverted" one; or if Tocqueville's concept of despotism is treated as having been anticipated in the eighteenth-century theories of "benevolent despotism"—when those theories had never presupposed the democratization of society.[8] Tocqueville's groping for a name was a rejection of "form analysis" and a search for the character of modernity with the ambiguities of freedom, individualism, mobility, and equality that democracy and revolution had brought. To understand how they could produce despotism required a reversal in images: instead of society being a projection of the despot, the despot was a projection of society. Society produces a despotism in which the despot is a side effect. He is not invisible; rather he does not exist. To find "him" we must look, not to the state directly, but to civil society and the "social condition" that defined it as modern.

Although Tocqueville would typically describe this condition as "democratic" or one of "equality," it is important to bear in mind his own caveat:

"The thing is new; it is necessary to try and define it since I am unable to name it."[9] It is not distorting to say of his account of despotism that it is equally about the politics of modernity and its unique dynamic ("an imperious necessity"), as well as about its unique expression of power. The context of modernity is not defined by political participation but "certain habits, ideas, and vices," which a "long revolution" has "nurtured and rendered general." Despotism emerges in a society that has reincarnated revolution by acquiring a taste for "rapid movement," by becoming accustomed to swiftly changing its leaders, opinions, and laws.[10]

## II

> *Thus every day [the paternalistic power] renders voluntary action* [libre arbitre] *rarer and less useful and restricts the activity of free will to a smaller space; and little by little it robs each citizen of the use of these faculties.*
>
> Tocqueville[11]

Despotism is for Tocqueville an "ideal" representation of a postpolitical regime. He claims to be presenting its "image," something "imagined." It is, one could say, a series of images, of imaginaries depicting the condition of depoliticized man, of the citizen as archaic, of beings who are totally immersed in private concerns. It is where the members feel a need for guidance, yet they also want to feel free. The perfect expression of these conflicting desires is the wish for a strong centralized government based on elections. For then the citizens can "relax": "In this system the citizens suspend their dependence just long enough to choose their master and then resume it."[12] Despotism does not abolish political life by imitating the Greek tyrant who forbade men to congregate in the civic square. Despotism is possible because political life has shriveled while at the same time majority rule had conditioned society to being receptive to a power coeval with society itself. The majority had approached omnipotence, not as something willed, but through the pervasiveness of those common convictions it represented and which allowed for nothing outside of it. It had invaded the "mind" of society and struck at the "soul."[13] The ethos that supported majority rule was an intimation of totality.

With despotism as its climax volume 2 is revealed to be an inquiry into the depoliticizing tendencies within democracy. At its best, as in the practice of *political* liberty, democracy gambles that the source of its dynamism, the self-interested individual, can be taught to care for common affairs, even if the only way he can care is self-interested. But over and beyond the difficulties of cultivating "self-interest rightly understood" so that it recognizes a common interest is the disproportion between the often boring routines of political life and the high excitement of a society in which challenging opportunities for wealth and endeavor are continually being generated. Democracy is not overthrown politically but steadily absorbed into all aspects of social and mental life. At the same time, while the demands of economic life strain individuals to the utmost of their abilities, the attenuated, undemanding political life causes civic skills to languish and critical thinking to become rarer.[14]

## III

*I want to imagine under what new guise despotism may appear in the world.*

Tocqueville[15]

What did Tocqueville "see" when he imagined the new society without a name? Although he does in fact call it "democratic despotism," the democracy of despotism is the namelessness implied in its emblem "the people" and in the anonymity of its ideology of equality. While remaining true to modern theory's promise of benevolent power, Tocqueville's democratic despotism is a representation of a side of modern power that none of the theorists of modern power, Bacon, Hobbes, or Marx, had intimated. This noncoercive power is silent and irresistible, with no apparent center of direction. It is not, as some later interpreters of Tocqueville were to claim, an anticipation of the totalitarian regime of mass society. Neither excitable nor mobilizable, much less eager for collective self-sacrifice, Tocqueville's populace is passive, even introspective, distracted by its anxious craving for small pleasures. It is "a vast multitude of similar and equal men endlessly revolving around themselves in search of petty and vulgar pleasures with which to stuff their souls." Enclosing himself in a small cocoon of family and friends, each gradually surrenders the development of his own potentialities. "Above him stands elevated a huge, tutelary power [that is] absolute." It sees to all of society's needs, exercises a benign paternalism over all of the details of life, and keeps men in a condition of perpetual childhood. Its sway is stultifying rather than tyrannical, depersonalized and pervasive, a despotism tirelessly attentive to details and content with slow, cumulative effects rather than grand architectonic designs.[16] "I do not fear that their leaders will be tyrants but schoolmasters."[17]

The essence of despotism turns out to be the evils of banality rather than Hannah Arendt's "the banality of evil." It would be oppressive without being experienced as oppression. "The nature of absolute power in democratic eras is neither cruel nor savage, but fussy and meddlesome."[18]

Banality is not ordinarily a political category. It announces a politics dissociated from the political, from "treating in common common things."[19] It would be, peculiarly, a politics without a specific institutional focus, such as a royal court, a legislature, an electoral process, much less a New England town meeting. Banality points to a politics expressed primarily through cultural forms of everyday life and the unremarkable strivings of ordinary and mostly upright individuals rather than the solemn dramaturgy reserved for the theater created by political institutions. Individualism signifies not individuality but the citizen manqué. The individual is made socially equal by democracy, and activated, while being freed from it politically—freedom as private pleasures and public passivity. The release of the ordinary and the resulting energization of it bring new dangers in new disguises. Its evil does not lie in the ethical or aesthetic shortcomings of ordinariness but in a mentality that individualism breeds that allows despotism to take hold insensibly, almost effortlessly.

## IV

*Is it sufficient to see things separately or should we uncover the hidden link which connects them?*

Tocqueville[20]

Civil society was both the repository of Tocqueville's hopes for political vitalization and the source of his fears. The hopes took him back to America. In the only chapters of volume 2 unqualifiedly favorable to American democracy he returned to the idea of association, expanding it from a defense against majority tyranny into a counterinstitution in which the practice of civic ideals would be preserved and the despotic tendencies of egalitarianism resisted. Instead of the negative contribution of associations as "intermediary bodies" defending local authorities against the incursions of the centralizing state—the teaching of volume 1—Tocqueville discovers in the United States a vast array of voluntary or "civil" associations many of which, strictly speaking, are nonpolitical. Americans, Tocqueville declared, create associations for every conceivable purpose from building roads to promoting temperance, from cultivating intellectual interests to establishing joint business ventures. The virtue of associations is partly that they preempt actions that the state might otherwise be entreated/tempted to undertake but, equally important, that they serve to overcome the isolation and loneliness that despotism exploits as "the surest guarantee of its own permanence."[21] Citizens learn to work together and to trust each other through contacts developed in the course of attempting to effect some common purpose.

Yet, Tocqueville insists, by themselves private ("civil") associations cannot effectively nurture political life unless strong connections are developed between them and political associations. It is the latter alone that can provide the example of how working together creates new powers; and so political associations serve to inspire citizens to invent their own collaborations: "Thus politics generalizes the taste and habits of association."[22]

The fate of the political in modern society thus depended on the vitality of certain segments of civil society, which, Tocqueville acknowledged, required inventiveness, indeed, a "new science."[23] Civil and political associations were "artificial"—not, as Aristotle claimed, "natural." To get the modern citizen to engage in "common action" requires "a great deal of art."[24] The reason why associations had to be contrived was that they ran counter to individualism, one of the strongest tendencies and most cherished values of the modern democrat. Individualism encourages a general indifference to civic life and mutual suspicion and isolation; it is a major factor in disposing society toward despotism. Thus the crucial question was whether the character of civil society would be set by individualism or by association.

Associations and a free press (Tocqueville links the two) were the only institutions discussed in volume 2 that are recommended as antidotes to despotism—and to equality. They are essential elements of "political liberty," which "is the only effective remedy for combatting the evils that equality can produce."[25] Tocqueville's fixation on the evils of equality served to obscure one of the main claims he put forward in defending associations, that the experience of cooperation worked to lower the barriers between human beings. "From the moment common affairs are treated in common . . . the cold passions which divide men are repressed, pride has to disguise itself, and scorn remain hidden. Egoism becomes afraid of itself."[26]

Whether associations could effectively discharge the heavy burden of combatting individualism and vitalizing public life would depend not only on the kind of powers they would be matched against but upon the character of the civil society surrounding them. As we shall see, associations were both overmatched in the powers they were to contend with and compromised by the affinities between the new culture of civil society and the culture of the new powers.

## V

> *I have shown how the Americans are continually driven toward trade and industry. Their origins, their social condition, their political institutions, even the place in which they live carries them irresistibly in that direction. For now they form an association, almost exclusively industrial and commercial, which is placed in the midst of a new and immense country and whose principal aim is to exploit it. That is the characteristic trait which, in our times, distinguishes Americans most especially from all other nations.*
>
> Tocqueville[27]

What, then, is the experience of civil society such that it could become a breeding ground for a novel phenomenon whose name Tocqueville was uncertain about but to which he assigned the traditional name of despotism? Some new circumstances would have had to emerge within civil society to render it congenial, even receptive to the one form of power that had been almost universally condemned since antiquity as the essence of the antipolitical.

In ancient Greece tyranny was often preceded by intense political activity by the Many protesting unjust actions by aristocrats or wealthy oligarchs. Tyranny was thus the consequence, negative or positive, of aroused political consciousness. Modern despotism, in Tocqueville's view, was a likely consequence of civil society either losing its zeal for "political liberty" and lapsing into apoliticism, favoring individual isolation over social ties and communal concerns; or civil society having embraced egalitarianism before acquiring the experience of political liberty. Whether the society was depoliticized (post-political) or merely apolitical, in either condition it was complementary to the centralizing tendencies of state power. Thus if state and civil society become smoothly continuous, if manners, *moeurs*, and beliefs shape social relationships and attitudes so as to discourage active political involvement by the citizenry while simultaneously encouraging state power, then the matrix exists for a new form of despotism. Despotism would change its physiognomy and cease to be an alien power violently superimposed on a stunned and resentful society. It becomes, instead, institutionalized, grounded in a congenial—because depoliticized—culture and camouflaged by modernity. It is a "democratic" despotism whose theoretical possibility was signaled by Tocqueville's silent elimination of "the New England factor." Without its participatory elements, other elements of democracy's culture can be reassembled—the nonresistant ones, as it were—to become supports for political democracy's opposite. Elements such as consensus are inverted and become conformism. Self-interest when rightly understood had included civic involvements; now it sheds them and evolves into the egoism of isolated beings. Equality, instead of serving as the symbol of the triumph of the Many, conspires unwittingly at their equal subjection.

## VI

*I have shown how democracy favors the development of industry and multiplies endlessly the number of industrialists.*

*Thus, if one traces things back to their source, it appears that aristocracy emerges naturally from the midst of democracy.*

Tocqueville[28]

How could this come about? The answer lies in an area with which Tocqueville was far more concerned than the vast majority of his commentators have given him credit. That civil society might harbor the potential for a new kind of despotism was related in part to its democratization but also, and in at least equal degree, to the rapidly increasing influence of industrialization and of "the science of industry," its theoretical accompaniment.

The importance assumed by industrialization in volume 2 might seem surprising in a writer who had none of the economic sophistication of a Marx and who would be chided by critics for his lack of attention to economics. Tocqueville was not interested in economic theory but in industrialism as a cultural determinant and political influence—that is, as a phenomenon of power. His concerns had little connection with classical economics but they were at the center of a well-defined and contemporary discourse in France to which Saint-Simon and the Saint-Simonian school, Comte, and a number of early socialist writers were contributors.

What renders his discussion unique is that it combines elements drawn from three different economies. Tocqueville's travels to America, England, and Ireland had exposed him to capitalist economies at different stages of development. In the United States he had observed a highly decentralized economy of numerous small entrepreneurs and landholders that was commensurate with an equally decentralized political system and a nigh invisible state.[29] While in England he had visited Manchester, the same highly industrialized city that Engels would indelibly describe a decade later, and, like Engels, Tocqueville would be appalled by the degradation of the factory workers. He would be positively impressed that Britain's robust economy was balanced off by a strong political system, which, while centralized, preserved a flourishing local politics, a politically influential aristocracy that absorbed new social elements, and a culture that continued to nurture the habits of political liberty. France, in contrast, presented the spectacle of a premodern economy and an ultramodern state. Although industrialization was clearly taking hold, peasant proprietorship of the land rather than the technologically advanced factory was the principal economic unit. A significant factor in the French economy was the extensive regulation, control, and sponsorship of industrialization by the state. Tocqueville made use of all three economies. America, where individual entrepreneurship was the dominant norm, supplied Tocqueville with the elements of what might be called the culture of high-energy materialism in its pure form, that is, without the state playing a major role. From Manchester he drew his picture of a highly developed industrialism. France would contribute the state as the dominant partner in the collaboration with industry.

The striking quality of Tocqueville's formulation lies in his depiction of an American entrepreneurial culture into which, insensibly, democracy has begun to merge. He does nothing less than show how certain democratic values and achievements could enable democracy to become the auxiliary of capitalism. The value of equality serves to spread the taste for well-being throughout the whole society and to dignify work, while keeping the desires for physical comfort and pleasure at a modest level that does not interfere with work or threaten society.[30] He portrays an entrepreneurial culture that has incorporated certain qualities associated with democracy—energy, optimism, receptiveness to change, and risk taking[31]—while eviscerating the practices associated with popular sovereignty, majority rule, participatory politics, and political community. It is democracy depoliticized by a massive channeling away of energy and skill. But there is also the question of the political or, rather, the antipolitical implications of the power relationships within industry. That question Tocqueville explores in a chapter entitled, "How Aristocracy Could Emerge from Industry."

The division of labor prescribed by an "industrial theory," Tocqueville notes, has become "more powerful than *moeurs* and laws." It operates to diminish the capacities of the worker while enlarging those of the manager. While industry advances, the worker becomes "weaker, more limited, and more dependent."[32] Although the worker is confined to the same minute operations, the manager "surveys a vast whole, and his mind expands in proportion as the others' contracts. . . . Increasingly the one resembles the administrator of a vast empire, the other a brute." What has been created is "an exception, a monster," a new "aristocracy," that is perhaps the "hardest" ever known.[33] Despite that characterization Tocqueville treated the owners as a distinctly secondary element. In part this was because he identified the industrial form of modern power with the structure of industry rather than with the class that owned and operated it. In part, too, the capitalist struck him as the representative of a stunted class. Its composition was too fluid; it lacked traditions; it was unable to found family dynasties because wealth and inherited privilege had become dissociated; in short, capitalists lacked the potential for genuine corporateness. At bottom it seemed a furtive aristocracy, its own timidity preventing it from flaunting its wealth before a suspicious, egalitarian society. Harsh though its factory rule might be, it was, as a class, "one of the most constrained and least dangerous."[34] And most unpolitical.

Thus far America has been spared the full political implications of industrialization, not because that society was underdeveloped economically but because of its head start in consolidating participatory institutions before developing an entrepreneurial culture. For the moment the two coexisted. In France, however, industrialization was prior to and more firmly entrenched in the nation's culture than democratic participation. The democratic elements that did exist in French culture worked to the advantage of state power, enabling it to exploit democratic sentiments in order to legitimate its use of the "new force" that "industry has created in our day." Although industrialists have "despotic" power over society, they are continually soliciting favors from the state that furthers their dependence. The result was a situation in which "industry leads us and governments lead industry."[35] At the same time, the magnitude of poverty in a society which has become democratized as well as industrialized works to the advantage of the state as it assumes the welfare functions formerly belonging to private agencies. The upshot is that the rich, whose emblem of real power is the "industrial enterprise," and the poor, whose emblem of potential power is the democratic suffrage, are both drawn into dependency on the state.[36]

Industrialism represents a doubling of power, not only the power to produce abundantly and cheaply while imposing a new discipline on society[37] but also the power resulting from collaboration between the state and industry. As a consequence, modern despotism is unimaginable without the presence of modern industry and its combination of a power to attract human desires, while subjecting human desires to "regular habits" and human energies to "uniform motions." "One may say that it is the very violence of their desires that renders the American so methodical."[38]

The democratization of the economy in the form of a wider diffusion of private property works to the further advantage of the state. A property-owning citizenry tends to be fearful of social disorders at the historical moment when their busy lives and aroused appetite for well-being leave little time and less inclination for political activity.[39] "The love of public tranquillity is often the only political passion that the people retain, and it becomes the more active and powerful to the extent that the others are weakened and die."[40] The democratization of economic life, like culture, works against political democratization, making it appear unprofitable and redundant.

Political economy thus reveals a depoliticized state rather than the depoliticized economy emphasized by the economists. The power that accrues to the state has been depoliticized: it operates through administration, but administration is not the source of power but its refraction. "[I]n democratic countries there is always the danger that revolutionary instincts will be softened and regularized without being extinguished and *will be transformed gradually into governmental mores and administrative habits.*"[41] Administration, which prescribes "rules" and "applies" them to specific circumstances and which had once been the instrument devised by centralizing monarchs, has now found its true master in popular sovereignty. Popular sovereignty, the ultimate, all-powerful master whose secret, which the world knows, is that it cannot act, has found its correlative. Like popular sovereignty, administration is anonymous; it administers rules but cannot act; it promises to place neutrality above politicalness; it is centered but unregal.

## VII

> *[A] great revolution has taken place in the world. Industrial wealth, once a germ, has spread over all Europe; the industrial class has expanded and enriched itself from the ruin of all the other classes; it has grown in numbers, in importance, in wealth; it grows endlessly. . . . [H]aving once been the exception, it threatens to become the main class.*
>
> Tocqueville[42]

Tocqueville's despotism reflects a shift in theoretical focus from democratic participation in the political to a preoccupation with the liberal culture emerging from the intersection of democracy and economy. Culture will register a corresponding shift, from being communal to being competitive, frantic, and anxiety-ridden in a Hobbesian quest for an ever elusive "felicity." The clue to the new preoccupation is in the chapter title, "How the Americans Combat Individualism by Free Institutions."[43] The institutions in question are "civil and political associations"—that is, the institutions most closely identified with democracy are brought to bear against individualism, the value most closely identified with a culture in which "freedom and industry" exist in "a necessary relationship . . . particularly among democratic nations."[44]

> It is a strange thing to see with what feverish ardor the American pursues well-being. . . . Americans attach themselves to worldly goods as if assured that they will never die. . . . They seize everything but without taking hold of anything. . . . Death finally intervenes and stops him before he has become wearied of this futile pursuit of a complete felicity which always eludes him.[45]

As democratic man becomes ever more immersed in a free economy, he is continually "coming up against the competition of all" and as a result he begins to experience a sense of powerlessness. Suddenly he becomes aware of widespread inequalities. Equality now appears elusive. Despite economic "abundance" a "remarkable melancholy" settles upon him. In France suicide appears on the increase; in America it is rare but "madness is more common than anywhere else."[46] The relatively high level of prosperity induces a loss of interest in political affairs but a heightened fear of social anarchy. "Good order" becomes a strong priority and serves to justify harsh measures.[47]

Despotism, in Tocqueville's depiction, is not the result of a crisis produced by political democracy but a crisis in its liberal variant. The glory of liberalism was its defense of individual rights, constitutional limitations on power, and political accountability of elected officials. Tocqueville located the crisis at the confluence where individualism, or the right of the individual to determine his or her conception of personal happiness, merged with self-interest, the guiding principle of conduct of economic life that each acted always with an eye to advancing or protecting his or her particular interests. That combination seemingly left no significant scope for political life.

The slim thread on which Tocqueville had hung his hopes for the revival of political life—the true antithesis to despotism—was that self-interest could be educated. His assumption was that privatization had already begun to marginalize public life. Accordingly, the individual who emerges in Tocqueville's pages possesses few of the civic impulses he had in volume 1; in volume 2 these have gradually atrophied to the point where *homo popularis* has become the grist of despotism. In part the change reflected a shift in focus, from the New England *poleis* to civil society and to what might be called the cultural economy of the bourgeois *agon* made possible by lowering the barriers to acquiring wealth and "moving up" in the world.

In Tocqueville's formulation it is not the pursuit of wealth per se or the vast opportunities for private happiness that alone account for antipolitical tendencies within democracy. Political disengagement is a "considered" (*réfléchi*) decision on the part of the individual "to isolate himself from the mass of his fellows and to retire into a circle of family and friends."[48]

In volume 2 Tocqueville gives the name of individualism to that phenomenon. His conception of individualism is developed by contrasting the loose ties among democratic peoples with the close bonds among aristocrats and those dependent on them ("a little fatherland for all its members").[49] By the logic of his own theory, however, the contrast could easily have been between the communal democracy of volume 1 and the democratic but apolitical civil society of volume 2. The problem he himself had opened concerned the two divergent paths a democracy might follow: either toward self-government or toward the abdication of the responsibility of caring for the political.

In a curious way Tocqueville tends to lose sight of the individual because of his concern to develop the notion of "individualism" and the closely related idea of *egoisme* as a preliminary to showing how the disposition of the one toward political withdrawal and of the other toward self-obsession renders them both the natural allies of despotism. If, however, we recall Tocqueville's individual American democrat, the being who believes in and lives his religion, his moral code, his political principles, it is possible to see more in Tocqueville's notion of individualism. What makes individualism a crucial concern is not only its moral obtuseness when compared with an idealized version of aristocratic paternalism. It was the fact of it being an "ism." In individualism the profoundly ideological character of modern democracy is exposed and, with it, the tensions between modernity and democracy.

Tocqueville's instinct was sure when he recognized that the dominant notions concerning the individual represented not only distinct modes of conduct but also the equally distinct convictions normalizing them. Like individualism, the concept of ideology was of recent coinage, having been in circulation for about a half century.[50] Although Tocqueville did not employ the term, it is no stretch of usage to apply it to his conception of individualism. Individualism is "the philosophical method of Americans," the demotic version of Cartesianism and the operationalizing of its consequences. Descartes's hermetic moment and its defiant conclusion, "je pense, donc je suis, " is mimicked: "Equality develops in each man the desire to judge everything by himself."[51] It becomes at once expressive of loss, disconnectedness, and isolation from others and, at the same time, is aggressively self-assertive: "in most mental operations each American calls upon the individual resources of his own reason."[52] The market serves as the secular equivalent to Luther's "priesthood of all believers." What is striking in Tocqueville's portrait is the credulous nature of the self-reliant man. The modern individual, when he stops short of the nihilism of *egoisme*, is not a cynic or skeptic. He is a *convinced* individual who believes as dogmatically in his own uniqueness as he does in the sanctity of his individual soul and its preciousness in the eyes of God.

For Tocqueville Americans shared a distinct system of beliefs—about politics, society, morality, and religion. The unifying center of the system, what gives it structure, is a passionate conviction about equality. "Equality suggests to the human mind several ideas which it would not incorporate by itself and it modifies nearly all those ideas which it has incorporated."[53] Thus equality functions as a kind of cynosure, radiating its influence throughout the society so that a culture is formed bearing its seal. The ideology of equality not only unifies beliefs but structures how democratic man sees and comprehends the world and expresses his desires and preferences, whether these involve personal matters, cultural tastes, politics, or religious beliefs.[54]

Tocqueville detected the influence of the American ideology in the themes favored by poets and in the constraints imposed on the imagination. Poetry, in Tocqueville's formulation, "was the search for the representation of the ideal." Democratic poetry, however, reflects "the love of material pleasures, the idea of improvement, competition, the beckoning of success." Although the poetic imagination may soar, "doubt brings the poetic imagination back to earth and confines it to a world visible and real."[55] Denied the themes stimulated by a society in which there were marked differences between men, the democratic poet will be fed upon "ideas of progress and the indefinite perfectibility of the human race."[56] "Democracy, which closes the past to poetry, opens the future."[57]

The paradox of individualism is that, while seeming to favor individual differences and a cult of variety, it is, in actuality, a social creation, a product of the difference-denying culture of equality. "In the United States the majority is in charge of furnishing individuals with a collection of ready-made opinions and thus relieves them of the obligation of forming their own."[58] The power of the ideology lies in this double creation: the democrat acts and believes as though he were wholly self-centered, yet he is, at the same time, a fervent believer in collectivities. The democratic imagination may be limited and impoverished when it focuses on the individual because he is so small, but "it expands indefinitely when it thinks of the State."[59] The individual believes fervently in his nation and its providential favor and, more immediately, in the essential rightness of the majority. Ideological conviction converts the majority into an immaterial power operating continuously but without uttering its name. It presides over what Durkheim would later call "collective representations," the widely shared belief in certain images of collectivity that appear "real" to the believers because of the cultural likeness that one believer bears to another. "To the extent that citizens become more alike . . . the disposition to believe in the mass increases, and more and more opinion leads the world."[60]

"Opinion" is a crucial element in Tocqueville's conception of the ideology of democracy. It tends to be underappreciated because of the temptation of later commentators to read into it certain late-twentieth-century notions of "public opinion" and to treat it simply as the statistical expression of mass preferences. "Opinion" was a serious notion for Tocqueville, conveying the passion of a religious conviction. "There is a large number of theories on matters of philosophy, morality, or politics which everyone accepts because of faith in the public." Indeed, religion is described as a subset of opinion: "religion holds sway less as a matter of revealed doctrine than as part of common opinion. . . . [O]ne could predict that faith in common opinion will become a kind of religion with the majority as its prophet."[61] Tocqueville wanted to emphasize the *power* of shared beliefs arising from a peculiar combination of unargued (though not simplistic) ideas—Tocqueville called them "dogmatic beliefs"—and strong passions. The potency of ideology can be appreciated if it is remembered that consensus is its offshoot and it is consensus that unifies a society. "Dogmatic beliefs" are necessary: "without common ideas, common action is not possible, and without common action men might still exist, but not a collectivity [*un corps social*]."[62]

Tocqueville's depiction of the modern individual created by the revolution of equality is not like that of the Benthamites in England—J.S. Mill was a significant exception—or the followers of Say in France who, in their theories of rational behavior, so thoroughly "economized" the actor that he appeared to be unshaped by ideology. At best, ideology was merely one of the interests or preferences of *homo economicus*. Tocqueville, however, creates a liberal individual who was the creature not only of interests but of beliefs, the carrier of an "ism," individualism, which was more far-reaching than its name implied, more than the "egoism" of its final, perverted destiny. Individualism was a product of that same distinct set of beliefs and assumptions that served as the main foundation of modern democratic culture—not as it was presently embodied in America or France but in that distillation of elements from each society that Tocqueville selected and then transported to the same theoretical plane as "democracy" and now as "despotism."

## VIII

> *I think that nowhere in the civilized world is there a country less concerned with philosophy than the United States.*
>
> Tocqueville[63]

The iconic representation of the American ideology was Descartes or, in Tocqueville's language, Cartesianism. Its role as a major mytheme is heralded in the title of the opening chapter of volume 2, "The Philosophical Method of the Americans."[64] When Tocqueville describes the American mentality as Cartesian, he is attempting to identify a quality that reflects a widespread way of thinking in a society of equals and similars. It is a social usage equivalent to a "method." Americans might be too busy to actually read Descartes but "they follow his maxims because the same social condition disposes their minds to adopt them."[65] The Cartesian parallels between how Americans think and how they act are displayed by Tocqueville's description, first, of American individualism in action—

> new families arise endlessly from nothing, others fall back into it . . . the woof of time is continually broken and the traces of generations erased. Those who have gone before are easily forgotten and no one has any idea of those who will follow. One's interests are in what is near at hand.[66]

—and then his comparison of it with his description of the philosophical method of Americans:

> To escape from the systematic mentality, from the judgment of habits, family maxims, class beliefs, and even to a degree from national prejudices; to treat tradition only as useful information and to accept existing facts only as a useful basis for going beyond them and improving them; to seek by themselves and in themselves alone the reason for things, concentrating on results rather than getting entangled in means and attending to substance rather than forms.[67]

Earlier I have called attention to Tocqueville's abhorrence of the Cartesian principle of doubt; now, ironically, Descartes signifies the opposite: the kind of belief that, in its cultural forms, approximates dogma. Doubly ironical, modernity's despotism is prefigured not in the tyrant but in the philosopher who rules not because he is a ruler, an anointed guardian-king, or because his ideas have somehow directly influenced society. Rather, in Tocqueville's formulation, he seems a prefiguring of society, floating harmlessly through the history of philosophy until society will have crystallized in a certain fashion so that his ideas become a Rosetta stone, a hieroglyph that explains the structure of social beliefs, even in societies such as the United States that scarcely know his name. Perhaps, however, Cartesianism is the disguise for the ideology of the French Revolution.

## IX

> *It is easy to see, however, that nearly all Americans direct their thinking by the same rules. . . . [They] follow [Descartes's] maxims because the same social condition disposes their minds to adopt them.*
>
> Tocqueville[68]

Cartesianism "clicks" at a certain moment because of social needs and political developments. In France of the eighteenth century, when men began "to become more equal and more like each other," then "the philosophical method" of Descartes became widespread. That method, Tocqueville emphasized, was "not just French but democratic,"—that is, it made sense, ideological common sense, of the conditions brought about by the spread of equality.

What makes Descartes an iconic figure turns out to be a peculiar combination of seemingly incongruous elements of individualism, revolution, and uniformity. Cartesian doubt is directed at the conventional truths that sustain/burden a history-conscious society. The test of new truths is whether they strike the individual as "clear and distinct." He, and not some social authority, is the final judge. The way to truth, however, demands conformity, the subordination of the mind to certain rules that impose order upon the mind. The individual has been set free but the mind, which begins by rejecting authority, has already chosen conformity: he submits because of the unprecedented powers which modern, desacralized truth promises and because method has seemingly not come at the expense of freedom. Method does not dictate ends, and hence it does not appear to restrict the uses to which knowledge may be put or to dictate what matters are worth inquiring into.

The doubting of accepted beliefs forms the philosophical analogue to revolution. Once doubting becomes a practice, once risk taking is methodized, its consequences are not confined to beliefs. Inevitably the practice of doubt calls into question the authorities legitimated by beliefs; revolution, as the practice of overthrowing authorities, becomes the political analogue to philosophical doubt. "[The French] were the first to generalize and to emphasize how a philosophic method could easily be used to attack everything ancient and open the way for new things."[69] The revolutionaries had appealed to the laws of nature in order to provide a universal rather than a historical foundation for the universal rights of man and the citizen, while denying validity to the historical exceptionalities of blood, rank, and privilege.

## X

Descartes had sought isolation in order to seek truth. The self sets about fashioning an abstract self by suspending its traditional beliefs and subjecting those elements of its own identity to the principle of radical doubt. The "way of method" seemed to offer the hope of truth freed from prejudice. It produced, instead, its own ideology, that of the sovereign individual. Cartesianism is not the cause of individualism but the expression of similar tendencies whose pervasive recurrence justifies a common label, "the modern." Protestant dissent sanctifies the individual conscience; political economy installs the individual as the best judge of his own interests; and political liberalism defends individual rights.

Descartes prefigures not only the ideology of individualism and the social condition of isolation but also what might be called "the theoretization of everyday life." Marx, in a note to his doctoral dissertation, described a world where philosophy was becoming more worldly and the world more philosophical.[70] Although Tocqueville's Americans are prereflective, they try nonetheless to make their world more philosophical, "to adjust the practice of human affairs to theory."[71] Social authorities are, for the American, always distant. And so he must think for himself, to confront beings and things without the givenness of prior connections, without preordained social inscriptions. Given its fluidity and mobility the everyday life of democracy becomes more dehistoricized; it necessarily becomes more theoretical. Memory is replaced by modes of knowing indifferent to historical time: economics is historyless. But the economy imposed by Ockham's razor is an empirical fact before it becomes a theoretical injunction.

> Having acquired the habit of general ideas from the matters which occupy him the most and involve his interests [democratic man] applies that habit to everything else, and it is thus that the need to discover common rules for all things and to group a large number of objects under the same form, and to explain a group of facts by a single cause becomes an ardent and often blind passion of the human mind.[72]

When abstracted individuals observe each other, they perceive only similarities and so they proceed to generalize, not from an aesthetic of elegant minimalism but from the natural impulses of an unstocked but impatient mind. They are in a hurry for each has to make his or her own way in the world without benefit of prolonged reflection, leisurely learning, or customary lore. Theory enables them to encompass a lot by means of very little.[73] In the jargon of the late twentieth century, theory is empowering as well as cost-effective.

In France, according to Tocqueville, however, Cartesianism proved to be explosively revolutionary. Democratic man in the age of mediocrity and self-interest could not aspire to virtue or greatness, but he could believe. Nothing impressed Tocqueville more than the American's capacity for belief—in a handful of moral maxims but especially in an assortment of uncomplicated religious dogmas. Belief tends to be uncritical for it is not about "ideas" but convictions that free the mind for other matters and allow, even encourage, it to devote its energies to those material things that premoderns considered to be the opposite of spiritual concerns.

Tocqueville's conception of belief was subtly different from the conception of consensus he had advanced in volume I. Consensus serves as a kind of "involuntary" and "instinctive" social contract. It is the "agreement" of "a large number of citizens" to remain under "the same government."[74] While consensus deals with what is settled and is made possible by a shared cognitive structure,[75] ideology contains a dynamic, expansive element deriving from the continuous attempt to comprehend/stabilize the world of change through generalizations.

## XI

*In aristocratic centuries the sciences are expected to please the mind, but in democracies the body.*

Tocqueville[76]

The prominence of ideology in modern political and social life imparts a peculiar importance to ideas that seems incongruous with the materialism that Tocqueville found so oppressive in America and France. The widespread reliance on "general ideas," "dogmatic beliefs," and "consensus" all contribute to create a kind of ethos of ideas that naturally begs for comparison with the popular influence of religion during the sixteenth and seventeenth centuries. But that comparison does not do full justice to what is uniquely modern, the theoretical character of popular discourse. Generalization-as-consensus—with its uncanny power of silently inducing millions of scattered individuals, unprogrammed by deep ties of family, place, or class, to express the same general convictions (a *universalis consensus* )—was the ultimate political expression of the theoretization of everyday life.

One of the most striking differences between the two installments of *Democracy* concerned the status of theory. In volume 1 Tocqueville declared flatly that "the American mind avoids general ideas; it is not directed toward theoretical discoveries." American politics, as well as industry, was carried on without reference to theory, and even in the law no "great writers" were searching out "the general principles of laws"—a comment that did not endear him to Justice Story.[77] But these characterizations were composed before Tocqueville discovered/constructed the Cartesian mind in America and before he was able to discriminate among various types of theory.

Although the Cartesianism of American thinking and the role of ideas in American culture were consistent with the admiration for the theoretical quality of New England political thinking expressed in volume 1, there remains an important sense in which volume 2 could be entitled "The Discovery of American Theory." What Tocqueville discovered and proceeded to explore can be described fairly as American pragmatism—not as a school but as a popular philosophy, not as *philo* + *sophia* (love of wisdom) but as *philo* + *praxis* (love of practical action). For the first time there appeared, surprisingly, a popularly based theoretical culture. This had profound consequences for the status of theory and its practice. Theoretical knowledge was no longer solely the creation of knowledge-elites working in demos-proof enclaves and further shielded by an aura of esoterica. Theoretical knowledge was now imbued by the pragmatics of survival and practical necessities, by a generalized ideology that would be pointedly democratic only as long as it remained civic, and by a way of life that made up by experiments what it lacked in precedents. The theoretical element in American pragmatic knowledge was its self-conscious resolve about remaining theoryless while in actuality engaged not in abandoning theory but in narrowing its scope. "It is easy to see how in a [democratic] society . . . the human mind should insensibly be led to neglect theory and that, in contrast, it should drive with unparalleled energy toward practical application, or at least toward that aspect of theory which is necessary for application."[78]

The theoretical culture developed by democracy would have a profound effect on the practice of theory as traditionally understood. From the time of Plato's Academy and Aristotle's Lyceum the theorist's search for the highest forms of knowledge was thought to require a certain autonomy and distance from society that would allow for the development of the kind of culture most hospitable to the theoretical life (*bios theoretikos, vita contemplativa*).[79] Not coincidentally, theorists were consistently critical of democracy and usually depicted its way of life as inherently antagonistic to the search for theoretical knowledge. Democracy signified the contamination and eventual absorption of theory by ideology or, as the ancients called it, "opinion" (*doxa*).

In America modern theory confronted for the first time a wholly democratic culture. An entire people was engaged in making its own politics, society, economy—in short, its own civilization. There were no aristocratic patrons or wealthy sponsors interested in underwriting the disinterested pursuit of truth, only a survivalist imperative that dictated a culture of practicality. To be sure, Bacon and Hobbes had earlier constructed a modernity in which truth need not apologize for being interest-laden or practical, but their appeals were formed for a predemocratic modernity where restricted entry to the ruling classes was still the norm, even though those classes were slowly being opened to pedigreeless men of knowledge, wealth, or practical acumen.

Not the least of the anomalies that Tocqueville found in America was a democracy with strong traditions of learning and an unsatisfied appetite for knowledge. Instead of meeting resistance, modern theory encountered pragmatism—"working" knowledge, not "idle" speculation. Americans displayed a marked affinity for the "real and tangible" and "a scorn of tradition and forms." Their distrust of utopian speculation was rooted not in conservative fears of change but in a scientific temper. They preferred to remain "close to the facts and to study them in themselves."[80] The mix of modern theory with American pragmatism was explosive in its potential for a society that imagined itself as a continuous beginning. Tocqueville, however, was momentarily attracted by the contrast between American pragmatism and French revolutionary ideologism. He noted that American political theory displayed the same practical bent as American scientific theorists, a quality Tocqueville applauded by contrasting it with the intoxication with theories on a grand scale, as occurred among eighteenth-century French revolutionaries. It was important, Tocqueville maintained, for a democratic people constantly to be reminded of the importance of bringing the practical requirements and detailed operations of government to bear as a kind of sobriety test for political speculation.[81]

That advice typifies once more Tocqueville's tactical use of particularity to combat the generalizing tendencies of democratic and revolutionary thinking. But it brought Tocqueville face-to-face with a dilemma. If theory does not remain in touch with the practical realities of governance, it is tempted toward radical and utopian speculation—a fear that Tocqueville would voice throughout the rest of his lifetime. On the other hand, if theory focused exclusively on what is at hand in the "real" world, it turns into shallow pragmatism, which Tocqueville identified with a bourgeois mentality. What would be lost, Tocqueville feared, was what democracy most needed, a critical theoretical voice, not hostile but disinterested. In a democracy, unfortunately, the critic was quickly typed as a threat and marginalized as an outsider: "you are forever a stranger among your own kind . . . an impure being."[82]

The problem, in part, was resolved by Tocqueville who fashioned aristocracy into the theoretical equivalency for critical distance and used its historical demise as proof of his own disinterestedness. Tocqueville defended his decision in a letter to his English translator: "I have written in a country and for a country where the cause of equality has now triumphed, leaving no possible return to aristocracy. In this state of affairs, I have felt duty-bound to give special emphasis to the bad tendencies which equality can nourish and thereby seek to prevent my contemporaries from surrendering to them."[83]

But the other problem, of encouraging a closer connection between theory and factual reality, faced the difficulty of determining what countervailing facts might look like and where they could be found in a society in which everything was slanted toward uniformity and sameness. What that suggested was a stark choice: either the search within a democratic society for a nondemocratic form of theory that could constitute facts differently, assigning them a different order of significance from that of the predominant ways of thinking or, failing that, a counterfactual theory. Because there seemed to be no practical alternative to egalitarian democracy, the character of theory had to be shaped by tactical considerations. The possibility then looming was that the politics of theory might dictate the theory of politics.

Tocqueville decided to defend the idea of theory in its more traditional form. He began by dividing "science"—a term that he used to cover virtually all forms of systematic knowledge—into three parts: the theoretical, the partly theoretical, and the practical. Each is dependent on a particular kind of culture for its support and nurture, but only one, the purely theoretical, appears socially unconditioned. The "permanent agitation" characteristic of modern democratic society, as well as its insatiable appetite for physical and material gratifications, was inhospitable to the contemplative life and to the purely theoretical, while the "egotistic, mercantile, and industrial" taste for scientific knowledge made democracy favor scientific knowledge or, more precisely, those forms of scientific knowledge that promised ready practical applications.[84] In modern times "the human mind has to be coerced into [pure] theory"; "the small number" who are drawn by the "proud" and "disinterested" love of truth will appear anomalous. The purity of pure theory, its dedication to the search for "the abstract sources of truth," is more at home in aristocratic cultures. The theorist, like the aristocrat, is associated with the "lofty" and "sublime." He stands "above the crowd" in his disdain for the merely practical.[85]

The point of the contrast between the status and character of theory in an aristocratic culture and in a democratic culture was partly to claim that under the Old Regime the aristocracy encouraged a purer type of theory but partly to underscore the radical changes brought about by modernity. Prior to the era of the bourgeoisie, theorists had cultivated a certain detachment. Theorizing, they said, was disinterested but far from being uncritical. Like the aristocrat, the theorist had to establish distance as a condition of contributing to society's enlightenment. Modernity reversed these understandings, elevating the practical over the abstract, the interested over the disinterested. At stake was not only the nature of theory but the encouragement given to tendencies within modernity, especially tendencies toward despotism. When the bias against disinterested thought becomes a cultural axiom, part of the *moeurs*, critical thought is pinched from two directions: accused either of being "unreal" because disinterested, or partisan because all thought is tainted by interest. The popular form of antitheory is exemplified in the notorious American dislike of criticism by outsiders. This distrust of distance is reinforced by the important role of consensus in a democracy; by the religious beliefs, whose power is measured by their unquestioned status; and, not least, by the great value placed in individual judgment. Heterodox ideas are not suppressed but isolated by the very virtues that Tocqueville found admirable among Americans, their moral strictness, trusting cooperation, pride in their achievements as a nation—in short, the *moeurs* that supported the great project of free self-government.

As in so many of his uses of aristocracy, Tocqueville's aristocratic conception of theory was not intended to bind theory to elitism—he was already beginning to distrust the theorist-intellectual—but to preserve/invent a cultural form that could allow for a critical, even oppositional perspective on the all-pervasive culture of democracy. The cultural threat posed by democracy was banality or mediocrity. Banality was the necessary expression of a society in which differences, rarities, and the exceptional were fast becoming incomprehensible and things were possessed or consumed rather than savored. The nature of modernity demanded modes of theoretical resistance that would call attention to what modernity was unable to see. Outwardly directed toward the practical and in a hurry, it could not pause for introspection into "the inner being of a democratic society." "How can thought be halted to dwell on a single point when everything around it is on the move?"[86] Theory had not only to seek out a nonmodern vantage point but a different tempo from the hurried, experimental tempo of pragmatic, practical theory. "Men who live in times of equality have a great deal of curiosity but little leisure."[87] To be able to see into modernity and differently from it required a slower pace; accordingly, Tocqueville likens theory to meditation. "Nothing is more necessary to the culture of the higher sciences, or to the lofty part of all sciences than meditation and nothing is less conducive to meditation than the inner being of a democratic society."[88]

But that would be difficult. If Americans were commendably suspicious of abstract theorizing, they were also lamentably deficient in their appreciation of theorizing that did not seem to serve some immediate purpose—and this despite the high value they placed on education and their strong faith in the progressive character of the mind and the perfectibility of man. In the past the vast majority of mankind had been indifferent to or completely ignorant of formal knowledge. Democratic man is eager for knowledge, not from love but from ambition. The whole society is in constant motion, its members kindled by "immense ambitions" unhampered by any limits of status or origins.[89] A society in a perpetual state of hurry was not so much anti-intellectual as unreflective. "[T]he mental habits conducive to action are not always conducive to thought." The democrat favors time-saving "abridgments" of knowledge and formulas, which can be applied mechanically.[90] Democracy subordinates thought to action; and, because it is a democracy, the subordination is practically total.

The thrust of a democratized culture thus works to sharpen the age-old distinction between theoretical and practical knowledge and to jeopardize the future of theory in its more traditional form. Democracy effects a revolution in the realm of action: it "produces" action. Action is no longer the preserve of a few kings, courtiers, generals, judges, and bishops; nor is it captured in a singular event that takes place in a reserved space; nor by a mode that preens itself dramaturgically. Action becomes ubiquitous, democratized. Everyone has projects, schemes, goals; some are bigger but few are grand and all seem monotonous variations on the theme of wealth. At the same time, modernity has made knowledge, even scientific knowledge, more widely available and accessible. Bacon's aphorism, that knowledge is power, is no longer an aspiration but a cultural assumption. One result has been to transform society by knowledge, as Bacon had hoped; another has been to transform knowledge by society. "The world is not led by long and knowledgeable demonstrations; instead it is the daily résumé of the changing passions of the crowd, the passing chance and the cleverness at seizing it that decide matters."[91]

Cartesianism is the name for revolutionary modernism that is at war with the old; or, rather, it conceives a new form of war against the old, a war that relies on theory to make its war a just one. At stake is the identity of the modern. What defines it, draws boundaries around it, is the death of the Old Order. The manner of that death injects an element of the problematic, of the transient, in the triumph of the New. The death of the Old has been made possible by the unique power of modern knowledge, the knowledge of how to produce change virtually at will. When the Old is gone or reduced to insignificance, modernity will have lost its defining contrast and placed its own identity in jeopardy. It will be forced to make itself its object, revolutionizing itself, not once as in one great uprising against the Old, but continuously. When modernity will have sublimated revolution, incorporated it, then modernity as such will have consumed itself.

That theme forms a major part of what is perhaps the most crucial chapter in volume 2, "Why Great Revolutions Will Become Rare." Great revolutions will no longer occur because change will have become so continuous that revolutionary conditions will not have time to fester. The ironical sign of the age of change, of the realization of the unlimited, is that "among democratic peoples those who cultivate the sciences are always fearful of losing themselves in utopias."[92]

The fate of modernity provides a clue to an unstated, repressed reason why Tocqueville relied so heavily on the contrast between aristocracy and democracy in volume 2. Aristocracy encourages resistance to modernity's plunge into an abyss of its own creation, the meaninglessness of existence when the

Whirl of endless change is installed as King. Aristocracy encourages resistance not in the name of an all but extinct social class but as an alternative form of theory.

Alternative to what?

## XII

> *That a large democratic republic existed on American soil was a palpable, uncontestable, and implacable fact of the nineteenth century. This undeniable presence was visible proof that a democratic republic was no merely Utopian idea. Yet the proof generated a mystery. What was required for such an experiment to succeed? And why had the Americans been able to prove the impossible?*
>
> Robert A. Dahl[93]

Although it would only be toward the end of the century that pragmatism would announce its presence as a full-fledged academic philosophy, its lineaments had been identified and substantially explained by Tocqueville.[94] Unlike Cartesianism, it was not a war against the old for there was no old to war against. Pragmatism was the "native" philosophy, as natural to Americans as their traits of self-reliance and their all round practical skills. It was a philosophy whose emphasis on the specific and concrete and on trial-and-error seemed the effortless ideological complement to the expansive American condition wherein all mistakes were remediable and all of nature and society presented endless opportunities for new beginnings. The conclusion seemed inescapable. America—inexhaustible, prosperous, classless, free—was a utopia.

Unlike all previous philosophies, which merely yearned for utopia, pragmatism could assume it. Because America was a realized utopia, it had no need of theories except an antitheoretical theory. Pragmatism, with its impatience with theory and affinity for method, emerged as the antiutopian ideology of a realized utopia, its true public philosophy in which the empirical becomes utopianized rather than the utopian becoming empirically realized: "I believe that rarely will it happen in a democratic society that a man will conceive in a single act a system of ideas that is far removed from those accepted by his contemporaries; and if such an innovator were to appear, I suspect that he would have great difficulty in gaining a hearing, much less in being believed."[95]

Pragmatism was at once the successor to the natural law–natural rights ideology of the American Revolution and, at the same time, the embodiment of a new ideology that was both progressive and antirevolutionary, favorable to material change but resistant to radical reform of cultural symbols and protective of earned inequalities: "It is not that the [American] mind is lazy; it is in constant motion but it is more concerned with infinite variations upon the consequences of known principles and in discovering new consequences than in searching for new principles."[96]

Pragmatism was the expression of a democracy that worked best when its problems were discrete, manageable, and when there was a strong consensus about leaving "fundamentals" untouched. For wrongs would then seem like finite "errors," easily diagnosed, and quickly put right. There was no "wrong in general" (Marx), stubbornly resistive of ad hoc remedies.[97]

An experimental philosophy is sorely tested, however, when anomalies assume systemic proportions that contradict the system's "fundamental law." The crisis gathering in antebellum American society exposed the limits of the public philosophy of democracy. Instead of being the philosophy of democracy *simpliciter*, pragmatism was the ideological expression of cognitive dissonance in a democracy that conceived itself as the embodiment of freedom and equality while it practiced slavery and genocide openly. Slavery, secession, and genocide proved to be beyond the reach of the pragmatic politics. Once darkness fell, utopia became nightmarish and democracy resembled a clumsy experiment, faltering despite ideal circumstances.

If slavery and genocide could not be accounted for under the terms of the public philosophy by which American democracy understood itself, the theoretical terms that Tocqueville himself fashioned to represent American democracy were not much better. When it came to racism, slavery, and genocide, Tocqueville's critical juxtaposition of aristocracy to democracy, privilege to equality, and elitism to self-government seemed at odds with his own strong condemnation of those practices. Similarly, neither pragmatical philosophy nor aristocratic sensibility were able to come to grips with another and equally glaring anomaly.

As we have noted earlier, Tocqueville saw a new aristocracy emerging from the factory system and he emphasizes that phenomenon in a particularly telling contrast: "Just as the masses of the nation are turning to democracy, the particular class which is engaged in industry is becoming more aristocratic."[98]

If the "masses" are "turning" to democracy that would mean, among many things, that they were becoming citizens and members of the sovereign body of a democracy. If, as Tocqueville himself had maintained, the new aristocracy of factory owners was presiding over the production of a species of social inferiority, of "brutes," then the formative experience of the new citizens was far from being a preparation for civic life.[99]

# CHAPTER XVIII
# OLD NEW WORLD, NEW OLD WORLD

## I

*A closer examination of the subject and five years of meditation have not lessened my fears but have changed their object.*
Tocqueville[1]

Toward the end of volume 2 a strange reversal sets in as Tocqueville characterizes the Old World in terms that seem more appropriate to the New. He refers to the Old as "this new society," "only now being born" and as a world where "time has not yet settled its form"[2]—as though he wanted to put a seal on his effort to blend a New World, whose theoretical significance he had settled, with an unsettled Old World becoming new, the one receding, the other struggling into focus. As a result of the temporal switch, in which the New was older and the Old was newer, the conclusion to the volume seems less confident. Rather than claiming to have grasped the full outline of the city, Tocqueville projects a panorama of "great dangers" and "mighty evils."[3]

The emergent world appears full of contradictions because its main tendencies, toward equality, democracy and even centralization, are continually changing appearances and implications. Thus one version of equality has rendered most men equally powerful (the American theme of volume 1) yet another version has left them equally powerless (the French theme of volume 2).

Contradiction is not a tension between abstract ideas; it divides behavior. The democrat is forever carping at state officials but he "loves" the power of the state.[4] The contradictions identified by Tocqueville are not like those of Hegel, sublated and synthesized. They form instead an unresolved problematic and contribute to the paradoxical character of Tocqueville's effort to complete a theory for a political world no longer capable of settling into a form because revolutionary impulses have become normalized as "habits and ideas." Yet, if revolutionary impulses form a "permanent" condition, the citizenry may eventually find instability intolerable and react against it. They will yearn for tranquillity but, infected by revolution, they may exhibit "a very disordered love for order" and yield rights to the state in return for social peace.[5]

A world of crosscurrents, powerful tendencies and countertendencies might, with effort, be rendered intelligible, although at the price of making its theory seem unsystematic and its author irresolute. To make a world that appears both humanly unintelligible yet systematic, under control, was the privilege of God, the symbol of theory's limits. Yet Tocqueville would make a final gesture at theoretical closure. He will greatly expand the theory of centralization and sever it from America and, by implication, from any positive lessons drawn from decentralization. In keeping with his notion of democracy as a changing form, he will treat it as a "social condition" rather than a mode of action. If there is closure at the end, it will be in the claim that a certain logic immanent in both democracy and despotism attracts one to the other and sets the stage for the ultimate political question of what should be done to prevent democracy and despotism from combining.

Tocqueville introduces his attempt at theoretical closure by telling his readers that if they were to lift their eyes from "the details of human affairs" and try "to grasp in its totality the huge tableau, they would be astonished" at the spectacle. The "huge tableau" is centered upon the convergence of two revolutions that seemingly contradict each other. "[O]ne continually weakens power, the other constantly reinforces it." One is the revolution that has overthrown monarchies and established the freedom of the individual. In the process, however, it has encouraged, and even legitimized, a certain excess in governability among the citizenry, an eagerness to be ruled and, in its extreme form, to be submissive. The second revolution has produced overgovernment, centralization on a massive universal scale. "Wars, revolutions, and conquests have promoted its development; all men have worked to increase it."[6] The two revolutions are "intimately linked together; they have a common origin and after following a different course, they finally lead men to the same place."[7] The "same place" is represented by the state.

The new model of democracy offers the state a fresh basis in a domesticated democracy that yields its former tendencies toward lawlessness. In exchange, the state adopts a sensibility that makes it more attentive to the needs and aspirations of the general populace, without surrendering its prerogatives.

Democracy absorbed into the state system becomes one of the elements that distinguishes the modern state without necessarily democratizing it. In order to assume a place in the modern state, democracy must accommodate by accepting a more perfunctory, less participatory conception of the political. The democratic state is made possible by the emergence of a democratic "consciousness," which, without realizing it, promotes its own subjugation. In contrast to the "aristocratic imagination," which finds the idea of uniformity "strange" and instinctively resists it, the democrat is attracted to the idea of "a uniform rule equally imposed on all members of the "body social" and welcomes "the notion of a single central power."[8] The crucial political defect of a culture of uniformity is at the same time its necessary condition: it accustoms men "to make their will totally and continually abstract."[9] Like equality, abstraction signifies the erasure of differences, the indifference to context. The abstractness of similars exerts a social force, radiating outward, permeating all relationships, even thought itself: "In politics, as in philosophy and religion, the mind of democratic peoples is very receptive to simple and general ideas. . . . Complicated systems put them off."[10]

Democracy works to reinforce the long revolution in governance that had seen personal rule give way to impersonal administration. The simplifying, suppressing of differences—decontextualizing that enabled administration to operate more efficiently—was symbiotic with the spread of egalitarianism. Centralization, Tocqueville insisted, did not originate with the French Revolution; the revolution merely "perfected . . . the taste for centralization and the mania for regulation," which had appeared centuries earlier.[11] The prerevolutionary monarchy had fairly consistently attempted to strengthen its bureaucracy, extend the powers of its agents throughout the nation, render regulatory rules uniform, and reduce the authority not only of the nobility but of local bodies and officials. The process of what might be called "the systematization of the state" was resumed during and after the revolution and achieved its apogee during Napoleon's regime: legal codification, improvement in the quality of administrators, support for technical education, and concentration of political power in his own hands. While centralization and the technical sciences of policy and administration were shaping the modes of governance, equality was becoming part of the political equation, first by "the absolute power" of kings and then by "violent revolution."[12]

"In our time," Tocqueville noted, "all of the governments of Europe have prodigiously perfected the science of administration. They do much more and they do everything more orderly, speedily, and with less expense."[13] The changing nature of governance was evident in other ways that Tocqueville did not discuss. The systematic cultivation of administration, not simply as a means of governance but as its major element,[14] acquired impressive intellectual and theoretical support: theories of "benevolent despotism," neomercantilism (Colbert in France, Hamilton in the United States, and Fichte in Germany), the emergence of cameralism and the idea of professional training for state service. Tocqueville's near contemporaries—Saint-Simon, Comte, and Hegel—were developing a political discourse that identified administrative centralization as the unique attribute of the state. It represented power held to a new standard of accountability, not to legislatures or electorates but to reason or, more precisely, to efficient reason.

## II

> *The instinct for centralization has been the single fixed point amid the remarkable flux in the lives and thinking [of modern ruling groups].*
>
> Tocqueville[15]

> *I maintain that there is no country in Europe where public administration has not only become more centralized, but more inquisitive and more detailed; everywhere it penetrates more than formerly into private matters; it regulates more actions and smaller ones by rules, and increasingly it establishes itself beside and above the individual in order to help, advise, and constrain him.*
>
> Tocqueville[16]

Although the centralized state is, for Tocqueville, the most visible representation of the convergent revolutions of democracy and administration, it is not the chief agent but the beneficiary. Centralization gains new momentum and support because of a profound cultural revolution that has altered human values, sensibilities, needs, and desires. This understanding lies behind such typical Tocquevillisms as: "all democratic peoples are drawn toward centralization of powers."[17] A modern culture represents an unorchestrated effect in which political ideas concerning democracy, equality, individualism, and popular sovereignty as well as certain prejudices against privilege, nondemocratic powers, and exceptionality become intermingled to create a "community of feeling . . . a secret and permanent bond of sympathy" between the individual and the state.[18]

State power is thus a reflection of an absolutism immanent in society, in a distinctive and pervasive culture that nourishes certain reflexes or responses so that one can speak of a society in the grip of a mentalité. Tocqueville refers to it as "the natural bent of the minds and hearts."[19]

Equality is the unifying element that joins the two revolutions into a cultural whole. Tocqueville is careful to distinguish between, on the one hand, an equality that has been brought about by "violent revolution" involving class warfare and, on the other, an equality that, as in America, was preceded by a long experience of political liberty.[20] Revolutionary equality was clearly a representation of French experience, but it also embodies a criticism of the depoliticization accompanying the particular political modernity prepared by the French Revolution. Revolutionary equality causes a retrogression in the level of political maturity and, as we shall see shortly, in political imagination. It is brought about when equality is achieved by contestation with aristocracy, a contestation that pits a dynamic of similarity against the defense of difference, *les semblables* versus *les dissemblables*.[21] The triumph of similarity over dissimilarity makes possible a uniquely modern power, "the unity, ubiquity, and omnipotence of the social power." It is represented not in a Rousseauean "general will" but by a state that is uniquely the product of a democratic culture.[22]

## III

*Le pouvoir social* is Tocqueville's version of modern power; or, more precisely, social power complements the modern power ushered in by the scientific and technological revolutions and heralded by Bacon, Hobbes, and Descartes. Social power, Tocqueville's great discovery, is power that culture has collectivized and, in the process, depoliticized. Where nothing else in the social landscape stands out in relief there looms "the huge and imposing image of the people itself."[23] "[T]he social power is always stronger and individuals weaker when a democratic people has arrived at equality by a long and painful social struggle than in a democratic society where the citizens have always been equal."[24] Each is simultaneously a part of a theoretically omnipotent sovereignty and each remains a fragmented, powerless being. Social power is uniquely the power of collectivity but, paradoxically, it is not power available to the demos. It supports popular government rather than self-government, and this America "completely proves." The Americans enjoy self-government because they were able to borrow from "the English aristocracy the idea of individual rights and the taste for local liberties" without in the process having "to struggle against aristocracy."[25] In contrast, revolutionary equality does not foster the habits of political liberty; its concerns are not to develop the political education of citizens but to annihilate social distinctions. When citizens become more alike than dissimilar, their natural inclination (*les instincts*) is to look toward the center and place their trust in the "single, all-powerful government" that now bears their name.

The enlargement of state powers is accompanied by the systematic cultivation of administrative knowledge and skills. The long-term result will be "an enormous difference between the intellectual capacity" of the rulers and that of each subject.[26] Thus the democratic state is a contradiction in terms that conceals the decline in political sophistication from an age that understood what was needed to combat centralized power: "But it requires a great deal of intelligence, knowledge, and skill to organize and maintain in these conditions secondary powers and to create among independent but individually weak citizens free associations able to fight against tyranny without destroying order."[27]

The practical remedies that Tocqueville proposed—encouraging civil associations, a free press, reviving local government, strengthening the judiciary so as to withstand the encroachments of administrative tribunals, and defending private rights—have the quality of a rearguard action.[28] Unlike the tendencies they were supposed to combat, they seem disconnected both from the powerful forces shaping modernity and from the power historically grounded in locality (communal liberty). They stand out as anomalous, and Tocqueville has to console himself with the possibility that buried deep in the idea of equality itself is a latent political impulse: "in the depths of the mind and heart of each man equality lodges some vague notion and some instinctive inclination toward political freedom, thus preparing the remedy for the malady which it has created. That is what I cling to."[29]

## IV

Tocqueville's conception of social power includes an important precondition. It depends on equality taking possession of a people "who have never known or have not known for a long time what freedom is."[30] Social power takes advantage of the limited resources available to modern memory and the mentalité produced and fostered by equality. The new collective mentalité is revealed in the limits of what it is capable of imagining. The limits of imagination are set not only by what is now conceivable but by what has been forgotten. In the immediate aftermath of a democratic revolution, the collective imagination expands as inherited constraints are erased or relaxed. Men find it "natural" to imagine a condition in which all men have equal political rights and all the traditional signs of privilege have vanished. Over time what was once a liberating dynamic settles into a mentalité. A mentalité is a disposition that emerges when a dramatic challenge turns into a banalized reality. For example, the once revolutionary conception of natural rights have become so naturalized as to be familiar, taken for granted. And it is equally normal for certain institutions or relationships to disappear from human memories: "As for particular privileges granted to towns, families, or individuals, the idea itself has been lost. It never enters their heads that one cannot apply uniformly the same law to all parts of the same State and to all men who live there."[31]

The "social imaginary"—to use a late-twentieth-century formulation—is exclusionist even as it proclaims its own universality. It is also self-subverting. When an idea such as equality dominates an age, the image of equality that men carry stands for a certain state of affairs they can imagine—for example, one where all men are equal in their political rights. But once the original demand for a more inclusive equality becomes commonplace, a different sort of political imagination silently emerges—not because the right has been fully realized but because it has become inert. The idea of "inherent rights" ceases to "fire" or "strike" the imagination. It recedes from the political imaginary and is consigned eventually to the politically archaic. There it slumbers alongside the idea of intermediary powers.[32] It is not that the members of society "forget" or lose their memories but that certain states of affairs have been dimmed out. "When equality develops among a people who have never known liberty or long forgotten it," then old habits and new habits and doctrines are "attracted" to each other and their intermingling produces, in this case, a fatal result: "all powers seem, of their own accord, to rush toward the center."[33]

Once the idea of equal rights has been broadly realized within the received understanding, the effect of equality is diverted elsewhere, creating a new imaginary, and new limitations on the political imagination. As equal rights lose their saliency, men come to accept occasional, even serious, encroachments. Equality becomes a cultural force that destroys not only privilege but forgets the point/ceases to respect differences of education, manners, tastes, and beliefs. "In the midst of general uniformity the slightest dissimilarity seems shocking, and to the degree that uniformity is more complete, the more insupportable it seems."[34] Equality encourages a different, even contradictory, imaginary with an aesthetic sensibility that favors uniformity, order, tranquillity. The culture of equality thus creates a symbiotic relationship, "a secret and permanent sympathy," with state power that thrives on legislating and administering citizens who are "lost in a crowd."[35]

## V

The final pages of *Democracy* are headed "General View of the Subject." Their tentative tone forms a revealing contrast to the confident tone of Tocqueville's traveler ascending the hill in the "Conclusion" to volume 1. There he had described himself as "approaching the end" of his discussion of the future destiny of the United States, as though he were contemplating a finished labor, both for the theorizing subject and for the theorized object. "Now," he had written, "I want to join all [of the previous parts of the work] into a single perspective [*un seul point de vue*]." What he is about to write will be less detailed than the particular discussions of the volume but it will be "surer," and although "each object" will be "less distinct," the "general facts will be grasped with greater certitude."[36]

In volume 2, however, he refers not to the "end" of his work but "to leaving forever the vocation that I have come to follow." And while he "would have preferred . . . to have been able to grasp in one last glance" the particulars of "the new world" and "the general influence of equality on the destiny of mankind," the difficulty of the undertaking stops him: "in the presence of so vast a subject my vision becomes clouded and my judgment reels." Instead of a completed labor and a realized object he finds that he is faced with the task of "portraying" and "judging" a new society that has "only just come into existence," one that continues to be shaped by a revolution that is "far from over" and that has not yet fully extricated itself from the debris of a decaying world. He seems confident only that the revolution in "the social condition, laws, ideas, and feelings of men" is incomparably greater than anything that has previously taken place in the world's history.[37]

What is incomplete about the world is the revolution for equality. How far would it go? Tocqueville's valedictory, as we have noted, is resigned but edged with bitterness as he surveys a future that promises to bring the triumph of banality: "virtually all extremes will be softened and blunted." His judgment exudes a godlike quality, and self-consciously "I sweep my glance over this countless multitude of similar beings among whom nothing is elevated or too abased."[38]

Tocqueville dares not only to set his judgment against God's but to voice his resentments at what God alone could have wrought: the uniformity of society, the mediocrity of men's ambitions, the relaxing of distinctions of "race, class, and country" in favor of "the great bond of humanity," the elevation of "social utility" from a necessity to the dominant norm, and the inversion of the ideal of action from one in which the human spirit was advanced by "the powerful impulses furnished by the few" to one where the impetus comes from the combined but tiny efforts of a large mass of nameless individuals.[39]

## VI

The lines are drawn. What strikes Tocqueville as "decay" and what he finds "painful," God sees as just and finds pleasing. God wants the lot of the Many to be improved and He prefers a benign condition in which prosperity, enlightenment, and morality are diffused to a condition of contrasting extremes.

And what of the world had equality overthrown? Tocqueville says that although he has struggled "to enter into God's point of view, and to consider and judge human affairs" as God would, even to accepting God's judgment that equality, while less exalted, is more "just," yet he will not forsake the *ancien régime*, even as he reiterates his belief that aristocracy cannot be revived and even as he urges members of his social class to abandon their dreams of a restoration of the old order. But these disclaimers are made only after first declaring—in a measured choice of words—that "no one on earth could assert in an absolute and general way that the new state of society is superior to the old."[40]

As he builds his peroration to the final paragraphs, however, Tocqueville inserts a hopeful note. Although he "sees . . . great perils" and "great evils," he is "increasingly confirmed" in his belief that for "democratic nations to be virtuous [*honnêtes*] and prosperous" they need only "will it." Providence has not created mankind to be entirely enslaved nor fully free: "It has, to be sure, traced around each man a preordained circle from which he cannot escape; but within those vast limits man is powerful and free, and the same for peoples."[41]

Equality appears as the outer limits of the social circle that contains mankind yet it is still within human powers to shape equality toward "servitude or liberty, enlightenment or barbarism, prosperity or misery."[42]

The ambivalence that pervades the closing pages of *Democracy* appears all the more striking because it is combined with a style of theorizing that can only be described as self-consciously prophetic. Tocqueville lays down one sweeping judgment after another regarding the egalitarian fate of modern societies, as though he is determined to prove that the modern theorist can grasp only those general facts and, at the same time, to assert that generality defines the modern world. Modernity is simultaneously the superfluity of the general and the dearth of the particular. Tocqueville's ambivalence thus becomes the signifier for the kind of freedom that is possible to modern man as he becomes encircled by equality. Equality's telos is toward centralization and hence the political has to be reconceived, not primarily as the citizenly practice of self-government but as an unrelenting struggle against conformity.

# CHAPTER XIX
# TOCQUEVILLEAN DEMOCRACY

## I

> *We live in an epoch that has seen the most rapid changes at work in the human mind; yet it could happen that soon the principal opinions of mankind will be more stable than they have been in the previous centuries of our history. That time has not yet come but it may be approaching.*
>
> Tocqueville[1]

The final section (part 4) of *Democracy in America* trails an air of willed finality as though its author, after having balanced his ambivalencies for several hundreds of pages, can no longer postpone a final judgment about his subject. In part 3, however, immediately prior to the act of closure Tocqueville had summarized his ambivalencies in a series of chapters that could be entitled an "inconclusion."

Typically when Tocqueville sensed that theory was taking him in a direction that might expose the tensions among his own beliefs, he sought refuge in ambivalence. The supreme expression was the metaphor of himself mediating between two worlds: one dying, the other emerging; one an affirmation of his loyalties, the other of his submission to necessity. The metaphor of location was also a means of posing or arranging the self while he repositioned his theory. Now, as his work neared completion, the mediator found that while the ambivalencies had become clearer, they had also deepened. Tocqueville's choice of location preserved without resolving the personal conflict of being at once antirevolutionary and protheory.

The specific textual location of these concerns is in chapters 21–26 of part 3. Their thematic structure is political rather than social; they deal with some of the most strikingly modern forms of power and their impending or actual transformations. The most famous discussion is chapter 21 on "Why Great Revolutions Will Become Rare." The five chapters that follow it explore the likely influence of democracy on the character of armies and warfare. Thus we have two of the great and distinctively modern forms of power: the democratic mass revolution and the democratic mass army. In chapter 21 Tocqueville proceeds to join the fate of great political and social revolutions with the fate of great theoretical revolutions, predicting that great theories would become as rare as great revolutions, that both would become casualties of the spread of egalitarianism.

There was an undeclared text hidden beneath his claim that the same banalizing social forces that were eliminating the possibility of great revolutions also discouraged the type of great theoretical innovation that could alter a whole intellectual climate. As Tocqueville well knew, in the past some great theoretical innovations had been associated with revolutionary destructiveness. One might wish for Pascal but be presented with Rousseau. Worse, one might be tempted by Rousseau because of deep admiration for grand theoretical gestures. Or, worse still, one might lament a world from which revolution has disappeared because that, too, would mean that another and even more heroic modality of human action had been lost. Modern citizens may become immune to "those great and powerful public emotions which may trouble the members of society but also develop and renew them."[2]

Tocqueville's ambivalencies, which might have produced mere indecisiveness, found instead a creative outlet. They produced an "inconclusion," remarkable not as a recording of its author's indecisiveness but for its perceptiveness. Tocqueville was attempting to portray the passage of modernity, the effects registered when societies abruptly, even violently, renounce their past, leaving behind the shards of an antiquity of their own making—a past civilization whose reconstruction then proves to be as contested in imagination as its existence had been in actuality. The reconstruction of the past would simultaneously be a hunt for its other in the present. Among the passing, the end of heroics; among the quarry of the present, the emergence of its caricature, individualism. Unlike the premodern hero, who stands for a special particularity, uniqueness, modern individualism is portrayed by Tocqueville as the creature of certain generalizable postulates, notably of equality of rights and dignity. The individual is presented as the collective writ small, a reproducible object rather than a creative subject. All along its line of advance, modernity encounters the particular and leaves behind a massive generalization: the extraordinary of revolution turns into the banality of change; the heroics of battle turn first into lengthy wars, then into total wars in which whole populations are mobilized; actors diminished; public opinion is elevated; theory is pragmatic.

Tocqueville's prediction about the end of revolution, like late-twentieth-century predictions about the end of ideology and of history, might be expected to receive a rapturous welcome from conservatives. His contemporaries had been taught by thinkers such as de Maistre and de Bonald that the philosophes and their forerunners bore the major responsibility for the catastrophe of 1789. But Tocqueville saw the emerging stability of public opinion as a precensor stifling theoretical activity before it was even conceived. He ends the chapter equivocally, even nostalgically:

> Some believe that the new societies are going to change their appearance daily but my fear is that they will end by being too unalterably fixed in the same institutions, prejudices, *moeurs*; that mankind will halt and remain within self-imposed limits; that the mind will yield and fold endlessly in on itself without producing any new idea; that mankind will exhaust itself in trivial, lonely, and sterile activities, and that for all of its perpetual movement, humanity will cease to advance.[3]

During the seventeenth and eighteenth centuries philosophers and intellectuals had seriously believed that the theoretical writings of Bacon, Descartes, Hobbes, Spinoza, Locke, Rousseau, and Kant had not only revolutionized humankind's opinions of nature, of human nature, and of the human understanding, but had contributed mightily to the revolutionary climate of 1688, 1776, and 1789 and its aftermath.

Tocqueville was well aware that "grand theory" had played an important role in discrediting the *ancien régime* and legitimizing revolution. So he leaves such theories unlamented and instead refers vaguely to "innovators" and to the rare instance of "a man who suddenly conceives a system of ideas far removed from those entertained by his contemporaries."[4] That type becomes vestigial in the new circumstances, which encourage and reward methodical and practical theorizing. As theory moves closer to everyday needs and concerns, the distinction between theory and ideology lessens. Ideology is theory enlisted in the service of interests. Theory becomes a nonvocation amid the liberation of energies encouraged by democracy and the new opportunities created by equality. "One meets with few ideas in a democratic nation. Life goes on amid movement and noise. Men are so absorbed in action they have little time to think. . . . They are perpetually acting and each action absorbs their soul; the fire that goes into their work prevents them from being fired by ideas."[5]

A reader has to be attentive in order to discover Tocqueville's recipe for the ideal conditions for "great intellectual revolutions." It is, like a concealed weapon, hidden in a footnote. Great revolutions require a condition somewhere between "complete equality for all citizens and the absolute separation of classes." A "caste regime" would cause the "imagination to slumber" because the necessary stimulus of "movement" would be lacking. A regime of equality brings abundant movement in the form of continuous agitation, but it is accompanied by social isolation and a sense of individual weakness. The ideal condition, "glorious and troubled," requires just enough social mobility to stir the mind and, more important, enough inequality to make it possible for "great power [to be exerted] over minds and other men and thus the few are able to modify the beliefs of all" and "new ideas suddenly change the face of the world."[6]

The democratization of action and opportunity, the extension of political rights, and the diffusion of property all work to bring a new culture into being and a new being into culture: people work differently, listen, hear, remember, and think differently. Everyone now has a stake in preserving the status quo. No one is tempted to heroics because the stakes are Lilliputian: there is little that is worth snatching and all fear for the loss of their property.[7] No longer bewitched by the imagery of ivory-tower detachment, thought acquires a broader reach and quickly becomes the arbiter and source of belief. Ideology becomes to popular belief what applied theory had become for industry, commerce, and technology: a formulary. The further result is a new public, one that has "opinions," which form characteristics, quickly harden, and acquire weight. The paradox of a free society takes shape: individuals who are at liberty to form and express their own beliefs hold tenaciously to the same convictions while around them intellectual creations change as rapidly as fashions. "Once an opinion has taken root in American soil there is no earthly power that can eradicate it."[8] Intellectual changes may succeed each other in dizzy fashion but because the notion of authority has virtually disappeared, none has any greater claim than another. The politically innovative theorist has little chance of a hearing and as a result "sudden intellectual revolutions" will be "rare."[9] Society may reach a point where "every new theory is viewed as a threat, every innovation as a vexation, every social improvement as the first step toward revolution."[10]

In this condition a dissociation takes place between ordinary human actions and common beliefs. A postrevolutionary culture presents a peculiar combination of "a society that is constantly on the move" but loath to alter its "fundamental" moral or religious beliefs, constitutional laws, and political institutions.[11] "There are two astonishing things about the United States: the great instability of most human conduct and the remarkable fixity of certain principles."[12]

The tableau that Tocqueville was sketching was not intended to represent a torporous society of sleepwalkers. The twin pulls of dynamism and caution are tugging constantly at the individual, leaving him in a state of tension from which he seeks relief by further activity. "While equality encourages men to change, it also entices them toward interests and tastes that require stability for their satisfaction; it pushes them on and holds them back at the same time; it spurs them on and keeps their feet on the ground; it inflames their desires and limits their powers."[13]

In proposing a modernity that becomes distanced from theory and revolution, the two principal wellsprings of its own being, Tocqueville argued that the uniqueness of the modern revolution was that it had largely put an end to the kinds of grievance that had inspired recent upheavals. The implications of that claim only become clear when we realize that Tocqueville did not restrict the meaning of "great revolutions" to the upheaval begun in 1789 in the name of the universal political rights of man. It included as well the irresistible movement toward equality of social condition, the spread of uniform cultural values, the broad diffusion of property ownership, and the ready availability of opportunities for increasing individual wealth. Although Tocqueville emphasized that the democratization of property was the key to the marginalization of revolutionary politics, the actual means of that development were cultural. Commerce and industry, which Tocqueville took to be the principal activities of modern society, encourage habits of "moderation, compromise, and even temper. . . . I know of nothing more opposed to revolutionary morality than commercial morality. Commerce is the natural enemy of all violent passions."[14]

That Tocqueville may have misread the bourgeois preoccupation with social order as denoting a general conservatism and overlooked the radical changes which that class introduced in tastes, modes of consumption, attitudes toward nature, notions of education, and the reform of governmental functions and of the selection of its personnel is probably true. It is, however, less significant than his preoccupation with culture and civil society. His change of emphasis—from participatory practices as the center of a flourishing politics to associations as defensive in an apolitical setting—can be read as a corollary to his realization that culture offers a means of blocking the growth of democratic politics and, at the same time, of shaping the opinions, attitudes, and values of the various institutions and associations of civil society. Religion, schools, family, newspapers, clubs, the arts, and theater are all cultural artifacts, but they, in turn, are typically shaped by the Few: by priests, teachers, parents, writers, editors, organizers, artists, and performers. Culture, in other words, is "natural" elitism. Along with commerce, industry, and science, these elites are the modern successors of aristocracy—although Nietzsche preferred to lump them all as "priests." Unlike the early modern aristocrats, late modern elites depend on mass constituencies for their survival and so they display an attentiveness lacking in aristocracies, especially in caste-oriented ones. Their function becomes the redirection of the demos, away from politics toward personal satisfactions. All that is needed to produce a politically neutralized demos is a combination of structured work haunted (but not demoralized) by unemployment; public education that provides the utensils to consume popular culture; and representative government that regulates mass politics according to a timetable of periodic elections leaving the rest to commentary by the clerks.

## II

> *In democratic societies it is very difficult to get men to listen when one is not talking about themselves. They do not hear what is being said to them because they are always deeply preoccupied with what they are doing.*
>
> Tocqueville[15]

That Tocqueville would appeal to later politicians and writers of varying ideological constituencies suggests that *Democracy* was a consensus-promoting rather than a divisive book. That conclusion can be fairly drawn from the work and from its later reputation. But I have tried to suggest that, especially in volume 2, Tocqueville's emphasis drew him away from the civic democracy symbolized by New England and toward a fixation with the culture of equality and suggestions for its control. In that light, Tocqueville's contribution to consensus building assumes an additional quality, which helps to explain its appeal. Reading Tocqueville can crystallize a wide range of objections to democracy and encourage an attitude of vigilance about its alleged dangers that serves to unite liberals, conservatives, and social scientists.

Because Tocqueville has become something of a canonical figure, especially in the United States and more recently in France, interpretations tend to shy away from the possibility that there might be a bizarre character to some of his formulations. His curious views about women, corporations, or theology are usually downplayed. Other pronouncements of his are treated as oracles rather than as an imaginary more reflective perhaps of his own genealogy than of actual political tendencies in the United States.

One such Tocquevillean imaginary claimed an elective affinity between democracy and centralization. That alleged conjunction did not rest on any evidence but depended instead on constructing two ideal types and then finding, *mirabile dictu!*, that they existed in a predestined state of symbiosis. What was actually being configured by Tocqueville was a conjunction between the two historical antagonists of aristocracy: the aristocracy-crushing revolution by which democracy gained entrance into modern Europe and the towering presence of a centralized state, which the prerevolutionary monarchy had created at the expense of aristocracy. Logically and ideologically, neither democracy nor centralization entails the other: the centralized state is typically based on a hierarchy of command and so its practice is diametrically opposed to democracy. The common element that Tocqueville claimed to have found was uniformity: the state was alleged to have a natural appetite for treating its citizens according to the same rule, thereby enabling it to govern more efficiently than if it were obliged to frame regulations that would correspond to actual differences of circumstance, status, or class. Yet by Tocqueville's own account democratic societies displayed a veritable mania for change: in opinions, status, class, occupation, and residence. Thus the social thrust of democracy actually worked at cross-purposes to the uniformist state. Instead of a natural union, we have Tocqueville forcing an unlikely connivance between a uniformitarian state and a volatile society.

Accordingly, Tocqueville's construction is seductive because of its combination of mythical and theoretical elements that melds the imaginative power of the one with the logic of the other. The mythmaker projects his fears upon the object, an equalizing society, so that its elemental desires justify his fears; the theory builder constructs a logically coherent model of the object and then breathes into his creation the force of reality, unaware that he, the incomparable generalizer, has transformed the object into a mirror image of his own thought processes, attributing to it a mentality that closely resembles his own:

> In politics, moreover, as in philosophy and religion, democratic peoples relish simple and general ideas. Complicated systems repel them, and they take pleasure in imagining a great nation in which all of the citizens resemble a single model and are directed by a single power.
>
> After the idea of a single central power the idea of uniform legislation appears most spontaneously to the minds of men in the centuries of equality.[16]

For the state to pursue the course Tocqueville plotted for it, for it to grasp the potential of democracy as an accomplice of its own ambitions, for it to be able to maintain its course unswervingly amid the crosscurrents of parliamentary and party politics demanded a resourcefulness, relentlessness, consistency, and clear-eyed sense of purpose in state actors that Tocqueville never accounts for and Machiavelli had only fantasized. Granted that Tocqueville had unforgettably illumined the anonymity of state power, yet the interest-oriented politics, whose pervasiveness he railed against even before his election to the Chamber of Deputies, tended in practice to compromise and corrupt rather than elevate the state and to produce laws reflective of a mosaic of purposes and cross-purposes rather than a simplifying and uniform rule.

In one of his notes written while drafting the introduction to *Democracy*, Tocqueville complained of the difficulty in "distinguishing what is democratic from what is revolutionary . . . because examples are lacking. There is no European nation in which democracy has been established, and America is an exceptional situation."[17] What is at stake is not Tocqueville's interpretation of the United States but the implications of severing democracy from revolution. To the twentieth-century observer, that severance seems not only right but urgent. Marxism and its variants of Leninism, Stalinism, Maoism, and countless other versions in Southeast Asia, Africa, and Central America have proved that any politics with a "mass base" is irreconcilable with constitutional government: either it is easily mobilized for demagogic purposes, such as the suppression of individual rights, or it is likely to produce an ungovernable populace unable to restrain its desires when, for example, fiscal austerity is called for.

But it may be that that claim, despite its plausibility, does not quite dispose of the stakes in the historical association between democracy and revolution or the theoretical and ideological connections between theories of revolution and concepts such as "the consent of the governed," "majority rule," and "the sovereignty of the people."

Democracy's historical association with revolution—in the English civil wars of the 1640s, and in the American and French revolutions of the last quarter of the eighteenth century—while not the dominant force of those vast complex movements was an element or, better, an irritant that exposed the age-old contradiction at the center of virtually all of the theory and practice of Western governments. During much of Western history, beginning with the Hebrews and Greeks, theory, public rhetoric and civic rituals all proclaimed that the main justifying principle of all political forms was that those who ruled were obligated to use their power and authority for the good of all, for the humble and poor as well as the rich and powerful. Actual experience proved otherwise. Every embodiment of the political, whether monarchical, aristocratic, or republican, favored the Few at the expense of the Many.

Ever since antiquity the force (*kratos*) brought to bear by the demos has been distinction-destroying, boundary-transgressing. Ever since antiquity historians, philosophers, politicians, and literary men and women have refined an entire vocabulary to describe the lawless character of the demotic power: turbulent, rebellious, leveling, Shakespeare's "the blunt monster with uncounted heads, / The still-discordant wavering multitude,"[18] a force of nature threatening to return civilized society to a state of nature.

Democracy first emerges not as a system of government but as a movement of protest against the material consequences of exclusionary politics. It gathers identity as ordinary beings come to recognize that they must learn how to take and exercise power. Revolution, precisely because it shatters or rejects many of the established forms of politics while relying upon the physical forces represented by the Many, first forged a link between a self-activating, self-conscious demos and the actual exercise of political power, between a demos acting by itself and for itself. Revolution is the awesome route by which the demos forces entry into the public world and first experiences the political. Democracy is thus inseparable from revolution, which is why Tocqueville had difficulty locating a nonrevolutionary democracy—and so, in volume 1 he created an America severed from its revolutionary roots and in volume 2 he relocated his nonrevolutionary America on an abstract apolitical plane where, except for the anomaly of civil associations, it all but disappeared into equality. Largely dissociated from the participatory, which was democracy's version of the political, equality could then be represented as the "ideal" antipolitical, as the total privatization of life and accessory to the complete realization of the antipolitical in the omnicompetent state.

In the end volume 2 of *Democracy* appears as the perfect parody of democracy and Tocqueville as unmindful of the significance of his own discovery: that American politics, with its mix of participatory, democratic, and religious elements was importantly premodern, while its socioeconomic culture was furiously modernizing.

# CHAPTER XX THE PENITENTIARY TEMPTATION

## I

*We want to penetrate the mysteries of the American discipline and see if the secret springs of the system can be discovered.*
Tocqueville and Beaumont[1]

The image of Tocqueville as the discoverer of modern democracy *and* the representative of a liberal-conservative consensus blurs when we take into account that two books emerged from the American journey: one about American democracy—and France—the other about American prisons. When Tocqueville and Beaumont had applied for permission to travel to the United States, the reason offered was to study American prisons. Later commentators have frequently described their request as a "pretext" or an "official" reason, as though the study of prisons was not in keeping with Tocqueville's historic status as one of the great theorists of modern democracy. The prison project may seem less anomalous if we recall that prior to his voyage Tocqueville's career, like Beaumont's, was that of a public prosecutor. An inquiry into prisons coauthored by two young prosecutors places their project in an "official" and intrinsically "state-oriented" context. Its audience was professional and bureaucratic; its theme, the authority of the state to imprison and punish, was prior to democracy historically and perhaps logically as well.

In contrast to *Democracy in America*, with its broad theoretical perspective grounded in a tradition of humanistic politics, *The Penitentiary System in the United States and Its Application to France* was cast in a newer technical genre, with research as its starting point and policy recommendations as its goal. When these newer theoretical tendencies were brought to bear upon the topic of prison reform, one result was a radical transformation of the idea of culture from being an expression of traditionalism to becoming an object of fabrication in the service of administrative control.

*The Penitentiary System* was the fulfillment of the original project that Tocqueville and Beaumont had outlined in their official request.[2] It was published in 1833, one year after their return and two years before the appearance of *Democracy*. Although its reception was not comparable, *The Penitentiary*

*System* went through two subsequent editions, appeared in translation in America as early as 1833 and shortly thereafter in the major European languages. It was awarded a prize by the French Academy of Moral and Political Sciences.[3]

One reason for its later neglect has been the common assumption among scholars that the volume, although formally coauthored, was mainly the work of Beaumont.[4] However, recent scholarship has restored Tocqueville as a genuine collaborator. Beaumont prepared the text for publication, but Tocqueville contributed to the research for the volume and to its final content. Moreover, Tocqueville continued to be actively involved in prison reform during the 1840s; his speeches as well as his writings on the subject were, on the whole, consistent with the views set out in *The Penitentiary System.*[5]

Another and perhaps more compelling reason for its neglect is that, prima facie, it seems unrelated to Tocqueville's political thought. The assumption that penology is an administrative subject rather than a political problem is, however, less certain now than it may have been before the appearance of Michel Foucault's *Discipline and Punish.* Although Foucault made only passing reference to Tocqueville and Beaumont, any subsequent reading of *The Penitentiary System* is inevitably post-Foucauldian.[6] Foucault taught his readers to be attentive to the ways by which the human body became an object of techniques of incarceration. Carcerary practices served to discipline the person while fostering a conception of body that promoted the ends of social control and political repression.

In what follows, the debts to Foucault will be apparent but the concerns somewhat different. I want to inquire into the political status of the penitentiary itself and the theoretical status of *The Penitentiary System*, especially when compared with *Democracy.* If chronology were strictly observed, *The Penitentiary System* would be discussed first. Reversing their temporal order allows a major theme of *Democracy*, despotism, to appear more ambiguous, not as an unqualified object of liberal abhorrence but as the projection of certain conflicting elements within modern political thinking that were turning liberalism against itself, alienating it from its revolutionary origins and democratic associations while moving it insensibly toward retrieving the *étatiste* ideology developed by prerevolutionary reformers of the French monarchy.[7] *The Penitentiary System* flirts with a new and antidemocratic theory of despotism that serves, paradoxically, as the precursor of the conception of democratic despotism which *Democracy* will recoil against but not before exposing a distinctively modern or liberal temptation.

## II

The temptation was related to the frustration arising from, on the one hand, the enlarged conceptions of power characteristic of the modern imagination and assumed by it to be available in reality and, on the other hand, the compromises and stalemates resulting from the conflicting political influences emanating from the wide range of organized interests spawned by the modern economy. In imagination modern notions of experimentation were joined to modern forms of power—technological, military, and administrative—to support a claim that conditions (social and economic) could be effectively controlled so that "pure" solutions to carefully delineated problems were possible. Modern politics, however, had settled on a highly porous process that undermined the possibility of objective solutions.

Enter the idea of prison where, in theory, conditions were subject to "design"—itself a theoretical idea—and its objects to total control, both spatially and temporally. The result: "pure" power and wholly opposite to the unlimited space, frenzied time, and near anarchical subjects of *Democracy*. That philosophy of the prison was summed up by Tocqueville himself in a letter of 1836: "Isolate the detainees in prison, separate them during the night by means of solitary cells, subject them to absolute silence during the day when they are forced to assemble; in a word, prohibit every communication between souls and minds as between their bodies: that is what I would consider the first principle of the science [of prisons]."[8]

One consequence of reading Foucault's work (although it was not one he considered) is to appreciate that, save for Plato's *Laws*, the canonical writers in the Western tradition of political theory gave only the slightest attention, if any, to the practices of punishment and none of the early modern theorists before the eighteenth century took notice of the institution of the prison. The prison was thus assumed to be outside of what was properly political. The reason is not obscure. The vast majority of criminals came from the lower social strata and therefore not "in" the domain of the political to begin with. They could not vote or hold office and were often illiterate. And because many of them were without work and others were debtors, their existence was inconsequential to economic life. Thus prisons housed those who were politically unrepresented, largely without rights, only minimally defended by the law, economically powerless, socially superfluous, and intellectually voiceless. They were "natural" experimental objects.

In the last quarter of the eighteenth century that population was discovered theoretically. Questions of proper punishment, the purpose of imprisonment, the organization of prisons, and laws governing debtors and the poor were widely discussed by European intellectuals and occasionally taken up by lawmakers. The criminal and the criminally disposed poor, the politically excluded and legally vulnerable easily became "pure" objects of theory and policy, their identities unmediated by protective categories such as "citizen," or the "man" of natural law and natural rights.

The imprisoned criminal, the lawbreaker, becomes the symbol of modernity's counterrevolutionary turn because he or she is perceived not only as the product of revolution but as a potential agent of its return. Criminals are alternately described as "lazy" and as unable to find work. Their emergent marginality is a reflection of a new economy that first displaces the future criminals, then tries to adapt them to the rhythms of the factory, but finds it necessary, periodically, to "throw" them out of work in order to revamp "the economy" prior to introducing technology whose effects include rendering the unemployed worker useless. And because most criminals will have lower-class origins, their control will be a major means of driving a wedge between the law-abiding bourgeoisie and the lawless class and of promoting greater comity between bourgeois and aristocratic elites. The criminal becomes the scapegoat for the temerity of the demos; what remains is to turn the sovereign people into its own warden.

"Object" is, then, an accurate designation of the status of prisoners. Inmates had no defenders, only a constituency divided between reformers, who thought that behavior could be changed from criminal to socially productive, and conformers who believed that, at best, criminals might be made law-abiding. Object is accurate, too, because it is defined and constructed by state power: hunted, prosecuted, sentenced, administered, then released by its order—pure objects of pure power.

In no society, except the United States, could it be said that a released criminal was "returned" to the political community, no matter how acceptable his work habits or social conduct might prove to be. The criminal—the object outside the political—thus becomes revelatory of the liberal thought that had emerged from the Enlightenment and its intellectual revolutions, confident that if state power were to apply the theoretically informed prescriptions of prison reformers, better individuals and a better society would result. The uncontested symbol of these beliefs was Jeremy Bentham who spent a good portion of his life seeking payment from the English government for his Panopticon prison scheme, a scheme that, equally symbolical, he extended to include reform of the work habits of the poor.[9] "But for George the Third [he complained] all the prisoners in England would, years ago, have been under my management . . . [and] all the paupers in the country would, long ago, have been under my management."[10]

Prison reform thus becomes one road by which liberals find their way back to the state. It signifies the emergence of administration as the mode of action for resolving social problems by institutionalizing them, establishing structures that serve to prolong not the original problem but its solutions. It is also liberalism's way of reconciliation with the Old Regime by adopting and adapting its structure of power and its ideology of paternalism and benevolence. When directed at criminal behavior, state administration can be represented as disinterested, as the exception that transcends liberalism's invention, the fragmented politics of interests.

## III

> *There is one people who, for forty years, have courageously followed the path of experiments, trying everything which has not been previously attempted, unbeholden to any system, but not passionate for any theory, always separating the question of principles from the difficulties of execution.*
>
> Tocqueville[11]

*The Penitentiary System* was a voyage of discovery, a *theoria*, made to the United States but not to the same land as *Democracy in America*. On this journey the travelers would not wonder at town meeting democracy but at the achievements of prison reformers who had made America "the classic soil of the penitentiary regime."[12] Theirs was to be a report about antidemocracies in America. In contrast to the considerable objections Tocqueville would express later about American democracy, *The Penitentiary System* report was less critical. It claimed, with few reservations, to have found a solution in the New World to a problem that the Old World had been unable to solve. The problem, while it required a political approach, had to be conceived in different, even nonpolitical terms. This was because the problem was not the one with which most political theorists had been preoccupied, the problem of justice. Rather it concerned justice's aftermath, with what happened to those who are assumed to have been justly judged in violation of the norms of justice, those who enter the postjustice world of the prison.

France's penitentiary system, Tocqueville and Beaumont charged, was not simply bad; "it was no system at all." The shortcomings of current prisons, they claimed, could not be solved by detailed recommendations worthy of "a bureau of charity" but required the outlook of "l'homme d'État."[13] The statesman, so centuries of political theory had taught, should look upon society as a "whole"; that political "look" enabled him to surmount the parochialisms of class or region. The penitentiary, too, seemed a natural if ambiguous whole. Its denizens were to be administered rather than governed.

In their project the meaning of the political "whole" took shape, not around such concepts as "civil society" or "community," or "citizen," but a penitentiary "system." That formulation was further testimony to modernity's growing fascination with unified and bounded structures, such as market, corporation, army, bureaucracy, and education. A penal system signified a freestanding construction, connected only by formal authority-relations to the conventional political world. It also signified totality, a world unto itself, not an Aristotelian whole of different contributing parts but of individuals whose criminality unwittingly enhances the ends of collectivity: "The moral reformation of an individual is of great moment to a religious man; for the political man it is a small one; or, stated better, an institution is political only if it is acting in the collective interest; it loses that character if it profits only a small number."[14]

That perspective welcomed the seeming homogeneity and manageability of a morally uncomplicated whole. But wholeness ought not to encourage solidarity among the confined; if discovered, it had to be destroyed. In the later words of Tocqueville's parliamentary report of 1843:

> It is necessary to recognize that at this moment there exists among us an organized society of criminals. All of the members of that society know one another; they support one another; they associate every day to disturb the public peace. They form a small nation in the midst of the large one. It is that society which should be scattered . . . and reduced, if possible, to a single being against all of the upright men united in defense of order.[15]

## IV

> *In our own day we too often lose sight of the necessity of making prisons intimidating.*
>
> Tocqueville[16]

Considered as a theoretical text, *The Penitentiary System* is a complex work, not because it is profound—it is not—but because superimposed upon its official concern of prison reform is another text. The latter is a reprise of the eighteenth-century struggles between order and revolution. It attempted to enlist prison reform in the antirevolutionary cause while associating the reformist proposals of its opponents with the utopian mentality of revolutionary theory.

In reading *The Penitentiary System* one cannot help being struck by the critical, even contemptuous, attitude displayed toward the theoretical approaches of contemporaries to prison reform, the "canaille pénitentiaire," Tocqueville called them.[17] Their "imagination has had a steady diet of general ideas and large theories" that prevented them from "descending to the vulgar details that practice demands."[18] *The Penitentiary System* is sprinkled with references to "vain theories," to the gap between theory and practice, and to the need to replace speculation with careful observations.[19] Its special scorn is directed at "philanthropists," at those who had boundless sympathy for criminals and little for their victims and who had an unshakable faith in the rehabilitative potential of criminals. The type was described so as to leave little doubt as to its historical antecedents. The nineteenth-century philanthropist was cut from the same cloth as the eighteenth-century philosophe:

> In the United States there is a number of philosophical minds that are stuffed with theories and systems and who are impatient to put them into practice and who, if they were masters, to make themselves the law of the land, obliterating all of the old customs by the stroke of a pen and substituting the products of their own genius and the decrees of their wisdom.[20]

Before leaving France Tocqueville and Beaumont feel compelled to declare that theirs is to be an antitheoretical project: "[I]t is not theories which are to be the object of our researches. These are not lacking in France, and they are to be found in the books of all ages and all societies; but we want facts."[21]

From Burke's *Reflections* until the late twentieth century the French Revolution was assigned a certain fixed character among some political writers as an alliance, or mesalliance, between theory and radicalism. *The Penitentiary System* accepted that characterization: radical prison reformers not only retained the French revolutionary faith in the power of theory to effect broad changes, but in their solicitude for criminals they perpetuated the revolution's alliance with the lower classes. They wanted to turn prisons into "pleasant abodes."[22]

Accordingly, Tocqueville and Beaumont favored a "system" of "rigorous punishments" to make the prisoners "better" without "softening their situation."[23] Punishment was to be the means of asserting the primacy of the social order. "In the regime imposed on the criminal in prison, it is still society that must be borne in mind."[24] "We believe," Tocqueville and Beaumont declared, that "society has the right to do anything necessary to preserve itself and the established order" against the "assembled criminals," all of whose instincts were "vicious."[25] Later in the Chamber of Deputies Tocqueville would defend his prison reforms by claiming them to be an ideal combination of "reform" and "repression."[26]

## V

Their formulation of the penitentiary problem had both a wide and a wider frame. The wide frame focused on the relationship between types of imprisonment and their effects on the moral reform of prisoners, especially on the rates of recidivism. The wider frame was laid out in the opening sentences of the preface to *The Penitentiary System*:

> The society of our day is experiencing a malaise that seems to us to be related to two causes. One is chiefly moral: there is an active element of the mind that does not know where to discharge itself, an energy which, lacking food, consumes society for want of another prey. The other is chiefly material: it is the deprivation of a working populace that lacks work and bread and whose corruption, begun in distress, ends in imprisonment. The first evil pertains to the intellectual wealth of the population; the second to the poverty of the poor class.[27]

Of the two "plagues," the authors concluded, the first depended more on circumstances than men, but for the second, despite many efforts at solution, it remained uncertain whether social institutions could actually be arranged so as to produce the desired results. Tocqueville and Beaumont force penitentiary reform into serving as a test of revolutionary ideology: of whether it was within the power of society to design an institutional order that could eradicate a grave social evil, in this case by reforming criminals. Those who believed in that possibility were the lineal descendants of revolutionaries who had actually consumed society "for want of another prey."

Tocqueville and Beaumont singled out Bentham, Edward Livingston, an American, and the French reformer, Charles Lucas, and lumped them with the "philanthropists."[28] Their minds "have been fed on philosophical reveries" while "their extreme sensibility requires illusions." "[T]heir point of departure is abstraction more or less divorced from reality." Their thinking illustrates "the dangers of a theory pushed to its extreme consequences"[29] and of an overly solicitous concern for the criminals to the neglect of the interests of society. Those reformers, according to Tocqueville and Beaumont, conceive the penitentiary as "a utopia sprung from the head of philosophers but the more likely result is to increase the number of human deviants."[30]

Although *The Penitentiary System* adopts a stance against the revolution, it does not refight the old battles with the old discourses that appealed to the past, to hierarchy and privilege. Instead it adopts some of the French Revolution's own ideology and, more important, it capitalizes on the impulse to experimentation that the revolution had encouraged and appropriates some of the ideas of the new *science sociale*.

## VI

> *The discipline in* [le système de l'emprisonnement individuel] *can be reduced to some simple and uniform rules which, once formulated, are easily followed. . . . [W]hen prisoners are separated from one another by walls, they cannot offer resistance or join in disorder; once the system is well established, the administration of the prison well chosen, things proceed by themselves, obedient to the first direction imparted to them.*
>
> Tocqueville[31]

In choosing the terrain of the penitentiary Tocqueville and Beaumont were drawn into a distinctive realm of discourse defined by their opponents and, paradoxically, reinforced by American penitentiary practices. The radical reformers had defined the prison as a total system and that conception seemed so perfectly descriptive of the isolated character of prisons as to make it virtually impossible to discuss reform in different terms. Their discourse was dominated by the vocabulary of despotism and the imagery of Old Testament Yahwehism, most notably represented by Bentham's Panopticon. The name, Bentham explained, came "from the two Greek words, —one of which signified everything, the other a place of sight." The prison was to be built so that "a functionary, standing or sitting on the central point, had it in his power to commence and conclude a survey of the whole establishment in the twinkling of an eye."[32]

While first observing Sing Sing, Tocqueville wrote revealingly to a relative about his mixed feelings of admiration and abhorrence. The regime embodied "arbitrary power without limits" and a degree of authority that should not be allowed to any individual. Yet there was the undeniable fact that "repression produced such complete obedience and useful work." He was convinced that "force alone" could not achieve the results he was observing.[33] The fascination was for an institution in which "force" was in the system rather than in a person.

In addressing prison reform from an antirevolutionary bias, Tocqueville and Beaumont adapted the same totalistic approach, including elements of the Panopticon, to project a counterutopia that was at one with the form and structure of the theory. The despotism of the penitentiary is reproduced in the experimental structure of the theory; its abstract form corresponds to the isolated condition intended to make each prisoner an abstraction from the society of criminals. The counterutopia is founded on a paradox: not only do its authors despair of perfecting its "citizens," but they insist that those members of the prison population who appear to be the most "law-abiding" are in reality the most dangerous. Many French prison directors, Tocqueville declared to the Chamber of Deputies, reported that those prisoners who seemed the best behaved were invariably the most corrupt. "Their intelligence easily persuades them that they cannot escape the rigors of discipline while the vileness of their hearts helps them to submit. The most docile of all are the recidivists."[34]

In order to promote its political objectives without seeming to share the radical faith in theory, *The Penitentiary System* chose an intellectual approach that simultaneously hid its own theoretical character and assumed a form of theory more suitable to a politics at the opposite pole from the politics associated with the Tocqueville of *Democracy*. Prisons, by their forbidding walled exteriors and their physical distance from society acquire an abstract quality, which gains in credibility by virtue of the actual separation of the inmates from ordinary society, that is, from the influence of *moeurs* and customs, which Tocqueville later extolled as the essence of social order. As an abstract entity, a pure society of the impure, the prison invited the sort of austere moral experimentalism most opposed to the rich conservative sociologism of *Democracy*. "Institutions, *moeurs*, political circumstances are what influence the morality of men in society; the prison system affects only the morality of men in prison."[35]

Although the fact was not noted by Tocqueville and Beaumont, there had been no carceral institutions in the United States—either for criminals or the insane—until the Jacksonian era.[36] Establishing a prison could seem akin to dictating to a tabula rasa: there would be a prison system where before there had been only unsystematic practices. The new prisoner, in contrast, was a *tabula inscripta*. Because the inmates themselves chose to inscribe immoral principles on their "souls," they had renounced their moral immunity and could be treated as experimental subjects to test the indelibility of the inscriptions.

Beginning with their architecture and extending to organization and administration, the penal institutions located at Baltimore, Philadelphia (Cherry Hill), Auburn, and Sing Sing were represented as systematic orders self-consciously founded upon explicit and often similar principles but with sufficient variations as to allow for quantitative comparisons of costs, mortality rates, productivity, and rates of successful rehabilitation. Except for the morality of prisoners, no topic held more fascination for Tocqueville and Beaumont than work: how it was to be organized; whether prisoners were to be paid for their work and whether they should be allowed to spend it in prison; whether the management of work should be handled by private entrepreneurs.[37] Prisoners were the natural stuff of a controlled experiment in a political economy.

When Tocqueville and Beaumont turn to the American systems, it is apparent that they, too, are infected by experimentalism. "[T]he penitentiary system of the United States," they declared, "can offer a theory whose first experiments have succeeded."[38] The French government, therefore, should commence reform by establishing "a model penitentiary" based on American principles, especially of "absolute silence."[39] The rhetoric of *The Penitentiary System* is infected by the same urge for uniformity that had been charged against the French Revolution by its opponents: "political geometers" Burke had called them. *Democracy* would make a similar accusation against American egalitarians yet *The Penitentiary System* displays no Burkean or Montesquieuean sensibility, no deference to principles of complexity when they recommend penitentiary systems for the "extreme practical simplicity" of their principle of isolation: "if one supposes that two perverse beings who occupy the same place will corrupt each other, then one separates them."[40] They praise the cellular system for substituting "a uniform regime" for the "confusion" resulting when different classes of offenders are mixed together. For the penitentiary system, "when once put into practice . . . , is powerful in maintaining order and regularity; it rests on a surveillance of all every moment. Then work [of the inmates] is always more energetic and productive."[41]

The distinctive, if somewhat paradoxical, position that Tocqueville and Beaumont staked out would stand the Enlightenment on its head. They accepted the idea of radical reform of prisons but, at the same time, doubted the possibility of genuine rehabilitation of prisoners because there was no way of assuring that the changes in behavior effected during imprisonment would carry over once the prisoner was returned to society.

But how could there be such a change when the prison and society represented two completely different systems of culture? That dilemma exposed the fragility of culture once it became an object of self-consciousness. In its earlier eighteenth-century conception among writers such as Montesquieu, Hume, and Burke, culture was identified with habit, custom—in short, with uncritical practice of received ways. "Prejudice," Burke declared, "renders a man's virtue his habit; and not a series of unconnected acts. Through just prejudice, his duty becomes a part of his nature."[42] Culture was thus a great undisturbed unconscious which those who most valued it unintentionally disturbed by calling attention to its power. Once habit, custom, and unreflective usage became the stuff of theory, they lost their naive nature and ineluctably were succeeded by created forms of social conduct fashioned to serve as their functional equivalents. The great unconscious would be replaced by the politics of cultural control.

## VII

> *Although American society provides the example of the most extended liberty, the prisons of that same country offer the spectacle of the most complete despotism.*
>
> Tocqueville[43]

Montesquieu's genius was in seeing despotism not only as a conception of the most repressive and antipolitical of regimes, but as a possible theoretical form: a temptation on the part of the theorist to exert absolute power over the structure of his theory by suppressing differences and ignoring traditional beliefs and practices, all in the name of a rationally consistent system.[44] Montesquieuean theory protects itself against the lures of despotism, both in its inner structure and its political recommendations, by making cultural complexity the norm for both theory and practice. Despotic rule could only function, theoretically or in practice, by using repression to simplify the political world. Montesquieu responded by reconceiving the political through the imagery of the labyrinth, the ultimate emblem of complexity. In practice this meant keeping alive social and cultural diversities and inherited formalities as stumbling blocks to the efficiency-minded.

In America Tocqueville and Beaumont found no national, centralized system of prisons, as in France, but several distinct types of prison reform being tried out in various states. The theoretical problem was how to adapt the heterogeneous experience represented by localized systems to the homogeneity required by France's national, centralized system. Were prisons like political institutions, dependent on cultural mores? Or were prisons different from what we might call the ordinary political, such that the problem posed by historically distinct cultures could be bypassed as irrelevant because the objective has been defined to be not the reproduction of the "outside" society but the creation, virtually ab nihilo, of a unique penitentiary culture?

> Whence comes our near absolute repugnance toward using corporal punishment against prisoners? It is because one wants to treat men who are in prison as though they were still in society. Society and the prison are not, however, composed of the same elements. In general one could say that all of the inclinations of free men are toward the good, while all of the passions of the condemned criminals drive them violently toward evil. . . . "The Rights of Man" . . . are not valid in prison.[45]

In this formulation the penitentiary is socially isolated and politically decontextualized. The penitentiary systems in the states examined by Tocqueville and Beaumont were presented, not as the potential stuff of generalizations, but as the site of experiments from which one could construct a model: the United States was the place where "all of the theories have been tried."

## VIII

> *The best system . . . combines the principle of moral reform with economy of expense.*
>
> Tocqueville and Beaumont[46]

What if experimentalism were a way for theorizing to hide from itself by claiming that it was dealing with facts and practical matters and by renaming American penal reforms "experiments"? If the infliction of pain could be redirected at the mind rather than the body and thus be brought into the experimental domain in which theory dwelt, then theory could dissociate itself from complicity in a system where physical coercion was deemed essential to discipline. Here are Tocqueville and Beaumont writing about the regime of silence and isolation at the penal facility they most admired:

> "[T]he punishment [at Philadelphia] inflicted [on the prisoner] produces in the depths of his soul a terror more profound than chains or beatings. Isn't this the way that an enlightened and humane society should want to punish? Here the punishment is simultaneously the mildest and the most terrible that has ever been invented. It is not only focused on the human mind but it exerts an incredible dominion over it.[47]

The types of prisons selected for examination in *The Penitentiary System* appear as systematic experiments in total arrangements. Ideas about punishment, discipline, work, pay, health, instruction, prison architecture, and supervision are described as though they represented virtual laboratory conditions imposed by authority.[48] Some penitentiaries had the prisoners eat in a common mess hall, but under "perfect silence"; other institutions had the prisoner take his meals silently and alone in his cell, an arrangement favored by the two Frenchmen; still others imposed silence and isolation only during the night; in some the prisoners exercised in a common area, in others each had a "private" courtyard. Some systems favored the convicts working together in a common room but with strict silence; other systems required the prisoner to work alone in his cells and in silence. Tocqueville and Beaumont favored the latter, although they acknowledged it to be more expensive.[49] The existence of different types of prisons allowed not only for the comparison of practices but of costs. The study of such regimes held almost unlimited possibilities for quantification.

The role of *moeurs*, which was to figure crucially in Tocqueville's account in *Democracy*, was not omitted but inverted. In *Democracy moeurs* were identified as a major barrier to majority tyranny, part of an assemblage of beliefs, customs, and practices that had, in unpremeditated Montesquieuean fashion, melded into a system of constraints. Penitentiary *moeurs*, in contrast, had to be constructed and imposed. In that respect they were closer in spirit to the *moeurs* proposed in volume 2 of *Democracy.*

The first requirement was to sort out the human material beforehand, not throw it together pell-mell as in the French *maisons centrales,* where convicts were indiscriminately mixed regardless of age and types of offenses. The experimental approach was predicated on excluding from the new-model penitentiary the inmates who had been sentenced to death or to lifetime imprisonment. The penitentiary's mission was to be confined to those who had temporarily been expelled from society. Precisely because they were to be returned to society, their treatment had to be all the more systematic. They had to be stripped of society's protections and contemplated as unmediated objects of power. Experience showed, however, that mere physical punishment had only short-term effects. Accepting reform as the option meant that one had to define punishment in moral and cultural terms. Reformation of the criminal would thus require a regime of reculturation. Because, however, the issue was not *civisme* but recidivism—that is, freed convicts who could be relied on to resume contact with the criminal culture—the implication seemed to be that before they could be reformed/recultured, they had to be decultured.

The word most often used in *The Penitentiary System* to describe deculturation was the same that was typically used to describe the "breaking" of animals, *dompté* (mastered). Never once did Tocqueville or Beaumont suggest that prisoners were citizens entitled to legal protection or that incarceration should be accompanied with some element of civic education. Although Tocqueville, in particular, commented upon the harshness of American prison discipline, *The Penitentiary System* did not inquire into possible connections between prison brutality and a society whose ethos was supposedly democratic in the extreme. The project did not, as in *Democracy,* require protecting the individual from the majority by appealing to the reader-citizen but counseling authority on how to protect the law-abiding majority from the minority of lawless individuals.

## IX

> *[D]espotism . . . sees in men's isolation the surest guarantee of its own duration, and it usually devotes all its attention to isolate them.*
>
> Tocqueville, *Democracy in America*[50]

In their investigations as well as in their final report Tocqueville and Beaumont focused entirely on the so-called cellular system, by which a separate cell was assigned to each prisoner. Individual physical isolation was established as the starting point for a whole system of isolation: moral, communicative, social, economic, and political. Their conception of a penitentiary system begins from the basis of an individualism that is to be deliberately imposed as a means of breaking the "organized society" formed within prisons. Prisoners should be "reduced to individuals" and forced to face "all the upright men united to defend order."[51] Prisoners should not know each other, nor speak because of "the contagion of mutual communication."[52]

## X

> *What is the main end proposed for a penitentiary regime? It is the improvement of the guilty. It is the hope of reentry into society offered to the condemned as reward for his moral reform.*
>
> Beaumont and Tocqueville[53]

Tocqueville and Beaumont never believed for a moment that the penitentiary could achieve what Bentham claimed, "grind rogues into honest men." Their more modest hope was that a prisoner should leave prison no worse than when he entered and, at best, a moral calculator.[54] "Perhaps he does not depart prison an honest man but he has acquired honest habits. . . . [H]is morality is not based on honor but on interest. . . . He is at least obedient to the laws."[55]

On the face of it, the pessimism of *The Penitentiary System* seems at odds with the heroic measures of reform proposed. Its understanding was expressed in the language of morality and deeply imbued with religious metaphors and categories. The recommendations placed a heavy emphasis on religious instruction for inmates, even to the point of mimicking monastic practices.[56] A penitentiary system, Tocqueville and Beaumont reminded their readers, was where criminals were punished in "expiation" of their crimes.[57] "The moral reform of the wicked . . . can only result from a long isolation, deep meditations, and habits of work."[58] The psychological harshness of *The Penitentiary System*'s regime as contrasted with its distaste for physical punishment was rooted in an understanding of criminality as a disorder of the "soul," which "society was powerless to pardon." Society cannot reach the soul; its pardon merely frees the prisoner. In contrast, "when God grants grace, He pardons the soul."[59] Paradoxically, because the penitentiary can only alter the behavior of prisoners, its power must be absolute.

More than a decade later, in his speech to the Chamber of Deputies, Tocqueville was even more passionate about the religious character of reformed penitentiary practices and was prepared to strike at the soul and change it: "What do we want? We want to have a powerful effect on the soul itself, on the mind, but no longer by corporal punishment, as in the Middle Ages. We want to raise the mind to more just ideas, the soul to more honest feelings. In a sense we want to change the point of view from which the inmate views human relations."[60]

## XI

The criminal stands opposed to the noncriminal, not merely because the one is guilty of a crime and the other is not; rather the latter has an aura of almost theological innocence while "the criminal is stained with all vices and immoralities."[61] The social essence of criminal depravity is that it is "a contagion" so "dangerous" that the criminal must be isolated not only from society but from other criminals if there is to be any hope of his reform.[62] Communication among inmates is the medium by which the communicable disease of criminality is transmitted and is the direct cause of the sexual depravities about which Tocqueville and Beaumont were greatly exercised.[63] Their dilemma was that if prisoners were allowed to mingle, "passions" would be aroused, homosexual intercourse might follow, and, in the case of young boys, pederasty. On the other hand, isolation encouraged masturbation.[64] Fortunately, there were ingenious architectural innovations that enabled the prisoners to be observed without their knowledge.[65]

As the name implied, a penitentiary was to be the site of repentance.[66] Tocqueville and Beaumont were deeply impressed by the powerful influence of American clergymen for their major role in the moral reeducation of the condemned. The clergy's presence focuses the drama of repentance and rehabilitation: they conduct the assault on the soul of the prisoner.

*The Penitentiary System* offers a vivid picture of what its authors imagine to be the experience of the inmate in the Philadelphia institution and its "disciplinary order of things" based on solitary isolation. "Full of terrible specters . . . agitated by a thousand fears and torments," the prisoner may resist but usually in about two days "the most rebellious inmate" submits. He will have overcome "the terrors which have pushed him toward madness or despair": "he will have debated with himself in a setting of a remorseful conscience and an agitated soul, and he will have fallen into dejection and sought in work distraction from his evils; from that moment he will have been broken [*dompté*] and become forever submissive to the rules of the prison."[67]

In 1844 Tocqueville presented a defense of a report, and an accompanying bill, on prison reform, which he had prepared for a parliamentary prison commission. The most revealing moment came when he was compelled to defend the cellular system and its principle of isolation from the charge that it drove inmates insane. In reply he argued that the system was like religion in that it aimed at "the soul" of the prisoner in order to make him moral. There was, Tocqueville acknowledged, a "bad side of the system." On rare occasions "the resulting stimulation produces alarming symptoms," and the soul may become "troubled" and eventually insane. However, he insisted, "it is not necessary to be too preoccupied with this undoubtedly very great evil, for it is one which is redeemed by even greater benefits." He went on to add that a prison where "man is exposed to the temptation to speak stimulates the development of this deadly disease more than any other."[68]

## XII

The role of religion in reculturating the condemned had little to do with religion in any theological or fideistic sense. It had everything to do with the political purpose of extirpating the spirit of rebellion by instructing prisoners on "how to obey."[69] Its unstated premise was similar to the antirevolutionary subtext of *Democracy*, only now, because of the clearly defined social character of prisoners, it was more directly expressed. The French Revolution was viewed by Tocqueville and his class as importantly, although not totally, a revolt of the *sans-culottes*, an uprising of the dregs of society—in short, the antecedents of the criminal population of the nineteenth century. The practices of atomization—silence and isolation—were intended to stifle any solidarity among the prisoners. In particular, all possibilities for conviviality among the inmates were to be discouraged. There were to be no canteens where prisoners might mix; the money earned by work was not to be spent on "luxuries" inside the prison. Tocqueville and Beaumont did not contain their disgust at a prison where convicts freely conversed during meals. "[N]early all had the stigmata of corruption and vice printed on their faces" as they laughed and drank as though at "a huge cabaret."[70]

In a letter from America Beaumont wrote of a revelatory moment in their visit to Sing Sing where they observed 900 inmates, unchained, cheerfully working in "absolute silence" and supervised by a mere 30 guards. Beaumont presents the scene as a case study in potential rebellion. The guards, aware of being outnumbered, "must at each instant fear to see a revolt break out," and so they restrain their use of punishment. "They understand that every oppression of theirs might bring on a rebellion." Yet, despite the "various elements of order," the explanation did not seem obvious until one perceived the principle at work: "All strength is born of association, and 30 individuals united through perpetual communication by ideas, by plans, in common, by concerted schemes, have more real power than 900 whose isolation makes them weak."[71]

Accordingly the prison becomes a nonsociety, perfectly atomized by silence and isolation, a caricature of a monastery vowed to silence. "They are joined but no moral bond exists among them. They see but do not know each other. They are in society without communicating together . . . their bodies are together but their souls isolated."[72]

At the same time that communal elements are being discouraged among the potential rebels, the depiction of their character, the emphasis on the "moral contagion" of their vices, the depravity of their morals, all have the effect of evoking, indeed, uniting an ideal moral community outside among those threatened by the-not-so-human beings inside.[73] The prison structure and the measures taken against prisoners have an atomizing effect inside, but they have the opposite effect of magically creating solidarity in a society whose rulers had only recently advised them, "enrichez-vous." The regime of atomization is justified by "the greater interest, that of society as a whole." The punishment of the guilty is a way of "addressing society." "The social interest, which is but the interest of the virtuous mass, demands that the wicked should be punished with severity."[74]

## XIII

*Isolate the detainees in prison, separate them during the night by means of solitary cells, subject them to absolute silence during the day when they are forced to assemble; in a word, prohibit every communication between souls and minds as between their bodies; that is what I would consider the first principle of the science.*

Tocqueville[75]

In *Democracy* Tocqueville would shape despotism to configure with democratic societies by claiming that democratic culture of equality, individualism, and acquisitiveness might eventually undermine civic life and allow society to accommodate easily to centralized rule. The impression that Tocqueville left was that for democracy to evolve into despotism would not require a wrenching transformation, only the erosion of its civic life. In *The Penitentiary System*, however, democracy and despotism were pictured as opposites: "While American society furnishes an example of the most extensive liberty, its prisons offer the spectacle of the most complete despotism."[76]

Despite the contrast, however, despotism evokes little of the repugnance and disapproval so apparent in *Democracy*. Rather the opposite: the major principles of the American penitentiary systems—silence, isolation, brutality—were strongly despotic, yet these, with the exception of brutality, formed the basis of the reforms that Tocqueville and Beaumont recommended. Their presence suggests the incorporation into modern ideologies of liberalism, conservatism, and constitutionalism of a countertendency whose presence is disguised.

The ingredients that are said to prepare and support democratic despotism in *Democracy* are also the main elements in reforms proposed for the penitentiary regime. The notion of individualism with its ethos of privatization and isolation, which Tocqueville would later condemn as a breeding ground for despotism, were to be the constitutive principles of the organizational structure recommended for the penitentiary, even to determining its cellular-based architecture. When viewed from *The Penitentiary System*, Tocqueville's later disapproval of individualism seems ironical: "Individualism is by origin democratic, and it threatens to develop to the extent that conditions are equal."[77] Similarly, uniformity and equality, which Tocqueville would later argue were congenial to despotic centralization, were defended as principles that justified the uniform treatment and equal punishment of prisoners. And in claiming that close surveillance would almost render obsolete the use of corporal punishment, *The Penitentiary System* anticipated the basic principle of democratic despotism, that it strikes the mind and leaves the body alone. And not least, Tocqueville, the opponent of centralization, endorsed the principle that a penitentiary must be based on a highly centralized structure of authority.[78]

The penitentiary stands as the quintessentially modern form of despotism: scientific in conception, administrative in its mode of rule, and, above all, depersonalized and hence not offensive to the sensibilities of modern individualism. It announces the modern principle that is to replace personal rule by monarchs and aristocrats: power can no longer be visible, personal. Bentham described "the keeper" of his Panopticon as "concealed from the observation of the prisoners, unless where he thinks fit to show himself: hence, on their part, the sentiment of an invisible omnipresence."[79] Virtually the same formulation was employed by Tocqueville and Beaumont, a tribute to the influence of Bentham and an echo of the theology of the hidden God.[80]

It is instructive in this connection to point to the eerie resemblance between the penitentiary principles advocated by Tocqueville and Beaumont and the classic and bitter description of despotism in Montesquieu's *Esprit des lois*:

> Despotic government has fear for its principle. . . . Everything turns on two or three ideas. . . . When you are training a beast . . . you program [*vous frappez*] his brain with two or three movements, no more. . . . Such a State will be best situated when it can see itself as alone in the world, when it is surrounded by deserts and separated

> from societies it calls barbarians. . . . While the principle of despotic government is fear, its end is tranquillity; but this is not peace but the silence of cities that the enemy is about to occupy. . . . In these States religion has more influence than in any other; it is fear added to fear.[81]

The allure of penitentiary despotism reflected the modern fears, shared by liberals and conservatives alike, about the working class. Unemployed workers were viewed as latent criminals whose moral depravity would come to the surface once the discipline of work was no longer there to contain it. Tocqueville and Beaumont were astonished and delighted to observe the Philadelphia convicts working of their own "free will" and finding "pleasure" in work despite receiving no pay.[82]

Perhaps the criminal appeared dangerous to Tocqueville and Beaumont because, like the enslaved African, he embodied the possibility of revolt. Along with women and slaves, he represented a significant social group denied full citizenship and a measure of hope within the new economic order of capitalism. The worker was used to mark the point at which modernity redefined its revolutionary genealogy: thus far and no farther. Unlike women or negroes, in excluding the worker from political life, modernity was employing a principle not of nature but of art. The factory worker was the "creature" of modernity in the double sense of that word.

The worker became the symbol of modernity's need to suppress the logic of its own promise in order to accommodate the logic of capitalism, a logic that had its own *petitio principii.* Capitalism, like aristocracy, reproduced social inequalities—of rewards, opportunities, powers, and life chances—as a matter of course. The worker who embodied the contradiction between the new regime's professions of equality and its systemically induced inequalities unintentionally promoted a solidarity among the remnants of the old regime and representatives of the new regime. By arousing a common fear of equality, the worker united the two classes, which, as a result of the French Revolution, had experienced opposite reversals of fortune: the aristocracy, which had lost social and political preeminence, and the bourgeoisie, which had acquired economic power and was steadily increasing its social and political influence.

The consolidation of modernity thus became increasingly dialectical as it ingested some lessons of premodernity regarding inequality. Recall that in their travel application, Tocqueville and Beaumont had posed the paradox of why societies committed to progress were nonetheless plagued by progressively higher crime rates.[83] In Tocqueville and Beaumont's presentation, the United States penitentiary system functions as a model of antimodernity: stern, repressive, authoritarian, priest-ridden. The American penitentiary stands in silent accusation of French society: having unselectively absorbed modernity, France was now finding that the political and social beliefs fostered by the revolution were preventing reform.

Like the depersonalized despotism depicted later in *Democracy*, the despotism of *The Penitentiary System* was strongly permeated by mythic elements, which, however, were concentrated in a single individual of heroic proportions and only later transferred to a collective system. In America, Tocqueville and Beaumont had discovered a living example of a selfless despot, a man who impressed them not only by his achievements but by "the firmness of his character" and "the power of his will."[84] In *Democracy* despotism would be viewed as issuing from a democratic culture of equality; in *The Penitentiary System* the despot is the means of establishing a culture that will combat the moral and religious excesses embodied in the mores bequeathed by the revolution.

## XIV

There is an elaborate, even heraldic flourish to the introduction of the despot in *The Penitentiary System* as the authors profess to be perplexed in trying to explain how the system at Auburn was suddenly reformed—as though confronted with explaining the Spartan constitution without Lycurgus. "We see the famous system of Auburn grow instantaneously and emerge from an ingenious combination of elements that seem, at first glance, incompatible: isolation and joining together. But what we do not see clearly is the creator of the system, for it must have been the case that someone got the idea first."[85]

That fanfare preceded Elam Lynds, one of the most remarkable Americans encountered by the two Frenchmen.[86] In his journals Tocqueville had described Lynds as "the father of the actual penitentiary system" and also a man of "clearly despotic tendencies."[87] He was renowned for his cruelty, fearlessness, incorruptibility, and absolute authority. "Bending the prisoner to a *passive obedience*," he insisted, was "above all necessary." Lynds was a Calvinist version of Dostoyevsky's Grand Inquisitor, not hesitating to employ the sternest measures, including the whip, while holding to the bleakest view of redemption. Coldly skeptical that prisoners could be genuinely reformed, he would concede only that "once they have been thoroughly broken to the yoke of discipline" they might become productive workers.[88]

Despite the initial impression of a simple hardware store owner, "a truly common man" whose "speech has that same vulgar quality," Tocqueville and Beaumont were soon struck by the force of his "intelligence and singular energy."[89] "According to me," Lynds opined to his interviewers, "the director of a prison, especially if he is an innovator, should be armed with an absolute and assured authority." Then, in a revealing reversal of predicates, Lynds compared unfavorably the situation of the reformer in America with that in France: "Here we are enslaved to a constantly changing public opinion. . . . [One] has simultaneously to court the favor of the public while pressing his undertaking to the end. In France his position is less difficult."[90]

The few later scholars who have taken note of Tocqueville's conversations with Lynds have remarked on the fascination exercised by the latter. Although Tocqueville and Beaumont disapproved of Lynds's readiness to employ the whip, the particulars of some of their final recommendations were clearly influenced by his unabashed defense of the penitentiary as a despotism and his pessimism regarding lasting rehabilitation.

The truly intriguing questions are, Why were they so plainly tempted by the despotic model in the first place and why did they hesitate to follow through?

## XV

That they did hesitate is strongly suggested by the anticlimactic, almost apologetic character of their final recommendations. "We are not presenting a system; we have only raised a question whose solution is of vital interest to society."[91] "We have never had the idea that France could suddenly attempt a general revolution in its system of prisons and suddenly erect new ones and instantaneously allocate enormous sums . . . to that objective alone."[92]

The crucial phrase, "general revolution," provides the clue to the questions raised here. For one reared in the Montesquieuean belief that the ultimate political contrast was between a society ruled by a despot and a society whose identity resided in a traditional political culture of long but unpremeditated preparation, one could only blanche before the despotic temptation—unless one was contemplating a society composed of the depraved and the antisocial. But why was despotism contemplated when it was reasonable to presume that in the aftermath of the Enlightenment society would enthusiastically approve of penal reform? In part, Tocqueville and Beaumont did follow that prescription.

In their closing pages they exhorted intellectuals and politicians to launch a national debate on the question. However, the same political culture that supported public discussion was depicted by Tocqueville and Beaumont as the main obstacle to reform. "In our *moeurs* and in the actual state of French thinking there are moral obstacles" that did not exist in the United States.[93] The crux of the problem was that the mores of French society were the product of The Revolution. Unlike the law-abiding Americans, the French did not have "that spirit of submission to order." Rather, "In France, in the mind of the masses, there is an unfortunate tendency to violate rules; and this inclination to insubordination appears to us of a kind that further limits prison discipline."[94]

At the heart of the matter was the different status of religion—precisely the topic that Tocqueville was to elevate into a prime, if not *the* prime, explanation for the stability and morality of American democracy. A penitentiary based on American principles of isolation, silence, work, and strict discipline emerged not only as the ideal form of incarceration but as an implicit critique of the political and moral culture outside. In America the prison reform movement "has been essentially religious." Religion was "one of the fundamental elements of discipline and reform. . . . Its influence alone produces complete regeneration." From top to bottom, from the administrators of American prisons to its guards, the influence of religiously inspired *moeurs* was at work. "The inmate in the United States penitentiaries breathes in a religious atmosphere that surrounds him on all sides, and he is more amenable to its influence because his own early education predisposes him toward it."[95]

Unfortunately the American system cannot be imported in toto because the French public would not tolerate the clergy playing the dominant role in the reculturation of inmates; nor would it support the corporal punishment used to enforce silence. One could only hope that French anticlericalism would abate; it was, after all, not "natural" for a society to exist without religious beliefs.[96]

The difficulties in that position, as well as the manipulative politics that, from desperation, it encouraged, were evident in a speech Tocqueville gave in 1844. With more than a touch of sophistry he argued that because the French Revolution had attempted to apply Christian principles of improvement, not to believe in the possibility of reforming the prisoner was tantamount to "paganism." All of Europe believed that there can be "rehabilitation following atonement": "Isn't the greater glory of the French Revolution to have secularized Christianity somewhat by its results, to have taken its maxims from the religious sphere in order to make them inform the practical sphere of legislation?"[97]

## XVI

With the exception of a few paragraphs that Tocqueville used as illustrative of the American inability to carry reforms to a completion,[98] the topic of prisons was not discussed in either volume of *Democracy*. That omission calls attention to a curious combination in America: on the one hand, an experimental approach to the principal institution of nonfreedom, which, by its embodiment of complete control over powerless objects, furnished a rare opportunity for the "perfect" realization of an "idea" of reforming human beings by the negation of freedom; and, on the other, the "outside society," whose unparalleled natural wealth and boundless opportunities for converting it into personal property were joined with a society of nearly perfect freedom of action and self-government—in short, a virtual utopia. Why did the American imagination give rise to, or feel the need for, approaching the problem of prisons as an exercise in negative utopianism? Was it the fascination for its opposite or the expression of rage at a utopia of freedom and opportunity that allowed no appeals from its judgments and no consolation prizes for failure?

# PART FIVE

## *Second Journey to America*

# CHAPTER XXI
# THE POLITICAL EDUCATION OF THE BOURGEOISIE

## I

Flushed with the success of *Democracy in America*, Tocqueville proclaimed himself "a liberal of a new kind." A few years later, wearied by the frustrations of parliamentary politics, his professions of liberalism seemed more protestation, even defensive: "I am a liberal and nothing more. I was so before 1830; I still am."[1]

The change in tone reflected the chastening effect of his new career upon his political hopes and its impact on the theoretical vocation that, up till now, had defined his way in the world. During the years between the final installment of *Democracy* (1840) and the revolutionary events of 1848 Tocqueville was deeply involved in parliamentary and intellectual politics. His published writings were directed at events of the time, many of them connected with his parliamentary role. It precluded him from affecting the detachment of the *theoros*-traveler atop the heights or proclaiming himself a mediator between contrasting worlds.

In engaging the new phenomenon of democratic equality in *Democracy*, he had sought a basis for a new public philosophy and to be its expositor. A theoretical position above the fray signified an honest effort to fight free of parochial allegiances of class and partisan politics. It was not a claim about being neutral but about the degree of political disengagement that was demanded in order to achieve theoretical truth about the possibilities for France's becoming a free and genuine political society within the limits of the nation's intense historical experiences of the past half century and the irreversible tendencies that had resulted. Now, however, whatever he chose to write about the political would necessarily be from the midst of politics. His political stands made of a *theoros* a partisan.

Yet he was not a party man in any strict sense. Although he took sides he shied away from polemics; he tried to preserve detachment and perspective and, above all, to elevate current issues to a loftier theoretical plane. Partisanship is not necessarily the enemy of truth or the sign of its absence. Partisanship is not only inevitable in liberal politics but the accompaniment to one of liberalism's great achievements, the legitimation of opposition. The concept of opposition is, in reality, liberalism's contribution to the solution of theory's perennial problem of how to counter the inherent tendency of any regime to rule in favor of its constitutive class or group. But even when correctives are operative, a free politics distorts as a matter of course. (An unfree regime, we might add, distorts not as a matter of course but of principle.) There is ambiguity in almost every substantive political problem, and if not in the problem, then in the solution proposed, and if not there, then in the motives of those who are proposing or opposing it. Tocqueville had his strain of partisanship, especially in his marked reluctance to give thoughtful consideration to the views of opponents, a reluctance that was in part tactical and in part psychological, dictated by the uncongenial ideas and interests he chose to defend and the ideas and interests he ventured to provoke by defending the French Revolution and appealing to the bourgeoisie.

## II

The personal and political tensions to which Tocqueville exposed himself can be conveyed through Bakhtin's distinction between epic heroes and "popular masks." We catch a glimpse of the tensions between the heroic and the political when a fellow deputy and close friend of Tocqueville once suggested that, as a token of their loyalties, they both take seats with the right of the Chamber. Tocqueville took this as an affront to the sincerity of his liberal commitments, as though he could not be both liberal and aristocrat. In a heated response he insisted on an identity that united principle and person. He described caustically "the enormous difficulty there is in understanding that a man who carries my name could truly love liberty and did not secretly have the desire to disguise by his actions the professions of liberal faith that the necessity of circumstances has wrung from him."[2] In Tocqueville's version of the two masks, the hero would gamble that as a politician he could assume a popular mask yet remain a hero of principle.

In Bakhtin's formula the hero struggles to achieve the great and complete action, fully realized: "As for me," Tocqueville declaimed, "I think that it is only by taking a stand on the country's most elevated ideas and passions that a government can attain to the greatness of the political [*la politique*]."[3] Popular masks, in contrast, change, respond, and are forever contemporary. Modern politics, Tocqueville lamented, is "extremely *mobile*." "Fifty years of revolution have shaken our religious beliefs, obscured notions of good and evil, cast all opinions into doubt."[4] For Bakhtin the hero always dies; popular masks never perish. For Tocqueville: "I fear that great men and events are disappearing; and that the destiny of our generation should not be to agitate endlessly without glory in the midst of this annoying anthill. . . . I cannot adequately express what is disagreeable about a practical political life passed among half believers, changing ideas, and mediocre men with whom it is necessary to act daily despite the disgust they inspire."[5]

Tocqueville would himself don a mask and proceed to rummage through the recent past to salvage cultural materials for political reconstruction, even if it meant that those materials symbolized all that was most opposed to his own heritage and to some of his deepest political convictions. He would dedicate himself to persuading the bourgeoisie to set aside its passions for the marketplace and Bourse in order to revitalize the political. He would be its educator.

In *Democracy* Tocqueville typically combined theoretical analysis with mythical modes of representation (*mytheoreticus*). Now, in addressing the issues of the day through journal articles, speeches, and newspaper pieces, Tocqueville aspired to the mythical but produced, instead, a hybrid of theoretical analysis and ideological representations, a discourse of truth combined with a discourse of partisanship.

## III

In past centuries the political had been exalted or sanctified by various myths: of gods, heroes, revelations, autochthonous peoples, divine right, ancient constitutions, original contracts, and Founding Fathers. In the age of individualism and interest politics, the political was being reconfigured more as ideology than as myth. The appearance of modern ideology is one of aggregated ideas that, in their intention of being more or less systematic, are mimetic of theology, philosophy, and political theories; but, unlike those quasi-professionalized intellectual forms, ideology is crucially shaped by the aim of becoming integral to the belief systems of society by winning over large and heterogeneous audiences. The emergence of modern ideologies disrupts the preexisting relationship between theory and myth. Early modern theorists, while retaining theory's hegemony, appropriated mythical elements (e.g., Machiavelli's depiction of *Fortuna*; Hobbes's "great Leviathan" created by covenants that "resemble that Fiat, or the *Let us make man*, pronounced by God in the Creation"; or Burke's state contract that "is but a clause in the great primaeval contract of eternal society").[6] Modernity signifies the moment when ideology displaces myth as theory's way of making contact with and exploiting popular beliefs. While myth fantasizes power, ideology is once removed from myth by its affiliations with theory and once removed from theory by its borrowings from myth. Because of the skeptical element that infects ideology by virtue of its affiliation with theory, myth's fantasies of power become ideology's penchant for mock power.

Mock power is power expressed in the grandiose terms characteristic of myth but undercut by ideology's own account of the extraordinary powers possessed by its enemies. Modern ideology's form of mock power would be where a people who had once overthrown established powers, are declared sovereign, but the actual exercise of power is controlled by others. The tasks of exposing mock power and demythologizing actual power would be divided among the newly emerging social sciences of political economy, administration, and sociology. Social science signified the replacement of myths of mock power by the sciences of "real" power and the self-conscious construction of ideology to serve as a substitute for religion by incorporating the consolations of belief while denying real power to believers (Saint-Simon, Fourier, and Comte).

For Tocqueville, while the location of the developing crisis was political and ideological, its resolution implied the containment of social science in order to prevent economy and bureaucracy from dictating the ideology of the political. Accordingly Tocqueville would claim that the lack of "beliefs" reflected the crisis in "the political *moeurs* of the country itself."[7] He would attempt the task of reconstructing a political culture for a politics with which, at best, he had lukewarm attachment and for a dominant class he mostly despised. It would mean the theorist-traveler would descend into the city, attempting to theorize, not from above and for a whole, but amid the swirl of parliamentary forces and festering postrevolutionary antagonisms to address and instruct a particular class, a part of the whole. He attempted to redefine the political ideology of that class and persuade it to embrace it.[8] But that would mean reexamining the revolutionary myth that had accompanied the rise of that class and restating its ideology as myth— while suppressing both the demise of his own class and refusing political recognition to the working classes.

## IV

> *There is not in France and, I do not hesitate to say, in Europe, another man who, in a more public way has made it clear that the old aristocratic society has disappeared forever and that for the men of our day there is only the task of organizing on its ruins, progressively and prudently, a new and democratic society . . . without abandoning monarchy. . . . I am a new man.*
>
> Tocqueville[9]

Tocqueville's countryman and fellow aristocrat, Henri de Saint-Simon, had declared that the political education of the bourgeoisie was the central question left by the French Revolution.[10] That perception would later seem so obvious that it obscured the curious character of the formulation. In earlier centuries when political theorists had attempted to instruct rulers or potential rulers on how to govern, it had never occurred to theorists that the task would be to cajole a reluctant dominant class into ruling. The traditional problem had been to teach restraint by emphasizing the inhibitions of virtue, not to arouse the politically indifferent.

The French Revolution, Tocqueville pointed out, had handed over the task of governance to the bourgeoisie but instead of developing a "regular, peaceful, though active and effective, public life," the class devoted itself exclusively to private interests and allowed itself to be corrupted into passivity.[11] The revolutions of 1789 and 1830, in effect, had anointed the bourgeoisie as the modern custodian of the political and confronted it with the perennial challenge to any ruling group: of overcoming the favoritism and biases inherent in the social forces and classes that had made its triumph possible.

In volume 1 of *Democracy* he had identified the dangers of modernity with its relentless drive toward equality and had made it his fundamental commitment to defend liberty against the onslaughts of equality. Now his analysis began to build on a theme from volume 2 of *Democracy*. The danger lay not in the threat to liberty from an egalitarian-minded majority but in the privatization of liberty at a time when France was attempting what no other European country had, "of trying to combine three elements traditionally separate: representative government, administrative centralization, and equality."[12]

As Tocqueville recognized, whatever its alleged excesses, equality was potentially the stake that related individuals to each other, thus providing a potential bond of commonality and collective identity. It was an element in stabilizing values such as national solidarity and consensus. In contrast, modern liberty, as formulated in Mill's essay *On Liberty*, was bent toward individualizing and welcoming dissent and eccentricity. The classic French formulation was provided by Constant:

> For forty years I have defended the same principle: liberty in everything: in religion, philosophy, literature, industry, politics; and by liberty I mean the triumph of individuality: as much over the authority which seeks to govern despotically as over the masses who demand the right to enslave the minority to the majority. . . . The majority has [the right] to constrain the minority to respect order; whatever does not disturb order, whatever is merely internal [to individuals], like opinion, [and] does not injure others, either by provoking real violence, or by opposing a contrary demonstration; everything which in the form of skill [*industrie*], allows a rival skill to be

exercised freely, is individual and ought not to be a legitimate subject for the power of society [*pouvoir social*].[13]

The promise of freedom, solemnized at first as the foundation of a modern society, seemed to be evolving into an apologetic for transforming a cohesive society of obligations into a divisive society of competitors by opening various avenues of opportunity, commercial, financial, industrial, intellectual, or bureaucratic: *les carrières ouverte aux tous les talents.*[14] Representative government, in turn, was acquiring the appearance of a vast machine for producing favors to local or "special" interests.[15] Its operations seemed to reproduce economic competition on the political plane. The regime of liberty, however, seemed unable to generate a political culture, a system of *moeurs* for a society of citizens, or a public space for discussion of "ideas" or "men" rather than "interests, canals, and railroads."[16] The great question was, How could a genuinely political culture be developed for a society dominated by individuals whose most powerful preoccupation was economic but who also displayed a strong impulse toward withdrawal into private concerns?

One might say that the question reflected a division within the liberal self and its conception of freedom. When the individual is free to enter into the public world either of finance, industry, and commerce or of politics, the self subordinates to the rational pursuit of its interests, objectifying itself. There, under the discipline of the market, interest takes precedence over self. In contrast, when the individual withdraws and seeks to cultivate the concerns and pleasures of private life, self is foremost, interest is subjectified. The political becomes the third domain. Interests, rationalized as economic behavior, transfer their intramural competition from economy to polity. There they vie for public subsidies and legalized advantage. In the process a hidden politics flourishes separate from the "open" politics of public debate and contesting party programs. The separation between the two reflects a bifurcation that runs throughout politics and the citizenry. Politics serves to transmute materialized interests into immaterial ideals, which can then be directed at divided and largely privatized selves in the hope of attracting both material "contributions" from "private" citizens and ideal support from "public" citizens.

## V

If Marx was the self-appointed political tutor to the working classes, Tocqueville attempted to play a comparable role to the bourgeoisie. But where Marx conceived his task as one of awakening the workers to a consciousness of their own class interest, Tocqueville assumed the more daunting project of gaining the attention of a class with a finely developed sense of self-interest and then persuading it that political rule required, in some degree, the transcending of class and personal interests. He would undertake to instruct this ruling class in the unnatural ways of the common interest, a formidable project for a class that, while it appeared indifferent about politics, was actually developing a political economy that enabled it to exercise power from a distance, to employ proxies, and to rule indirectly by means of economic power.

In 1843 Tocqueville published a series of *Letters on the Domestic Situation in France* in the review *Siècle*; and in 1844 another series of articles followed in the journal *Commerce*. There he presented himself as a defender of the true principles of 1789. By a return to origins—traumatic for him, triumphant for the bourgeoisie—he hoped to inspire the bourgeoisie to an act of collective remembrance, recovering a great moment when its identity was political. The reincorporation of a moment of altruism, heroics, and common endeavor—but not of revolutionary destruction and class hatreds—could reverse "the extinction of public life" and combat the lethargy enveloping the society.[17] "Who does not see that among us human activity has changed its end, that the dominant passion, the mother passion, has changed course? From the political it has become industrial. Who does not perceive that our contemporaries have little concern for liberty and governance but care greatly about wealth and well-being?"[18]

The provocative terms in which Tocqueville formulated his project were not, however, the prelude to a radical analysis. The problem, as he conceived it, was of a social class that had accomplished a successful political revolution and now displayed little enthusiasm for developing the politics that the French Revolution had made possible. The bourgeoisie seemed both satisfied with the results of the revolution and fearful of its implications. The approach he adopted was didactic rather than policy-specific; his concern was to elevate bourgeois-liberal thinking to an authentically political plane, not to divide or to challenge the postrevolutionary distribution of power or the hegemony of the middle classes. Toward that end and to reassure his readers, he described a high-minded party that would have limited ideal objectives: it would be conservative and concentrated on conserving public life.[19]

To attract the bourgeois to a conception of politics as a high calling, Tocqueville proceeded in a highly tactical way to construct a political myth of the revolution tailored to the political role he would have the bourgeoisie play. Tocqueville's approach to the revolution was circumspect. "There are," he explained, "many ways of being revolutionary." His version was circumscribed and highly selective. He described it as "liberal revolutionary." Its exemplar was the Constituent Assembly of 1789, which he contrasted to the tyrannical and centralizing Convention and to the military revolution of Napoleon. "For our part we date our politics from '89, not '92 or 1800."[20] To ensure that his revolution would not be confused with violent overthrow, he repeatedly coupled it with the revolution of 1830, which had led to the present constitutional system.[21] His aim was to establish revolution as a unifying myth and this required a particular and highly idealized construction of events which, more than any other, had divided Frenchmen:

> What distinguished the Revolution of 1789 from all the others, what sets it apart and above, is that it was accomplished, not to promote the exclusive supremacy of one class, one party, one interest, one opinion, but to assure to each class, party, interest, and opinion the general freedom to think and, so far as public order allows, the liberty to act. It intended to create for all citizens, whatever their position, birth, or fortune certain rights. . . . [I]t wanted to open to all the road which, by effort and merit, leads to wealth and power.[22]

The great end of Tocqueville's efforts can be seen as an attempt to give liberalism, that child of fiendishly abstract doctrines—first of natural right, then of classical political economy, and finally of utilitarian individualism—a cultural and historical grounding, a foundation myth to elevate the political above the ideology of a class. For Tocqueville all societies required a unifying set of beliefs, a central political myth, and a shared set of moral practices. Because the French Revolution had destroyed most traditional beliefs in hierarchy, privileged classes, and institutional religion, a new identity had to be carved. He would set out on a bold, perhaps hopeless, project of sanitizing the revolution by bracketing its fury and terror and replacing it with a unifying myth of the nation. Included in the myth was religion, the revolution's historical antagonist. Admittedly, to accomplish this unlikely union of opposites required a certain political dexterity, if not disingenuousness: one had to distill "the principles of the revolution" and sharply distinguish them from "revolutionary habits."[23] The struggles of the eighteenth century, Tocqueville claimed, had given rise to certain passions, habits, and ideas whose unfortunate residue in the mores of later generations worked against the possibility of a political revival. Foremost was the animosity toward the church that resulted in denying politics a much needed source of moral authority. A further impediment was the suspicions against all forms of "superiority," a leftover from the struggles against aristocracy.[24]

Tocqueville proceeded to construct a revolution that represented not the class struggle of his 1835 essay or the revolution of his later masterwork on the Old Regime, but a politician's assessment of the habits, passions, anxieties, and beliefs of a political culture deposited by the revolution. His starting point depended heavily on the construct developed in *Democracy* of an apolitical condition, a politics without a public, that prepared the way for despotism. French politics, he declared, was enveloped by a malaise of apathy, which left it petty, egotistical, unprincipled, passively agreeing to be administered rather than governed. "[T]he passions of patriotic devotion, liberty, independence, human fraternity, those great and noble passions which were the life and glory of the revolution of 1789" have been exhausted. "The nation has not abandoned certain political opinions" derived from the revolution but "it has abandoned politics."[25] The citizen "considers political life an alien thing whose care he disregards" as he concentrates on "his personal and individual interest." The political life remaining "seems only an opportunity to satisfy particular interests."[26] Tocqueville traced the origins of alienation back to the revolution and its destruction of a system that had integrated interests around hierarchical principles. In place of hierarchy the revolution created a society of peasant proprietors, small entrepreneurs, and manufacturers and replaced hierarchy with equality and individual property rights. The result was a striking homogeneity of interests throughout society. The politics generated by those interests was notable not for its injustices but for "the extinction of political life."[27]

Tocqueville's portrait was of an estranged political with no common interests and no interest in the common. Actual politics appears as the reflection of a civil society dissolved into "particular interests." Floating above politics is its alienated opposite, the political, the symbol of "common ideas, common political passions, a common patriotism on which the government could be supported in putting each thing in its place and upholding the supremacy of the state over localities."[28] A liberal constitution had produced a politics freed of the political.

The project of political revival involved Tocqueville in a strategy of dispelling the fears of the middle class and the new peasant landholders. If they could be persuaded that a revolutionary outbreak was hardly possible, then they might be budged from supporting a simplistic politics of order and persuaded to take the plunge into political life and, in the process, become accepting of conflicts as normal. In a series of *Letters on the Domestic Situation in France* (1843), he offered a rather curious argument that "revolution only happens when a country wants it" and, because revolution was so widely feared, there was little chance of it. His stronger claim—stronger within the limited political audience he addressed—was that the revolution had so thoroughly eliminated inequalities that the only remaining ones were those of marriage, heredity, family, and property; and it was unthinkable that these could be abolished without "attacking the institutions which rule all societies; it would not simply be a departure from a constitution but from humanity as well."[29]

On one particular dimension Tocqueville's discussion was, uncharacteristically, unequivocal. There was, he emphasized repeatedly, no need for further democratization of French institutions. Current practices were in that respect, if not in others, adequate for the state of the French "social condition" and of its *moeurs.* At a time when the public was worried about agitation among the workers, what was needed was not "more democracy" in the electoral requirements but "more morality."[30]

## VI

> *The Business of Government to secure to every Man his own, and to prevent the Crafty, Strong, and Rapacious, from pressing upon or circumventing the Weak, Industrious, and Unwary.*
>
> *Letters of Cato*[31]

In *Democracy* Tocqueville claimed that the Americans had demonstrated "invincibly" that "the middle classes can govern the State."[32] Although that conclusion may have been doubly wishful thinking with France in mind and Federalist rather than Jacksonian America as the evidence of middle-class *virtù,* it reflected a fundamental misjudgment on Tocqueville's part and a misunderstanding of what ruling meant in the age of the bourgeoisie. Tocqueville reasoned that because the bourgeoisie had become the dominant social class, it had inherited responsibility for the political and must discharge it in the time-honored manner: by "serving" as the governing class and "ruling" in the literal sense. In order to perform as a political class, the bourgeoisie would have to break with its economic reflexes and cultivate disinterestedness.

Tocqueville's analysis accepted as his starting point the liberal self-understanding that insisted on a clear distinction between politics and economics. Jean-Baptiste Say provided one of its classic formulations:

> For a long time the political [*la politique*] in the strict sense of the science of the organization of societies has been confused with political economy which teaches how the wealth which satisfies the needs of society is formed, distributed, and consumed. However, this wealth is essentially independent of political organization. If political liberty is more favorable to the development of wealth, the effect is indirect, in much the same way that it is more favorable to education.[33]

What would justice be like in the era of the bourgeoisie, of that class which proclaimed equal rights for all but whose political economy acknowledged that the production of social inequalities was the inevitable by-product of a free economy? The naturalistic conception of politics as an agonal contest among the strong set the problematic for the premodern practice of justice as a dispensation to those who were unequal in power. Each should be secured in what was properly his or rightly due him. The later icon of justice as a woman, blindfolded and weighing the scales equally, marked an advance over justice as a concession of the strong, although an ironic one; parties to a dispute were rarely equal and rarely women; even when the scales were equally weighted and justice did not place the status of the contending parties in the balance, the powerful would be heard if not seen.

Had justice to retie or slip its blindfold and look at the parties with an unblinded (woman's?) eye? What changes would have to take place in conceptions of the political for unblinded justice to prevail?

## VII

> *How could any virtue or good faith survive in a society whose basic maxim is that economics has nothing to do with justice, that it is totally separate from it, that the idea of economic justice is an economic utopia.*
>
> P.-J. Proudhon[34]

Although the defense of the system of justice and the property rights of employers would become defining political matters for Tocqueville, the idea of justice did not figure importantly in any of his theoretical inquiries. Like some of his liberal contemporaries, he assumed that because impartial judicial procedures had been written into law, the problem of justice had largely been settled. While he recognized that great revolutions do not halt at the same time or place for all groups and that a large population of poor, sick, and uneducated had hardly benefited at all from the changes that had accompanied modern revolutions, that insight did not stimulate him to develop a theory of justice. The great question was whether the economy, which liberal political economy had delineated as a distinct domain with sharply defined boundaries and distinctive, though unlegislated, "laws" of its own, was to be politicized, subjected to requirements of justice arrived at politically; or whether the political would be economized, its practices and norms subjected to criteria inspired by political economy and reshaped accordingly.

In a move that was tantamount to the economizing of the political, liberal thinking shifted responsibility for the well-being of the society to the unseen hand of the economy. Nowhere was this more evident than in the use of economic status to deny equal political status. According to the liberal Constant, economic fact takes precedence over political right: "Those who are kept in poverty by eternal dependence and who are condemned by it to daily labour, are neither more knowledgeable than children about public affairs, nor more interested than foreigners in national prosperity. . . . Property alone makes men capable of exercising political rights."[35] When translated into politics political economy amounted to "bourgeoisification," not because the bourgeois achievers threw themselves into politics but rather because they preferred to rule indirectly through political employees. What had been an *agon* was transformed into a strategy for exploiting legal forms and parliamentary processes by means of a new form of political agency that substituted politicians for retainers.

While liberals theorized individual freedom and constitutional limitations on the powers of government, others were beginning to theorize against the prevalence of misery and for expanding state power into the domain of economic "laws." Justice became a major focus of thinkers and social movements protesting the consequences resulting from modernity's equation that liberal politics plus classical economics equals a political economy. None of the terms of that equation were about equality, while its conclusion, political economy, acknowledged inequality to be inherent in the structure of the modern market economy. In reaction to the usurpation of the political by economy and the rejection of the traditional role of the political as the protector of commonality, theorists in France increasingly employed the "social" as a term of criticism for emerging capitalism and postrevolutionary politics. Usages such as "social science," "socialism," and "social justice" testified to a widespread perception that the political no longer represented the interests of society as a whole, that it signified partiality as well as weakness, and that some more inclusive, just, and communal conception was needed. Conversely, liberal theory tended to repress the "social" and to concentrate on the more manageable project of controlling access to the political.

The push to extend the scope of justice and enlarge the political by socializing both justice and the political might be described, as it shortly would be in France, as social democratic rather than liberal. Its representatives demanded a politics open to excluded groups, including women and workers, and the use of state power to reduce the sufferings caused by inequality, even to promote employment. In short, to assert the political as an active force in the domain of economy.

In response liberalism could rightly claim to be unrivaled in its inclusiveness, at least in theory. Owing primarily to eighteenth-century liberal thinkers, universal equality of rights had become a distinctive element in modernity's self-definition. The modern natural rights argument in the American Declaration of Independence or the French Declaration of the Rights of Man and of the Citizen was directed at ridding societies of privilege and inherited inequalities. What, then, could be more universally inclusive than "the rights of man"? Although their political economy accepted inequality and periodic exclusions (e.g., unemployment), liberals denied that either one was the result of any deliberate policy of discrimination and, instead, contended that they were occasioned by the nature of the economy, by scarcity of resources, and, in an updating of Machiavelli's eternal struggle between *fortuna* and *virtù*, by what Constant called "the multiple contingencies of chance, or because some worked harder than others."[36]

For Tocqueville universality had seemed unthreatening under the conditions prevailing in the United States. Unlimited economic opportunities, abundance rather than scarcity of resources, and the virtual absence of significant class divisions ("no proletarians in America") encouraged him to be somewhat tolerant toward the prospect of a democratized political life. Yet in *Democracy* he had also maintained that the modern idea of rights would, of necessity, be driven by self-interest, that the momentum of equality would not permit its champions to be content with equal political rights, and that inevitably they would demand equal distribution of property.[37] Tocqueville did not raise the possibility that under conditions of economic scarcity, the same self-interest that made men treasure their political rights might also make them loath to extend them to the social classes whose self-interest they feared.

Was universality, then, to be modernity's proud badge of identity or its historical embarrassment? Perhaps both—and its exposed flank. When universality of rights is asserted amid clear evidence to the contrary, it serves to provoke a claim that something is being "hidden," that "behind" the declarations of universality were tacit agreements or "deals" that violated the letter or spirit of publicly proclaimed principles of right and justice. Universality thus becomes suspect and gives rise among both victims and victimizers to a politics of suspicion and to strongly ideological accusations.

## VIII

Tocqueville had predicted in *Democracy* that the impending triumph of equality would remove the cause of revolutionary resentment. Ironically, the advance of equality seemed instead to sharpen the allures of inequality and to alarm the defenders of modern universality into seeking refuge in a formalistic conception of equality and a more traditional notion of inequality as "inherent" in the nature of man and society. A clear expression of this position was Tocqueville's own *Memoir on Pauperism* (1835).

The *Memoir* was a sustained attack on current attempts to alleviate poverty by establishing a "right" to public charity and a defense of the notion that inequality was the sign of inferiority. "The idea of rights," Tocqueville asserted, "elevates and sustains the human spirit" like nothing else because it raises the recipient to "the same level as the one who grants it." In contrast, "the right of the poor to obtain society's help is unique." "[I]nstead of elevating the heart" of the recipient, "it lowers him" to the status of a "suppliant." "What is the achievement of this right if not a notarized manifestation of misery, of weakness, of misconduct on the part of the recipient?" Unlike "ordinary rights" that are gained by virtue of "some personal advantage acquired over their fellow men," the right to public charity "is accorded by reason of a recognized inferiority."[38]

Tocqueville's *Memoir* reveals how *ancien régime* notions of natural inferiority might resonate with capitalist economics and be absorbed into liberalism. A system of "public welfare," Tocqueville declared, will "dry up the sources of savings, will stop the accumulation of capital, will retard the development of trade, [and] will benumb human industry and activity." The demagogic expression of the melding of the Old Order with the New was to conjure up the specter of 1789: the end result of welfare policies, Tocqueville predicted, will be "a violent revolution" by the legions of poor, who "will find it easier to plunder [the haves] of all their property at one stroke than to ask for their help."[39]

Tocqueville treated the idea of social class as a faithful rendition of human inequalities, due not so much to "nature," as he had suggested in *Democracy*,[40] but to modernity's surrogate for nature, the "laws" of economy; accordingly, the alleviation of abject poverty fell primarily to Christian charity rather than to the state and the objects of charity were to be treated as dependents on private benevolence rather than as citizens. Philanthropy is the symbolic act by which dependency is privatized and superiority publicized: the act of stooping to distribute largesse to the powerless, of (dis)interest pointedly calling attention to its transgression of the regnant norm of self-interest. Philanthropy: virtue in the age of the bourgeoisie but also testimony to *ancienneté*'s marginalized role in the moral economy of liberalism.

Philanthropy is more intimately connected with Tocqueville's way of theorizing than an association of it with charity would suggest. The norm of disinterestedness, which had figured prominently in Tocqueville's ideal of political action, represented an attempt to apply to politics another philanthropy, one distinctive of theoretical activity: the theorist as truth teller, truth as philanthropic gesture. In 1843 he had tried to rally a political opposition around the banner of disinterestedness, saying that in the struggle the opposition would be armed only with "ardent convictions" and "disinterested passions."[41]

In *Democracy* there is a revealing example of the sort of philanthropic politics produced when theoretical disinterestedness combines with social superiority. It occurs in the course of Tocqueville's most extended discussion of rights. For more than a half century theorists had been engaging in changing the entire discourse about human rights, using notions of utility or of natural rights or principles of justice to argue either for the extension of political rights to all adult males or their restriction to the propertied and educated. In contrast, Tocqueville's approach remained rooted in Old Regime paternalism and moralism. Rights, he averred, were "nothing other than the concept of virtue applied to the political world."[42] Virtue, he explained, is demonstrated by obeying superiors.[43] "Certain rights"—a phrase which Tocqueville did not elaborate beyond alluding to property rights—should be given to "all." To those who might be skeptical that "all" could be trusted to exercise their rights virtuously, Tocqueville offered the example of how children are taught/made to learn the proper notion of right. At first the child is unable to distinguish his possessions from those of others. "What takes place with a child and his toys happens later with the man and all of the belongings that are his."[44] The really "dangerous" moment comes, however, when a people is given political rights after having been deprived of them. Tocqueville describes what occurs at such "a time of crisis": "A child may kill when he is ignorant of the value of life; he carries off other people's property before he knows that his own may be snatched from him. The man of the people, at the moment when he receives political rights, is in the same position as regards those rights as the child is toward the whole of nature."[45] With that teaching as guide, when class tensions seek political expression, when the "child" incarnated as "man of the people" demands rights, then disinterestedness responds not by expanding equality but by summoning the repressive element in philanthropy's understanding of the political: deference, order, and authority, the political that distrusts as it diminishes the citizen.

## IX

In probing those concerns Tocqueville helped to develop a set of markers delineating liberalism from democracy and socialism. As the project took shape what had begun as the quest for a unifying myth ended in ideology. The extended quotation cited earlier had exposed a glaring fault line, between the universality of "certain rights" for "all citizens" and inequality, "the road which by effort and merit, leads to wealth and power." Universality as the new road to inequality represented a defining moment: the choice of a less inclusive, more selective liberalism. The net effect was to consolidate an ideological rampart rather than to advance a public philosophy. As a consequence, Tocqueville can be accounted a contributor to the secular decline in the estimation of democracy that set in among the influential social classes and political elites of the nineteenth and twentieth centuries and helped to drive socialists toward more desperate remedies. Although Tocqueville might exhort his friends to join with him in pursuing "something really new" in politics, in the next breath he would add that this meant "fleeing with all our might from the nonsense" being spouted on the left by Lamartine, one of the leaders in the struggle for social reforms.[46] He could identify the phenomenon that threatened the fundamental principle of democracy, which he himself had done most to publicize: "Everywhere equality is extending its sway except in industry, which is organized more and more in an aristocratic form."[47] That insight was crowded out by another that interested him more because it played upon the fears he shared with the bourgeoisie while appealing to the heroic impulses that were his alone.

The workers, he warned, would organize their growing numbers into a revolutionary force. Moreover, a section of the republican party drew its support from the lower classes, which wanted to change the social order even more than the form of government.[48] That prospect, far from prodding him into thinking about how the new inequalities might have stalled democracy at a predemocratic stage, suggested a new means of political revival. In the growing anger of the working classes, he first glimpsed the same possibility as his later compatriot, Georges Sorel, that proletarian anger might stiffen the resolve of the bourgeoisie and inaugurate an era of authentic politics. But where Sorel would propose a "myth of the general strike" as a means of focusing the energies and idealism of the workers, Tocqueville would incorporate religion into the new ideology. He wanted to revive the hegemony of religion without seeking to restore "the debris of another age," as Tocqueville called the old system of throne and altar.[49] Tocqueville's religion was more than an anodyne against mass disorder. He looked upon it as simultaneously the principal source of popular morality and as its opposite, a powerful antidote to the modern banalization of everyday life. "[I]n the midst of this swarm of petty matters, small interests, small ambitions, the horizon of our thoughts and sentiments threatens to grow ever narrower." The mind and feelings need "objects greater than ourselves."[50]

During the 1840s he defended the autonomy of church schools, the academic freedom of Catholic teachers critical of modernist philosophies, and the rights of religious associations. His foremost concern was not religiosity but order, the principal value of the Old Regime and increasingly that of an anxious middle class. "Belief," he declared, assures "that element of morality, stability, and tranquillity of life that alone makes [liberty] grand and fruitful."[51] The French Revolution had destroyed all of the other embodiments of hierarchy and authority; if religion decays then order will depend on "soldiers and prisons."[52]

His invocation of religion in the name of "stability" and order represented a moment of hesitation before his own teaching in *Democracy* that conflict and occasional disorder were an inseparable part of a free politics. By enlisting religion in support of the political, he meant to persuade the bourgeoisie that a political order could be liberal and strong. It was not at all clear, however, that the bourgeoisie did not prefer the state to be strong only when occasions demanded it. Tocqueville was resisting the possibility that in the new society a culture of political apathy was not a denial of the political but the expression of its intermittent relevance; the bourgeoisie's commitment to political action during the revolution was, like revolution itself, an extraordinary deviation or rupture but not a life-form. The old political would become relevant when public order itself was jeopardized: then the bourgeoisie could be galvanized to counter revolution.

## X

While Tocqueville's foray into political education was a response to the modern phenomenon of bourgeois ascendancy, its limitations reflected the premodern understanding that political education, like the higher truths of statecraft, philosophy, and theology, was a matter for the few. That assumption had begun to crumble nearly two centuries earlier, most notably because of the Protestant revolution, which demoted the priest and elevated the congregation. Beginning in mid-seventeenth-century England the civic body, too, began slowly to enlarge. Revolutionary movements spread from the body of believers to the body politic. The people, a more unwieldy and complex presence, made its appearance as an actor. Before that century was over, the claim that the people were the true sovereign had become a commonplace in the polemics of the age. The new actor was accompanied by new ideas and new demands: about natural rights, legal protection for all citizens, expansion of the suffrage, more frequent elections of representatives, and the culminating idea of popular sovereignty. A demotic political culture gave signs of emerging. To the theoretically minded, however, that prospect provoked the question of whether the idea of political education was suddenly reduced to an oxymoron.

Modernity's early theoretical response was to seek ways of neutralizing the demos while enlisting its allegiance. The desperation of that strategy was expressed in one of Hobbes's fantastic metaphors. He imagined "men" as agreeing to accept "Artificiall Chains" of law "fastened at one end" to "the Soveraigne Power and at the other end to their own Ears."[53] But if the "ear" of "men" was to respond in the desired way, obediently, it had to be prepared. Hobbes took the task to be a comparatively easy one. He simply assumed that the common people had no culture, only minds "like clean paper, fit to receive whatsoever by Publique Authority shall be imprinted in them."[54]

Although Hobbes recognized the people as an important object of thought, he could not conceive it as an active political subject. A dogmatic nominalist,

Hobbes maintained that the people could not act as a corporate entity, because such entities were wholly fictitious. Accordingly, in Hobbes's scenario it is not "the people" but individuals who sign the covenant surrendering all rights and powers to authority. When Hobbes had need of a corporate conception of the people, however, he did not hesitate to smuggle it back if only for the restricted purpose of indoctrinating them with the proper beliefs about authority. Despite his animus against Catholicism he incorporated its notion of a uniform belief system imposed by authority upon an essentially passive body of believers. The attraction of that model was its efficiency: a uniform culture imposed on uniformly empty minds producing uniform obedience.

Hobbes's obtuseness in refusing to recognize that the people, instead of being a tabula rasa, was freshly inscribed with revolutionary notions and infused with revolutionary passion, a development repeated later in America in the 1770s and in France in 1789, nonetheless, represented, a decisive turning point in political theory. Hobbes was the first modern secular thinker—theologians had done the same for centuries—to conceptualize, indeed to reify, the idea of culture as a system of beliefs "cultivated" by authority, that is, disseminated throughout the society so that its members would tend to act in predictable ways. Culture was, in Hobbes's words, the "means or Conduit" for promoting uniformity of belief and predictable conduct. Culture thus became objectified as a discrete system that, like a legal or educational system, could be acted upon and managed in accordance with the sovereign's wishes.[55]

Hobbes's solution for cultural control would be undermined by the very forms of scientific knowledge and technological innovation he admired. These distinctive modern modes of power would radically challenge and alter the traditional assumptions about political education with its reliance on simple communication between teacher and pupil. New means of teaching, such as newspapers, journals, broadsides, pamphlets, theater, art, and music vastly expanded the number of those who could or should be instructed. Virtue, knowledge, and action had now to be conceived in terms of vast numbers who would participate rather than rule. This raised a perplexing problem. The virtue of the Many had traditionally been conceived in passive terms or, at best, of unthinking support. Modernity complicated all of that. Modern skepticism proceeded to extend the idea of the "critical" from the ruling circle of the Few to anyone who was able to avail himself or herself of the means of disseminating ideas. Plebeian theorists, such as Rousseau and Paine, emerged as political teachers. Although modernity did not invent the idea of the critical, it did invest it with new powers. The critical would have strong links to notions of revolt. Indeed, disobedience, freedom to criticize, and the right to revolution were integral to the teachings of modern political theorists such as Locke, Paine, and Jefferson. Civic virtue was being expanded to include not only support but opposition and dissent, not only from the oppressed but from the disinherited and the disaffected, from Paine but also from de Maistre.

The revolutionary heritage of modernity meant that the task of political education could no longer be based on the premodern assumption that education was synonymous with the transmission of knowledge or political truths. But if revolutionary modernity rejected the theoretically based political truths of the Platos, Aristotles, and Machiavellis, it also canceled the claims of Montesquieu, Rousseau, and Burke to the effect that although it might no longer be possible for an elitist political education grounded in truth, there could be a popular political culture of historical preservation based on settled customs, habits, and traditional practices. The quickened tempos of modernity and its revolutionary spasms undermined both the culture of truth and the culture of mores, each of which assumed certain temporal continuities. Political culture was being reduced to "beliefs"—and modern beliefs, by definition, were continuously contested and left uncertain, hence impermanent.

# CHAPTER XXII
# *SOUVENIRS*: RECOLLECTIONS IN/TRANQUILLITY

## I

> *[T]he* work, *whether of the artist or the philosopher, invents the man who has created it, who is supposed to have created it.*
>
> Nietzsche[1]

Chronologically *Souvenirs* represents an intermediate point between Tocqueville's first great work, *Democracy in America*, and his last, *The Old Régime*. Politically it spans the beginning, apogee, and end of his political career. Tocqueville wrote *Souvenirs* during 1850–51, after he had been forced from office in October 1849. He continued to serve as a deputy until Louis Napoleon's coup of 2 December 1851. It is clear from the existing manuscript that when Tocqueville first undertook the project, he assumed his political retirement to be temporary; he ceased writing one month before the coup. The intervening confusion may have made him hesitant to publish immediately. With the rapid consolidation of the Bonapartist despotism and the institution of censorship, publication was no longer feasible. The fact that *Souvenirs* was never published in his lifetime attaches a presumption of incompleteness.[2]

Although Tocqueville describes the revolutionary events of February 1848 and the abortive revolts of June 1848 and June 1849, he chose not to include either the counterrevolutionary response that culminated in Napoleon's coup of December 1851 or the despotism that soon followed. The manuscript breaks off abruptly, as though in deference to events still unfolding. In another sense, however, the manuscript, while incomplete, was finished. The author's political career was ended and his theoretical position in disarray. The parallel between the disintegration of national and personal identity is complete when France submits to a new tyranny and Tocqueville is forced into political oblivion. *Souvenirs* is the trace of that suspended moment.

Of all of Tocqueville's works, *Souvenirs* is the most self-dramatizing. Tocqueville is at once author and actor in the events being portrayed and thus enjoys a privilege few actors have, of performing on a stage of their own design. What is staged is part recording, part re-view, and a virtual pun on the double meaning of "recall" (*se souvenir*), either as summons or as remembrance of how the actors and events appeared to him at the time. In remembering past actions and events from the vantage point of the distance he now has—*Souvenirs* was completed from afar, in Sorrento—he can superimpose on remembrance a theoretical layer of understanding. Tocqueville will depict himself, not simply autobiographically, but as a symbolic actor whose being constitutes the site where a political crisis and a personal crisis converge, propelling society toward an uncertain future while provoking Tocqueville into a moment of self-discovery and political deliverance—even a rare, if fleeting, experience of certitude and fulfillment.

*Souvenirs* is not, in a simple sense, self-serving. Tocqueville tries to recreate his confusions, not smooth them out or even resolve them. Accordingly, he claims only limited prescience and abstains from portraying an author/actor who is omniscient about the causes behind the events or about their outcome.[3] "I was never able then to discern fully [where truth, honor, and men of goodwill were] and I declare that even now I am unable to do it well."[4] Those words hint at a debacle, the nature of which becomes clearer if *Souvenirs* is supplemented by Tocqueville's contemporaneous correspondence with his most intimate friends. His constant lament, in both the correspondence and in *Souvenirs*, is his inability to "see," to grasp theoretically where events were heading and what actions were needed. Instead,

> that obscurity, more and more profound, which spreads over the tableau, always so obscure, that we call the future. Put yourself in the position of a voyager who sails on a moonless December night shrouded in fog; then tell me what little pleasure he would have in observing through his window the passing view. . . . This man is France. It is such a night that surrounds us. The men who have spyglasses do not see any further than those who have only their naked eyes . . . in the meantime they arrive together at the abyss.[5]

Tocqueville's impasse was a product of a set of political conditions significantly different from those traditionally postulated or assumed by political writers. To theorists as contrasting as Plato and Machiavelli the challenge was to shape or cajole actors into becoming the instrument of theoretical truth. Tocqueville's project was far more complex. He longed to be the actor-instrument of his own theory in a political medium largely unknown to political theorists before the nineteenth century. It should be remembered that while parliamentary politics existed in England and congressional-presidential politics in the United States, France had just begun the practice and, unlike England and the United States, political party organization barely existed.[6] Tocqueville was attempting to combine theory and action in a new parliamentary setting complicated, first, by the presence of monarchy, then by a presidency, and repeatedly by revolutionary upheavals of a uniquely modern kind. Previous to Tocqueville, the only political theorist whose reference point could be called consistently parliamentary was Edmund Burke. While the latter's political thinking was addressed to a milieu defined by parliamentary politics, it did not have to deal with revolution at home; and unlike Tocqueville, who would eventually experience politics under conditions approximating universal male suffrage, Burke's political setting was considerably narrower. The unreformed electorate was small and corrupted; it was not until late in the eighteenth century that the Commons permitted its debates to be published. Burke could effectively appeal to the element of *ancienneté* Tocqueville's politics lacked, the living presence of an "ancient constitution."

## II

Revolution is perhaps the most complex collective experience to render theoretically. It appears as movement for large-scale change that grips a whole society, yet it seems out of control, centerless. No one form of discourse seems capable of comprehending its contradictions, ambiguities, or crosscurrents. It may unsettle without being decisive. At a minimum revolution signifies both the breakdown, or breakup, of an established version of the political and a demand for its reconstitution. Revolution also creates on a large-scale what Tocqueville most dreaded, uncertainty.

Not surprisingly *Souvenirs* is the most enigmatic of Tocqueville's major writings,[7] yet its obscure, even puzzling qualities tend to be overlooked possibly because *Souvenirs* seems less a theoretical work than a participant's memoir, an insider's observations of the revolution of 1848, and more suited to be documentary material for the historian and biographer. Tocqueville himself disclaimed any intention "to compose a history of the revolution of 1848"[8] and avowed that the work was written only for himself. Instead of writing history he would try to combine an explanation of events and their meaning with a parallel attempt to understand the reasons for his own actions and inactions. The self for which *Souvenirs* is being written, however, is a chastened self who had sought to combine two roles but now is finding one closed off. In December 1850, while finishing *Souvenirs*, he wrote to a friend that "I am better at thinking than at action, and if anything of mine survives in this world it will bear the traces more of what I have written than the recollection of what I have done."[9] Earlier, however, in a letter of April 1848 to Beaumont, Tocqueville had been emphatic about where his commitments lay. "Politics has become our career. . . . Perhaps there will now be a moment when action could be glorious. . . . It seems to me that we are about to begin a new political life."[10]

In contrast to Machiavelli's *Prince* —a work also colored by the resentment of an embittered ex-officeholder—*Souvenirs* would provide no recipes for successful actions. Tocqueville is mostly preoccupied with, even fixated upon, unsuccessful actions, especially with his own failure before 1848 to establish (what might be called) his positive theory of a new kind of liberalism. Ironically, the driving force behind that defeat had been anticipated by Tocqueville's own analysis, his "theoretical theory," which had warned that the dynamics of inequality would not halt with political equality. To be both vindicated and defeated by the same events is grist enough for intense introspection. The reader should consider that he or she may be an uninvited guest and, bearing in mind the words with which Tocqueville began his reminiscences, "Removed for the moment from the theater of affairs . . . ," remember as well that while all politicians desire public vindication, fallen politicians privately seek revenge.

## III

> *I wrongly believed that I would find again on the [parliamentary] tribune the success which my book had met.*
>
> Tocqueville[11]

*Souvenirs* lacks the finality of the typical political memoir: it is uncertain about the eventual course of the events it records, about whether France will manage to preserve a republican form, or will suffer a social revolution, or succumb to despotic rule. Only one matter appears settled. Tocqueville's personal political project had failed. *Souvenirs* is the epitaph to a half-dozen years of effort on Tocqueville's part to change French political life by applying the theoretical principles derived from observing democracy in the United States and formulated with France always "in mind." The unstated question for a reader of *Souvenirs* is, however, which America did he now have in mind?

In 1848 Tocqueville injected *Democracy* into the developing revolutionary situation in the preface written for the twelfth edition. From being an achievement that belonged to his past, he restores *Democracy* to immediacy, elevated to the status of an *Ur*-text, and given a certain emphasis so as to persuade an audience of its direct relevance. He claimed that because of that work he was not surprised by the momentous events taking place. To make his meaning clear, he drew attention to a passage where he had warned that the democratic movement would not halt before threatening "the middle classes and the rich." He owned the work to have been "prophetic": "actual circumstances have given the book a topical interest and practicality which it did not have when it first appeared."[12] Because France was now a republic, the overriding question was whether it would enjoy a "tranquil," "regular" republic respectful of "the sacred rights of property and family" or face a radical democracy bent on destroying those values. America is touted as the republic that has "solved" the problems inherent in democracy. It is "not only the most prosperous but the most stable of all the peoples in the world." Private property and other rights are "better guaranteed" there than anywhere else on earth. The current stakes, he warned, involve not just France but "all the nations around us."[13] The preface makes no explicit mention of socialism; perhaps none was needed.

*Souvenirs* forms part of a cycle in the tactical uses of America and in the status of *Democracy in America.* In his writings during the years immediately preceding the outbreak of revolution in 1848, Tocqueville used American democracy to oppose socialism, to emphasize the value of religion for mass control, and to exemplify the importance of private property as the basis of political order. America had served as the example of how revolution could be combatted by democracy. While he had appealed to the American example in support of the cause of moderate liberal reforms and the revitalization of *civisme*, that emphasis, which had become noticeably attenuated as 1848 loomed nearer, now disappears. Participatory America, the America of civil associations and local democracy, is suppressed theoretically at the very moment that comparable developments are emerging and acquiring crucial importance in France. When participatory democracy appears in France in the form of producers' cooperatives, mutual-aid societies, workingmen's associations, local political clubs, and discussion circles, Tocqueville's response is consistently hostile.[14] Thus, when he is about to run for reelection, he instructs his political agent to exploit the fears of those who will be most threatened "by the ultrademocratic doctrines of the free commune, of offices open to all without conditions, of the capacity of everyone to do everything."[15] When participatory politics is mixed up with revolutionary ferment, it appears threatening and is suppressed. Sadly, the uses of *Democracy* will come full circle a few years later in *The Old Regime*, where Tocqueville belatedly retrieves the America of participatory democracy and fashions it into an implicit criticism of the despotism of Louis Napoleon.

As a work of theory *Souvenirs* marks a midpassage in Tocqueville's changing attitudes, particularly toward democracy and revolution. *Democracy* had represented the future as qualified promise and might even be read as futuristic for its hopeful prophecies about equality. In contrast, *The Old Regime* would reverse directions and compose elegiacally an inegalitarian past; *Souvenirs* would be about the present as threat or, more precisely, where the future, represented by radical equality, collides with an antirevolutionary present in a moment prepared by a revolutionary past. Events of 1848 would furnish Tocqueville, who had come to despise "the long parliamentary comedy,"[16] with a substitute target: workers demanding admission into public life as actors and socialist theories attacking the foundations of the bourgeois hegemony. Those challenges would force him closer to the repressive spirit of *The Penitentiary System* than to the modernist sympathies of *Democracy in America.* The year 1848 may have been, as a historian of an earlier generation put it, a turning point on which the century forgot to turn; but Tocqueville, for one, made a turn—to the right. Or, more precisely, the combination of secretly welcoming the revolution that appeared to have overthrown the bourgeois political system and of opposing a worker's revolution produced the odd phenomenon of a counterrevolutionary who welcomed revolution and who believed for one brief moment, following the bloody suppression of the worker revolt of June 1848, that a turning point had occurred.

## IV

"[T]hese recollections," Tocqueville tells himself, "are to be a relaxation of my mind, not a literary work."[17] Why should a work dealing with exciting, tumultuous events be the stuff of relaxation? What is being relaxed in the course of being recollected? How should *Souvenirs* be approached if it was apparently not meant to be read by others—as a soliloquy perhaps rather than a record?

A start might be made by describing *Souvenirs* as a work that crisscrosses between the recording of public events and actions and the recording of personal reactions to events and actors. What is relaxed is the boundary between the personal and the public. The inhibitions which that boundary had enforced are lowered. Likewise the boundary between theory and autobiography is dissolved in soliloquy, thereby allowing a meditation in which the habits of the confessional shape the course of self-examination. The cause of the relaxation of boundaries was the same as that for the personal, political, and theoretical: failure. Relaxation may also intimate that certain close connections have been "relaxed." In that sense *Souvenirs* records a moment when the carefully expressed and suppressed connections between the political, the theoretical, and the personal lie exposed and in confusion.

Tocqueville stipulates that events he was about to recollect were to be "retraced only for myself."[18] He describes the activity of recollection as "trying to recover the trace of my actions, of my ideas, and of my impressions over the course of that revolution."[19] The concern to retrieve personal experience of a recent past lends to the *Souvenirs* the initial appearance of an interior monologue, ofttimes meditative and confessional, rarely apologetic, occasionally defensive, and consistently disdainful of dialogue with his opponents. The impulse to privatize public events, including his own public actions, was inspired by a personal crisis of political identity culminating in a painful decision to abandon the political and theoretical self-image that he had fashioned by *Democracy in America* and that critical acclaim had reinforced. So Tocqueville writes that despite the difficulties of composing a sincere account, "I will try, nevertheless, to find myself again in this labyrinth."[20] The verb employed by Tocqueville, *retrouver*, has various shades of meaning (to recover, regain) that suggest the pain of prior loss and an attempt to reestablish the self by seeking it in events that then and afterward struck him as confused, even mysterious, a "labyrinth." Elusiveness lends to recovery a tinge of desperation. So Tocqueville clutches at the imagery of a "mirror." A mirror serves to hold a select number of objects in place, to control them momentarily; or, additionally, a mirror might catch the "true" self unawares, without its protective masks.[21]

## V

> *sincère*, adj. Qui s'exprime sans déguiser sa pensée.
>
> Larousse

The intimate, shielded character of *Souvenirs* allows for intimacies that Tocqueville had previously reserved for private correspondence and papers. One obvious feature of his personal writings is they are less guarded, particularly in respect to his political opinions. These are on some occasions more conservative and on others more liberal, but consistently more contemptuous of parliamentary politics than in his public utterances and occasional essays; and they openly display his frustrated ambitions for power and glory. *Souvenirs* frees Tocqueville to vent in private publicly suppressed grievances and resentments, to drop some of his public masks. He complains that because he had been "cruelly misunderstood," his true abilities had never found their proper outlet and his self-confidence had been sapped: "[E]ven today my most ghastly memory of those days is of the constant uncertainty in which I was forced to live regarding the best course of action for the day."[22] The expression of resentment is to be guided by a norm different from the truthfulness of the historian, one more appropriate to his double role as author and actor. "I wish that the expression of my recollections should be sincere."[23]

Why, in a work intended solely for his own eyes, should Tocqueville feel obliged to declare his sincerity? He defines the question as an aristocrat might, as one of honor. He feels compelled to add in a marginal note: "I confess that I have been honest more by instinct than principle. I would have found it very difficult to live as a rogue."[24] Thus, being honest by nature, he can pledge to make an honest effort to avoid flattering himself or his friends. The guarantee of his sincerity is the promise to himself that the work would remain "entirely secret."[25] After reading Tocqueville's mostly acid portraits of his friends as well as his enemies, a reader of *Souvenirs* might easily agree that, indeed, he had avoided flattering any of them. Sincerity signified more than honesty, however. It allowed for pride and for self-praise of actions of his own that could not be shared with a public of strangers.[26] Freed from the pressure to conform to the public persona trailing the author of *Democracy*, he could interrogate privately the public self, scrutinize his past commitments with a new eye, and work out a new identity, or, at least, become reconciled to living in times when no genuinely political identity was realizable.

The secrecy guaranteeing the sincerity of the *Souvenirs* was only one level of secrecy and sincerity. "I wish to reveal sincerely what are the hidden motives that caused them, myself as well as others, to act and, having understood them, to expose them."[27] To "expose" in private cannot bring public vindication; it may serve self-justification and symbolic revenge. Then the staging of events and actors on a private stage serves as the means of exploiting the private in order to compensate an aggrieved self, which feels deprived of its fair share of public recognition and blames that on a political setting congenial to his contemporaries but frustrating to one of his qualities and antecedents. Consequently their failure could vindicate his own.[28] Accordingly Tocqueville's procedure was not to analyze actions so much as to expose the weakness of actors overwhelmed by events. Events, in turn, are rendered as tableaux of confusion: deputies shouting, political leaders strutting but ineffectual, crowds menacing, malodorous, and uncertain, royalty insulted and helpless. The only constants are the shallow support for the political system and the moral and political failings of its operatives.

*Souvenirs* is also the record of a political triumph that is deeply personal and of which the public was unaware. It is the triumph of a political actor who finally makes up his mind to act. Despite some strong reservations, he is given a cause to which he can commit himself. He will be the defender of "order," of that primordial state of assured expectations that all political theorists, save the most resolute of anarchists, have proposed as a first principle. By itself, as an abstraction, order is a vacuous notion: stability or repression? That question suggests another motive for Tocqueville's secrecy. He opposed the February revolution but he welcomed the destruction of "the parliamentary world."[29] At the level of rejecting the existing system he was complicit with those he detested. Paradoxically, he is freed to act with decisiveness for a variety of reasons: because his own political prescription for a limited democracy has been discredited by events even as his prophecy of the irresistible march toward ever greater equality threatens to be fulfilled; because he is liberated by the failure of a liberal politics conceived as a rearguard action against the historical inevitability of democratic equality depicted in his own theory; and, finally, because the threat of socialism and the working class has lifted Tocqueville's personal curse of ambivalence. If he felt uncertain of his allies, he was confident of the identity of the enemy.

The decision to act seemed the fulfillment of Tocqueville's dream of heroic action, action that involved large stakes and high risks and tested character. It announced the central agonistics of *Souvenirs* between two forms of action pitted against each other, heroic action in defense of the fundamental order of society and revolutionary action to which Tocqueville begrudged the name heroic.

## VI

> *I do not know if it is because of the latest circumstances in which I find myself or the great seriousness which the age presents to thought, or the solitude in which I live. . . . I have never felt more painfully the weight of the obscurity which veils everything in the other world.*
>
> Tocqueville to Corcelle, 1 August 1850[30]

*Souvenirs* is filled with tensions arising from the interplay between the personal, the political, and theoretical. Each of the three elements is accorded an unusual intensity: the personal because of a crisis in the author's political identity; the political because of the new revolutionary challenge mounted by the workers; and the theoretical because of the peculiarity of the revolution of 1848 as an anticlimax rather than a seismic upheaval.

The *Souvenirs* records the emergence of a different Tocqueville from the one who had boldly set himself against the interests and thinking of most members of his social class to argue in *Democracy in America* for the irreversible and universal character of the movement toward democracy and equality. The theoretical action represented by *Democracy* and the "peace overtures" extended to the French Revolution in his speeches and essays of the 1840s were consistent with his chosen role of mediator and can be described as attempting to bind up, possibly even heal, historical wounds inflicted by the movement toward equality. The newly incarnated Tocqueville will tacitly discard the role of mediator-healer, even though he sees his society as "cut in two" by the threat of socialism.[31] Socialism stands for the opposite, which his liberalism and conception of the political cannot or will not mediate. To him it represents not a New World in which inequality, represented by the privileged, moneyed, and educated Few, might accommodate a measure of equality to the unprivileged, moneyless, and uneducated Many; it is, instead, an Inverted World in which equality appeared as repressive of inequality as inequality had once been of equality. Instead of viewing socialism, as some contemporaries were, as an attempt to extend the range of what was politically and economically shareable, he will choose to be the defender of order, even as the revolutionary situation was rendering that cliché less abstract and more illiberal: "I decided then to throw myself boldly into the arena, and to devote my fortune, person, and peace of mind to the defense, not of any form of government but of the laws which constitute society itself."[32]

The reasons for siding with reaction were numerous and deep-seated. Not the least was the incompatibility between Tocqueville's temperament and ideals and the parliamentary politics of his age. Certainly strong elements of class snobbery figured: unless a person impressed him as a rare being, Tocqueville confides, "I do not, so to speak, see him." He takes a certain satisfaction in recalling his inability to remember the faces of mediocre men and being forced to inquire about the names of those he meets daily—only to promptly forget them. "I honor them, for they lead the world, but they bore me profoundly." The distaste for the common is extended to public discourse. "[T]he discussion of matters which are of little interest is disagreeable to me, but of those which interest me greatly, sad; the truth is for me a thing so rare and precious that, when once I find it, I do not care to put it at risk in a debate."[33] Against the bourgeoisie, as against the proletariat, Tocqueville presents himself as the signifier of differentiation—by lineage, class, and upbringing—confronting the undifferentiated.

By the late twentieth century postmodernity would have forgotten that its highly prized value of "difference" was once the property of traditionalists and elitists like Burke and Tocqueville.

The consistency of the Tocqueville of the *Souvenirs* derives from the exact opposite of the theme that had supplied coherence to *Democracy.* Now consistency consists in repeatedly denouncing political and social equality, and (as he put it) in voting "without hesitation" for all measures that would "establish order and discipline in society and defeat the revolutionary and socialist party." He commits himself to opposing these expressions of egalitarianism with the zeal of one who finally felt free to voice his true convictions.[34] Although in the *Souvenirs* he occasionally indulged in wistful thinking about the revival of the aristocracy, more often than not he knew that that prospect was about as promising as an efflorescence of civic virtue among the bourgeoisie. The stark consequence of Tocqueville's self-examination is the revelation of a political man with no politics to which he could attach himself, who drifts toward the plane where the political is so rarefied as to be virtually devoid of politics of the quotidian variety; who finds an allegiance beyond petty politics, in the "nation," "order," and the domain of foreign affairs, and who is fatefully drawn, if temporarily, toward repression, toward the antipolitical.

Unlike his personal and political situation when he wrote *Democracy in America,* there was in 1848 no natural distance between himself and the political society he is observing, no natural contrast between the "old" and the "new world." The absence of historical and spatial distance makes possible the tensions, even the agony of *Souvenirs.* These were not the result alone of the stresses and anxieties produced by a revolutionary situation but of a personal political identity forced to choose only to find the choices almost equally repugnant: "my true cause is lost."[35]

Tocqueville had heroized American democracy, making its achievements match its scale; and by extension, he heroized his own theoretical achievement as an epical encounter with the gathering power of equality. Neither the contents of the theory nor the heroic postures of its author provided a helpful preparation for the actual encounter with a politics that combined the forms most likely to offend aristocratic sensibilities: monarchy, bourgeois parliamentarism, the reduction of politics to party politics, and capitalism as legitimized greed. The forms had shrunk the possibilities of action, limiting them to rhetorical displays and behind-the-scenes negotiations on behalf of parochial interests.

The political self that he had constructed theoretically, through *Democracy in America,* began to disintegrate under the twin impact of worker revolutionaries seeking to reform a system and of their bourgeois opponents seeking to oppose them—and this upon a self only minimally committed to the system. In America, Tocqueville lamented, "I had spent the best days of my youth in the midst of a society which seemed to grow more in prosperity as it became freer." He then recalled the translation of that experience into his personal political creed: "from that I conceived the idea of a moderate, regularized liberty, constrained by religion [*croyances*], customs [*moeurs*], and laws." That conception of controlled liberty became the "passion. of my whole life," but now "I recognize clearly that it is necessary to renounce it."[36] He had failed in the attempt to combine liberal and traditional elements and to educate the bourgeoisie in the necessity of restraining self- and class interest so as to develop a political role commensurate with their social and economic power.

Yet, ironically, what finally punctured the heroic ideal was precisely the kind of political situation that, more than any other, should have provided the stuff of heroics. Revolution usually arouses expectations of some sort of decisive results, such as the triumph of a new social class or the toppling of a dynasty, and of some memorable deeds, such as the storming of a symbolic stronghold. The typical experiences recorded in *Souvenirs* are of ineffectualness and uncertainty, rendering it less a recollection of actions than of unheroic reactions, of his and of his contemporaries, to an extraordinary situation. No individual or party appears able to control what is happening, much less direct it. As a result the stereotype of revolution as a decisive turning point is continually subverted by events that are revolutionary yet indecisive and by actions that rarely deserve the name. The system seems to dissolve rather than be overthrown. Devoid of authentic action, overcrowded with mere "events," revolution might have been disposed of by treating it ironically—and Tocqueville often resorted to that device; but that solution only served to undercut his characteristically heroic standard of what constituted the proper subject of theory and of action.[37] The deflation of the revolution was carried over into Tocqueville's attempt to theorize revolution by historicizing it as merely the most recent installment in a dreary series of irresolute attempts at a political settlement. Yet that effort at devaluation is repeatedly called into question by Tocqueville's own insistence that the emergence of socialism, both as theory and political movement, was unprecedented in the annals of revolution. He wanted to assert that 1848 was both an installment in a preestablished sequence and a unique moment. This would enable him to deny that what was unique, socialism, was a political phenomenon, as were the preceding revolutions of 1789, 1815, and 1830. That, in turn, enabled him to ignore the vast array of political forms invented by ordinary people during the years before and after 1848—except for the festivals, which he pilloried. Thus the concept of "social" revolution serves to suppress the political fact that popular participation was being invented.

In attempting to portray the complexities of revolution manqué and the accompanying political confusion and, at the same time, seek for some redeeming epical dimension while denying it to the obvious candidate, Tocqueville deploys a variety of genres: introspective memoir, chronicle, vignette with a didactic aim—and theory.[38] The multiple genres allowed for flexibility, permitting scope not only for Tocqueville's previously displayed skill in projecting outsized historical panoramas and his painterly talent for assembling striking tableaux but also for an unsuspected gift for political portraiture, sometimes satirical, mostly critical, even destructive, seldom affectionate: his portrait gallery of feckless actors is introduced to illustrate the foibles of the system and explain the unconsummated character of the revolution. The stated purpose served by these various genres is to enable the author to sit in judgment on himself, on others, and on the political system as a whole. The judgments are not cool; they form a partisan, sometimes bitter, soliloquy in which the narrator recalls his yearnings to play the hero but finds himself performing as a politician. The tensions are also played out between the principal genres employed by Tocqueville: between the historian, who will recount what has happened; the theorist, who will try to project its meaning by establishing a signifying context of important ideas, such as freedom, socialism, order, and society; and the political actor, who seeks justification or excuse for what he has or might have done.

## VII

> *One needs to have spent years in the midst of party politics and the whirlwind which drives it to understand how far men mutually push each other from their intended aims and how the destiny of the world marches by the effect, although often contrary to the desires of those who produced it, like the kite which flies by the opposed action of wind and twine.*
>
> Tocqueville[39]

At the outset Tocqueville affixes to *Souvenirs* the character of a self-examination, an unmediated attempt at self-understanding: "I am condemned in the midst of my solitude to contemplate myself directly." It is not, however, a Cartesian meditation about a being that has deliberately privatized itself, divesting it of its prior public roles. *Souvenirs* is a private document about a being who had fashioned an essentially public identity and invested it in a conception of the political, which was then overwhelmed by the events being recalled, the same events that reduced him to political insignificance. Tocqueville confirms the point by revising the direct contemplation of himself saying, "or rather to summon before me the contemporary events in which I was an actor or which I had observed."[40] That abrupt shift, from direct self-contemplation to "summon[ing] events" in which he had been an actor, as well as the equally disjunctive categories of events in which he had acted and those which he had observed suggest a shift from a focus upon self-examination to constructing a series of tableaux that allow Tocqueville to see himself indirectly, by reflection. Tocqueville does not say that he will discuss his own actions per se but instead, like a character in a play, the "events" in which he was an "actor." That formula hints at a lack of personal efficacy in "the theater of affairs," at conformity to a script composed by someone else or imposed by no one at all. However, as the language of Tocqueville's next sentence suggests, efficacy denied in the events engaged in can be reclaimed by events recollected: remembering as the enforcement of retroactive control. In describing the best use he can make of his involuntary leisure Tocqueville employs some forceful imagery that hints at an element of violence necessitated by the daunting task of recollecting confusion and indecision and then finding that confusion has reappeared at the point where theory tries to combine with memory: "to retrace those events, to portray the men who had taken part in them before my eyes, and to grasp and, if I am able, thus engrave in my memory the confused features which formed the uncertain physiognomy of my times."[41]

What seems most striking about that passage is its anxious tone, the recurring fear of loss of control, and of its intellectual accomplice, doubt. Events must be captured or fixed because of the uncertainty in the broader context surrounding them. By *retracing* (i.e., tracing over), *portraying, grasping,* and *engraving* the events in "memory," he seeks through the distance provided by solitude to lend events a clarity/stability lacking when they were elements of the public swirl in which one had been immersed. His language discloses a continuing tension between theory, historical understanding, and action that threatens the attempt to stabilize. "Grasping" is typically associated with the theoretical activity of conceptualizing; "memory" and "portraying," with history, that is, with modes of ordering the past. "The confused features" of the "times" suggests the unstable flux associated with revolution, with what can only be sorted out or arranged at leisure, either by the theorist or the historian, but constitutes the immediatism of the actor who, too, wants to stabilize and reestablish order yet is uncertain of how those abstractions are to be realized concretely. The ordering modalities of history and theory in *Souvenirs* prefigure the thematic that was to define the substance of Tocqueville's new political program and the energy for his actions: "to reestablish order and discipline in society and to crush the revolutionary and socialist party."[42]

Tocqueville will find it important later in *Souvenirs* to remind himself of a hard-won insight, "my mind is such that it fears danger less than doubt"[43]. His uncertainty, combined with his remark that *Souvenirs* was begun in "solitude," evokes echoes of his old adversary, Descartes, and of the isolation in which the Cartesian *Discourse on Method* had originated. Descartes had relied upon the *cogito* (I think) to supply a firm starting point, *ergo sum* (therefore I am) from which to arrive at reliable knowledge, "clear and distinct ideas." Tocqueville started from the "confusion," personal and theoretical, of his thinking when he first attempted to recall the revolutionary days. Unlike Descartes his strategy is not only to look *into* himself but also *at* himself. The *Souvenirs,* he declares, "will be a mirror in which I will amuse myself by looking at my contemporaries and myself, and not a painting intended for the public."[44] He, not the public, is to judge.

That formulation, in which the mirror stands for truthfulness or verisimilitude, cannot but seem disingenuous. What is held up before his mirror is not randomly selected. In its own way it is as composed as a painted portrait. It is at best a personal painting for a private showing—as Tocqueville all but concedes in the extended marginal note he affixed to the passage.[45] "All paintings done of friends in their presence or shown publicly are faulty. The only true portraits are those intended not to be shown."[46] After the single reference, Tocqueville ceases to employ the mirror metaphor, possibly because it does not convey thoughtfulness and seems to exclude theoretical perspective, whereas a painting or tableau, like a theory, is a composition that presupposes perspective and demands premeditation. In the variant of the manuscript the visual metaphors reveal the theoretical impulse asserting itself, even to invoking the ancient ideal of theory as contemplation: "the only end I see for myself in composing [the work] is to procure solitary pleasure for myself, the pleasure of contemplating a true tableau of human affairs, of seeing man in the reality of his virtue and vices, his nature, of understanding and of judging him."[47]

In likening his construction to a tableau, Tocqueville seemingly chose an odd medium. The events he portrayed were revolutionary and, by nature, unstable, fluctuating, rising, falling, in constant motion. A tableau is a means of centering and then of fixing its objects. The medium may have been ill-suited to its message, but the choice responded to a different need, of resolving the meaning of its subject, containing it. But at a price: how to connect a series of tableaux so as to preserve the dynamics of revolutionary events? One possibility is that Tocqueville meant his tableaux to serve as a series of vantage points, each pointed toward the same event but revealing different aspects of it. Or, alternatively, does the discreteness of each tableau identify the problem that revolution brings to one caught within it, of disjointedness, of things no longer fitting together because the old connecting links have snapped—in short, of all those aspects which metaphors of "process" or "flow" elide?

There was also a theoretical challenge, one forced on Tocqueville by the threat of the workers and the ineptitude of the bourgeoisie. Before the revolution of 1848 Tocqueville had believed that 1789 had eventually resulted in a settlement. The new character of revolution in 1848 upset that assumption and required as well a reconsideration of the meaning of the revolution of 1830, the latter having been viewed earlier by Tocqueville as merely the aftershock of 1789. Revolutions that produced unstable political arrangements and a dominant but apolitical social class seemed to signify that the phenomenon of revolution was undergoing a significant challenge. Theorizing revolution in a new way—not as events building to a climax within a delimited temporal span, but as a sequence with no apparent terminus—led to fresh questions. How was the inconclusiveness of revolution, its serial character, related to the rise of the new politics of interest represented by the bourgeoisie and the accompanying decline of the politics represented by *ancienneté*? Was the new politics the expression of larger social forces that were rendering change a regularity instead of an exception and, if so, what was revolution being contrasted with now that *ancienneté* was fading?

Clearly Tocqueville had sketched two distinct projects. The first, of observing actions and actors, produced, almost relentlessly, portraits of actors too small for the setting. Politicians who had been formed by "a milieu of regular movement and the constraints of constitutional liberty" could not cope with "une grande révolution" and its "grande aventure."[48] *Democracy in America* had concluded that the American political regime owed its modest success to the fact that it was not the creature of a democratic revolution. In the *The Old Regime* he would portray the destruction of an undemocratic regime by a popular revolution, which perpetuated the worst feature of that regime, state centralization. *Souvenirs* is, in contrast, a drama in which everyone fails—revolutionaries as well as legitimists and republicans—and democracy is accounted as one of the major causes of those failures. The result is a work in the dramaturgy of anticlimax, a stillborn epic in which there are few, if any, heroes on the side where Tocqueville might have acknowledged heroics, and none on the revolutionary side, only seedy characters and an envious rabble moved by "the worst human passions." Their lack of stature makes Tocqueville's actors suitable to miniature frames. Even the scale of revolution in February 1848 is found wanting: no "general seething" of the kind he had observed in 1830. It is awarded a sardonic epitaph: "This time they did not overthrow the government but let it collapse."[49] The fury of the crowd, likewise, did not measure up.[50] Even as spectacle, the revolution falls short: "low tragedy performed by provincial actors."[51] On the basis of such ruminations *Souvenirs* could have been subtitled, "A Memoir of Aristocratic *Ressentiment*."

The deflation of actors and events was in keeping with the foreshortened temporal dimensions by which Tocqueville frames his recollections. He promises himself to go back "no further than the revolution of 1848" and no farther forward than 30 October 1849, the precise date of his "departure" (*ma sortie*) from office.[52] Only within those "limits" will the events be "painted," either as he observed them *or* because of their "*grandeur*." No sooner does Tocqueville announce the limits of his recollections then he proceeds to violate them in order to allow for a second project. The signal of that intention had been the word *grandeur*, the quality of great actions or spectacles which Tocqueville had frequently incorporated into the theoretical structure of *Democracy*: in his description of physical nature, his eulogy of the Puritans and the Founding Fathers, in his panoramic surveys of the course of equality, or his imaginary of democratic despotism. *Grandeur*, with its aura of the heroic, was precisely what he would refuse to revolutionary events in which, or because, workers had become major actors. Collective action would be denied the "deed"; it was visualized as "movement," as anonymous, hulking, formless misery but far from being insignificant.

Along with the dramatic appearance of the people as a political actor, the February revolution of 1848 had produced the abdication of the monarch, the declaration of the republic, the proclamation of a right to work, and the establishment of "national workshops" for ending unemployment. Yet Tocqueville claimed to be able to recall only "two or three spectacles which had *grandeur*."[53] The rest were ineffectual events rather than actions, events as actions manqués. The distinction between action and event is fleshed out when Tocqueville adds (after the remark just quoted) that the moment, when armed workers proceeded to occupy the Chamber and the deputies fled, lacked greatness (*grandeur*) "absolument." Why did this "event," which Tocqueville acknowledged would significantly influence "the destiny of France" as well as his own future, fall short of being an "action"? His explanation was that "the form" or appearance assumed by this "great unexpected event" detracted from the impression the event had left on him. It was, in other words, second-rate spectacle.The workers had decked out their deed inappropriately, with the result that "the terrible originality of the facts [of what they had done] remained hidden." The deed seemed inauthentic because mimetic. The workers had imitated "the acts and words" of the revolutionaries of 1789 and had thus behaved more like theatrical players following a script about the French Revolution than political actors venturing to "continue it." The workers had acted from borrowed passion, seeking "to warm themselves in the passions of their fathers" but unable to muster either "enthusiasm" or "fury." The unintended effect of Tocqueville's account is ironical: he, the representative of a class that had made a fetish of inherited forms and of the respect due them, castigating the workers for having affirmed their own tradition, while missing the pathos—which he shared—of continuity grappling with change.

Tocqueville remarked that while he was able to see "the terrible ending" of the charade, he "could not take the actors very seriously."[54] He was "moved" instead by the spectacle of the royal princess and her child having to suffer the insults of the mob.[55] When royalty left the Chamber, Tocqueville, motivated by "the public interest" rather than personal affection, ran after them in hopes of offering protection. It turned out that his help was unneeded, but the episode adds yet another layer of secret revelations: if princes were truly "like God," Tocqueville confides, and able to see into men's hearts, they would have been pleased by the gallantry of his intention. However, he concludes, "they will never know, for no one saw me and I have never told anyone."[56] His public performance, like the revolutionary workers', had fallen short; neither had successfully forced the kind of showdown that *grandeur* demands.

The same shortcoming had afflicted the politicians when faced with the February revolutionaries. They had persuaded themselves that the best tactic was to temporize. "I had always believed," Tocqueville insisted, that "the movement" could not be controlled "gradually or peaceably" but only "suddenly by a great battle fought out in Paris."[57]

In a preliminary way one can say that *Souvenirs* is an incomplete confrontation between two forms of action, heroic and revolutionary. As we have noted many times, Tocqueville was deeply enamored of actions that involved risk, large stakes, and remarkable abilities and his frequent use of metaphors that referred to the stage or to theater were clearly more congenial to representing singular heroes than anonymous masses. Among those actors on the side of order, the only ones *Souvenirs* depicted as heroic were, without exception, not politicians but military men engaged in crushing the revolution.[58] At the same time, he refuses to allow that the revolutionaries were, in any sense heroic actors, even though they might be said not only to have fulfilled the relevant criteria but to have gone further: their actions were contesting the limits of the political and attempting to extend its boundaries, certainly an objective not devoid of *grandeur*.

The larger question was why he refused to see those actions as political, specifically as the expression and extension of highly diverse forms of participation. The voluntary associations that ordinary citizens had developed after 1830, and which now were being used to defend the republic, to preserve universal manhood suffrage, and to ensure freedom of the press and of association as well as the right to work, would seem to share a close kinship with the American model. But that conclusion is, in one crucial aspect, wrong. If one returns to the relevant passages in *Democracy* it is apparent that Tocqueville had been careful to give a confined, even conservative interpretation to democratic participation. He was nearly as enthusiastic about "civil" as about political associations, while in his treatment of political associations more often than not he emphasized their local and mundane character, thus restricting their scope and potentialities. Participation was welcomed as long as it did not serve as an accessory of large-scale collective mobilization.

## VIII

> *During the first days that followed the 24th of February, I did not seek out any politicians. . . . I did not feel the need nor, to speak truthfully, did I have the taste for it. . . . I felt that we were in the midst of one of those great democratic floods. . . . I spent all my time, therefore, in the streets with the victors, as though I had been an adorer of fortune. It is true that I did not render homage to the new sovereign or ask favors of it. I did not even speak to it but confined myself to listening to it and observing it.*
>
> Tocqueville[59]

If revolutionary events were to be saved from ineffectual actors and the "terrible originality" of the revolutionaries exposed, it had to be achieved by theoretical means. A theory of revolution, however, could not be confined within either of the temporal limits Tocqueville had initially postulated or confined to a single tableau. Its scale needed enlarging, temporally or historically, so that theoretical means might accomplish what the actors themselves could not—namely, investing events with a certain seriousness. To endow *gravitas* and award significance is to settle meaning, to interrupt the endlessness of history. Accordingly, the portraits of failed actors and the sketches of fizzled events contrast with the theoretical achievement that, in transcending them, attains the *political* grandeur both had lacked. The function of grandeur is to affirm the possibility of enduring meaning. The theoretical strategy which makes that possible is one that historicizes the actions of politicians and revolutionaries, linking their contemporary context to one that is theoretically constructed in order to lend actions a meaning different from what they might have had or did have in the actor's own minds. That strategy produced a theoretical retrospective, a context for uniting past revolutions, establishing the threshold of the contemporary revolution, and fixing, rather than projecting, its meaning: "The constitutional monarchy had succeeded the old regime; the republic the monarchy; the empire the republic; the restoration the empire; then came the July Monarchy. After each successive mutation it was said that the French Revolution, having achieved what was presumptuously called its work, was ended . . . and here is the French Revolution beginning again, for it is still the same one."[60]

Tocqueville would not claim that he could foresee where or if the revolution would stop. "Other prophets" predicted a social transformation more thoroughgoing than any yet experienced; still others foresaw a "chronic and incurable" anarchy. "As for me I am unable to say; I do not know when this long voyage will end; I am weary of successively mistaking some misty mirages for the shore, and I often ask myself whether the safe ground we have been seeking for so long really exists or whether it isn't our destiny to wander the seas forever?"[61]

Tocqueville's longing for the revolution to end was the expression of a fundamental fact about *Souvenirs*: that the cause of the February revolution, except at the level of broad interpretation, remained theoretically incomprehensible to him. He all but confesses this under the guise of explaining it:

> It is a waste of time to search for the secret conspiracies which have brought about events of this kind. Revolutions which are brought about by popular emotion are typically more desired than premeditated. Those who boast of having plotted them have only tried to exploit them. They are born spontaneously from a general sickness of the spirit brought suddenly to a state of crisis by a fortuitous circumstance that no one had foreseen; and as for the pretended inventors or leaders of these revolutions, they invent and lead nothing; their only merit is like that of adventurers who have discovered most of the unknown lands. They have the courage to go straight ahead as long as the wind pushes them.[62]

In that passage Tocqueville identifies the February revolution as a particular type of revolution, one distinguished by "popular emotion."[63] His choice of words to characterize it are revealing: it was spontaneous, yet "born from a general sickness of the spirit [*esprit*] brought suddenly to a state of crisis by a fortuitous circumstance that no one had foreseen." Arguably, Tocqueville meant no more than that it would be difficult to specify the precise triggering event that produced the outbreak, although that explanation fails to indicate whether this difficulty is peculiar to revolutions driven by "popular emotion." Further, Tocqueville was certainly aware that some events might qualify as flash points—for example, the suspension of Michelet's course of lectures or the banning of a so-called public banquet planned by republicans. It is possible that Tocqueville meant that there had to be some explosive event related to the socialist character of the revolution. Or, alternatively, Tocqueville may have been terrified by the irrationality of a revolution whose consequences were hugely disproportionate to *any* triggering event.

*Souvenirs* purports, then, to be a recollection of a "spontaneous" phenomenon whose causes are unknowable and unpremeditated, and its direction uncontrolled. Those categories of ascription might have served a tactical purpose. The actors, the ideas, the politics, even the rituals of the revolutionaries, can, literally, be belittled, diminished by the very events they see themselves activating. Tocqueville the theorist can assert his superiority by encapsulating the revolution in a historical sequence and explaining it by "general" causes, while claiming simultaneously that he had prophesied the coming of the revolution. In order to substantiate his prophetic powers, he violated his self-imposed temporal boundaries by referring to two documents, one a manifesto he had prepared for a party group, the other a parliamentary speech. Both predate February 1848 and both express fear of an impending revolution. In recalling the two texts, Tocqueville claims that he is satisfied that their prophetic character can be established "without difficulty," for the event "justified him more promptly and completely than he had foreseen."[64] Although he admitted that he had neither expected the revolution which did occur nor predicted "the accidents that had triggered it," "I did perceive . . . more clearly than any other the general causes that inclined the July Monarchy toward its ruin."[65]

Each text warns that revolution was likely if public corruption remained unchecked, but the emphasis of the selected extracts was on the threat he perceived from a new type of revolution. Although issuing from "the old democratic malady" of egalitarianism, the new revolution, unlike 1789, aimed at the rights of property.[66] And property, Tocqueville noted not without malice, was more vulnerable now than in 1789 because the power of the aristocracy had been eliminated. The larger point was that changes had been taking place in the relative power of the major social classes such that nothing now stood between the rabble and the wealth of the bourgeoisie, an outcome for which the bourgeoisie had mainly its own shortsightedness to blame.

In *Democracy* he had entertained the possibility of an attack on property but he had visualized it as a demand extending the principle of equality from political to property rights. In France, however, the workers had neither political rights nor the ample opportunities for acquiring property generally available to Americans. As a consequence revolution appeared in a different form, as social rather than political. In the second of the two documents (27 January 1848) he had warned that the apparent calm on "the surface of society" disguised the dangerous "passions" stirring among the workers. These have gone undetected, Tocqueville had declared, because passions, that were once "political" have become "social" and portended a "most formidable revolution."[67]

Now, as we noted in the previous chapter, the "social" had been employed by the left as a synonym for commonality and collectivity; and it was used to demand the enlargement of the scope of the political. It was not immediately evident all that Tocqueville meant to subsume under the antithesis of "social" and "political," but, clearly, the social included private property, material interests, and class distinctions. These categories, which liberals tended to individualize, social-ism conflates in criticism of "the rich" and then inflates its own identity in opposition until, in Tocqueville's eyes, it appears as self-interest writ large, collectivized, and simplified. It mobilizes the potential for homogeneity in the material aspirations solely of the working poor, a class that vastly outnumbers the other classes. Although Tocqueville clearly recognized that materialism was a strong motivation among the propertied, he considered it a stabilizing force, because they wanted to conserve what they had. Equally important, unlike the strong anticlericalism among workers and socialists and the occasional advocates of sexual liberation and women's rights among some socialists, the propertied idealized their materialism by defending religion and family. In contrast to the materialism of the social, Tocqueville's political stands for the ideal, the legal or constitutional, the civic-spirited, and the social and intellectual diversity that freedom encourages. In the first of his prerevolutionary documents, the party manifesto, Tocqueville had looked forward with anticipation to a kind of showdown, as it were, between the political and the social. "Soon," he predicted, "there will be a political struggle between those who possess and those who do not." He even prophesied that it would produce a heroic political struggle: "the great battlefield will be property. . . . Then we will see great [*grandes*] public agitations and great [*grands*] parties."[68] For that political dénouement to have materialized, however, the bourgeoisie would have had to transcend its "social" character.[69] That desperate fantasy can be seen as the Tocquevillean formulation of liberalism's utopian moment when it would leap, as Marx might have put it sardonically, from the realm of self-interest to that of civic virtue, from being an economic class to becoming a political class as well. As matters turned out, the upper bourgeoisie were not required to leap beyond self-interest, only to accept despotism in exchange for order.

Although the distinction between the political and the social was strategically important in enabling Tocqueville to elucidate the nature of the socialists' threat, the point was blunted by the necessity for Tocqueville to partially veil what, beyond private property, was included under the social. Was the defense of class privilege as crucial as the protection of private property? And given that by Tocqueville's own showing, social conditions were the critical element in moderating the politics of American democracy, how was it possible to criticize the Montagnards for advocating political means, universal manhood suffrage, to offset social power—for example, property qualifications for suffrage that simultaneously disfranchised the poor and empowered the propertied classes? Possibly what was being signaled here was the tacit agreement on the part of liberal thinkers with the formulation that Marx, Tocqueville's near contemporary, was promoting: that political arrangements are derivative of private property power—but only as long as the arrangements mediate that connection by providing politically significant elements of popular involvement and genuine solicitude for the common well-being. When property relinquishes that element in favor of despotism, the equation is reversed and property becomes dependent on unpolitical power. Paradoxically, it was the representatives of the social, the workers and their allies, who were contending for the primacy of the political, defending it as the means for reducing the inequalities of power and of the quality of life-forms rooted in social conditions.

## IX

> *[I]t is especially in the midst of this universal anarchy and upheaval that the need is felt to be attached for the moment to at least some simulacrum of tradition or some shards of authority in order to save what remains of a partially shattered constitution, or to complete its disappearance.*
>
> Tocqueville[70]

Although Tocqueville deployed his distinction between the political and the social to privilege a certain meaning to the confrontations of February and of the months thereafter, there was another thematic contrast whose recurrence throughout *Souvenirs* establishes continuity between it and *Democracy* and, in turn, would attain apotheosis in *The Old Regime*: the antithesis of modernity and what I have called *ancienneté.*

Unlike the antithesis of political-social, whose force was weakened because there was no obvious bearer or even defender of the political, the opposition/contrast of *ancienneté* with modernity had its obvious representatives in the aristocracy and the bourgeoisie, respectively.[71] But to which camp did the working classes belong, or the artisans, or the newly prominent intellectuals?[72] Not by Tocqueville's reckoning with *les anciens,* and yet the sense in which, as dependent classes, they could plausibly be grouped with the bourgeoisie suggests a category that was meant to be cultural and historical as well as political. And because *ancienneté* united, if only abstractly, political and class enemies it confused, if it did not weaken, the contrast between the political and the social. Unlike the opposition between the political and the social, which culminated in an actual confrontation of political order with the "social" revolutionaries, there could be no pitched battle between *ancienneté* and modernity, only for the one a desperate clutching at souvenirs of the past, cherishing each of its token appearances, and for the other the savoring of acceptance.[73] Thus, while *Souvenirs* records the victory of order over anarchy, it simultaneously mourns the final defeat of *ancienneté* by modernity.

Accordingly, *Souvenirs* can be read as an embittered archaism. No matter what the outcome in the struggle between two versions of modernity, one represented by the bourgeoisie the other by socialism, *ancienneté* remained the counterideal to both antagonists. Once it had been capable of enmity, now it was their critic, reduced to fighting by theoretical means against individualism, self-interest, political parties, centralization, the "literary spirit" and urban-centered life. Hence, amid the unequivocal moments Tocqueville preserved ambivalence, between a repressed sympathy toward a revolution that attacked the bourgeoisie and overt support for the counterrevolution's suppression of an emergent democracy. Ambivalence serves to conceal the persistence, even the depths, of his reactionary sympathies, although a rightward drift would be unmistakable in some of the tableaux.

In the several references that Tocqueville makes to the "modern," the defining element of change is given a new character, no longer occasional or exceptional or restricted, but pervasive, irreversible, heralding a qualitatively new condition. Change is endowed with a mythical force comparable in power with equality, though lacking the aura of a "providential fact." Tocqueville describes despairingly "the mobility of all things, institutions, ideas, *moeurs*, and men in an unstable society which had been shaken by seven great revolutions in less than sixty years, without counting a multitude of small, secondary upheavals."[74]

"Society" appears not as the sum of structures that absorbs and shapes change, but as passive, merely the most convenient symbol of the widest generality, the body whose every part is vulnerable to change. Change ramifies, bringing dislocation, disappearance, instability. Eventually, while society is absorbed with change, change is absorbing society.

That change had acquired a broadened scope for political theorists of Tocqueville's era, regardless of their social pedigrees, was directly traceable to the trauma of the French Revolution. The revolution had revealed undreamed of dimensions and magnitudes, even velocities of change: a governing class had been permanently displaced; the future of monarchy was left uncertain but its power fatally weakened; the hold of the church had been loosened and unbelief was beginning to spread among the lower classes; and those same classes had emerged to enlarge the boundaries of public space, raising the question of whether they would first be taught patriotism in place of piety, nationalism instead of fealty, and their revolutionary ardor converted into a force for national expansionism or, instead, educated into becoming the agents of their own transformation.

While many theorists engaged the meaning of the French Revolution and tried to draw lessons from it, there were several who believed that the revolution was only one of the distinctive forms of power shaping societies, endangering their stability, and stamping them as modern. The two forms mentioned most often were science and its practical applications ("invention") and industry. The oddity of Tocqueville's conception of the modern was that science hardly figured in it, and industry and technology fared only marginally better. For near contemporary writers such as Saint-Simon, Comte, and, later, Marx, modernity *was* defined by the continuing revolutionizing effects of these "forces." The challenge, as Saint-Simon and Comte saw it, was to master the revolution and the power of science and industry; for Marx it was to liberate revolutionary force of the proletariat, science, and industry. "Revolution" was clearly becoming an integral concept, which bundled together the French Revolution, the Industrial Revolution, scientific discovery, and technological invention. Thus the concept of change was being revolutionized in an effort to emphasize the profundity and scale of the social transformations taking place. Now, as the "basis" of society, change was, paradoxically, being made into the substitute for the concept of order. A certain disruptiveness seemed as necessary to the perpetuation of society as order once had been deemed to be.

Although each of those theorists could be said to have had a strong streak of technoscientific determinism, they also shared an element of unease were the new powers to continue uncontrolled. Hesitancy was not, however, a trait congenial to the new temper. Instead, the transformative potential attributed to modern powers encouraged a belief in a mythic future of unlimited possibilities. Those powers, in effect, signified nothing less than that the large scales—which Tocqueville had believed were unique to the New World with its endless land and rich natural resources that alone made it possible to accommodate the driving energies of modernity—were now becoming the property of an Old World without the natural advantages of the New. Tocqueville's *ancienneté* would be importantly shaped by an abhorrence of the emergence of large scale in its many guises: as mass movement, electoral politics, the popularization of ideas as ideology, centralization, egalitarianism, and the despotic tendency—and all concurring within a constricted space.

The text of *Souvenirs* is "illustrated" by numerous symbolic references to a past where aristocracy and hierarchy were accepted as normal, where traditional values of honor, privilege, and deference to rank set the moral and political tone of society. Tocqueville reports his sadness at viewing the ancient oaks, which once towered above the boulevards of Paris, now toppled by the insurgents and reduced to barricades; how he wept at the sight of an old aristocratic kinsman buckling on "his little ceremonial sword with its silver hilt" and setting out to join his dependents who had come to Paris to do battle with the revolutionists; and lamented as he thrilled to a moment when "nearly all the old aristocracy of all degrees . . . remembered at that moment that they were part of a warrior and ruling caste, and everywhere they gave an example of resolution and vigor; such is the great vitality of these old aristocratic bodies. For they preserve a trace of themselves even after they seem to have been reduced to dust only to rise again from the shadow of death before sinking back forever."[75]

The contrast between modernity and *ancienneté* was personalized in a diptych that Tocqueville constructs: on the one side, the porter of his house, who was rumored to have threatened to murder Tocqueville, and, on the other, his faithful valet Eugene. The one, a former soldier, is described as "a little cracked in the head, a drunkard," and layabout who, when he wasn't abusing his wife, idled away the hours in a tavern. "It could be said that this man was a socialist by birth, or rather by temperament." The "brave" Eugene is the embodiment of *ancienneté*'s ideals among the lower orders, "unquestionably not a socialist, either in theory or temperament." Eugene is praised for lacking that "restlessness of mind," which was "the general sickness of the age," and for being contented with his lot and never overreaching his native capacity. He had taken a brief leave from his duties in the now loyal National Guard to inquire about his master's needs. The pleasantries that Tocqueville exchanged with Eugene end after the latter has removed his own uniform, cleaned his master's boots, and brushed his clothes. Eugene then dons his uniform, asks if there is any further need of his services, and returns to his duty of suppressing the rebellion.[76]

*Ancienneté*'s ideal of a society of ranks based on mutual respect among unequals linked a number of ideals—of national *grandeur*, heroic action, disinterested but passionate actors, a believing populace, of freedom as the necessary condition for the unique to flourish. *Ancienneté* shaped Tocqueville's conception of theory as the historicizing of the forces contending for hegemony over the present. *Ancienneté* is pitted against a strange power that had originated in a profound but dirempted revolutionary experience, part achievement and part trauma. That power was temporarily repressed only to reappear periodically. The revolution of February 1848 was "a new facet of the Revolution" of 1789.[77] In contrast to the recurrent, seemingly endless possibilism of modern revolutionary changes, *ancienneté* might be called a theory of finitude. It was attuned to the characteristics of "old peoples" and to the "limits" of what was possible in "old societies," where, unlike America, there were always "too many men and too few places."[78] The overriding concern of the politics of *ancienneté* is to stabilize and contain a society based on privilege and inequalities whose legitimacy requires a theoretical gaze that furtively looks backward.

*Ancienneté* might be described as elongated past time with its tightly structured space at a premium. Modernity seemed the reverse: short of present time, time compressed by the hurry into the future, but in desperate need of unclaimed space to accommodate the sudden release of energies that translate into forces and aggregates of power greater than any known to the past. Modern political doctrines tended accordingly to be doctrines of collective power:

democracy, revolution, popular sovereignty, majority rule, state centralization. Hence, socialism, Tocqueville claimed, should not have come as a surprise: "Shouldn't it have been perceived for a long time that the people had unceasingly enlarged and raised its condition, that its importance, its education, its desires, its power have increased steadily?"[79] And consistent with these developments there was now the democratization of theory: "And as the French in their political passions are as argumentative as they are unreachable by arguments, they busied themselves endlessly at those popular meeting places [i.e., the political clubs] by concocting theories on which they could later base their acts of violence."[80]

## X

Tocqueville claimed to have foreseen the coming of revolution, yet he admitted to being wholly unsure of its long-term implications. To admit to being unable to see the shape of a future he had prophesied was to state the limits or, better, the limitations of his vision insofar as it was shaped by a particular sensibility. Tocqueville had claimed that his liberalism accepted the results of the revolution of 1789 or at least a thin version of them. However, the events of 1815, 1830, and 1848 were also characterized by him as revolutions, when, by his own deflationary account, they might simply have been subsumed under the rubric of "change." The restricted scope of their consequences qualified them as episodes of modernity rather than as successive revolutions. In that reading, modernity would signify the acceleration of superficial change and, with the dizzy succession of political forms, a deceleration in radical substantive change. Tocqueville came close to that understanding in a letter of July 1848. Writing to an intimate he confided: "It is not that I believe in an uninterrupted succession of revolutions. I believe, on the contrary, in rather long intervals of order, tranquillity, of prosperity; but in the firm and definitive establishment of a good political and social state, how can one still believe in that?"[81]

Unlike his comments in that letter, *Souvenirs* was an internal dialogue meant only for an author who had been forced to withdraw from the political world. Unlike a theoretical formulation, meditations were not expected to furnish a basis or directive for actions. In that mood Tocqueville could contemplate rather than confront a "social" phenomenon, "unique" but without greatness, which, more than any other, represented the rejection of all his efforts and hopes for political reconstruction. The theoretical or ideological novelty of socialism and the workers as would-be political actors shattered the conception of the political on which he had staked his career, not because socialism proposed a new conception of political life but because, in his eyes, its reliance on state action would exacerbate the historical malady of overcentralization, which was already choking out politics in France. If socialism was understood to stand not only for the extension of democracy into society and economy, but for the expansion of state power as the principal means for promoting socialist objectives, then Tocqueville's fears concerning the tendencies of both socialism and democracy might appear justifiable.[82] Yet if democracy were to be denied the instrumentality of the state to remedy social grievances and injustices, was political democracy pointless except perhaps as an unrealizable ideal whose function was as an inhibition upon the rhetoric rather than upon the actions of ruling elites?

# CHAPTER XXIII
# *SOUVENIRS*: SOCIALISM AND THE CRISIS OF THE POLITICAL

## I

*Socialism will remain the central character and the most formidable memory of the February revolution.*

Tocqueville[1]

Because Tocqueville had read, written, and spoken about socialism on several occasions in the years immediately preceding 1848, *Souvenirs* might have seemed the opportune moment for a measured theoretical engagement. That it did not happen seems all the more surprising in light of the terms he used in describing socialism and identifying its novel character. Socialism represented more than a political theory or a political party. "[I]t aspired to found a social science, a philosophy, I might almost say a religion to be learned and followed by all of mankind. This was the really new part of the old picture."[2] "Science," "philosophy," "religion"—all of the major forms of belief encompassing both intellectual elite (science, philosophy) and ordinary beings (religion). The combination of elements was rendered all the more formidable and menacing because it was inciting the politically excluded.

Earlier he had welcomed the passion and agitation created by the organized workers' movement, hoping that it might generally revitalize a torporific political society and its petty politics.[3] When it appeared, however, that workers' organizations had adopted socialist ideas and succeeded in generating a potential revolutionary force, the intensity of Tocqueville's reaction suggested that the foundations of his beliefs, conceptual as well as political, were profoundly threatened. He responded by defending the existing boundaries of the political and hardening an already exclusionary conception. When Tocqueville complained during these years that he could no longer "see" theoretically,[4] one reason was the emergence of a phenomenon to which he would not concede any common political ground or common historical antecedents. He could not, in a literal sense, comprehend it theoretically. Socialism was a reversion to the prepolitical: "the insurrection was of such a nature that any negotiation with it seemed at once impossible and from the first moment it allowed no other alternative than to conquer or to perish."[5]

The effect of refusing to engage socialism dialogically—to speak about it but not to it—was to blur the line between the ideological and the theoretical, enabling partisanship to crowd out perspective. There is a telling anecdote Tocqueville inserts in a context where he describes how "the crowd" became active and tried to form a provisional government. He recalls a conversation with a physician who operated an asylum for the insane. Although *un sympathisant,* the doctor confided that he had treated several of the revolutionary leaders, a revelation that leads Tocqueville to muse, "I have always thought that in revolutions, especially in democratic revolutions, madmen—not those who are given that name metaphorically, but genuine madmen—have played a very considerable political role." He also thought that the physician should have been locked up with his patients.[6] Tocqueville depoliticizes what might seem an important moment by placing the actions beyond the political pale, literally in a context of insanity.

## II

"Socialism" was a neologism that first made its appearance during the 1820s but the ideological intensity of Tocqueville's *theoretical* reaction, with its insistent antithesis of the political and the social, has its origins in the transformation taking place in his own conceptions of the "social." I want to suggest that Tocqueville held two distinct and contrasting conceptions of the social and that the first of them appeared to wax, the second to wane in the course of the revolution. One of these conceptions I call mythical, the other (at the risk of an anachronism) the social-scientific conception of the social. The mythical is first expressed by Tocqueville in a youthful letter of 1830 before "socialism" attained wide usage:

> [In advanced civilizations] society is all-pervasive; the individual takes the trouble to be born; for the rest society takes him in its arms like a nurse; it watches over his education; it opens before him the roads to fortune; it sustains him on the march; it takes away from him all perils; he advances in peace under the eyes of this second Providence; this tutelary power which has protected him during his life watches finally over the disposition of his ashes; this is the fate of civilized man.[7]

The nightmarish image of an all-embracing tutelary power is one that, as we have seen, resurfaced in the conception of "democratic despotism" developed in *Democracy in America.* That imaginary depicted a huge concentration of power resulting from the withdrawal of individuals into their private cocoons.

Despotic power was made possible by the atomization of social power. Social power, the power of social authorities, is absorbed into a benevolent, centralized state that then attends to the needs of all. When socialism emerged as a revolutionary force, Tocqueville, with scarcely any modification, sublimated into socialism the presocialist image of a tutelary society and the slightly later image of democratic despotism. The specter of a gigantic power standing athwart a society of helpless individuals, unlike the image of democratic despotism, was the projected power of a revolution, or, more precisely, of a social revolution.

Tocqueville's mythic language was uncovering the presence of a new form of power. If the concept of political power was as old as Thucydides or as young as Machiavelli, and that of economic power as old as Harrington or as young as Marx, the concept of social power may be said to be as old as the Scottish thinkers of the eighteenth century and as young as Tocqueville. For social power to be absorbed to form despotism, it had to exist and then be absorbable. These possibilities were implicit in a quasi–social science construct that Tocqueville had developed in the first volume of *Democracy*, five years before the second volume in which the famous representation of democratic despotism would be sketched.

The progenitive idea of an all-encompassing despotism was elaborated in the course of Tocqueville's attempt to convey the totally pervasive ethos of democracy in the United States, which, he insisted, could not be appreciated by an analysis of political institutions alone. What made popular sovereignty a reality instead of a rhetorical fiction was, Tocqueville contended, "the omnipotence of social power." Tocqueville's crucial formulation followed directly after his claim that "once a people begins to touch electoral requirements, it is predictable that sooner or later it will abolish them completely. That is one of the most invariable rules governing society. . . . [F]or after each new concession, the forces of democracy are strengthened. . . . There is no stopping point until universal suffrage is reached." Tocqueville then tries to locate the novel character of the dynamic of equality in the fact of its being a power internal to society rather than external as represented in one of the traditional metaphors of absolutism: in some countries, he noted, the directing power takes a form "external to the social body," but in America power takes a radically different turn because there is no outside, no external Archimedean point: "society acts by itself on itself. The only existing power is within it. . . . The people rules over the American political world as God rules over the universe. It is the cause and end of all things; everything emerges from it and everything is absorbed back into it."[8]

Despite language that seemed to assimilate the "action" of society to that of individual actors, it is precisely the opposite that Tocqueville was suggesting. Social power was a form in which there was no one directing or performing agent, no unified group. Instead a myriad of uncoordinated behaviors created a pressure, which operated as an undifferentiated force because the behavior in question was that of roughly equal and similar beings. The difference between the social power that Tocqueville discovered in the United States and what he experienced in France was the difference between social power inhibited by moral, religious, and political beliefs and social power that was being revolutionized and unified by an ideology.[9]

In keeping with his mythic formula, Tocqueville describes the revolutionaries in graphic, menacing, almost preternatural terms: they are "greedy, blind, vulgar," mad, revolting in appearance, frenzied, and transgressive—Tocqueville is shaken by the active role of women in the revolutionary struggles.[10] The social character of the extraordinary power generated by the revolution, its active presence in the innermost fibers of working people, was vividly etched in Tocqueville's memory by an incident in which his path was "obstinately" blocked by an old woman and her vegetable cart. When he demanded passage, she struck him. "The hideous and terrible expression on her face filled me with horror, painted as it was with all the fury of demagogic passions and rage of civil war." That "small fact," Tocqueville confides, was a "great symptom" because it demonstrated to "the attentive eye" how in "moments of violent crisis" actions that seemingly have no relation to politics can nonetheless assume "a singular character of violence and disorder." Times of "great public emotions form a kind of violent atmosphere in the midst of which all private passions heat up and boil."[11]

That the poor should come to represent menace during revolutionary times, or alarm an aristocrat, is not surprising. But the mythical expression of those fears in the concept of the "social" suggests that some fundamental structures of society, which had previously served to repress the demotic powers welling up from below, were no longer holding.

Before the advent of socialist theories of the early nineteenth century, the principal theoretical response to class conflict visualized society as an ordered structure of distinctions. Social order was the work of a variety of institutions that instructed, regulated, and shaped the lives of members who were otherwise sharply differentiated by birth, wealth, status, education, and legal rights. Accordingly, society divided into ranks, orders, estates, and local authorities, and these were crisscrossed by family and church. These controlling structures were supported and legitimated by complex systems of value—law, custom, religious doctrines, and moral beliefs—which social authorities were expected to uphold. Typically, private property and economic relationships generally were categorized as social institutions.[12] The totality of this complex was what early modern writers had in mind by "society." As a rule, society was considered to be somewhat less plastic than political arrangements and, although of divine origin, more like a natural fact. That conception contrasted with Hobbes's, for whom the creation of state authority made it possible for society to exist. Locke and Rousseau followed that same sequence. Beginning with Montesquieu and later including Hume and Burke, a conservative tradition took shape around the notion of society as some primordial substratum that evolved insensibly into multiple but complementary codes of understandings regarding beliefs, norms, and behaviors. The distinguishing characteristics of society, according to that conception, were the work of anonymous authors (society's origins were typically described as "lost in the mists of time") and resulted in the dispersion of power over time and throughout space. It was never legislated into existence and never centered: "To be attached to the subdivision," in Burke's words, "to love the little platoon we belong to in society, is the first principle . . . of public affections."[13]

The theoretical strategy at work in the conceptualization of society was originally devised to oppose despotism. In Montesquieu's classic formulation, despotism was essentially a radical simplification of power. He visualized it as issuing from a single center and acting directly on individuals in a society wherein the infrastructure of ranks, privileges, and other differences had been eliminated. The positive teaching of this theory was that social inequalities represented diffused powers and were the guarantors of limited governmental power and personal freedom. By this version of Aristotelian theory, the proper relationship of the state to society was one of dependency, of centralized authority being grounded or "rooted" in local society and respectful of its authorities. Society stood for decentralized authority, cultural complexity, a social order of ranked differences; the state, in contrast, was represented as a dangerous simplifying, centering tendency, an order of uniformity. Reformers were, accordingly, warned off from their naive belief that a "living" political constitution, with its inexhaustible complexities, could be legislated into existence. Joseph de Maistre, the great French theorist of reaction, remarked contemptuously that Tom Paine's various constitutional projects assumed that a constitution was a simple matter of a few axioms, which could be reduced to a pocket-sized document.

By the same reasoning, however, the dependence of state upon society meant that the inequalities characterizing society would be reflected back into the political system. In this context the meaning of the French Revolution was to challenge that equation by reconstituting political institutions and using the powers of the state to eliminate the inequalities perpetuated locally though aristocratic and ecclesiastical privileges. But the unintended consequence of dissolving or weakening those social powers was that class struggle emerged more starkly, unmediated by entrenched social hierarchies. Although the state remained as the principal means of reforming society, that potential would clearly be realized or frustrated depending on which of the social powers was controlling or influencing the state. If society's inequalities of power were perceived as reducible to class, it seemed utopian to expect the state to eradicate inequalities when its own powers were a reflection of them—hence the great struggles over electoral reforms throughout most of the nineteenth century and the appeal of the leveling formula, "one man, one vote."

In an important sense, the eighteenth-century French contests were carried forward into *Democracy in America.* Tocqueville had followed a conservative social tradition both in the importance he had attached to the concept of "the social condition" (*l'état social*) in explaining the stability of the new republic and in the distinctly secondary status he assigned the state. Far from forming a contrast to the social, political arrangements were declared to be "the expression" of the social condition.[14] The usage reappears in *Souvenirs,* where society is said to "serve as the basis" of government.[15] That relationship prompted Tocqueville to declare that "the February revolution must not be social," meaning that the revolution had already succeeded politically, because a republic was established, but now in reforming the conditions of labor, the state was weakening social power in the form of capital or property rights and extending its own control over society and thereby shifting the republic to a different foundation than property.

However partisan his views might seem, Tocqueville's fears were not imaginary nor was his analysis misplaced. The theorists of socialism had made the social the main site for contesting the nature of the political and theorized the social into two polarized classes; and they had helped to educate the working class into becoming an actor.[16] The effort was revolutionary in the specific sense of organizing power outside the official arrangement of the political. The results were evident in Tocqueville's account of the so-called June Days of 1848. Tocqueville declared this popular outbreak to be "the greatest and most singular" insurrection in French or "any other history," partly because of the large numbers involved and partly because "the insurgents fought without a battle cry, without leaders, without flags, and yet with a marvellous unity and military skill that astonished the oldest officers." That the primal chaos could spontaneously take shape and act in unison without apparent leadership was made all the more remarkable by its objective:

> What distinguished it from other events of this kind which have succeeded one another among us for sixty years is that it did not aim to change the form of government but to alter the order of society. It was not, in fact, a political fight (in the

> meaning that up to now we have given that word) but class combat, a kind of slave war [*guerre servile*]. . . . [T]hat terrible insurrection was not the undertaking of a certain number of conspirators but the insurrection of one whole population against another.[17]

## III

Within the context created by the intensification of class conflict, the value of consensus, so crucial to Tocqueville's liberalism, suddenly appeared vapid. Consensus stood for common beliefs about, and common perceptions of, the sociopolitical world. The natural conclusion was that consensual beliefs were elements of a common culture.

The emphasis on belief betrayed the religious genealogy of consensus. Missing from this conception of society as a body of believers was the idea of civic skills or practices, especially the practices of deliberation among citizens leading to actions. While Tocqueville had introduced the notion of consensus primarily as a means of overcoming differences, it now appeared, at best, as a necessary illusion, an idealized unity for a divided society, and, at worst, exposed as a cover-up for a competitive society of vastly unequal social rewards. What was at stake was not solely the status of consensus but the revelation of the desperate importance of culture. When consensus is presented as a natural process—that is, not the result of manipulation but the natural extension of society's culture—it is tacit admission that the modern political, the political in the setting of sharp class divisions without official class distinctions, needs, beyond periodic elections, continuously to cultivate support and diffuse opposition. The actuality of a culture of consensus is indirect, to make the antipolitical effects of a market economy appear as contingent when measured against the enduring and pervasive presence of "society"—when, thanks to a culture of consensus, the society is, as Lord Balfour once put it, "so at one that it can safely afford to bicker." While society supports the political by socializing, civilizing, and inhibiting its members, it also compensates for an unrobust political life and for the antipolitical effects of self-interest by instilling the values of nationalism and patriotism.

The radical nature of socialism's challenge, its incompatibility with Tocqueville's political, produced a hardening of the categories of Tocqueville's theory, as well as a redistribution of emphasis that would signify the declining status of the political as the regulative principle of society and, along with it, the displacement of political theory itself. Major concepts, such as participation, which had been considered sufficiently flexible in *Democracy* to accommodate populist elements, now symbolize constraint, delimiting the theoretical boundaries of the political while defending the established limits of politics. Equality, which had been attributed not only to American politics but to its culture, education, religion, and a variety of social relations, including those between the sexes, was now restricted to a conception of political equality that justified an electorate radically smaller than the general citizenry. Tocqueville similarly treated the concept of social class as a faithful reflection of the inequalities among human beings, due not so much to "nature," as he had tended to argue in *Democracy*,[18] but to modernity's surrogate for nature, the "laws" of a "free" economy; accordingly the evils of abject poverty would be assigned primarily to Christian charity rather than political action and the objects of poverty treated as dependents on private benevolence rather than as citizens.

In *Democracy* Tocqueville declared that he had "deduced" the abstract consequence that "within a certain time" men would become "equal in all respects."[19] Doubtless that deduction was intended to startle his contemporaries into considering actions that might mitigate the impact of equality; nevertheless, it is doubtful that he envisioned the equalization of property or wealth. The whole point of the American experience, after all, was that private property and the pursuit of wealth were not necessarily jeopardized by democracy and, equally important, that a democracy based on a neo-Athenian conception of citizenship could comfortably coexist, even flourish, notwithstanding the members' devotion to private property and the pursuit of riches.

Socialism upset those assumptions by transforming into an immediate practical demand what Tocqueville had contemplated as a gradual development toward a formal equality. And while socialists had criticized private property, the institution that Tocqueville had excluded from his "deduction," their immediate objective was to use the state to guarantee employment. A possible implication of "the right to work" was the enlargement of the scope of the political and the entitlements of citizenships, as well as the substitution of right for dependency. But Tocqueville resisted that implication, and with a broad brush characterized "all of them [as] . . . aiming lower than the government and straining to strike society itself—which provides the basis of government—[they] took the common name of socialism."[20]

The aspect of socialism that aroused genuine wonder in Tocqueville, though it stopped short of eliciting the kind of awe that had stimulated the vision of *Democracy*, was not the misery of the workers but the power and dramaturgy of their movement. Repeatedly he is drawn to describing the colorful spectacles staged by the revolutionaries—descriptions that unconsciously evoke the ancient origins of theory in the spectacle (*theoria*) accompanying Athenian religious festivals.[21] The distinctive nature of the workers' power struck at the conception of an elaborate pluralist "society," which a conservative social science had constructed to ward off the consolidation of power, either in society or in the state. It was that sensitive boundary between the state and society that, in Tocqueville's eyes, the socialists threatened to erase rather than merely violate. His fears and their threat were epitomized in the union of ideas, and potential power, represented by the slogan adopted by the revolutionaries, "the Democratic and Social Republic." He countered that attempt to expand the political with his own slogan, "the February revolution must be Christian and democratic"—that is, a qualified democracy restrained by the most powerful form of social morality available.[22]

In his analysis, the dynamic of socialism had been ignited by a novel combination: "a mixture of greedy desires and false theory had made the insurrection [of June] so formidable after having nurtured it."[23] That had to be the explanation because, as he pointed out on other occasions, the workers were actually enjoying an unprecedented level of well-being.[24] The improvement in the education, material lot, and importance of the working class, Tocqueville argued, made it virtually inevitable that the people should have dreamed of using their power to escape poverty and "inferiority." But being ignorant of the limits to the level of prosperity in "old societies" and having found that the changes in political institutions had not improved their condition the people drew the inevitable conclusion, "it was not the constitution of government" at fault, but "the immutable laws which constitute society itself." By this chain of speculations they were led to believe that they had a right as well to change those "laws," and so they turned against property. Tocqueville concedes that the workers had not actually demanded the abolition of private property; however, he reasons that since property was the last obstacle in the path toward perfect equality, they must have have considered it.[25]

Tocqueville's insistence that the revolutionary element in socialism was social, not political, enabled him to ignore the intense and diverse forms of politics being created by ordinary citizens, the vast majority of whom had been excluded from politics before 1848. Recently historians have referred to "the great political mobilization of 1848" and described it as "the first mass political experience since the French Revolution of 1789–99."[26] The slogan, "democratic and social republic," meant to convey a commitment to popular participation and a determination to use the power made available by the establishment of political freedoms to shape the state into an instrument for improving the social condition of workers, peasants, and artisans.[27] What Tocqueville ignored, although his American experience might have sensitized him to it, was that "socialism" connoted not only the right to work, the right to form producer and consumer cooperatives, but also meant "sociability," sharing ideas, expressing grievances, and inventing strategies in a convivial setting. The February revolt that established the republic and enacted guarantees of freedom of assembly, association, and expression encouraged a veritable explosion of associations, clubs, and discussion groups throughout many of the French provinces.[28]

A new civic culture was in the making and attempting nothing less than the democratization of republicanism. One historian has described it as "the descent of politics towards the masses."[29] The social and the political were being intermixed and the energy and enthusiasm of the revolutionaries threatened to overwhelm the political pastiche being assembled by the so-called party of order. Tocqueville's refusal to admit that socialism was political amounted to a theoretical act of *political* suppression, which, by treating the widespread political activity among the populace as threat, unconsciously mimicked the actions by which the regime was, in fact, suppressing opposition.[30]

Following his election to the Constituent Assembly (April 1848) Tocqueville admitted that he had overreacted in wanting to win the election "to escape from the hands of the people in order to seize boldly the government and by a great effort secure it."[31] That the stakes were political was clearly understood by the government and it proceeded to clamp down on the activities of socialists and worker organizations because they were both "political"[32] in wanting to share in the use of public power and "antisocial" because they were preaching insubordination to their social superiors. Accordingly, the authorities forbade anyone to shout "*social*," or "Long live the democratic and social republic."[33]

A substantial price would be paid for blocking the aspirations and development of the workers as a *political* class. It would help to distort socialism into the narrowly economistic movement that both liberals and conservatives deplored and feared. Not surprisingly, at first strong support for Bonaparte developed among the workers, especially as he appeared to favor retention of universal suffrage.

## IV

> *ancienneté.* État de ce qui est vieux, ancien. Priorité d'âge.
> Larousse

Tocqueville had originally seized upon the distinction between the "social" and the "political" as a means for identifying the objectives of the revolutionaries. Plausibly, the revolutionaries were defending democratic forms of political action and thereby contributing to the revitalization of the political while Tocqueville would narrow the political and subordinate it to the social. He abandoned the moderated democratic and traditionalist elements that had distinguished his brand of liberalism in order to embrace the liberalism configured around political economy and its apologia for industrialism, private property, and rule by the middle class. The strategy of the social marked the moment when he dropped one mask and adopted another.

That interpretation is supported by Tocqueville's emphatic defense of private property and individual freedom, his opposition to governmental "interference" in economic relations, and his castigation of socialists and workers for "their false notions on political economy" and ignorance of "the real conditions of production and of social prosperity."[34] In that vein he warned against "substituting the State's foresight for the individual's foresight" and conjured up a vision of a "regimented, regulated, formalized society where the State takes responsibility for everything and where the individual is nothing."[35] All of these were standard principles of political economy liberalism.

However, as though to retrieve an old mask, Tocqueville balked at converting *tout court* to political economy liberalism.[36] He embarked instead on a tortuous effort at modifying that hybrid by injecting elements of *ancienneté* that lent a sociopolitical shading to certain economic categories.[37] Thus, he defends private property as a bulwark in a society of privilege rather than as the constituent element of an entrepreneurial society, calling it "the foundation of our social order and of all the privileges which covered it and which, so to speak, concealed the privilege of property."[38]

A crucial text is a speech of September 1848 in which Tocqueville spoke against the famous amendment that would have had the state guarantee the right to work to every able-bodied member.[39] Tocqueville used the occasion to attack socialism, but his defense of private property was notable for its employment of the idiom of traditionalism and for its appeal to premodern values, such as glory, while decrying materialism. In the course of denying the socialists' claim to be the ideological descendants of 1789, he insisted that their commitment to state intervention in the economy and to "ultracentralizing doctrines"[40] revealed that their true genealogy was in the *étatisme* of the Old Regime.[41] The revolution of 1789 was, he argued, about the individual right to private property, but the values of that event transcended the bourgeois interpretation of it. Tocqueville proceeded to heroize 1789 in order to contrast its appeal "to higher and finer things . . . love of country, national honor, virtue, generosity, disinterestedness, and glory" with the socialists' appeal to "man's material passions" and their hope of "unlimited consumption for everybody." Thus, he transfers the aristocratic ideals of the Old Regime to the bourgeois revolutionaries who had overthrown it, while simultaneously identifying the evils of the old monarchy with the new revolutionaries whom he charged with attempting to undo the French Revolution. In a disingenuous aside he concedes that "undoubtedly the French Revolution waged a cruel, energetic war against some proprietors," yet, he was quick to add, "No people have treated [the principle of private property] more magnificently."

A difference between *Democracy* and *Souvenirs* is that in the former Tocqueville could view economic relations in a consistently political light, even subordinate them; for, despite the spirited democratic politics of the United States, there did not appear to be significant class conflicts centered around the political and economic power of the wealthy few. In contrast, his attempt to inject archaic elements of heroism, traditionalism, and religion and the republican virtue of disinterestedness into the French setting, with its corrupt political culture, profound disagreements over political forms, intensifying class conflict, and a socialist movement demanding political democratization and economic reforms, revealed just how discordant those archaic elements were proving to be for a liberalism increasingly wedded to a specific economic doctrine. The discordancy was produced by the attempt of liberals to combine the celebration of change as inevitable in a free economy with the insistence on social order, political stability, and cultural coherence as the necessary preconditions of economic growth. If Tocqueville's archaisms seem merely quixotic, they nonetheless force the question of what order might mean under conditions of rapid, incessant change and even to reveal an answer in the practices of interest politics and its conception of the politically acceptable.

Despite his assertion that the revolution of 1848 was a consequence of the restriction of politics to "the middle class," which monopolized "all political power to the legal exclusion of all below them and, in practice, of all above," Tocqueville's *ancienneté*, when faced with popular pressures for a more expanded political, chooses to be accomplice to liberal resistance. The thought of exploiting the American example to support greater popular participation never arose. Instead Tocqueville made a point of contrasting American emphasis on private property with socialism's threat. The worries expressed in *Democracy*, that individualism might undermine civic life, and his denunciation of self-interest as responsible for the catastrophic decline in the quality of French public life,[42] were not renounced nor were they reconciled with his defense of property and a free economy. He substituted instead a depoliticized version of the United States, extolling it as the shining example of a society zealously committed to private property and democracy, to the extension of "the sphere of individual independence," "equality in liberty," and the assignment of "the greatest possible value to every man."[43] The American lesson was that one should "assure to the poor all the legal equality and all the well-being compatible with the existence of the right of individual property, and with the inequality of conditions which flow from that right."[44] In some notes he had made in 1847 Tocqueville envisioned a political party dedicated to conserving "political life" but warned that "It is not necessary to flatter the people and it is not necessary to thoughtlessly load them with more political rights which they are not capable of exercising."[45]

*Ancienneté* thus comes in the end to reinforce liberalism's insistence that to install individual freedom as the principal social value means justifying inequality as freedom's inevitable by-product. Freedom and equality are thus constructed as antagonists, freedom and inequality as allies. The traditionalist's conception of society as an unequal ordering of ranks, privileges, and obligations is not so much displaced as overlain by a conception of an order of inequalities secured by individual property rights. Commonality is reduced to the principle that rights ought to be accorded to all but subject to the qualification that legal equality must not jeopardize "the inequality of conditions" produced by the rights of private property. The attempt to republicanize liberalism faltered: virtue was no match for individual self-interest.

## V

> *Do not enlarge the circle of rights, but enlarge the horizon.*
>
> Tocqueville[46]

> *This love, which demands a continuous preference for the public interest over one's own . . . is singular to democracies. In them alone, government is entrusted to each citizen. But government is like every thing else in the world; in order to preserve it, one must love it.*
>
> Montesquieu[47]

Tocqueville's overtures toward political economy liberalism were a response to the profound change in the role of political theory effected by socialism and "its men of theory."[48] He had selected, as the most novel feature of 1848, the appearance of socialist theories and the unprecedented alliance of theory with the people. He was responding to the fact that for the first time in Western history the people as workers enjoyed a theoretical advocate. That development was important because it accompanied the explosion of popular political activity during the revolutionary years. Theory could now squarely put to the test whether liberalism was committed to a participatory conception of citizenship when it championed the idea of popular sovereignty or whether the idea of governments and constitutions "based" on the people was merely a useful fiction for disguising new forms of privilege and preserving old modes of passivity.

Prior to the appearance of socialist doctrines, the role to which theorists had aspired, virtually without exception, was that of educators and counselors to rulers and ruling classes. Although in the course of the eighteenth century deviant writers like Rousseau and Paine attempted to voice popular needs and aspirations, they had not visualized the people as a self-motivated actor but as a constituent power summoned to ratify a political constitution and then, save for an occasional reappearance to confirm amendments, disbanding into private life until recalled: the demos as Cincinnatus.

The American and French revolutions challenged those formulations by raising the prospect of the demos as a regular actor rather than an episodic force that intervened only when its burdens and suffering had become unbearable. In France the working classes had made but not won the revolution of 1789, yet as Tocqueville recognized, that memory of themselves as actors continued to exercise a powerful hold over the popular imagination during 1848. Socialist theory, in articulating the concept of class, concretized the idea of "the people" and used it to challenge the liberal claim to be both the inheritor of 1789 and the defender of a completed revolution. In analyzing socialism, Tocqueville's power-packed language conveyed the realization that, while socialism was theoretical, it was also a new species of ideas, one that would, as Marx put it, "grip" the masses:[49]

> [O]ne ought to see [in the events of June] only a brutal and blind, but powerful, effort of the workers to escape the necessities of their condition which had been described to them as illegitimate oppression and to force a road to that imagined well-being which had been taught to them from afar as a right. . . . These poor people have been told that the wealth of the rich was in some way the result of a theft committed against themselves. They were assured that inequality of fortune was as contrary to morality and society as it was to nature. . . . That obscure and erroneous notion of right, mixed with brute force, acquired an energy, tenacity, and power that it would otherwise never have had.[50]

The crucial element that Tocqueville saw socialism introducing was a catalytic one. "It was socialist theories . . . which later ignited the real passions, embittered jealousies, and eventually stirred up warfare among the classes." Although "the passions" of the workers may have been "less disorderly" at the beginning than might have been feared, that was not true of "the ideas of the people" on the morrow of the revolution. Their ideas displayed "an extraordinary agitation and an unheard of disorder." Clearly amazed, Tocqueville described the scene following 25 February when, as it were, the people seemed intoxicated with theory and caught up in a theoretic bacchanal:

> A thousand strange systems issued with impetuous force from the minds of innovators and spread among the troubled minds of the crowd.

> [E]ach proposed his own plan; this one produced his in the newspapers; the other [put] his on placards which soon covered the walls; and another spoke in the open air. One claimed to destroy inequality of fortune, another inequality of intellect, the third undertook to erase the oldest of inequalities, that between man and woman; one indicted poverty on some specific counts and offered some remedies for the evil of work which has tormented mankind from the beginning of its existence."[51]

If that description is juxtaposed to Tocqueville's concern to proclaim the unique qualities that made his own theoretical acumen possible, the unique reveals itself as a protest against the threatened democratization of yet another preserve of exclusion. Amid the chaos Tocqueville had perceived a revolution taking place in the political character of theory, not only new theorists and new theories, but a different kind of alliance between knowledge and action. In his eyes, the political was being displaced by—rather than on—the social, and hence the aim of theory was "lower" than the state, and, as a further consequence, political forms were becoming merely instrumental, as "means but not as an end." The invasion of the social heralded a new vocabulary and however repellant its carriers, the subject of theory could not be the same:

> This natural anxiety in the minds of the people, this inevitable agitation of its desires and thoughts, these needs, these instincts of the crowd formed, in a certain way, the material on which the innovators embroidered so many monstrous or grotesque figures. Their work could be seen as ridiculous but the basic stuff on which they worked is the most serious object for philosophers and statesmen to contemplate.[52]

The measured, meditative tone of those remarks is indicative of a major tension that pervades *Souvenirs.* In referring to the people "as the most serious object for philosophers and statesmen to contemplate," the tone of the passage could be described as contemplative, theoretical, concerned with the truth. It alternates, however, with agitated, even venomous, tirades against socialists, workers, women, and, not least, against the bourgeoisie and their politicians: there the tone is the opposite of measured, concerned not with truth but with *revanchisme.*

Implicit in the tensions was the question of whether the two roles Tocqueville had chosen were compatible. At issue is not whether theorists should abstain from judgments or advice concerning politics but whether the theorist and the politician can be combined without damaging both. Or, put differently, the problem is, in part, location, the difficulty of theorizing from *within* politics, from behind the constraints imposed by changing tactical considerations and the necessarily partisan character of politics. Rather than theory paralyzing action, the reverse may be true. All theories operate with a simplified picture of the world; but politics is notorious for its moral ambiguities, empirical complexities, and its long list of politicians who have failed because, unlike the theorist, they are rarely praised for admitting past errors.

There is also a difficulty that stems from the contrast, not between "word" and "deed," but between different forms of action, one highly symbolical, moving freely within the constraints of its own choosing; the other necessarily consequentialist in its thinking and constrained by public procedures and expectations. The following from *Democracy* is illustrative of a grand type of theoretical action, sweeping, provocative, and—inconsequential, yet also displaying a rigidity that would be fatal if practiced by a politician: "Societies, like other organized bodies, follow certain fixed rules from which they are unable to escape. They are made up of certain elements that are found everywhere and at all times."[53] In *Democracy* Tocqueville had begun to mingle the two modes of action in a special task he had assigned to both "philosophers and the men in power." He appealed to them to combat the tendencies of democracy, especially the dangerous combination of "doubt and democracy," by holding before their society "a distant aim as the object of human efforts." Both should teach men how to resist the petty desires and pursuit of immediate gratifications, which were the vices encouraged by democratic equality. "Little by little" and "insensibly" men would then be led back to "religious faith."[54]

Clearly his model was a prerevolutionary Catholic establishment which no longer existed even in France. Even less plausible was the notion that "philosophers" would freely collaborate with clerics or that in a democracy, where politicians were subject to periodic elections, a politician would devote himself to the task of promoting distant and intangible goals. Thus the price to be paid for mixing politics and theory is not solely in warped theoretical conclusions but in practical misjudgments as well. Certainly the stiffening of Tocqueville's conception of the political in the face of worker demands for inclusion in the so-called legal country of the voters resulted in the worst of both worlds, a rigid liberalism in theory and a reactionary politics.

In contrast to the rigidity of his practical politics, when contemplating socialism purely theoretically Tocqueville was capable of a more open attitude. One remarkable passage reveals Tocqueville struggling to get clear of the ebb-and-flow of revolutionary and counterrevolutionary politics in order to make theoretical sense of the phenomenon of socialism. He all but concedes that the socialists had succeeded in establishing a fundamental theoretical point of enormous practical significance. They had undermined the belief that private property was the necessary constitutive principle of society. The result, in his own formulation, was that he had come to appreciate that the boundaries of possibility in the political world had been dramatically and suddenly enlarged.

Just how difficult it was for him to accept his own conclusion is evidenced by the tortuous route his meditation then takes. Socialists, he first argues, had been rightly derided for believing that "the laws constitutive of our modern society will be greatly modified in the long run." That seemingly firm judgment is followed by a bewildering series of qualifications, assertions, and further retractions whose effect is to undermine the solidity of the very principle, property, for whose defense he had based his decision to act. First he hesitates, admitting that some of those "laws" have in fact been modified; then in the next breath he affirms the solidity of those same laws but on pragmatic grounds, declaring that their destruction would be "impracticable." That conclusion is promptly upset by a remarkable admission, which undercuts the very notion of enduring laws of society:

> I will say nothing more [on the subject] for the more I study the former condition of the world and see in greater detail that same world in our time; when I consider the immense diversity one encounters, not only among the laws, but among the principles of law, and the different forms taken and retained . . . by the rights of property on this earth, I am tempted to believe that what one calls necessary institutions are often only the institutions to which one has become accustomed, and that in matters of the social constitution the field of possibilities is vaster than men living in their particular societies imagine.[55]

## VI

> *The moment had come when it was a question of deciding if one wished only to be an observer of this singular revolution or become involved in events.*
>
> Tocqueville[56]

The personal-theoretical drama of the *Souvenirs* is staged around a decisive moment shortly after the February revolution. Although Tocqueville portrays it as the moment when bourgeois liberalism is forced to face the revolutionary challenge of socialism, as his analysis unfolds the confrontation gets blurred, not from any softening toward socialism but because of his intense revulsion at, yet complicity with, the bourgeoisification of liberalism. Tocqueville's alienation from both socialism and bourgeois liberalism originated in his conviction that both ideologies shared certain elements. In earlier conflicts of the century, he believed, the political stakes seemed uppermost to the contending groups, but in 1848 both sides understood the other through the language of material class interests. As the lines between them became more sharply drawn, the less significant political life seemed—at least if one refused, as Tocqueville had, to recognize the political values of democratic socialists. The result was that, although Tocqueville would publicly side with the bourgeoisie, he privately viewed its politics as differing not in kind from the socialists' but in quantity: theirs was a politics writ small, of individual self-interest; that of the workers' was collective interest, hence large. For Tocqueville the specter of socialism had the effect of driving deeper the wedge between the corrupt politics of self-interest he considered natural to the bourgeoisie and his ideal of a politics dominated by a public-spirited class, performing on a political stage congenial to great actions, and supported by a postrevolutionary consensus about the point where the revolution of 1789 had stopped and became a unifying myth.

Tocqueville represented his encounter with revolutionary socialism as the experience of a phenomenon that was at once bizarre and threatening, some strange outside force gathering itself for an assault on the political. When he was able to observe from close range the party of revolutionary socialists represented by the Mountain (Montagnards) in the National Assembly, it produced the exclamation, "For me it was like the discovery of a new world." That formula, unlike comparable remarks that he had made several times about America, was chilling rather than stimulating. He comments that while we often console ourselves with the homily that although we may be ignorant of foreign countries, at least we know our own. That, he declares, is "wrong, for one will always find some region one has not visited before and some races of men who are new to you." Thus the *moeurs* of the Montagnards impressed him as foreign, even their "idiom" belonged to no familiar category.[57] Yet so profound was his revulsion at bourgeois parliamentarism that the confrontation with socialism, instead of producing despair had the opposite effect. He was relieved that the revolution had exposed the bankruptcy of bourgeois politics and, in so doing, had released him from an obligation he had never wholeheartedly embraced. "In the depths of my own heart," Tocqueville confessed,

> I discovered . . . a sense of relief, mixed up with all of the sadness and fears which the revolution had occasioned. I suffered from this terrible event for my country but it was clear that I did not suffer for myself; on the contrary, it seemed to me that I breathed more freely than before the catastrophe. I had always felt myself diminished and oppressed in the midst of the parliamentary world which had just been destroyed. . . . [T]here was no longer any room for uncertainty of mind: here lay the salvation of the country, there its ruin.[58]

## VII

The paradoxical position in which Tocqueville found himself was that, while his polemics against socialism were pitched at a heroic, embattled level, his portrait of actual events and actors was antiheroic. If events were to be redeemed from the mediocrity that seemed the curse of modernity and acquire a significance worth their reexamination, it had to be both a theoretical and a personal accomplishment, one that would redeem theory and truth from the entanglement with the flux of partisan politics and reveal the indispensable role of personal qualities in the achievement, the selfsame qualities that had proved to be a handicap in his political career. At the same time he would formulate a conception of the prerequisites for a theorist that would allow him to retain the duality of theorist-actor by claiming that the theorist with political experience is better able to understand events than either the untheoretical actor or the politically inexperienced theorist.

In his explanation of revolutionary outbreaks Tocqueville developed a distinction he had first sketched in *Democracy* where he had described God as the paradigmatic theorist who could simultaneously conceive of the general and the particular, while mortal theorists were limited to one or the other at one time. In *Souvenirs* the distinction is tailored to fit the problem of revolution and to promote a conception of theory, which, once more, turned on unique qualities, not surprisingly ones that Tocqueville could claim.

Tocqueville's starting point borrowed from the earlier formulation, only now the distinction was between general and accidental causes, between the long-run tendencies that prepare the way for revolution and give it a course, and the particular incident, often trivial or accidental, that ignites the revolution. The distinction does not, however, rest on a contrast between the divine and the human understanding but between types of human understanding applied to revolution. There are "the men of letters who have written history without having taken part in public affairs" and "political men who have always occupied themselves with bringing about events without giving thought to describing them" and who dwell "in the midst of disconnected daily events" and want to attribute every event to "particular incidents." The true form of understanding is theoretical. It is ascribed to the type of "historian" who is "always in search of general causes." Because Tocqueville is reluctant to abandon the combination of theorist and actor, the "pure" historian is not Tocqueville's ideal. It is, instead, the historian who has acquired both the political experience, which the man of letters ordinarily lacks, and the generalizing skill, which the typical politician does not cultivate.[59]

Tocqueville then pushes the distinction further in order to attack those "absolute systems" of thought which claim that "all the events of history depend upon some first great causes." The resulting conception of events and their causes is then connected to a predestined chain that "suppresses the human element from human history."[60] Although Tocqueville probably had Comte in mind and possibly the Saint-Simonians, that conception of strict limitations on human action had respectable theological antecedents among Calvinists and Jansenists. It is, in that sense, a continuation of the difficulty first raised by Tocqueville in *Democracy* when he had voiced the hope that the same God who willed the march of equality did not mean to extinguish inequality and uniqueness. The formulation that followed was remarkable for its casting of aristocratic resentment in the language of explanation.

It begins with an antimonarchical formula. He rejects the monocausal conception (sc. monarchical) as "too narrow" despite its "pretended greatness," and as specious for its show of mathematical exactitude. Then follows a case for the aristocratic categories of the rare, the exceptional, the individual. The vanity of the theoretical monocausalists has blinded them to the accidental and the inexplicable in historical facts. Yet chance is not sovereign. It accomplishes what has often been prepared beforehand by antecedent facts, by which Tocqueville meant the kind of historical particularism and cultural diversity Montesquieu had celebrated and which included formative and particularizing influences such as the institutional peculiarities of a society, the caliber of the governing elites, intellectual styles, and the state of customs and morals.[61] The February revolution, Tocqueville declares, was just such a combination of general causes and certain specific accidents.

That formulation in which theory comes to the rescue of action and defends its possibility was, when read closely, a source of questions rather than solutions. Does the "human element" refer to action or to ideas? What is the relationship between "general causes" and "the human element"? Do general causes loom larger when actors are ineffectual? And are "general causes" a way of asserting the superiority of theory and the theorist by suggesting that theoretical knowledge of general causes connects the theorist with the powers that are shaping the broad contours of history?

As Tocqueville attempts to demonstrate, or to convince himself, that he combines uniquely the ability both to grasp general causes and to identify the accidents that actually triggered the February outbreak, he mimics the powers he had attributed to God. Among the particular causes Tocqueville emphasizes the personal failings of Louis-Philippe and the stupidities and moral shortcomings of bourgeois politicians. In describing these accidental factors Tocqueville attaches to the actors attributes of powerlessness: "weakness," "vacillation," and "lack of energy." That vocabulary of the ineffectual contrasts with the power-packed language he uses in the list of general causes: the growth of industry, which drew workers to Paris but then could not furnish them with employment; a multitude aroused by the material pleasures encouraged by the regime and by "the democratic disease of envy"; economic and political theories that gained wide popularity among the masses by teaching that "human misery was due to the workings of the laws and not of Providence" and that "poverty could be suppressed by altering social conditions"; pervasive contempt for the governing class, which weakened the will of those who had most to lose from its overthrow; the centralization of power that made the capture of Paris the key to seizing control of government; and, not least of the powerful forces at work, "the mobility of all things" that resulted in an "unstable society," one that had undergone seven major revolutions in less than sixty years.[62]

The picture sketched by these general causes is of a demoralized society in an advanced condition of decay, challenged by forces mostly outside of the official, class-defined circle of politics, and reaping the consequences of its failure to nurture a civic-minded culture.

The transfer of *grandeur* from action to theory is achieved in part by the huge scope of events encompassed by the theory and in part by attributing to theory the power of prophecy, a power to foresee revolution and to determine the meaning of past revolutions in relation to the present, but not beyond. Theory and the theorist both are not, however, preexisting forms and vocations, like medicine or the law, but are defined by the qualities unique to the person who chooses them.

Once Tocqueville leaves off his somewhat disjointed efforts at justifying the *Souvenirs*, the theoretical cast to his project and the role of theorist of revolution begin to emerge. These are established before he undertakes to describe his own intervention in events. His starting point is reminiscent of earlier imageries he had employed, of the traveler ascending the hill adopted in *Democracy*, or of being born between two worlds. Once more the truth of what he will say is facilitated by his distance from his object. The earlier images seemed striking, even authentic,when introduced in the context of describing a truly foreign society. When they are employed in *Souvenirs* to describe contemporary events in which he had participated, however, the imagery seems strained, as though under the guise of distance he was confessing his own involuntary marginalization and alienation. The basis for his present claim of distance was not the same as his earlier one that he was situated between worlds. It is, instead, a parochial one, that he had his roots in one of those worlds, the nearly vanished world of the traditional countryside. He noted that although "his life" had been lived during the July Monarchy, he had lived "apart." "I could have neither the same interests nor the same cares" as the king, Tocqueville remarks; and then he concludes by identifying the special insight his detachment/alienation has given him "that allowed me to penetrate through the mechanism of institutions and the welter of small daily details to observe the state of habits and opinions in the country. There I would clearly see several of the signs appearing that ordinarily signify the approach of revolutions."[63]

Tocqueville's reference to "the country" is not casual; it connotes an older, more rural, prerevolutionary, and deferential culture than is found in the revolutionary capital of Paris. The "country" also signifies the ancestral estate to which Tocqueville will return repeatedly in order to get away from Paris, regain perspective, and renew contact with the local sources of his political and psychological support.

Once distance is achieved, he turns to the task of establishing grandeur. He begins by confessing that he is unable to "retrace distinctly" the events of the revolutionary years. Even though they are "near" they remain "confused." The confusion he describes is not the result of huge, swirling forces but of their opposite, of the antiheroic, the banal: "I lose the thread of my recollections in midst of the labyrinth of petty incidents, of small ideas, petty passions, of personal view and contradictory projects in which the life of public men of that time was exhausted."[64]

Theory fears being lost in the "labyrinth" of detail: the labyrinth, which, for Montesquieu, was a positive metaphor signifying a social complexity that confused power and discouraged it from directly attaining its objectives. For Tocqueville the labyrinth of revolutionary events confuses theoretical vision, in-sight. To combat it, Tocqueville resorts to language almost exactly parallel to his description of the traveler climbing the hill. Although the petty details appeared obscure, "the general physiognomy of the times" remained "vividly present." Tocqueville attributes the vivacity with which he recalled the general features of the time to his having been drawn to them by "curiosity mixed with dread": "I perceived very clearly the special features which characterized it."[65] What he dreads is a permanent state of revolution, of which 1848 is the most recent expression. That conclusion was a tacit admission of the failure of his own political project of establishing 1789 as an ending.

The theoretical character of *Democracy* had been expressed spatially, in the grasp of the politics of a huge land mass which the theorist had traveled. The theorist of the *Souvenirs* was stationary, and, accordingly, his theoreticity is temporal: "Our history, from 1789 to 1830, viewed from afar and as a whole. . . . " The present is to be understood by temporalizing it, relating it to a certain past that can be visualized pictorially as "a tableau of a deadly struggle" between the "old regime" and "the new France." Although the struggle ended in the triumph of the middle class and a decisive defeat not only of the old regime but of its supporting culture of social customs, political traditions, and hierarchical values, the victory of the bourgeoisie was not secure. The revolution of 1789 had established the dominance of the new class, yet it was not the final episode, only the beginning of a *révolution en chaine*, "always the same one, despite varying fortunes and passions," of which "our fathers saw the beginning" but "we, in all likelihood, will not see the end."[66]

*Democracy* had devoted an entire chapter to the question whether great revolutions, such as 1789, would become a rarity. The context in which he had conceived the problem indicated an important shift had taken place in the understanding of revolution. The revolution of 1789 had been dramatized by numerous theorists—Burke, de Maistre, Saint-Simon, and Comte—as pitting overthrow and anarchy against order and stability. But Tocqueville formulated the question in a way that placed revolution in a preexisting context of change. In the second volume of *Democracy* he had argued that although a democratic society is always changing, that does not mean it is in the grip of "endless revolution." Modern revolutions, he believed, are the product of the drive for equality; because democratic societies will have already achieved that condition, with the rich being few and politically "invisible" and wealth changing hands rapidly, revolutionary upheavals would be rare. The middle class, by concentrating on a "narrow" range of interests, further ensures social stability while the methodical character of commercial and industrial societies discourages revolutionary passions.[67] The would-be revolutionary would find himself, therefore, addressing the politically deaf, "his poetry and their prose." So convinced was the younger Tocqueville that the future was unlikely to bring revolutions that he confided to his readers that what he feared most was "endless agitation" that produced no *grandeur* of ideas or actions.[68]

Tocqueville's first attempt to comprehend revolution had related it to democracy. Once democracy was established, the concentrated impulse to destroy the political order became diffused in social, cultural, and economic "changes." The quickening pace and ubiquity of change caused the old to disappear, leaving the impression of revolution without the experience of destruction or the respite of a settlement. Given that formulation, what stake did Tocqueville have in clinging to the category of "revolution" when it seemed to have been displaced by the normalization of significant change? That Tocqueville could collapse revolution into change was a tribute to the tenacity of a memory that pictured predemocratic societies as so stable and unchanging that the actual experience of democratic social and political change was disorienting.

As noted previously, during the 1840s Tocqueville had written several newspaper articles in which he tried to give 1789 the status of a definitive event, the last great revolution, whose outcome settled certain major problems. In this way Tocqueville had hoped to incorporate 1789 into his brand of liberalism where it could serve to establish an outer boundary separating liberalism from socialism and further democratization. When, however, 1848 seemed to transform 1789 from a final chapter on revolutions into their prologue, it seemed a confirmation of his warning in *Democracy* about the difficulty of halting the march of equality at the boundaries represented by property rights. Despite, or perhaps because of the difficulty, he confronted and rejected the demand for the further extension of political rights beyond the middle class. When that demand was joined to socialist proposals for government programs to provide employment, Tocqueville took a stand against both socialism and democratization. In *Democracy* he had defended a conception of political liberty that included the participatory practices of local politics and civil associations, but in the aftermath of the February revolution he opposed aid to workers' cooperatives.[69] His conception of liberty, with its strong feudal flavor deriving from Montesquieuean corporatism, depended on the presence of a supporting culture in which functional equivalents of aristocratic values rooted in local status were decisive. Tocqueville could render American democracy as tolerable by depicting it as a democracy qualified by the equivalents of aristocratic institutions. In the narrative Tocqueville now constructs, that possibility has been nullified by a revolution that eliminated an aristocratic presence from politics: "Our history from 1789 to 1830, seen from a distance and as a whole, appeared to me like a tableau of a deadly struggle extending over 41 years between the old regime, its traditions, memories, its hopes and its men as represented by the aristocracy, and the new France led by the middle class."[70]

Tocqueville reserved his bitterest comment for a society in which all political passions had subsided save one: "only one passion remained deeply rooted in France: hatred of the old regime and distrust of the old privileged classes who represented it in the eyes of the people."[71]

The revolution of 1830 had replaced the legitimist king with the bourgeois king, Louis Philippe. The triumph of the middle class had been complete: "all political power, all franchises, all prerogatives, and the entire government" were "confined" and "concentrated" within "the narrow limits of the bourgeoisie." Those "beneath" as well as those "above" were excluded. "Not only was [the bourgeoisie] the sole directive force over society but its exploiter [*la fermière*]." Tocqueville does not indict the bourgeoisie for injustice or illiberalism but for subordinating political life to class interests to a degree that no aristocracy would have dared. "In its egoism" it lent "an air of private enterprise" to governmental power. Its representatives "thought no more of pubic affairs than to turn them to their private profit and in its petty profits forgetting the nation." Ultimately the bourgeoisie gave to political life "the air of a joint-stock company in which all of the operations are for the benefit of the shareholders."[72]

The bourgeoisie, which Tocqueville had once hoped to educate politically, is now viewed sourly as a class with a few commendable qualities, notably energy and industriousness, while its political vices—"often dishonest, timid, comfort-loving, and mediocre"—disable the bourgeoisie from achieving a regime of "virtue" or "greatness." If it had truly allied with either the people or the aristocracy the bourgeoisie might have worked prodigies. Instead its vices had joined those of Louis Philippe in "a marriage of vices."[73] Thus the revolution of 1830 had destroyed political freedom and corrupted politics. What remained as an object of commitment was the defense of order and the nation—of what endures, the political equivalents of an ontological principle.

## VIII

*By modern I understand not only those moral philosophers who have written in the past fifty years, but those who immediately preceded them and who belonged to that generation which had broken decisively with the Middle Ages.*

*. . . it seems to me that Christianity accomplished a revolution, or if you prefer, a very considerable change.*

Tocqueville[74]

However diverse its forms, all revolutions are about change, but change is not necessarily, or even "normally," about revolution. Modernity, however diverse the interpretations of it, is typically associated with changes in modes of thinking and sensibility and, above all, with the large-scale alterations of the environment in which people live, work, associate, and make plans. Because change disrupts habits it demands adaptation and within that demand is a prescription for the response. Unlike previous eras in which change figures importantly, modernity is uniquely the era in which change has been institutionalized, captured, and imprisoned in processes—of education, industry, and invention—designed, paradoxically, to perpetuate change. Modernity has also been the theater of revolutions: 1640, 1688, 1776, 1789, 1848, 1917, and 1947. In acute self-consciousness of its double progeny, change and revolution, modernity's politics has been preoccupied with warding off revolution by normalizing change, making it an object of policy, and tending it by endless adjustments and transitions (e.g., from underdevelopment to developing). Is change, then, a mere subtext of revolution, or is it the other way round, that rapid, intense, and incessant change tends to normalize revolution? Is it that the conventional contrast between the two was based on the association of revolutions with violence and change with peaceful "transition," and can that facile contrast be maintained once one takes account of the chapters in *Capital* on "Machinery and Modern Industry" or "The So-Called Primitive Accumulation," where Marx recounts the violent dislocations occasioned by the founding of modern economies?[75]

As we have noted earlier, Tocqueville wavered between treating 1848 as revolution or as change, or as failed revolution and successful change.[76] In *Democracy* he had associated change with the natural fluidity of a democratic society, with the endless opportunities for bettering one's condition, and with the consequences of the exuberant energies released by egalitarianism. The instabilities were, he insisted, superficial: the deeper certainties of political fundamentals and religious belief remained mostly steadfast, thereby keeping doubt at bay. "America," like "democracy," was shaped by Tocqueville's sharpening sense of the nature of the political crisis peculiar to modernity. The culture of stability required by the political was being undermined by change and its inevitable accompaniment of skepticism. Tocqueville's conception of the political, which had manifested a growing narrowness throughout the 1840s, now seemed haunted by a fear that the tempos conducive to the emergence of the political had been dangerously accelerated. A fluid, unanchored, indeterminate political seemed to have emerged, self-contradictory and potentially anarchic: all politics and no political. Stability required "slow time" for continuity, tradition, and moral principles to take hold. Unable to conceive of a political without a basis in the unchanging, he clung to religion hoping that it would provide the cultural anchor for containing the dynamics of mediocrity. In *Democracy* that had meant accepting the demise of heroism for the assurances of mediocrity, but in revolutionary France religion signified more than belief. It meant siding with the institution that, historically, was the arch-symbol of antidemocracy and counterrevolution. In allying property and religion Tocqueville was assuming that a defense of property was the same as a defense of the status quo. However, because the institution of property had changed from a feudal to a capitalist form, the actuality was an alliance of opposites: the dynamics of acquisitiveness and innovation with the conservatism of Catholicism. For the church, struggling to overcome popular anticlericalism, the alliance could not but be compromising and incite rather than pacify the masses.

In *Democracy* Tocqueville had located the driving force of change in an adventurous temperament drawn to risk taking and to the new as a matter of course.[77] Without quite realizing it at the time, Tocqueville had drawn the portrait of an as yet unfrightened bourgeoisie. *Souvenirs* presents a different moment, when a bourgeois whose timidity was already commonplace is challenged on both the political and economic planes by socialism. While Tocqueville judged the workers to be misguided, seeing them less as agents of change than as a brute force blinded by envy and premodern in its ignorance, he gave special attention to a new and unmistakably modern actor, one that had made the violation of boundaries its defining mode. The Parisian intellectuals, a class with no counterpart in America, represented a new mentality, post-Enlightenment and high modern, uniting novelty and fashion with sedition. The "literary man," as Tocqueville scornfully called the habitué of Parisian salons and cafés, was responsible for the socialist ideologies and naturally sympathetic to the revolution. Such a type was his friend Ampère: "he was much inclined to carry the spirit of the salons into literature, and the spirit of literature into politics."

> What I call the literary spirit in politics consists in seeking what is ingenious and new rather than what is true, in loving what makes for an interesting spectacle rather than what is useful, in showing a nice sensibility for the fine performance and speech of actors, independently of the consequences of the play, and, finally, to judge by impressions rather than reasons.[78]

The threat posed by a new sensibility—attracted to the surface of things, to appearance rather than substance, and profoundly allergic to boredom—was not primarily the aestheticization of politics but a certain form of aestheticism. Certainly in *Democracy* an aesthetic of the rare inspired by the visual arts had played a major part in Tocqueville's efforts to preserve aristocracy, if only as a sensibility. Although he doubted that a modernist aesthetic could edify democratic man—recall his unfavorable contrast in *Democracy* between the spiritual aesthetic of Raphael and the scientific aesthetic of David—his antimodernism was expressed more pointedly in his attack on individualism and in his concern to find checks to self-interest than in any hostility toward the sciences as such. It is possible that their insignificant influence upon Tocqueville's thinking was less a matter of intellectual taste than of political suspicions. While traditionalists rarely appealed to it, socialist writers had seized upon science and exploited it to legitimize their claims. In Tocqueville's imagination each of these distinctively modern elements—ideology, literary modernism, and science—became interconnected and then distilled into the uniquely modern version of despotism.

That response—the transfiguration first of democracy, then of socialism into the formation of modern despotism—inadvertently drew attention to two striking omissions from that construction, the total exclusion of traditionalist elements and the absence of an aesthetic. Despotism as an advanced stage of modernity, a form virtually acultural, independent of laws and *moeurs*, devoid of an aesthetic, and conceived as somehow above the power of change or perhaps with change controlled by Saint-Simonian experts and a centralized bureaucracy.[79] The alternative which Tocqueville falls back on to counter modern despotism and socialist revolution is the idea of order, one of the most venerable and persistent in the history of Western political theories. The concept of order was developed in response to the question of what enables a society to cohere given its composition of the diverse powers represented in different classes, occupations, and statuses. Premodern thinkers, such as Augustine, Aquinas, and Hooker had concluded that order was a macrocosm, a reflection of the numerous smaller orders represented in the graduated "ranks" of power such as rulers, nobility, ecclesiastics, warriors, burghers, artisans, merchants, and peasants. The usual conclusion was that the larger order was assured if each of the lesser orders remained in its proper place in the hierarchical scheme. Beginning with the seventeenth-century doctrines of equality and consent as the basis of legitimate rule and continuing through the revolutionary overthrow of established orders, the concept lost its *grandeur* but not its urgency.[80]

Under ordinary circumstances order is the ordinary, the taken-for-granted. One needs reminding of what it stands for, the crucial and seemingly neutral requirements of peace and legality that assure expectations, the irreducible condition if there is to be politics at all. In revolutionary times, when the ordinary routines that are order become disordered, an otherwise vacuous notion suddenly acquires the clarity of an imperative armed with a mandate—for repression. Louis Napoleon's remark following his coup of December 1851, "I only departed from legality in order to return to the law,"[81] points to the elasticity of a notion that extends from the extralegal to the legal—and to its impoverishment when compared with premodern notions. The modern notion, however, has its own complexities. The Old Regime notion of order conceived it in terms of both a sharply differentiated social order, which had its accurate reflection in a sharply differentiated political order of "three estates." The modern liberal conception represented order as differentiated socially (upper, middle, and lower classes) yet insisted that that order, largely the result of the workings of the economy, should not be reflected officially into the political order: the latter signified a formal order of impartiality.

Under the pressure of revolutionary events Tocqueville restored an element of *grandeur* to the notion. Order became the site of a metapolitics, the domestic counterpart of foreign policy, superior to all interests except that of the nation. Accordingly, order is outfitted with its own version of *raison d'état* to justify whatever is necessary to save the nation. In its abstract simplicity the politics of order gave Tocqueville the occasion to dissociate himself from republicanism, which had become a central demand of left liberals and socialists.[82] Tocqueville placed his decision to side with the forces of order in the context of his deepening antipathy toward representative government with its corrupt politics of interests and politically inept bourgeoisie: "the class which governed had become, by its indifference, its egoism, its vices, incapable and unworthy of governing." The impotence of government was not so much the result of competing interests but of its narrow base in the "exclusive interests and egoistic passions of a single class,"[83] a claim that not only echoed that of the socialists but resembled the indictment leveled against the aristocracy by the bourgeoisie in the eighteenth century. For Tocqueville order became a refuge that permitted him to take sides while appealing to the principle of disinterestedness. The commitment to order also reveals why Tocqueville could distinguish himself from both the revolutionary and the counterrevolutionary. Both types fight against domination, albeit different versions. Order wants only to suppress disorder, while protesting that, because of its impartial character, it cannot represent domination.

## IX

While the February revolution had a liberating effect on Tocqueville and represented, in his eyes, a turning point in his lifelong struggle against the demons of doubt, he also experienced a rejuvenating moment that captured the ambiguities in his attempt to combine liberalism and *ancienneté.* Soon after the February revolution and the formation of a provisional government, elections for a Constituent Assembly were called. Following his decision to stand for reelection, Tocqueville returned to his rural constituency and ancestral home. In a setting with few large towns he encountered none of "the demagogic agitation" among workers, but he did note that a "universal terror" had served to unite landowners, large and small, in a solid opposition, with property as their "bond of fraternity" and Paris, the loathed "central power," as the enemy. There was also "not the trace . . . of political opinions." In that atmosphere, curiously apolitical yet charged with the kind of passions that should have been reassuring, Tocqueville presents it, nevertheless, as a moment of political and personal dissociation. He recalls that he had steeled himself for defeat by discovering a certain "tranquillity and clarity of mind, a respect for myself and a contempt for the follies of the times." In the theater of his memory Tocqueville recreates a striking series of tableaux, of a campaign notable for the *hauteur* that he displayed toward his electors ("I do not come to solicit your votes" but "to place myself in the service of my country"); for his refusal to respond to the "insolent questions" put to him by a local political club; and for the heroic bombast of his speeches ("with these perils there is glory and it is because there are perils and glory that I am here").[84]

Between descriptions of the campaign and the election, which he won easily, Tocqueville inserts a recollection that summarized the political journey that had brought him to a point where he could shed his political allegiances and seek other emotional and symbolic sources of renewal for the coming struggle against an aroused demos. He found it in revisiting his ancestral estate.

He describes the overpowering sadness he experienced upon surveying an empty chateau, with its dusty rooms and stopped clock and, like Ulysses, finding "none but my old dog" to welcome him. As he recalls the happy and carefree years spent in "the ancient abode of my forefathers," his reverie takes on the resentful tone of the internal émigré: "I can say that it was there and then I best understood all the bitterness of revolutions." Tocqueville immediately connects that passage with a recollection of his triumphal march to the polls, supported by a local populace, which, though always well disposed toward him, was now "more respectful." That deference is then contrasted with the placards proclaiming a "crude equality," which covered the walls at the local polling place. According to custom, all of the voters gathered first at the local church before marching to the polls. Tocqueville's description of the scene reenacts an earlier triumph of the lone traveler who ascends the hill to gain an overview of America—but that purely theoretic deed is surpassed by the triumph of the politically realized actor who will shortly ascend to even greater heights: "At the top of the hill which commands [his ancestral seat of] Tocqueville," the army of voters halted and asked him to speak. He responded by urging them to do their duty. Subsequently "they did," with the result that nearly all of them gave their vote "to the same candidate."[85]

The exhilaration of an *ancienneté* revisited could not conceal the curious character of the elements Tocqueville was attempting to combine: traditionalist elements terrified by socialism, passions that were apolitical, and the bourgeoisie, frightened but without passion, and only tenuously committed to the republic. The problem was not whether the elements were uncombinable but rather what—other than the "fraternity" of property—they could be combined for. The answer would not be long in coming: the traditionalists and large sections of the bourgeoisie would form a "party of order" in support of the Bonapartist despotism. In contrast, the opposition to absolutism, ironically, was rooted in the vigorous political life that had flourished under the July Monarchy, not only in Paris but in many regions of the country. Political clubs, associations, newspapers, and worker organizations—all of which would soon be suppressed or censored—represented precisely what Tocqueville had admired in America. There was passion aplenty, strong political opinions, willingness to risk and to sacrifice, especially among the workers and women.[86] Tocqueville observed much of this but refused to see any possibilities of political revival. Instead, upon returning to take his seat and noting the sharply reduced number of representatives sympathetic to the revolution, he was moved to remark that although there may have been more wicked revolutionaries than those of February, "I do not think that there has ever been any more stupid." But, as he proceeds to list their stupidities, what he considers blunders might be construed as evidence of the sort of civic virtues glaringly absent among his allies. The revolutionaries might have won the Assembly, he declares, if they had taken advantage of universal suffrage to call elections when the upper classes were bewildered and the people "astonished" rather than "discontented"; or, if they had established a dictatorship, they might have held power for some time. Instead they innocently trusted themselves to the nation and then did all they could to alienate the nation; they took on the air of schoolmasters to the nation while making themselves dependent on it Their idealism is then punctured by his cynicism: "they foolishly imagined that it was enough to appeal to the crowd to take part in political life to attach it to their cause, and that to make them love the republic, it was enough to extend rights unaccompanied by profits."[87]

## X

*You know my ideas well enough to know that I grant institutions only a secondary influence on the destiny of men.*

Tocqueville[88]

If there was any assignment in the Constituent Assembly ideally suited for one who had made a theoretical study of political institutions and who had acquired extensive knowledge of comparative practices, it would have been the Constitutional Committee established to draw up a new constitution for the nation following the February revolution. Tocqueville was appointed to it. The first comments of *Souvenirs* about his colleagues on the committee disparage their lack of theoretical sophistication: some of them had spent their lives in "administration" and had "never seen, studied, or understood any system but monarchy." Other members had "hardly raised themselves above practical matters." Although charged with "realizing the theories which they had always ignored or combatted," they remained trapped within monarchical ideas or they handled republican ideas "like novices."

Tocqueville conceded that the task confronting the committee was overwhelming but his main complaint was that the members never had the opportunity for "general discussion" of "the constitution as a whole" or "to trace back and find *les idées mères.*"[89] He finds that, measured against the heroic standard of the American Founding Fathers, they "hardly resembled [those] men, so sure of their purpose and so well informed about the means to take for realizing it . . . [who] drafted the Constitution of America."[90] For his part, when it came to defending a proposal for a bicameral legislature, Tocqueville proved he remembered the *Federalist* by arguing for "a somewhat complicated system of counterpoised" powers rather than a "simple" system of a "single homogeneous power . . . without boundaries" and "irresistible."[91] The proposal was defeated, leaving Tocqueville "discouraged" about continuing the "struggle." Subsequently, when the crucial debate took place over the mode of election and the powers of the new office of president, Tocqueville participated hesitantly, reluctant "to fight", even though he held well-developed views on the matters. Despite reservations and widespread concern that the office would be won by Bonaparte, he supported direct election and strong presidential power.[92] "Socialism was at the gates"; hence, it was more urgent "to put a powerful chief at the head of the republic than to organize a republican constitution."[93]

*Souvenirs* makes little effort to defend its author's feeble showing on the committee, admitting that he had been ineffectual and lacked the determination to press his own arguments. Tocqueville is apologetic as well for the speeches he had given in support of popular election of the president and of the prohibition against reelection.[94] Perhaps the best that can be said in defense of his performance is that it reflected fairly his lack of faith in written constitutions. Even in *Democracy* he had displayed a noticeable lack of interest in the formal structure of the national governmental system. His attitude was fairly summed up in his refusal to take a stand on an amendment that would have made constitutional change a difficult process. Amending should be easy rather than difficult for, according to his curious argument, "it [is] better to treat the French people like madmen whom one should not tie down for fear that they will become enraged by the restraint."[95]

Spite, of course, does not rescue an unconvincing apologetic, yet at bottom Tocqueville's views about constitutional safeguards reflected the struggle in his own mind. He could not accept that revolution signified at the very least a break, a disruption of previous habits and beliefs. A constitution might be a piece of paper, but it was also the beginning of the effort at reconstituting a political culture around a republic and, by establishing universal manhood suffrage, it acknowledged that the political could no longer countenance an exclusionary politics. Tocqueville, in response, insisted that culture could not be reconstituted that easily because too much of the past culture of centralization would persist. While he might support a strong president because of the socialist danger, he also feared that the old "monarchical memories and habits" of the country might produce a popularly elected "pretender to the crown." At the same time he suspected that the current support of republicanism was uncertain because too many monarchical reflexes were being carried over.[96] He remained a confirmed Montesquieuean: unless a governmental structure faithfully mirrored the prevailing social *moeurs*, it would not be effective. There were echoes of de Maistre in Tocqueville's ridicule of those who placed their confidence in "the all-powerfulness of institutions" and in "the precious piece of paper" with its "recipe" for "all our evils": "There is nothing I am more convinced of than that political societies are not what their laws make of them but rather of what prepares them ahead of time are the sentiments, beliefs, ideas, habits of the heart and mind of the men who compose them, as well as what their disposition and education have made of them."[97]

Clearly, for Tocqueville culture had to stand for stabilities if it is to perform its political function of control. The implication was that a rapidly changing culture was a political oxymoron, an anticipation of anarchy. Given that conception of the conditions required of a political culture, it was not surprising that material interests were absent from Tocqueville's list of cultural elements, even though Tocqueville recognized their crucial importance to liberals, conservatives, and socialists alike. Although at some level he acknowledged the importance of property and work, he refused them any honored place in either the ideal world of beliefs ("habits of the heart and mind") or in the equally ideal world of the political. In the end Tocqueville's formulation creates the suspicion that in the revolutionary context of 1848 Tocqueville's worries about "culture" served more to excuse inaction than to advance analysis.

What form of politics, then, might be worthy of action and commitment if the politics of material interests were disparaged as unpolitical? As early as 1843 Tocqueville had formulated his answer in a speech to the Chamber of Deputies. "Public life," he asserted, "has withdrawn from the terrain of domestic politics in order to enter and settle increasingly in the theater of foreign politics." The phenomenon could be "easily explained":

> By substituting interests for opinions, by fragmenting the parties, by making of them a kind of political mist, by disgusting, if I may dare to say it, the country itself, by reducing its domestic politics to boredom, without grandeur, you have necessarily pushed it, in spite of itself, toward the external. That was inevitable; for it is indeed necessary that political life among a free people is practiced somewhere.[98]

In June 1849 Tocqueville got his chance to escape the petty politics of the Assembly and to pursue political *grandeur* of "the external" as foreign minister in the Barrot cabinet.

## XI

> *I felt a peace of mind and a singular calmness when facing greater [responsibilities. . . . [I]t is a great deal easier for me to be obliging and even eager when I feel myself singled out* [hors de pair] *above the crowd.*
>
> Tocqueville[99]

> *At this moment [he wrote to a friend who was serving as his emissary to the Holy See during the crisis over the political status of the Vatican] we hold in our hands the greatest affairs of our times. It is crucial not to become puffed up with pride—God save us from that, but on the contrary to repress the expression of personality in view of the great and sacred nature of the undertaking.*
>
> Tocqueville[100]

*Democracy* had been the work of an unknown eager to enter politics; *Souvenirs* was written by a politician who, at the pinnacle of his success, was forced out of office and, eventually, from political life. What is the closing note Tocqueville chooses? Where has he situated himself politically—to what "end" is the ending?

The final paragraph describes how, as foreign minister, the author's diplomacy brought a successful conclusion to the European conflicts that had kept "the peace of the world in suspense." *Souvenirs* then halts abruptly with Tocqueville's final *souvenir*, "the Cabinet fell."[101] Those words, which seem both anticlimactic and climactic, may have carried a special meaning for Tocqueville. The fact that he offered no comment on the fall of the Barrot ministry raises the possibility that none was called for. Given the intimate nature of the document, it was the logical personal stopping point. The revolution had given him the political opening he sought and the personal fulfillment he longed for. In his own eyes, his diplomatic success marked the moment of political vindication, reversing two decades of futile efforts to make a mark as a political actor.

Foreign affairs represented not only a personal stopping point but a certain destiny, a point of convergence for the authentication of the political and theoretical, as well as the personal. Far from being irrelevant to Tocqueville the political theorist, foreign affairs served to make manifest and to clarify some of his deepest and most abiding concerns, not the least of them being to obstruct the expansion of democracy, to suppress revolutionary movements, and to find in nationalism an alternative to interest politics. Its significance was foreshadowed as early as 1840 in a parliamentary speech on the Eastern Question.[102] Describing the travails of the Ottoman Empire as "a huge tableau" of a world being "transformed" by upheavals over "an immense space," he declared that a great nation cannot merely watch but must actively intervene even if it meant war. "A government that cannot make war is a detestable government." War would recapture the "energy" and "passion" that had once enabled France to stand alone against "the old powers of Europe."

Energy, passion, patriotism, and war were the ingredients by which Tocqueville attempted to combat the two principal sources of the political malaise afflicting the society, the pursuit of particular interests and the revolutionary movement. An aggressive foreign policy would naturally rally men to subordinate petty interests to the interests of the nation. To defeat revolution, he proposed the transformation or, better, the transubstantiation of the French Revolution into "France," to absorb the passion of the revolutionary people into the passion of the nation conceived as a mystical body.[103] His personal achievement would remain linked to combatting revolution, not in the pit of domestic politics but in the more rarefied realm of foreign policy.[104] Foreign policy became the means of redeeming action, of affording heroics an opportunity for grand gestures in "one of the greatest theaters in the world."[105]

In a passage that he marked for deletion, Tocqueville reports a speech he gave at the first meeting with "our ambassadors." After indicating his awareness of the fact that France could no longer dominate the Continent, he specified the neighboring countries in which France had a "right" to exercise not only a "great but a preponderant influence," and emphasized that he would risk "everything," including war, to preserve that influence:

> I shall not hide from you that, at this moment, [war] would be very difficult and perilous for us; the social order might collapse under the strain, burying our fortunes and our lives under its ruins. Count on it, nevertheless, that in the case to which I am referring, we would go to war. Rest assured that if the president of the Assembly did not support me, I would resign.[106]

Foreign affairs exerted a theoretical attraction at a time when politics was roiled by intense class conflicts and ideological polarization. In the age of interest politics, foreign policy and its close adjunct, warfare, become the locus of a displaced political, and it falls to the few who are called to conduct it to view themselves as the real bearers of the political. Ideally, it promised a refuge for the political, external to domestic politics and, at the same time, exempt from the uniformizing reach of bureaucratism. It comprised disinterestedness, patriotism, action taken from the perspective of the whole nation, and, above all, where thought and action were encouraged to contemplate the *grandeur* of nonmaterial objectives in a setting uniquely unencumbered by popular participation, a controlled theater where the "audience" sees and hears only what the actors allow. To one who believed that the political had been all but lost to modernity, foreign policy seemed not only a fitting culmination to a career but a reward for a lifetime of devotion to the political.

Traditionally foreign policy has been the domain most resistant to democratizing, the most remote from popular participation, the preserve of statecraft and of *arcana imperii* where elites could display their unique abilities in the practice of the higher politics of *raison d'état.* Foreign policy appears as the last and most authentic preserve of the premodern political, of an *ancienneté,* where interest is idealized into a univocal and mythical form, the national interest, and thus reclaims an archaic objectivity. In *Democracy* Tocqueville had remarked that foreign policy does not make use of the virtues peculiar to democracy but requires "most of those which it lacks," notably the ability to execute complex strategies, to persevere, and to plan "in secret." By those criteria aristocracy was superior because in foreign policy its interests were not likely to be "distinct" from those of the people.[107]

Although he confessed to having been awed and not a little frightened by "the number and *grandeur* of the difficulties," he soon found himself exulting in the heady experience of power. He includes himself among "those whose will affects the destiny of an entire people."[108] The form that, in his solitude, he gives to that recollected experience is theoretical: being in charge of an entire nation's relations with the world was truly a summit experience, unlike the provincial politics of the elected deputy. This was the real *political* hill he had always longed to climb. Once atop it he experienced again the same reduction of the world to a manageable size: "affairs do not always become more difficult by becoming larger. . . . On the contrary. Their complexity does not grow with their importance. It even happens that often they take on a simpler aspect in the measure that their consequences become wider and more formidable."[109]

Along with the mental exhilaration from the "grandeur of the objects," a moment when the perspective of theorist and actor seemed to coincide, Tocqueville also felt the greatest personal satisfaction at a newfound "self-confidence." It allowed him to resist the temptation to be insolent or haughty. It was now easy for him to be affable when he felt "above" rather than "in the crowd" and to delight in flattering his colleagues while ignoring their advice.[110]

Yet, as Tocqueville makes clear, he intended to enlist foreign policy in the struggle against revolutionary forces. Upon assuming office, he found part of Europe still "aflame" with the passions of 1848. He concluded that the French revolutionary past would make it difficult for the nation to undertake the role of "restorer of the general order in Europe" and "even more impossible" for

France to side with the forces of change, the "innovators," for this would have meant allying with "extravagant" and incompetent allies. It might also risk setting France "aflame" once more with "revolutionary doctrines" and "passions." In a passage that he marked for omission, he declares he had decided to adopt a maxim: to break absolutely with the revolutionary party abroad while promising himself "not to disown the principles of our revolution of liberty, equality, and toleration." Thus, while "waging war on revolution," France would not lose its "liberal appearance" (*l'air libéral*).[111] Notwithstanding, he urged other governments to deny amnesty to any of their subjects who had taken refuge in Switzerland and to refuse them, "whatever their culpability," the right to return home. He also recalls having made sure that France would exclude all refugees of 1848 who might seek passage through France on their way to asylum in Britain or America. He found the refusal of the Swiss to follow his recommendations in keeping with "the natural tendencies of democracies" to confuse foreign and domestic policies.[112] Foreign policy is thus made continuous with domestic "order," its counterpart in the metapolitics of repression.

Later political theorists mostly ignored Tocqueville's tenure as foreign minister, and historians have pretty much rated it as brief and inglorious.[113] His greatest fiasco was to attempt to restore papal sovereignty in the face of liberal efforts to end the temporal power of the pope, a topic that went unmentioned in *Souvenirs.* Ironically, one of the main contributors to Tocqueville's failures was the ineptness of some of the aristocratic diplomats he had appointed. In the end, it was frustration rather than triumph that summed up the episode. As he wrote to Beaumont, "what a miserable thing it is to direct the foreign affairs of a people who have a memory of great force but, in reality, a limited power and do not want to and cannot risk anything. It would be better to plant cabbages."[114]

## XII

*I did not believe then any more than I believe now that republican government is best suited to the needs of France; strictly speaking what I mean by republican government is an elected executive power. For a people whose habits, tradition,* moeurs, *have assured so great a place to executive power, its instability, during agitated times, will always be a cause of revolution; and in calm times, of great uneasiness. . . . And yet I sincerely wished to maintain the republic.*

Tocqueville[115]

*I will never serve you in overthrowing the republic but will willingly work to assure you a great place in it.*

Tocqueville's report of a conversation with Louis Napoleon[116]

Throughout the history of political theories there have been so many encounters, real and imagined, between theorists and rulers as to form a highly stylized genre. Among the more famous are Socrates' performing his self-appointed role as gadfly to Athenian democracy; Plato's efforts to educate a young Syracusan tyrant; Aristotle's service as tutor to the young prince Alexander (soon to be the Great); Machiavelli's attempt to win favor with the Medici by making a gift of *The Prince*; and Thomas More's presentation in his *Utopia* of the pros and cons of philosophers entering the service of kings—not long afterward More himself would, with grisly symbolism, be beheaded by the king he agreed to serve.

These various episodes might be choreographed as a duel between Knowledge and Power. More often than not the encounter is absurdly asymmetrical, a theorist with a tyrant, the power of Truth versus absolute power. In the late-twentieth-century academics expressed the inequalities of power in the plaintive catchphrase, "speaking truth to power." An encounter between contraries demands guile for a battle of tactics in which each tries to exploit the other and both are aware of the other's scheming. The Man of Knowledge schemes to have power serve the ends of truth, enforce justice, fashion a virtuous citizenry, and promote knowledge. In return he will confer dignity by lending power an aura of justification, immaterializing it. What does the Man of Power seek? Absolution? or disinterested advice? or a fig leaf for power?

Tocqueville's encounter was unique. As minister of foreign affairs, he faced the duly elected president who, it was widely assumed, aspired to become dictator. Tocqueville's encounter with Louis Napoleon had few of the elements for the Truth-versus-Power drama and more of those for its parody. The office occupied by Bonaparte had, after all, been designed by Tocqueville and his committee with the aim of creating a powerful counterpoise to socialism and revolution. True to his inclination, Tocqueville clothed his relationship with the would-be tyrant in multiple ambiguities, of defending the republic by not conspiring against it while becoming the friend of its enemy, a republic that he despised only slightly less than its form of politics. "I believe that of all his ministers, and perhaps of all of the men who did not want to take part in his conspiracy against the republic, I was the most advanced in his good graces, who saw him closest, and was best able to judge him."[117]

In Tocqueville's account, his strategy is not to use Napoleon but to contain him and, in the process, save a republic. Although recognizing that Napoleon presented "the greatest and most permanent danger" to the republic as well as to the ministry, Tocqueville, who claimed to "have studied him very attentively," was "convinced" that he and his colleagues could "establish ourselves firmly enough in his mind." In his assessment Tocqueville concluded that the president was "extraordinary," not because of his intelligence or character but because circumstances had conspired to "push . . . his mediocrity so high." Because Louis Napoleon was neither teachable nor pliable but ordinary, he was, Tocqueville reasoned, manipulable. It was not "impossible," therefore, "for us to enter partly into the designs of Louis Napoleon without departing from our own." One common bond was, according to Tocqueville, that both Napoleon and the ministry wished to be independent of the majority leaders of the Assembly. This tactical alliance was approved by Tocqueville, even though he was convinced at the time that Napoleon would be plotting to violate the constitutional prohibition against the reelection of the president.[118] Although Tocqueville had claimed to be most fearful of an elected president, he assured Napoleon nevertheless that he and his colleagues would work with him to amend the constitution.[119] Moreover, because revision was doubtful, Tocqueville was prepared to go "even further" and encourage Napoleon to run for reelection despite the constitution.[120] Tocqueville reports with obvious pride that soon he and the would-be heir of the emperor were exchanging favors: Tocqueville supplied jobs for some of the president's supporters, while the president signaled that he would forgive certain remarks of Tocqueville's closest friend, Beaumont, and not oppose the latter's appointment as ambassador to Austria. "All of my colleagues," Tocqueville remarks reproachfully, "did not imitate me in the care I gave to currying [*à capter*] the goodwill of the president without swerving from my opinions and duties."[121]

In *Souvenirs* Tocqueville made no attempt to describe the course by which Louis Napoleon would establish himself as emperor and institute a severely repressive regime. To be sure, those developments occurred after Tocqueville and his colleagues were forced to resign. Yet, in his final note about relations with Louis Napoleon, Tocqueville insists that the president "was drawing closer to us" when "the Roman affair" brought down the ministry. Although Tocqueville promises to explain why toward the end relations with the president were improving and those with the Assembly worsening, he never does. Similarly, the crucial "Roman affair," which proved to be the flash point that brought down the cabinet and may well have been Tocqueville's least glorious moment in office, is omitted from his account of his tenure as minister of foreign affairs.[122]

The failure of Tocqueville's strategy for preserving order with a republican veneer is presented by him as the defeat of someone who had hoped to establish a regime of "moderate liberty" and constitutionalism but was outwitted by a man who proceeded to establish a despotism. Yet there is an important sense in which that outcome was closer to Tocqueville's own political evolution than is suggested by the antithesis between moderate liberty and tyranny.

## XIII

Tocqueville wrote no conclusion to *Souvenirs*, perhaps because the dead end he had reached—personally, politically, and theoretically—provided an eloquent silence that served the same purpose. *Souvenirs* was haunted throughout by a sense of failure, or, more precisely, by a sense of weakness. There was the inability to come to terms with liberal parliamentary politics; Tocqueville could despise its pettiness, yet be exhilarated when he triumphed at the polls and was later made foreign secretary. Both his service at the ministry and earlier on the Constitutional Committee were accounted failures—although he only admitted to the latter. Tocqueville's penchant for projecting huge panoramas of power—the movement toward equality, democratic despotism, the refusal of 1789 to be interred once and for all, the power of socialist theories, and the threat of the working masses—first encouraged indecision, then support for repression and the cause of "order."

Weakness finds its correlative in force. That is, however, another way of testifying to the depths of the trauma produced by 1789. This was illustrated in one of *Souvenir*'s most striking vignettes where Tocqueville's most precious mark of identity is threatened—by a woman. Tocqueville described attending a dinner party whose host, perhaps unaware or perhaps not, of the political animosities between some of the guests, had seated Tocqueville with Georges Sand. Noting that "at that time Madame Sand was something of an *homme politique*," Tocqueville recalls that earlier a friend had asked Georges Sand her opinion of *Democracy in America*. Her reply was that she only read books presented to her by their authors. Tocqueville not surprisingly wants to even the score, especially with a woman who had adopted certain mannish modes of dress and, of course, the first name, and whose sympathies were with the forces of disorder, of transgression. He confesses that he was "greatly prejudiced against Madame Sand, for I detest women who write, especially those who make a system of disguising the weaknesses of their sex instead of interesting us by having us see them in their true character." Having disposed of her affectation of the style of *un homme*, he then turns to deflate the other pretension, equally masculine, of *le politique* (politician). He notes that while she had conversed most informatively about the revolutionaries, giving him an intimate view of the temper and organizational preparations of the Paris workers about which he had been ignorant, she had mistakenly predicted that, unless the ruling classes halted their provocative acts, a showdown would occur and Tocqueville and his kind would surely perish.[123] She had, in other words, shown some grasp of politics (*la politique*) but had failed as *le politique*, unable to grasp the deeper direction and meaning of events.

## XIV

*Souvenirs* formed the second installment in an unpremeditated trilogy about the political and its proper supporting culture. *Democracy* had explored the positive power of a political culture, though not one created ex nihilo; it had envisioned the possibility that, with the powerful support of religious beliefs, the political might be reconstituted so as to engage the modern temper, reconciling individualism and *civisme*, self-interest and the common good, liberty and law, while equivocating about the value of equality; the last component of the trilogy, *The Old Regime*, in contrast, would seek the recovery of the political on terms that combined a premodern understanding of inequality and an archaic conception of participatory politics, but it also recounts how an established political culture was destroyed by political modernization. That story, Tocqueville's last, would be haunted by a present that, in the despotism of Louis Napoleon, had abolished political life, replacing it with the pseudo-individualism of privatized lives and the pseudodemocracy of plebiscites.

*Souvenirs* records Tocqueville's resistance to the inevitability of equality, which *Democracy* had announced, and his doubts that the political could be reconstituted even on the basis of liberalism's restricted version of equality. Although *Souvenirs* attributes the dissolution of the political to the resurgence of equality, the new equality is seen as one element in a larger picture colored by failure to establish a civic culture, which he attributes primarily to the bourgeoisie. Together with the political shortcomings of the middle class, the emergence of socialism as an antipolitical movement spelled for Tocqueville a crucial turning point in the nature of politics. For one who had defined himself as a new kind of liberal, one question being posed by events was whether a politics based on his version of a liberal theory of the political was possible, not alone because of the political inadequacies of the bourgeoisie but because of the triumph of modernity over revolution itself, of relentless incremental change over radical rupture. The question being forced by Tocqueville on himself was, If his quarrel was becoming centered upon modernity, was liberalism the best means of defending against the baleful effects of modernity and, if not, was his version of liberalism, if not misconceived, then miscast?

While socialist theories were pressing for enlarged political and theoretical possibilities, the threat of socialist revolution drove Tocqueville to retreat even beyond retrenchment and support repressive measures that would forcibly shrink the political and transfer his theoretical from the introspective *Souvenirs* to the retrospective of investigating the past. Although that choice might seem to reject the imaginative, experimental, even playful modes of the Saint-Simonians, Fourier, and Proudhon in favor of the valedictory mode of Chateaubriand's *Memoirs from beyond the Grave*, the more sensitive question would be, Under tyranny what is the best mode for theorizing opposition?

# CHAPTER XXIV
## *THE OLD REGIME AND THE REVOLUTION: MYTHISTORICUS ET THEORETICUS*

### I

> *I am proud enough to believe that I am better suited than anyone else to bring to such a subject great intellectual freedom and to discuss men and things without passion or reticence.*
>
> Tocqueville[1]

> *I easily picture a great tableau before me, pierced with new insights. But when I try to reproduce it, the copy which actually emerges from my mind is so inferior to the original that I become upset by the difference between what I am doing and what I want to do.*
>
> Tocqueville[2]

Public calamity and personal humiliation formed the backdrop to the last, most tortured phase of Tocqueville's life; nonetheless, out of it came a masterpiece, *L'ancien régime et la Révolution.* Unlike *Democracy in America,* however, *The Old Regime* was written more in despair than hope. "The despotism [of Napoleon III]," he wrote to Beaumont, "will last a long time . . . because its only obstacle will be itself."[3]

*Democracy* was composed to gain entry to a political career; *The Old Regime* was written by a political outcast who felt honor-bound to resist any overtures to return. To one ally, he wrote of "the impossibility of being political men" and described himself as "a superannuated lover of liberty at a time when everyone longs for a master."[4] And to an American correspondent, he declared, "I have absolutely left public life and have decided not to reenter as along as there is in my country an order of things so contrary to everything that I have wished and hoped for," adding wistfully that he often looked "toward America" and considered himself "nearly a citizen."[5] All of the political values by which he lived seemed hopelessly out of touch with the new political realities where men cared only for their interests. More than estranged from the new order of things, he was close to being a broken man, his health and spirits "in need of rest and especially of solitude. . . . Thirteen years of public life, four years of revolution, and, more than anything, the sadness caused me by the spectacle of my country, and the prevision of its future, have shaken my constitution."[6]

Despotism also cast its shadow over the theoretical enterprise itself, accelerating the profound change taking place in the reading public. In bygone eras, Tocqueville lamented, the politically active and the enlightened classes were identical; when they became captivated by some great ideas, the other classes followed. Now, however, power had gravitated toward classes whose reading was restricted to newspapers. "We are left to declaim as much as we want, like academicians addressing a public academy." When a disturbing thought penetrated the public, however, suppression followed.[7]

Amid his enforced isolation, and the steady consolidation of the Bonapartist regime during the early 1850s, Tocqueville pondered what to do with the rest of his life, a question that became more pressing as his health deteriorated. What remained of a vocation was, by default, purely theoretical. He could no longer assume that he could be the enactor of his own ideas, that his actions could be the embodiment of his theory, or vice versa.[8] He might, of course, attempt once more to give theoretical expression to his conception of politics, but the brute fact was that the new regime had emasculated parliamentary institutions thereby eliminating the political forums, which in the past, and despite his disdain for them, had been presupposed in his conception of the theory-action relationship. Even if something like parliamentary politics were to survive, the existence of that particular form and its limitations, would have only confirmed Tocqueville's conviction of the futility of political involvement. While the modern world might, with difficulty, be understood, it could not be mastered; it seemed adrift, settled only in its recalcitrance to the efforts of thought to grasp its direction and of action to shape it.

## II

> *I believe that I have drawn from this study many new facts and insights which not only explain why this great Revolution has occurred in France and why it has had the character we have seen; but also why many events which have taken place since, and whence have come down to us a mass of habits, opinions, and inclinations which we believe to be new but which have their roots in the government of the Old Regime.*
>
> Tocqueville[9]

Tocqueville's constant lament was that he had lost his prophetic powers amid the "impenetrable obscurity which reigns in the political world."[10] He "could not see an inch in the surrounding darkness."[11] Darkness represented the suppression of politics and the secretive regime of cronies imposed by despotism.

Tocqueville's gloom at the "black night" and his excruciating estrangement from political life seemed to express what it might be like to live Nietzsche's eternal recurrence.

> I myself thought that [the democratic revolution] finally ended in 1830 because democracy, after having destroyed all privileges, had arrived where nothing remained except the privilege, so ancient and necessary, of property. I thought that, like the ocean, it had finally found its shore. Mistake! Today it is evident that the flood continues its course, that the sea rises; that not only have we not seen the end of the immense revolution which began before us but that the child who is born today will not see it. What is at stake is not a modification of the social body but its transformation. To arrive where? I do not really know.[12]

Denied knowledge of the present, of the temporal dimension crucial to action, and facing a one-dimensional regime repressive both of free political action and of theory, it seemed impossible for theory to be resumed on the basis of the old prospectivist assumption, of theory oriented toward the future while offering guidance to action in the present. In a letter he seemed resigned to a disconnection between theory and action:

> You are right that a bird's-eye view of affairs is often more favorable to the prediction of events than studying them in detail; but it is on condition that one is satisfied with very general truths, extending over a wide space of time. But as to knowing how men are likely to act tomorrow, how they will deal with coming events, all who are not in a position to know what is passing in their minds, must argue at random: even when you see clearly the interests of others, you cannot be sure of their taking the same view.[13]

Yet, toward the end of that letter and after returning to the difficulty of penetrating the thought and practices of present-day actors, Tocqueville gave the first hint of creating a different form of theory, predominantly retrospective rather than prospective, eliding the present in order to connect past and future: "I divert my mind as much as I can from the occurrences of the present to the contemplation of the past and of the future, which, though farther off, are less obscure."[14]

As we have seen in several other contexts, it was an article of faith for Tocqueville that 1789 continued as an active, even decisive, presence in French politics, never exorcised and with seemingly no end to its reincarnations. If, however, one could expose the anatomy of recurrence, truly understand why the French were hopelessly gripped by a compulsion to repeat, then one would have succeeded in grasping the nature of the forces shaping the political history of modern France. Bonapartism was the obvious symbol of continuity between 1789 and 1852. The Great Revolution had seemingly ended in the despotism of Emperor Napoleon I; 1848 had culminated in the despotism of Louis Napoleon and the Second Empire. Egalitarianism, now empowered by theories of popular sovereignty, had made both despotisms possible. The consolidation of Louis Napoleon's power—with the support of universal suffrage—was a crucial, if allusive, element in Tocqueville's numerous references to "darkness" and "obscurity" and the cause of his inability to "see" into the future. The obliteration of the social and political differences that had given theoretical vision its points of reference and politics its centers of resistance had left an undifferentiated society, an unpolitical night. Sightless amid sameness.

If, as Tocqueville insisted, "the issue of political domination" outweighed all others,[15] what did it mean, for someone who had once declared that no one was less revolutionary than he, to attempt to compose a *political* theory? How could one restore light, a political mode of seeing, while living amid the suppression of politics, the darkness of despotism, and to whom should it be addressed? And what would be the appropriate form for comprehending revolution and despotism, the most *overpowering* and now interconnected modalities of power?

Some light is shed on these matters by a letter written while Tocqueville was deeply involved in his researches. The letter is striking for its attempt to balance the equivocal and the unequivocal. He tells his close friend, Corcelle, that, although he will not write *un livre de circonstance*, "it does not follow that a clear meaning is not to be drawn from the historical study as I have undertaken it; that it should leave the opinions and sentiments of the author in the dark, and the mind of the reader uncertain of the judgment he ought to have on the events and men." A reader is, however, more likely to become "reflective" if the author does not "dogmatically" tell him what to think. Tocqueville concludes by saying that, when the work is finished, "No one, rest assured, will be in doubt about the purpose I have set for myself."[16] This was to be a political theory written for antipolitical times and under the political and personal conditions of inner exile. It would of necessity be a highly tactical work, *politique*, full of indirection, allusions, metaphors, disguises, a political education in the guise of a historical narrative.[17] That *The Old Regime* is not the book he set out to write lends some plausibility to these conjectures.

In 1851 his original intention was to focus on the Great Revolution and his first researches and preliminary sketches dealt mainly with that phenomenon. At some point, probably early in 1854, the earlier focus was replaced by one centered upon the Old Regime.[18] He had shifted emphasis from a living tradition to a dead one.The title he had originally chosen, *The Revolution*, was replaced by *The Old Regime and the Revolution*, a choice that apparently was not entirely his.[19] Aware that he had not achieved his original objective with publication, he declared his intention to "resume the whole suggested by the broad title [*La Révolution*] which I chose originally."[20] Instead, he left behind a sketch of the concluding part of that project indicating his intention to cover the revolutionary events, the Consulate, and the Empire.

It might be reasonable to conclude that his worsening health and eventual death explain why the project could not be completed; however, that explanation does not resolve the question of why he broke off his original studies on the revolution in order to focus upon the re-creation of an archaic world located somewhere between the late Middle Ages and the first half of the eighteenth century and to insist that its extinction had occurred long before the French Revolution that claimed to have destroyed it. The decision to concentrate upon the prerevolutionary world may have been political, prompted by events in his own postrevolutionary world. The original project, of exploring the connections between revolution and despotism in the era of the first Napoleon, had its gestation at a time of great political uncertainty concerning the future form of French politics. In the *Souvenirs* Tocqueville had remarked of the second Napoleon that "he will create nothing, but he will endure." The likely durability of the new regime was overwhelmingly confirmed by the plebiscite of November 1852 based on "universal" suffrage. A few weeks later the Second Empire was proclaimed. After four years of turmoil a settled, perhaps irreversible, context had emerged, a system of reference defined by the bipolarity of revolution and despotism.

Although it might have been possible for Tocqueville to have drawn contemporary political implications from the original bipolarity culminating in the first Napoleon, the fatal weakness of the discarded subject was that he could not generate a conception of an alternative regime from the historical materials within that temporal span. Without an alternative there could be no teaching. The new emphasis which would treat the French Revolution as the terminus ad quem rather than the terminus a quo, could be the way of dispelling darkness. But if the darkness *was* the revolution, could it be dispelled other than by working through it? This could mean identifying certain tendencies such as common citizenship, and civil rights, and public deliberation that promoted freedom and broadened the political. These had been proclaimed during the revolutionary era and could serve to connect present and past.

## III

> *The French Revolution will only appear as darkness if it is considered by itself; it is in the times which preceded it that one must seek the only light which can illuminate it.*
>
> Tocqueville[21]

Later students have assumed that the liberal/conservative Tocqueville, unlike his more radical contemporaries, the Saint-Simonians, Fourierists, and Proudhon, could never have been tempted to construct a utopia. That assumption is correct insofar as it compares Tocqueville with utopians whose futuristic schemes required a sharp rupture with the past. Radical utopians could dismiss, in toto, the past because they were captivated by the boundless possibilities they perceived in the integration of science and technological innovation with industrial organization. There is, however, no necessary connection between utopianism and antihistoricism, or between utopianism and perfectionism, or, more arguably, between utopianism (e.g., of the Kropotkin variety) and the requirement of a complete blueprint for society. Tocqueville could conceive a utopian element whose basis was in history, not beyond it, and whose character was ambiguous rather than flawless. To retrieve a utopian element rather than project an ideal totality would allow for the presence of imperfect beings and arrangements, a utopian element within a fallen world of flawed beings.

Retrieving a particular past would, necessarily, be a historical task; identifying its significance a theoretical one. Tocqueville's *Old Regime* can plausibly claim to be a new theoretical form, combining theoretical and conceptual approaches in the service of a nontotalistic ideal that was unique among his contemporaries for being a political rather than a technoeconomic vision and, for that reason, a utopia for fallible beings. It would be a utopia conceived as a solution to the problem of class antagonisms that his younger contemporary Marx was investigating—and encouraging. Instead of looking to the rational exploitation of productive power as the means of eliminating classes and class conflicts, Tocqueville looked to forms of politics whose raison d'être presupposed a steady modulation, rather than the disappearance, of class distinctions.

The fusion of political purpose, historical research, and theoretical form produced a dual structure of critique and ideal, a counterparadigm standing in judgment upon the paradigm of revolution and despotism most recently traced in the trajectory from 1848 to Louis Napoleon. Hence the dualism of the title, *The Old Regime and the Revolution. L'ancien régime* fulfilled a political purpose that could not be accomplished by concentrating primarily upon *la Révolution.* It would provide a detailed picture of political liberty as the way of life in prerevolutionary centuries—hence an example of the practices for resisting despotism, not by pitched battle, but by following time-hallowed means of resolving the everyday needs of communities in which people differed by rank, wealth, and education. The relationship between the two, between the counterparadigm of a premodern regime and the revolutionary paradigm, was not static but tragic. The Old Regime was destined to collapse, mainly from self-inflicted wounds, into the revolutionary regime, leaving scarcely a trace—except in the revival of a centralized bureaucracy, the nemesis that, in Tocqueville's view, had defeated the promise of both the Old Order and the New.

Traditionally the question of the form of *The Old Regime* has been settled by categorizing it as a history, a narrative about the reemergence of administrative centralization, the disintegration of the political culture supported by religion and aristocracy, and the spread of subversive beliefs among the ruling and enlightened classes.[22] Tocqueville seemed to echo the occupational woes typical of the historian when he wrote feelingly of his "abyss of despair" at "this mountain of notes which overwhelms me."[23] Certainly *The Old Regime* is remarkable for being prepared by extensive archival research; and this in no small measure is why it continues to find favor among professional historians. Nonetheless, to the degree that history is measured by Rankean standards, *The Old Regime* does not comfortably qualify. There are very few exact dates for the developments described and almost no effort to pause over, much less to weigh, conflicting evidence. At a time when several of his illustrious contemporaries were engaged in writing histories of the revolution, Tocqueville makes no reference to any individual historian.[24] Instead, during the composition of the work he writes hortatory notes to himself intended to evoke that moment of uniqueness, personal and political, that he had always regarded as essential to achieving theoretical greatness: "A new view, were I am really able to approach it with a fresh mind: especially now that I am detached from my time and my country."[25] The consciousness that has deliberately ransomed itself to the past and, in good faith, immersed itself in extensive research into old records, manuscripts, state papers, *cahiers*, and pamphlets—so diligently that its labors would be hailed as innovative model of historical research and its results held up as a classic study of the most crucial epoch of modern French history—nonetheless found itself straining against the constraints imposed in writing a narrative or causally structured history. Not least were the limitations of history as a means of political education.

The foremost difficulty, however, arose from the nature of the question and the appropriate political solution once the answer was revealed. The question concerned the various forms assumed by a power that had first irrupted in 1789, culminated in despotism, and then had disappeared subterranean-fashion only to emerge in 1830, vanish again to surface once more in 1848, only to exhaust itself in 1852 and collapse into another despotism. The answer would be that political stability and freedom posed an impossible demand under conditions that combined a democratic conception of popular sovereignty with a strongly centralized, highly bureaucratized state. The demands for extending equality would drive the state to greater and greater penetration of everyday life. Stability could then be achieved only at the expense of free politics. The society that had been deprived of free politics had to relearn its political lessons by retracing its own regression toward political underdevelopment.

The lessons were to be extracted from the encounter between a modernizing administration and a traditional society, between a monoculture and a polyculture. Question, answer, teaching: a tantalizing mix of elements needing the skills of the historian in order to locate the relevant actors, institutions, and policies; the judgment of the theorist to weigh the political implications; and a third element, something between history and theory, to better convey a political teaching in dark times. What is the third element and how does it take shape in Tocqueville's new form? Is it to be differentiated from theory or incorporated?

If Tocqueville's reservations about history had to do with its limitations as a method of political understanding, his concerns about theory had to do with excess. The historian could detail the actions of revolutionaries as they set about deliberately to transform an entire society by virtually obliterating the preexisting civilization, yet there remained something confounding, mysterious, about the sheer enormity of an undertaking that was beyond the powers of the actors to control. The historian could come to an understanding of what had happened only to find inexplicable the relationship between what actors had intended and the full range of what had actually happened. There was, however, something more unfathomable, perhaps more immoral, in the case of thinkers rationally justifying the action *beforehand*, and of taking it for granted that actors could limit the consequences of actions taken to achieve a theoretical prescription. The destructive role of theorists deeply troubled Tocqueville and helped to produce a "fear of theory" that contrasts with the self-consciously Promethean conception embraced by Marx. Tocqueville conceived of revolutionary ideology as an explosive mix of opposites, of abstract ideas and mass passion. More precisely it was a fear of that version of modern theory wherein the line between theory and ideology was deliberately blurred in the interest of uniting radical ideas with revolutionary will.[26]

He responded in two ways. One was to outline—once more—a new "political science" focused on mass movements of opinion rather than antimajoritarian devices. The second, which was fulfilled in *The Old Regime*, was to formulate theory as an archaeology of loss that sifts the debris left by a philosophically inspired act of world destruction and pieces together/recreates the old order of things—an act of piety with, however, an edge of defiance.

The act of piety is served by archival research, which, instead of simply lending factual support, provides access to or, better, restores life to lifeless forms. When Tocqueville traveled to Germany to observe firsthand a society where "the institutions of the Middle Ages are scarcely destroyed and where there is left countless debris in the customs, *moeurs*, and social and economic condition," it was as much a pilgrimage as a research effort with the past serving less as an archive than as an object of communion.[27] While plotting out *The Old Regime* Tocqueville wrote of how he and his wife retreated and "renounced the living and dwell only in the company of our illustrious dead whose books will be our only society."[28]

Then, from the autopsy of the old, Tocqueville prepares for the stranger world of a living tradition, of the revolutionary idea and its mentality of total destruction:

> My subject consists in the successive changes in the social condition, the institutions, the public opinion and manners of the French, as the Revolution advanced. As yet I have discovered only one way of finding this out: it is to live over every moment of the Revolution with its contemporaries by reading not what has been said *of* them, or what they said afterward of themselves . . . but what they themselves said at the time, and, as much as possible, what they really thought. . . . By these means I certainly attain my object, which is to live gradually through the period.[29]

*The Old Regime* of the historians discounts not only Tocqueville's intentions but his specific disclaimers as well. In the same letter in which he complains of "the mountain" of facts he has assembled, he begs his correspondent for counsel on when it is appropriate to restrain the use of facts so that the reader would not lose sight of the "general ideas," which are his real purpose. Toward that end he wants a subject that allows him "to mix [facts] with general ideas so that the ideas reflect the facts."[30] That would require not a Rankean "recital of facts" but "a new form," not a history but an attempt to render comprehensible "the cause, character, extent of the great events which furnish the main links of the chain to our own time."[31] Provisionally, Tocqueville's "new form" might be called historical political theory or theoretical political history. But those labels would be only a modest stab at its complexities.

A helpful clue to Tocqueville's thinking about the most suitable form for his new project is a long letter written in December 1850 while completing

*Souvenirs.* In casting about for the right formulation of "a great work," something that would be "a great subject of political literature," Tocqueville stipulated that it had to be a work congenial with his talents and temperament, one that would "seize" him and arouse an "impassioned pleasure." One possibility was a synthetic work on the French Revolution that would focus on the rise and fall of the Empire, thus allowing him to make "one tableau" out of all of the "detached pictures." An alternative was a shorter work that would focus on the Empire and, particularly on "the *true* nature of the man" who founded it; this would not be a history but rather "an ensemble of reflections and judgments." As matters turned out Tocqueville executed neither of these projects: instead of tracing the forward trajectory of the revolution through the Empire, he reversed its course and went backward from the revolution to prerevolutionary France.

What is revealing about these false starts is the worried and uncertain tone that enters when he emphasizes the importance of formulating a project suited to his own strengths and purpose and of identifying the appropriate methods. His qualms arose from the realization that the project demanded "a solid and continuous basis in facts." The "principal merit of the historian is to know how to connect the tissue of facts, and I don't know if this skill is within my grasp. Up to now I have been better at judging facts than at recounting them." In describing "the immense difficulties" attending the second proposal, he identified as the "most troubling" that it would require a "mixture of history properly speaking and historical philosophy" in the manner of "the inimitable" Montesquieu's work on the greatness and decadence of the Romans: history provides the "canvas" and philosophy the "color."[32] In another letter when referring to the same combination, Tocqueville employs the phrase "philosophy of history" to distinguish what he means by philosophy.[33] What did he mean by "history" and "philosophy of history"?[34]

Although Tocqueville never defined either term, history seems to have meant, in part, legal-type evidence mustered to support a claim and, in part, archaeology, a recovered artifact that received its broad meaning from a "philosophy." The latter was closely connected to *grandeur* and allowed for an epical vision of actions or events that had been "not only great but extraordinary, even unique."[35] It embodied a special way of seeing that recalled the ancient origins of *theoria*, from *theorein*, to see. "Seeing" Tocqueville likened to looking through a lorgnette: one end magnifies the object, the other reduces it. "I would prefer to place the eye on the end which enlarges; in my life I have always needed to look in this way at whatever I am doing in order to make something worth doing."[36] By the same token, what is temporally distant is made vivid, brought near, by its contrast with the uncanny air of unreality that envelopes, and distances, what is temporally close at hand. On his "parliamentary life" he muses:

> Is it true that there really were political assemblies in France? That the nation passionately cared for what was said there? These men, these institutions, these forms—were they not shadows without reality? These passions, experiences, fears, friendships, and hatreds which swirled around and agitated us, did they belong to the times that we have really seen or are they memories that we have learned while reading the history of past times? Truthfully, I have been tempted to believe this, for what truly lives leaves some trace and I do not see any of what we have imagined to understand or feel.[37]

## IV

Although his frequent travels to Germany had familiarized him with the ideas of Kant, Schiller, and Hegel, it would be incorrect to assume that Tocqueville meant to emulate the systematic philosophies of history associated with those writers. What he did share with them was an approach to history as epic, history as dealing in large scales, spatially broad and sufficient temporally to serve the dramatization of hypostatized concepts, such as Right, Peace, and Freedom. Temporally *The Old Regime* moves freely back and forth, from nineteenth-century France to the eighteenth century, and from thence to mediaeval France and forward to prerevolutionary France. Initially Tocqueville envisaged the spatial scope of the French Revolution as encompassing a vast European-wide panorama.

Some further light is shed on these matters in the letter to Kergorlay cited earlier. After disclaiming the aim of a history in the usual sense, he says his objectives could be realized in "an ensemble of reflections and judgments on that history."[38] "Ensemble" signified selected images grouped according to a theory that connects, interprets, and judges. As we have noted several times, Tocqueville's writings were notable for their concern to evoke in the reader the kind of impressions associated with painting or, better, heroic painting. A theory, for him, was an assemblage of tableaus, remarkable for their striking juxtapositions, chronological sweep, and conceptual scope. "[T]he composition of a book is like that of a tableau. The important thing is not the perfection that one could give to a part, but the exact relation of all of the parts, out of which emerges the general effect."[39] Thus, under the direction of the theoretical the dramatic and the pictorial vie/mix with the historical, but in the process expose the lack of congeniality between the demands of political *grandeur*, with its inclination toward the mythical, and the cautionary modes of factual history and theoretical reasoning which cannot legitimate without qualifying.

For reasons which I hope become stronger when I discuss the substance of *The Old Regime*, I propose to consider the work as embodying a novel form, part history, part myth, with theory as the governing element. Toward that end I borrow the phrase *mythistoricus* from Cornford's classic study of Thucydides to emphasize that just as Thucydides combined a respect for factual evidence with mythical modes that, despite his intentions, he did not wholly exorcise,[40] so Tocqueville combines attested historical facts with mythic elements in an endeavor guided by political objectives and informed by theoretical strategies. The similarities between the theoretically inclined historian of the Peloponnesian War and the historically inclined theorist of the Old Regime are at times so striking as to suggest conscious imitation.[41] What connects them is a shared fascination for the extraordinary.

Consider the antilogical rhythm of a passage near the end of *The Old Regime*. It begins,"When I consider this nation in itself I find it more extraordinary than any of the events of its history"; then it continues: no nation has been so "full of contrasts and so extreme in all its actions, more led by feelings and less by principles, always worse or better than expected, one time above and another time below the common level of humanity." It is a nation of stay-at-homes, content to follow routines, but when routines are disrupted "it will push to the ends of the world and dare all things." It has an "aptitude for everything but excels only in warfare, adoring chance, force, success, the clamor of noise rather than true glory; more capable of heroism than of virtue . . . more able to conceive immense designs than to achieve great undertakings; the most brilliant and the most dangerous of European nations."[42]

The passage, with its paired contrasts, is structurally an echo of the speech that Thucydides has a Corinthian address to the Spartans. The difference is that where Thucydides has his speaker contrast Spartan qualities with those of the Athenians Tocqueville endows the French with both of the contrasting qualities.[43] Although it may seem that Thucydides and Tocqueville were warning against extremes and implying that great virtues had to be moderated by restraint, that impression would be misleading. Both writers were examining the forms of greatness and exposing their tragic character. At that point analysis has entered the domain of myth, the domain where excess of virtue and vice, power and weakness rather than moderation, prevails. Tocqueville's conception of the political, with its elements of *grandeur*, heroic action, and its exalted standard of virtue, invites myth. Similarly, his conception of theory, unlike that of Comte or Bentham, was not shaped by the ambition of founding a school but, like Thucydides, by the determination to perform a memorable deed.

In *Souvenirs* Tocqueville had looked with contempt upon the new powers represented by socialism and mass democratization and denied them the status of the heroic; in *The Old Regime* the revolution approaches a Thucydidean *grandeur* as he envelops certain of its moments with an aura of the extraordinary that preserves for a later generation a stirring picture of ancestral greatness. Like the preternatural *kinesis* that Thucydides records, the upheaval that had shaken the whole Greek world and ended by shattering Athenian power, Tocqueville will express "astonishment" at "the prodigious grandeur" of the revolution and depict it as "a spectacle which has never been seen before on the earth."[44] Where Thucydides had portrayed the Athenians as the supreme overreachers who challenged all limits to their hegemony, "born into the world to take no rest themselves and to give none to others," Tocqueville would see the revolution as a phenomenon that overrode all restraints, "immoderate, violent, radical, desperate, audacious, often mad, yet powerful and effective."[45] And like Thucydides' portraits of virtuous actors, of Pericles and Themistocles, Tocqueville would praise the Convention, "a time of youth, enthusiasm, pride, and generous and sincere passions"[46] and preserve the moments when men were "passionately dedicated to the public good" and "absorbed in the contemplation of a grand design."[47]

## V

In Tocqueville's thinking the mythical does not form around "the traditional tale," which scholars of our day have declared to be the nucleus of the classic myths of the ancient world.[48] Typically ancient myths (*mythoi*) are contrasted with modern skeptical rationalism (*logos*) and classified as "nonfactual storytelling."[49] This approach implies that once the intellectual horizon associated with modern science and the eighteenth-century Enlightenment has been legitimated, it seems odd that a sophisticated thinker should simultaneously acknowledge that horizon, even adopt some of its main principles and yet persist in the old and discredited ways.

Of necessity a modern myth is chastened into incorporating certain limitations if it is to avoid the magical: it is myth subdued, inhibited. Typically it will not furnish solutions to practical problems but rather attempt to circumscribe a world, remote yet vaguely familiar so that the desired meanings can be communicated. The meanings begin as mythistorical images that *reveal* as they are described in historical detail (desired meaning "arises" from historical fact or vice versa), then become mytheoretical (the mythistorical images are combined into generalized implications), and culminate as mythpolitical, an indirect teaching about the origins of the present political condition of society.[50] In myth the truth regarding what has happened is disclosed not by reduction to "what was the case" but by enlargement, by the long-run consequence of a past event or action such that it reappears as a decisive element in a present that, by virtue of a succession of other reappearances, gradually acquires coherence and tendency. For example, the mythical element appears in the service of Tocqueville's strategy of startling his readers as the first step toward getting them to recognize their present servitude and then to exploit the momentum until a climax is reached. He calls their attention to "one of the strangest features of the French Revolution": "the contrast between the benevolence of the theories [of the philosophes] and the violence of the deeds" committed by the revolutionaries.[51] To grasp how that incongruity was possible, readers are invited to picture a course of events in which the political experience acquired over generations gradually atrophies, leaving a world emptied of political life, "estranged from its own affairs," and embittered against the prevailing institutions. The "political world divides into two separate and disconnected provinces," one of administration, the other of abstract ideas propounded by politically naive philosophes. On the eve of its destruction the "actual society" will still be "traditional, confused, and irregular, its laws diverse and contradictory." But "above it" there gradually takes shape an "imaginary society in which everything appeared simple and coordinated, uniform, equitable, and in conformity with reason." And "gradually the imagination of the crowd deserted" the existing city and took "refuge" in "the ideal city."[52]

To the modern mind reared on a sharp distinction between "reason" and "the fabulous," mythical thinking is a contradiction in terms. The modern identifies reason with the critical thinking that musters logic and fact to discredit "stories" of the dimly seen, the uncanny, that which moves in mysterious yet powerful ways. Ever since the seventeenth century reason had become ever more closely identified with scientific thinking. Despite that development, which saw some of the most influential political theorists declaring scientific modes of reasoning to be exemplary of theorizing, an embarrassing number relied upon mythical representations that bore little or no relation to "facts." Foremost among the myths was one that traced the beginnings of society to a state of nature (Locke) and the origins of the state to an "original contract" (Hobbes). Rousseau's *Discourse on the Origins of Inequality* is an extended myth about the origins of society, the appearance of property and inequality, and the invention of political domination. Possibly the most persistent and influential of all mythical constructions is Adam Smith's "theory" of "the" market ruled by an unobservable power, an "unseen hand" that coordinates millions of selfish actions into a benevolent system that no one intended. In late modern times theory utilizes the mythical as a propaedeutic or preliminary to "rigorous argument" (e.g., about rights), or uses it to establish imaginary situations (such as Rawls's "original position")—which, though not strictly "true" anticipate the true in a pretheoretical form.

What is most striking about these traces of myth is that all of them were or are invoked not as illustration but as representations of what is deemed most fundamental to society—to basic laws or constitutions and rights, to the "foundations" of "the" economy. It may reflect a certain unease that modernization, instead of being perceived as a goal, is being experienced as a process without beginning or end, and hence vulnerable to meaninglessness. The attraction of myth lies in the meaning that emerges as the myth locates *a* past that contains the explanation of how certain things began. Myth introduces connection where there had been only disconnection. Recall that early modern theorists, such as Hobbes and Locke, who described in detail a state of nature and an original contract, created their myths in the contexts of societies that had broken with historical or traditional institutional arrangements after experiencing revolutions. The myth of an original contract furnished the starting point for inventing a new political past and reestablishing connection. The state of nature and the contract exemplify what Cassirer designated an "absolute past," a condition or era that is given and does not require an exploration that goes behind it. For Tocqueville the absolute past will be located somewhere in the late Middle Ages.

## VI

> *The communities of the Middle Ages were, in truth, aristocratic bodies which (and it is, in part, here that their greatness lay) contained only small fragments of democracy.*
>
> Tocqueville[53]

The standard contrast between *mythos* and *logos*, with its either/or formula, stifles the poignancy Tocqueville frequently expressed in the conception of himself as stranded between two worlds—one dying, the other yet to be born. When he was about to begin his last work he states, as a virtual precondition, that for the contemplated work to succeed its author has to be fated to be at "the point of division" between the old and the new in order to appreciate the contrast.[54] The source of poignancy, and of the *mythos*, is the loss of a past integral to the present: "in the time where we once had political assemblies in France."[55] The forces of the present cause a certain past to recede with unprecedented rapidity, in the process separating it not only from the present but from the future. Modernizing, as a matter of course, makes a place for its innovations by disconnecting the old patterns of relationships and substituting its creations or simply abandoning the old connections. For Tocqueville modernizing means the founding of centralized and bureaucratized power, its complicity with egalitarianism, and, eventually, the triumph of administration over political governance.

Although the past is irretrievable for any practical political purpose—that is what modernizing means—it can be recreated for a pedagogical political purpose. If it exists only when described, explained, or understood, there is little or no temptation to mythicize the past. If, however, the past is to be conceived as relevant to the *modern* present, its re-creation can hardly avoid mythical terms.

The idea of the present signifies a boundary that requires modern myth to employ anachronistic elements if it is to retrieve certain sensitive meanings, which, to defend its supremacy, the present proscribes or ridicules.

The present prescribes the terms of relevance and wants to enforce an appositive past congenial with the categories of the present. The present is especially avid in suppressing that past whose defeat was the condition for its own emergence: "[the French Revolution] has entirely destroyed or is in process of destroying (for it is still at work) everything in the old society that was derived from aristocratic and feudal institutions, everything that was in any way related to them, everything which bore, however slight, the *least* imprint of them."[56]

Poignancy is about loss, not as the idle embellishment of myth but as its modern core. "At the bottom of this soul of mine is a great and profound sadness, one of those sadnesses without remedy, because although one suffers from it, one would not want to recover from it. It clings to whatever there is of the best. It is sadness which gives me the clear view of my time and my country."[57] Sadness and loss are not solely about mourning a vanished social order but about missed opportunities for avoiding a calamity few truly wanted. The lack of political intelligence and moral courage at critical moments was not due to the accident that feckless politicians happened to be in power but to an atrophied political sensibility that was a direct consequence of a long process of depoliticization. Tocqueville feels compelled to remind a vanishing nobility of "the arguments which are so familiar to classes with long experience in public affairs and who possess the science of government." Instead of entertaining the doctrine of "natural equality," the nobility should have made the case for its privileges: "only an aristocracy can preserve the people from the oppression of tyranny and the misery of revolutions; the privileges which seem to serve only the interests of those who possess them form the best guarantee for assuring the tranquillity and well-being even of those who do not possess them."[58]

The *mythos-logos* dichotomy further fails to take account of the modern's alienation from the premodern that occurs at a moment of uncertainty, when modernity is busy discovering, or inventing itself, while numerous reminders of the premodern persist. "My contemporaries and I are more and more marching along routes so different, and sometimes so contrary that we rarely meet in the same feelings and thoughts."[59] The modern is intent on explaining how its *logos* has become potentially omnipotent and what worlds have now become possible, but the premodern wonders why its power is diminishing and its world disappearing. "I have no traditions, no party, no *cause* unless it is that of liberty and human dignity."[60]

Although modernization was an element in the experience of loss, its processlike character or conception introduces a facile quality that obscures the trauma of violent destructiveness, which is evident on virtually every page of Tocqueville's unfinished volume. In the finished volume the trauma of reliving the French Revolution is registered in the rejection of a chronological account or continuous narrative. He keeps disrupting the narrative flow because of a belief that the old order did not die a "natural" death, but rather its allotted span was shortened unnaturally by what for him was the unfathomable fury of the revolution. In recounting the revolution, as he had intended, the trauma asserts itself in the form of Tocqueville becoming possessed by the past. Myth becomes a means not only of dealing with loss but of conveying the experience of traumatic loss, of loss unresolved.[61] And that is why Tocqueville will introduce imagery in which he likens his work to that of a doctor performing an autopsy: autopsies are superfluous when the corpse has died a "natural" death, fulfilled its allotted span. True autopsies are performed upon a victim, for one whose demise seems suspect, its allotted span cut unnaturally short.

Tocqueville did not self-consciously set about constructing a myth, much less attempt to foist one upon the public. Nor did he suddenly "lapse" into mythical modes of thinking. As we have seen in the previous chapter, elements of the mythical were already present in his fearful descriptions of democracy, equality, and socialism as "forces," unnatural, powerful, and allied. We have also noted that a certain "fear of theory" occasioned by the destructive power of revolutionary ideas was combined with a loss of confidence in the regenerative power of antirevolutionary theories, such as those of Burke or de Maistre, to penetrate the "darkness" of his times. Mythic modes are a means of reoccupying, remythologizing terrain previously held by theory.[62] For Tocqueville this meant attempting to discredit the theories associated with writers such as the physiocrats and philosophes whose ideas had allegedly inspired and given theoretical legitimacy to the French Revolution. In this respect myth seeks to combat abstraction by supplying a context for the unique, thereby defeating the abstract universals so dear to the Enlightenment—and to the centralizing mentality.

## VII

One of the basic assumptions in the analysis of myth is that myth is a response to fear of powers previously controlled or suppressed by a superior power. Hence the question for Tocqueville: what mythical power has lost its hegemony and become weakened, allowing new mythical powers to emerge? After the church and religion had been overthrown, Tocqueville declared, "it would be impossible to predict to what unheard of temerity the spirit of the [revolutionary] innovators might be carried once they were freed from all of the restraints which religion, customs, and laws imposed on the imagination of men."[63] In *The Old Regime*, the novel and extraordinary concentrations of power represented by revolution and despotism were made possible by the prior weakening of the hallowed trinity of king, nobility, and clergy.[64] Each of those powers had claimed a sacred origin for their authority. Their decline implied a weakening of the divine power from which each drew. Although—as Tocqueville would emphasize—the monarchy appeared to have increased its control at the expense of the nobility, events disclosed that a new and fantastic form was emerging, a centralized state, virtually all-powerful yet fragile. That remarkable development in the scale of power became all the more menacing in light of the singular character of the revolution reflected in "the terrible expression it bore." The revolutionaries who would command the powers of the state were in the grip of "a new religion" whose peculiarity was that it had been made possible by the triumph of *irréligion*. Before the French Revolution had irrupted, virtually all classes in France had become infected by an irrational hostility toward all religion, not only toward the established church. *Irréligion* was far more than a matter of disbelief: it was a force that "deranged men's minds" and "disposed" them to "singular extremes." Its power was explained in mythical imagery. "When religion deserted their souls," they were not left "empty" or weakened. New "sentiments and ideas" filled the vacuum and "did not allow them at first to collapse." In the early stages of the revolution this ideological zeal moved the French to perform prodigies of virtue, turning them away from "individual egotism" to "sacrifice" and a "heroism" and "*grandeur* " without precedent in the annals of history.[65]

The closing paragraph of Tocqueville's chapter, on how *irréligion* dominated French character in the eighteenth century, has the marks of a myth of origins. It relates how a new species of beings, veritable titans, emerged from the emptiness created by a preternatural catastrophe:

> But in the French Revolution, the religious laws having been abolished at the same time that the civil laws were overthrown, the human mind entirely lost its bearing; it no longer knew what to cling to or where to halt; revolutionaries of an unknown

species made their appearance and carried their audacity to the point of madness; no novelty could surprise them, no scruple inhibit them. It is not that these new beings were the isolated and ephemeral creation of the moment, destined to pass away with it; they have since formed a race which has perpetuated itself and spread throughout all parts of the civilized world; and which has everywhere retained the same physiognomy, the same passions, the same character. We have found it in the world when we were born; it is still before our eyes.[66]

## VIII

> *At this instant I think that I have before my eyes all of the mighty movement which has carried us from the* Ancien Régime *to our present state. I think that I see it begin, rush on, slacken, and stop. The Revolution, viewed as a whole, is as yet an indistinct, undefined object, but so vast that it excites and enlarges the imagination.*
>
> Tocqueville[67]

In its *grandeur* the subject presented a complicated mix of qualities: huge, menacing, demanding the heroic not only in the deeds of the actors being portrayed but in "the great work" envisioned by the author. *Grandeur* can then assume a certain overpowering quality especially when contrasted with the diminished world of the present: "When I look at myself, at my pygmy condition, confronting this mountain to climb, and I compare my actual puniness with the *grandeur* and length of the work that is in my mind, I find my enterprise quite vain and even ridiculous. But . . . isn't this the whole human history?"[68] In a letter in which Tocqueville asserts the unique character of the French Revolution, he also confesses that there is something incomprehensible, inexplicable at the center of it. "I feel that it is an unknown entity . . . as though it were a foreign body which prevents me from touching or seeing it." I cannot, Tocqueville notes, raise "the veil"—and, of course, he will not actually engage the revolution, only its preliminaries. He will approach its "threshold" but not venture beyond except in some unfinished pages. Mythical powers are never ordinary, but extraordinary in their potential for harm: "There have been violent revolutions before in the world but the immoderate character of these revolutionaries, violent, radical, desperate, audacious, often mad yet powerful and effective, has no precedent it seems to me in the great social upheavals of past centuries. Where does this new race come from? What has produced them? What makes them so effective? What perpetuates it?[69]

"Modern" myth does not recount the actions of a Zeus or a Yahweh, that is, of personified supernatural powers. Rather power is naturalized, even secularized and impersonalized; yet, as the nineteenth century was beginning to recognize, knowing the origins of powers, even being the originator of them, does not assure control. Constitutions, laws, and regulatory institutions are perhaps but latter-day versions of the rituals that the ancients invoked to propitiate their "powers and dominations." Europe's nineteenth century was possibly the first century to experience colossal power issuing from human inventions: the power of industry, of technological invention, of mass armies, of nationalism, of widespread economic depressions, and mass revolutions. There were prophets aplenty to warn of the dangers posed by these new and potentially uncontrollable forces—Burke, Saint-Simon, Herder, and Marx among them. Each of these writers could be said to have injected an element of the mythical into their theories: recall Burke's "primeval contract" between the living and the dead, Marx's rhapsode to the earth-transforming powers of Modern Industry. Their myths became a weapon in the struggle to control the future by defining the present according to terms that combined warning and prediction, fear and hope. Tocqueville, however, would be far less confident of the power of *mytheoreticus* except as retrospective. After completing *The Old Régime*, he confides to Beaumont that he is under no illusion that he can affect action, much less effect it. Once "there were times when books were political acts," but now the public only wants diversion.[70]

Reduced to a book, *mytheoreticus et politicus* thus becomes an entry in the story of modern powerlessness. When theory uncouples from action, it amounts to a confession of helplessness regarding the future, conceding it to the forms of theory aspiring to imitate the sciences. In contrast to predictive theories in the natural sciences, and in contrast, too, to the Tocqueville for whom theory and prophecy had once been combined, *mytheoreticus* is unable to penetrate the future and, repulsed, it grubs in the past in search of sources of political renewal. "Until now," Tocqueville wrote to a friend, "[the French Revolution] has been shown aboveground; I have turned it over to show what was underneath."[71] Despite the efforts of the *mytheoros* to avoid submitting to the historian's standards, the mythical elements cannot be "pure" because he cannot recover a prehistorical innocence by going behind history. *Mytheoreticus* can only mythicize the findings, the debris that historical research alone is able to identify and classify. However, if history teaches any political lesson, it is that history is irreversible.[72] If no resurrection of the past is possible, and the future cannot be foreseen, the *political* task becomes to provide a prolegomenon that would teach the knowledge necessary for humankind to grasp a condition dominated by revolution and despotism but without being able to reverse it.

Why this impotence in the face of tyranny, when modernity itself was the creature of revolution and when the right to overthrow tyranny was one of the most venerable traditions of Western political thought? The problem was not a new one for Tocqueville. One of the unresolved dilemmas of *Democracy in America* was its feeble response to democratic despotism, the specter of its own imagination. Yet how could resistance be justified when despotism could trace its legitimacy to the same demotic basis as the "right" of revolution?

In the modern world mythical thinking was encouraged by a paradoxical development that discouraged theoretical thinking and seemed to alter radically the "right" to resist. Modern theorists such as Locke, Jefferson, and Paine had tried to arm the demos with truth only to discover truth returning as ideology and the demos as the *sans-culottes.* Theory was becoming marginalized by the power of "ideas."[73] Instead of ideas being theory's reflection by serving as the stuff of consensus and of stability, as Tocqueville had hoped in *Democracy,* ideas had become a mobilizing power, the stuff of dissensus, antitheoretical. The power of ideology took the form of "great movements" of opinion over long stretches of time and in the minds of vast numbers of individuals. The political world was not to be conceived as *sustained* by a generally shared body of stable beliefs but as being continually redefined in shifting patterns of opinions.

What supported the political world rendered the theorist helpless: an amorphous aggregate that could not be seen or even heard, a democracy of privatized members, activated as supporters, passive as citizens, a political world broad but shallow, its politics narrow, even furtive: "Politics, which used to be transacted in open day, has now become a secret process into which none can penetrate except the two or three alchemists who are engaged in its preparation."[74]

As politics became more "democratic," it became more labyrinthine, but as long as the fiction of the sovereign people held sway, the right of revolution appeared as a contradiction in terms. And, as the last half of the nineteenth century began to unfold, terrorism and conspiratorialism sought to resolve the contradiction, only to confirm it: terrorism as impotence, the violence that feeds on its own failures.

For Tocqueville it was not politics alone that was hidden. The invasion of the political realm by the "social" and by mass ideologies and movements was symptomatic of the decline in the restraining power of religion. The weakening of the spiritual was evidence of what had troubled Tocqueville ever since his discovery of the relentless crush of equality and of what he would only confide to his private correspondence. This was the fear that God had withdrawn from the world and become a *deus absconditus,* thus allowing a new power to well up from the lower depths: "[T]his revolution has been prepared by the most civilized classes of the nation but carried out by the most barbarous and rudest classes."[75]

## IX

In April 1852 Tocqueville was presented with an opportunity to express publicly his reflections on thought and action and to suggest why or how theory was being displaced by ideologies and action by movements.[76] The occasion, his presidential address to the Academy of Moral and Political Sciences, took place in the aftermath of the plebiscite that had overwhelmingly confirmed Bonaparte and led to the inauguration of a new constitution.

The speech might have been memorable as the first and only occasion when Tocqueville presented a considered view of "political science." Instead the address is diffuse and hesitant, revealing mainly for Tocqueville's difficulties in establishing any political role for theory in a world where politics and political action were adapting to the new force created by (nearly) universal manhood suffrage. A huge electorate had come into existence, responsive to ideas tailored to its plebeian understanding and sensibilities, and, as Bonapartist plebiscites would show, mobilizable and manipulable. In addition to the discouraging political situation, his inability to compose more than a formalistic conception was probably affected by what Tocqueville privately referred to as the "moral isolation" that had left him "outside the intellectual community of [his] time and country."[77]

At the outset of his address Tocqueville posed a question that seemed to echo the concerns of many of his contemporaries: is there a science of politics? In fact, he never returned to that question, at least not in the terms current among his contemporaries. Instead of their question—Is it possible to establish the study of politics on a scientific basis by applying the methods of science to political phenomena with the aim of discovering the "laws" operating in that domain?—Tocqueville began from a more traditional, premodern starting point that associated "science" with so-called perennial knowledge, the wisdom attributed to the great political philosophers and historians. Science, in that conception, referred to general moral and political principles whose validity was attested universally and by "the test of time" rather than by careful methods of investigation, verification, and revision. As represented, for example, in the laws of nature and the corollary of natural rights, scientific knowledge was an important part of what Tocqueville understood by theory. However, the two were not identical in Tocqueville's own practice. Science, understood as universal truth, was independent of historical contexts. That, he argued, explained the present situation where political actors were largely indifferent to political science. Most of them believed that politics was so fluid and varied as to make it impractical to base the praxis of governance upon theories or maxims.[78] While admitting that politicians had little traffic with theories,[79] he maintained that the actor's dismissal of theory was too sweeping and he attempted a defense, albeit a modest one, of a theoretical political science that would blend moral philosophy and political history. His concoction would be more abstract than the latter but more concrete than the former.

Tocqueville sought to define the relevance of theory by proposing a distinction between the "fixed" and the "mobile" parts of politics. The fixed part referred to man's nature, his instincts, faculties, and needs, which were unchanging even though the objects of human endeavor did change. The task of philosophy and history was to reveal man's nature and to teach "what the laws are that are most appropriate to the general and permanent condition of mankind," while the "art of government" would deal with the practical daily decisions arising from the "mobile" part of politics. As Tocqueville proceeded to enumerate the types of theories produced in the past, it became apparent that theory and action were in a virtual state of divorce: in Tocqueville's typology there had been theories that had concentrated on the question of the best political system;[80] others that had dealt with international law; and still others that focused on a particular aspect of society, such as its economy or penal system.[81] Without remarking on the scientific quality of any of the past theories Tocqueville merely noted, without specifying, that a relatively small number of *idées mères* had been produced and that a few of these were true and a few false. With this desultory, and possibly obligatory, discussion behind him Tocqueville could turn to his real concern: what was the point of theory now that the association with action had been severed? What was its efficacy and, equally problematic, what was its form?

Tocqueville approached the questions cautiously, noting that although the number of theoretical truths was small, a handful of theorists had exerted significant "influence" or "power." For his example he chose, revealingly, the theorists who had written prior to and during the French Revolution. Clearly he had the philosophes in mind, not as individual thinkers but as representatives of a broad and influential current of ideas. The conclusion he drew from that episode was that civilized nations were distinguished by the influence of political science over politics. The role of this science was not to furnish practical directives to actors but to shape a milieu of "general ideas" that enveloped actors, lawmakers, and citizens: "Political science forms around each society a kind of intellectual atmosphere which the governed and the governing breathe in the principles of their conduct, often without knowing it. Only the barbarians do not recognize this in their politics or practice."[82]

While Tocqueville's formulation seemed to suggest that if theory had any function it was educational rather than action-oriented, helping to mold the climate of opinion rather than making direct overtures toward power or promoting specific policies, he virtually collapsed any distinction between theory and what might be called regime ideology. Theory's role, he declared, was to help stabilize the political and social order rather than criticize it, as the thinkers prior to the revolution had done.

The pessimism of this retrenched and unheroic view of theory was muted in his presidential address, at least in the portion of it he actually delivered. By chance there is extant a fragment that Tocqueville chose to suppress but which conveys his mood more faithfully. The first few sentences of the relevant passage suggest resentment at the inconsequential lot of theory in the age of mass movement and a stronger note that encourages the few who remain dedicated to the theoretical vocation. The conclusion, however, is bleak, suggesting that a certain understanding of theory and action had reached a dead end. The danger of theory, of what theory could accomplish when allied with the masses, made the case for a view of theory as inaction:

> The greatest publicists the world has produced have preceded or followed periods of public liberties. [Aristotle, Montesquieu, and Rousseau are then mentioned.] Their books have made us what we are, but we would probably be incapable of writing them today. Invariably ideas play no part in unfolding events; actual practice avoids the sciences, and politics ends by being only a game of chance where, moreover, the dice are often loaded.[83]

"The greatest publicists," who "have made us what we are," had written in periods when "public liberties" either did not exist or had been suppressed, yet "we" are said to be "incapable" of writing great political "books" and the political actors pay no heed to ideas. This formulation with its parallel between the theorists' inefficacy and the actors' indifference to theory points toward an ambivalence that colored Tocqueville's conception and execution of his project on the *ancien régime*. By its choice of subject and the parallels between past and present that it inevitably evoked, *The Old Regime* created political expectations in advance of its exposition. At the politically sensitive moment of the mid 1850s it might even appear as a provocation because most readers would know beforehand that the revolution of 1789 had followed a course ending in the despotism of Napoleon Bonaparte; and most citizens knew that the revolution of 1848 had instigated a chain of events ending in the despotism of Louis Napoleon. The two shared a common name and lineage and, potentially, a common symbolism. To some the name Napoleon stood for the betrayal of revolutionary hopes, to others for order and national salvation. The coincidences of history were easily assumed to be continuities, and this produced a kind of natural echo chamber, encouraging a contemporary resonance and innuendo to the politics of the past.

The political expectations aroused by the subject matter were bound to be heightened by the reputation of the author. In western Europe and the

United States Tocqueville's name was closely identified with the cause of liberty and liberal constitutionalism. And as the creator of the concept of "democratic despotism," no one could fairly doubt the depths of his opposition to the Bonapartist regime. It was not unreasonable, therefore, to expect a theorist of Tocqueville's stature to expose the nature of the political derangement causing French politics to lurch from the extremes of revolution to those of tyranny. And having exposed the causes it was plausible to hope that he would suggest how France might overcome or at least temper the historical forces controlling its destiny: formulations about the origins of the French Revolution have consequences for promoting triumphs over it. Perhaps, despite the dangers, he might offer some clues about the course to be followed by those who cherish liberty and find themselves deprived of freedom with no legal means for peaceful and orderly redress. But given the pessimism about the influence of theory expressed in the Address of 1852, either he would have to abandon that earlier formulation or create a new form of theory with a different orientation toward action.

## X

> *to penetrate to the heart of this "old order" . . . that the Revolution has hidden from us.*
>
> Tocqueville[84]

The preface to *The Old Regime* occupies a special status that provides insights into Tocqueville's theoretical strategies and political aims. A theoretical strategy might be defined broadly as an attempt to set limits to what the text should be interpreted to mean or not mean. If successful, the reader's interpretation would coincide with the author's intentions.

The major portion of the preface was written while the main text was in press.[85] As the last part of the work to be written but the first to be read, it affords the author an opening advantage, a unique opportunity to influence the public's overall interpretation, not only of the text but of the author's motives. In the preface he advises readers that he has not hesitated to point out the "mistakes" and "miscalculations" of the Old Regime as well as to diagnose "not only the disease of which the sick man died, but also how he might have avoided dying."[86] A later reader could conclude that Tocqueville was presenting a counterfactual history. Tocqueville promises to demonstrate not only how the Old Regime, although "sick," might have been saved but also that, viewed from the antipolitical present of despotism, things would have been better if it had survived. To "save" the Old Regime might take several forms: from resuscitating elements of the political from their *ancien* embodiments to preserving the Old Regime as a theoretical ideal, a counter-paradigm, a critical presence standing in judgment over the operative system of postrevolutionary despotism.

These possibilities are suggested because *The Old Regime* describes no single regime but several: an Old Regime that had its roots in the communalism of the late Middle Ages; an early modern monarchy attempting to assert its authority over the nobility; and an Old Regime in which administration was superseding governance. The preface provides a general guide to negotiating these complexities while indicating what is to be taken as the core teaching of the work and, equally important, delimiting its range of desired implications. Accordingly the preface develops around two connected themes, the political intentions of the work and the directions intended to guide the reader's understanding of the text.

Tocqueville begins the preface by advising the reader that what follows is not a history but a "study" (*une étude*) of the French Revolution. Elsewhere, in the unfinished manuscript of the second volume, he reminds himself that "I am discussing history not narrating it."[87] Despite its vagueness, that description suggests that he is attempting the "new form," the "mixture" of "philosophy and history" to which he had alluded in his correspondence. I want to suggest that the preface allows us to see how that mixture generates a mythical element.

Early on he carefully reassures/impresses the reader that while the work is not a conventional history it is based, nonetheless, on careful and extensive historical research. Tocqueville's immediate concern was to encourage the reader into a frame of mind different from that fostered by unnamed historians whose works, he notes with a touch of maliciousness, are "too brilliant" (*trop d'éclat*) for him to "dream" of producing a competing work.[88] As he immediately makes clear, he wants readers who, assured of the factual veracity of his account, will be responsive to visual metaphors, to heroic scales, and to the evocation of struggle, danger, overpowering forces, and great consequences. So, straightaway, he presents the myth of the revolution:

> In 1789 the French made the greatest effort to which any people has ever committed itself to cut, so to speak, their destiny in two, and to separate by an abyss what they had been heretofore from what they wished to be henceforth. Toward this end they took every sort of precaution to transport nothing from the past into their new order; they imposed upon themselves every type of constraint to fashion themselves other than their fathers; they overlooked nothing in making themselves unrecognizable.[89]

It is precisely the myth of the Great Revolution as the Grand Caesura that Tocqueville attempts to deflate or, more accurately, to demythologize. "I have always thought," he confides, "that the revolutionaries were much less successful in that remarkable undertaking than outsiders believed or they themselves first believed. . . . [U]nconsciously they retained from the old order most of the sentiments, habits, even the ideas by which they conducted the Revolution that destroyed it, and that without wishing it, they made use of its debris to construct the edifice of the new society."[90] Thus the true nature of the French Revolution was not understood by the revolutionaries themselves: what they had perpetuated was what they believed they had destroyed forever. In reality they had mainly swept away the empty forms whose substance had been hollowed out well before 1789. Their destruction exposed the work of an earlier revolution that had begun the transformation of the political and social structure of the *ancien régime.*

By this formulation Tocqueville meant not only to deflate the myth of a revolutionary break but to defeat rival myths about the revolution. Here Tocqueville criticizes Burke and de Maistre for having overdramatized the revolution as "satanic" and "monstrous"[91] and denying any continuities between the prerevolutionary order and the revolutionary regimes. They were, ironically, conservative counterrevolutionaries who would not recognize that the revolution had a past in which the Old Regime was complicit.

The crucial political objective of Tocqueville's attempt at diminishing the revolution's claim to have created a new world was to discredit the images of a revolutionary eschatology, of a climactic moment when the entire course of things was redirected. By the same token, the conservative myth that had idealized the *ancien régime* and demonized the revolution, had also missed the point. By showing that the revolutionaries had resurrected the worst achievement of the Old Regime, he meant to strike a heavy blow at revolutionary hope, at the idea that a popular revolution could remake the world without reproducing the hated institutions of the past and, equally tragic, while turning a blind eye to the political achievements inextricably connected with the vices of the past. Thus, *mytheoreticus et historicus* reverses the prevailing perspective. Despite some achievements, the revolution, instead of being forward-looking and progressive, will be revealed to be, at best, ambivalent, and at worst retrogressive, even antidemocratic.

Tocqueville did not disclose in the preface precisely what of the old order's debris the revolution preserved, but he added an important element to his strategy of demythologization by indicating that "the" revolution was not to be identified solely with either the simple image of a grand mass uprising which overthrew the previous order of things or even with the "revolutionary era" of the 1790s. He loosened "revolution" from its singular association with radical mass action and hinted at a broader application that extends the work of revolution and its temporal span deeper into the prerevolutionary past. Later he would refer to it as "the first revolution." The peculiarity of that first revolution is that it has neither precise beginning—because no revolution had been preconceived—nor ending, because it was still going on. Tactically that move suggests that Tocqueville was *not* concerned primarily to establish the causes of the revolution of 1789 but to define the meaning of French politics of the past two centuries, from roughly the mid-seventeenth century to the mid-nineteenth.[92] This meant contesting the "name" of revolution, denying a monopoly to its defenders, and even appropriating it to make clear "what the proper name of the ideas of 1789 should be."[93]

Significantly, the announcement that he intends to attack the revolutionary myth is followed by a recital of the types of supporting evidence he had for his thesis: famous books of the period as well as books "with very little art," a mass of public documents by which Frenchmen had tried to make their views known before the revolution, and governmental archives. This enables him to claim a knowledge of the old order superior to that of its contemporaries because he had before "his eyes" what "they were never allowed to see."[94] The logic of facts is thus mobilized to discredit the heroic image of 1789. The history unearthed by the historian, often in the form of minutiae, makes available a kind of truth that can dispel a grandiose myth. "I shall dare to say this because I hold the facts in my hand": historical fact as a logic of belittlement, of reduction in meaning. The Old Regime, in launching a "first revolution" of the state against society and attempting to modernize through enlightened methods of administrative regulation, had ended by destroying itself and preparing the way for the second or real revolution. "The old regime has furnished the Revolution with several of its forms; the Revolution has merely added its genius for atrocities."[95]

Revolutionary theory, Tocqueville would claim, achieved an astonishing success because of the vacuum created by depoliticization. The French had once possessed political judgment, the ability of appreciating and defending the force of "certain particular facts," but those skills had atrophied in the years immediately before the revolution. France stood out as "the one European country where political life had been extinguished for the longest time and most completely." The discontinuity in French political experience allowed "the abstract principles and very general theories" of the philosophes to fill the void and determine the course of the revolution.[96]

At the same time that Tocqueville demythologized the achievement of the revolutionaries, he remythologized their display of heroic endeavor, preserving it as a lesson for unheroic times. Where the revolutionaries had failed to separate France from its political past, their extraordinary endeavor now served to highlight for Tocqueville's times the contrast between past and present political virtue. There was, thus, one exceptional moment, one part of the myth that Tocqueville's demythologizing makes a special point of sparing:

> I shall begin in the company of those of that first epoch of '89 when the love of equality and of liberty shared their hearts; when they wanted to found not only democratic institutions but free institutions; not only to destroy privileges but to recognize and consecrate rights; a time of youth, of enthusiasm, of pride, of generous and sincere passions, when, in spite of its mistakes, men will forever preserve its memory; and a time which, for years to come, will trouble the sleep of all those who want to corrupt and enslave them.[97]

The bracketing of a special moment of the French Revolution was the prelude to remythologizing it in a tableau, which is then succeeded by another and sharply contrasting tableau of "the course of this same revolution" when Frenchmen "forgot" liberty in favor of becoming "equal servants to the master of the world." In the process, power became concentrated, while "empty images" of "the sovereignty of the people" replaced precious local liberties with the decisions of ignorant voters. The "means of self-government" secured by freedom of thought, speech, and writing, all that "was most precious and noble in the conquests of '89," was afterward taken away in the "great name" of '89.[98] A remythologizing theory will then retrieve and enlarge what history's demythologizing had exposed as hollow imagery. And in the process theory educates, rehistoricizing its readers, reawakening their political sensibilities as the author dissects the mistakes and exposes the misjudgments of the actors.

The complex interpretative strategy embodied in the new form had to avoid the impression that 1789 and its political radicalism had not profoundly changed the nation. Yet—to pile complexity upon complexity—Tocqueville's political strategy of challenging the existing regime required that he not denigrate the heroism of the revolution insofar as it offered dramatic proof that opposition to tyranny was a possibility. That element of the strategy is preserved in a passage from the uncompleted second volume. It provides a remarkable summary of the continuities in Tocqueville's conceptions of civic virtue and of authentic political action:

> When I consider the French Revolution, I am amazed at the prodigious *grandeur* of the event, at the glare it cast to the corners of the earth. . . . No moment in history has ever witnessed on earth so large a number of men [as in the National Assembly of 1789] so passionately dedicated to the public good, so really forgetful of their own interests, so absorbed in the contemplation of a grand design, so ready to risk. . . . There are undertakings which only the French nation can conceive, magnanimous resolutions which this nation alone dares to take."[99]

Tocqueville's political purpose becomes more sharply focused when he remarks that he wrote his book with "passion"— the signature of a pure political act—but without "prejudice." He declares that he has deliberately adopted an interpretive strategy, which while examining "our old society in its various aspects . . . never lost sight of the new order." Tocqueville admits that he has tried to produce a work that will be "instructive" and that, accordingly, he has emphasized both the political vices that destroyed the old society and continue to work their "harm" as well as the "manly virtues" that are vital and yet "almost extinct."[100] But he promises more than moral instruction: he will reveal the political truth *interred* in the Old Regime. His archival research is described as "penetrating to the heart of that *ancien régime*" and of "having found 'the old order' all alive."[101] In a startling passage he compares his new theoretical form to the conduct of an autopsy that will use/perpetuate the remains of the dead to instruct the living: "I have wanted to see not only to what illness the sick man succumbed but how he might have avoided death. I have acted like those doctors who, in each dead organ, attempt to surprise the laws of life."[102]

What were those "laws of life" that had animated the old order? What purpose for a later and different age would be served by knowledge of them? The questions were posed but not directly answered. Instead Tocqueville's response followed a circuitous route. After apologizing to those who might feel wounded by his "honest" and "disinterested" criticism—an apology meant primarily for the surviving members of the old nobility—he remarks that some (members of the apolitical bourgeoisie?) may criticize his book for displaying "a very unfashionable taste for liberty at a time when it is scarcely shared by any one in France." That preference, he continued, represents "a very old leaning of mine." That remark prepared the way for a further revelation of his political intentions by means of yet another parallel, one that pits the continuities in his own political commitments against the continuities of revolution and Napoleonic despotism. He begs the reader's indulgence while he repeats "almost textually" what he had written twenty years earlier in *Democracy in America.*

His main purpose in recalling *Democracy* was strategic. That text was adduced as proof for his claim to being a longtime friend of liberty, and it allows him to elaborate on his conception of liberty. He does not quote verbatim from *Democracy* but summarizes its most vivid construct and restates, with a greater emphasis than in the original text, one of the principal themes. The construct is democratic despotism. The implication was that it would importantly figure in a work that promised to reveal resemblances to "the France of our own days."[103] By asserting the prescience of *Democracy*, Tocqueville was reasserting his powers as a prophet and the prophetic truth of *Democracy.*

A truth that had at one time pointed forward and identified the conditions conducive to a democratic despotism was a truth that now would serve a theory that looked backward to a predemocratic order and defended its relevance to the present when democratic despotism had become a reality.

The Tocqueville who had repeatedly acknowledged that the days of aristocratic power had passed now states that in *Democracy* he had discerned "three very clear truths about the future": that the men of our time were being impelled by an unknown and irresistible force toward "the destruction of aristocracy"; that societies in which aristocracy does not, or cannot, exist will experience the greatest difficulty in avoiding absolute rule; and that the effects of despotism will be more pronounced in those societies because the absence or disappearance of aristocracy exacerbates the vices to which they are especially prone.[104]

Most striking about the list of truths is its omission of the principal truths that had given *Democracy* its distinctive character and the transformation of others. Instead of the "providential fact" of a long historical development which, in *Democracy*, had lent a tincture of sanctity to equality and democracy, there is a simple reference to "force" whose very anonymity suggests illegitimacy. Even though Tocqueville had recognized that aristocracy had never truly taken hold in the United States and that the distinguishing feature of the American founding was that it was not the result of an antifeudal, antiaristocratic revolution, now, in his distillation of *Democracy*, aristocracy assumes center stage. Tocqueville even suggests that an antifeudal, antiaristocratic revolution would be unable to secure democracy, or at least not a democracy that was both moderate and egalitarian. The purpose of Tocqueville's revisionism was to prepare his readers for a reconstructed world in which the role of the aristocracy was pivotal to both the flourishing and eventual demise of that world. And, more strikingly, that the participatory practices assumed to be unique to democracy, an assumption that *Democracy* had helped to promote, had depended on the aristocracy and could not survive its decline.

That Tocqueville was intent on appropriating the idea of participatory politics for an inegalitarian ideal needs to be borne in mind. Otherwise one can be misled by the declamatory passage, "What sort of person would be so base as to prefer to depend upon the caprices of one of his *semblables* than to follow the laws which he himself has contributed to establish." That Rousseauean-sounding passage concludes with an important qualification that reflects its author's long-standing reservations about demos-based democracy: the preference for living under laws one has helped to establish holds only "if the nation seemed to him to have the virtues necessary to make good use of its liberty."[105] Tocqueville was giving ample notice that freedom would be reconceived, not as embodied, for example in the revolutionary Declaration of the Rights of Man and Citizen of 1791, but as embedded in a premodern context where inequalities of rank and privilege were paramount. That conclusion is prefigured in Tocqueville's silence about equality, the *idée mère* of *Democracy.* Not until the very end of his gloss is equality mentioned, and then only in association with despotism: "I do not shrink from asserting that the common level of heart and mind will never be so low as when equality and despotism are joined"[106]—and he will demonstrate that they had been joined in the revolution. Equality and despotism are thus fatefully allied against inequalities, and determined to level and deplete a polytheistic world.[107]

The remainder of his exegesis of *Democracy* is devoted to painting a vivid picture of life under a despotism. The imaginary pictured in *Democracy,* including the chiaroscuro of darkness and light, required no new touches to serve as a likeness of the real world of the 1850s. He emphasizes, as he had twenty years earlier, how despotism exploits the modern preoccupations, with private interests, narrow individualism, material comfort, all of the distractions that turn men's energies and attention from "public affairs" and hurry them toward "the privacy and darkness" that prove so congenial to the designs of despotism. Only freedom, Tocqueville asserts, can "rescue the citizens from isolation" and give them "the warmth" that "draws them together."[108]

Yet something crucial has occurred in Tocqueville's thinking. His return to *Democracy* was a return to *political* democracy and to the contrast it presented to bourgeois liberalism; he makes no reference to the rights of property. It is a democracy relocated in, and imbued with, the values of *ancienneté.* In *Democracy* he had drawn analogies between American local democracy and France's *corps intermédiaires,* thus injecting a feudal element into democracy. Now he will find a democratic element in feudal institutions as he contrasts a society in which human beings are connected by the "bond of castes, classes, corporations, [and] families" with a society of "narrow individualism" wherein people are "preoccupied with their particular interests" and "public virtue" has been "suffocated." Despotism encourages an individualism driven by the fear of failure and the knowledge that no one will care about the casualties. Under despotism the scramble for wealth is the dominant passion: society becomes more sharply defined by economic activity. At the same time despotism destroys the ties of commonality, thus ensuring that the political will cease to be cared for: "it drains the citizenry of all common passion, all mutual need, all necessity of acting in concert, all occasion of common action; it walls them, so to speak, into private life. Already they have tended to remain apart: it isolates them; already they were becoming cooler toward each other: it freezes them."[109]

Almost casually Tocqueville remarks that under despotism where "men's imagination" is preoccupied with money rather than public affairs, "men tremble at the very idea of revolutions."[110] That mention of resistance provokes the question, Can a teaching about resistance be collected from among the archaic materials in *The Old Regime*?

# CHAPTER XXV
## *THE OLD REGIME*: MODERNIZATION AND THE POLITICS OF LOSS

### I

> *Never forget the philosophical character of the French Revolution, its principal characteristic, although a transitory one.*
>
> Tocqueville[1]

In its preface Tocqueville posed two questions that form much of the framework of *The Old Regime*: Why did the revolution erupt in France rather than elsewhere in Europe and why did it follow the violently destructive course it did? And why did the seemingly impregnable French monarchy and its supporting social order collapse so quickly?

Tocqueville's opening chapter begins polemically with a double challenge: first, to theoreticians, such as Burke and de Maistre, who had interpreted the French Revolution as a sudden irruption against the traditional political and religious values and institutions of Christian Europe, and, second, to the politicians and statesmen who struggled unsuccessfully to stem the revolutionary movement.[2] Both theorists and actors had been humbled by the phenomenon they had attempted, in their different ways, to master: "There is nothing more appropriate than the history of our Revolution for reminding philosophers and statesmen of a sense of modesty; for there have never been greater events, originating from so far back, better prepared, and yet less foreseen."[3]

To drive home his point and to locate more squarely his own project, he insisted that long before 1789 the signs of an impending revolution were everywhere to be seen, yet those who, above all others, should have been politically percipient proved to be blind or ignorant: "as to that great science of government, which learns to grasp the general movement of society, to appraise what is passing in the minds of the people and to foresee its results, it was as wholly ignorant as the people themselves."[4]

These criticisms announce the presence of an *agon*. Its aim is to establish the superiority of his own judgments, theoretical and political, to those of earlier actors and later "philosophers." It is not historians but political theorists and actors who are his rivals. Tocqueville had carefully noted at the end of the first chapter that he enjoyed an advantage in perspective denied to those who had written or acted in closer proximity to the actual events: "today we are placed at the precise point from which we can best perceive and judge this great subject. We are far enough from the Revolution to feel only slightly the passions which troubled the views of those who have made it but near enough to be able to enter into the spirit of those who led it and to understand it."[5]

Although that formulation recalled the claims to a privileged perspective that he had advanced for *Democracy*, there were some notable differences. Earlier the claim of distance was employed to defend his disinterestedness by denying that he had a class interest in defending aristocracy, insisting that the society of privilege was dead, beyond recall. Now, as we have noted, the preface defends the critical importance of aristocracy in the defense of freedom. That served to prepare the way for a later analysis that correlates the loss of public freedoms with the decline of the political role and influence of the aristocracy. The analysis does not attribute the decline to factors beyond human control—no "providential facts"—but rather to errors of judgment, moral weakness, and a decayed political sensibility.

*The Old Regime* would also reverse *Democracy's* perspective. In *Democracy* he had prophesied the future of the Old World by observing the New, foretold it to be more egalitarian and democratic, and sought only to moderate its defects while admitting its virtues. Now he sees the Old World as the embodiment of democratic despotism, the worst possibility of *Democracy* realized, the form of regime that, as Aristotle had noted long ago, was not easily moderated, nor were its small virtues balanced off against its horrendous vices. How, then, to undo his own prophecy?

In *The Old Regime* Tocqueville chooses to uncover (rather than discover) the origins of the present despotism. He exhumes the world of political, social, and economic inequalities whose destruction had been the principal aim of the revolutionaries and whose suppression formed the main bond between all classes, save for the aristocracy. His reconstruction will "restore" the aristocracy and justify it by arguing that it was the crucial element in a salutary scheme of inequalities. That broader scheme, as embodied in traditional local and provincial institutions, is offered by Tocqueville as the basis for a viable alternative to despotism. Historical communities of inequality were to serve as demonstrations that an alternative system of power was possible. They could be made to reveal how power could be scaled differently: diffused yet sufficient to discharge functions limited in scale and scope, each of its elements (nobility, local clergy, bourgeoisie, and local officials) too powerful to be ignored yet not powerful enough to impose its will continuously and hence compelled to promote a politics of class cooperation, capable of resisting central power yet too weak to pose a general threat to society at large.

The striking claim is that inequalities represent the necessary condition for politics— the exact contrary to the claims of the French Revolution's theorists that politics should be the expression of political equals. For Tocqueville gradations of power expressed the actual texture of society, guaranteeing that diversity and difference will appear and be sustained. Because all classes (save the peasantry) were assured some powers, politics emerged in the practices of negotiating cooperation. The representatives of different powers—landed property, rank, trade, ecclesiastic—participated, though not on equal terms. That world forms the counterparadigm to the world ushered in by the revolution. And yet, as Tocqueville recognized in the unfinished volume, that ideal was unrealizable for the basic reason that among Frenchmen "hatred of the old regime" exceeded all other hatreds and in his own day the fear that it might be restored outweighed all other fears.[6]

To make a case for the significance of a regime that is both hated and feared is not to make a case for its relevance; and to make a case for its relevance is not to argue for its restoration. The strategy he adopts is, in part, to compromise the revolution by showing that it had been built on certain foundations laid by the hated Old Regime—foundations that deserve to be hated because they had been instrumental in destroying what was best, and most relevant, in the Old Regime. Tocqueville attempts to pin down the connection between the old and new regimes by drawing a distinction between the enduring substance of the revolution and its ephemeral manifestations. The "most lasting" results of the revolution are certain "opinions" regarding "the condition of society" and certain "principles of civil and political laws," such as "natural equality"; the abolition of certain privileges of castes, classes, and professions; the sovereignty of the people, "the omnipotence of the social power"; and the uniformity of laws. Tocqueville viewed these principles as testimony to the crucial role of ideas in the preparation for revolution: they were not only the "causes of the French Revolution" but "its substance" and "the most fundamental, most enduring, and the truest part as far as time is concerned."[7] Each of the principles contradicted those of the counterparadigm that Tocqueville constructed from the Old Regime.

The contrasts between two theories and their accompanying practices serve to introduce the crucial question: how could a people, especially its enlightened classes, living under the society and rule of the Old Regime, come to adopt the revolutionary paradigm even though it meant ruination for many? The remarkable power ascribed to theoretical ideas was a preliminary to setting up his major target, the responsibility of theorists for the catastrophe, and a first indication of the terms on which he would engage the French Revolution. The destructive power attributed to revolutionary theories signals that the reader is about to be introduced to a world wherein ideas had become connected and unified by a theory, their separate claims inflated by combination, their power to dismiss, condemn, or elevate magnified beyond anything previously known. The extreme abstractness, which he attributes to revolutionary theory—to its ideas of natural right, the sovereignty of the people, the equality of all, and the absolute rejection of all traditional institutions and beliefs—and his refusal to discriminate among competing theories, allows Tocqueville to compact them into a form of myth rather than deal with them as arguments.

Those powers are to be contested on the terrain of the present as well as the past. This requires that the counterparadigm be an idealization, an inflation of meaning, not of powers. It was too weak to survive the centralizing and equalizing powers that challenged it. If the triumphant powers in their contemporary incarnation are to be challenged on the mythical level, the counterparadigm must be supplemented by powers more attuned to the present. The second part of Tocqueville's strategy is to identify forms of power that transcend differences, powers that unify. These turn out to be the mythical elements of religion, the enemy of the revolution, and nationalism, the creature of the revolution. In order to incorporate religion into his competing myth, Tocqueville must show that it is compatible with a postrevolutionary, yet nonreactionary society. He denies that the revolution destroyed religion and maintains that the church's antirevolutionary stance was a passing phase. He goes further, claiming that by eliminating the political role of the clergy, the revolutionaries helped to "purify" religious belief and prepare the way for its revival, especially among the masses.

Although in private correspondence Tocqueville frequently complained that Christianity provided a poor training for citizenship, he never perceived an implicit antagonism between the values of diversity as expressed in local power and, the centralized, hierarchical structure of the Catholic Church with its emphasis on unity of dogma. Nor did he see any tension between local diversity and class differences, on one side, and, on the other, the overriding of these, or at least their subordination, to the nation's greatness and glory, which he insisted were displayed in the revolution.The cultural role that Tocqueville reserved for religion and nationalism repeated what he had argued in *Democracy*, that in an age of self-interest, whether bourgeois or proletarian, the myths of religion and nationalism seemed the only ideological elements capable of holding class-ridden societies together. As the key elements in a myth of cultural unity, however, they seem contradictory, at least in spirit, to the provincial character of premodern power and more congenial with the myth of centered power shared alike by revolutionaries and royal administrators.

At the level of myth Tocqueville claims that a mutual attraction developed between the egalitarianism of revolutionary theory and the benevolent uniformitarianism of the prerevolutionary bureaucrat. He sets about establishing the affinity between the overthrowers and the overthrown by insisting that the most ominous and enduring legacy of the revolution contradicted a widespread belief that the revolution, by eliminating monarchy and aristocracy, had weakened "political power." To dispel that illusion, Tocqueville constructs a series of tableaux illustrating the political misjudgments of the revolutionary actors who had mistaken empty forms for actual powers, while the surviving forms of real power were mistaken for new constructions. The revolution had made "it look as though living bodies were being torn asunder; in fact, it was only corpses being carved up."[8] Instead of dismantling the main power structure of the Old Regime, the revolutionaries "involuntarily" relied on it "to construct the edifice of the new society."[9] The prerevolutionary destruction of the "old social structure," including its traditions and *moeurs*, and the "emptying the human mind of all of the ideas on which respect and obedience had been founded," combined to allow a "new power to emerge spontaneously from the ruins created by the Revolution." Tocqueville wants to evoke astonishment at this novel power, which could "empty" the mind of a whole people of the habits and beliefs accumulated over centuries.

Having set an atmosphere in which ignorance and confusion reign and men are attempting to shape powers of huge proportions, an atmosphere wherein *mythos* is more at home than *logos*, Tocqueville assists his readers in imagining this awesome, centered power by "removing the debris" left by the destructive force of the revolution: "You perceive an immense central power which has attracted to itself and absorbed into its unity all the particles of authority and influence which heretofore had been dispersed among a crowd of secondary powers, orders, classes, professions, families, and individuals, dispersed as it were throughout the social organism. The world had never witnessed such a power since the fall of the Roman empire."[10]

Was there an older myth being unearthed, the archetypal myth of the dissolution of centralized power, only now inverted to recount the dissolution of decentralized power?

## II

> *The whole earth had one language and few words . . . and [men] said, "Come let us build ourselves a city, and a tower with its top in the heavens, and let us make a name for ourselves, lest we be scattered abroad upon the face of the whole earth." [God, threatened by the unified power of mankind, intervened to] confuse their language, that they may not understand one another's speech. . . . [He] scattered them abroad . . . and they left off building the city.*
>
> Genesis[11]

Tocqueville reverses the story of Babel to recount how local power is drained away and reconstituted as concentrated power. His myth takes shape as the antithesis between polytheism and monotheism, between a decentered world with a plenitude of modest powers and a powerfully centered but depleted world. The French Revolution had obliterated a condition in which power was scattered, decentralized, apportioned among various classes, localities, and professions. The remnants of those powers and authorities may have survived the revolution as mere "debris," much like the irrelevance of the surviving Roman cultic gods once Christianity had begun to take hold, while the new form of power, "simple, regular, and grandiose," and formerly "invisible to the eyes of the crowd," is now exposed for all to see, "especially to the eye of princes." (Louis Napoleon would carry the title of prince.) The work of the revolution continues to be imitated by those who seek to eliminate "immunities" and "privileges," who "mingle ranks and equalize conditions, substitute bureaucracy for aristocracy, uniform rules for local immunities, unified government for a diversity of powers."[12]

Tocqueville's *mythos* should be understood as post-Christian. Recall his worries that God had abandoned the world to the forces of equality and his exclusion of Providence from his account of the revolution. Tocqueville feared that God has either abandoned the world or that His weakness has allowed the world to be turned upside down. Political polytheism is the expression of fear now turned into resentment and directed against the political version of monotheism, unified and monopolized power, despotism supported or worshipped by democracy. Monotheism, as distinct from the "sociological" function of religion, is thus complicit in the preparation for revolution.

In the unfinished portion of his work where he developed the discrepancy between "the magnitude of the events" and the ineptness and "singular imbecility" of the actors, he concludes on a bitter note: "and I marvel at the power of God who, with levers as short as these, can set the whole mass of human societies in motion."[13]

## III

Tocqueville's new form combines theory and myth to assert a political role, a *mytheoros* to accompany *mytheoreticus.* Once again he drew upon notions first advanced in *Democracy.* There he had described God as the master theorist because He could simultaneously grasp the general and the particular, the abstract and the concrete while the human mind could do one or the other but not both. Tocqueville had also noted the similarities between the theoretical abstractness he associated with Cartesianism and the theological conception that isolated man from his national and historical context. In *The Old Regime* he asserts that although "the French Revolution was a political revolution, it operated in the manner, and assumed some of the features, of a religious revolution." Among the features he singles out are its proselytizing mission, which spread revolutionary propaganda abroad to diverse societies. At a "deeper" level he finds a more fundamental similarity in "the general and abstract character" of religions, which, he pointedly notes, was not present in the civic-oriented pagan religions: "The principal aim [of Christianity] is to regulate the general relations between man and God, the general rights and duties of men toward each other, independently of the particular form of society." He then insists that the French Revolution "has operated in precisely the same way" toward the things of this world. "It has considered the citizen in an abstract fashion, apart from all particular societies" and "independently of country and time." The crucial question then becomes, by what means has a type of humanity been prepared that would lend itself to the rule of abstraction, generality, and a certain sameness—and thus allow those identifying marks of the theoretical to become a practice?[14]

To answer that question was, for Tocqueville, to embark on a course that would describe how the prerevolutionary world of particularities had been destroyed by a generalizing and centralizing power. How, in other words, the theorist-god had abandoned historicized particularity to allow the hegemony of power that is dehistoricized and abstract. To describe that chain of events was, by the same token, to restore and preserve the actuality of particularity and plenitude. The two interrelated objectives that Tocqueville set were to explain the revolution as having been prepared by a long process of dehistoricization and, by the methods of explanation, to rehistoricize the political consciousness of his contemporaries. This meant challenging the accepted meaning of their political identity. The revolution had become enshrined as the founding event that had radically redefined the nation's political identity in libertarian and egalitarian terms. It was also the liberatory moment when modernity acquired authority.

For these profound changes to take hold, the nation had to be prepared for them beforehand. Earlier centuries, Tocqueville noted, had "agitators" who sought unsuccessfully to change "particular customs" by appealing to "general laws of human society." For similar arguments to foster revolutions successfully, "certain changes" had to occur in "the conditions, customs, and *moeurs*" to render "the human spirit receptive."[15] Those changes involved nothing less than the emptying of a world of richly pluralistic and decentralized political forms and their supporting cultures and the eventual replacement of the "democratic" character of mediaeval "communities" with a culture of "dependence." Instead of local assemblies popularly elected, there were sham elections and rule by "a small oligarchy." The loss of municipal liberties was, Tocqueville declared, the most "shameful" aspect of the Old Regime. That loss was the accompaniment to a broad modernizing tendency, which resulted in the elimination of all the bodies of local law and peculiar customs, as well as provincial legislatures, self-governing municipalities, parlements (i.e., courts), and class privileges. The work of the Old Regime made Frenchmen "look exactly alike" and left "a glacial body more compact and homogeneous than perhaps any hitherto seen in the world."[16] This had been made possible by the destruction of complex patterns of cooperation and civility between unequals, a commonality amid differences: "all common passion, all mutual need, every necessity of understanding one another, every occasion for common action."[17]

It was not just the disappearance of institutions that would matter but the steady loss of political skills over a long period of time. Depoliticization was the other side of the coin of dehistoricization: "It is no small enterprise to bring together fellow citizens, who had lived together for centuries as strangers or enemies, and to teach them how to conduct their affairs in common once more."[18] The crucial consequence for a society in which political ignorance became widespread was that a revolution which should have been foreseen was not. Its members, regardless of class, were no longer capable of "reading" events. The extreme depoliticization that had occurred also explained why the revolution first appeared in France and why it took the awful forms it had:

> France being the one country in Europe where all political life had been extinguished for the longest time and most thoroughly, where individuals had most lost the practice of public affairs, the habit of reading the meaning of events, the experience of popular movements, and even the notion of a people, it is easy to imagine how all Frenchmen could fall all at once into a terrible revolution without seeing it and with those most threatened by it leading the march and opening and widening the road which led to it.[19]

The modernization of France and its entrance into modernity were the culmination of a lengthy process in which, according to Tocqueville, the steady penetration of local life by the central administration and its agents, the intendants, was accompanied by the emergence of a "new nobility" of "humble birth." The later revolutionaries, misled by the dazzle of pomp and privilege, failed to perceive the dynamic elements that for more than a century had steadily undermined the old order and stifled its vitalities. Before the French Revolution "the central power . . . had already succeeded in destroying all intermediary powers, and between it and individuals there yawned an immense void."[20] It had performed the work of revolution, not in the name of liberty but in accordance with a new logic, that of the tutelary state. These developments were summarized by one of the chapter titles in *The Old Regime*: "What Is Today Called Administrative Tutelage Is an Institution of the Old Regime."[21]

Thus a new power came into being and, while Tocqueville had identified the conditions which had made it possible, there remained something uncanny about the subversive character of the forces at work as well about the great power that had come into existence before the revolution and would survive it. For, although the power of the tutelary state was enormous, it was, Tocqueville insisted, "fragile." It lacked a genuinely political culture. It could absorb local powers and privileges but not recreate the webs of respect, affection, and cooperation by which the local powers had been constituted. It could not, as it were, diminish its citizens by encouraging the privatization of virtue and ability and then expect either its citizens or its own functionaries to display the qualities of loyalty, dedication, disinterestedness, and political skill needed by a political order. Nonetheless, a formidable centralized power had been created, and, even though it seemed suspended in midair, it was able to impose its will and suppress opposition.

The political monotheism represented by the centralized state reflects the wavering religious convictions of Tocqueville. He wanted the assurance of order that a benevolent power could extend but he also wanted a god who, while solicitous of common humanity, was not to be its political ally. One result is a love/hate fascination with Napoleon I, the political monotheist extraordinaire, who performs the impossible deed of bringing the revolution to a halt and, at the same time, harnessing its élan to create a military and imperialist power unmatched in Europe, while destroying liberty at home, perfecting centralization, and establishing the model of modern despotism for his nephew. Despite his antipathies, there is more than a trace of a proto-Nietzschean admiration for the power of a single man who, in the age of anonymous masses, can dominate an entire era and set the the impress of his mind on a whole society. Tocqueville attributes to him "the most extraordinary quality" of the same mental powers associated with God: "the power to comprehend effortlessly the great affairs of the world and immediately without difficulty focus on the smallest details."[22] Here is Tocqueville's portrait of that supreme incarnation of political monotheism:

> I want to survey the effort of this almost divine intelligence vulgarly employed to repress human liberties; to watch this intelligent and perfected organization of force, such as only the greatest geniuses in the midst of the most enlightened centuries could conceive; to see, under the weight of this admirable machine, a flattened and choking society becoming sterile . . . souls shrinking, great men ceasing to appear; an immense and flat horizon where, from whatever side we turn, appears nothing but the colossal figure of the Emperor himself.[23]

## IV

> *Providence which, doubtless wanting to give the spectacle of our passions and of our misfortunes as a lesson to the world, allowed the moment when the Revolution began to coincide with a great drought and an extraordinary winter.*
>
> Tocqueville[24]

The truly uncanny was the French Revolution itself. In Tocqueville's account the revolution was the result of developments that began to interlock but which no one planned or anticipated and which, if had they been understood, would not have been encouraged. He gives numerous examples of a kind of creeping chaos that allowed one blunder, miscalculation, or act of hubris to feed another. Thus, in the name of the reform of abuses, the state launched "a great administrative revolution" to remodel, simplify, and uniformize "all the rules and administrative habits" of the entire society. The result was massive confusion and, more importantly, widespread resentment because the effort to introduce more equal rules by abolishing exemptions had the unintended effect of making people more conscious of existing disparities. Consequently, to a nation bewildered and resentful, only "one last blow" was needed to topple the regime.[25]

Of all the unlikely occurrences none was more striking and less rationally accountable than the various ways by which the monarchy and the nobility had unintentionally succeeded in fatally weakening each other. Each undermined the crucial support that the other had lent to its own structure of power. Administrative centralization, by replacing the local institutions in which the nobility had played a major role and had mingled regularly with the other classes, isolated the nobility and left it vulnerable. The monarchy had lured the nobles into surrendering their political and social functions in exchange for the retention of certain class privileges, thereby eroding as well any justification for their special status. Mankind resents privileges, Tocqueville emphasized, only when they are divorced from political or social responsibilities. The French nobility had allowed itself to become a caste, a development hurried along when many of its members neglected their ancestral estates, and the attached civic responsibilities, for the attractions of Paris. Meanwhile, the peasantry and lower classes were abandoned by the aristocracy only to be radicalized by the example of a monarchy that went about discrediting established institutions and relationships that had endured for centuries.[26] The rage of the lower classes was further fed by the humanitarian idealism propagated by the literati, who, in turn, were encouraged by support from the aristocracy.[27]

Throughout Tocqueville's account of a world being destroyed, irony becomes the measure of helplessness, of the impossibility of halting the movement underway. The Old Regime unwittingly prepared the work of the French Revolution, and the revolutionaries consolidated and perpetuated the worst achievement of the Old Regime. At times the revolution appears not so much an overthrow as an exchange of forms: kings and their ministers are replaced by revolutionary tyrants and their acolytes; abstract rights are substituted for empty privileges; and the army of functionaries remains. The irony is compounded in Tocqueville's famous thesis that in the last two decades before the revolution France had been experiencing an unprecedented prosperity. Instead of easing discontents, material progress aroused greater expectations, and "the French found their situation insupportable just when it had become better."[28] The force of the irony is derived from the contrast between small-minded actors and the earth-shaking events they unwittingly set in motion.[29]

Irony allows the ironist to claim a measure of superiority over the earlier theorists and statesmen as he marshals the unintended consequences of policies and describes how their accumulation finally engulfs the actors. Irony is also a means of weaving a web of complicity, which joins all parties to a common but involuntary fate. He exposes the hidden connections of a fatally disconnected society: no one, neither contemporaries nor later commentators, seemed able to "see" what was really taking place.

Save for the one important exception of the intellectuals, there are no villains in Tocqueville's account. There were fools in abundance, greedy and shortsighted nobles, narrow-minded bourgeoisie, and "statesmen" whose "cleverness" extended no further than "a thorough grasp of all of the details of public administration."[30] The role of social classes is given considerable weight but the conception of class is notable for its portrait of actors who were highly self-conscious of class and consistently obtuse in their understanding of long-term class interests. The bourgeoisie, in addition to its political ineptness, displayed an inordinate passion for local offices, avidly buying them—and enjoying the accompanying tax exemptions—instead of employing wealth for productive purposes. In due course they became as isolated as the nobility from other classes, especially from the peasantry.[31]

Nonetheless, Tocqueville's account wavers between describing powerful tendencies set in motion unintentionally and criticizing the main actors for failing to do the morally right thing. Thus, while he remarks of the nobility's desertion of the countryside that "the principal and permanent cause of this fact was not in the will of certain men but in the slow and unceasing action of [the central] institutions,"[32] elsewhere in recounting the overly harsh actions of governmental agents he remarks, plaintively, that instead of sending vagabonds to the workhouses it would have been better "to open the hearts of the wealthy."[33]

## V

*Have all ages been like ours? And have men always had before their eyes, as in our time, a world in which nothing is connected.*
Tocqueville, *Democracy in America*[34]

No class, group, or governmental institution emerges as blameless, except for the peasantry which is depicted as resentful but passive. Tocqueville leaves no doubt, however, that those who actually held positions of political and social authority—the king, his ministers, the bureaucracy, and the nobility—bore the major responsibility for promoting conditions favorable to revolution.[35] The fundamental indictment was that in a variety of ways these actors either kept the social classes isolated from each other or did little or nothing to bring them together or, worse, when it suited them, played off each class against the others.[36] The condition was not one of atomization or Durkheimean anomie, but rather of "collective individualism," a pseudopluralism in which classes splintered into small, virtually self-contained societies and "the legitimate pride of the citizen was forgotten." Thus the nobles split into "infinite divisions" and devoted their energies to protecting their privileges, often against each other, and imposing various burdens, such as forced labor, onto the peasantry. If only the rich had supported the peasant instead of abandoning him, Tocqueville lamented.[37] The middle class separated into numerous small bodies, each jealous of its prerogatives and so determined not to remain identified with the common people that they aided the king in stripping townspeople of their political rights.[38] When, in the early stages of the revolution, the attempt was made to establish representative institutions that would promote class collaboration, "the different classes merely made first contact at their sorest points and came together only to tear one another to pieces."[39]

Toward the end of *The Old Regime* Tocqueville asserts that "classes alone occupy history."[40] That remark has been interpreted by some later commentators as evidence that he had recognized the centrality of the same phenomenon as Marx and most socialist thinkers. Although classes were the principal actors in Tocqueville's account, they were portrayed and understood in terms exactly the opposite of those used by Marx.[41] The striking contrast between Tocqueville's limited attention to the economic role of classes and Marx's preoccupation with it is reflected in contrasting metaphors. Marx typically invoked metaphors of separation: workers became separated from their products and tools, from their rural origins and, not least, from control over the routines of work. That metaphor crops up in later discussions of liberal economists: in its corporate forms capitalism separates those who own from those who actually control and, of course, managerial hierarchies from the work force. In the economic setting the metaphor of separation is essentially a way of confining the implications of power and powerlessness to "the economic domain" rather than connecting them to civic consequences.

Although Tocqueville employs metaphors of separation, they portray classes almost exclusively in political terms. His central story is that in the beginning there was class cooperation and interaction, only later, conflict and separation. Although his account is sympathetic toward the economic grievances of the peasant, its major emphasis is on political life. Consequently classes appear as political actors who, because they differ in social origins and economic interests, find it natural to work together and seek a common interest. The picture not only contrasts with Marx's focus on class conflict and irreconcilable interests, but with that of the fearful Tocqueville of the *Souvenirs* who despaired of the political being able to flourish amid antagonistic class differences. It also contrasts with the situation described in *Democracy*, of a flourishing political life and deeply engaged citizenry in an essentially classless society. In showing the actors in the class-ridden society of *The Old Regime* as authentically political, Tocqueville's account was as much, if not more, about the future of the political as it was about its past. There is continuity, from his alarm over the rise of "the social" in the *Souvenirs*, to his reference in *The Old Regime* to "the omnipotence of the social power" as one of the lasting principles of the French Revolution, and to his indictment of the "economists." *The Old Regime* is a reaffirmation of his commitment to retrieving the political but, in contrast to its context in *Democracy*, the political is cautiously restated in a reactionary setting. That attempt at recovering the political might appear to contemporaries as a venture in archaism but it might also be read as a hint how the social question might be handled differently. Instead of approaching it through the one-sided misrepresentations of class warfare or the neutral abstractions of expert policy, the emphasis could be on creating settings where representatives of the various social classes would meet regularly and over time develop a civic culture for coping with class differences.

## VI

> *In this abyss of isolation and misery in which the peasant lived he was shut in and impenetrable. . . . Nonetheless, the ideas current in the age were, from all sides, already penetrating these coarse minds; they entered there by circuitous and subterranean paths, and in these narrow and dark spaces assumed strange shapes.*
>
> Tocqueville[42]

As we have noted, one major exception to Tocqueville's principle was that no individual actor or class had sought deliberately to bring about the destruction of the Old Regime. The "men of letters" were the exception.[43] Predictably, philosophes, such as Voltaire and Rousseau, were singled out.[44] More surprisingly, Tocqueville reserved his strongest hostility for the eighteenth-century forerunners of Adam Smith and the classical economists, the Physiocrats, whom he pronounced to have been more influential than the philosophes.

With that declaration *mytheoreticus* has identified the form of theory to which it is the alternative. Defenders of "enlightened despotism," the Physiocrats were the equivalent of theologians of political monotheism. The combination of abstract rationalism and dogmatic style effected a radical change in perceptions causing traditional institutions to appear as bizarre and their elimination more like reclaiming empty space.[45] Their political economy was identified as the perfect representation of revolutionary theory, not as it appeared in the streets but in the councils of state. The "Economists'" defense of enlightened despotism as the most efficient method of reform proved dangerous when, through the strategically placed minister, Turgot, their ideas came to shape state policies.[46] Enlightened despotism, and its ideal of the state as the disinterested servant of society, is declared by Tocqueville to be the direct ideological forerunner of "democratic despotism."[47]

"The French Revolution was made by general theories, closely connected and forming a single body of doctrine."[48] Tocqueville's extended treatment of the Enlightenment writers was indicative both of the decisive influence that he believed ideas in general had on virtually all classes in the years before and after the revolution and of the unprecedented influence in particular of abstract theories.[49] The numerous references to "theory," "theorists," and to the role of the false "aristocracy" of philosophes and Physiocrats suggest a preoccupation with basic questions about the proper political role of the theorist and of the true nature of political theory—questions that, as we have seen, began to emerge in his attack upon socialism in the *Souvenirs* and in his address on political science.[50] The heavy responsibility that Tocqueville assigned this group, the lengthy discussion devoted to its role, and the biting tone of his comments suggest not so much an analysis as a deliberate confrontation over the nature of political theory and the political preparation of the theorist. That impression is confirmed by the striking opening sentence of the chapter devoted to describing "How toward the middle of the eighteenth century the men of letters became the chief politicians of the country." When translated literally that sentence recalls *Democracy in America* but reverses the imagery of the traveler ascending the hill and observing the receding clarity of the city below: "I now lose from view the remote and general facts which prepared the way for the great Revolution which I wish to portray. I come to particular and more recent facts which finally succeeded in determining its place, its birth, and its character."[51]

The passage is also significant for the recurrence of the parallel between general and particular facts. In *Democracy* the mastery of both was a sign of the divine intelligence. In *The Old Regime* the distinction is given a paradoxical twist. The "remote and general facts" of the past will be painted with animation and specificity, for the old is the particular and the synonym for diversity, multiplicity, and polytheistic powers, while the "particular and more recent facts," the men of letters, will embody the absolute opposite to "particular facts": they will be the representatives of "abstract principles and very general theories," the supreme antipositivists in their indifference to "particular facts," the ideologists of political monotheism.[52]

Tocqueville's intense focus on the theorists of the Enlightenment reflected his long-standing conviction that modern politics was unique for the dynamic that conjoined "ideas" with popular passions to produce mass "movements."[53] Clearly for ideas to have the effects he had witnessed in 1848 and he was now discovering in the eighteenth century, the state of society and the character of the teachings must have complementary structures. Because critical ideas were no novelty even before the eighteenth century, for an explosion to occur, certain corresponding qualities had to have existed between, on the one side, the state of society and its political condition and, on the other side, the character of theory.

In his Address of 1852, noted earlier, he had cast about for a formulation that might serve as an alternative to the version of theory being developed by predominantly socialist writers. He proposed a "political science" to assist statecraft in the age of emerging mass social movements. Its specialty would chart the direction of large-scale shifts in popular ideas and consciousness. That conception resurfaces briefly in *The Old Regime* but as a political science that had not discerned the direction of things and, in the process, failed the prerevolutionary statesmen.[54] His own evolution toward a more political theoretical position and a less political-science-oriented conception grew out of his worries about whether and how his current project could affect men and events. During the years when *The Old Regime* was in gestation Tocqueville frequently expressed a fear that the public had lost interest in politics and that his labors would be fruitless. However, following the enthusiastic reception of the book he became more hopeful. Writing to a former colleague he explained that "since the movement of the masses, even of the grossest kind, originates in ideas, and often in very metaphysical and abstract ideas . . . it is always useful to place one's ideas in circulation in the hope that if they are true, they will gradually be transformed into passion and facts."[55]

What had changed Tocqueville's estimation of possibilities was the experience of reflecting on the revolutionary role played by the Enlightenment writers. The reference to "the grossest kind" of ideas and "very metaphysical and abstract ideas" is a sure sign of whom he had in mind and of the kinship with the untutored Cartesianism he had discovered in America. While suggesting that ideas still mattered, he was careful to distinguish between crude and abstract ideas and ideas that are "true" and "gradually" attract a following.

True ideas working gradually: who will be their object and with what practical implications? An indication was given in a letter written near the end of his life: "I believe that the superior classes could be persuaded and aroused again; and I think that once that was accomplished, they would exercise a sufficiently strong, but lesser, influence over the people; but that could be done only very slowly, and with the help of a multitude of sharp blows at their minds."[56]

How to persuade and arouse "the superior classes"? That question takes us back to one posed earlier but not pursued: what sorts of conditions present in prerevolutionary France had made all social classes receptive to highly abstract and radical doctrines? Tocqueville's answer was: by the eighteenth century the French people had allowed themselves, by one means or another, to become politically ignorant, depoliticized. Into that void rushed the Enlightenment writers with "general and abstract theories" ideally suited to a society choked with resentments, floundering in the thicket of administrative rules, and palpably oppressed by real grievances but severely lacking in the kind of political experience that produces balanced judgments and careful assessments of consequences. Men dwelt in "an ideal city of the imagination" where "everything appeared simple and coordinated, uniform, equitable, and in conformity with reason."[57] Unlike their English counterparts, the representatives of theory rarely mixed with men of affairs, but instead frequented the salons of the aristocracy and bourgeoisie where they encountered men who were also shut off from public life. As a result the publicists were as politically naive as their audience, political innocents who were "wholly unacquainted with politics," men of "pure theory" who never doubted their ability to pronounce judgment on the most intractable and obscure political problems and never hesitated to advance their views with a sublime disregard for facts.[58] A dangerous situation developed where "public passions became disguised in philosophy and political life was violently mixed with literature." Inevitably "general theories were transformed into political passions and political actions."[59]

Thus the lines were drawn between Tocqueville's *mythistoricus et politicus* and the theorists of revolution: he stands for precisely what they lacked, political and historical sensibility. Their lack was summed up as indifference toward "political liberty," Tocqueville's foremost political value.[60] Political liberty is to be cherished "independently of its benefits" and especially of any material goods. "It is the delight in being able to speak, act, breathe without constraints save only those of God and the laws."[61]

That conception of liberty seems, like many of Tocqueville's conceptions, vague; yet it is not elusive and once its referents are identified it becomes full with the plenitude of a lost polytheistic world. To recapture that world and then to reveal it to have been a world where political liberty had flourished and the word "democracy" might justifiably be applied to its politics define the project of *mythistoricus et politicus.* That will mean identifying *mythos* not as the antithesis to *theoria* but its supplement. What, then, is *mytheoreticus*? What sort of practice is it? How does a *mytheoros* proceed?

## VII

*I began this study of the old society full of prejudices against it; I have ended full of respect.*

Tocqueville[62]

*The feudal government . . . had been a government in which arbitrariness, violence, and great freedom were mixed together. Under its laws actions had often been constrained, yet speech was nearly always independent and proud.*

Tocqueville[63]

*Mytheoreticus* begins by rejecting the imagery of the traveler who ascends the hill to gain his synoptic view of the whole and, in the process, loses sight of particularity. In a letter of 1856 to Gobineau, Tocqueville remarks that in writing *The Old Regime* he had reversed the conventional approach to the French Revolution and, instead of viewing it from the top he had viewed it from "underneath."[64] Accordingly, the text itself is sprinkled with metaphors about digging "beneath the debris" or "below the surface." To be sure, archaeological metaphors had their literal counterpart in the archival research he had conducted but, as he explained to a correspondent, their real point was "to recompose ideally a world forever destroyed" and "nearly as difficult to reconstruct and understand as the antediluvian epochs."[65]

The world he will describe vaguely as "feudal" might also be described as archaic, for Tocqueville repeatedly insists that the values and customs from that past often persisted into the age immediately prior to the revolution. To "recompose ideally" would not mean presenting an idyllic world of virtuous actors and unflawed institutions. As he remarked of the parlement, the judicial bodies that "irregularly" intervened and disrupted the course of royal administration were "doubtless more preoccupied with themselves than with the public good [*la chose publique*]." Nonetheless,"it was a great evil which limited a still greater one."[66] It was, then, a fallen world. The "political liberty" that he claimed for it was, when contrasted with the Economists' combination of abstract natural right doctrine and administrative rule, unnatural. Political liberty, he insisted, encourages "necessary connections and mutual ties of dependence" yet "does not render men alike."[67] The Economists, with their "system of reform, so vast and so tightly interconnected in its parts," looked to "the State not only to command the nation but to fashion it in a certain way and to form the mind of the citizens according to a certain predetermined model."[68] The prerevolutionary world, in contrast, with its "privileges, prejudices, and false ideas," its asymmetries and irregularities, nonetheless "maintained the spirit of independence among a great number of subjects and disposed them to stiffen against the abuses of authority."[69] The nobles are depicted as the defenders of local institutions, their shield against the incursions of the monarchical state and the arrogance of its agents. In his eyes, the old nobility epitomized a class whose status and privileges had been earned by the political and social duties it performed and by the responsibilities it shouldered on behalf of communities.

In re-creating the nobility as the political class, Tocqueville finally had the opportunity not only to justify the institution most symbolic of inequality but to disclose the identity of the guardian class he had been compelled to repress throughout his political career. Although the nobility had been broken and it was politically impossible to restore its former power Tocqueville takes great pains to insist that if the nobility had been more astute politically it could have survived and continued to play an important political role. In support of that claim he repeatedly invokes the example of the English aristocracy, emphasizing its flexibility and openness to the recruitment of new members. Its continuing political influence argues that it is still possible to combine *ancienneté* and modernity. However important the American model of political pluralism to Tocqueville's re-creation of feudal pluralism in France, the idealization of the English aristocracy—and of British politics in general—was equally crucial to the political agenda of *The Old Regime*.[70]

As "the point of most resistance" to central power Tocqueville would have the nobility transcend historical traditions to become symbolic figures of a *mythpoliticus*.[71] They are the key actors in a project of political education launched from a reactionary starting point. Tocqueville's account of the nobility does not so much preach resistance as illustrate it. Resistance is conceived as defensive, embedded in daily life, anticlimactic protest, and concerned to preserve the status quo by avoiding bringing matters to a head: "Most of the means of defense . . . were beyond the reach [of the common people]; to be able to use them it was necessary to have a place in society where one could be seen and make one's voice heard. But outside the common people there was not a man in France who, if he had the heart for it, could not wrangle over his obedience and resist while yielding."[72]

Unlike Marx Tocqueville abhors collective action, in part because he fears that the demos, with its lack of experience in the "means of defense," naturally responds to oppression by the only means available, violence. So he seeks instead to identify instances of "independence," that is, classes or groups that, because they are not dependent, can resist "while yielding." In that vein he recalls that under "the ancient constitution" clerics had owned their own land; this had enabled them to be free from papal domination and to be able to instruct parishioners in "civic values."[73] The clergy may have been intolerant and opinionated but it was also "the enemy of despotism, and as favorable toward civil liberty and as enamoured of political liberty as the third estate or the nobility." Tocqueville even managed to discern an element of independence among the bourgeoisie, although he could not resist adding that this was the result of "many of their vices." The bourgeoisie had splintered into small associations and, while each had jealously guarded its interests, each also displayed a sense of "common dignity and common privileges." Their corporations resembled tiny polities where none could hide in anonymity. "Each man found himself in a very tiny theater, it is true, but brightly illuminated, and with a public always ready to applaud or to hiss." The world before centralization was one "where the art of stifling the sound of all resistance had not reached the perfection it has today. France had not yet become the muffled place in which we now live."[74]

The complexity of Tocqueville's allusions to resistance comes from the fact that the same institutions that could offer resistance to the center were also the main carriers of authority: the same reason that made them natural resisters also made them the opponents of rebels. As long as France remained strongly diversified the protests of local powers would remain localized, restricted; but once local authorities everywhere became infected by the same abstract political and moral doctrines, their protests would become grounded in homogeneity of outlook and protest would be ready to explode into revolution.[75]

The political plenitude of a polytheistic world acquired its supreme expression in Tocqueville's account of the political life-forms that flourished in abundance before the advent of monotheistic centralization. France had once been a varied mosaic of parishes, municipalities, local councils, provincial assemblies, and a complex system of justice that made France "a free people." All of the major social groupings of aristocracy, bourgeoisie, and artisans came together to deliberate about common affairs, to vote taxes, and to transact public business. Men from the most varied social backgrounds and degrees of influence could assemble and deliberate because they were joined together by prior customary ties of obligation.

Tocqueville's pronouncement, that the old parishes of France enjoyed "the most extreme democracy" and strongly reminded him of the rural communities in America,[76] signified the fulfillment of a lifelong and often repressed quest: finally, in a world of privilege, inequality, and injustice he had come upon the best practicable realization of the political, an admittedly "deformed" regime of political liberty where, nonetheless, "originality" and "the taste for glory" were not extinct and "there was far more liberty than in our own day."[77]

The model was not unrealizable. In order "to show what provincial liberty could achieve under the 'old order,'" he devoted an appendix to discussing the representative assemblies of the provinces and primarily one in Languedoc. Tocqueville depicts an assembly composed of respected men of substance from the clergy, nobility, and bourgeoisie who represent a model of careful deliberation on the affairs of their province. Public works were administered by agents chosen by the assembly, not by the king. Taxes were levied according to local methods and all classes cooperated on a footing of "the most perfect equality." The clergy "lived in perfect understanding with the men of the third estate. . . . The nobles, while strong enough to maintain their rank, were not strong enough to rule alone. . . . During the whole of the past century Languedoc was administered by the bourgeoisie, controlled by the nobles, and assisted by the bishops." Tocqueville laid particular emphasis upon the province's ability to respond to changing values. The "spirit of the new age" that was demanding greater equality had begun quietly to "permeate" the old institutions, modifying without radically altering them. "This might have been done everywhere else."[78] Languedoc, the realized version of the counterparadigm, illustrates how the Old Regime might have been saved, how it was adapting to "the necessities of modern civilization." Tocqueville even went so far as to conclude that the French Revolution had not been inevitable: the "old social edifice" would have fallen, though gradually, by "slow degrees" and "spontaneously."[79]

## VIII

*[In May 1788] the time had not yet come when despotism could appeal to democracy by maintaining order and equality.*
Tocqueville[80]

Languedoc stands out as the realization of Tocqueville's ideal of *ancienneté*, but it is equally striking for the celebration of political arrangements that exclude the common people in general and the peasantry in particular. This was in keeping with Tocqueville's portrait of the premodern political world where all of the varied political life-forms uniformly excluded all of the social strata below the bourgeoisie. Thus the common people were consigned to a kind of darkness, outside the pale of political life. They remain unpoliticized, Tocqueville notes, except for one isolated moment, their "participation" in the religious struggles of the sixteenth century. Then the "common people" had been idealistic, whereas the upper classes had acted primarily from motives of ambition and profit. Those roles, he emphasized, were reversed in the first stage of the French Revolution when the "enlightened classes" were moved by altruism and the common people by "rage and covetousness."[81] Tocqueville's description of that experience clearly anticipates his later hope that the enduring religiosity of the countryside and its peasantry might provide the cultural basis for a stable, nonrevolutionary regime of the enlightened classes.

But he was also looking back toward 1848 and redescribing his fears of an aggrieved demos of urban workers and artisans inflamed by politically irresponsible men of ideas. The prerevolutionary government, he notes, made the mistake of speaking publicly about the injustices of the poor as though the latter were not listening. Admittedly the bourgeoisie and aristocracy had publicly expressed contempt for the poor, yet Tocqueville looked back on any sustained effort to investigate the injustices visited upon the poor as a provocation. He reminded his readers that the French become "barbarous" when gripped by "violent passions."[82] Tocqueville acknowledges the common people as historical actors only when he attributes the violence of the French Revolution to "the most barbarous and rudest classes of the nation." Over the centuries they had become brutalized and when the enlightened classes had taught them to hate inequality, the common people "applied" the "theories" in a savage effort to root out all traces of it.[83]

For Marx the final showdown would see a self-conscious proletariat, educated by the communist party to the causes of its exploitation, facing off against a small capitalist class struggling to preserve power, which it was incapable of developing rationally. For Tocqueville the crucial struggle was between the small number with a passion for political liberty and the masses, who with their passion for equality, were the natural allies of the benevolent, uniformity-minded, and centralized state. In his eyes the struggle was heavily weighted in favor of the latter. The passion for liberty waxes and wanes; it tends to be ephemeral because its devotees are inexperienced and easily frightened. In contrast, the idea of equality fuses the savage and primal force of the lower classes toward a moment of resolution, which because of its vagueness is elusive yet potentially incendiary: "the passion for equality is always the same, always attached to the same end with the same stubborn and often blind ardor, ready to sacrifice everything to those who permit it to satisfy [the passion], and grant to a government that favors and flatters it the customs, ideas, and laws which despotism needs in order to rule."[84]

## IX

The title of Tocqueville's great work, with its juxtaposition of *ancienneté* and modernity, foretold the antithesis that recurs throughout and endows *The Old Regime* with a long-term significance equal to that of *Democracy in America.* To exaggerate only slightly: *Democracy* had been written about America but with one eye on the future of France; *The Old Regime* was written for France and could have had an eye toward the future of the United States. The story he unfolds can be read as a story of the antipolitical consequences of modernization. He conceived the connection between revolution and despotism, which formed the principal thematic of the work, as contingent rather than necessary. When a revolution inspired by democratic ideals irrupts in a society previously depoliticized, the likely result will be "democratic despotism." However, as the example of the English revolution of 1688 demonstrated, if a society preserves most of its traditional political institutions during a revolution, the revolutionaries are unlikely to attack the system of social relations.[85] In that formulation the crucial variable is whether politicization has been shaped by class contact or class conflict. The great contribution of local institutions to politicization was made possible by a settled location where members of different classes—doubtless the poor and workers excepted—met regularly to discuss common affairs, adjudicate disputes, and voice grievances. And where the economic was subordinated to the political, "the practice of common affairs . . . alone is capable of tearing men away from the cult of money and the petty daily anxieties of their particular interests" and of getting them "to perceive and feel at every moment the presence of the fatherland above and around them."[86]

His account of the centralization of administration, with its effort to advance the welfare of the population by state regulations and to promote justice by uniform laws, is more than an anticipation of Max Weber's famous account of bureaucratic rationality. For the distinctively modern element in the "new power" of the state was the presence of policy makers, such as Turgot and Necker, men steeped in the new science of economics taught by the Physiocrats. "Of all the men of that time, it was the economists who would seem least out of place in our own age." While the other writers of that age seemed alien, "when I read the books of the economists, I seem to have lived with them and just finished talking to them."[87] When Tocqueville declares that "the destructive theories of socialism . . . are contemporary with the first economists," he means to call attention to the latters' indifference to rank, tradition, and customary practices. In the name of logical reasoning, abstract economic theory abolishes the quirks of traditional society: theory is the revolution before the fact. Socialism and centralization are declared to be "products of the same soil" and are to each other what "the wild fruit" is to the "cultivated fruit."[88]

Modernity combined rationalism, administration, governing as policy making, economics as the substance of policy and a new language of the antipolitical with a strong passion for social equality, no interest in political liberty, hatred of "all the ancient powers derived from feudalism," and suspicion of whatever "tended toward aristocracy."[89] From the new vantage point supplied by a Bonapartist despotism supported by universal suffrage, Tocqueville restates his conception of democratic despotism, this time with less emphasis on privatization than on its formally democratic character:

> That particular form of tyranny which has been named democratic despotism, and of which the Middle Ages had no idea, was already familiar [to the economists]. No more hierarchy in society, no distinct classes, no fixed ranks. [Instead] one people composed of individuals who were nearly similar and entirely equal; this confused mass recognized as the only legitimate sovereign, but carefully deprived of all the means which would enable it to direct and even to oversee its own government. Above it a sole authority [*mandataire*], charged with doing everything in its name but without consultation. To control that agent was to have public reason without organs, to check it only by revolutions but not laws; by formal right only an instrument but in reality a master.[90]

To Tocqueville what is striking about modern conceptions of socialism and democracy is that their aim is equality, not repoliticization, an aim that can be realized without reinvigorating civic life. Socialism is committed to a strong state with the power to reorganize social and economic relations; but to encourage democratic practices of self-government seems beside the point, or, worse, might result in the weakening of state power and hence of its ability to solve "the social problem." Accordingly, Tocqueville suggests, it makes more sense for socialism to embrace despotism as the most effective method of introducing radical social reform.[91] Similarly, political equality does not encourage contact between dissimilars through "the practice of common affairs" but obscures their differences by endowing each with the same abstract status of citizen and provides no clues about the responsibilities of those with great social power and influence. "Individualism" and self-interest may be efficient engines of materialism but they are corrosive of the civic values that produce "great citizens."[92]

## X

In the closing tentative sentences of *The Old Regime*, Tocqueville writes that "perhaps" he might "soon" cross the "threshold" to examine the French Revolution "itself." Then "I shall dare to judge the society which emerged from it."[93] At the beginning of *The Old Regime*, Tocqueville had left a reader in little doubt what that judgment would be. There he had promised to identify the "mistakes" and "miscalculations" of the revolutionaries and show that after 1788—that brief moment when moderate leadership had been as dedicated to political liberty as to equality—the French Revolution was launched on a course in which the passion for equality predominated. Frenchmen then would accept the suspension of the basic political liberties—"freedom of thought, speech, and writing"—and become "equal slaves of the master of the world."[94] Now, in the concluding chapter, he looked back and claimed to have accomplished his original purpose of dispelling "the darkness of night" that enveloped the revolution if one tried to understand it as an isolated event. Without describing in detail the outbreak of the revolution, or even its causes, he had, instead, given it a specific course, a progression toward despotism. The fundamental character of that course, and the originality of the theory, was that it had been set beforehand.

The darkness had been dispelled by light from the prerevolutionary past to reveal—what? A combination of intellectual pathology, political inexperience, and egalitarian passions? While that conclusion might fit with the treatment of the revolution as a progression to despotism and even satisfy the political purpose of establishing a political parallel between revolutionary events and their Napoleonic end points, it supplied little or no assistance in resolving the grand question, What resources could be drawn upon to theorize a post-despotic arrangement? *The Old Regime* had tried to place the best face possible on the late feudal system of communal liberties, provincial assemblies, and lawcourts controlled by the nobility. He had identified "democratic" elements, lauded the independence of the leading elements, and even praised the resistance of local powers to central authorities. But in the end he had to concede that that system could only have survived by continually changing. There was no assurance that the changes would have preserved what had been politically valuable in the system, especially when its virtues had depended on a political culture of inherited inequalities.

It would seem, then, that the only place where the resources for political reconstruction could be found was in the French Revolution itself. This suggests that, like the projected second volume, *The Old Regime* is also unfinished—politically and theoretically. Or to put it slightly differently, that the incompleteness of *The Old Regime* signifies the political and theoretical limitations of *ancienneté*. And further, that the unpublished work on the revolution "itself" holds important clues about how Tocqueville intended to build on certain aspects of it and to incorporate elements of modernity. There is warrant for these possibilities in some of Tocqueville's remarks in the second volume. After noting that "certain ingenious minds of our day have undertaken to rehabilitate the old regime," he insists that hatred of the old regime remained intense and declares that "for me the test is over and the system has been judged. It was impossible to make the French return to the old order of things."[95] Further, Tocqueville must have known that the elements of political liberty that he repeatedly singled out—freedom of thought, speech, and press—were not the achievements of the Old Regime and owed no small debt to the reviled philosophes. In his notes to the second volume he criticizes those of his contemporaries who were "as blind and also stupid in their systematic and absolute denigration of . . . the philosophy of the eighteenth century" as the men of that century had been blindly infatuated with it.[96]

## XI

> *[A reviewer of* The Old Regime*] seems to me to have understood that this new work is linked to* Democracy *which he is very familiar with. No one has done quite right what would have been particularly gratifying to me; for the unity of my life and my thought is, above all, the thing that I most want to preserve in the eyes of the public. The man is as interested in that as the writer.*
>
> Tocqueville[97]

While working on *The Old Regime*, Tocqueville maintained a substantial correspondence with Americans that extended from 1852 to 1858, the year before his death. In one letter he describes himself as "partly an American citizen."[98] It forms a sad footnote, for Tocqueville senses a theoretical failure and yet another political defeat. At first his letters evince mild concern over the slavery crisis in the United States; then concern turns to dismay as he takes stock of the corruption in American politics and the low level of ability among its politicians; and, finally, anxiety turns to alarm before the growth of violence and lawlessness of a people who combine passion and savagery with the tastes, vices, and vigor of civilized men. He writes to his American correspondents that Europeans, who once had embraced democracy because of what they had been taught, now feel both betrayed because of the contradiction between slavery and democracy, and fearful because great power appears to be in the hands of a violent and semicivilized people. "You have become, on this side of the ocean, the *puer robustus* of Hobbes . . . an unpredictable and dangerous force."[99] He closed one letter with the "ardent desire that the great experiment of Self Government that is being carried on in America will not fail."[100] Despite his stated reservations about democracy, his public reputation as a theorist was bound up with the success of the New World experiment. By the time he was preparing the introduction to The *Old Regime* and invoking *Democracy* for inspiration against despotism, Tocqueville was clearly becoming alarmed at the actuality of American democracy. Tocqueville had invested a lifetime defending the American system as proof that "liberal ideas and institutions" could be the basis of a stable system as well as a morally and politically virtuous one.[101]

In the light of this correspondence and the apparent stability of the Bonapartist despotism, certain motifs in *The Old Regime* assume a sharper definition. As previously noted, Tocqueville had made a pointed reference to *Democracy*, not in order to recommend some feature of the American democracy but to teach a lesson about the crucial importance of aristocracy; and at several junctures in *The Old Regime* he had reinforced that point by extolling the contemporary example of the English aristocracy and the British political system in general. This shift toward a more explicit defense of an aristocratic principle and a cooler view of democracy, while in no sense a turnabout, had its justifying and symbolic moment. In preparation for the second volume of *The Old Regime* but still smarting from his inglorious departure from political life, he went to England in 1856 in order to examine the British Museum's collection of French revolutionary publications. Upon his return there in 1857, "he was pounced upon and lionized by members of society, and for a month he basked in popularity." Then the British navy made special arrangements for a warship to conduct him to France.[102]

## XII

> *I have never been able to force myself to reread* Democracy *after it appeared except when it has been necessary to make the corrections which later editions allowed.*
>
> Tocqueville[103]

After 1848 the democracy of *Democracy in America* was no longer an instructive example, at least not for the Tocqueville who had personally experienced revolution and dictatorship and then reexperienced them while sifting through the archives of revolution. The "spirit of liberty," he noted, had "never taken hold among the inferior classes"[104] Far from displaying a blindness to social conflicts and an overemphasis on political considerations—often alleged to be the vices of liberal thinkers—Tocqueville was guilty of overlooking the political possibilities.[105]

The French Revolution had, among other things, signified multiplicity's challenge to the unity of the privilege-ridden political space symbolized by monarchy and aristocracy. That invasion was the culmination of a revolution that had been occurring at least a half century before 1789 and had involved the emergence of a multitude of political sites—in meetings, associations, a wider and more diversified writing and reading public. The idea of the political was being dissolved and reconstituted in ways that signified it would not be permanently settled—a development that, while he lamented it, Tocqueville had also glimpsed in his frequent references to the persistent recurrence of revolution.

What was at stake in the simultaneity of multiple conflicts and the burgeoning of politics in diverse forms was the rejection of a certain generality resting on permanent social distinctions and along with it the entire pre- and early modern attempt to combine a political based on exclusion with a rhetoric of "the common good" and "general welfare."[106] While the Bonapartist dictatorship worked to crush political multiplicity in the name of a general order, it also attempted to reassure the bourgeoisie, create support among the working classes, and retain the allegiance of the peasantry. Modern power seemed to be groping toward some as yet unsettled combination of elements of a broadly inclusive public and a narrow, virtually private sphere of decision making. Insofar as It could be said to have a direction, it was toward the depoliticization both of citizens and their rulers and away from the early modern liberal conception of a public politics (e.g., Locke, Montesquieu, the *Federalist*, and Jefferson) and of a measured reduction in the distance between ruler and ruled.

How was the crisis in the political registered in Tocqueville's thinking? A clue is to be found in one of his notes to the unfinished volume on the French Revolution: "An examination of the legal system of the Constituent Assembly by throwing into relief its divergent character, liberalism and democracy, leads me, bitterly, back to the present."[107] The divergence between liberalism and democracy was given fuller expression in other fragments, but these can be reduced to two principal claims. The first was that an "absolute ruler" who governs by laws and institutions that favor "the condition of the people" ought not to be described as democratic. "The natural meaning" of democracy is where "the people take a more or less large part in the government."[108] That formulation, while it tacitly denied democratic legitimation to Louis Napoleon and his plebiscitary practices, was not introduced in order to oppose despotism with a conception of democratic participation. Instead, Tocqueville implied that popular participation had been compromised by the phenomenon of mass support of despotism. That implication was developed in the fragments devoted to political liberty.

## XIII

> *Revolutions and misery can teach even the greediest and most cowardly peoples that despotism is miserable. But who will give men a taste for liberty, if they have never known it or have lost it? Who will make them appreciate its noble pleasures? Who will make them love it for its own sake, if that love is not naturally in their hearts?*
>
> Tocqueville[109]

Tocqueville was no stranger to the idea of political liberty. He had defended it throughout his public life: as the most precious of all political values, the core of his conception of liberalism, and a crucial point marking the divergence between liberalism and democracy. Political liberty included not only the right to express one's ideas and beliefs but to participate in local political life. In *The Old Regime* he identified political liberty with the system of local, provincial, and corporate institutions. Participation in the political life of a traditional society was, however, understood as participation by social unequals. Tocquevillean participation was premised on the value of independence, which depended on the economic and social resources that supplied an individual or class with the power to protest and defend. In *Democracy*, however, the interdependence of individuals more or less equal in their powers had been the key element in participation: citizens recognized the need of pooling their individually modest resources, not to protest but to deliberate about practical objectives. Upon investigating the stages by which the revolutionaries had succeeded in discrediting the idea of inequality and elevating equality, Tocqueville reacted by narrowing the meaning of participation and its circle of participants. Because participation contains the potential threat of aggregated popular power, Tocqueville shapes political liberty with an antimaterialist and predominantly aristocratic cast, presupposing a virtue that is born and bred in the few and more at home in Plato's *Republic* than even in austere New England.

Political liberty was foremost the free expression of ideas understood as the work of disinterested thinkers addressing an audience able to appreciate the nobility of *la chose publique.* Liberty is not to be loved for its "practical advantages" or the "material goods" it brings but for the "instinctive taste" it nourishes. It is not only on "intellectual grounds" that free men hate absolute power; it is also "instinctive." Their "brave" rejection of arbitrary rule and a willingness to risk comes from "a taste for independence, a taste that, to some extent, is disinterested, instinctive, and involuntary." The "manly and noble pleasure" of speaking and acting without restraint rests ultimately on having a "taste" for freedom. In contrast, the "reasoned and interested taste for liberty"—which Tocqueville all but labeled the bourgeois conception of liberty—represents the calculation of advantage, a "view of the benefits" that will accrue. But the "instinctive tendency, irresistible and hardly conscious, born of the hidden sources of all great human passions . . . exists only in the hearts of very few" and is independent of "tangible benefits." Tocqueville caps the point in a note exhorting himself: "Never forget that in your thoughts."[110]

Tocqueville's formulation can be read as a late and beleaguered expression of the republican tradition of civic virtue—although, as "the best and the brightest" would claim, not the last.[111] The well-being and fate of a political society was believed to rest principally with a relatively small group of public-spirited and experienced "wise men" whose patrician origins were the guarantors of disinterestedness. Meanwhile, the pressure for equality, for extending material, social, and cultural advantages to those created unequal by an institutionalized system of material rewards, is represented as an attack on freedom by an ignorant demos for whom the politics that is beyond their grasp should properly be out of their reach.

The conception of political liberty and its antiegalitarianism sums up a persistent tendency toward the aestheticization of politics that was evident throughout Tocqueville's life. It had taken several forms: the disdain for materialism; the longing for *grandeur* and disdain for massiveness; the criticism of uniformity, homogeneity, and anonymity as representing the categories of the administrative, the economic, and the social; the attraction to sweeping panoramas, spectacles, tableaux, myth. Aestheticism is, in part, a response to the loss occasioned by the political invasion of grossness and symbolized in the appearance of "numbers," of persons who do not require discrimination or individual identification and who, because they lack, or are unable to acquire, distinctions, can only be assembled as a "mass," as that which is shapeless and graceless because it lacks discriminating traditions of culture. Mobilized mass stands for the monstrous, the uncultivated grown wild. Literally, it crowds out the rare, that which requires careful cultivation and demarcation.

With the collapse of hierarchical notions of order, a process speeded by the advance of secularization, Tocqueville's liberalism was pressed to find functional equivalents for containing the resentments of inequality. To the end, and despite his outrage at the reactionary politics of the church, especially for its support of the Bonapartist despotism,[112] he hoped that liberalism and religion could be allies and, bolstered by nationalism and patriotism, could help to unify a society riven by inequality and class conflicts. Religion, nationalism, patriotism: items on a diminishing list of counters available to resist equality and enlist the masses in the mystification of politics.

# CHAPTER XXVI
# POSTDEMOCRACY

## I

*I believe that the revolutions which have forcibly diverted me from the road that I was following, have, in spite of myself, put me back on the road that I should always have followed.*

Tocqueville[1]

*The same person will speak differently when in a salon, in a book, at the tribune, to a friend and to a thousand listeners, to an academic public and to passersby in the street. The basic sentiments and ideas may be the same, but the form of the thought, the animation of the speech, the nature of the language, and the choice of expressions will vary in each case.*

Tocqueville[2]

Most commentators have proceeded as though there was nothing problematical about Tocqueville himself, that he was simply the author of his books, a subject representing itself by a theory. Perhaps, however, this bundle of contradictions, poses, anachronisms, absurdities, and willfulness, this "Tocqueville," represented not a single authorial self but a named being struggling, over time, to hold together an uncertain assemblage of wayward phenomena, of diverse impulses and frustrated ambitions. "It is difficult," Tocqueville once confided to Beaumont in the course of a political campaign, "to show one of *my faces*" without creating a false impression.[3]

The variety of texts that carry the same name, "Tocqueville," may correspond to several Tocquevilles. Tocqueville *simpliciter* dissolves into a writer who found that the success of his first work had given him a public identity inseparable from the United States but who, except for a brief interlude late in his life, displayed only slight or occasional interest in that country; a young lawyer who gained instant acclaim with *Democracy in America*, though previously he had never published anything consequential and seemed more interested in a political career; a politician who, having failed in his first try for elective office, came to hate elections and to find public speaking an excruciating ordeal; a parliamentarian who, after winning a seat in the Chamber of Deputies, quickly fell to complaining about the anonymity and pettiness of parliamentary life, yet who earlier in *Democracy* had praised politics for its broadening effects and for the exhilaration that came from working with others for common goals; an aristocrat who repeatedly declared that aristocracy no longer mattered politically, yet who in his writings reconstituted that class as a ghostly but crucial element in the structure of his theory; a political hero manqué who spouted an embarrassing amount of romantic mush about his longing for the opportunity to perform great and noble public deeds and about how that ambition was being repeatedly foiled by the triviality of parliamentarism, but who, when an actual revolutionary caesura opened in 1848, chose, instead, to retreat to a spectator's box and to comment, meanspiritedly, on the efforts of his contemporaries to cope with extraordinary events; the parliamentary politician who rose to become minister of foreign affairs by virtue of the sort of political deals he despised, only to fall from power after a brief and mostly inglorious performance; and, finally, the theorist who, when confronted with the fulfillment of his direst political fears and the perfect materialization of one of his most renowned concepts, "democratic despotism," responded to the despotism of Louis Napoleon by secluding himself in historical archives, exhuming the past, and emerging with a work that seemed to refuse engagement with the political present and only tangentially with its chosen past: *The Old Regime and the Revolution* breaks off on the eve of the French Revolution, as though its author found it too painful to confront, even in his imagination, a revolution waged against an authority that no longer existed.

Then there was the penultimate Tocqueville who early in life had voyaged to America and returned to warn his countrymen that they must accommodate to the irresistible tide of democracy, but who, after a lifetime of near silence about America, suddenly rouses himself to a renewed interest in America, follows its desperate debates over slavery, fears that if the cause of freedom is lost in America, its future in Europe will be lost as well, and, as though in a last effort to resolve a lifetime of ambivalence about democracy, declares himself at the end to be "half-Yankee."[4] Finally, there were and are the Tocquevilles of we commentators.

In a letter of 1856, three years before he died, Tocqueville confided to a friend, "The unity of my life and thought is the most important thing which I need to maintain before the public eye; the man is as involved in that as the writer."[5] In the light of what Tocqueville's life and thought encompassed, his anxieties about the coherence of his life are not surprising. If we think of Tocqueville's theory as extending over a lifetime, it appears overmatched by the magnitude of its chosen encounters. The theory was a registry of responses to the uniqueness of modernity: events and experiences of almost preternatural size and power and of change without mutation; the otherness of America, an overpowering landscape and a society that seemed classless and pastless; the several revolutions in France; and, finally, despotism. A protean world that kept producing novel forms of culture and rule, while multiplying the obstacles to coherence and stability, threatened either to overwhelm any theoretical attempt to comprehend it, or to lure the theorist into believing that his theory could unite the truths of a self-subverting world while avoiding the same effect on the theory.

## II

> *Human destiny is in general sad, especially in regard to the ordinary vexations that are aggravated as life goes on. The more one proceeds down this road, the more this aspect of the moral world is distorted and solitude increases. Along the way one loses cherished objects until in the end one is without friends or faculties. One leaves only the debris of one's self. And, worst of all, early on one knows it to be inevitable. It leaves man as the most unfortunate being created by God, if the justice of God were only exercised in this world and were not open to other interpretations.*
>
> Tocqueville[6]

When combined, Tocqueville's distinctive vocabulary, his choice of a theoretical route different from that of his contemporaries, and a belief in his own chosenness create an impression of theoretical extravagance and are likely to produce an unforgiving estimate of him. Tocqueville seems possessed by a simplistic faith in the power of the theorist both to transcend the limitations of language and to negotiate its traps.

That judgment would be not as much right as inevitable. For Tocqueville does not merely invite a postmodern reading. He courts it. He appears as the perfect case of the illusion of "the theorist as hero," the creator of The Great Text that will set the world right, if only the world will take heed. In the outlook of the prestructuralist critic, such excess was corrigible because it was naively assumed that there was nothing that prevented an author from deciding what to include, delete, or emphasize or from taking a hundred other decisions that, in principle, might enable him to eliminate the imperfections in his work and to make it accord with his intentions. Barring incompetence or error, an author should be able to say what he or she intends, nothing more nor less.

But ever since Barthes and Foucault demolished the myth of the "sovereign author" who imposed his will and intentions upon the text, much critical attention has been given to singling out the pitfalls of language as the principal cause for the defeat of theoretical intentions. Theorists produce textual consequences they had not intended and statements that, like the return of the repressed, emerge to vex the stability of the theory. Apparently the nature of language makes it cleverer at insinuating countertextual meanings than authors are in eradicating them. Language appears as the handiwork of a Cartesian demon, malevolent but artful, the real creator-god of meaning—which is why some deconstructionists have maintained that language, not the author, writes the text.

Tocqueville once described himself as "the last of his species."[7] The reference was, in part, to his aristocratic origins, but mainly it was a protest against the way that parliamentarism trivialized politics. Accordingly he presents himself as the ideal victim for the deconstructionist block. For Tocqueville thought that politics was sacred, not as Bossuet had, as "politique tirée des propres paroles de l'Écriture sainte," but because it held the possibility of being theoretically or truthfully constituted.

In this as in so many other of his theoretical claims Tocqueville seems a throwback to early modern (e.g., Hobbes) and ancient modes of theorizing. His illusions appear to embody the myths of a whole tradition and to culminate a genealogy of illusion.

But what would the world have to be like for a nonsovereign, appropriately humble, illusion-free theory to make sense and be preferable? Or is that ideal itself an illusion? The questions have prompted the choice of Tocqueville as a theorist who helps us to see into the many forms of the postmodern political predicament. And this not in spite of his illusions and extravagances but because of them. The absurdity that cavorts at the edges of Tocqueville's thinking and tempts it into posturing is the effect of a condition in which the political is becoming absurd—that is, dangerous—because while politics is being trivialized the magnitude and variety of the powers available to postmodern ruling groups are unprecedented. In the self-consciously postmodern world of "the cool," it would be difficult to find any resonance for Tocqueville's conception of the *grandeur* of the political as the noblest of human settings, of public life as the highest calling, and of the public good as the supreme object of political action. Political virtue, either of elites or of citizens, has become a curiosity, or, rather a prurient curiosity. Perhaps, then, Tocquevillean *grandeur*, instead of being dismissed as romantic posturing, might be viewed as a valuable measure, not of how impossibly high Tocqueville set his political sights, but how distressingly low the theorists and politicians of interest politics have set theirs.

Precisely because of the odd and surprising mix of contingent elements that attaches to the being we have come to call "Tocqueville," he was able to see differently and more deeply than many of his contemporaries—and not just, as he put it, able to see "further." Tocqueville has valuable things to say about modernity, the importance and complexity of political cultures, the conditions necessary for a genuinely political life, the political consequences of rapid change and extreme social mobility, the difference between a politics arising out of and directed against nature and one shaped by and directed against history. In large measure he was able to see differently and further because of a premodern or "archaic" stratum which made him supremely sensitive to the inhospitable aspects of the modern world. He would not only write about the *l'ancien regime* and forever carry its birthmarks; he cultivated it and made it integral to his vision of the present. At a time when a great number of theoretical minds were struggling desperately to rid themselves of inheritance—Marx of his Judaism and Hegelianism, Mill of his Benthamism, and Nietzsche of Christianity—Tocqueville was attempting to incorporate his and to make it a vital part of the analysis and, ultimately, of the theoretical imagination.

## III

In gaining some familiarity with the range of Tocqueville's theories against the background—or foreground—of his political lives, it is possible to gauge whether the theories matched the political and theoretical intentions of its author or whether there was slippage, loss of control, unanticipated, even unwanted, revelations that made Tocqueville the first victim of his own theorizing. Initially the world revealed by his theory jeopardized and eventually defeated his political program for the renewal of French political life. The sense in which Tocqueville "failed" matters. More than any other political writer after Rousseau and before Gramsci, he made the revival of the political his primary concern. For that project to become politically anachronistic and theoretically absurd; for theory to theorize its own disconfirmation so as to find a world and lose a theory is to find one's self in the world heralded by some of Tocqueville's contemporaries and accepted as home by their successors in the social sciences. For the latter the truest theory is one whose values find confirmation in the world's practice.[8]

Tocqueville's claim, that he stood between two worlds, might strike later readers as pretentious and yet the element of truth in the posturing lent a specific thematic structure to his thinking, a set of categories, and a characteristic way of analyzing reflectively. Thematically the most important element was the archaic. It gave a distinctive cast to his thinking, shaping it to see into and through modernity.

Usually the archaic refers to a practice or belief that has survived the time to which it "properly belongs." Most of Tocqueville's archaisms derived from the Old Regime, which had governed France before the Great Revolution. The principal archaisms in Tocqueville's theory were "feudalism," "aristocracy," and "political liberty."[9] As an element in a theoretical strategy, archaism aims at unsettling the present, bringing it to a temporary pause, insisting that it historicize its self-understanding. But the present instinctively resists historicization.[10] It wants nothing more than to interpret itself by itself, that is, by its own notions and categories, by its own self-confirming narrative. The intrusion forces the present out of its self-contained hermeneutical circle. Archaism can accomplish this effect because, unlike the present, it has been stripped of its context. It confronts the present like some displaced refugee caught between times and without place. Precisely because it cannot represent the abandoned past to a present whose identity is staked on the death of the past, the archaic trails an odor of death, an unwelcome reminder to the present that change not only brings new things into the world but causes other things to languish and disappear. The archaic forces the modern into self-questioning, slowing the urge to totalize. While premodern societies fetishized the past and were in constant fear of losing it, modernizing societies seek to escape by fetishizing the future.

Tocqueville's archaism was the product of a tension between his awareness that he was prone to fantasize a restoration of a certain past and a recognition both of its impossibility and of the imprudence of openly acknowledging it. He resolves the conflicts by attempting to enlarge modernity's understanding of progress to include the experience of loss. When archaism is thrust into the conversation of liberal democracy, it causes notions of equality to be viewed phenomenologically: not just as the acquisition of rights or of a common status among citizens but as the erasure of differences, of "becoming distanced more and more from the ideas and sentiments peculiar to a class, a profession, or a family."[11]

Modernity and equality thus conceal a specific trauma. A regime of equality is not simply a leveled condition where all have been reduced to the same economic and social plane—as antidemocratic critics, citing Tocqueville, have maintained. Equality signifies a condition in which human beings draw apart as certain bonds of identity slacken: bonds of generations, families, religion, economic obligations, and political communities. Archaism is a protest against what it exposes as the principal form of destructiveness inherent in modernity, the disconnectedness of existence. Tocqueville's conception of a democratic modernity was as much a warning about individualism as about the threat of the masses, and this despite the apparent affinity between individualism and liberty.[12] The vulnerability of democracy-modernity is revealed in its drift toward self-caricature: the free but privatized individual turns out to be the jargon by which identity conceals from itself that it is identical and, as such, the condition of despotism rather than its polar opposite.

Thus democracy is poised to become for our times what aristocracy was for Tocqueville's, the archaic remains of a superseded past. Unlike Tocqueville's aristocracy, however, the passing of democracy, if that is what is happening, is not being experienced as loss, as entrance into a time of postdemocracy, but as freedom from an impossible obligation.[13]

Tocqueville speaks to this condition not as the prophet of democracy but as the critic of modern ambivalencies, not when he speaks authoritatively but hesitantly, not of what has happened in the past or of what is happening now but of the novel character of what is coming to be, of what is emerging. The advent of modernity means that thereafter what will come to be will have been deprived of the past as a reference point: "Everyone recognizes [Tocqueville wrote] that the whole political system which Europe had followed for forty years has changed; that all of the old alliances are loosened or destroyed as new interests and forces have come into play; and that the past is no guide to the future."[14]

The theme of a deepening divide between past and present recurs throughout most of his writings and may be said to be a comment upon his own fate. We might think of Tocqueville as representing a point of intersection for three mutually hostile historical tendencies. He is both the representative and the theorist of the premodern, of the traditional society, of *ancienneté.* He is also the critical theorist of the modern, of Enlightenment, democracy, and revolution. Finally, he is the theorist of the postpolitical and the postdemocratic.[15] The first represents an archaic, predemocratic moment; the second, an apocalyptic moment of radical change followed by periodic aftershocks, the third, the domestication of democracy and the emergence of a uniquely postmodern regime.

Returning to *Democracy*'s imagery of the "abyss," imagine Tocqueville standing at its edge. The edge of the abyss is not the moment when one chooses but a condition from which one recoils but cannot retreat. The condition is not an either/or dilemma because it is not a spatial problem, as the notion of an abyss first implies, but a temporal one. A second image, this time of a theory that represents a dividing line, entails not a theory that *is* a dividing line but one that represents its own acute self-consciousness of a world that has wandered, marched, or happened into a different "time," from a time when privilege ruled the public, social, and cultural life of society to a time when anonymity reigns.[16] That self-consciousness might be described as a growing awareness of being condemned to live when change has co-opted revolution to create a continuum of fabrication: once revolutions were fomented, now change is "produced." Revolution abandons the clandestine; it is not plotted in the café or lavatory but in the boardroom and laboratory.

The modern emerges and then accelerates, until finally the process of producing the new becomes a matter of course, precisely the opposite of what the new was believed to be. The new becomes the prosaic.

This can be stated in somewhat different terms that may bring out the unresolved problem in Tocqueville between the New World and the Old. If a comparison is made between the impressions that he committed to his notebooks of his travels into the sparsely settled interior of the New World and the impressions of the revolutionary events of 1848 that he recorded in his *Souvenirs*, two strikingly different versions of modernity emerge. The American wilderness is the scene of the struggle to subdue nature. The westward migrations are a triumph over natural space but the subjugation of nature effectively marked the destruction of a certain notion of time as well, one in which nature and history had cooperated by sharing certain metaphors of slow growth, customary ways, timeless values. Premodernity: when time was slow and plentiful. America, the home of spatial plenty, was the triumph of an ironical notion of the timeless. There it was the growing scarcity of time, its shortage, the exhaustion of time in the conquest of space by beings in a hurry. Past time is no longer of consequence, and the present and the future are continually collapsing into each other. Once space has been conquered, however, time returns as measurable moments, as deliberately compressed into process. Modern time is the displacement of cultural time by economic time, by time homogenized. Frederick Taylor is its Moses, Henry Ford its Aaron, Detroit the promised land.

The intellectual is the symbol of the impending transformation of modern time. In ancient times he was the thinker as the creator of timeless worlds; in modern times, when time is quick, he is Promethean, the overthrower of old, time-bound worlds; he is Marx, yet he is also Hegel, the figure who, in self-conception, is outside changing time even as he claims to be attuned to it.

The outside as a metaphor of intellectual distance, hence of the condition for disinterested theorizing, collapses under the pressure to restore culture in a form that will promote social stability while adapting to a new version of timelessness in which process sheds any relationship to teleology and becomes its opposite: instead of "development" or the fulfillment of potential, culture is end-less process, the formalized method by which artifacts are produced continuously—but conditionally. The condition is destruction. Its symbol is the idea of "the latest," whose appearance is conditional upon the new artifact rendering an existing one obsolete. The intellectual cannot stand outside the process of production except by choosing to be irrelevant. Even that most rarefied embodiment of intellectualism, the theorist, is drawn into the process of production, either by joining a "program" at a "research university" or by becoming a pundit–performance theorist.

## IV

*I want to imagine under what novel features despotism could happen in the world.*

Tocqueville[17]

If the Old Regime was the regime of *ancienneté* and democracy the regime that ushered in modernity, what political regime follows modernity? The Tocquevillean answer is: very possibly a despotism. That answer naturally invites reference to Hitler and Stalin and to their mass support and seems proof of Tocqueville's prescience. What could be clearer instances of democratic despotism, of what one acclaimed study labeled "totalitarian democracy"?[18] Or what could be more misleading. Tocqueville's conception depended on precisely what was absent in the prior history of both the Soviet Union and Nazi Germany: prolonged exposure to the experience of democracy, not simply to its catchwords or to a brief and thin experience of Weimar electoral politics and of cultural experiment. Despotism in Tocqueville's formulation signifies simultaneously the conquest of democracy and the mimicry of it. It is postdemocratic; the key to its distinctive character is not harshness but the opposite, not regimentation but privatization, not Brezhnev drabness but glitter and lavish consumption.

In support of the suggestion that Tocqueville's democratic despotism contains an outline of a postmodern, postdemocratic possibility, recall his claim that the "species of oppression which threatens democratic peoples" would not resemble anything that had occurred before. No word, he wrote could exactly capture his meaning: "the old words 'despotism' and 'tyranny' do not fit." Nor will democratic despotism fit the political category of "mixed government," by which ancient, mediaeval, and early modern theorists meant a system that combined important features of the good regimes—that is, monarchy, aristocracy, and "polity" or limited democracy (Aristotle's rule by a propertied middle class). Nor was it to be understood as a species of the "perverted" forms of tyranny, oligarchy, and mob rule.[19] Democratic despotism was the product of a new time. Its appearance was impossible earlier because the enabling conditions were unavailable and certain predispositions were as yet unformed. The administrative means were lacking for ruling large numbers of people, superimposing a mass culture on cultural diversities, and overriding local authorities. Ideas of freedom had not yet legitimated a universal chase after "small and vulgar pleasures" and a yearning for the joys of private life.[20] Nor an ethos of democratic equality, which would condition men and women to submit to uniform rules that applied to everyone.

There is a sense in which democratic despotism is not a "form" at all. Save for an omnipresent bureaucracy, it has little in common with the highly personalized tyrannies of the twentieth century and their charismatic leaders. Tocqueville's despot appears as faceless and nameless, a shadowy presence, enveloping rather than domineering. How he attained to power is never discussed but, significantly, there is no suggestion that he would seize it by a coup. Rather he seems to combine superbureaucrat with mediocre politician, as though he might easily disappear into the system, as though despotism is the archetype of the impersonal, which overcomes even the despot. The despot is not required to be heroic, but simply administer a society of stunted individuals who have embraced lives emptied of political responsibility. Because postdemocratic man wants to be led while feeling free, rule will, accordingly, be "milder" than traditional tyrannies although wider in scope. It would "degrade" rather than "torment."[21] Moreover, a society in which the public has been educated, and where power and wealth appear to be diffused, where public *moeurs* have become "more humane and gentle," the despot will not feel threatened but inclined to be solicitous of the welfare of his citizens.

For Tocqueville despotism did not qualify as democratic simply because the despot appealed to certain notions associated with democracy. Democratic despotism presupposed a society whose members had experienced democracy and importantly were shaped by some of its values, such as self-interest and equality, and by some of its practices, such as administrative centralization. What is crucial to the appearance of despotism is the virtual disappearance of the culture of participation and its replacement by a culture of privatism, isolation, and what Tocqueville could not have foreseen, consumerism. The importance of the democratic experience in preparing the way for despotism consists not only in its *positive* contributions but in elements of loss.

If, as Tocqueville believed, self-government would be the crucial loss, how might that loss be concealed or, better, sublimated so that it appears to be flourishing? If despotism signifies, at the minimum, the destruction of the political in its modern form, we need to ask, What was that form? The answer is not obscure. The modern political was expressed as the concept of popular sovereignty, the idea that the citizenry should rule. That idea, however, assumed a politically engaged citizenry capable of disinterestedness. Without that assumption, democracy becomes all-purpose, infinitely plastic, and the question becomes, Who controls the meanings of democracy and, thereby, its fate?

For democracy to be exploited a semblance of popular sovereignty has to be preserved. One example: throughout the nineteenth century and until the Great Depression of 1929 most classical economists had viewed politics and political notions as antithetical to the economic. Now economic discourse is comfortable in referring to "consumer sovereignty" and attributing to it a "force" that commands the market to respond to the wants of ordinary citizens. A purchase is a vote and the consumer is to the economy as the citizen is to the polity. Accordingly, the original notion, its assumptions subtly changed by the economizing context, is returned to the political domain, which, meanwhile, has become increasingly directed by corporate economic powers that have become politically self-conscious. As the imprint of the economic upon the political increases, the political is discovered to be more comprehensible by economic modes of analysis. Concepts of popular sovereignty collapse into theories of "rational choice" and "voter preference," while voter surveys become indistinguishable from consumer research.

The evolution that saw electoral politics become assimilated to the practices of the marketplace—candidates marketed as products, elections reduced to slogans and advertisements, voters maneuvered into the position where *caveat emptor* becomes their most reliable guide—suggests a conclusion, that postmodern despotism consists of the collapse of politics into economics and the emergence of a new form, the economic polity. The regime is, as Tocqueville suggested, benign, power transmuted into solicitude, popular sovereignty into consumerism, mutuality into mutual funds, and the democracy of citizens into shareholder democracy. If postmodernity signifies the sovereignty of economy, not only as the domain where the most dazzling deeds are performed, where real power is to be had, where the fate of society as a whole is ultimately decided, then, as the successor to conceptions of government or of the state, it is plausible to believe that it may be subject to vicissitudes and alteration. Would a depoliticized form, an economic polity, respond to crisis by assuming the characteristics of a "democratic" despotism?

The historical conjuncture that found modern power and democracy expanding together posed the question of whether the "political moment" within democracy, but by no means synonymous with it, could be preserved and cultivated, or whether democracy would gradually shed its civic potentialities and become simply a cultural subset with a functional role in the maintenance and reproduction of modern power. Stated slightly differently, the question came down to whether the "masses" were to be prepared for citizenship or for a work force. Modernity might be described as the moment of that choice, postmodernity as its decision.

Far from being valued as symbolizing an aspiration toward the democratization of power and a participatory society of political equals—democracy as subject—democracy would come to be regarded by late-modern power elites as object, an indispensable yet malleable myth for promoting American political and economic interests among premodern and post-totalitarian societies. At home, democracy is touted not as self-government by an involved citizenry but as economic opportunity. Opportunity serves as the means of implicating the populace in antidemocracy, in a politicoeconomic system characterized by the dominating power of hierarchical organizations, widening class differentials, and a society where the hereditary element is confined to successive generations of the defenseless poor. Democracy is perpetuated as philanthropic gesture, contemptuously institutionalized as welfare, and denigrated as populism.

# NOTES

## Introduction

1. For a thoughtful study of Tocqueville's ideas and relevant contemporaries, see Roger Boesche, *The Strange Liberalism of Alexis de Tocqueville* (Ithaca: Cornell University Press, 1987); Alan S. Kahan, *Aristocratic Liberalism: The Social and Political Thought of Jacob Burckhardt, John Stuart Mill, and Alexis de Tocqueville* (Oxford: Oxford University Press, 1992); Lucien Jaume, *L'individu effacé, ou le paradoxe du libéralisme français* (Paris: Fayard, 1999). For studies of Tocqueville in a broader context, see Bruce James Smith, *Politics and Remembrance: Republican Themes in Machiavelli, Burke, and Tocqueville* (Princeton: Princeton University Press, 1985). Tocqueville figures importantly in Claude Lefort's thoughtful study, *Democracy and Political Theory* (Minneapolis: University of Minnesota Press, 1988). Unfortunately the stimulating volume by Mark Reinhardt came too late to my attention: *The Art of Being Free: Taking Liberties with Tocqueville, Marx, and Arendt* (Ithaca: Cornell University Press, 1997). For a critical but highly suggestive (somewhat Foucauldian) reading of Tocqueville, see William Connolly, "Tocqueville, Territory, and Violence," *Theory, Culture and Society* 2 (1994): 19–41. The best general survey is Jack Lively, *The Social and Political Thought of Alexis de Tocqueville* (Oxford: Clarendon Press, 1962).

2. In France there has been a growing scholarly interest in what kind of liberalism Tocqueville represented. See André Jardin, *Histoire du libéralisme politique: De la crise de l'absolutisme à la Constitution de 1875* (Paris: Hachette, 1985). In addition to the study by Jaume, *L'individu effacé,* see Françoise Mélonio, *Tocqueville and the French* (Charlottesville: University Press of Virginia, 1998). Also Jean-Claude Lamberti, *Tocqueville et les deux démocraties* (Paris: Presses Universitaires de France, 1983), pp. 102–3; published in translation by Harvard University Press, 1989 and the earlier study R. Pierre-Marcel, *Essai politique sur Alexis de Tocqueville* (Alcan: Paris, 1910).

3. Like many who write on theory and action, I owe my earliest interest in the problem to Hannah Arendt's discussion in *The Human Condition* (Chicago: University of Chicago Press, 1958).

4. François Furet would be an important exception. See his essay, "Tocqueville, est-il historien de la Révolution française?" *Annales,* no. 25 (1970): 435–451.

5. Herodotus described Solon's travels abroad as a *theoria* (I.30). See also Norma Thompson, *Herodotus and the Origins of the Political Community: Arion's Leap* (New Haven: Yale University Press, 1996), pp. 5–6.

6. Tocqueville was an inveterate traveler. In addition to his travels to North America, he visited Sicily, Italy, England, Ireland, Algeria, and (as yet ununited) Germany.

7. In the course of a letter of 1852 to his father, Tocqueville protested vehemently against any attempt that implied he favored Bonaparte's government: "I have never desired power, only reputation. Mine is mixed with liberal ideas and institutions. To associate me, even indirectly, with a government which is destroying them in my country, to permit it to be believed that I shall seek a reconciliation with it, is to diminish me in the public's estimation. . . . The one essential is the respect which is attached to a

consistent life, all of whose parts are bound together and which remain, from beginning to end, all of a piece." *OC,* XIV, 283. The sentiments, even the language, are virtually the same as those in a letter to his fiancée almost twenty years earlier. See *OC,* XIV, 387.

8. To Marie Mottley (his fiancée), 26 Dec. 1837, *OC,* XIV, 410.

9. *OC,* III (2), 720.

10. In *Les libéraux français, 1814–1875* (Paris: Aubier, 1985), Louis Girard devotes a scant three pages to Tocqueville.

11. *OC,* VI, 408.

12. Hannah Arendt explicitly followed Tocqueville on the threat of equality to freedom. See *On Revolution* (New York: Viking, 1965), p. 23. Tocqueville's influence appears throughout Arendt's discussion of the French and American revolutions.

13. Tocqueville's most extended discussion of aristocracy and the anticipation of most of his later views on that subject appeared in "État social et politique de la France avant et depuis 1789." *OC,* II (1), 31–66. The relative neglect of the essay is owed in part to an editorial decision to include it with *L'ancien régime et la Révolution* in Tocqueville's collected works. The essay first appeared in 1836 before Tocqueville had begun to work on the second installment of *Democracy.* One of the notable features of the essay was his attempt to broaden the meaning of "aristocracy" to approximate a meritocracy.

## Chapter I
## Modern Theory and Modern Power

1. To Corcelle, 23 Sept. 1851, *OC,* XV (2), 48.

2. See William H. McNeill, *The Pursuit of Power: Technology, Armed Force, and Society since A.D. 1000* (Chicago: University of Chicago Press, 1982); Michael Mann, *The Sources of Social Power* (Cambridge: Cambridge University Press, 1986), 1:373ff.

3. Jean-Jacques Rousseau, *Du contrat social,* ed. C. E. Vaughan (1918; Manchester: Manchester University Press 1947), I.vi, pp. 12–13.

4. See George Rudé, *Paris and London in the Eighteenth Century: Studies in Popular Protest* (New York: Viking, 1971), and *The Crowd in History, 1730–1848* (New York: Wiley, 1964).

5. There is a vast literature on the subject of liberalism and reform. I have found the following particularly useful: Elie Halévy, *The Growth of Philosophic Radicalism,* tr. Mary Morris (London: Faber, 1928); Charles F. Bahmueller, *The National Charity Company: Jeremy Bentham's Silent Revolution* (Berkeley: University of California Press, 1981); Gertrude Himmelfarb, "The Haunted House of Jeremy Bentham," in *Victorian Minds* (New York: Knopf, 1968), pp. 32–81; Eric Hobsbawm, *The Age of Revolution, 1789–1848* (London: Weidenfeld & Nicolson, 1962), especially ch. 8–10; François Furet, *Revolutionary France, 1770–1880,* tr. Antonia Nevill (Oxford: Blackwell, 1988); Mélonio, *Tocqueville and the French*; Kahan, *Aristocratic Liberalism.*

6. Cited in Joseph Hamburger, *Intellectuals in Politics: John Stuart Mill and the Philosophic Radicals* (New Haven: Yale University Press, 1965), p. 270 (emphasis in original).

7. Mill, *Considerations on Representative Government,* ch. 5.

8. Karl Marx and Friedrich Engels, *The Manifesto of the Communist Party,* in *Birth of the Communist Manifesto,* ed. Dirk Struik (New York: International Publishers, 1971), pp. 94, 95.

9. Ibid., pt. 2, pp. 111–12 (on technical education and the end of politics); Friedrich

Engels, *Anti-Dühring*, tr. E. Burns (New York: International Publishers, n.d.), pp. 208, 313–15, 317–18, 328–9, 331.

10. Marx and Engels, *The Manifesto of the Communist Party*, p. 92.

11. Ibid., p. 95.

12. Thomas Hobbes, *Leviathan*, ed. Michael Oakeshott (Oxford: Blackwell, n.d.), p. 186.

13. Francis Bacon, *De Augmentis*, VII. 2, in *The Works of Francis Bacon*, ed. S. Spedding, R. L. Ellis, and D. D. Heath, 14 vols. (London: Longmans, 1874), 5:12. See Antonio Pérez-Ramos, *Francis Bacon's Idea of Science and the Makers' Knowledge Tradition* (Oxford: Clarendon Press, 1988), especially pp. 106ff.

14. Polybius, *The Histories*, VI.2.11–18.

15. See the discussion in Pérez-Ramos, *Francis Bacon's Idea of Science and the Makers' Knowledge Tradition*, pp. 83ff.

16. Francis Bacon, *Advancement of Learning*, in *Selected Writings of Francies Bacon*, ed. Hugh Dick (New York: Modern Library, Random House, 1955), bk. 1, p. 189.

17. Francis Bacon, "Thoughts and Conclusions," in *The Philosophy of Francis Bacon*, ed. Benjamin Farrington (Chicago: University of Chicago Press, 1964), p. 99.

18. Hobbes, *Leviathan*, ed. Oakeshott, ch. XI, p. 161.

19. Richard Rorty, "Habermas and Lyotard on Postmodernity," in *Habermas and Modernity*, ed. Richard Bernstein (Cambridge, Mass.: MIT Press, 1985), p. 169.

20. The locus classicus is C. B. Macpherson, *The Political Theory of Possessive Individualism: Hobbes to Locke* (Oxford: Clarendon Press, 1962). See also Margaret Jacobs, *The Newtonians and the English Revolution, 1689–1720* (Ithaca: Cornell University Press, 1976), pp. 23–27.

21. On the general topic of the emergence of the ancient/modern split, see Richard F. Jones, *Ancients and Moderns: A Study of the Rise of the Scientific Movement in Seventeenth Century England*, 2nd ed. (Berkeley: University of California Press, 1965).

22. There are several useful essays in *The Intellectual Revolution of the Seventeenth Century*, ed. Charles Webster (London: Routledge, 1974), especially nos. 16–25.

23. Francis Bacon, *Novum Organon*, I.40, *Works*, 4:89–90.

24. Francis Bacon, *The Great Instauration*, preface, *Works*, 4:14.

25. Bacon, *Novum Organon*, I.74, *Works*, 4:110.

26. Thomas Hobbes, *Body, Mind, and Citizen*, ed. Richard Peters (New York: Crowell-Collier, 1962), p. 27.

27. *OC*, I (2), 47.

28. Cited in Farrington, *The Philosophy of Francis Bacon*, p. 28.

29. Thomas Hobbes, *Leviathan*, ed. C. B. Macpherson (Harmondsworth: Penguin, 1968), ch. 5, p. 114 (references hereafter are to this edition). Hobbes, *De Corpore*, in *Body, Mind, and Citizen*, p. 28, or Hobbes, *The English Works of Thomas Hobbes of Malmesbury*, ed. William Molesworth, 11 vols. (London: John Bohn, 1839–45), 1: ch. 1.7.

30. Thomas Hobbes, *Elements of Law*, ed. F. Tönnies. (Cambridge: Cambridge University Press, 1928), I.13, pp. 50–512.

31. Bacon, *Novum Organon*, I.cxiii, *Works*, 4:102.

32. *Works of Francis Bacon*, 3:231.

33. Bacon, *Novum Organon*, bk.I.xc, *Works*, 4:90.

34. See Roger Hahn, *The Anatomy of a Scientific Institution: The Paris Academy of Sciences, 1666–1803* (Berkeley: University of California Press, 1971). For an earlier period,

James E. King, *Science and Rationalism in the Government of Louis XIV, 1661–1683* (New York: Octagon, 1972). Also relevant is Keith Michael Baker's fine study, *Condorcet: From Natural Science to Social Mathematics* (Chicago: University of Chicago Press, 1975). On Bacon and the efforts to institutionalize scientific research prior to and during the "Puritan" revolution, see Charles Webster, *The Great Instauration: Science, Medicine and Reform, 1626–1660* (London: Duckworth, 1975). See also Steven Shapin and Simon Schaffer, *Leviathan and the Air-Pump: Hobbes, Boyle, and the Experimental Life* (Princeton: Princeton University Press, 1985); Steven Shapin, *A Social History of Truth: Civility and Science in Seventeenth-Century England* (Chicago: University of Chicago Press, 1994), which traces the origins of the practices of English experimental philosophy in the conventions and values of "gentlemanly conversation." Also Jacob, *The Newtonians and the English Revolution, 1689–1720*; J. R. Jacob, *Robert Boyle and the English Revolution* (New York: Burt Franklin, 1977); and especially Barbara J. Shapiro, *Probability and Certainty in Seventeenth-Century England* (Princeton: Princeton University Press, 1983), explore the convergence between certain concepts and ideas—and their interrelationships—of natural scientists and thinkers concerned with religious, historical, legal, and literary matters.

35. Bacon, *The Great Instauration*, *Works*, 4:29.

36. The opening lines of *Leviathan* are: "Nature, (the Art whereby God hath made and governes the World) is by the *Art* of man, as in many other things, so in this also imitated, that it can make an artificial Animal" (introduction, p. 81). Hobbes continues: art can also imitate nature and create an "Artificiall Man" in the form "that great Leviathan called a Commonwealth or State."

37. The tension between unpredictable and predictable power was reflected and left unresolved in Locke's discussion of "the federative power" but especially in his treatment of the prerogative: "*Prerogative is nothing but the Power of doing publick good without a Rule*" (emphasis in original). John Locke, *Two Treatises of Government*, ed. Peter Laslett, rev. ed. (New York: Mentor, 1965), II. 166.

38. Ibid., II.124–26.

39. Ibid., II.49.

40. Shakespeare, *All's Well That Ends Well*, II.iii.1.

41. Bacon, *Novum Organon*, I.xc, *Works*, 4:89–90; Hobbes, *Leviathan*, ch. 30, pp. 384–85. See also Sheldon S. Wolin, *Hobbes* (Los Angeles: William Andrews Clark Memorial Library, University of California, 1970), pp. 48–49.

42. Hobbes, *Leviathan*, ch. 11, p. 160.

43. Hobbes, *De corpore*, ch. 15, in *Body, Man and Citizen*, p. 130.

44. Although there are countless fine studies of ancient politics and culture, a useful starting point in earlier scholarship is Werner Jaeger, *Paideia*, tr. Gilbert Highet, 3 vols. (New York: Oxford University Press, 1945). Among recent scholars I have found the following highly instructive: Pierre Vidal-Naquet, *The Black Hunter. Forms of Thought and Forms of Society in the Greek World*, tr. Andrew Szegedy (Baltimore: Johns Hopkins University Press, 1986); Jean-Pierre Vernant, *Myth and Society in Ancient Greece*, tr. Janet Lloyd (Sussex: Harvester Press and Humanities Press, 1980); Nicole Loraux, *The Invention of Athens: The Funeral Oration in the Classical City*, tr. Alan Sheridan (Cambridge: Harvard University Press, 1986); Josiah Ober, *Mass and Elite in Democratic Athens: Rhetoric, Ideology, and the Power of the People* (Princeton: Princeton University Press, 1989); and Roger Chartier, *The Cultural Origins of the French Revolution*, tr. Lydia G. Cochrane (Durham, N.C.: Duke University Press, 1991).

45. Francis Bacon, *Of the Interpretation of Nature*, in *Selected Writings of Francis Bacon*, p. 151.

46. The term "laymen" was originally applied to distinguish those who were not clerics; later it was used to separate the knowledge of ordinary persons from that of experts.

47. Francis Bacon, *The Refutation of Philosophies*, in *The Philosophy of Francis Bacon*, p. 108.

48. Rousseau was the exception but he was largely outside the modern scientific movement.

49. Hobbes, *Leviathan*, ch. 30, p. 387.

50. In addition to Macpherson's discussion, *The Political Theory of Possessive Individualism*, pp. 78ff. and 95ff, see Hobbes's distinction between the new and the old nobility in *De Homine*, ch. 13, in *Man and Citizen: Thomas Hobbes*, ed. Bernard Gert (New York: Anchor Doubleday, 1972), p. 66.

51. James Mill, *Essay on Government* (Cambridge: Cambridge University Press, 1937), pp. 45, 49–50. The best theoretical discussion of representation is Hanna F. Pitkin, *The Concept of Representation* (Berkeley: University of California Press, 1967).

52. Francis Bacon, "The Masculine Birth of Time," in *The Philosophy of Francis Bacon*, p. 72.

53. René Descartes, *Discourse on Method*, in *The Philosophical Works of Descartes*, tr. Elizabeth S. Haldane and G. R. T. Ross, 2 vols. (Cambridge: Cambridge University Press, 1979), 1: 87–89.

## Chapter II
## *Theoria*: The Theoretical Journey

1. To Eugene Stoffels, 1844, in *Memoirs, Letters, and Remains of Alexis de Tocqueville*, 2 vols. (Boston: Tickner and Fields, 1862), 1:395.

2. One of the first recorded instances of political associations being attached to *theoria* is in Herodotus, *Histories*, I.29–30. He declares that the reason why Solon, the former archon and lawgiver, traveled abroad was not only to inquire about the practices of other peoples but to allow the Athenians time to absorb the controversial political and social reforms he had recently instituted. It might be noted that the idea of a theoretical journey assumes a somewhat different character when the journey is the result of exile. That experience tends to be associated with revolutionary theorists, e.g., Locke and Marx, and radical thinkers such as Hobbes. See the suggestive study by Hans Blumenberg, *Shipwreck with Spectator*, tr. Steven Randall (Cambridge, Mass.: MIT Press, 1997).

3. Philo, *On Abraham*, 65, in *Philo*, tr. F. H. Colson, 12 vols. (Cambridge, Mass.: Harvard University Press, 1935), 6:37.

4. Aristotle, *Nicomachean Ethics*, bk. VI.

5. Plato, *Republic*, VI.511c–e; *Laws*, XII.951c–952d.

6. Thomas More, *Utopia*, in *Complete Works of St. Thomas More*, vol. 4, ed. Edward Surtz and J. H. Hexter (New Haven: Yale University Press, 1965), bk. I, p. 53.

7. Ibid., pp. 110–11. The quotation is the title of book II of *Utopia.*

8. Locke, *Two Treatises of Government*, I.147.

9. Locke did attempt to "confirm" aspects of his state of nature by referring to the accounts of travelers to the New World but his free interpretation of that "evidence" is not far removed from More's use of travelers' tales.

10. For a different approach to the contrasts between utopian political theories and other forms of ideal societies see J. C. Davis, *Utopia and the Ideal Society: A Study of English Utopian Writings, 1516–1700* (Cambridge: Cambridge University Press, 1981).

11. In the early stages of the *Republic*, II.368d, Socrates discusses how "seeing" is made easier by first having a larger model.

12. Montesquieu, *Lettres persanes*, "Quelques réflexions," in *Oeuvres complètes*, ed. Roger Callois, 2 vols. (Paris: Pléiade, Gallimard, 1949), 1:129.

13. Ibid., p. 133.

14. Ibid., p. 130.

15. Montesquieu, *Ésprit des lois*, XIV.13, *Oeuvres*, 2:487.

16. More did attempt to furnish his Utopia with historical connections to Europe and much of the irony of his description depended on it.

17. Montesquieu did not develop a conception of revolution as a widespread social upheaval involving the radical transformation of political and social relationships within a relatively compressed time span. Rather he was concerned with important changes that occurred slowly over a relatively long time. See his discussion of the "revolutions" brought about by changes in the Roman laws of inheritance and in French civil laws. *Esprit des lois*, bks. XXVII–XXVIII. Note the interesting epigraph of Ovid, which Montesquieu used at the beginning of book XXVIII: "My imagination brings me to speak of forms changing into new bodies." Also Melvin Richter's helpful discussion in *The Political Theory of Montesquieu* (Cambridge: Cambridge University Press, 1977), pp. 29–30.

18. Montesquieu, *Considérations sur les causes de la grandeur des Romans et de leur décadence*, ch. 8, *Oeuvres*, 2:114.

19. Montesquieu, *Esprit des lois*, XXV.11, *Oeuvres*, 2:745.

20. Ibid., V.14, *Oeuvres*, 2:297.

21. Hobbes, *Leviathan*, ch. 30, p. 379. It is virtually impossible to exaggerate Hobbes's difficulties in trying to prevent the basic habits of civility from becoming overwhelmed by the power potential inherent in modern man. In this regard the crucial text is chapter 11 of *Leviathan.* Hobbes begins it as if he intends a discussion of "manners," "those qualities of man-kind that concern their living together in Peace and Unity" (p. 160). He then subverts that conception by promptly introducing in highly dramatic terms man's "perpetuall and restlesse desire of Power after power that ceaseth onely in Death" (p. 161). The tension is left unresolved.

22. Montesquieu, *Esprit des lois*, I.2, *Oeuvres*, 2:235.

23. Ibid., I.3, *Oeuvres*, 2:236–37.

24. This is, I think, a fair interpretation of Montesquieu's preface to the *Esprit.* See especially *Oeuvres*, 2:230–31.

25. Cited in Peter Gay, *The Enlightenment: An Interpretation* (New York: Knopf, 1969), 2:515.

26. See Nannerl O. Keohane, *Philosophy and the State in France: The Renaissance to the Enlightenment* (Princeton: Princeton University Press, 1980), pp. 346–50; Franklin L. Ford, *Robe and Sword* (New York: Harper and Row, 1953), chs. 10 and 12; Elie Carcassonne, *Montesquieu et le problème de la constitution française au XVIIIe siècle* (Paris, 1926).

27. Hobbes, *Leviathan*, ch. 13, pp. 187, 188.

28. Ibid., p. 187.

29. Hobbes's attack on monopolies and corporations is particularly revealing for he regards these as forms of a "body politique" and hence by nature a rival to the body that

establishes sovereign authority. "The variety of Bodies Politique is almost infinite." Ibid., ch. 22, p. 279.

30. Plato, *Republic*, tr. F. M. Cornford (New York: Oxford University Press, 1945), V.472e.

31. Hobbes, *Leviathan*, ch. 31, pp. 407–8.

32. Hobbes, *De corpore*, I.1.7, in *English Works*, vol. 1.

33. Ernst Bloch, *Thomas Münzer als Theologe der Revolution* (Munich: Kurt Wolff, 1921); George Hunston Williams, *The Radical Reformation* (Philadelphia: Westminster Press, 1962), p. 362ff.

34. Christopher Hill, *Intellectual Origins of the English Revolution* (Oxford: Oxford University Press, 1965), and *Antichrist in Seventeenth-Century England* (Oxford: Oxford University Press, 1971); William M. Lamont, *Godly Rule: Politics and Religion, 1603–60* (London: Macmillan, 1969); James Holstun, *A Rational Millennium: Puritan Utopias of Seventeenth-Century England and America* (Oxford: Oxford University Press, 1987).

35. Hobbes, *Leviathan*, review and conclusion, p. 728.

36. Hobbes, *De Cive: The English Version*, ed. Howard Warrender (Oxford: Clarendon Press, 1983), p. 32.

37. Aristotle, *Politics*, V.1301a19 ff.; Polybius, *The Histories*, VI.5 ff.; Cicero, *De re publica*, II.xxv.

38. Locke, *Two Treatises of Government*, I. preface. See J. P. Kenyon, "The Revolution of 1688: Resistance and Contract," in *Historical Perspectives: Studies in English Thought and Society in Honor of J. H. Plumb*, ed. Neil McKendrick (London: European Publications, 1974), pp. 43–69; Richard Ashcraft, *Revolutionary Politics and Locke's "Two Treatises of Government"* (Princeton: Princeton University Press, 1986). There are also some helpful discussions by Lawrence Stone and Christopher Hill, among others, in *Three British Revolutions: 1641, 1688, 1776*, ed. J.G.A. Pocock (Princeton: Princeton University Press, 1980).

39. Locke, *Two Treatises of Government*, II.157.

40. *Souvenirs, OC*, XII, 84–85, 87.

41. *The Federalist*, ed. Jacob E. Cooke (Middletown, Conn.: Wesleyan University Press, 1961), no. 14, pp. 88, 89.

42. Lynn Hunt, *Politics, Culture, and Class in the French Revolution* (Berkeley: University of California Press, 1984), especially ch. 2; Mona Ozouf, *Festivals and the French Revolution* (Cambridge: Harvard University Press, 1988).

43. To Beaumont, 22 Nov. 1855, OC, VIII (3), 350.

44. Montesquieu, *Esprit des lois*, XIX.16, *Oeuvres*, 2:566.

45. Ibid.

46. Edmund Burke, "Thoughts on French Affairs," in *The Works of the Right Honourable Edmund Burke* (Oxford: Oxford University Press, 1934), 4:328.

47. Edmund Burke, *Reflections on the Revolution in France*, Everyman edition (London: Dent, 1910), p. 31.

48. Thomas Paine, *The Rights of Man*, in *The Complete Writings of Thomas* Paine, ed. Philip S. Foner, 2 vols. (New York: Citadel Press, 1945), 1:341–42.

49. Ibid., pp. 361–62.

50. Edmund Burke, *An Appeal from the New Whigs to the Old, Works*, 5:134.

51. Paine, *Rights of Man*, 1:265.

52. Ibid., pp. 368–73.

53. Edmund Burke, "Speech on the Petition of the Unitarians," *Works*, 3:319; Burke, *Reflections on the Revolution in France*, p. 87.

54. This is not to say that historical thinking begins in the eighteenth century but that the union of historical and theoretical begins to take hold. For the shaping of English historical thought in the seventeenth century, especially by controversies regarding the common law, see J.G.A. Pocock, *The Ancient Constitution and the Feudal Law* (Cambridge: Cambridge University Press, 1957).

55. See Herbert J. Marcuse, *Reason and Revolution: Hegel and the Rise of Social Theory* (New York: Oxford University Press, 1941), pp. 323ff. Also Albert Salomon, *In Praise of Enlightenment* (Cleveland: World Publishing, 1963), pp. 201ff. See also Roger Boesche, "Why Could Tocqueville Predict So Well?" *Political Theory* II, no. 1 (1983):79–104.

56. See Steven Lukes, *Emile Durkheim, His Life and Work* (New York: Harper and Row, 1972), pp. 322–23, 542–46 and my discussion in *Politics and Vision* (Boston: Little, Brown, 1960), pp. 364ff.

57. See Henry Guerlac, "Some Aspects of Science during the French Revolution," *Scientific Monthly* 80 (1955):93–101.

58. Frank E. Manuel, *The Prophets of Paris* (Cambridge: Harvard University Press, 1962), chs. 3–4, 6. Still valuable is the older study by Élie Halévy, *L'ère des tyrannies. Études sur le socialisme et la guerre*, 2nd ed. (Paris: Gallimard, 1938), pp. 15–94.

59. Saint-Simon's *Nouveau Christianisme* is the clearest version of religion as the opiate of the people. For Durkheim, see his *Elementary Forms of the Religious Life*, tr. Joseph Ward Swain (1912; New York: Free Press, 1965), especially pp. 463ff.

## Chapter III
## Discovering Democracy

1. Adam Smith, *Lectures on Jurisprudence*, ed. R. L. Meek, D. D. Raphael, and P. G. Stein (Oxford: Oxford University Press, 1978), p. 226.

2. Jean Bodin, *Six Books of the Commonwealth*, tr. M. J. Tooley (Oxford: Blackwell, n.d.), VI.4, pp. 192–93.

3. On the idea of democracy in ancient Greece, see Christian Meier, *Entstehung des Begriffs "Demokratie"* (Frankfurt am Main: Suhrkamp, 1981); Eric Havelock, *The Liberal Temper in Greek Politics* (London: Cape, 1957); Cynthia Farrar, *The Origins of Democratic Thinking* (Cambridge: Cambridge University Press, 1988). See also my "Transgression, Equality, Voice," in *Demokratia: A Conversation on Democracies, Ancient and Modern*, ed. Josiah Ober and Charles Hedrick (Princeton: Princeton University Press: 1996), pp. 63–90.

4. Bodin, *Six Books*, p. 193.

5. Sir Thomas Elyot, *The Book Named the Governor*, ed. S. E. Lehmberg (London: Dent and Dutton, 1962), p. 2.

6. Ibid., pp. 2–3, 6–7.

7. Jacob Talmon, *The Rise of Totalitarian Democracy* (Boston: Beacon Press, 1952). Seymour Martin Lipset, "Working-Class Authoritarianism," in *Political Man* (Garden City, N.Y.: Doubleday, 1960), pp. 87–126. On the problem in Hannah Arendt's writings, see my "Hannah Arendt: Democracy and the Political," in *Hannah Arendt: Critical Essays*, ed. Lewis P. Hinchman and Sandra K. Hinchman (Albany: State University of New York Press, 1994), pp. 289–306.

8. John Adams, *A Defense of the Constitutions of Government of the United States of America, 1787–1788* in *Selected Writings of John and John Quincy Adams*, ed. Adrienne Koch and William Peden (New York: Knopf, 1946), p. 83.

9. For a useful and critical survey, see Lauro Martines, *Power and Imagination: City-States in Renaissance Italy* (New York: Vintage Books, 1980).

10. Hobbes, *Leviathan*, ch. 8, p. 134.

11. Machiavelli, *The Prince*, ch. 9. See also Aristotle, *Politics*, IV.13.1297$^{b}$1.

12. *Federalist*, no. 55, p. 374.

13. Hobbes and Locke both admit democracy to be a possible choice but Hobbes dismisses it as less effective in maintaining "peace" and "security." Hobbes, *Leviathan*, ch. 19, pp. 241ff. Locke is even more dismissive but, revealingly, he goes out of his way to emphasize that a "commonwealth," which is the term he chooses for his recommended system, is "not a Democracy." Locke, *Two Treatises of Government*, II.133.This virtual silence, it needs to be emphasized, was in an era when democratic ideas were very much in the air.

14. The contemporary scholar who has done most to promote the idea of republicanism is J.G.A. Pocock. See his *The Machiavellian Moment: Florentine Political Thought and the Atlantic Republican Tradition* (Princeton: Princeton, University Press, 1975). His most persistent American critic has been Joyce Appleby, *Liberalism and Republicanism in the Historical Imagination* (Cambridge, Mass.: Harvard University Press, 1992); see p. 341, n. 4 with its references to her exchanges with Pocock.

15. *OC*, Vol. V(1), 202–3.

16. Aristotle, *Politics*, tr. Ernest Barker (Oxford: Clarendon Press, 1946), I.1.1252$^{a}$5; III.7.1279$^{a}$25–31.

17. Thomas Smith, *De republica Anglorum*, ed. L. Alston (Cambridge: Cambridge University Press, 1906), I.16, pp. 30, 46.

18. Ibid., I.16.46.

19. *The Book Named the Governor*, p. 1.

20. Plato, *Republic*, IV.420c.

21. *The Book Named the Governor* , p. 1.

22. According to Elyot true public well-being would be present only if various artisans did not attempt to share in judicial and military offices. Ibid., pp. 4–5.

23. Karl Marx, *Critique of Hegel's "Philosophy of Right,"* tr. Joseph O'Malley (Cambridge: Cambridge University Press, 1970), pp. 29–30.

24. On the ideological character of the Reformation, see Donald Kelley, *The Beginning of Ideology: Consciousness and Society in the French Reformation* (Cambridge: Cambridge University Press, 1981); for England, see Christopher Hill, *The World Turned Upside Down* (Harmondsworth: Penguin, 1975).

25. Putney Debates (1647), in *Puritanism and Liberty*, ed. A.S.P. Woodhouse (London: Dent, 1958), p. 56.

26. Ibid.

27. Richard Overton, *An Arrow against All Tyrants*, in *The Levellers in the English Revolution*, ed. G. E. Aylmer (Ithaca: Cornell University Press, 1975), p. 69.

28. "England's Miserie and Remedie" (1645), in *Divine Right and Democracy*, ed. David Wooton (Harmondsworth: Penguin, 1986), p. 276.

29. See Zera S. Fink, *The Classical Republicans: An Essay in the Recovery of a Pattern of Thought in Seventeenth-Century England* (Evanston, Ill.: Northwestern University

Press, 1945); Caroline Robbins, *The Eighteenth-Century Commonwealthman* (Cambridge, Mass.: Harvard University Press, 1959); Pocock, *The Machiavellian Moment* and also his introduction to *The Political Works of James Harrington* (Cambridge: Cambridge University Press, 1975); Gisela Bock, Quentin Skinner, and Maurizio Viroli, eds., *Machiavelli and Republicanism* (Cambridge: Cambridge University Press, 1990), especially the essays by Judith Shklar on Montesquieu and Blair Worden on Milton; and for the United States, see Appleby, *Capitalism and a New Social Order*; Lance Banning, *The Jeffersonian Persuasion: Evolution of a Party Ideology* (Ithaca: Cornell University Press, 1978); Gordon Wood, *The Creation of the American Republic, 1776–1787* (Chapel Hill: University of North Carolina Press, 1969), and *The Radicalism of the American Revolution* (New York: Knopf, 1992). In the earlier volume Wood had tended to distinguish democracy from republicanism (see especially pp. 223–24) but in the later volume he insists that the two were inseparable, a claim that allows him to declare that "The republican revolution was the greatest utopian movement in American history" (p. 229).

30. Pocock, *The Political Works of James Harrington*, p. 209.

31. Ibid., p. 212.

32. "His Majesty's Answers to the Nineteen Propositions of Parliament" (1642), in *The Stuart Constitution*, ed. J. P. Kenyon (Cambridge: Cambridge University Press, 1966), pp. 21–22.

33. Pocock, *The Political Works of James Harrington*, p. 165.

34. Michel Foucault, *Discipline and Punish: The Birth of the Prison*, tr. Alan Sheridan (New York: Pantheon, 1977), especially pt. 3.

35. *Federalist*, no. 10, p. 62.

36. On the importance of equality in the revolutionary ideology, see Wood, *The Radicalism of the American Revolution.*

37. These developments would be reflected in Alexander Hamilton's contemptuous dismissal of local and state politics as petty when contrasted with national politics. *Federalist*, no. 17, pp. 106–10. For the historical background to the nationalization of politics during the revolutionary era, see Jack Rakove, *The Beginnings of National Politics: An Interpretive History of the Continental Congress* (Baltimore: Johns Hopkins University Press, 1979).

38. *Federalist*, no. 72, p. 489.

39. Pocock, *The Political Works of James Harrington*, p. 797. This quotation is from a dialogue, *Valerius and Publicola.*

40. *Federalist*, no. 68, p. 461.

41. Ibid., pp. 458, 459.

42. The standard source for the ideas of those opposing the new constitution is the great edition, *Complete Anti-Federalist*, ed. Herbert J. Storing, 7 vols. (Chicago: University of Chicago Press, 1981). There is also a useful abridged version, *The Anti-Federalist*, ed. Murray Dry (Chicago: University of Chicago Press, 1985).

43. Modern commentators have tended to treat as a problem of "federalism" (i.e., of the relationship between the rival jurisdictions of the central government and the various state governments) what was originally a controversy between republicanism and democracy.

44. To Eugène Stoffels, Jan. 1835, *OC*, XIII (1), p. 373.

45. Tocqueville's close reading of the *Federalist* is amply documented in George Wilson Pierson, *Tocqueville in America* (Baltimore: Johns Hopkins University Press, 1996), pp. 602ff. This volume is a reprint of *Tocqueville and Beaumont in America* (Oxford:

Oxford University Press, 1938). See also James T. Schleifer, *The Making of Tocqueville's "Democracy in America"* (Chapel Hill: University of North Carolina Press, 1980), ch. 7.

46. See Marvin Meyers, *The Jacksonian Persuasion: Politics and Beliefs* (New York: Vintage, Random House, 1960), pp. 33–56.

47. *OC*, I (1), 29.

48. *OC*, V (1), 278. From a journal entry of 26 Dec. 1831.

## Chapter IV
## Self and Structure

1. To Madame Swetchine, 7 Jan. 1856, *OC*, XV (2), 268.

2. The popularity of the two *vitae* owes most to Hannah Arendt's *The Human Condition.* There are valuable discussions in A. J. Festugière, *Contemplation et vie contemplative selon Plato* (Paris: Vrin, 1975), and Werner Jaeger, *Aristotle: Fundamentals of the History of His Development*, 2nd ed., tr. Richard Robinson (Oxford: Oxford University Press, 1948), especially pp. 426ff. The contrasts between the two lives are not to be confused with those arising from the distinction between "theory" and "practice." There are discussions of the distinction in Jürgen Habermas, *Theory and Practice*, tr. John Viertel (Boston: Beacon Press, 1973); Richard Bernstein, *Praxis and Action* (Philadelphia: University of Pennsylvania Press, 1971); the essays collected in Paulus Engelhardt, *Zur Theorie der Praxis* (Mainz: Matthias-Grünewald Verlag, 1970); and Terence Ball, ed., *Political Theory and Praxis: New Perspectives* (Minneapolis: University of Minnesota Press, 1977). For a history, see Nicholas Lobkowicz, *Theory and Practice: History of a Concept from Aristotle to Marx* (Notre Dame, Ind.: University of Notre Dame Press, 1967).

3. In Plato's *Republic* the philosophers interrupt their studies once in order to devote themselves fully to ruling for a limited period and then resume their philosophical pursuits.

4. Aristotle, *Metaphysics*, tr. Hippocrates G. Apostle (Bloomington: Indiana University Press, 1973), XII.9.30–35.

5. Cicero, *De re publica*, tr. Clinton W. Keyes (Cambridge: Harvard University Press, 1951), I.ii.2 (p. 15). Translation slightly modified.

6. "Discours de réception à l'Académie française," 21 Apr. 1842, *OC* (B), IX, 4.

7. *OC*, VI (1), 344, 346.

8. Blaise Pascal, *Pensées*, tr. W. F. Trotter (London: Dent, 1948), no. 77 (p. 23).

9. René Descartes, "Rules for the Direction of the Mind," in Descartes, *Philosophical Writings*, ed. N. K. Smith (New York: Random House, 1958), p. 13.

10. *OC*, I (2), 13. Tocqueville's association of Descartes with revolutionary Europe of the eighteenth century was not repeated in *L'ancien régime.* The philosophes were given that role and Descartes was not mentioned.

11. *Federalist*, no. 9 (Hamilton), p. 51; no. 47 (Madison), p. 324.

12. Descartes, *Discourse on the Method*, in *Philosophical Works*, 1:91.

13. René Descartes, "Principles of Philosophy," pt. 1, principles 1 and 2, in *Philosophical Works*, 1:219.

14. Descartes, *Philosophical Works*, 1:81, 82.

15. Descartes, "Rules for the Direction of the Mind," in *Philosophical Writings*, pp. 13, 21.

16. *OC*, V (1), 183.

17. *OC*, I (2), 27.

18. *Principles of Cartesian Philosophy*, tr. Harry Wedeck (New York: Philosophical Library, 1961), p. 18.

19. To Charles Stoffels, 22 Oct. 1831, in Alexis de Tocqueville, *Selected Letters on Politics and Society*, ed. Roger Boesche, tr. James Toupin (Berkeley: University of California Press, 1985), p. 64; to Corcelle, 1 Aug. 1850, *OC*, XV (2), 29.

20. On the "necessary truths," see *OC*, I (2), 27.

21. To Corcelle, 1 Aug. 1850, *OC*, XV (2), 29.

22. To P.-P. Royer-Collard, 6 Apr. 1838, *OC*, XI, 59.

23. André Jardin, *Alexis de Tocqueville* (Paris: Hachette, 1984), pp. 62ff. The experience which Tocqueville recounted to Mme Swetchine was alluded to many years before in a letter to Chales Stoffels. See the text in Tocqueville, *Selected Letters*, pp. 63–64.

24. 26 Feb. 1857, *OC*, XV (2), 314–16.

25. *OC*, I (2), 27, 28.

26. *OC*, I (1), 241.

27. Descartes, *Discourse on the Merthod*, in *Philosophical Works*, 1:81.

28. There are numerous references to Pascal throughout Tocqueville's writings. Beaumont noted in the memoir which he included in his edition of Tocqueville's works that his friend had closely studied Pascal's style. The influence of Pascal upon Tocqueville is discussed at length in Peter Augustine Lawler, *The Restless Mind: Alexis de Tocqueville on the Origin and Perpetuation of Human Liberty* (Lanham, Md.: Rowman and Littlefield, 1993), especially pp. 73ff.

29. Descartes, *Discourse on the Method*, in *Philosophical Works*, 1:100–101.

30. *OC*, I (2), 78.

31. *Pensées*, no. 1.

32. *OC*, I (2), 81. Compare Pascal, *Pensées*, nos. 194, p. 55; 205, p. 61.

33. Descartes, *Discourse on the Method*, in *Philosophical Works*, 1:91.

34. 19 Oct. 1836, *OC*, VI (1), 314. Late in life Tocqueville described himself in much the same way as in the letter to Mill. To Beaumont, 16 Nov. 1857, *OC*, VIII (3), 511–12. Compare Descartes: "those who proceed very slowly may, provided they always follow the straight road, really advance much faster than those who, though they run, forsake it." *Discourse on Method*, in *Philosophical Works*, 1:82.

35. See Descartes, *Discourse on Method*, in *Philosophical Works*, 1:83–84, 87–90.

36. Pascal's description of the *esprit de finesse* could be applied to Tocqueville without much modification: "in the intuitive mind principles are found in common use, and are before the eyes of everybody. One has only to look, and no effort is necessary; it is only a question of good eyesight, but it must be good, for the principles are so subtle and so numerous, that it is almost impossible but that some escape notice." *Pensées*, I.1.

37. The gist of what follows was first developed in my essay, "Archaism, Modernity, and *Democracy in America*." It can be found in *The Presence of the Past: Essays on the State and the Constitution* (Baltimore: Johns Hopkins University Press, 1989), pp. 66–81.

38. To Reeve, 22 Mar. 1837, *OC*, VI (1), 37–38. See also the letter to Beaumont, 3 Mar. 1853, *OC*, VIII (3); Pierson, *Tocqueville in America*, pp. 454–55; and Tocqueville's preface to the second volume of *Democracy in America*, pp. 37–38. The letter to Reeve also casts interesting light on Tocqueville's critical review of a book that had been modeled after *Democracy*. He attributed the weakness of the book, *Democracy in Switzerland*, to the biases of an author who had suffered personally from the recent Swiss revolution. See *OC*, I (2), 351–53.

39. *OC*, I (1), 27.
40. *OC*, V (1), 203.
41. *OC*, I (2), 11.
42. *OC*, V (1), 235.
43. *OC*, I (2), 49.
44. *OC*, I (1), 267.
45. *OC*, I (1), 266–67.
46. *OC*, I (2), 49.
47. Descartes, *Discourse on Method*, in *Philosophical Works*, 1:87.
48. Descartes was careful to exempt from his skepticism "the laws and customs of my country" and the religion in which he had been raised. Ibid., pp. 95–96.
49. Tocqueville even recommended a Cartesian strategy for establishing probabilities in the face of doubts. And like Descartes he argued that it was better to strike out "quickly and vigorously onto a bad path than to remain in uncertainty or act weakly." To Charles Stoffels, 22 Oct. 1831, in Tocqueville, *Selected Letters*, p. 64. Compare Descartes, *Discourse on Method*, in *Philosophical Works*, 1:96.
50. *OC*, V (2), 38.
51. Lamberti, *Tocqueville et les deux démocraties*, p. 96.
52. "Tocqueville on Democracy in America (Vol. II)," in John Stuart Mill, *Essays on Politics and Culture*, ed. Gertrude Himmelfarb (New York: Doubleday, 1963), p. 215.
53. Schleifer, *The Making of Tocqueville's "Democracy in America,"* p. 281.
54. 1 Nov. 1833, *OC*, VIII (1), 136.
55. *OC*, I (2), 77.
56. *OC*, I (2), 251.
57. The crucial discussion is in part 1, chapter 5: *OC*, I (1), especially 69–98.
58. *OC*, I (2), 239.
59. Some confusion is created by the customary practice of publishing *Democracy* in two volumes. Originally it was published in two parts, each of which appeared in two volumes. Even the one volume Mayer edition (in English) presents the work as though it were two volumes.
60. *OC*, I (2), 7.
61. 18 Dec. 1840, *OC*, VI (1), 330.
62. John Stuart Mill, "M. de Tocqueville on Democracy in America," in *Mill's Ethical Writings*, ed. J. B. Schneewind (New York: Collier Books, 1965), p. 107.
63. Seymour Drescher, *Dilemmas of Democracy: Tocqueville and Modernization* (Pittsburgh: University of Pittsburgh Press, 1968), p. 252.
64. *OC*, I (1), 92–93.
65. *OC*, I (2), 200.
66. Compare the following from a thoughtful study of Tocqueville: "I assume that Tocqueville's thought consists of a network of interconnected themes with no fixed order of primacy among them." Doris S. Goldstein, *Trial of Faith: Religion and Politics in Tocqueville's Thought* (New York: Elsevier, 1975), p. x.
67. *OC*, I (1), 1.
68. Although Tocqueville did not use the phrase "political culture," it corresponds closely to the complex formation he referred to repeatedly as "ideas, manners, habits, and *moeurs*."
69. *OC*, I (1), 294.

70. *OC*, I (2), 43.

71. *OC*, I (2), 228.

72. To Baron Edouard de Tocqueville, 10 July 1838, *OC* (B), VII, 166–68 (emphasis in original). Cited in Schleifer, *The Making of Tocqueville's "Democracy in America,"* p. 163.

73. *OC*, I (1), 14.

## Chapter V
## Doubt and Disconnection

1. To Tocqueville and Beaumont, *OC*, VII, 25.

2. To Louis de Kergorlay, Jan. 1835, *OC*, XIII (1), 374.

3. 25 Oct. 1829, *OC*, VIII (1), 93.

4. For the details of Tocqueville's family background, see Jardin, *Alexis de Tocqueville*, pp. 9–56; and R. R. Palmer, introduction to *The Two Tocquevilles, Father and Son: Hervé and Alexis de Tocqueville on the Coming of the French Revolution* (Princeton: Princeton University Press, 1987).

5. Kergorlay to Tocqueville, 8 Sept. 1830, *OC*, XIII (1), 213–15; Pierson, *Tocqueville in America*, pp. 30–31; Edward Gargan, *Alexis de Tocqueville: The Critical Years, 1848–1851* (Washington, D.C.: Catholic University Press, 1955), pp. 15–18; Jardin, *Alexis de Tocqueville*, pp. 87–88.

6. Gargan, *Alexis de Tocqueville*, p. 9, n. 24; Pierson, *Tocqueville in America*, p. 29.

7. 14 March 1831, *OC*, VIII (1), 106.

8. Pierson, *Tocqueville in America*, p. 29.

9. To Charles Stoffels, 21 Feb. 1831, *OC* (B), II, 413.

10. To Kergorlay, 23 July 1827, *OC*, XIII (1), 107, 108.

11. Palmer, *The Two Tocquevilles*, pp. 3, 7.

12. 6 June 1831, *OC*, VIII (1), 107–8.

13. 14 Oct. 1831, *OC*, V (1), 183.

14. *OC*, I (1), 256.

15. To Kergorlay, 29 June 1831, *OC*, XIII (1), 232–33.

16. Entry for 27 Dec. 1831, *OC*, V (1), 276.

17. Entry for 29 Oct. 1831, *OC*, V (1), 186 (emphasis in original).

18. On the difficulties of marrying outside one's class, see *OC*, I (2), 214–15.

19. *OC*, V (1), 93, 234–35, 240, 266, 279, 280, 281–82.

20. To Stoffels, 18 Oct. 1831, *OC* (B), II, 422.

21. *OC*, I (2), 200, 204–5.

22. Tocqueville's shock was apparent in his much criticized claim that in America aristocracy had once enjoyed a foothold but legislation preventing the inheritance of large estates had eliminated that possibility and, along with it, the "spirit of family." The "aristocratic tendency which might have shaped" the young republic gave way instead to "an irresistible democratic tendency." To Kergorlay, 29 June 1831, *OC*, XIII (1), 232.

23. *OC*, V (1), 279.

24. Cited in Schleifer, *The Making of Democracy in America*, p. 149; *OC*, I (1), 417.

25. *OC*, I (2), 338.

26. *OC*, V (1), 160–61.

27. Tocqueville's discussions of individualism occupy a major place in Lamberti, *Tocqueville et les deux démocraties.*

28. To Stoffels, 21 Apr. 1830, cited in Gargan, *Alexis de Tocqueville*, p. 4, n. 7. Compare Rousseau, *Émile*, especially bk. II.
29. 26 Feb. 1857, *OC*, XV (2), 314–15.
30. *OC*, I (1), 4.
31. *OC*, V (1), 123–24.
32. To Eugène Stoffels, 21 Feb. 1835, *OC* (B), II, 428; also *OC*, I (1), 294.
33. To Reeve, 15 Sept. 1839, *OC*, VI (1), 48; to Mill, June 1835, *OC*, VI (1), 294.
34. Cited in Pierson, *Tocqueville in America*, p. 453.
35. *OC*, V (1), 208–9.
36. *OC*, V (1), 123–24.
37. *OC*, I (2), 237.
38. *OC*, I (1), 10.
39. 28 July 1831, *OC* (B), II, 415, 418.
40. *OC*, I (1), 5.

## Chapter VI
### ". . . the theory of what is great"

1. From letters to Charles Stoffels, Nov. 1830 and Feb. 1831, as cited in Pierson, *Tocqueville in America*, pp. 31–32. See also letter to Stoffels, 21 Feb. 1831, *OC* (B), V, 414.
2. Aristotle, *Politics*, 1252ᵃ1. I have followed the translation by Carnes Lord, *Aristotle: The Politics* (Chicago: University of Chicago Press, 1984).
3. Jan. 1835, *OC*, XIII (1), 374. The letter in *OC* is cited as having been written to Kergorlay, but Jardin has corrected this in his *Alexis de Tocqueville*, p. 92.
4. Jardin, *Alexis de Tocqueville*, pp. 187–88.
5. 20 Nov. 1838, *OC*, XI, 74.
6. *OC*, V (1), 103.
7. To Stoffels, 21 Feb. 1831, *OC* (B), II, 414.
8. Cited in Jardin, *Alexis de Tocqueville*, pp. 108–9.
9. 24 Oct. 1831, cited in Ibid., p. 170.
10. *OC*, V (1), 123–24, 118–19, 208–9, 234–36.
11. Cited in Pierson, *Tocqueville in America*, p. 81.
12. *OC*, V (1), 206, 235, 257.
13. To Kergorlay, 18 May 1832, *OC*, XIII (1), 235.
14. To Royer-Collard, 6 Apr. 1838, *OC*, XI, 61.
15. Claude Lévi-Strauss, *Triste Tropique*, tr. John Russell (New York: Atheneum, 1955, 1964), p. 374. Copyright © 1955 by Librarie Plon. Translation copyright © 1973 by Jonathan Cape Limited. Reprinted by permission of Georges Borchardt, Inc., for the author.
16. *OC*, V, (1), 206.
17. *Esprit des lois*, preface, *OC*, II, 230.
18. 24 Jan. 1832, cited in Jardin, *Alexis de Tocqueville*, p. 170.
19. Cited in Pierson, *Tocqueville in America*, p. 151. On Tocqueville's despair: *OC*, V (1), 269; VI (1), 47–48; *OC* (B), II, 427–28; Pierson, *Tocqueville in America*, p. 245.
20. *OC*, V (1), 234, 206, 286.
21. *OC*, V (1), 346–47. Tocqueville's essay has been translated by George Lawrence in Alexis de Tocqueville, *Journey to America*, ed. J.-P. Mayer (New Haven: Yale University Press, 1962), pp. 328–76.

22. *OC*, V (1), 89.
23. *OC*, V (1), 193, 234.
24. To Royer-Collard, 6 Apr. 1838, *OC*, XI, 61 (emphasis in original).
25. *OC*, V (1), 235.
26. *OC*, VIII (1), 421.
27. To Stoffels, 12 Jan. 1833, *OC* (B), V, 425–26.
28. To Corcelle, 14 July 1842, *OC*, XV (1), 158.
29. To Corcelle, 19 Oct. 1839, *OC*, XV (1), 139.
30. *OC*, V, (1), 197.
31. 20 Aug. 1837, *OC*, XI, 40.
32. To Royer-Collard, 20 Aug. 1837, *OC*, XI, 40.
33. *OC*, V (1), 205–6, 234–35, 256, 257.
34. *OC*, V (1), 289.
35. *OC*, I (1), 15.
36. Cited in Pierson, *Tocqueville in America*, p. 115.
37. 18 Dec. 1840, *OC*, VI (1), 330.
38. *OC*, V (1), 202, 203.
39. On the original idea of a book, *Tocqueville in America*, see Pierson, pp. 31–32.
40. 4 Nov. or 3 Dec. 1836, *OC*, VIII (1), 176.
41. To Beaumont, 22 Nov. 1836, *OC*, VIII (1), 175.
42. *OC*, I (1), 1.
43. To Kergorlay, 4 Dec. 1836, *OC*, XIII (1), 423.
44. *OC*, I (1), 1.
45. *OC*, I (1), 12.
46. Cited in Pierson, *Tocqueville in America*, p. 748. Before his discussion of "the three races" Tocqueville remarks, "These matters are marginal to my subject; they are American without being democratic, and it is above all democracy that I have wanted to portray." *OC*, I (1), 331.
47. *OC*, I (2), 41.
48. *OC*, I (1), 326.
49. Schleifer, *The Making of Tocqueville's "Democracy in America,"* p. 267.
50. For a defense of the notion that there are "standard" conceptions of basic political terms and criteria for their correct use, see Quentin Skinner, "Language and Political Change," in *Political Innovation and Conceptual Change*, ed. Terence Ball, James Farr, and Russell L. Hanson (Cambridge: Cambridge University Press, 1989), pp. 8–10.
51. These were masterfully discussed by Furet, *Revolutionary France, 1770–1880.*
52. To Kergorlay, 18 Oct 1847, OC, XIII (2), 209.
53. Ibid.
54. Ibid.
55. *OC*, V (1), 278.
56. *OC*, I (1), 9.
57. Tocqueville wrote that the heroic character of the American Revolution had been "greatly exaggerated" and owed more to geography than to "valor" or "patriotism." He added that it was ridiculous to compare the American with the French Revolution: the French had held off "the whole of Europe" while dealing with counterrevolution at home. *OC*, I (1), 114.
58. To Eugene Stoffels, 21 Feb. 1835, *OC* (B), II, 428–29.

## Chapter VII
## Myth and Political Impressionism

1. Friedrich Nietzsche, *Thus Spoke Zarathustra*, tr. R. J. Hollingdale (1961; Baltimore: Penguin, 1969), p. 161.

2. See Bentham's attack on Blackstone, *A Fragment on Government*, ed. F. C. Montague (London: Oxford University Press, 1891). For Marx, see *Capital*, tr. Ben Fowkes, 3 vols. (Harmondsworth: Penguin, 1976), I: prefaces to the first and second edition and ch. 1, "The Commodity."

3. *OC*, I (2), 258, 261.

4. See especially the opening pages of Marx and Engels, *The Manifesto of the Communist Party*.

5. *The German Ideology*, ed. S. Ryazanskaya (London: Lawrence and Wishart, 1965), preface and pt. 1, pp. 23ff.

6. *OC*, I (2), 78.

7. *On the Reasonableness of Christianity as Delivered in the Scriptures*, ed. George W. Ewing (Chicago: Regnery, 1965), sec. 243, p. 179.

8. *OC*, I (1), 361–64.

9. *OC*, V (1), 129.

10. To Beaumont, 8 Aug. 1855, *OC*, VIII (3), 331.

11. *OC*, I (1), 425–26.

12. *OC*, I (1), 39–40.

13. *OC*, I (1), 34.

14. Ibid.

15. *OC*, I (1), 43.

16. *OC*, I (2), 293.

17. *OC*, I (1), 27.

18. Cited in Julian Barnes, "Prince of Poets," *New York Review of Books* 36, no. 7 (8 Nov. 1989): 10–14 at p. 10.

19. *OC*, II (1), 73 (emphasis added).

20. To Reeve, 15 Nov. 1839, *OC*, VI (1), 99.

21. *OC*, I (2), 57.

22. *OC*, I (1), 13.

23. Cited from Tocqueville's notes in Pierson, *Tocqueville in America*, p. 302.

24. See the examples in ibid., pp. 755ff.

25. *OC*, I (1), 12.

26. *OC*, I (1), 13.

27. To Beaumont, 26 Dec. 1850, *OC*, VIII (2), 343.

28. Tocqueville was not using "philosophy" in a technical or academic sense. More often it stood for general principles, especially regarding morals.

29. Compare Macaulay 's essay "Hallam" of 1828: "History, at least in its state of real perfection, is a compound of poetry and philosophy." *Critical and Historical Essays*, ed. A. J. Grieve, 2 vols. (London: Dent, 1907), 1:1. Similar views can be found in Wilhelm von Humboldt's essay, "On the Task of the Historian" (1821).

30. Shakespeare, *Henry VIII*, V.iii.50.

31. *OC*, I (1), 344.

32. *OC*, I (2), 102.

33. *OC*, I (1), 1.

34. *OC,* I (1), 1.
35. *OC,* I (2), 103–4.
36. 7 May 1835, cited in Jardin, *Alexis de Tocqueville,* p. 225.
37. To Count Molé, cited by J.-P. Mayer, ed., in Alexis de Tocqueville, *Journey to England and Ireland* (Garden City, N.Y.: Doubleday, 1968), p. xviii.
38. To Tocqueville, 1835, *OC,* VI (1), 298.
39. *OC,* VI (1), 99.
40. 29 June 1831, *OC,* XIII (1), 235.
41. *OC,* V (2), 64.
42. *OC,* V (2), 69.
43. To Comtesse de Circourt, 18 Sept. 1852, *OC* (B), VI, 197.
44. To Beaumont, 8 July 1838, *OC,* VIII (1), 311–12 (emphasis in original).
45. To Corcelle, 2 Sept. 1849, *OC,* XV (1), 374.
46. *OC,* V (1), 209.

## Chapter VIII
## The Spectacle of America

1. C. Kerenyi, *The Religion of the Greeks and Romans,* tr. C. Holme (New York: Dutton, 1962), p. 151.
2. Plato, *Republic,* 327a (tr. Cornford).
3. Plato, *Republic,* tr. Paul Shorey, 2 vols. (Cambridge, Mass.: Harvard University Press, 1963), 475e.
4. *OC,* I (1), 17.
5. *OC,* I (1), 174.
6. See the letters cited in Jardin, *Alexis de Tocqueville,* p. 113.
7. *OC,* I (1), 25.
8. *OC,* V (1), 209.
9. *OC,* I (1), 293.
10. *OC,* I (1), 11.
11. *OC,* I (1), 299.
12. From an unedited letter of 1831 to Chabrol, cited in Jardin, *Alexis de Tocqueville,* 113.
13. *OC,* I (2), 336.
14. *OC,* I (1), 422.
15. *OC,* I (2), 336–37.
16. *OC,* I (2), 336.
17. *OC,* I (2), 108.
18. *OC,* I (2), 107–8.
19. *OC,* I (2), 162.
20. "Political and Social Condition of France before and since 1789," *OC,* II (1), 62.
21. *OC,* I (2), 22.
22. To J. S. Mill, 10 Feb. 1836, *OC,* VI (1), 307.
23. Plato, *Politics,* 259c.
24. *Oxford Universal Dictionary,* s.v. "generality."
25. Cited in Schleifer, *The Making of Tocqueville's "Democracy in America,"* p. 164.
26. Tocqueville mused about the problem during his travels in America. In a notebook entry he replayed the eighteenth-century controversy in which the claims of natu-

ral reason and its general or universal truths were pitted against the defense of tradition as the primary source of moral and political truths. In a strongly Pascalian vein he wrote: "Reason like virtue does not vary in different climates nor with the temperaments or nature of places. It is one and inflexible. All the people who take it as regulative of their actions must have great points of resemblance." In contrast, a people that follows "a certain ideal perfection, when it is concerned to do as its fathers did, and to do the best possible," will increasingly appear as different from other societies. *OC*, V (1), 190–91.

27. *OC*, I (2), pt. 1, chs. 17, 20; pt. 2, ch. 17.

28. From a note written while completing the last part of *Democracy*. Cited in Schleifer, *The Making of Tocqueville's "Democracy in America,"* p. 165.

29. Schleifer, *The Making of Tocqueville's "Democracy in America,"* p. 165.

30. *OC*, I (2), 437.

31. *OC*, I (2), 338.

32. *OC*, I (2), 437.

33. *OC*, I (2), 20.

34. On these institutions, see Roland E. Mousnier, *The Institutions of France under the Absolute Monarchy, 1598–1789*, tr. Arthur Goldhammer, 2 vols. (Chicago: University of Chicago Press, 1984), 2:302ff. Also Franklin L. Ford, *Robe and Sword* (1953; New York: Harper & Row, 1965).

35. *OC*, I (1), 279–80.

36. On the *corps intermédiaries*, see the influential chapter of Montesquieu, *Esprit des lois*, II.4.

37. To Kergorlay, 13 Nov. 1833, *OC* (B), V, 320.

38. June 1835, *OC*, V (1), 293.

39. "The Over-Soul," in *Works of Ralph Waldo Emerson*, 4 vols. in one (New York: Tudor Publishing, n.d.), 1:173.

40. See Tocqueville's reflections on the French fad of preserving revolutionary memorabilia in *OC*, VII, 297.

41. *OC*, I (2), 21.

42. Aristotle, *Politics*, VI.4.1319$^{b}$27.

43. Hobbes, *Leviathan*, ch. 18, p. 237. "As in the presence of the Master, the Servants are equall, and without any honour at all; So are the Subjects, in the presence of the Soveraign" (p. 238).

44. Cited in Lamberti, *Tocqueville et les deux démocraties*, p. 55.

45. To Kergorlay, 29 June 1831, *OC*, XIII (1), 232.

46. To Kergorlay, 15 Dec. 1850, *OC*, XIII (2), 230–1.

47. To Corcelle, 2 June 1839, *OC*, V (1), 109.

48. *OC*, I (2), 118, 123.

49. *OC*, I (2), 89, 90.

50. *OC*, I (1), 32.

51. *OC*, I (1), 31, 34.

52. *OC*, I (1), 293.

53. *OC*, I (1) 32.

54. *OC*, I (1), 28, 31 (emphasis in original).

55. *OC*, I (1), 25.

56. *OC*, I (1), 41.

57. *OC*, I (1), 84–85.

58. *OC*, I (1), 153.

59. *OC*, I (1), 120, 159.

60. To Eugene Stoffels, 21 Feb. 1835, *OC* (B), II, 427–29.

61. See Lamberti, *Tocqueville et les deux démocraties*, p. 40. The most influential treatment of Tocqueville as a sociologist was Raymond Aron, *Main Currents in Sociological Thought*, tr. Richard Howard and Helen Weaver, 2 vols. (New York: Doubleday, 1968), 1:303–33.

62. *OC*, V (1), 89, 90.

63. *OC*, I (1), 44.

## Chapter IX
## Social Contract versus Political Culture

1. To Kergorlay, 10 Nov. 1836, *OC*, XIII (1), 418.

2. Among contemporary American historians there continues to be a running battle regarding the importance of "theories" during the last half of the eighteenth century. One of the most striking aspects in some historians is that they begin emphasizing the importance of ideas but then, subsequently, they take pains to point out that "behavior" or "concrete events" were more important determinants. For recent formulations, see Wood, *The Creation of the American Republic, 1776–1787*, pp. 288ff and more recently, *The Radicalism of the American Revolution*, pp. 169ff. Also, Bernard Bailyn, *The Ideological Origins of the American Revolution* (Cambridge, Mass.: Harvard University Press, 1967), pp. 22ff., and "The Central Themes of the American Revolution," *Essays on the American Revolution*, ed., Stephen G. Kurtz and James H. Hutson (New York: Norton, 1973), pp. 6–7. George Mace, *Locke, Hobbes, and the Federalist Papers: An Essay on the Genesis of the American Political Heritage* (Carbondale: Southern Illinois University Press, 1979), does not attempt to assess the influence of Locke and Hobbes but to argue the merits of the *Federalist*.

3. Jean-Jacques Rousseau, *On the Social Contract*, ed. Roger Masters, tr. Judith Masters (New York: St. Martin's Press, 1978), II.7, p. 68.

4. Hobbes, *Leviathan*, ch. 17, p. 227; Locke, *Two Treatises of Government*, II.97; Rousseau, *Social Contract*, I.6, p. 53.

5. One reflection of this development is evident in the *Federalist* where all of the references to "contract" relate to business transactions, including the discussion of the "contract clause" of the proposed constitution.

6. The classic discussion of these matters is Macpherson's *The Political Theory of Possessive Individualism*. My formulation deliberately reproduces the masculine emphasis and exclusion of women among contract theorists. For feminist criticisms of contract theory, see Susan M. Okin, *Women in Western Political Thought* (Princeton: Princeton University Press, 1978), and Carole Pateman, *The Sexual Contract* (Stanford: Stanford University Press, 1988).

7. Shakespeare, *Sonnet*, cxxiv.

8. Locke, *Two Treatises of Government*, I.xi.106.

9. Ibid., II.1.1.

10. Hobbes, *Leviathan*, ch. 21, p. 265 (see also ch. 18, p. 229); ch. 16, p. 217.

11. Premodern contract theories had avoided these difficulties by pointedly avoiding investing the right of resistance in "the people." Instead the right was assigned to specified magistrates or corporate bodies. One of the most famous examples was the *Vindiciae contra tyrannos* of 1576.

12. Hobbes, *Leviathan*, ch. 30, p. 379.

13. The classic work on tacit knowledge is Michael Polanyi, *The Tacit Dimension* (London: Routledge and Kegan Paul, 1967). See also Michael Oakeshott, *Rationalism in Politics* (New York: Basic Books, 1962), especially pp. 1–36, 80–136; and my "Paradigms and Political Theories," in *Politics and Experience: Essays Presented to Michael Oakeshott*, eds. Preston King and B. C. Parekh (Cambridge: Cambridge University Press, 1968), pp. 125–52. The persistence of the problem is reflected in John Rawls's stipulation that those in the "original position" who choose the basic terms of engagement are assumed to have certain basic knowledge.

14. Montesquieu, *Esprit des lois*, III.3, *Oeuvres*, 2:252.

15. A recent attempt at presenting a democratic Rousseau is in James Miller, *Rousseau: Dreamer of Democracy* (New Haven: Yale University Press, 1984). See also Rousseau's *Social Contract*, III.4.

16. Rousseau, *Social Contract*, II.7, p. 69.

17. Ibid., p. 68. For an acute discussion of the role of the Legislator, see Raymond Polin, *La politique de la solitude* (Paris: Sirey, 1971), pp. 221–42.

18. Jean-Jacques Rousseau, *Confessions*, VIII, in *Oeuvres complètes*, 4 vols. to date, Éditions de la Pléiade (Paris: Gallimard, 1959–69), 404–5. Some notion of the radical change in the scale of virtue, so to speak, can be gained by contrasting Machiavelli's attempt to instruct a single prince in the *virtù* of military action with Rousseau's attempt to instill civic virtue in an entire people.

19. On the Spartan element, see Judith Shklar, *Rousseau: Man and Citizen* (Cambridge: Cambridge University Press, 1979), pp. 7, 127–28. On the Calvinist element, see Miller, *Rousseau: Dreamer of Democracy*.

20. Rousseau, *Du contrat social*, II.3, p. 24.

21. Rousseau described the social order as a "sacred right" (*un droit sacré* ) and referred to the "sanctity of the contract." Ibid., I.1, p. 4;I.7, p. 15.

22. Ibid., I.6, p. 14.

23. Ibid.

24. Ibid., II.12, p. 47.

25. Jean-Jacques Rousseau, *Government of Poland*, in *The Political Writings of Jean-Jacques Rousseau*, ed. C. E. Vaughan, 2 vols. (1915; Oxford: Blackwell, 1962), 2:427ff.

26. "One who dares to undertake the founding of a people should feel that he is capable of changing human nature, so to speak; of transforming each individual, who by himself is a perfect and solitary whole, into a part of a larger whole from which the individual receives, in a sense, his life and being." Rousseau, *Social Contract*, II.7, p. 69.

27. Rousseau, *Contrat social*, II.7, p. 37. In translating *le vrai politique*, I have followed the translation by Judith R. Masters in Rousseau, *Social Contract*, p. 70. In the chapter Rousseau is intent upon distinguishing the theoretical knowledge required by the legislator from the practical knowledge of the politician. The combination of legislator-theorist has a long history beginning with Plato's *Laws*.

28. For a recent discussion of Montesquieu's influence upon Tocqueville, see Anne M. Cohler, *Montesquieu's Comparative Politics and the Spirit of American Constitutionalism* (Lawrence: University of Kansas Press, 1988), pp. 170ff.

29. Montesquieu's views on rulers are also scattered throughout the fragments collected under *Mes pensées*. For examples, see Montesquieu's *Oeuvres complètes*, 2:1154–55, 1430ff., 1437ff.

30. *OC*, I (1), 167.

31. *OC,* I (1), 168.
32. *OC,* I (1), 328.
33. The authorship of the work in question, *The Fundamental Constitutions of Carolina,* has been disputed as to whether it is solely the work of Locke or a collaboration between him and Shaftesbury. For details see Locke, *Two Treatises of Government,* p. 42.
34. *OC,* V (1), 282–83.
35. *OC,* I (1), 114–15.
36. *OC,* I (1), 115.
37. *OC,* I (1), 11.
38. *OC,* I (1), 121.
39. *OC,* I (1), 5.
40. *OC,* I (1), 11.
41. *OC,* I (2), 339.
42. *OC,* I (1), 4.
43. *OC,* I (1), 425–26.
44. *OC,* I (1), 336.
45. *OC,* I (2), 328.
46. *OC,* I (1), 5.
47. *OC,* I (2), 337.
48. *OC,* I (1), 338.
49. *OC,* I (2), 339.
50. Ibid.
51. See Tocqueville's letter to E. Stoffels, 21 Feb. 1835, *OC,* II (B), 428–29.
52. *OC,* I (1), 323, 324.
53. *OC,* I (1), 324.
54. *OC,* I (1), 262.
55. *OC,* I (2), 303.
56. Aristotle, *Nicomachean Ethics,* tr. J.A.K. Thomson (Harmondsworth: Penguin, 1953), I.2 (p. 26).
57. *OC,* I (1), 329.
58. *Federalist,* no. 9 (Hamilton), p. 51; no. 31 (Hamilton), p. 195; no. 47 (Madison), p. 324.
59. Aristotle, *Politics* , I.1.1252$^{a}$1–5.
60. Ibid., IV.4.1291$^{b}$30–1292$^{a}$38.
61. Ibid., IV.11.1295$^{a}$25–1295$^{b}$34.
62. *OC,* I (2), 336.
63. *OC,* I (2), 338.
64. *OC,* I (1), 255–56. See also *OC,* I (1), 7–8.
65. *OC,* I (1), 256.
66. Tocqueville's note to himself cited in Schleifer, *The Making of Tocqueville's "Democracy in America,"* p. 242.
67. *OC,* I (2), 347.
68. The theme of moderate government had a central place in Montesquieu's political science. See my discussion of the texts in "Montesquieu and Publius: The Crisis of Reason in the *Federalist,*" in *Presence of the Past,* pp. 100–119.
69. *OC,* I (2), 334, 338.
70. *OC,* I (1), 255–56.
71. *OC,* I (1), 139. See Plato, *Laws,* III.701d–e.

72. *OC*, I (1), 5, 6.

73. Cited in Schleifer, *The Making of Tocqueville's "Democracy in America,"* p. 184.

74. *OC*, I (1), 253.

75. Montesquieu, *Esprit des lois*, IV.6, *Oeuvres*, 2:267.

76. Ibid., V.3–4, *Oeuvres*, 2:274–76.

77. Representative of the genre is Walter Isaacson and Evan Thomas, *The Wise Men: Six Friends and the World They Made* (New York: Simon and Schuster, 1986).

78. See Eric Hobsbawm, *The Age of Revolution, 1789–1848* (London: Weidenfeld and Nicolson, 1962), pp. 69, 73–76; Simon Schama, *Citizens: A Chronicle of the French Revolution* (New York: Knopf, 1989), pp. 760–63.

79. *OC*, V (1), 178.

80. *OC*, V, (1), 278.

81. Montesquieu, *Esprit des lois*, III.3–4.

82. Ibid., III.3, p. 252.

83. *OC*, V (1), 278.

84. "The Americans do not have virtue but principles." *OC*, V (1), 206.

85. *OC*, V (1), 179.

86. *OC*, I (2), 334–35.

87. *OC*, I (1), 255.

88. *OC*, I (1), 70.

89. *OC*, I (2), 113, 114.

90. *OC*, I (1), 322.

91. *OC*, I (1), 171, 172.

92. *OC*, I (1), 414–15.

93. *OC*, I (1), 56.

94. *OC*, I (1), 177.

95. *OC*, I (1), 414.

## Chapter X
## The Culture of the Political: "the rituals of practice"

1. *OC*, I (1), 316.

2. *OC*, V (1), 199.

3. These have been edited by Mayer and translated as *Journey to America* by Lawrence. They form part of *OC*, V (1). They were not published during Tocqueville's lifetime and appeared only in abbreviated form in Beaumont's edition of Tocqueville's works. For details, see the editors's introduction to *OC*, V (1), and Pierson, *Tocqueville in America*, p. 826.

4. The first edition bears the date of 1833 but apparently it had circulated in official circles in 1832.

5. *OC*, V (1), 197–203.

6. *OC*, V (1), 282–3.

7. *OC*, V (2), 379.

8. *OC*, V (1), 370.

9. *OC*, V (1), 336.

10. *OC*, I (1), 21.

11. *OC*, V (1), 370.

12. *OC*, I (1), 23–25.

13. *OC*, V (1), 346–47.
14. *OC*, V (1), 353.
15. *OC*, I (1), 316–17.
16. *OC*, I (1), 23, 25.
17. *OC*, I (1), 11.
18. *OC*, V (1), 206.
19. *OC*, I (2), 67.
20. *OC*, I (1), 254.
21. Ibid.
22. *OC*, I (1), 253–54.
23. *OC*, I (1), 215.
24. *OC*, I (1), 31.
25. *OC*, I (1), 28, 31 (emphasis in original).
26. *OC*, I (1), 32.
27. *OC*, I (1), 41.
28. *OC*, I (1), 84–85.
29. *OC*, I (1), 153.
30. *OC*, I (1), 120, 159.
31. *OC*, I (1), 31–37.
32. *OC*, I (1), 28, 31, 38.
33. *OC*, I (2), 304.
34. *OC*, I (2), 305.
35. *OC*, I (1), 34.
36. *OC*, I (1), 30, 34, 38.
37. *OC*, I (1), 42.
38. *OC*, I (1), 41.
39. *OC*, I (1), 59.
40. Ibid.
41. *OC*, I (1), 247.
42. *OC*, I (1), 59.
43. *OC*, I (1), 247.
44. *OC*, I (1), 412, 413.
45. Among early modern theorists, see the author(s) of the *Vindiciae contra tyrannos* and Johannes Althusius. In the nineteenth century and early twentieth the major figures in this tradition were Otto von Gierke, J. N. Figgis, Frederick Maitland, and Sir Ernest Barker. The best discussion of the earlier tradition can be found in the works of Antony J. Black, *Monarchy and Community: Political Ideas in the Later Conciliar Controversy, 1430–1450* (Cambridge: Cambridge University Press, 1970); *Council and Commune: The Conciliar Movement and the Council of Basle* (London: Burns & Oates, 1979), especially pp. 194ff.; and an overview in *Guilds and Society in European Political Thought from the Twelfth Century to the Present* (London: Methuen, 1984). Black has also edited selections from von Gierke, *Community in Historical Perspective* (Cambridge: Cambridge University Press, 1990).
46. The classic study remains George Troeltsch, *The Social Teachings of the Christian Churches*, tr. Olive Wyon, 2 vols. (London: Allen and Unwin, 1931). See especially the second volume where the distinction between church and sect is developed.
47. *OC*, I (1), 58.
48. Ibid.

49. Ibid.
50. *OC*, I (1), 67.
51. *OC*, I (1), 171.
52. *OC*, I (1), 66.
53. *OC*, I (1), 66, 39.
54. *OC*, I (1), 253.
55. *OC*, I (1), 238.
56. *OC*, I (1), 67.
57. *OC*, I (1), 66.
58. *OC*, I (2), 111.
59. Cited in Schleifer, *The Making of "Democracy in America,"* p. 229.
60. *OC*, I (1), 254.
61. *OC*, I (1), 58–59.
62. *OC*, I (1), 80.
63. *OC*, I (1), 81.
64. *OC*, I (2), 127.
65. *OC*, I (1), 246–47.
66. To Chabrol, 9 June 1831, cited in Pierson, *Tocqueville in America*, p. 129 (emphasis in original).
67. *OC*, I (1), 249.
68. *OC*, I (2), 105.
69. *OC*, I (2), 105.
70. *OC*, I (2), 106.
71. Tocqueville was critical of the "extreme" division of labor in economic life, saying that it "materialized" men and left them soulless. *OC*, I (1), 421.
72. *OC*, I (1), 66, 67.
73. *OC*, I (1), 93 (Tocqueville emphasized "political" in the original).
74. *OC*, I (1), 95.
75. *OC*, I (1), 247.
76. *OC*, I (1), 66–67.
77. *OC*, I (2), 304.
78. *OC*, I (1), 50, 51.
79. *OC*, I (2), 110.
80. *OC*, I (2), 138, 223–24.
81. *OC*, I (1), 166.
82. *OC*, I (1), 322–23.
83. This appears most strikingly in Rousseau's conception of a civil religion. See *Du contrat social*, IV.8.
84. *OC*, V (1), 206.
85. *OC*, I (2), 304–5.
86. To Kergorlay, 29 June 1831, *OC*, XIII (1), 235.
87. *OC*, I (1), 323. Tocqueville would repeat this same language when he was about to begin work on *L'ancien régime*. See his letter to Corcelle, 17 Sept. 1853, *OC*, XV (2), 81. A detailed discussion of the concept can be found in Lively, *The Social and Political thought of Alexis de Tocqueville*, 52–70, 236–39.
88. *OC*, I (1), 321.
89. *OC*, I (1), 281.
90. *OC*, I (1), 286.

91. *OC*, I (1), 300. Although Tocqueville did not elaborate on the connection between his usage of *moeurs* and *mores* we might note that among the ancient Roman republicans the phrase *mos maiorum* (*mos* is the singular of *mores*), which stood for ancestral custom, was an important element in the ideology of the *optimates* or ruling aristocracy. It was frequently invoked as an appeal to ancient precedents and practices against the claims of newer social elements and their demands for greater inclusion. It was captured in a fragment of Ennius much favored by Cicero, "On the customs and men of old the Roman state is founded." Cited in Donald Earl, *The Moral and Political Tradition of Rome* (Ithaca: Cornell University Press, 1967), p. 28; see also pp. 30–38.

92. This aspect of Tocqueville's formulation has been used by Robert Bellah et al., *Habits of the Heart: Individualism and Commitment in American Life* (Berkeley: University of California Press, 1985).

93. *OC*, I (1), 300, 317–18.

94. *OC*, I (1), 443–44.

95. *OC*, I (1), 281.

96. *OC*, I (1), 45.

97. Ibid.

98. *OC*, I (1), 51.

99. *OC*, I (1), 47.

100. *OC*, I (1), 48.

101. *OC*, I (1), 50.

102. *OC*, I (1), 48.

103. *OC*, I (1), 51.

104. *OC*, I (1), 52.

105. *OC*, I (1), 507–8.

106. *OC*, I (1), 322.

107. *OC*, I (1), 249.

108. *OC*, I (1), 59.

109. *OC*, I (1), 342.

## Chapter XI
## Feudal America

1. *OC*, I (1), 429.

2. Ibid.

3. *OC*, V (1), 195.

4. *OC*, I (1), 160–61.

5. *OC*, I (1), 161.

6. *OC*, I (1), 274.

7. The most suggestive and influential work, which drew heavily on Tocqueville, was Louis Hartz's *The Liberal Tradition in America* (New York: Harcourt, Brace, 1955).

8. The expression of feudalism among various southern writers is treated at length in ibid., especially pp. 145–200. There are some suggestive comments on the planter economy in Joyce Appleby, *Capitalism and a New Social Order: The Republican Vision of the 1790s* (New York: New York University Press, 1984). The "society of fealties" is a phrase used by Mousnier, *The Institutions of France under the Absolute Monarchy, 1598–1789: Society and the State*, 1:99.

9. Tocqueville's letter to Kergorlay of 29 June 1831 stresses the importance of revising the Napoleonic system of centralized control over local governments. *OC*, XIII (1), 233–34.

10. *The Discourses*, ed. Bernard Crick, tr. Leslie J. Walker, with revisions by Brian Richardson (Harmondsworth: Penguin, 1974), I.1, p. 101. In his famous exhortation at the end of *The Prince* where Machiavelli exhorts the Medici to liberate and unite Italy, he describes its present condition as "more scattered than the Athenians" (*che gli Ateniesi fussero dispersi*). *Il Principe*, ed. L. Arthur Burd (Oxford: Clarendon Press, 1891, 1968), ch. 26.

11. Machiavelli, *Il Principe*, ch. 5, p. 205.

12. Hobbes, *Leviathan*, ch. 25.

13. *OC*, V (1), 90.

14. *OC*, I (1), 98.

15. *OC*, I (2), 329.

16. *OC*, I (1), 275–80. Toward the end of his account of the ideology of lawyers Tocqueville acknowledged that "it is especially in England that one can see in a striking way this legal type which I am attempting to depict." *OC*, I (1), 279.

17. *OC*, I (2), 330.

18. "[T]he rich (industrialists) do not have a corporate spirit or common objects, neither common hopes nor traditions. There are limbs but no body." *OC*, I (2), 166.

19. *OC*, I (2), 166, 167.

20. See my essays, "Montesquieu and Publius: The Crisis of Reason in the *Federalist*" and "E pluribus unum: The Representation of Difference and the Constitution of Collectivity," in *Presence of the Past*, pp. 100–119, 120–36.

21. *OC*, I (1), 326, 327.

22. *OC*, I (1), 327, 328.

23. *OC*, I (1), 308, 309.

24. *OC*, I (1), 304, 305.

25. *OC*, I (1), 305.

26. *OC*, I (1), 304.

27. *OC*, I (1), 305.

28. *OC*, V (1), 97–102; *OC*, I (1), 40–42, 306.

29. *OC*, I (1), 302, 303.

30. *OC*, I (2), 117.

31. *OC*, I (2), 123.

32. *OC*, I (1), 195, 197–98.

33. *Federalist*, no. 17, p. 108.

34. Ibid., pp. 108–9; no. 45, pp. 310–11.

35. *OC*, I (2), 122–23.

36. *OC*, I (2), 125–26.

37. *OC*, I (1), 171.

38. Ibid.

39. *OC*, I (1), 189.

40. *OC*, I (2), 113–17; *Federalist*, no. 10, p. 61. See in this connection: J.A.W. Gunn, *Politics and the Public Interest in the Seventeenth Century* (London: Routledge, 1969). David Hume's essay, "Of Parties in General," is crucial to understanding the ideology of "factions." See David Miller, *Philosophy and Ideology in Hume's Political Thought*

(Oxford: Clarendon Press, 1981), pp. 173ff. For the background to *Federalist* thinking, see Douglas Adair, *Fame and the Founding Fathers*, ed. Trevor Colbourn (New York: Norton, 1974), especially essays 3 and 4. Madison's emphasis on the value of social fragmentation is illustrated by the following: "Whilst all authority in [the federal republic] will be derived from and dependent upon the society, the society itself will be broken into so many parts, interests, and classes of citizens that the rights of individuals or of the minority, will be in little danger from interested combinations of the majority." Note in the quotation how Madison begins from an assumption of a unified society when he wants to establish legitimate authority but slides to a "broken" one when he wants to block the majority.

## Chapter XII
## Majority Rule or Majority Politics

1. Aristotle, *Politics*, VIII.7.1279b8–10.

2. *OC*, I (1), 176.

3. Aristotle, *Politics*, III.7.1279a32–1279b10; V.5.1304b20–35.

4. For a highly suggestive exploration of the political in ancient Greece and its contrasts and comparisons with modern understandings see Christian Meier, *The Greek Discovery of Politics*, tr. David McLintock (Cambridge, Mass.: Harvard University Press, 1990), pp. 13–25.

5. Aristotle, *Politics*, III.7.1279a22–1279b10.

6. Cicero, *De re publica*, I.xxxiv.53.

7. See the fine study by Ober, *Mass and Elite in Democratic Athens: Rhetoric, Ideology, and the Power of the People*.

8. One of the rare defenses of democracy, although not advocating it, can be found in Cicero's *De re publica*, I.xxxi–xxxii.

9. For a stimulating application of the notion of ideology to the Protestant Reformation in France, see Donald R. Kelley, *The Beginning of Ideology: Consciousness and Society in the French Reformation* (Cambridge: Cambridge University Press, 1981).

10. Locke, *Two Treatises of Government*, II.212.

11. Ibid., II.95.

12. In my reference to "goods," I am following the interpretation that locates Locke's origins of private property in the state of nature. See C. B. Macpherson, *The Political Theory of Possessive Individualism* (Oxford: Oxford University Press, 1962), pp. 197ff; Leo Strauss, *Natural Right and History* (Chicago: University of Chicago Press, 1953), pp. 234ff.; and see James Tully, *A Discourse of Property* (Cambridge: Cambridge University Press, 1980).

13. Locke, *Two Treatises of Government*, II.96.

14. Locke emphasized that one of the major justifications for rebellion was if the executive interfered with elections or altered the legislature. Ibid., II.216, 222.

15. Ibid., II.132. Locke did not endorse democracy but he did incorporate several ideas advanced by democrats during the civil wars. See Ashcraft, *Revolutionary Politics and Locke's "Two Treatises of Government,"* ch. 4.

16. For a Tocquevillean contrast between the two revolutions that emphasizes the American success and the French failure in stabilizing revolution, see Patrice Higonnet, *Sister Republics: The Origins of French and American Republicanism* (Cambridge, Mass.: Harvard University Press, 1988).

17. For the reception abroad of the American Revolution and constitution making, see R. R. Palmer, *The Age of the Democratic Revolution: A Political History of Europe and America, 1760–1800* (Princeton: Princeton University Press, 1959), 1:206–10, 239–82.

18. Locke, *Two Treatises of Government*, II.98.

19. Ibid., II.96.

20. See the valuable study by Gunn, *Politics and the Public Interest in the Seventeenth Century*, and Albert O. Hirschman, *The Passions and the Interests: Political Arguments for Capitalism before Its Triumph* (Princeton: Princeton University Press, 1977), especially pt. 1.

21. *A Letter concerning Toleration*, p. 155. I have used the text included in J. W. Gough's edition of *The Second Treatise of Civil Government* (Oxford: Blackwell, 1948). Locke was far less tolerant of disagreement about political "fundamentals." See *Letter*, pp. 154–56.

22. *Federalist*, no. 10, p. 59.

23. Ibid., pp. 58–59.

24. Ibid.

25. On these matters, see Richard Hofstadter, *The Idea of a Party System: The Rise of Legitimate Opposition in the United States, 1780–1840* (Berkeley: University of California Press, 1970), pp. 56–63.

26. *Federalist*, no. 85, p. 592.

27. *Federalist*, no. 10, p. 64; no. 51, p. 351; no. 62, p. 418; no. 63, p. 425.

28. I have followed the text in Marvin Meyers, ed., *The Mind of the Founder* (Indianapolis: Bobbs-Merrill, 1973), p. 529.

29. *OC*, I (1), 177.

30. *OC*, I (1), 257.

31. *OC*, I (1), 271, n. 6.

32. *OC*, I (1), 258.

33. *OC*, I (1), 261.

34. In his discussion of the current controversy over the chartering of the national bank, Tocqueville did see a "blind democratic instinct" at work in the opposition, but he also described the main struggle as one between "the provinces and the central power." *OC*, I (1), 406–7. Tocqueville's remarks suggest a certain perplexity when what he sees as feudal elements in the state and local opposition to a national bank colliding with the centralizing program of an American "aristocrat" like Nicholas Biddle.

35. *OC*, I (1), 265–67.

36. *OC*, I (1), 265.

37. *OC*, I (1), 271.

38. *OC*, I (1), pt. 2, ch. 5 and pp. 260–61, 269–70.

39. Cited in Wood, *The Radicalism of the American Revolution*, p. 299. (emphasis in original).

40. Jefferson was notoriously hostile to parties. Wood, *The Radicalism of the American Revolution*, p. 298. See also Edmund S. Morgan, *Inventing the People: The Rise of Popular Sovereignty in England and America* (New York: Norton, 1988), pp. 304–5.

41. See Hofstadter, *The Idea of a Party System*, pp. 74ff.

42. *OC*, I (1), 171.

43. *OC*, I (1), 178.

44. The same distinction was being developed almost contemporaneously by Marx. See in particular the essay of 1844 "Critical Marginal Notes on the Article 'The King of

Prussia and Social Reform. By a Prussian,'" in Karl Marx and Frederick Engels, *Collected Works* (New York: International Publishers, 1975), 3:189–206.

45. *OC*, I (1), 178, 179.

46. I have adopted a literal translation of *grand* and *petit* instead of the customary rendering "great" and "small" because it brings out both the element of contempt Tocqueville had for the latter and the element of *grandeur* he was always searching for and which he would discover even among actors and movements he detested.

47. *OC*, I (1), 179.

48. *OC*, I (1), 181.

49. *Federalist*, no. 72, p. 489. See also the fine title-essay in Adair's *Fame and the Founding Fathers*, pp. 3–26.

50. *OC*, I (1), 409–11.

51. *OC*, I (1), 69.

52. *OC*, I (1), 401.

53. *OC*, I (1), 162ff.

54. *OC*, I (1), 137.

55. Ibid.

56. *OC*, I (1), 139–40.

57. *OC*, I (2), 110.

58. *OC*, I (1), 194–95.

59. *OC*, I (2), 330.

60. See Ozouf, *Festivals and the French Revolution.*

61. *OC*, I (1), 166.

62. *OC*, I (1), 383–84.

63. *OC*, I (1), 246–47.

## Chapter XIII
## Centralization and Dissolution

1. *OC*, I (1), 412.

2. *OC*, I (1), 87–88.

3. *OC*, I (1), 88.

4. *OC*, I (1), 70.

5. *OC*, I (1), 90.

6. *OC*, I (1), 92–93; Schleifer, *The Making of Tocqueville's "Democracy in America,"* pp. 127–28, 183–84.

7. *OC*, I (1), 88.

8. *OC*, I (1), 70, 72.

9. OC, V (2), 49. Tocqueville's mention of a third volume refers to the fact that the first installment of *Democracy* was in two volumes.

10. Leonard D. White, *The "Federalists": A Study in Administrative History* (New York: Macmillan, 1948), pp. 267–90, 507–16.

11. *OC*, I (1), 271.

12. In the second volume of *Democracy* Tocqueville dropped the association of centralization with state legislatures. For the evidence in this matter see Schleifer, *The Making of Tocqueville's "Democracy in America,"* pp. 166–68.

13. *OC*, I (1), 394.

14. On the growing weakness of the federal government, see *OC*, I (1), 401, 411.

15. *OC*, I (1), 407.
16. *OC*, I (1), 405–6.
17. *OC*, I (1), 389, 390.
18. *OC*, I (1), 393.
19. *OC*, I (1), 390–4.
20. *OC*, I (1), 390.
21. *OC*, I (1), 390–1.
22. *OC*, I (1), 331.
23. There are surprisingly few analyses of this chapter by political theorists. An exception is Ralph Lerner, *The Thinking Revolutionary: Principle and Practice in the New Republic* (Ithaca: Cornell University Press, 1987), pp. 174–91. See David Brion Davis, *The Problem of Slavery in Western Culture* (Ithaca: Cornell University Press, 1966), and Robert William Fogel, *Without Contract or Consent: The Rise and Fall of American Slavery* (New York: Norton, 1989), pp. 263, 308.
24. Schleifer, *The Making of Tocqueville's "Democracy in America,"* p. 66ff; Jean-Claude Lamberti, *Tocqueville and the Two Democracies*, tr. Arthur Goldhammer (Cambridge, Mass.: Harvard University Press, 1989), p. 228.
25. In his interviews with Americans, the question of slavery appears several times, which suggests that the topic was present virtually from the outset. The references are conveniently indexed under "Negroes" in Mayer's English edition of *Journey to America*.
26. *OC*, I (1), 357.
27. *OC*, I (1), 379.
28. See Hartz, *The Liberal Tradition in America*, pp. 167ff; and for objections, see Anne Norton, *Alternative Americas* (Chicago: University of Chicago Press, 1986), pp. 3–4, and Rogers M. Smith, *Civic Ideals: Conflicting Visions of Citizenship in U.S. History* (New Haven: Yale University Press, 1997), pp. 17ff.
29. *OC*, V (1), 98.
30. *OC*, I (1), 372.
31. *OC*, I (1), 346.
32. *OC*, V (1), 149.
33. *OC*, V (1), 99.
34. *OC*, I (1), 331.
35. From the evidence of Tocqueville's unpublished notes, Schleifer has concluded that Tocqueville had been even more convinced of the dissolution of the Union than he let on in *Democracy*. See *The Making of Tocqueville's "Democracy in America,"* pp. 103–11.
36. *OC*, I (1), 166–72.
37. *OC*, I (1), 412.
38. Ibid.
39. *OC*, I (1), 412, 413.
40. *OC*, I (1), 417.
41. *OC*, I (1), 392–93.
42. *OC*, I (1), 332.
43. *OC*, I (1), 355.
44. *OC*, I (1), 332–34.
45. *OC*, I (1), 377. Tocqueville played a leading role in the movement, which aimed at abolishing slavery in the French West Indies. He did not advocate an immediate end to slavery but a policy of gradualism. It provided for a "preparatory period" in which slaves were required to work in the labor force and for a fixed period were to be denied

the right to own land. The guiding principle was not to prepare the slave for citizenship but for incorporation into the work force. There is a helpful discussion of these matters in Drescher, *Dilemmas of Democracy*, ch. 6. Tocqueville's speeches and writings on the subject are conveniently assembled in Drescher, *Tocqueville and Beaumont on Social Reform*, pt. 3.

46. Later historians have mostly denied Tocqueville's account and argued that the slaves developed and perpetuated a distinctive culture. See, for example, Eugene Genovese, *Roll, Jordan, Roll: The World the Slaves Made* (New York: Pantheon, 1972).

47. *OC*, I (1), 376.

48. *OC*, I (1), 293.

49. *OC*, V (1), 123–24.

50. *OC*, I (1), 317; V (1), 353.

51. *OC*, V (1), 209.

52. *OC*, V (1), 353.

53. *OC*, V (1), 354.

54. *OC*, I (1), 430.

55. *OC*, I (1), 426, 428–29.

56. *OC*, I (1), 430, 431.

## Chapter XIV
## The Image of Democracy

1. *OC*, I (1), 323.

2. *OC*, I (1), 249, 317.

3. Later, in writing *L'ancien régime*, Tocqueville would discover in the provincial institutions of Languedoc a French equivalent of New England.

4. *OC*, I (1), 202.

5. *OC*, I (1), 12.

6. *OC*, I (2), 262.

7. "In New England, where education and liberty are the offsprings of morality and religion, where society, already old and well established, has been able to form rules and habits, and yet escape from all the superiorities which wealth and birth have always created among men," the inhabitants have "become accustomed to respect intellectual and moral superiority and to submit to them without resentment." But, Tocqueville continued, as one traveled south the principles of morality, liberty, and religion were less happily combined. Worst of all were the "new states" of the southwestern United States: they were "agglomerations of adventurers and speculators." *OC*, I (1), 206–7.

8. *OC*, I (1), 421.

9. *OC*, I (1), 92.

10. *OC*, I (1), 274.

11. These are at the beginning of ch. 5, in *Democracy in America*, vol. 1, pt. 2.

12. *OC*, I (1), 202.

13. *OC*, I (1), 247.

14. Ibid.

15. *OC*, I (1), 243.

16. *OC*, I (1), 245.

17. *OC*, I (1), 203–4.

18. *OC*, I (1), 204–5.
19. *OC*, I (1), 268.
20. *OC*, I (1), 177.
21. *OC*, I (1), 51.
22. *OC*, I (1), 177.
23. *OC*, I (1), 297.
24. *OC*, I (1), 329.
25. *OC*, I (1), 324.
26. *OC*, I (1), 241.
27. "The Americans have certainly not solved this problem [of organizing democracy] but they have furnished some useful lessons to those who wish to resolve it." *OC*, I (I), 326.
28. *OC*, I (1), 207.
29. *OC*, I (1), 412.
30. Ibid.
31. *OC*, I (1), 413–17.
32. *OC*, I (1), 325.
33. *OC*, I (1), 412, 413.
34. *OC*, I (1), 324.
35. *OC*, I (1), 325–26.
36. *OC*, I (1), 323.
37. *OC*, I (1), 300, 319, n. 8.
38. *OC*, I (1), 322.
39. Ibid.
40. *OC*, I (1), 323.

## Chapter XV
## Tragic Hero, Popular Mask

1. To Beaumont, 9 July 1837, *OC*, VIII (1), 208.
2. See J. P. Mayer, *Alexis de Tocqueville: A Biographical Essay in Political Science*, tr. M. M. Bozman and C. Hahn (New York: Viking, 1940), p. 36 and especially the edition of *Democracy*, ed. Phillips Bradley (New York: Knopf, 1945), 1:xxiff. Also helpful is René Rémond, *Les Etats-Unis devant l'opinion française, 1815–1852*, 2 vols. (Paris: Librarie Armand Colin, 1962), 1:377ff.
3. "My intention was to describe in a second part the influence which is exercised in America by equality of conditions and the government of democracy upon civil society, customs, ideas, and *moeurs*; but I began to feel less zeal for carrying out this project." *OC*, I (1), 12.
4. To Royer-Collard, 23 June 1838, *OC*, XI, 64.
5. There is a fine discussion of that journey and its influence in Seymour Drescher, *Tocqueville and England* (Cambridge, Mass.: Harvard University Press, 1964).
6. To Beaumont, 13 Aug. 1833, *OC*, VIII (1), 126.
7. This theme is played out in Henry James's *The American*. A Tocquevillean American encounters French aristocracy.
8. Lamberti cites a crucial passage from Tocqueville's notes that had been intended as a preface to volume 2. There Tocqueville asserts that he has created two ideal repre-

sentations, one of democracy, the other of aristocracy, and that he had deliberately pressed their consequences to the limits. He intended to leave it to the reader to determine Tocqueville's own opinion. *Tocqueville and the Two Democracies,* p. 25.

9. To Beaumont, 8 Oct. 1839, *OC,* VIII (1), 380.

10. To Mill, 9 Nov. 1836, *OC,* VI (1), 314; to Beaumont, 8 July 1838, *OC,* VIII (1), 310.

11. To Beaumont, 8 July 1838, *OC,* VIII (1), 310; to Edouard de Tocqueville, Nov. 1840, *OC* (B), VI, 106–8.

12. *OC,* I (2), 49.

13. To Royer-Collard, 6 Apr. 1838, *OC,* XI, 59. See also the letter to Beaumont, 26 May 1837, *OC,* VIII (1), 191–92.

14. To Mill, 18 Dec. 1840, *OC,* VI (1), 330.

15. Seymour Drescher, "Tocqueville's Two *Démocraties,*" *Journal of the History of Ideas* 25 (April–June, 1964): 201–16. Drescher's title somewhat overstates the claims he actually makes. These have more to do with emphasis than with a diremption. For example, that volume 1 emphasizes the dynamic threat of democracy (pp. 203–4) while volume 2 stresses stagnation; that centralization moves to the foreground of volume 2 (p. 212). See also Schleifer, *The Making of Tocqueville's "Democracy in America,"* pp. 281ff. and Lamberti, *Tocqueville and the Two Democracies,* pp. 51, 52.

16. Schleifer's chapter on the second volume is entitled "Tocqueville's Return to America." See also the earlier article by the great scholar of Tocqueville, George W. Pierson, "Le 'second voyage' de Tocqueville en Amérique," *Livre du Centenaire* (1959): pp. 71–86.

17. *OC,* I (1), 289.

18. To Royer-Collard, 15 Aug 1838, *OC,* XI, 67.

19. Levi-Strauss, *Tristes Tropiques,* p. 384.

20. The idea of *un promeneur* may have been an allusion to Rousseau's *Réveries du promeneur solitaire.*

21. To Kergorlay, 4 July 1837, *OC,* XIII (1), 459–60.

22. 10 Nov. 1836, *OC,* XIII (1), 418.

23. 5 Aug. 1836, *OC,* XIII (1), 388–89; 22 Apr. 1838, *OC,* VIII (1), 292; 8 Aug. 1838, *OC,* XIII (2), 41. David Brian Davis, *Slavery and Human Progress* (New York: Oxford University Press, 1984)

24. To Beaumont, 22 Apr. 1838, *OC,* VIII (1), 293; *OC,* XI, 21.

25. 18 Mar. 1838, *OC,* XIII (2), 26, 27.

26. *OC,* I (2), 152. Tocqueville would defend *un matérialisme honnête* against an extreme asceticism. To Kergorlay, 5 Aug. 1836, *OC,* XIII (1), 388.

27. Machiavelli's influence on Tocqueville has largely gone unremarked, probably because of the latter's dismissive remarks in his correspondence. Nonetheless, Machiavelli's mark is apparent in the military discussions in *Democracy,* vol. 2, pt. 3, chs. 22–26. Tocqueville appears to have missed the Florentine's deep concern with political renewal and to have been unacquainted with the *Discorsi.* See my discussion of Machiavelli in *Politics and Vision,* pp. 195–238.

28. To Royer-Collard, 25 Aug. 1836, *OC,* XI, 19–21; to Kergorlay, 5 Aug. 1836, *OC,* XIII (1), 389.

29. Machiavelli might have added the qualification that American Christianity did not directly encourage the military virtues necessary to a republic. Tocqueville believed that in a war democracy might be effective in the short run but not in a protracted struggle. *OC,* I (1), 231–33; *OC,* I (2), 270–92.

30. To Corcelle, 11 Mar. 1839, *OC*, XV (1), 135.
31. To Corcelle, 18 Sept. 1839, *OC*, XV (1), 135.
32. 9 July 1837, *OC*, VIII (1), 207, 208.
33. *OC*, III (2), 46.
34. 20 Nov. 1838, *OC*, XI, 74.
35. 6 Jan. 1839, *OC*, VIII (1), 331.
36. 4 Oct. 1838, *OC*, XIII (1), 479.
37. To Royer-Collard, 15 Aug. 1840, *OC*, XI, 89–90.
38. To Beaumont, 22 Apr. 1838, *OC*, VIII (1), 292.
39. To Corcelle, 19 Mar. 1838, *OC*, XV (1), 97.
40. To Royer-Collard, 14 Nov. 1837, *OC*, XI, 52–53.
41. M. M. Bakhtin, *The Dialogic Imagination: Four Essays*, ed. Michael Holquist, tr. Caryl Emerson and Michael Holquist (Austin: University of Texas Press, 1981) pp. 34–37.
42. Tocqueville's electoral letter can be found in *OC*, III (2), 41ff.
43. Letters of Sept. 12 and 14, 1837, *OC* (B), VI, 74–75, 76–77.
44. 12 Nov. 1837, *OC*, VIII (1), 262, 263.
45. To Beaumont, 22 Apr. 1838, *OC*, VIII (1), 292 and note.
46. To Beaumont, 21 Mar. 1838, *OC*, VIII (1), 284.
47. To Beaumont, 22 Apr. 1838, *OC*, VIII (1), 291–92.
48. To Stoffels, 7 Mar. 1839, *OC* (B.), V, 439.
49. To Stoffels, 14 July 1840, *OC* (B.), V, 442–43.
50. To Stoffels, Oct. 1843, *OC* (B), V, 450. For Tocqueville's irritation with politics, see his letter to Beaumont, 16 Nov. 1842, *OC*, VIII (1), 483; to Royer-Collard, 8 Aug. 1839, *OC*, XI, 81; to Stoffels, 3 Apr. 1844, *OC* (B), V, 451.
51. 27 Sept. 1841, *OC*, XI, 107.
52. 8 Aug. 1839, *OC*, XI, 79.

## Chapter XVI
## The Democratization of Culture

1. 15 Aug. 1838, *OC*, XI, 67. See also letters to Beaumont, 30 Sept. 1838, *OC*, VIII (1), 317; to Mill, *OC*, VI (1), 326. For a good discussion of the complexities of the structure of the second volume, see Lamberti, *Tocqueville and the Two Democracies*, pp. 168–92.
2. *OC*, I (2), 7.
3. 30 Aug. 1838, *OC*, XI, 71.
4. Cited in Drescher, *Dilemmas of Democracy*, p. 31, n. 11.
5. *OC*, I (2), 7.
6. *OC*, I (2), 299.
7. *OC*, I (2), 7. Schleifer has noted that in the original design of *Democracy*, Tocqueville had envisaged it divided into three parts, "political society," "civil society," and "religious society." *The Making of Tocqueville's "Democracy in America,"* pp. 7ff.
8. *OC*, I (2), 201, n. 1.
9. *OC*, I (2), 299.
10. *OC*, I (2), 18.
11. See Black, *Guilds and Society in European Political Thought from the Twelfth Century to the Present*.
12. *OC*, V (1), 279.

13. This is made more explicit in a draft of Tocqueville's preface to volume 2: "In order to make myself understood, I am constantly obliged to consider extreme states: aristocracy unalloyed with democracy, democracy unalloyed with aristocracy. At times I attribute to one or the other of these two principles effects more far-reaching than they generally produce, because in general they do not exist in isolation. The reader must judge for himself how much of what I say is my true opinion and how much is said in order to make myself understood." Cited in Lamberti, *Tocqueville and the Two Democracies*, p. 25.

14. *OC*, I (2), 324.

15. *OC*, I (2), 8.

16. The sole exception occurs in a footnote in which Tocqueville, anticipating his thesis of *L'ancien régime* asserts that the revolution did not create centralization. *OC*, I (1), 447–48.

17. *OC*, I (2), 72.

18. *OC*, I (2), 70.

19. For further discussion of myth, see my "Postmodern Politics and the Absence of Myth," *Social Research* 52, no. 2 (Summer 1985): 217–39.

20. *OC*, I (2), 70, 71.

21. *OC*, I (2), 90.

22. *OC*, I (2), 18.

23. The first chapter concerns "the philosophical method of the Americans"; the second deals with the main sources of belief among democratic peoples; the third and fourth chapters discuss the role of general ideas in America and France; the fifth and sixth concern religion; the seventh, "pantheism"; and the eighth, the idea of human perfectibility.

24. *OC*, I (1), 300.

25. Ibid.

26. *OC*, I (2), 25.

27. *OC*, I (2), 38.

28. See Francis Oakley, *Omnipotence, Covenant, and Order: An Excursion in the History of Ideas from Abelard to Leibniz* (Ithaca: Cornell University Press, 1984), pp. 93ff. Also the earlier work by Erik Peterson, *Theologische Traktate* (Munich: Hochland, 1951), pp. 45–147 ("Der Monotheismus als politisches Problem."). For the shift from a religious cosmology to a secular, individual-oriented society, see Stephen L. Collins, *From Divine Cosmos to Sovereign State* (Oxford: Oxford University Press, 1989).

29. *OC*, I (2), 298.

30. *OC*, I (2), 37, 38.

31. Ibid.

32. *OC*, I (2), 79.

33. *OC*, I (2), 22.

34. *OC*, I (2), 23.

35. *OC*, I (2), 22.

36. *OC*, I (2), 41, 42, 43.

37. On the matter of Tocqueville as a precursor of "ideal-type" analysis, it needs to be emphasized that unlike Weber's conception of ideal-types, which sought (not always successfully) to avoid including normative elements, Tocqueville's "aristocracy" and "democracy" are both loaded notions. My suggestion is that the perceptiveness of Tocqueville's uses of them depends on their normative character.

38. *OC*, I (2), 62, 63.
39. *OC*, I (2), 101–2.
40. *OC*, I (2), 44, 43.
41. *OC*, I (2), 43.
42. *OC*, I (2), 150.
43. *OC*, I (2), 150–51.
44. *OC*, I (2), 83.
45. *OC*, I (2), 335.
46. "Salutary fear" is evocative of the ancient argument that true courage requires an element of healthy fear, not great enough to paralyze the actor but sufficient to prevent foolhardiness. Tocqueville does not mention courage and, more important, even if he assumes it, he does so within the framework set by fear rather than (as the ancients did) the other way round. See Aristotle, *Nicomachean Ethics*, III. 6–7.1115a7–1116a15.
47. *OC*, I (2), 146.
48. *OC*, I (2), 147. Tocqueville's portrait of democratic desire has some of the same elements that Plato ascribed to the tyrant; but the latter is depicted as assailed by conflicting desires and reduced to inaction. Plato, *Republic*, IX.571ff.
49. *OC*, I (2), 148.
50. *OC*, I (2), 110.
51. *OC*, I (2), 103.
52. Ibid.
53. *OC*, I (2), 104.
54. *OC*, I (2), 103.
55. *OC*, I (2), 101.
56. *OC*, I (2), 104.
57. *OC*, I (2), 29.
58. Tocqueville was cooler toward American religiosity in his private correspondence. He was amused and astonished at the rituals of some of the smaller sects, and he expressed doubts about the depth of American religious beliefs. Although he admired the political effects of American religions, it is not at all clear that he succeeded in explaining them. For some of his reactions, see his letter to Kergorlay, 29 June 1831, *OC*, XIII (1), 225ff.; to his mother, 17 July 1831, *OC*, XIV, 115ff. The Kergorlay letter is mostly reproduced in Pierson, *Tocqueville in America*, pp. 152ff.
59. *OC*, I (1), 311, 312.
60. *OC*, I (1), 310; *OC*, I (2), 29.
61. *OC*, I (1), 308.
62. *OC*, I (1), 304.
63. This is a mytheme as old as Eusebius of Caeserea in his *De laudibus Constantia* (335/6 C.E.). See the edition by H. A. Drake, *In Praise of Constantine: A Historical Study and New Translation of Eusebius' Tricennial Orations* (Berkeley: University of California Press, 1976).
64. *OC*, I (2), 30–31.
65. *OC*, I (2), 320. This formulation will be repeated in *L'ancien régime*.
66. *OC*, I (2), 155.
67. *OC*, I (2), 156.
68. *OC*, I (2), 14.
69. To Stoffels, 29 July 1836, *OC* (B), V, 432.
70. *OC*, I (2), 80.

71. Ibid.
72. *OC*, I (2), 33.
73. Ibid.
74. *OC*, I (2), 151.
75. In a broad sense Tocqueville may be said to have anticipated Weber's observation that Americans practiced an "inner-worldly asceticism" that helps to produce an ascetic materialism. Max Weber, "The Protestant Sects and the Spirit of Capitalism," *From Max Weber*, ed. and tr. C. Wright Mills (New York: Oxford University Press, 1946), pp. 302–22.
76. *OC*, I (2), 140.
77. *OC*, I (2), 140–41.
78. *OC*, I (2), 150–51.
79. *OC*, I (2), 153.
80. *OC*, I (2), 217.
81. *OC*, V (1), 93.
82. The American woman was primarily the creation of volume 2. In volume 1 of *Democracy*, she is mentioned only in passing, and, although her role as moral educator was alluded to, there is no chapter or section devoted mainly to her. In volume 2, however, there is a block of five chapters (part 3, chs. 8–12) that deals exclusively with women or with their family roles.
83. *OC*, V (1), 46.
84. *OC*, I (2), 207.
85. Ibid.
86. *OC*, I (2), 206, 207.
87. *OC*, I (2), 220.
88. *OC*, I (2), 220–21.
89. *OC*, I (2), 106.
90. *OC*, I (1), 305.
91. *OC*, I (2), 222.
92. *OC*, V (1), 354.
93. *OC*, I (2), 208.
94. Ibid.
95. *OC*, I (2), 209.
96. *OC*, I (2), 222.
97. *OC*, I (2), 219.
98. *OC*, I (2), 216.
99. *OC*, I (2), 205.
100. *OC*, I (2), 220.
101. Ibid.
102. *OC*, I (2), 212, 214.
103. *OC*, I (2), 216.
104. *OC*, I (2), 217.
105. *OC*, I (2), 218.
106. There are, of course, exceptions to this rough classification. Rousseau was clearly closer to the conservative camp, as was John Stuart Mill in the essay on Coleridge.
107. The forerunner in the reification of culture could be said to be the Protestant Reformation. The reformers had clearly defined the contours of "religion," specifying

not only beliefs, practices, and institutions and the church's location in society and relation to political authority, but also rendering the belief systems transportable.

108. *OC*, I (2), 156, 157. Tocqueville's formulation appears like a Catholic version of Weber's thesis about the Protestant origins of the capitalist dynamic, except that Tocqueville was not concerned with the ways that religion might promote the development of a capitalist ethic of postponed gratifications but rather with the reverse: how a capitalist ethic might lead to a more religious outlook among the upper and middle classes. Weber's thesis in *The Protestant Ethic and the Spirit of Capitalism*, tr. Talcott Parsons (London: Allen and Unwin, 1930), would principally be an account of action, of how Calvinist anxieties came to be rechanneled into capital accumulation.

109. *OC*, I (2), 207.

110. *OC*, I (2), 74.

111. *OC*, I (2), 334.

112. *OC*, I (2), 355, 356. Tocqueville's review was presented to the Academy of Moral and Political Sciences. When Tocqueville mentions the United States in his review, he does not mention New England democracy as a worthy example; instead, he recommends the more conservative state constitution of New York. A translation can be found in *Democracy in America*, ed. J.-P. Mayer, tr. George Lawrence (Garden City, N.Y.: Doubleday, 1969).

## Chapter XVII
## Despotism and Utopia

1. *OC*, I (1), 262, 263.

2. There is an excellent discussion of despotism and its historical usages in Roger Boesche, *Theories of Tyranny from Plato to Arendt* (University Park: Pennsylvania State University Press, 1996), especially pp. 167–99. This work also has a careful account of Tocqueville's views on the subject, pp. 201–36. There is a valuable historical discussion of despotism by R. Koebner, "Despot and Despotism: Vicissitudes of a Political Term," *Journal of the Warburg and Courtauld Institutes* 14 (1951): 275–302. See also the helpful account by Melvin Richter, "Despotism," in *Dictionary of the History of Ideas*, 5 vols. (New York: Scribner's, 1974) 2:1–18, and the discussion of enlightened despotism and liberalism in Jardin, *Histoire du libéralisme politique*, pp. 37–58.

3. Montesquieu had argued that a prince who succeeds a republic acquired a greater potential for absolutism than one who might displace an aristocracy. Tocqueville echoes this at *OC*, I (2), 322. In the twentieth century Max Weber would draw on the older tradition of antiquity, in which democracy and tyranny were united in the figure of the demagogue, to develop the ideal type of "democratic Caesarism." Here the popular leader ascends to power by exploiting a mass plebiscite. See "Politics as a Vocation," in *From Max Weber: Essays in Sociology*, p. 106.

4. To be sure, Tocqueville refers to the possibility of a politician who cleverly exploits the modern "fear of anarchy" to establish a despotism, but this is only an incidental remark. Some interpreters have seized on it as a prophecy about Louis Napoleon's despotism. However, on the next page Tocqueville makes virtually the same "prophecy" about a "faction" seizing power. In both cases Tocqueville was merely posing possibilities that in no way formed the crux of his analysis, which concerned the decline and corruption of political life. See *OC*, I (2), 147–48.

5. *OC,* I (2), 322.
6. *OC,* I (2), 324.
7. Still useful is Alfred Cobban, *Dictatorship, Its History and Theory* (London: Cape, 1939); it can be supplemented by Boesche, *Theories of Tyranny from Plato to Arendt.*
8. I discuss benevolent despotism in Chapter 25 on *The Old Regime.*
9. *OC,* I (2), 324.
10. *OC,* I (2), 332, 333.
11. *OC,* I (2), 324.
12. *OC,* I (2), 325.
13. *OC,* I (1), 265, 266.
14. *OC,* I (2), 324.
15. Ibid.
16. Ibid.
17. *OC,* I (2), 323.
18. *OC,* I (2), 146.
19. *OC,* I (2), 147.
20. *OC,* I (2), 125.
21. *OC,* I (2), 109.
22. *OC,* I (2), 122.
23. *OC,* I (2), 114.
24. *OC,* I (2), 123.
25. *OC,* I (2), 112.
26. *OC,* I (2), 109, 110.
27. *OC,* I (2), 243.
28. *OC,* I (2), 164, 166.
29. *OC,* I (2), 163.
30. *OC,* I (2), 160, n. 1.
31. *OC,* I (2), 162.
32. Compare Marx's discussion of "alienated labor," where the laborer's products are taken from him and stand over and against him as an alien object. *Economic and Philosophical Manuscripts of 1844,* section on "Wages of Labor," in Marx and Engels, *Collected Works,* 3:237.
33. *OC,* I (2), 165, 166, 167.
34. *OC,* I (2), 167. Lamberti, *Tocqueville and the Two Democracies,* p. 51, cites several passages from Tocqueville's unpublished notes that portray the middle class as unable to govern. Lamberti argues that Tocqueville suppressed those opinions for fear of being accused of aristocratic prejudice. For a careful discussion of Tocqueville's views of the bourgeoisie, see Roger Boesche, *The Strange Liberalism of Alexis de Tocqueville* (Ithaca: Cornell University Press, 1987), chs. 4–5.
35. *OC,* I (2), 318–19.
36. *OC,* I (2), 314–18. For the phrase *entreprises industrielles,* see *OC,* I (2), 162.
37. *OC,* I (2), 236, 237.
38. *OC,* I (2), 237.
39. *OC,* I (2), 300.
40. *OC,* I (2), 301.
41. *OC,* I (2), 333 (emphasis added).
42. *OC,* I (2), 316.

43. *OC*, I (2), pt. 2, ch. 4, p. 109.
44. *OC*, I (2), 146.
45. *OC*, I (2), 142, 143.
46. *OC*, I (2), 144, 145.
47. *OC*, I (2), 147.
48. *OC*, I (2), 105.
49. *OC*, I (2), 106.
50. See Emmett Kennedy, *A Philosophy of the Age of Revolution: Destutt de Tracy and the Origins of "Ideology"* (Philadelphia: American Philosophical Society, 1978). For a careful study, which explores ideology as a relationship between historical processes and social consciousness, Kelley, *The Beginning of Ideology: Consciousness and Society in the French Reformation*, especially pp. 1–10, 299ff.
51. *OC*, I (2), 46.
52. *OC*, I (2), 11, 105.
53. *OC*, I (2), 39.
54. *OC*, I (2), 53ff.
55. *OC*, I (2), 76, 77.
56. *OC*, I (2), 77, 78.
57. *OC*, I (2), 79.
58. *OC*, I (2), 18.
59. *OC*, I (2), 58.
60. *OC*, I (2), 18.
61. *OC*, I (2), 18, 19.
62. *OC*, I (2), 16.
63. *OC*, I (2), 11.
64. The Lawrence translation of *la méthode* as "approach" obscures the Cartesian allusion. Curiously, Lamberti describes "Tocqueville's philosophy" as "Cartesian in its origins and principal conclusions" and "foundations," yet does not elaborate. Lamberti, *Tocqueville and the Two Democracies*, p. 157.
65. *OC*, I (2), 13.
66. *OC*, I (2), 106.
67. *OC*, I (2), 11.
68. *OC*, I (2), 11, 13.
69. *OC*, I (2), 14.
70. Marx and Engels, *Collected Works*, I:85.
71. *OC*, I (2), 25.
72. *OC*, I (2), 22.
73. *OC*, I (2), 23.
74. *OC*, I (1), 389.
75. "[A] society exists when men consider a great number of objects from the same point of view; when they have the same opinions about a great number of subjects; and when the same facts give rise to the same impressions and the same thoughts." *OC*, I (1), 390.
76. *OC*, I (2), 50.
77. *OC*, I (1), 315. For the Story episode, see Pierson, *Tocqueville in America*, pp. 730–35.
78. *OC*, I (2), 50.

79. For a close discussion, see Trond Berg Eriksen, "*Bios Theoretikos*": *Notes on Aristotle's "Ethica Nicomachea"* X, 6–8 (Oslo: Universitetsforlaget, 1976).
80. *OC*, I (2), 46.
81. *OC*, I (2), 25–26.
82. *OC*, I (1), 267.
83. To Reeve, 15 Nov. 1839, *OC*, VI, 47–48.
84. *OC*, I (2), 48, 50.
85. *OC*, I (2), 48, 49.
86. *OC*, I (2), 47.
87. *OC*, I (2), 23.
88. *OC*, I (2), 47.
89. *OC*, I (2), 51.
90. *OC*, I (2), 48, 50.
91. *OC*, I (2), 48.
92. *OC*, I (2), 46.
93. Robert A. Dahl, *Pluralist Democracy in the United States* (Chicago: Rand, McNally, 1967), p. 56.
94. Bruce Kuklick, *The Rise of American Philosophy: Cambridge, Massachusetts, 1860–1930* (New Haven: Yale University Press, 1977).
95. *OC*, I (2), 265.
96. *OC*, I (2), 264.
97. Karl Marx, *The Critique of Hegel's "Philosophy of Right" Introduction*, in Karl Marx, *Early Writings*, ed., T. B. Bottomore (New York: McGraw-Hill, 1964), p. 58.
98. *OC*, I (2), 166.
99. Frederick Winslow Taylor's *The Principles of Scientific Management* (1911); New York: Norton, 1967), pp. 45, 46, presented a worker who seems a lineal descendant of Tocqueville's brute. See Taylor's account of a conversation in which he instructs "the mentally sluggish type of worker" that if he wishes to make more money, he "has to do exactly as he's told from morning till night." The cover of the Norton edition features the unironical remark of a scholar that "Taylor's book is not merely the precursor of modern organization and decision theory, it is in many respects its origin."

## Chapter XVIII
## Old New World, New Old World

1. *OC*, I (2), 322.
2. *OC*, I (2), 336.
3. *OC*, I (2), 339.
4. *OC*, I (2), 302.
5. *OC*, I (2), 308.
6. *OC*, I (2), 319, 320.
7. *OC*, I (2), 320.
8. *OC*, I (2), 297.
9. *OC*, I (1), 87.
10. *OC*, I (2), 297.
11. *OC*, I (1), 447 (appendix K). Tocqueville's principal theses about centralization and the ambiguities of the French Revolution, which he developed later in *L'ancien régime*, were evident in the early pages of *Democracy*. See especially *OC*, I (1), 97–98 and

the entries under "uniformity" inspired by Tocqueville's journey to England and Ireland, *OC*, V (2), 35.

12. *OC*, I (2), 305.

13. *OC*, I (2), 314.

14. Perry Anderson, *Lineages of the Absolute State* (London: New Left Books, 1971); Lionel Rothkrug, *Opposition to Louis XIV: The Political and Social Origins of the French Enlightenment* (Princeton: Princeton University Press, 1965) especially chs. 1–3; Mousnier, *The Institutions of France under the Absolute Monarchy*, 2:15; Keohane, *Philosophy and the State in France*, chs. 2, 8; Leonard Krieger, *An Essay on the Theory of Enlightened Despotism* (Chicago: University of Chicago Press, 1975); Marc Raeff, *The Well-Ordered Police State: Social and Institutional Change through Law in the Germanies and Russia, 1600–1800* (New Haven: Yale University Press, 1983) pt. 1; Lynton K. Caldwell, *The Administrative Theories of Hamilton and Jefferson* (Chicago: University of Chicago Press, 1944); Leonard D. White, *The Federalists: A Study in Administrative History* (New York: Macmillan, 1948); Theda Skocpol, *States and Social Revolutions* (Cambridge: Cambridge University Press, 1979), especially chs. 4, 5; Joyce Appleby, *Liberalism and Republicanism in the Historical Imagination* (Cambridge, Mass., Harvard University Press, 1992), chs. 1, 3.

15. *OC*, I (2), 319.

16. *OC*, I (2), 313.

17. *OC*, I (2), 304. Typically, Tocqueville qualifies this claim by saying that not all democratic peoples are drawn toward centralization in the same way or at the same time, and that it depends on local circumstances.

18. *OC*, I (2), 302.

19. *OC*, I (2), 303.

20. *OC*, I (2), 304, 305.

21. Pierre Manent, *Tocqueville et la nature de la démocratie* (Paris: Julliard, 1982), p. 74, has shown the importance of "similarity" in Tocqueville's analysis. See *OC*, I (2), 21, 106, 172.

22. *OC*, I (2), 299.

23. *OC*, I (2), 298.

24. *OC*, I (2), 306.

25. Ibid.

26. *OC*, I (2), 307.

27. *OC*, I (2), 306.

28. See Tocqueville's remarks about associations (*OC*, I (2), 296), local government (329–30), press (330–31), judiciary (331–32), and private rights (332).

29. *OC*, I (2), 296.

30. *OC*, I (2), 304.

31. *OC*, I (2), 298.

32. *OC*, I (2), 297.

33. *OC*, I (2), 304.

34. *OC*, I (2), 302.

35. *OC*, I (2), 302, 298.

36. *OC*, I (1), 425.

37. *OC*, I (2), 336.

38. *OC*, I (2), 337.

39. Ibid.

40. *OC*, I (2), 338.
41. *OC*, I (2), 339.
42. Ibid.

## Chapter XIX
## Tocquevillean Democracy

1. *OC*, I (2), 268.
2. *OC*, I (2), 269.
3. *OC*, I (2), 269.
4. *OC*, I (2), 265.
5. *OC*, I (2), 266.
6. *OC*, I (2), 266, n. 1.
7. *OC*, I (2), 258–60.
8. *OC*, I (2), 264.
9. *OC*, I (2), 265.
10. *OC*, I (2), 269.
11. *OC*, I (2), 262.
12. *OC*, I (2), 264.
13. *OC*, I (2), 269.
14. *OC*, I (2), 260, 261.
15. *OC*, I (2), 266.
16. *OC*, I (2), 297.
17. *OC*, I (2), 42–43.
18. *King Henry IV*, pt. 2, introduction, p 18.

## Chapter XX
## The Penitentiary Temptation

1. *OC*, IV (1), 76.

2. There is a helpful introduction by Michelle Perrot in *OC*, IV (1) and invaluable notes accompanying the text. The great work by Pierson remains indispensable; see *Tocqueville in America*, chs. 9, 10, 18, 32, 35, and 54. Seymour Drescher's work is an important exception to the neglect of Tocqueville's thinking about prisons and his practical efforts at reform. See *The Dilemmas of Democracy*, ch. 5. The neglect has been partly remedied by Thomas L. Dumm's engaging *Democracy and Punishment: Disciplinary Origins of the United States* (Madison: University of Wisconsin Press, 1987). The beginnings of American penitentiaries are treated in David J. Rothman, *The Discovery of the Asylum: Social Order and Disorder in the New Republic* (Boston: Little, Brown, 1971), especially pp. 78–108. For discussions in France, see Gordon Wright, *Between the Guillotine and Liberty: Two Centuries of the Crime Problem in France* (New York: Oxford University Press, 1983), especially ch. 3.

3. For details, see Jardin, *Alexis de Tocqueville*, p. 179, and Phillips Bradley's introduction to his edition of *Democracy*, 1:xii and note.

4. See the useful discussion of the collaboration of Tocqueville and Beaumont in Seymour Drescher, ed., *Tocqueville and Beaumont on Social Reform* (New York: Harper, 1968), pp. 201–17.

5. One section of Drescher, *Tocqueville and Beaumont on Social Reform*, pt. 2, con-

tains an abridged version of a speech on prison reform by Tocqueville. Drescher also devotes a long appendix (pp. 201–17) to the collaboration between Tocqueville and Beaumont. On Tocqueville's part in the authorship of *The Penitentiary*, see the remarks of Perrot, *OC*, IV (1), 20–23.

6. Michel Foucault, *Discipline and Punish: The Birth of the Prison*, tr. Alan Sheridan (New York: Pantheon, 1977), p. 318, n. 6. Foucault's views on prisons were elaborated in more popular form in two discussions in *Power/Knowledge: Selected Interviews and Other Writings, 1972–1977*, ed. Colin Gordon (New York: Pantheon, 1980), pp. 1–54. I have critically discussed Foucault as a political thinker in "On the Theory and Practice of Power," in *After Foucault*, ed. Jonathan Arac (New Brunswick, N.J.: Rutgers University Press, 1988) pp. 179–201.

7. See C.B.A. Behrens, *The Ancien Régime* (London: Thames and Hudson, 1984), pp. 119–84; Keith M. Baker, *Condorcet: From Natural Philosophy to Social Mathematics* (Chicago: University of Chicago Press, 1975), pp. 18–33.

8. *OC*, IV (1), 30, cited in the editor's introduction. In the state of Wisconsin such a system was introduced in 1999.

9. Charles F. Bahmueller, *The National Charity Company: Jeremy Bentham's Silent Revolution* (Berkeley: University of California Press, 1981); Margaret Fry, "Bentham and English Legal Reform," in *Jeremy Bentham and the Law: A Symposium*, ed. George W, Keeton and George Schwarzenberger (London: Stevens, 1948), pp. 20–57; Elie Halévy, *The Growth of Philosophic Radicalism* (London: Faber, 1928).

10. "Panopticon Papers," in *A Bentham Reader*, ed. Mary P. Mack (New York: Pegasus, 1969), p. 195.

11. *OC*, IV (1), 66–67.

12. *OC*, IV (1), 67.

13. *OC*, IV (1), 53.

14. *OC*, IV (1), 205.

15. *OC*, IV (2), 135.

16. To Langlois, 17 Aug. 1838, *OC*, IV (2), 95.

17. For a fine account of Tocqueville's ideas on and role in prison reform politics, see Drescher, *Dilemmas of Democracy*, ch. 5.

18. *OC*, IV (1), 69.

19. *OC*, IV (1), 74, 122, 124, 171.

20. *OC*, IV, (1), 170.

21. *OC*, IV, (1), 67.

22. Cited in Drescher, *Dilemmas of Democracy*, p. 138, n. 18.

23. *OC*, IV (1), 53, 54.

24. *OC*, IV (1), 136.

25. *OC*, IV (1), 193.

26. Drescher, *Tocqueville and Beaumont on Social Reform*, p. 80.

27. *OC*, IV (1), 152.

28. Drescher, *Tocqueville and Beaumont on Social reform*, p. 80.

29. Recall in *Democracy* Tocqueville's plea to readers to be forgiving of an author who, in the interests of being understood, must draw all of the "theoretical consequences" from his ideas and must push to the edge of "the false and impracticable." *OC*, I (1), 13.

30. *OC*, IV (1), 197, 230, 231.

31. Speech, 1843, *OC*, IV (2), 134.

32. Mack, *A Bentham Reader*, pp. 196–97.
33. *OC*, IV (2), 15.
34. *OC*, IV (2), 141.
35. *OC*, IV (1), 212.
36. Rothman, *The Discovery of the Asylum*, p. xiii.
37. *OC*, IV (1), 61, 93, 174, 176, 183.
38. *OC*, IV (1), 232.
39. *OC*, IV (1), 233, 238, 246.
40. *OC*, IV (1), 231.
41. *OC*, IV (1), 223.
42. Burke, *Reflections on the Revolution in France*, p. 84.
43. Cited by editor, *OC*, IV (1), 43.
44. The crucial terms in Montesquieu's conception of theory are "reason," "law," and "relations." The discussion of them is scattered throughout the *Esprit* but some of the theoretically more important passages are: the author's foreword; preface; and bks. 1 and 2. Some of these matters are discussed in my "Montesquieu and Publius: The Crisis of Reason in the *Federalist*," *Presence of the Past*, ch. 6.
45. This is from a note in Beaumont's hand. See *OC*, IV (2), 519 (note 6 to p. 43)].
46. *OC*, IV (1), 54–55.
47. Cited in th editor's introduction, *OC*, IV (2), 37. Not long ago the State of California inaugurated a new prison at Pelican Bay that fulfills Tocqueville's ideal of absolute isolation of each inmate.
48. The wealth of prison experiments in the United States gives an ironic twist to the later boast that the American federal system allowed the states to serve as "laboratories" of social experiments.
49. *OC*, IV (1), 264.
50. *OC*, I (2), 109.
51. *OC*, IV (1), 39.
52. *OC*, IV (1), 229.
53. *OC*, IV (1), 79.
54. *OC*, IV (1), 197.
55. *OC*, IV (1), 206.
56. Writing to his cousin after observing the silence of the inmates at Sing Sing, Tocqueville describes it as reminiscent of "something similar among the Trappists." To Le Peletier d'Aunay, 7 June 1831, *OC*, IV (2), 15.
57. *OC*, IV (1), 171.
58. *OC*, IV (1), 93.
59. *OC*, IV (1), 204.
60. Drescher, *Tocqueville and Beaumont on Social Reform*, p. 84.
61. *OC*, IV (1), 126. "For an innocent man there is something worse than the cruelest solitude: it is the company of the wicked." *OC*, IV (1), 125.
62. *OC*, IV (1), 197.
63. "[O]ne of the most fertile sources of corruption" is "the conversation" among inmates. *OC*, IV (1), 58.
64. *OC*, IV (1), 122, 200. See the editor's note marked *** at *OC*, IV (1), 532.
65. Surveillance figured prominently in Tocqueville's speech (1844) on prison reform. See Drescher, *Tocqueville and Beaumont on Social Reform*, pp. 77, 80.
66. Pierson, *Tocqueville in America*, p. 96, suggested that the substitution of "peni-

tentiary" for "prison" was a Quaker contribution, the idea being to encourage penance through solitude. See also pp. 61–63.

67. *OC*, IV (1), 189–90.

68. Drescher, *Tocqueville and Beaumont on Social Reform*, p. 86.

69. *OC*, IV (1), 25.

70. *OC*, IV (1), 58–59.

71. Cited in Pierson, *Tocqueville in America*, p. 101.

72. *OC*, IV (1), 175–76.

73. Tocqueville's idea that the criminal serves the function of uniting the outside society anticipates Durkheim. See Émile Durkheim, *Les régles de la méthode sociologique*, 10th ed. (Paris: PUF, 1947), pp. 64–75.

74. *OC*, IV (1), 136.

75. Letter of 1836, *OC*, IV (2), 89.

76. *OC*, IV (1), 196.

77. *OC*, I (2), 105.

78. For an incisive discussion of the centralization theme in *The Penitentiary*, see Drescher, *Dilemmas of Democracy*, pp. 147ff. It should be noted that Tocqueville and Beaumont did recommend a measure of decentralization in the national prison system in the hope that it might encourage local pride among the *départements* as well as an added element of surveillance by the community. *OC*, IV (1), 238–41. They had been impressed by the American practice of encouraging the public to visit prisons. *OC*, IV (1), 181.

79. Bentham, "Panopticon Papers," p. 194.

80. *OC*, IV (1), 206.

81. Montesquieu, *Esprit des lois*, V.14, *Oeuvres* 2:292, 294. One should be reminded that John Stuart Mill allowed that despotism was justifiable as a temporary stage of tutelage for "backward" peoples. See his *Representative Government*, ch. 4.

82. *OC*, IV (2), 38.

83. *OC*, IV (1), 49.

84. *OC*, IV (1), 161.

85. *OC*, IV (1), 160.

86. Lynds is discussed in Pierson, *Tocqueville in America*, pp. 98–99, 206–10, and by the editor at *OC*, IV (1), 541 note ****. They reproduced their interview with Lynds in *The Penitentiary*, *OC*, IV (1), 342–45. It can also be found in *OC*, V (1), 63–67.

87. *OC*, V (1), 67.

88. *OC*, V (1), 65.

89. *OC*, V (1), 63, 65.

90. *OC*, V (1), 64.

91. *OC*, IV (1), 243.

92. *OC*, IV (1), 245.

93. *OC*, IV (1), 236–37.

94. *OC*, IV, (1), 235.

95. *OC*, IV (1), 236.

96. *OC*, IV (1), 234, 237.

97. Drescher, *Tocqueville and Beaumont on Social Reform*, p. 80. For a suggestive discussion of today's problems concerning prisons and of Tocqueville's views, see Thomas Dumm, *United States* (Ithaca: Cornell University Press, 1994).

98. *OC*, I (1), 261.

## Chapter XXI
## The Political Education of the Bourgeoisie

1. *OC*, III (2), 61, 72. The statement was made during the electoral campaign of 1842.
2. To Corcelle, 11 Mar., 1839, *OC*, XV (1), 126–27.
3. "Letters on the Internal Situation in France" (1843), *OC*, III (2), 116.
4. *OC*, III (2), 210. Notes for a speech, 1843 (?).
5. To Kergorlay, 12 Aug. 1839, *OC*, XII (2), 64. See also the letter to Corcelle, 15 Feb. 1839, *OC*, V (1), 115.
6. Hobbes, *Leviathan*, introduction, p. 82; Burke, *Reflections on the Revolution in France*, *Works*, 4:106.
7. *OC*, III (2), 134, 201.
8. M. M. Bakhtin, *The Dialogic Imagination: Four Essays*, p. 36.
9. *OC*, III (2), 52, 53.
10. Henri Comte de Saint-Simon, *Selected Writings*, ed. F.M.H. Markham (New York: Macmillan, 1952), pp. 69ff.
11. *OC*, III (2), 725–27.
12. *OC*, III (2), 129–30.
13. Cited in Jardin, *Histoire de libéralisme politique*, p. 232. For a different view of this passage and a mostly uncritical appreciation of Constant, see Stephen Holmes, *Benjamin Constant and the Making of Modern Liberalism* (New Haven: Yale University Press, 1984), pp. 176ff. On the transformation of the revolutionary ideas of 1789 and their adaptation to postrevolutionary France, see Jack Hayward, *After the French Revolution: Six Critics of Democracy and Nationalism* (Hemel Hempstead: Harvester Wheatsheaf, 1991). For a critique of the postrevolutionary weaknesses of French liberalism, see the unfinished but thoughtful study by George Armstrong Kelley, *The Humane Comedy: Constant, Tocqueville and French Liberalism* (Cambridge: Cambridge University Press, 1992).
14. *OC*, III (2), 202–4. In these passages Tocqueville emphasizes the importance of supplying bureaucratic jobs.
15. *OC*, III (2), 384–86.
16. *OC*, III (2), 487.
17. *OC*, III (2), 722.
18. *OC*, III (2), 101.
19. *OC*, III (2), 722.
20. *OC*, III (2), 584–85.
21. *OC*, III (2), 134. See his essay "On the Commemoration of the July Days," *OC*, III (2), 133–35.
22. *OC*, III (2), 119.
23. Ibid.
24. Ibid.
25. *OC*, III (2), 217.
26. *OC*, III (2), 198.
27. *OC*, III (2), 722.
28. Speech of 1844, *OC*, III (2), 487.
29. *OC*, III (2), 99.
30. *OC*, III (2), 209, 211.
31. Cited in Wood, *The Radicalism of the American Revolution*, p. 81.

32. *OC,* V (1), 258.
33. Cited in Jardin, *Histoire du libéralisme politique,* p. 188.
34. P. -J. Proudhon, "De la capacité politique des class ouvrières," in *Selected Writings of P.-J. Proudhon,* ed. Stewart Edwards, tr. Elizabeth Fraser (Garden City, N.Y.: Doubleday: 1969), p. 52.
35. Benjamin Constant, *Principles of Politics,* in *Political Writings,* ed. Biancamaria Fontana (Cambridge: Cambridge University Press, 1988), p. 214. All references to the *Principles* are from that edition.There is a helpful analysis of French liberalism in this period in Jardin, *Histoire du libéralisme politique,* pp. 226ff.
36. Constant, *Principles of Politics,* p. 262.
37. Ibid., pp. 215ff.
38. Tocqueville, "Memoir on Pauperism," in Drescher, *Tocqueville and Beaumont on Social Reform,* p. 17. Tocqueville's arguments drew heavily on the English administrative experience with poor-law legislation. Drescher's notes are invaluable here, as is his more extended discussion of sources in *Tocqueville and England.*
39. Tocqueville, "Memoir on Pauperism," p. 25.
40. *OC,* I (2), 43–44.
41. *OC,* III (2), 117.
42. *OC,* I (1), 248.
43. Thus Tocqueville refers to "the recognized right of a *semblable* to give him orders." *OC* (1), 248.
44. *OC,* I (1), 248.
45. *OC,* I (1), 250.
46. To Corcelle, 11 Mar. 1839, *OC,* XV (1), 128–29.
47. "Letters on the Domestic Situation in France," Jan. 1843, *OC,* III (2), 101–2, 106.
48. *OC,* III (2), 104.
49. *OC,* III (2), 519.
50. "Liberty of Teaching" (1844), *OC,* III (2), 519.
51. Speech of 1845, *OC,* III (2), 600.
52. *OC,* III (2), 551.
53. Hobbes, *Leviathan,* ch. 21, pp. 263–64.
54. Ibid., ch. 30, p. 379.
55. For Hobbes's discussion of religion as an instrument of cultural control, see ibid., ch. 12, especially p. 173.

## Chapter XXII
## *Souvenirs*: Recollections In/Tranquillity

1. Friedrich Nietzsche, *Beyond Good and Evil,* tr. Walter Kaufmann (New York: Random House, 1966), pt. 9, sec. 269, p. 218.
2. Tocqueville, in a letter of 15 Dec. 1850 to Kergorlay, notes that he will not publish *Souvenirs* because he does not wish to make a literary spectacle of himself. He also claims to be finishing it. *OC,* XIII (2), 229–30.
3. Tocqueville twice employs the metaphor of a "labyrinth," once to indicate his failure to comprehend fully certain revolutionary events and once as he attempts "to rediscover himself." OC, XII, 30, 102.
4. *OC,* XII, 104.

5. To Gobineau, 7 Jan. 1850, *OC*, IX, 101.

6. In a letter to Senior, 25 Aug. 1847, Tocqueville emphasized the "experiment" being tried in France of combining an elected assembly with a centralized executive. *OC*, VI (2), 99.

7. Among recent discussions of the *Souvenirs* that rely on the methods of literary deconstruction and the work of Hayden White and Michel Foucault are: L. E. Shiner, *The Secret Mirror: Literary Form and History in Tocqueville's Recollections* (Ithaca: Cornell University Press, 1988), Linda Orr, *Headless History: Nineteenth-Century Historiography of the Revolution* (Ithaca: Cornell University Press, 1990) and ch. 4.

8. *OC*, XII, 29.

9. To Kergorlay, 15 Dec. 1850, *OC*, XIII (2), 230.

10. *OC*, VIII (2), 12–13.

11. *OC*, XII, 102.

12. *OC*, I (1), xliii.

13. *OC*, I (2), xliv.

14. See Maurice Agulhon, *The Republican Experiment, 1848–1852*, tr. Janet Lloyd (Cambridge: Cambridge University Press, 1977), pp. 114–15.

15. To Paul Clamorgan, 7 Mar. 1848, in Tocqueville, *Selected Letters*, p. 203.

16. *OC*, XII, 40.

17. *OC*, XII, 29.

18. Ibid.

19. *OC*, XII, 100.

20. *OC*, XII, 102.

21. For a different interpretation of the mirror metaphor, one that adopts as Tocqueville's viewpoint that "the mirror captures what is true because, unlike painting or literature, it is not consciously arranged," see Shiner, *The Secret Mirror*, p. 95.

22. *OC*, XII, 104.

23. *OC*, XII, 29.

24. *OC*, XII, 30, n. 2.

25. *OC*, XII, 29.

26. *OC*, XII, 101.

27. *OC*, XII, 29.

28. For passages in *Souvenirs* that display Tocqueville in a less than flattering light see *OC*, XII, 104.

29. *OC*, XII, 102, 105.

30. *OC*, XV, 28–29.

31. *OC*, XII, 117.

32. *OC*, XII, 105.

33. *OC*, XII, 103. Perhaps the most telling passage in *Souvenirs* occurs in Tocqueville's comments about his cabinet role in maintaining good relations with the nobility among the Legitimist Party. After remarking that "my origins and upbringing gave me a greater facility for this that others did not possess," he continues: although "the French nobility has ceased to be a class, they have remained a kind of free masonry of which all of the members continue to recognize one another by certain invisible signs." Then follows a passage that Tocqueville eventually marked for omission where he says that the closeness of the invisible bonds among the nobility allowed him to be more at ease with aristocrats with whom he differed politically than with the bourgeoisie, whose "ideas and instincts" coincided with his own. *OC*, XII, 222–23 and 223, n. 1.

34. Tocqueville records an incident that reveals his hardening conservatism. It involved his friend Ampère whom he describes as superficial and criticizes for injecting "the literary *esprit* into politics." Tocqueville suggests that Ampère's contempt for the overthrown government was rooted in a sensibility that detested bigotry and could recognize disinterested and generous actions among the rebels—which Tocqueville mean-spiritedly attributed to Ampère's being "overcome by popular emotion." Tocqueville proceeded to lecture his friend for failing to see that the people had proved itself unfit for freedom. *OC*, XII, 88–89.

35. *OC*, XII, 86.

36. Ibid.

37. There are, to be sure, passages in the correspondence where Tocqueville refers to "a moment of crisis" at hand when "action could be glorious" (to Beaumont, 22 Apr. 1848, VIII *OC* (2), pp. 12–13); yet more characteristically are those where he despairs (*OC*, VIII (2), 76) or cautions that it is better to wait. *OC*, VII (2), 274–76.

38. While *Souvenirs* might be described as part memoir and part chronicle of events, it is not a "whole" of which those two genres are the "parts." The memoir is interspersed with theoretical reflections, and vice versa, and some of the reflections are antecedent to the events being recalled while others are subsequent. Nor is the work a chronicle by any strict historical standard. Tocqueville was aware that he had made some glaring omissions and it was in that context he denied that he had attempted a conventional history. *OC*, XII, 100.

39. *OC*, XII, 50.

40. *OC*, XII, 29.

41. Ibid. The variants of *indécise* (*la physionomie indécise*) are *troublée* and *agitée*. *OC*, XII, 295.

42. *OC*, XII, 279.

43. *OC*, XII, 105.

44. *OC*, XII, 29.

45. "Comparable memoirs could not be a mirror in which no failings could be found." Tocqueville then adds that he could not show his recollections to his friends without having to apologize for having displayed their weaknesses as well as his own. *OC*, XII, 295.

46. Ibid.

47. *OC*, XII, 295 variant h.

48. *OC*, XII, 100.

49. *OC*, XII, 61.

50. *OC*, XII, 60.

51. *OC*, XII, 75.

52. *OC*, XII, 29, 30.

53. *OC*, XII, 74.

54. *OC*, XII, 75.

55. For a somewhat different interpretation, see the fine account in Shiner, *The Secret Mirror*, pp. 65–66.

56. *OC*, XII, 76.

57. *OC*, XII, 117.

58. *OC*, XII, pt. 2, ch. 10.

59. *OC*, XII, 98.

60. *OC*, XII, 87.

61. Ibid.

62. *OC*, XII, 57.

63. Presumably to distinguish 1848 from the counterrevolution of 1814–15, which restored the monarchy, and from the revolt in 1830, which established the July Monarchy.

64. On one important count Tocqueville's prophecy proved to be at odds with his conclusions in *Souvenirs*. In the first document or manifesto he predicted that "Soon there will be a political struggle between those who possess and those who do not." This would lead to an epic struggle: "the great battle field will be property. . . . Then we shall see great public agitations and great parties." *OC*, XII, 37.

65. *OC*, XII, 41.

66. *OC*, XII, 37.

67. *OC*, XII, 37, 38. Apparently Tocqueville did not insert the actual text of the speeches. It was done by the editors of the first edition. See *OC*, XII, 40, n. 1. The second document, a speech of 27 January 1848 was also inserted by Tocqueville as an appendix to the twelfth edition of *Democracy*. The influence of Tocqueville's conception of the "social" upon Hannah Arendt has been critically examined in Hanna Pitkin's suggestive study, *The Attack of the Blob: Hannah Arendt's Concept of the Social* (Chicago: University of Chicago Press, 1998).

68. *OC*, XII, 37.

69. Oddly, when Tocqueville had served on the Constitutional Committee of the Constituent Assembly, he had lectured his colleagues on the importance of incorporating new concepts "more social than political, which should be placed at the beginning of the Constitution in order that it proceed from them, in a methodical manner." Cited in Gargan, *Alexis de Tocqueville: The Critical Years, 1848–1851*, pp. 95–96.

70. *OC*, XII, 69.

71. It is worth noting that Tocqueville's essay, "The Social and Political State of France before and after 1789," which was published in the *Westminster Review* in 1836, bore the French title "L'ancienne et la nouvelle France." See Furet, *Revolutionary France, 1770–1880*, p. 369.

72. Tocqueville made no attempt to distinguish among the various elements of the working classes (or in Hobsbawm's phrase, "the laboring poor"). The presence among the revolutionaries of artisans, "mechanics," and other handworkers—rather than of an undifferentiated "proletariat"—blurs the line between the traditional and the modern.

73. In a letter of 1844 Tocqueville described the work of a local historical restoration commission and its disputes about what to preserve from 1789. Half-ironically Tocqueville described the controversies as a continuation of "the struggle between the old and the new society." After the revolution of 1830 "the old society existed only in history." *OC*, VII, 299, 300.

74. *OC*, XII, 85.

75. *OC*, XII, 166–67, 177.

76. *OC*, XII, 168, 170–71. An essential element in Tocqueville's *ancienneté* is the role of the French peasant as a faithful soldier. See his admiring comments in a letter of 25 July 1855 to Senior, *OC*, VI (2), 183.

77. *OC*, XII, 95. I have used the variant at *OC*, XII, 300 (95c).

78. *OC*, XII, 69, 79, 95–96.

79. *OC*, XII, 95.

80. *OC*, XII, 131. "Théories" is the variant reading for "principes."

81. To Stoffels, 21 July 1848. I have used the translation in Tocqueville, *Selected Letters*, p. 215.

82. That same criticism was being voiced at the time by the "utopian socialists," such as Fourier, Cabet, and most notably by Tocqueville's colleague in the Constituent Assembly, J.-P. Proudhon.

## Chapter XXIII
## *Souvenirs*: Socialism and the Crisis of the Political

1. *OC*, XII, 95.

2. *OC*, XII, 92.

3. See especially "De la classe moyenne et du peuple," *OC*, III (2), 738–41. There is an interesting similarity between Tocqueville's hope that the threat of the workers would energize the bourgeoisie and Georges Sorel's conception of myth in *Reflexions sur la violence*, 10th ed. (Paris: Rivière, 1946), chs. 1–2.

4. "You ask for prophecies about politics; who would dare to offer one? The future is as black as the bottom of a kiln; and men who are gifted with the most perceptive eyes confess their inability to see anything." In this letter to Stoffels, 28 Apr. 1850, Tocqueville went on to say that what he could see was an endless revolution. *OC* (B), II, 460–61.

5. *OC*, XII, 158. One is reminded of the opposite claim in Carl Schmitt's famous formulation of the political: "The specific political distinction to which political actions and motives can be reduced is that between friend and enemy." *The Concept of the Political*, tr. George Schwab (New Brunswick, N.J.: Rutgers University Press, 1976), p. 26.

6. *OC*, XII, 139.

7. Letter of April 21, 1830, cited in Gargan, *Alexis de Tocqueville: The Critical Years, 1848–1851*, pp. 7–8.

8. *OC*, I (1), 156.

9. See Karl Marx and Friedrich Engels, *The German Ideology*, preface and section entitled "Feuerbach," in *Collected Works*, 5:23–93.

10. *OC*, XII, 152. Tocqueville is clearly unsettled by the spectacle of women passing ammunition and being "the last to yield." He ends with an incongruous simile: "they enjoyed this war as they might have enjoyed a lottery." Ibid.

11. *OC*, XII, 160.

12. The decontextualization of "the economy" and its subsequent autonomous status was the focus of the seminal work of Karl Polanyi. See his *The Great Transformation* (New York: Rinehart, 1944) and *Primitive, Archaic and Modern Economies*, ed. George Dalton (Garden City, N.Y.: Doubleday, 1968).

13. Burke, *Reflections on the Revolution in France*, in *Works*, IV, 50.

14. *OC*, I (1), 46–47.

15. *OC*, XII, 95.

16. Marx's *The Class Struggles in France, 1848–1850* (1850) developed a more complex class analysis of the revolution that was especially concerned with the role of the peasantry. *Collected Works*, 10:45–145.

17. *OC*, XII, 151, 152.

18. *OC*, I (2), 43–44.

19. *OC*, I (1), 52.

20. *OC*, XII, 95.

21. See C. Kerenyi, *The Religion of the Greeks and Romans*, tr. Christopher Holme (London: Thames and Hudson, 1962) pp. 141ff.

22. Tocqueville, "Speech on the Right to Work" (12 Sept. 1848), in Drescher, *Tocqueville and Beaumont on Social Reform*, pp. 181, 192.

23. *OC*, XII, 151.

24. In a letter to Senior of 10 Apr. 1848 Tocqueville wrote: "The revolution has not been powered by the misery of the working class. This misery surely exists in certain respects, but in general one could say that in no country or at any other time has the working class been in a better condition than in France." *OC*, VI (2), 101.

25. *OC*, XII, 90, 96.

26. Charles Tilly, "How Protest Modernized in France, 1845–55," in *The Dimensions of Quantitative Research in History*, ed. William O. Aydelotte, Allan G. Bogue, and Robert William Vogel (Princeton: Princeton University Press, 1972), p. 235; John M. Merriman, *The Agony of the Republic: The Repression of the Left in Revolutionary France, 1848–1851* (New Haven: Yale University Press, 1978), p. xx.

27. Merriman, *The Agony of the Republic*, p. xxi.

28. Ibid., pp. 57–58.

29. Maurice Agulhon as cited in ibid., p. 58.

30. See Tocqueville's sneering account of the Feast of Concord. *OC*, XII, pt. 2, ch. 8.

31. *OC*, XII, 129.

32. Merriman writes, "Such voluntary associations came to be condemned as 'political,' like the clubs, popular societies, and even secret societies, because they challenged fundamental notions of hierarchy, deference to social and economic superiors, and ultimately, the fundamental determination of power." *The Agony of the Republic*, p. 81.

33. Ibid., pp. 93–94.

34. *OC*, VI (2), 101.

35. Drescher, *Tocqueville and Beaumont*, pp. 195, 182.

36. Jardin, *Histoire de libéralisme politique*, p. 383, takes note of Tocqueville's critical view of liberal political economy and points out that Tocqueville had been reading Owen, Blanc, Saint-Simon, and Fourier.

37. The tension between Tocqueville's *ancienneté* and political economy was of long standing. Illustrative is his exchange with Nassau Senior in 1835. The latter had written to criticize Tocqueville's use of economic terms in the first volume of *Democracy*. Tocqueville responded by saying that Senior had mistaken what Tocqueville had meant by "le bien du pauvre." Tocqueville explained that whereas Senior understood *le bien* to refer to "wealth" or "riches," Tocqueville had meant "well-being" to include "respect, political rights, ease of obtaining justice, the pleasures of the mind, and a thousand other things which indirectly contribute to happiness." Tocqueville went on to take exception to Senior's claim that it was more rational for a man to prefer labor on the land as a worker than to want to own the land himself. There were, Tocqueville retorted, noneconomic values associated with the land that might cause a worker to prefer ownership to wage labor. Letter of 21 Feb. 1835, *OC*, VI (2), 70.

38. *OC*, XII, 90.

39. The speech is reproduced in Beaumont's edition and in translation in Drescher, *Tocqueville and Beaumont on Social Reform*, pp. 179–92.

40. *OC*, VI (2), 101.

41. Today, ironically, Tocqueville's admirers want to hand back 1789 to the left; they

see it as the antecedent of the Bolshevik Revolution—which is to say the socialists of Tocqueville were historically correct and Tocqueville politically incorrect as well as historically wrong. See François Furet, *Interpreting the French Revolution*, tr. Elborg Forster (Cambridge: Cambridge University Press, 1981), pt. 1, "The Revolution Is Over," and part 2, ch. 2, "De Tocqueville [*sic*] and the Problem of the French Revolution. Furet makes no reference to Tocqueville's writings related to 1848.

42. In *Democracy* Tocqueville had been more sympathetic toward the workers, partly because he was reacting against the "industrial science" of the Saint-Simonians. *OC*, I (2), 164–66.

43. Drescher, *Tocqueville and Beaumont on Social Reform*, p. 187.

44. Ibid., p. 178.

45. *OC*, III (2), 720, 727. In the draft of a manifesto of 1847 Tocqueville called for the slow extension of "the circle of political rights" and for the involvement of "the lower classes in politics in a regular and peaceful manner." Drescher, *Tocqueville and Beaumont on Social Reforms*, p. 178. The fact remains, however, that Tocqueville never voted for any proposal aimed at extending the suffrage.

46. *OC*, III (2), 720.

47. Montesquieu, *Esprit des lois*, IV. 5, p. 267.

48. *OC*, XII, 120.

49. Although Tocqueville remarked that religion had lost its hold on the masses, he did not connect that observation with the possibility that they had transferred their faith to socialism.

50. *OC*, XII, 151–52.

51. *OC*, XII, 95.

52. *OC*, XII, 95, 96.

53. *OC*, I (1), 216.

54. *OC*, I (2), 156, 157.

55. *OC*, XII, 96–97.

56. *OC*, XII, 100.

57. *OC*, XII, 120–21.

58. *OC*, XII, 102, 105.

59. The distinction also appears when Tocqueville suggests his superiority to the other members of the Constitutional Committee. He attributes their lack of a conception of a political system and its principles to their "administrative" background. *OC*, XII, 180. Ironically, after Tocqueville published *L'ancien régime*, Gobineau wrote him and described it as an "administrative" history. Tocqueville's irritation with that characterization was evident in his response. Letter of 12 May 1858, *OC*, IX, 293.

60. *OC*, XII, 84.

61. Ibid.

62. *OC*, XII, 84–85.

63. *OC*, XII, 36.

64. *OC*, XII, 30.

65. Ibid.

66. Ibid.

67. *OC*, I (2), 259, 260–61.

68. *OC*, I (2), 265, 269.

69. See Doris Goldstein, *Trial of Faith: Religion and Politics in Tocqueville's Thought* (New York: Elsevier, 1975), p. 61.

70. *OC*, XII, 30.
71. *OC*, XII, 210.
72. *OC*, XII, 30, 31.
73. *OC*, XII, 32.
74. To Gobineau, 5 Sept. 1843, *OC*, IX, 45.
75. Karl Marx, *Capital*, vol. 1, pt. 4, ch. 15; pt. 7, chs. 26–33.
76. See also his letter to Gobineau, 5 Sept. 1843, *OC*, IX, 45.
77. *OC*, I (2), 162.
78. *OC*, XII, 88.
79. Saint-Simonism was closely identified with the application of science to social and economic problems There is a vast literature on the movement. A useful starting point is Frank E. Manuel, *The New World of Henri St.Simon* (Cambridge, Mass.: Harvard University Press, 1956). One might also compare F. A. Hayek, *The Counter-Revolution of Science: Studies on the Abuse of Reason* (Glencoe, Ill.: Free Press, 1952) and its classic attack on Saint Simon's scientism with Friedrich Engels's appreciation of Saint Simon in *Socialism: Utopian and Scientific* (1880), pt. 1.
80. For Edmund Burke the idea of order had lost neither its *grandeur* nor its urgency. *Reflections on the Revolution in France*, *Works*, 4:35–36, 101–6. There is a useful discussion of earlier formulas of order in Preston King, *The Ideology of Order: A Comparative Analysis of Jean Bodin and Thomas Hobbes* (London: Allen and Unwin, 1974).
81. Cited in Agulhon, *The Republican Experiment*, p. 173.
82. *OC*, XII, 105. Agulhon notes that the republic from January 1849 to the coup of December 1851 was operated by men who, at best, tolerated the republic and wanted a monarchical restoration. *The Republican Experiment*, p. 191. Tocqueville could be counted among them.
83. *OC*, XII, 38–39, 63.
84. *OC*, XII, 107, 108, 110.
85. *OC*, XII, 114.
86. For details, see Agulhon, *The Republican Experiment*, pp. 88–89, 115; for their destruction under the dictatorship, see pp. 175–79. For a close sociological analysis of the attitudes of various sectors of the working class and artisans, see Roger Price, *The French Second Republic: A Social History* (Ithaca: Cornell University Press, 1972), pp. 72–82. Price's volume also contains a running critique of Marx's account of the same events.
87. *OC*, XII, 115, 115–16, 116.
88. To Corcelle, 17 Sept. 1853, *OC*, XV (2), 81.
89. *OC*, XII, 183–84.
90. *OC*, XII, 180.
91. *OC*, XII, 184–85.
92. Tocqueville did succeed in attaching a stipulation that if the election failed to give an absolute majority to a candidate, the Assembly would determine the winner. He had also proposed unsuccessfully an amendment that would have adopted the American system and have the president chosen by elected delegates.
93. *OC*, XII, 189.
94. *OC*, XII, 189, 190. Bonaparte had made it clear early on that he wished to be rid of the prohibition against reelection.
95. *OC*, XII, 191.
96. *OC*, XII, 188.
97. To Corcelle, 17 Sept. 1853, *OC* XV (2), 81.

98. *OC*, III (2), 344.
99. *OC*, XII, 235.
100. *OC*, XV (1), 252.
101. *OC*, XII, 263.
102. For Tocqueville's preministerial views on the Eastern question, see Mary Lawlor, *Alexis de Tocqueville in the Chamber of Deputies: His Views on Foreign and Colonial Policy* (Washington, D.C.: Catholic University of America Press, 1959), ch. 3.
103. *OC*, III (2), 290, 291–92, 298–99, 299–300, 306.
104. *Souvenirs* is actually divided into three parts. The first two are devoted to the revolution of 1848, the third to "mon ministére." He skips over the period from June 1849 to June 1849, saying that, if time permits, he will return to them. He does not. *OC*, XII, 196. Tocqueville's eagerness to leave a record of a personal triumph was reflected in the uneven proportions of the *Souvenirs*. Tocqueville devoted the third part of *Souvenirs* entirely to the Barrot ministry and his own service as foreign minister.
105. *OC*, XII, 235.
106. *OC*, XII, 243–44, n. 1.
107. *OC*, I (1), 238–39.
108. *OC*, XII, 234.
109. Ibid.
110. *OC*, XII, 235, 236–37.
111. *OC*, XII, 242, 243, n. 1.
112. *OC*, XII, 245–46.
113. See Jardin, *Alexis de Tocqueville*, pp. 411–21.
114. 12 Oct. 1849, *OC* VIII (2), 201.
115. *OC*, XII, 209.
116. *OC*, XII, 229–30.
117. *OC*, XII, 211.
118. *OC*, XII, 229.
119. *OC*, XII, 229–30.
120. *OC*, XII, 230. See the letter to Corcelle, 26 Oct. 1849, in which Tocqueville raises the possibility of breaking the political impasse by "irregularly" altering the Constitution. He concludes that the extreme political fragmentation prevents it. *OC*, XV (1), 472.
121. *OC*, XII, 231–32.
122. *OC*, XII, 232–33.
123. *OC*, XII, 150.

## Chapter XXIV
*The Old Regime and the Revolution: Mythistoricus et theoreticus*

1. To Kergorlay, 15 Dec. 1850, *OC*, XIII (2), 233.
2. To Freslon, 12 Jan. 1858, *OC* (B), VII, 478.
3. To Beaumont, 1 Feb. 1852, *OC*, VIII (3), 20. Evidently the phrase *l'ancien régime* was not used until 1790 and then in a letter from the king to Mirabeau. It meant "previous," not "archaic." See Simon Schama, *Citizens: A Chronicle of the French Revolution* (New York: Knopf, 1989), p. 63.
4. To Corcelle, 17 Dec 1852, *OC*, XV(2), 66; to Alexis Stoffels, 4 Jan. 1856, *OC* (B), 470.

5. To Jared Sparks, 11 Dec. 1852, *OC*, VII, 148. At the time Sparks was president of Harvard.

6. To von Bunsen, 23 May 1853, *OC*, VII, 332.

7. To Freslon, 12 Jan. 1858, *OC* (B), VII, 479–80. Senior once asked Tocqueville, "What do you consider your Golden Age?" Tocqueville answered, "The latter part of the seventeenth century. Men wrote then only for fame and they addressed a small and highly educated public." *Correspondence and Conversations of Alexis de Tocqueville with Nassau William Senior, from 1834 to 1859*, ed. M.C.M. Simpson, 2nd ed., 2 vols. (New York: A. M. Kelley, 1968), 1:141. As late as 1854 Tocqueville evidently still nursed hopes that a great writer might "imprint indelible traces" on the line of human progress. Ibid., 2:60 (18 Feb. 1854).

8. In a letter to Beaumont, 3 Oct 1853, *OC*, VIII (3), 154–55, in which Tocqueville reports that in reading a book about Frederick the Great of Prussia he was struck by the difference between "the mind which can write and the mind which acts."

9. To Hubert de Tocqueville, 7 Mar. 1854, *OC*, XIV, 295.

10. To Comtesse de Circourt, 19 June 1850, *OC* (B), VI, 149; to Beaumont, 28 Nov. 1849, *OC*, VIII (2), 253, and 19 Dec. 1849, *OC*, VIII (2), 261; to Stoffels, 28 Apr. 1850, *OC*, II (B), 460–61; to Corcelle, 1 Jan. 1853, *OC*, XV (2), 70.

11. To Comtesse de Circourt, 19 June 1850, *OC* (B), VI, 149. See also to Beaumont, *OC*, VIII (2), 233, 253, 408.

12. To Stoffels, 28 Apr. 1850, *OC*, II (B), 460–61.

13. To Corcelle, 23 Oct. 1854, *OC*, XV (2), 123–24.

14. To Corcelle, 23 Oct. 1854, *OC*, XV (2), 124.

15. To Corcelle, 23 Dec. 1855, *OC*, XV (2), 157.

16. 17 Sept. 1853, *OC*, XV (2), 80.

17. That Tocqueville had a highly tactical view of writing is confirmed in the letters of advice he gives to some of his correspondents. See *OC*, XIII (2), 185–86; *OC*, IX, 199–200.

18. The indispensable source for my discussion is Andre Jardin's introduction to *L'ancien régime et la Révolution*, *OC*, II (1), 17, and to the fragmentary remains of the original project, *OC*, II (2).

19. Jardin, *OC*, II (1), 20. See also Tocqueville's letters to Beaumont, 17 Feb. 1856, *OC*, VIII (3), 370–71; 6 March 1856, Ibid., 375; and 17 Mar. 1856, ibid., 379.

20. 22 March 1856, *OC*, VIII (3), 384.

21. *OC*, II (1), 249.

22. For a sensitive account, see Richard Herr, *Tocqueville and the Old Regime* (Princeton: Princeton University Press, 1962). Any student of Tocqueville is profoundly indebted to the work of François Furet. In addition to *Interpreting the French Revolution*, especially pp. 132–63, see his introduction (with Françoise Mélonio] to the recent English translation of *The Old Regime and the Revolution* (University of Chicago Press: Chicago, 1998). Also instructive is the essay on narrative history in *The Workshop of History*, tr. Jonathan Mandelbaum (Chicago: University of Chicago Press, 1984), pp. 54–67.

23. To Ampère, 1 Jan. 1854, *OC*, XI, 232.

24. That he was aware at least of one of them, Thiers, see the letter to Kergorlay, 15 Dec. 1850, *OC*, XIII (2), 231. In a letter to Rémusat of 22 July 1856 Tocqueville refers to his own well-known dislike of reading any book on a subject he himself was working on. *OC* (B), VI, 315. Also his letter to Hauranne of 1 Sept. 1856, *OC*, VI (B), 332.

25. *OC*, II (2), 331. See also Ibid., 28.

26. Compare Marx: "Just as philosophy finds its material weapons in the proletariat, so the proletariat finds its spiritual weapons in philosophy. . . . The head of [German] emancipation is philosophy, its heart is the proletariat." "A Contribution to the Critique of Hegel's 'Philosophy of Right.' Introduction," *Critique of Hegel's "Philosophy of Right,"* ed. Joseph O'Malley (Cambridge: Cambridge University Press, 1970), p. 142.

27. To Kergorlay, 2 July 1854, *OC*, XIII (2), 287.

28. To Corcelle, 17 Sept. 1853, *OC*, XV (2), 82.

29. To Kergorlay, 16 May 1858, *OC*, XIII(2), 337.

30. To Ampère, 1 Jan. 1852, *OC*, XI, 232.

31. To Beaumont, 26 Dec. 1850, *OC*, VIII (2), 343–44. Tocqueville was sensible of the criticism that he was insufficiently concerned with facts. See his tart reply to Sir George Cornwell Lewes, 15 Aug. 1856, *OC* (B), VII, 402–3.

32. To Kergorlay, 15 Dec. 1850, *OC*, XIII (2), 229–33.

33. To Beaumont, 26 Dec. 1850, *OC*, VIII (2), 343.

34. Curiously, Tocqueville's father wrote a work that he entitled *Histoire philosophique du règne de Louis XV.* It was published in 1847. The elder Tocqueville described his "philosophical history" as "not a metaphysical work. The facts are narrated in detail, and I have tried to group them in such a way as to bring out their consequences." Cited in Palmer, *The Two Tocquevilles, Father and Son*, p. 10.

35. To Kergorlay, 15 Dec. 1850, *OC*, XIII (2), 231.

36. To Beaumont, 8 Aug. 1855, *OC*, VIII (3), 331.

37. To Beaumont, 22 Nov. 1855, *OC*, VIII (3), 350.

38. *OC*, XIII (2), 232.

39. To A. M. Freslon, 9 June 1853, *OC* (B), VI, 208.

40. Francis Macdonald Cornford, *Thucydides, Mythistoricus* (1907; London: Routledge, 1965. It might be recalled that the arch-modernist Thomas Hobbes accompanied his translation of Thucydides with a highly laudatory account of Thucydides' work.

41. In addition to the parallels between Tocqueville and Thucydides discussed later in the text, both writers deal with large-scale disasters and indicate special moments when, with wiser decisions or better foresight, things might have taken a different and better course.

42. *OC*, II (1), 249.

43. The speaker declares that the Athenians are addicted to innovation, swiftness in conception and execution, while the Spartans are told that they have a genius for keeping what they have, lack inventiveness, and never go far enough in action. The complete passage is at I.70 of *The Peloponnesian War.*

44. *OC*, II (2), 115, 125.

45. Thucydides, *The Peloponnesian War*, tr. Crawley, ed. John H. Finley Jr. (New York: Random House, 1954), I.70 p. 40. Tocqueville, *OC*, XIII (2), 337.

46. *OC*, II (1), 72.

47. *OC*, II (2), 132–34. While Tocqueville looks back to Thucydides, the heroic character of myth in his thinking might also be considered with reference to Georges Sorel. The latter's *Reflections on Violence* (1906) is a call to heroism in service of an ideal that can never be realized; in its emphasis upon sacrifice it is also meant as an antidote to bourgeois pragmatism. Although Sorel, too, began from the revolution of 1789, the crucial contrast is, of course, that Sorel was appealing to the workers, Tocqueville to the elites. The following from *L'ancien régime* is suggestive: "The common people alone,

especially those in the countryside, nearly always lacked the means of resisting oppression except by violence." *OC*, I (1), 175.

48. See generally G. S. Kirk, *Myth: Its Meaning and Functions in Ancient and Other Cultures* (Berkeley: University of California Press, 1970).

49. Walter Burkert, *Structure and History in Greek Mythology and Ritual* (Berkeley: University of California Press, 1979), pp. 2–4. I have greatly benefited from Hans Blumenberg's magistral, *Work on Myth*, trans. Robert M. Wallace (Cambridge, Mass.: MIT Press, 1985).

50. The indirect mode of teaching was clearly set out in a letter of 1853 where Tocqueville first attacks the notion of "the all-powerfulness of institutions," the idea that "a precious piece of paper" could contain "a recipe" for "all our evils." The letter continues with his oft-cited formulation that what matters are "the sentiments, beliefs, ideas, habits of the heart and of the mind." Then he concludes with his credo about how one teaches this lesson: "If this truth does not permeate my entire work, if it does not lead readers to reflect, in this way, continuously on themselves, if it does not show them at each moment, without ever making a show of teaching it to them, what are the sentiments, *moeurs* which alone could lead to prosperity and public liberty, what are the vices and errors which inevitably lead away from it, I will not at all have attained the main—and so to speak—only end I have in mind." To Corcelle, 17 Sept. 1853, *OC* XV (2), 81.

51. *OC*, II (1), 246.

52. *OC*, II (1), 199.

53. *OC*, II (2), 124.

54. To Beaumont, 23 Mar. 1853, *OC*, VIII (3), 95.

55. *OC*, II (1), 107.

56. *OC*, II (1), 96 (emphasis in original).

57. To Ampère, 27 Jan. 1857, *OC*, XI, 364.

58. *OC*, II (2), 109.

59. To Mme Swetchine, 20 Oct. 1856, *OC*, XV (2), 298.

60. To Kergorlay, 15 Dec. 1850, *OC*, XIII (2), 233.

61. On these matters see Dominick LaCapra, "Lanzmann's *Shoah:* 'Here There Is No Why,'" *Critical Inquiry* 23, no. 2 (1997): 231–69.

62. Hans Blumenberg's main thesis is that "philosophy" and science reoccupy the ground once held by myth and that, as a consequence, they are compelled to address the same questions previously addressed by myth. See his remarkable *Legitimacy of the Modern World*, tr. Robert M. Wallace (Cambridge, Mass.: MIT Press, 1983).

63. *OC*, II (1), 245.

64. See the suggestive discussion in Georges Duby, *The Three Orders: Feudal Society Imagined*, tr. Arthur Goldhammer (Chicago: University of Chicago Press, 1980).

65. *OC*, II (1), 207, 208.

66. *OC*, II (1), 208.

67. Feb. 1857, in *Memoirs, Letters and Remains of Alexis de Tocqueville*, 2:349.

68. To Beaumont, 14 Jan. 1853, *OC*, VIII (3), 84.

69. To Kergorlay, 16 May 1858, *OC*, XIII (2), 337.

70. To Beaumont, 1 Feb. 1857, *OC*, VIII (3), 456.

71. To Gobineau, 30 July 1856, *OC*, IX, 268.

72. Tocqueville would recognize this when he reflected upon the redistribution of

land that had occurred as the result of the French Revolution. To Kergorlay, 22 July 1852, *OC*, XIII (2), 244. See also Jardin, *Alexis de Tocqueville*, p. 461.

73. To Bouchitté, 23 Sept. 1853, *OC* (B), VII, 299–300; to Barrot 18 July 1856, ibid., 395); to Baron de Tocqueville, 23 Feb. 1857 ibid., 436–37); to Corcelle, 17 Sept. 1853, *OC*, XV (2), 81.

74. To Senior, 21 Apr. 1854, in *Correspondence and Conversations*, 2:88.

75. *OC*, II (1), 246. The personal anguish created by the fear that God had withdrawn from the world is especially evident in his intense correspondence with Mme Swetchine during the 1850s. See *OC*, XV (2), 268, 275, 285, 314–15.

76. "Discours à la Séance Publique Annuelle," 3 April 1852, Académie des Sciences Morales et Politiques *OC* (B), IX, 116–33.

77. To Mme Swetchine, 7 Jan. 1856, *OC*, XV (2), 268.

78. "Discours," pp. 116–17.

79. Ibid., pp. 117–20.

80. Tocqueville listed the following: Thucydides, Plato, Aristotle, Machiavelli, Rousseau, and Montesquieu. Although that list seems curious and somewhat crude, the inclusion of Thucydides and Montesquieu was significant. Both represented "history" of the kind that appealed to Tocqueville and both would figure importantly in his conception of *L'ancien régime*.

81. Beccaria and Adam Smith were mentioned.

82. "Discours," pp. 124–25.

83. *OC* (B.), IX, 647. I have followed the translation of Gargan, *Alexis de Tocqueville: The Critical Years, 1848–1851*, pp. 236–37. A similar mood was expressed in Tocqueville's letter to Gobineau. *OC*, IX, 298. After noting that the reigning despotism had produced apathy rather than creativity among political writers, Tocqueville remarked that men no longer hate nor love with a passion, but worry instead about their investments. Ironically this same worry afflicted him. To Beaumont, 6 Dec. 1857, *OC*, VIII (3), 522. In the unpublished part of *L'ancien régime* Tocqueville discussed the sterility of political theory during periods of repression. *OC*, II (2), 345ff.

84. *OC*, II (1), 70.

85. See Herr, *Tocqueville and the Old Regime*, p. 30.

86. *OC*, II (1), 73.

87. *OC*, II (2), 48.

88. *OC*, II (1), 69.

89. Ibid.

90. Ibid.

91. *OC*, II (1), 80–81.

92. "Moreover, there is in this sickness of the French Revolution something peculiar that I am unable to describe adequately, nor to analyze its causes. It is a *virus* of a new and unknown species." To Kergorlay, 16 May 1858, *OC* XIII (2), 337.

93. *OC*, II (2), 200.

94. *OC*, II (1), 70, 71.

95. *OC*, II (1), 235.

96. *OC*, II (1), 245.

97. *OC*, II (1), 72.

98. Ibid.

99. *OC*, II (2), 115, 125, 133–34; see also 275, 281.

100. *OC*, II (1), 73.
101. *OC*, II (1), 70, 71.
102. *OC*, II (1), 73.
103. *OC*, II (1), 71.
104. *OC*, II (1), 73–74.
105. *OC*, II (1), 75.
106. Ibid.
107. A reader who, after finishing *L'ancien régime* wished to retrace Tocqueville's second journey to America would discover that many of its major theses had been anticipated in *Democracy.* Already the young Tocqueville was arguing that the French Revolution had two contradictory "impulses," liberty and despotism; that the revolutionaries hatred of monarchical power caused them to sweep away all trace of the old regime with the result that "the secondary" powers that had served as checks to centralized absolutism were eliminated as well; and that the growth of centralization had been well under way before 1789. What had not been foreshadowed was the role of prerevolutionary centralization in preparing the way to the French Revolution and the retroactive character imputed to the revolution itself. The new conception of revolution involved a radical revision of historical time with the projection of *ancienneté* forward into modernity and the retroaction of modernity backward into *ancienneté. OC*, I (1), 97–98 (the French Revolution as favoring both despotism and liberty while destroying local institutions), ibid., 447–48, note K (on centralization before the revolution); I (2), 310–11 (destruction of local institutions throughout Europe by revolution and counterrevolution).
108. *OC*, II (1), 74–75.
109. *OC*, II (1), 74.
110. Ibid.

## Chapter XXV
## *The Old Regime*: Modernization and the Politics of Loss

1. *OC*, II (2), 239.
2. Special mention is made of Frederick the Great of Prussia, the benevolent despot who had fancied himself a political theorist without realizing he was a practical "precursor." *OC*, II (1), 79.
3. *OC*, II (1), 79.
4. *OC*, II (1), 198.
5. *OC*, II (1), 82.
6. *OC*, II (2), 287.
7. *OC*, II (1), 84.
8. *OC*, II (1), 141. Tocqueville directed this remark at what he considered to be Burke's misrepresentation of the vitality of the prerevolutionary regime.
9. *OC*, II (1), 69.
10. *OC*, II (2), 85.
11. Genesis 11:11 (1–9).
12. *OC*, II (2), 86.
13. *OC*, II (2), 115–16.
14. *OC*, II (1), 88, 89, 90.
15. *OC*, II (1), 89.

16. *OC*, II (1), 43.

17. *OC*, II (1), 74. This passage occurs in the course of Tocqueville's gloss on *Democracy in America.*

18. *OC*, II (1), 167.

19. *OC*, II (1), 245.

20. *OC*, II (1), 135.

21. II.3.

22. *OC*, II (2), 308.

23. *OC*, II (2), 301. See also *OC*, II (2), 305; to Beaumont, 26 Dec. 1850, *OC*, VIII (2), 344; "Speech of 21 April 1842," *OC* (B), IX, 17, contains an early example of Tocqueville's ambivalence toward the first Napoleon.

24. *OC*, II (2), 127.

25. *OC*, II (1), 236ff.

26. *OC*, II (1), 178–79, 186.

27. *OC*, II (1), 188–90.

28. *OC*, II (1), 218–25.

29. "I am less struck by the genius of those who made the Revolution because they wanted it than by the singular imbecility of those who made it without wanting it. . . . When I turn to the [royal] court which had so great a share in the Revolution I see some of the most trivial scenes in history: hare-brained or incompetent ministers, dissolute priests, futile women, rash or greedy courtiers, and a king whose only virtues are useless or dangerous. Yet I see these paltry personages moving, pushing, precipitating immense events." *OC*, II (2), 115–16.

30. *OC*, II (1), 134–35.

31. *OC*, II (1), 153–56.

32. *OC*, II (1), 180.

33. *OC*, II (1), 187.

34. *Democracy in America*, *OC*, I (1), 10.

35. Among modern commentaries that have emphasized the central importance of social class in *L'ancien régime Dilemmas of Democracy*, are Drescher, pp. 239–40, and Kahan, *Aristocratic Liberalism*, pp. 26–29. For Tocqueville's acknowledgment that social conditions and class relations explain most of the great political problems, see his letter of 19 July 1857 to Lord Radnor, *OC* (B), VI, 390; and in a letter to Hubert de Tocqueville, 4 Apr. 1858, *OC* (B), VII, 497: "the great question of our time: the relationship between classes." It is difficult to claim, however, that Tocqueville employed a clear conception of class analysis; his main concern was with classes as political actors. This, I think, is the thrust of his remark that "doubtless one could counter [my argument] by pointing to individuals; but I am speaking of classes; they alone deserve the attention of history." *OC*, II (1), 179.

36. *OC*, II (1), 166–67.

37. *OC*, II (1), 178–80, 184–86.

38. *OC*, II (1), 156–58.

39. *OC*, II (1), 167.

40. *OC*, II (1), 179.

41. It is worth recalling that Marx never wrote an extended account of class. Although his writings are, of course, full of references to the notion, all that remains of the promised systematic account are a few pages in *Capital*, 3: ch. 52.

42. *OC*, II (1), 188.

43. Tocqueville's treatment of the prerevolutionary writers was clearly influenced by Burke's attack on them in his *Reflections on the Revolution in France*. For some comparisons, see François Furet, "Burke ou la fin d'une seule histoire de l'Europe," *Débat*, no. 39 (March–May, 1986), 56–66.

44. Rousseau, who hardly figures in *L'ancien régime* is characterized in the unfinished work as "the singular authority" in the first period of the French Revolution when the push was toward "pure democracy." *OC*, II (2), 107.

45. *OC*, II (1), 195.

46. There is a large literature on the Physiocrats. The following provide a useful introduction: Leonard Krieger, *Kings and Philosophers, 1689–1789* (New York: Norton, 1970) especially pt. 3, "The Philosopher Kings." There are many suggestive ideas in Keith Baker, *Condorcet: From Natural Philosophy to Social Mathematics* (Chicago: University of Chicago, 1975), ch. 4. See also Peter Gay, *The Enlightenment: An Interpretation*, 2 vols. (New York: Knopf, 1969), 2:344–68, 483–96.

47. *OC*, II (1), 209–10, 213.

48. *OC*, II (2), 198.

49. The phenomenon had received only glancing notice in Tocqueville's essay of 1836 on *The Social and Political Condition of France before and since 1789*. In that essay the men of letters were briefly described as a discontented section of the middle class. *OC* II (1), 31–66.

50. *OC*, II (1), 196.

51. *OC*, II (1), 193. The traveler motif is suggested even more strongly in the language of the second edition of *L'ancien régime*. See the variants in *OC*, II (1), 330.

52. *OC*, II (1), 245.

53. "Everything in politics is only the consequence and symptom" of "the ideas and sentiments reigning among a people." To Bouchitté, 23 Sept. 1853, *OC* (B), VII, 299–300. See also: to Corcelle, 17 Sept. 1853, *OC*, VI (B), 227–28, and to Hubert de Tocqueville, 23 Feb. 1857, *OC* (B), VII, 436–37.

54. *OC*, II (1), 198.

55. To Odillon Barrot, 18 July 1856, *OC* (B), VII, 395.

56. To Freslon, 12 Jan. 1858, *OC* (B), VII, 480. See also the letter to Beaumont, 27 Feb. 1858, *OC*, VIII (3), 544.

57. *OC*, II (1), 199.

58. *OC*, II (1), 193–96, 199, 211–12.

59. *OC*, II (1), 196.

60. *OC*, II (1), 209ff.

61. *OC*, II (1), 217.

62. *OC*, II (1), 173.

63. *OC*, II (2), 53.

64. 30 July 1856, *OC*, IX, 268.

65. To Mrs. Grote, 22 Nov. 1853, *OC* (B), VI, 243.

66. *OC*, II (1), 174.

67. *OC*, II (1), 146.

68. *OC*, II (1), 212.

69. *OC*, II (1), 169.

70. Among the numerous references to the British aristocracy, see *OC*, II (1), 94, 147–48, 159–60, 163. One of the most striking occurs in the unfinished volume where

Tocqueville waxes ecstatic over "the grand spectacle: "[English] *liberty* alone capable of struggling against [the French] *revolution.*" *OC,* II (2), 247.

71. *OC,* II (1), 170.

72. *OC,* II (1), 175.

73. In a powerful passage Tocqueville warns against the rootlessness of an ultramontanist clergy: "His only fatherland is the Church. . . . An excellent member of the Christian city but a mediocre citizen everywhere else." *OC,* II (1), 171.

74. *OC,* II (1), 172, 173–74.

75. This point is developed by Tocqueville in connection with the role of the parlements. In the unfinished volume he stresses their growing "uniformity" as both the "means" of the revolution and its "sign." He takes this as evidence that the nation was becoming "*semblable*" and that "the habitual instruments of power . . . were being turned against" the government. *OC,* II (2), 66, 67.

76. *OC,* II (1), 119–20.

77. *OC,* II (1), 175–77.

78. *OC,* II (1), 155, 260–61.

79. *OC,* II (1), 96.

80. *OC,* II (2), 68.

81. *OC,* II (1), 231.

82. *OC,* II (1), 226, 230.

83. *OC,* II (1), 246, 247.

84. *OC,* II (1), 248–49.

85. *OC,* II (1), 94.

86. *OC,* II (1), 75.

87. *OC,* II (1), 214.

88. His linking of socialism with economic theories hearkens back to 1848, but it is also an allusion to the Saint-Simonianism attributed to Louis Napoleon.

89. *OC,* II (1), 213–16.

90. *OC,* II (1), 213.

91. *OC,* II (1), 214.

92. *OC,* II (1), 75.

93. *OC,* II (1), 250.

94. *OC,* II (1), 72.

95. *OC,* II (2), 287.

96. *OC,* II (2), 348.

97. To Ampère, 26 Aug. 1856, *OC,* XI, 342.

98. To Sedgwick, 4 Dec. 1852, *OC,* VII, 146. See the same sentiments in his letter to Sparks, 11 Dec. 1852, *OC,* VII, 148.

99. This correspondence is contained in *OC,* VII. See especially the following pages: 146–47, 163–64, 177, 179, 182, 192.

100. To A.E.V. Childe, 2 Apr. 1857, *OC,* VII, 193.

101. To Sparks, 21 Aug. 1837, *OC,* VII, 66.

102. Herr, *Tocqueville and the Old Regime,* p. 98.

103. To Beaumont, 22 Feb. 1856, *OC,* VIII (3), 374.

104. *OC,* II (2), 342.

105. In a letter to Lord Radnor, 19 July 1857, Tocqueville claimed that nothing interested him more than the "social condition of mankind" and relations between classes; these explained most of the great problems. *OC* (B), V, 390.

106. Tocqueville's defense of generality appeared most strikingly in his parliamentary papers and speeches. See *OC*, III (2), 216 ("Political Notes"), 223 ("The General Condition of *Esprits*").

107. *OC*, II (2), 195. The exact same remark appears at *OC*, II (2), 198.

108. *OC*, II (2), 199.

109. *OC*, II (2), 344.

110. *OC*, II (2), 344–45.

111. For the classic exposition of republicanism, see Pocock, *The Machiavellian Moment.* And for applications to the United States, see Lance Banning, *The Jeffersonian Persuasion: Evolution of a Party Ideology* (Ithaca: Cornell University Press, 1978). For a criticism of Pocock, see Appleby, *Liberalism and Republicanism in the Historical Imagination*, especially pp. 277ff.

112. See the following letters to Corcelle: *OC*, XV (2), 55–56, 81.

## Chapter XXVI
## Postdemocracy

1. To A.E.V. Childe, 23 Jan. 1858, *OC*, VII, 222.

2. To Corcelle, 17 Sept. 1844, *OC*, XV (1), 195.

3. 7 May 1838, *OC*, VIII (1), 294 (emphasis in the original).

4. To Childe, 12 Dec. 1856, *OC*, VII, 185.

5. To Ampère, 26 Aug. 1856, *OC*, XI, 342.

6. To Corcelle, 6 Jan. 1857, *OC*, XV (2), 194.

7. To Royer-Collard, Feb. 1838, *OC*, XI, 57.

8. "It is a somewhat easier and probably more useful task [to] hold to the view that theories of politics should be drawn from the realities of political life" than to believe that "the realities of political life should be molded to fit one's theories of politics." Gabriel A. Almond and Sidney Verba, *The Civic Culture* (Boston: Little, Brown, 1965), p. 340.

9. *OC*, I (1), 417. Tocqueville consistently argued for a distinction between "aristocracy" and "nobility." The nobility represented a closed "caste" within the aristocracy; the latter, especially in its English version, was open to exceptional talent. See his essay on "France before the Revolution," *OC*, II (1), 37–39.

10. Historians once claimed that "contemporary history" was a contradiction in terms. Postmodernity has recognized it as a legitimate subject of historical inquiry.

11. *OC*, I (2), 237.

12. For a powerful Emersonian defense of a democratic individualism, see George Kateb, *The Inner Ocean: Individualism and Democratic Culture* (Ithaca: Cornell University Press, 1992).

13. For a thoughtful defense of a postmodernist approach to theory, see William E. Connolly, *Political Theory and Modernity* (New York: Basil Blackwell, 1988).

14. To T. Sedgwick, 18 May 1856, *OC*, VII, 164.

15. As an example of the postmodern as postpolitical, see Jean-François Lyotard, *The Post-Modern Condition: A Report on Knowledge*, tr. Geoff Bennington and Brian Massumi (Minneapolis: University of Minnesota Press, 1984). See also Aryeh Botwinick, *Postmodernism and Democratic Theory* (Philadelphia: Temple University Press, 1993), pp. 163–66.

16. Note that as a last gasp of privilege, it is de rigueur for advanced critics to attack the "privileged" position assigned an idea or concept as evidence of an undeveloped postmodern sensibility.

17. *OC*, I (2), 324.

18. Jacob Talmon, *The Rise of Totalitarian Democracy* (Boston: Beacon Press, 1952). Talmon's cast of suspects overlaps in part with those of *L'ancien régime*: the Physiocrats, philosophes, and Rousseau.

19. In the light of Tocqueville's periodic fascination with Roman emperors, it is plausible to regard it as one strand in his imaginary. The same could be said of Physiocracy's benevolent despot and of Napoleon I.

20. *OC*, I (2), 322, 324.

21. *OC*, I (2), 324–25, 326, 323.

# INDEX